1ST EDITION

GREAT AMERICAN LEARNING VACATIONS

Fodor's Travel Publications, Inc.
New York • Toronto • London • Sydney • Auckland

First Edition

ISBN 0–679–02597–9

Fodor's Great American Learning Vacations

Project Editor: Paula Consolo
Editors: Karen Cure, Caroline Haberfeld, Andrea Lehman, David Low, Conrad Little Paulus, Melanie Roth
Editorial Contributors: Hannah Borgeson, Bernard Burt, Fionn Davenport, Sean Elder, Lori P. Greene, Paul M. Konrad, David Low, Carole Martin, Kristin McGowan, Mary Myers, Mary King Nash, Irene Rawlings, Melissa Rivers, Melanie Roth, Ben Sandmel, Linda K. Schmidt, M.T. Schwartzman, John Sellers.
Creative Director: Fabrizio LaRocca

Cover Photographs: background, Mark J. Ferrari/Center for Whale Studies; left spot, Kay Chernush/Image Bank; middle spot, Julie Graber/Santa Fe Photographic Workshops; right spot, Dann Coffey/Image Bank.
Cover Design: Tigist Getachew

Special Sales

Fodor's Travel Publications are available at special discounts for bulk purchases for sales promotions or premiums. Special editions, including personalized covers, excerpts of existing guides, and corporate imprints, can be created in large quantities for special needs. For more information, contact your local bookseller or write to Special Markets, Fodor's Travel Publications, 201 East 50th Street, New York, NY 10022. Inquiries from Canada should be directed to your local Canadian bookseller or sent to Random House of Canada, Ltd., Marketing Department, 1265 Aerowood Drive, Mississauga, Ontario L4W 1B9. Inquiries from the United Kingdom should be sent to Fodor's Travel Publications, 20 Vauxhall Bridge Road, London SW1V 2SA, England.

MANUFACTURED IN THE UNITED STATES OF AMERICA

10 9 8 7 6 5 4 3 2 1

CONTENTS

INTRODUCTION *4*

Archaeological Digs *1*

Arts and Crafts Workshops *11*

Birding *38*

Campus Vacations *51*

Cooking Schools *60*

Cultural Tours *71*

Environmental Cruises *86*

Foreign-Language Immersion
Programs *103*

Garden Tours *114*

Music Programs *132*

Nature Camps *147*

New Age Centers *165*

Painting Workshops *182*

Photography Workshops and Tours *199*

Spas and Fitness Centers *217*

Volunteer Research Vacations *244*

Volunteer Vacations in Public and
Community Service *263*

Whale-Watching Cruises *278*

Writing Conferences and Workshops *288*

APPENDIX: WHERE THE PROGRAMS
ARE *313*

ow about spending your vacation making a quilt, weaving a rug, building a log cabin or an adobe hut, or maybe lapstraking a wooden sailboat? Or photographing bald eagles in Alaska's Chilkat River Valley or listening for Antillean nighthawks at dusk around Key West? Or learning from La Varenne's Anne Willan the path to a perfect puff pastry?

A growing group of Americans has learned that a vacation can be more than a trip to the beach—Americans who are taking advantage of the increasing number of learning programs that make it possible for ordinary folks to spend a week or two or three learning things that they previously had only fantasized about.

This guide will turn you on to hundreds of ways to do just that, enabling you to come away from your vacation with a lot more than a suntan. You might have cleared brush off the Appalachian Trail, worked alongside Jimmy Carter to build houses in south-central Los Angeles, star-watched at ancient observatories with an astrophysics professor, or helped scientists study the Great Lakes' declining loon population or survey

bottlenose dolphins in Monterey Bay. Instead of revisiting the same old tourist haunts, you might have learned Czech or Arabic in a total-immersion program. Or studied mountain dulcimer or fusion jazz, watercolor or Zen meditation. Or explored the riddles of creation at Dartmouth, Tin Pan Alley at Cornell, or underwater photography with Nikon.

Whether you're young or old, alone or traveling with your family or friends, this book will give you a lifetime of ideas for such great vacations, courses, and scheduled group trips in the United States that last between 5 and 14 days. Keep in mind that in addition to the programs described here, there are many others: shorter ones, longer ones, and many to other destinations, outside the United States as well as inside. Each chapter in this guide contains a comprehensive checklist of questions to help you choose the right program—from among those described here as well as others that you find out about on your own.

If you have special needs, don't forget to query the program directors before you sign up. If you're traveling with your family, for instance, be sure to ask whether youngsters may participate, or if there's something for them to do in the area.

If you're traveling solo, ask about the single-occupancy policy. When a workshop or program you're considering has separate prices for tuition, lodging, and meals, you obviously have the option of doing what suits you best. At other programs, there's a single all-inclusive price that includes tuition and room and board; most of the prices for these are per person based on double occupancy, and you will probably be paired with another single if you don't pay extra to have a room to yourself.

If you observe a special diet, ask whether the program can accommodate you. Some programs may be able to do so and some cannot, for various reasons. If the program that interests you is among them but is convenient to restaurants or accommodations with cooking facilities, find out whether a deduction can be made from the cost of the package.

If you use a wheelchair or need any other assistance, make sure that the program can give you what you require.

Finally, once you've made your decision, be sure to ask:

How much of a deposit is required and when is the balance due? Most schools and operators require you to put down a deposit by a particular day in order to reserve your spot, then pay in full sometime before the starting date.

What is the cancellation policy? You may get a full or partial refund if you cancel your reservation, and then again, you may not. Policies vary from full refunds offered up to 30 days before the program begins, to partial refunds offered up to 7 days before, and no refunds offered ever. Find out how far in advance you must cancel to get a full refund, and ask if any allowances will be made for cancellations due to medical emergencies. If cancellation insurance is available, take it. You'll receive a full refund if for any reason you can't show up as planned.

Are taxes included in the cost? Generally, they're not, although they can add substantially to the cost of your trip. Depending on the program, you should also ask about tipping—specifically, who customarily gets tipped and about how much that tip should be.

Every care has been taken to ensure the accuracy of the information in this guide, and all prices and dates quoted here are based on information supplied to us at press time. Still, trips and workshops that run one year often aren't available the next. In fact, cancellations can occur right up to departure date. Stay flexible and you are sure to find something that appeals at the time you want to travel. The publisher cannot accept responsibility for errors that may have occurred.

We at Fodor's would love to hear about your travel experiences. When a program fails to live up to its billing, please let us know—we'll investigate your complaint and revise our entries as the facts warrant. If a program proves better than our descriptions suggest, tell us that, too. Send your letters to the edi tors of Fodor's Travel Publications, 201 East 50th Street, New York, NY 10022. We'll look forward to hearing from you. And have a wonderful trip.

Karen Cure

Editorial Director

Archaeological Digs

By Andrea Lehman with research by Irene Rawlings

 magine standing on a bluff in the desert Southwest, holding a sandal woven from a yucca plant, knowing that sandal was worn by a person over 900 years ago. Imagine digging in a Maine potato field, looking for the tools used by the first European farmer who tried to break the rocky soil in 1677. Imagine looking through a pile of garbage for a piece of evidence—not for some sensational 20th-century news story but for a story that unfolded hundreds or even thousands of years ago.

All of these experiences are part of the rituals and rewards of archaeological digs—as everyday as bones and bowls and as exciting as Indiana Jones, minus the chase scenes and special effects. Archaeology is not just about collecting artifacts; it's about understanding people from times past. However, it's by examining artifacts, most often ordinary objects used in daily life, that archaeologists learn about how people lived. The programs profiled below allow you to work alongside professionals at archaeological sites, helping to excavate some of the same types of objects you see on display in museums—pottery, stone tools, and religious artifacts.

Most of these programs do not require any previous dig experience or knowledge of archaeological techniques. In fact, most have as part of their mission teaching the public about archaeology and its methods, along with conducting research and documenting, preserving, and protecting sites threatened by weather, construction, pothunters, or vandals. The only prerequisites are a willingness to learn and to perform some basic physical activities. Although not overly strenuous, some of these vacations may require hiking, shoveling, lifting, carrying, or pushing a wheelbarrow.

A typical day at an excavation begins early, especially if you're staying at the site. (Some sites are so remote that you must hike in and camp there, while others are so accessible you can drive right to the dig.) Once on location, you are briefed on what you're looking for and what you hope to accomplish that day. Each site varies, so different excavation techniques are used and different tasks performed: surveying a location to determine possible excavation sites, laying out a grid over a site you want to explore, carefully removing topsoil without disturbing artifacts, sifting to find small items, logging and recording the position of artifacts in the grid, removing pieces, and, finally, cleaning and storing them. Good programs rotate people through the tasks so you can experience them all. The whole process is slow and methodical: You watch, you listen, you ask questions, and you dig carefully, so as not to damage anything. It may seem to take forever, but at the end of the day there's always plenty of satisfied conversation about what was found and its relationship to the people you are studying.

Participants range in age from teens to senior citizens, though most programs have a minimum age of 17 or 18 and do not provide day care. To allow for enough attention from the professional archaeologists, groups are usually small (5 to 25), creating an atmosphere of camaraderie. You can expect to be in the field (and sometimes lab) for eight hours a day. Projects that run throughout "the season" start in the spring, as early as the weather permits, and run into the fall; others last only the short sessions that faculty, trip leaders, or volunteers are available. Some programs do offer off-season work, especially in the lab, but openings are very limited.

The biggest difference between programs is the peoples they study; digs cover all types of cultures, in all types of places, and at all points in time. The representative ones listed in this chapter are just that; if you're interested in a particular aspect of history (or prehistory), there's a good chance you'll find a program out there for you. Other significant differences between programs include the weather, the physical demands, and the "comfort factor." Only you can decide what you want; what's challenging and fun for one person could be daunting and uncomfortable for another. Ask for suggestions regarding appropriate dress for the time of year you will be on site; it could make all the difference.

So, is a dig for you? If you don't mind getting down and dirty, literally, and slowing your pace a bit, working on an excavation can be a rewarding and educational experience. Once you've found your first artifact and held it in your hand, you'll be hooked.

CHOOSING THE RIGHT DIG

Though it might at first seem that a dig is a dig is a dig, if you dig a little deeper you'll find that programs vary by as much as 3,000 miles and 10,000 years. Be sure to ask the questions that concern you.

What is the subject of the excavation, and what is the site? Archaeological digs are as different as the sites at which they're located and the cultures they're attempting to uncover. Not surprisingly, in this country, and especially in western states, many excavations focus on prehistoric or historic-period Native Americans. You might learn about the Anasazi, Apache, or Nez Percé

and dig at pueblos, cliff dwellings, or plains settlements. For those interested in more recent American history, other, typically eastern, excavations take place at such locations as Colonial villages and Civil War–era plantations with slave quarters.

What types of activities are offered? Chances are if you're looking for an archaeological dig, you're interested in, well, digging. But most programs also offer activities that put excavating in a broader context—lectures, tours of other historic sites, and trips to museums being the most common—as well as those that teach other archaeological skills, such as cleaning, analyzing, and cataloging the artifacts you discover. Decide whether you want to be out in the sun, trowel in hand, as much as possible, or if you want to sample different facets of the field. Many programs, especially those of at least a week, are designed to expose you to different activities and then allow you to tailor your day to suit your interests.

Where is the dig and what are the conditions (including weather) like? If, when you hear the phrase *archaeological excavation,* visions of hot, dry, dusty digs pop into your mind, you're probably not far off. Many programs are in the South, Southwest, Midwest, and West, and most are offered in summer, the prime research time. You're outside much of the day, far from the comforts of soda machines and swimming pools. (Isn't that what it's all about, after all?) Look for sunshades and ice water, afternoon lab breaks and afternoon thundershowers. For many, hot weather is no big deal, but if you can't stand the heat, stay out of the Sun Belt or opt for spring or fall sessions.

What kind of experience or skills are necessary? In almost all cases, the answer is none: no previous dig experience, no knowledge of archaeology, and not even any particular physical skills. The only requirement is the desire to learn, but it's best to check on this anyway. If the work is strenuous and you're out of shape, or if most of the other participants will have a level of knowledge you don't, you might want to reconsider.

How long has the program been in operation? Older doesn't necessarily mean better, but it can mean more organized. A few years of working with volunteers can help staff fine-tune how to train them.

What's the cost and what's included? Roughly speaking, archaeological digs come in two varieties: full-service and self-service. The majority of the programs listed here, most sponsored by government agencies, universities, museums, and archaeological societies, are the latter. Open to volunteers, they generally charge nothing, save the occasional small fee for supplies or association membership, but then nothing is included either. For self-service digs, you are responsible for your own meals, lodging, and transportation unless otherwise noted. Ask about transportation from the nearest airport to the site; sometimes it's supplied. Also ask whether there are camping fees.

Full-serve digs, on the other hand, charge a fee for participation ($500 to $1,500 for several days to several weeks); unless otherwise stated, those listed in this chapter include accommodations, meals, and transportation to the site from a nearby airport or other rendezvous point. Part of the fee covers the cost of the research project itself. These programs are usually operated by national organizations, most nonprofit, that are in the learning vacations business, offering a whole variety of projects beyond digs. In either full- or self-service digs, the program generally supplies the equipment and materials needed in the research.

This explanation oversimplifies the distinction between these two types a bit, and many programs fall somewhere in between. It's always best to check exactly what is and what isn't included, especially if particular items, such as tents and sleeping bags, are an issue for you.

What are the accommodations like? Most volunteer programs encourage or at least make arrangements for you to camp out. It's part of the whole experience: Just pitch a tent and pitch in. As a rule, you're closer to the site if you camp, so you can participate in evening activities and stay part of a group. However, for those who prefer not to rough it, programs almost always provide lists of reasonably priced local motels or even bed-and-breakfasts and nice hotels, especially at sites near cities or popular tourist attractions. Many bigger and more established programs have arrangements with nearby colleges to provide low-cost accommodations. Ongoing research sites often provide lodgings near the excavation, though they tend to be rustic—cabins, bunkhouses, and the like.

What's the food like? If you camp, your food is likely to be what you cook yourself; if you stay in a motel, you'll probably be eating in restaurants. Programs that offer lodging usually provide meals in a common dining hall.

How long can I stay? If you have never done anything like this before and want to try archaeology on to see how it fits, perhaps as part of a longer vacation, a program that enables you to stop in for a day or so is ideal. For more than a taste, you need a good week or longer. Programs that are designed in one- or two-week sessions have a learning curve and some flexibility built in. You not only have more time to perfect excavation techniques, but you also can learn more in the lab and at lectures and possibly develop your own small projects based on special interests. Some projects allow you to work a month or all season, staying over a number of sessions (where formal sessions are offered). Of course, to become truly knowledgeable takes more than a handful of weeks.

How far in advance do I need to book? Check the literature you receive for application deadlines. Most programs don't have them and take applicants as long as space is available, so try to sign up two to six months in advance. For programs with fees, check for cancellation deadlines and policies; changing your mind too close to dig time can cost you.

Do you have references from past participants? You may not choose to check references if you're only going for a few days, but if you're going for several weeks or more, a talk with someone who's gotten his or her hands dirty is invaluable. Ask not only whether a given program is well run but also what a day at the dig feels like; it'll help you decide if the dig is right for you.

MAJOR PLAYERS

EARTHWATCH Since 1972, Earthwatch has been providing scientists with the resources they need—funding and volunteers—to conduct significant research in varied fields, all of it with the aim of protecting the planet. Nearly 40,000 volunteers, known as the EarthCorps, have shared in the experience and the cost of mounting this research. Though many projects deal with the physical and biological sciences, a number each year fall in the human impacts categories, which include archaeological excavations in the United States and abroad. (Some are listed under Favorite Archaeological Digs, *see below.*)

Anyone 16 or over can take part, regardless of education, cultural background, or experience. You must be a member, and it helps to have a sense of adventure and a sense of humor. Participation is on a cost-shared basis, which means your fee helps fund the research in addition to covering your lodging and food. Typically, accommodations are rustic—permanent tents, bunkhouses, dormitories, or camping under the stars—and meals are usually prepared by a cook, though you might be asked to help. Costs are based on the total project cost; sessions in recent years have run about two or three weeks and from $1,000 to $1,500 (680 Mt. Auburn St., Box 403, Watertown, MA 02272-9924, tel. 617/926–8200 or 800/776–0188, fax 617/926–8532).

FOUR CORNERS SCHOOL Referring to itself as "the premier outdoor ed-venture classroom in the Southwest," Four Corners School has been conducting educational adventure programs throughout the Colorado Plateau for over a decade. Though many of its programs

have an archaeology component, only some involve actual excavation, such as the one that explores the 8,000-year-old secrets of Old Man Cave. Other programs are devoted to other archaeological activities—mapping and surveying sites or drawing and photographing features and artifacts—or they may simply be exhilarating quests to see rock art or ruins.

Programs generally run from 4 to 10 days and cost about $500 to $1,000, which covers supplies, food, lodging, and transportation during the program. Difficulty is rated on a scale of 1 (no camping or hiking) to 10 ("You must be crazy!"), but excavations tend to cluster in the lower half. Some might require camping at a primitive base camp and day hikes of 4 to 6 miles. Group sizes range from 8 to 25, and participants are generally 35 to 65, though students under 18 are welcome if supervised by an adult (Box 1029, Monticello, UT 84535, tel. 801/587–2156).

NATIONAL TRUST FOR HISTORIC PRESERVATION As its name suggests, the National Trust for Historic Preservation, a nonprofit organization created by an act of Congress, owns and maintains historic properties nationwide. During its weeklong Study Tour programs, you can work alongside architects and archaeologists at National Trust properties, uncovering material that provides information about the site and its history. Up to a half-dozen programs are offered each year in the summer and early fall. The focus is on U.S. history, mostly Civil War to the present. The programs also stress hands-on work, from excavating to analyzing artifacts, but lectures and tours of other area sites complement the experience.

To take part, you must become one of the 250,000 members of the National Trust ($15). The cost of each program is $500 to $800 and includes lodging (sometimes at the property), meals, activities, and transportation from the airport to the site. Groups are small, usually 5 to 15 participants (Study Tour Program, National Trust for Historic Preservation, 1785 Massachusetts Ave. NW, Washington, DC 20036, tel. 202/673–4138).

PASSPORT IN TIME Through this volunteer program of the U.S. Forest Service, individuals and families, young and old alike, work with professional archaeologists and historians on exciting heritage projects in national forests nationwide. Projects have been as varied as they are far-flung: stabilizing ancient cliff dwellings in New Mexico, excavating a 10,000-year-old village site in Minnesota, restoring a 19th-century hand-hewn log house in Florida, cleaning vandalized rock art in Colorado, surveying sites in the Utah wilderness, restoring mansions along the shores of California's Lake Tahoe, and excavating a 19th-century Chinese mining site in Oregon. They run from a weekend to a month, some even longer; and though there's no fee for the projects themselves, you'll have to cover your own expenses.

The "Passport in Time Traveler," a free newsletter announcing current projects and containing an application form, is published twice a year, in spring and fall. Look through it and apply for one that interests you. Don't be disappointed if you're not accepted to your first choice; though PIT tries to accommodate everyone, sometimes interest exceeds the number of available spaces (Passport in Time Clearinghouse, CEHP Inc., Box 18364, Washington, DC 20036, tel. 202/293–0922).

SCRAP The New Hampshire State Conservation and Rescue Archaeology Program, better known as SCRAP, is an adult participation program (minimum age 17) administered by the state's Division of Historical Resources. Its goal is to educate the public about archaeology and in so doing increase site discovery, reduce site destruction, recover information from sites about to be destroyed, and conduct original research. Part of SCRAP's mission is to debunk the image of the elitist archaeologist; toward that end, the staff tries not only to train participants but also to raise them to the level of colleagues. (In fact, New Hampshire was the first state in the country to legislate the training and certification of avocational archaeologists.) An example of the program's populist philosophy is its name: The acronym SCRAP was inspired by the Persian word for archaeologist, *bastanshanas,* whose literal translation is "one who collects garbage."

Though SCRAP also sponsors workshops, lab work, and independent research projects, the centerpiece of the program is the annual summer field school, which accepts college students as well as volunteers. Excavation sites change from year to year (the Connecticut River most recently), but fundamental recovery methods and ethics are always stressed. And while each project has a formal research design, there is room to tailor your work to your interests.

Details concerning lodging and meals vary, depending on the site. In previous years, the field school was organized in two-week sessions, with a fee of $100 a week for meals and tent camping (alternate housing could also be arranged). The program generally requests a $25 donation to help defray the cost of supplies (Summer Archaeology Field School, New Hampshire Division of Historical Resources, Box 2043, Concord, NH 03302-2043, tel. 603/271–3483).

UNIVERSITY RESEARCH EXPEDITIONS PROGRAM Somewhat similar to Earthwatch (*see above*), UREP creates teams of volunteers and scientists to conduct research about life on earth. As a member of a University of California research expedition, you provide labor and share in the cost of the project; in exchange, you gain new skills, new friends, and the excitement of discovery.

UREP's emphasis is on other cultures in other lands, but it offers some archaeological programs in the United States. Examples from recent years were titled Hawaii after Captain Cook and Pueblo Dwellers of the Southwest. Projects last two to three weeks, and accommodations and costs (actually a tax-deductible contribution to the university) vary with the destination, averaging about $1,300. The contribution covers meals and shared lodging, ground transportation, nonpersonal camping and field gear, and research equipment and supplies (University of California, Berkeley, CA 94720, tel. 510/642–6586).

```
┌─────────────────────────────────────┐
│            FAVORITE DIGS             │
└─────────────────────────────────────┘
```

┌─────────────────────────────────────┐
│   THE MID-ATLANTIC   │
└─────────────────────────────────────┘

VIRGINIA **Colonial Williamsburg.** In the same quaint reconstructed Colonial village where tourists visit originals or replicas of houses, forges, and taverns, an innovative program, Learning Weeks in Archaeology (for ages 16 and up), gives you a chance to dig up the real thing. Working under the guidance of Williamsburg archaeologists, you may unearth postholes or privies, buttons or bones; while you do, you'll be learning how to take field notes, map finds, identify artifacts, and analyze site remains. Tours and lectures supplement the hands-on work, enabling you to understand how scholars use what is found to re-create 18th-century life in Virginia's Colonial capital.

Four two-week sessions are held each year, with weekends free for you to explore Jamestown, Yorktown, the James River plantations, or, if you've had enough American history, Virginia Beach or Busch Gardens. (If you'd like to stay just one week, it's better to attend the first week of a session.) Sessions are held from spring to fall, and weather varies accordingly. May and late September have cooler temperatures (typically in the 70s), while summer brings the high 80s or warmer. Rain comes more often in the early session; by summer it's drier, with the exception of some late-afternoon thunderstorms. Since sites, which change from year to year, are in the Historic Area, you won't be roughing it: Terrain is flat and not rocky, there's no wildlife to worry about (not even ticks and mosquitoes), and rest rooms and vending machines are only a walk away.

You have to arrange your own accommodations and dining, with the exception of an opening reception, one luncheon, and a farewell dinner at one of Colonial Williamsburg's taverns. Lists of lodgings and restaurants are provided; though some are within walking distance of the Historic Area, a car is recommended so that you can fully enjoy local attractions. Generally, small groups of participants tend to eat and spend evenings together, and many are returnees. *Department of Archaeological Research, Colonial Williamsburg Foundation, Box 1776, Williamsburg, VA 23187-1776, tel. 804/220-7330. May–early Oct.: 6–12 days, $400–$600. Price does not include lodging or most meals, but does include admission tickets and tours.*

WEST VIRGINIA **St. Albans.** On the banks of the Kanawha River at St. Albans, volunteers can join with archaeologists sponsored by Marshall University in exploring the site's deep deposits, looking for evidence of the Adena tribe. The first excavations here, conducted between 1964 and 1968, exposed important early Archaic period levels. Subsequently, Woodland levels were found, with finds such as hearths and tools pointing to almost continuous occupation of the site for the past 10,000 years.

Volunteers are welcome for any length of time, and dates change from year to year. You must be at least 18 and must join the State Archaeological Society ($12). Conditions are generally warm (in the 80s) and humid. Dining and lodging arrangements are your responsibility. Within a mile or so are many fine hotels and motels, starting at $22 a night, as well as restaurants that are varied in both cuisine and price. Camping facilities are within 10 miles. *Dean Braley, 301 4th Ave., St. Albans, WV 25177, tel. 304/722-1704, or Jim Recknagel, 103 Riverview Dr., St. Albans, WV 25177, tel. 304/727-0418. June–July: no limit on stay, no charge but donation accepted.*

┌─────────────────────────────────────┐
│   THE SOUTH   │
└─────────────────────────────────────┘

ARKANSAS **Parkin Archeological Research Station.** In a flat, mostly agricultural area in northeast Arkansas, part of the Mississippi River floodplain, lies the Parkin site. Here a 17-acre Native American town on the St. Francis River, surrounded by a moat and a log palisade for protection, was occupied between 1350 and 1550. An ongoing archaeological research project conducted by the

Arkansas Archeological Survey is gathering information on the original residents and searching for additional evidence that the site was indeed the town of Casqui, visited by the expedition of Hernando de Soto in 1541. Evidence to support the theory is found not just in expedition accounts, which describe a town resembling the Parkin village, but also in the discovery at the site of Spanish artifacts of the type carried by the expedition: a brass bell, which was placed on a child at burial, and a glass chevron bead, used by the Spanish for trading.

The specific purposes of excavations change each field season, but general research topics include learning about the architecture of Native American houses, investigating plants and animals grown for food, searching for more evidence of contact with the de Soto expedition, investigating the moat and palisade, and determining how long the site was occupied. Current research focuses on recovering information about domestic structures and subsistence. The remains of house floors are abundant in the village area, as an estimated 2,000 people lived within the moat, and both botanical and animal remains are well preserved. Deposits are over 6 feet deep in some areas.

Volunteers, who must be at least 17, are invited to help excavate, working mainly with trowels and small hand tools. Excavated soil is then water screened on site. If it's raining or too hot—and it gets extremely hot in the summer (temperatures in the 90s are common, readings over 100°F occasional), with rain more frequent in early fall—work is done in the lab instead. You receive sunshades and ice water at the site.

You are on your own for dining and lodging. If you'd like to camp, you may do so for free, courtesy of the project, at a nearby state park. Otherwise, there are motels and restaurants about 15 miles away in Wynne and a small café, pizza shop, and grocery stores in Parkin. *Dr. Jeffrey M. Mitchem, Parkin Archeological State Park, Box 241, Parkin, AR 72373, tel. 501/755–2119. July–Oct.: no limit on stay, no charge.*

SOUTH CAROLINA **Stono Plantation.** Founded by the English in 1670, Charleston was the center of a flourishing plantation economy, and by the early 18th century, Stono Plantation—about 6 miles away and now within the Dill Wildlife Sanctuary on James Island—was home to the Hamiltons, a wealthy and politically active family who enjoyed an elegant lifestyle. It was Paul Hamilton, Sr., a loyalist, who named this 350-acre tract Stono and who ultimately lost it due to his allegiance to the Crown.

Here, in an area of fallow fields and secondary forest, the Charleston Museum is working with the College of Charleston to conduct investigations on all aspects of southern plantation life. Since excavations started in 1989, the site has revealed a planter's house, occupied from about 1790 to 1830, and adjacent yard areas, while the search continues for an 18th-century slave settlement. The site is also yielding data on prehistoric and historic-period Native American occupation.

Volunteers (minimum age 17) are invited to join the excavation alongside students from the College of Charleston, for whom the project is a formal archaeological field-study course. You can take part for a day or several weeks. After the digging in the heat (90°F) and humidity is over in July, work returns to the lab, where excavated materials are washed and sorted. Though it's not as exciting, volunteers are welcome in the lab as well.

You are responsible for your own room and board, though college dorms are often available for a modest fee. Accommodations and restaurants in the Charleston area are plentiful and diverse, and the city has a wealth of museums, historic sites, beaches, and forests to enjoy. *Ron Anthony, Charleston Museum, 360 Meeting St., Charleston, SC 29403-6297, tel. 803/722–2996, fax 803/722–1784. May–early July: no limit on stay, no charge.*

TENNESSEE **Andrew Jackson's Hermitage.** The focus of this Earthwatch plantation archaeology project is slavery, as excavations around the Greek Revival mansion belonging to the seventh president of the United States yield information on the lives of those who labored here. In 1994, Earth-Corps teams focused on areas occupied by those assigned to the mansion, kitchen, and stable. Work includes surveying and screening, washing, labeling, and sorting artifacts.

Volunteers (aged 16 or over) stay in a 1930s-era house east of Nashville and share cooking duties. *Earthwatch, 680 Mt. Auburn St., Box 403, Watertown, MA 02272-9924, tel. 617/926–8200 or 800/776–0188, fax 617/926–8532. Mid-June–mid-Aug.: 13 days, $1,195.*

THE MIDWEST

KANSAS **Kansas Archeology Training Program.** Established in 1974 under the joint sponsorship of the Kansas State Historical Society and the Kansas Anthropological Association, the Kansas Archeology Training Program (KATP) runs a 16-day field school the first two weeks in June. Whether you attend for as little as a day or for the full session, you can take part in original research and further your knowledge of archaeological methods and theory. Among the activities you're encouraged to experience are block excavation, site surveying, artifact processing in the lab, and soil flotation. Classes can be taken for college credit or just for fun.

Over the years, investigations have been conducted at a wide range of prehistoric and historic-period sites across the state, and attendance has grown from 50 to nearly 300. To take part, you must be at least 14, become a member of the Kansas Anthropological Association ($12), and pay a dig site fee ($15); other expenses, including food, lodging, and transportation, are your responsibility. *Virginia A. Wulfkuhle, Kansas State Historical Society, 120 W. 10th Ave., Topeka, KS 66612-1291, tel. 913/296–3813, fax 913/296–1005. June: 16 days maximum, $15 per day.*

NEBRASKA **Hudson-Meng Bison Kill Site.** About 10,000 years ago, over 600 bison died in an arroyo in what is now the Oglala National Grassland in western Nebraska, thus ensuring the survival of a small, and very lucky, band of nomadic hunters for another winter. The remains of the bison and scattered stone tools and projectile points have been found, and scientists are using the evidence from continuing excavations to piece together what happened. Did the hunters kill the bison by stampeding them over a cliff, or did the animals die of natural causes, such as a prairie fire or drifting snow? Why did so many die at the same time? How was the bison used in the everyday life of these people, and how does this bison, *Bison antiquus,* differ from the bison of today? In addition, researchers hope to uncover (pun intended) more information on ancient environments and on the continent's first inhabitants, the Paleo-Indians.

Northwestern Nebraska summers are hot—nearing 100°F in the day but cooling down to the upper 50s and 60s in the evening. Late-afternoon thunderstorms are not uncommon, and hail is possible. Spectacular scenery helps take your mind off the weather, however. On the edge of the hills and buttes of the Pine Ridge, forested by native ponderosa pine, the site overlooks open prairie and badlands to the north, with the Black Hills visible about 40 miles away.

Four 10-day work periods, with 2 days of training, can accommodate 10 volunteers each, but you must be 18 or older. Accommodations are strictly BYOT (Bring Your Own Tent). Although motels are available in Crawford, 20 miles away via gravel and dirt road, you're encouraged to stay on site to take advantage of evening programs offered during each session. Due to the small camping area available, mobile homes and campers are discouraged. Participants help with food preparation on a rotating basis. *Louis A. Redmond, Heritage Program Manager, Nebraska National Forest, 125 N. Main St., Chadron, NE 69337, tel. 308/432–0300, fax 308/432–0309. June–Aug.: 10 days, no charge.*

SOUTH DAKOTA **Earth-lodge villages.** Every year since 1983, the U.S. Army Corps of Engineers has selected archaeological sites for excavation by volunteers. The sites are generally chosen because they are threatened by erosion at reservoirs managed by the corps. In 1995, work returns for ten days in late June to two adjacent earth-lodge village sites on the east shore of Lake Francis Case, approximately 7 miles north of Chamberlain, off I–90 in south central South Dakota. Plans for succeeding years were not set at press time.

The Smithsonian Institution's Missouri River Basin Survey first identified and partially excavated the sites in the 1950s, and the corps's volunteer archaeological program began working here again in 1992.

If you're willing to commit at least eight hours total to the dig, you can volunteer. Children under 17 must be accompanied by a parent or guardian who's also volunteering. When work hours are over, you can attend slide programs and visit local museums and other archaeological sites. One word of warning: Summers are generally hot and humid next to the lake, and thunderstorms are to be expected.

The corps may offer free camping at a nearby recreation area, or you can find creature comforts in any of the many hotels and restaurants in Chamberlain or across the Missouri River in Oacoma. *U.S. Army Corps of Engineers, Omaha District, Planning Division, 215 N. 17th St., Omaha, NE 68102-4978, tel. 402/221–4603. Late June: 10 days, no charge.*

THE SOUTHWEST

ARIZONA **Raven Site Ruin.** Classic southwestern desert archaeology is at its best at the White Mountain Archaeological Center and its adjacent Raven Site Ruin excavation, named for the abundance of bird symbols found on ceramics and petroglyphs in the area. Here on a 5-acre knoll in eastern Arizona is an 800-room pueblo, occupied between AD 1000 and AD 1500. Despite damage by pothunters, the site is still rich in cultural material; it has more than 80 ceramic types, including White Mountain redwares,

vitreous Zuni glazed wares, and many other kinds used for trading. Excavations continue on more than 200 rooms at surface level and two kivas.

Flanked on all sides by mountain ranges, the high-desert landscape, some 6,500 feet in elevation, is covered with over 200 extinct volcanoes that are now surreal, grass-covered domes. Summer days tend to be hot (85°F to 90°F) and dry except for brief afternoon thunderstorms, but nights are cool (50°F to 55°F). Fabulous sunsets darken to a night sky so clear that the Milky Way looks like smoke.

Working alongside professional archaeologists (the participant-to-archaeologist ratio is about 6:1), you spend your day learning all three facets of archaeology: surveying, excavation, and analysis. The daylong program starts with an artifact orientation, followed by hands-on excavation at the ruin. After lunch, you might try a guided hike or horseback ride through the surrounding area, seeing and discovering prehistoric rock art panels. By midafternoon, it's off to the lab to clean and sort artifacts, reconstruct ceramic vessels, or catalog materials; the day ends with a lecture. If you elect to stay more than a day, there's dinner and, usually, an after-dinner campfire—the silence of the night broken by a coyote chorus in the nearby hills. Since only meals and lectures are at set times, your activities can be adapted to your interests, even in a day visit. If you stay longer, however, you can really focus on a particular area of research.

If you do opt to stay, you can lodge in the bunkhouse (private rooms are available for an extra fee). Although linen is provided, you need your own sleeping bag in May, September, and October. You can also camp with a tent or RV; however, only the state park 6 miles away has hookups. Reasonably priced motels can be found in Springerville and St. Johns. Meals are served in the chow hall. Children from 9 to 17 accompanied by an adult are welcome and are often very able and enthusiastic participants. *White Mountain Archaeological Center, Western Office, HC 30, St. Johns, AZ 85936, tel.*

602/333–5857. Early May–mid-Oct.: 1 day, $42 adults, $24 children 9–17; overnight, $66 adults, $44 children; 6 days, $390 adults, $260 children. Price includes lunch for day program, lodging and meals for overnight programs, and transportation from Springerville.

■**TEXAS** **Lubbock Lake Landmark.** With more than 100 archaeological sites ranging from 12,000-year-old Paleo-Indian settlements to the 19th-century remains of the origins of Lubbock, Texas, Lubbock Lake provides a rich area for archaeological study. An Earthwatch project is concentrating on Apache history in the 200 years prior to mid-17th-century European contact. Teams excavate and document sites used for everything from bison butchering to tool manufacture. You participate in digging, screening, mapping, sketching, photographing, and work at the Quaternary Research Center lab.

The southern high plains are home to coyotes, red foxes, prairie dogs, and more than 40 species of birds.

Participants are housed in permanent tents and fed by the camp cook. *Earthwatch, 680 Mt. Auburn St., Box 403, Watertown, MA 02272-9924, tel. 617/926–8200 or 800/776–0188, fax 617/926–8532. June–Aug.: 21 days, $1,345.*

SOURCES

■**ORGANIZATIONS** At Boston University, the **Archaeological Institute of America** (675 Commonwealth Ave., Boston, MA 02215-1401, tel. 617/353–9361), also known as AIA, has served both the public and the scholarly community for more than 100 years. It encourages and supports archaeological research, informs the public about archaeology, and protects the world's cultural heritage. **State archaeologists** and **state historic preservation offices,** often under the jurisdiction of a department of cultural resources and historic preservation, are excellent sources of information.

■**PERIODICALS** *Archaeology,* published by the AIA (*see above*), is a richly illustrated magazine with a circulation of 150,000. Several publications list upcoming excavation projects: *Earthwatch* (680 Mt. Auburn St., Box 403, Watertown, MA 02272-9924, tel. 617/926–8200) is Earthwatch's bimonthly magazine and comes with membership. The free "Passport In Time Traveler" (U.S. Forest Service, Box 18364, Washington, DC 20036, tel. 202/293–0922), Passport in Time's newsletter, is published in spring and fall.

■**BOOKS** *The Guide to Academic Travel* contains extensive information about worldwide academic learning vacations sponsored by schools, colleges, museums, educational and cultural organizations, and travel companies. AIA's *Fieldwork Opportunities Bulletin* provides a comprehensive directory of education opportunities in the field for both the student and the amateur archaeologist.

■**ALSO SEE** For more information, see the Volunteer Research Vacations and Volunteer Vacations in Public and Community Service chapters.

Arts and Crafts Workshops

By Andrea Lehman and Irene Rawlings

aybe you want to make a quilt, build a log cabin, weave a rug? Do you harbor a hankering to bind a book or be a blacksmith? How about lapstraking a wooden sailboat or applying paper-thin mahogany veneer to a dining room table you've just made by hand? Or maybe you want to learn historic crafts such as adobe building or blacksmithing, perhaps from a craftsperson in period costume at a living history site or heritage center.

There are literally hundreds of arts and crafts workshops nationwide that offer every specialty imaginable—from woodworking and bookbinding to fiber art and faux finishes, from basketmaking and ceramics to glass-blowing and haute couture. Some are at large crafts centers that attract students interested in a broad range of disciplines; other workshops are offered by individual craftspeople in their specialty. Some advertise extensively in glossy magazines. Others rely on simple word of mouth advertising. Many courses, like most of those described here, last between five and seven days. However, some courses last as long as a month, and weekend programs are widely available. (If that's all the time you have to spend, just contact any of the schools we describe.)

The cost varies widely as well, depending on what's included. A five-day workshop usually costs between $100 and $500 for tuition only; materials may or may not entail an additional fee (and that fee, when levied, varies wildly depending on whether it's buying you raffia to make a basket or 14-karat gold to use in a ring). Housing costs an extra $100 to $400, depending on the quarters. Some schools offer a complete package that includes tuition as well as room and board; these range from $425 to under $1,000 for five days, $465 to $1,350 for seven, and may or may not include materials. The weekend programs cost proportionately less. Prices for both housing alone and for complete packages usually cover only a double room; if you're set on having quarters to yourself (at one of the few programs that does make singles available), you'll usually pay more.

Your companions are an equally mixed bag, an interesting melange of thirtysomething professional singles, and baby boomers traveling with their teenaged children, along with a smattering of those vigorous seniors who, when introducing themselves, always manage to sneak in their age, e.g., "I'm Larry Kinkle—sixty-eight years young." Generally, there are more women than men—except in the workshops that concentrate on hefty subjects like boat building and log home construction.

Days start early at most crafts workshops; lectures, critiques, and studio time fills the rest of the day. In the course of the program, you not only acquire a whole new vocabulary and information about a range of techniques in the field covered by the workshop—you usually complete at least one piece. The souvenirs you bring home from an arts and crafts vacation won't sit around gathering dust. Long after you've unpacked your bags, washed your socks and gone back to the nine-to-five, you'll have precious handmade memories of your week in the woods, beside the ocean or perched high in the mountains. Every time you toss a salad in that hand-turned walnut bowl, wear that hand-knitted sweater or sleep under that colorful patchwork quilt, you'll remember. And the memory will bring you pleasure.

One caution. Since arts and crafts schools are often run by artistic, independent, free-spirited and, sometimes, eccentric people, it's best to verify schedules. In other words, make certain the master glassblower with whom you've always dreamed of studying hasn't dashed off to Venice to participate in an international competition or to Budapest to accept a design award. This seldom happens, but it doesn't hurt to check.

CHOOSING THE RIGHT WORKSHOP

For this chapter, we reviewed a large number of craft schools and determined our favorite based on quality, reliability and that intangible thing called "just plain fun."

When choosing a school, first decide what you want to learn and what level of skill you want to attain in the time your vacation allows. Then decide how far you want to travel. Some crafts are very regional. For example, if you want to learn how to carve a santo, weave a huerga or embroider a colcha, you'd best head for New Mexico. You can only learn how to carve totem poles in the Pacific Northwest or Alaska. Wyoming is the best place to learn how to make that rugged cowboy furniture that's so popular. For Adirondack chairs, it's upstate New York.

Courses in some crafts, like glassblowing or ceramics, are conducted all over the country and, indeed, all over the world. In these cases, you need to be more specific about your needs. Do you want to create art glass—the kind you see in museums or galleries—or are you more interested in making a dramatic statement with your dinnerware? Your choice of school and instructor necessarily will depend on what you want out of the class.

Once you've narrowed your search for a program, be sure to ask a few questions to help you compare similar programs and find the one that's right for you.

Is it a large school with many topics or a single-subject program? Some craft schools teach a wide variety of subjects, others just a single subject. The biggest advantage of the larger schools is the exciting flow of ideas between instructors and students and among students of different disciplines that naturally seems to occur at the dinner table or by the campfire in the evenings. The primary advantage of the smaller, single-subject schools is the personal and undivided attention of the instructor.

How big are the classes? Do you want individual instruction or the camaraderie of working with others in a classroom situation? Some craft centers accept as few as one or two students, others are geared more to classes of twenty or more.

What's the cost and what's included? There is frequently one cost for tuition and a separate fee for accommodations—we give them both where lodging is on-site and tuition only when that's not the case. When complete packages are available, we give that fee instead; unless otherwise noted, they include tuition, room, and board. In both instances, materials may or may not be included; be sure to inquire about any additional fee, because it can be hefty if your chosen course entails work with pricey substances. Tools are usually included, but not always, so it's a good idea to ask about that, too. When on-premises accommodations are not part of the vacation package, all of the schools are glad to recommend attractive, reasonably priced places to stay that are nearby, usually within walking distance.

What are the accommodations like? You might stay in a B&B, a dorm in a cabin or lodge, or even a great 19th-century resort; lodging styles range from no-frills or rustic to quaint to downright posh. Campsites are often available.

What is the food like? In general the cuisine is pretty basic; but there are exceptions. Vegetarian fare may predominate. In other situations you have the option of lodging in a place with a small kitchenette, so that you can cook what you want to eat.

Is this a school or camp for singles or are families welcome? Are other activities available nearby for your family if they are not as enchanted as you are by, let's say, buildng the perfect Adirondack chair.

How long has the workshop been in business? New schools can be good, but longevity is a sign that students over the years have given it a thumbs-up. In addition, a program that has been around for a while will have worked out the kinks and handled any challenges that you're apt to throw its way.

Do you have references from past guests? Willingness to provide names is another green light. Follow up with a telephone call by all means; speaking with someone who has actually been there may help you resolve any questions you may have when you're ready to decide between two equally appealing programs.

Is laundry service available? The answer to this question, while not a deciding factor in where you go, will probably help you determine what to pack.

How far in advance do I need to book? Plan as far ahead as you can so that you get the dates, course, housing, and instructors you want. This is especially true when the course you have your heart set on taking is taught by a visiting instructor who puts in limited appearance on the crafts-workshop circuit.

FAVORITE WORKSHOPS

THE NORTHEAST

MAINE Haystack Mountain School of Crafts. Haystack Mountain fits in perfectly on Deer Isle, long regarded as an artists' colony by Downeasters and lobstermen

from the mainland. The campus, designed by Edward Larrabee Barnes and built in 1962, was modeled on the weathered gray-shingled buildings typical of the Maine coast. A short drive across the high bridge over Eggemoggin Reach brings you to the campus, which has panoramic views of Blue Hill Bay and the islands beyond.

The Haystack community is made up of approximately 80 participants, comprised of staff, students, and an internationally respected faculty. Classes in clay, wood, glass, quilts, fiber, baskets, metals, jewelry making, and book arts are open to craftworkers at all levels from beginning to advanced. The one-, two-, and three-week classes, which run from early June until the beginning of September, are conducted by artists who are well-established, award-winning professionals. Each summer it's a different group: You might find ceramic sculptor Anne Currier, whose work is in the permanent collection of the American Craft Museum, or wood-designer Frank E. Cummings III, featured in *National Geographic*'s *Craftsmen in America*. Classes have a maximum of 20 students, with one instructor.

Days start early with a hearty breakfast served cafeteria-style in the airy, wood-beamed dining room. Classes last until noon, when there's a casual lunch. Afternoons are divided between lectures, classes, critiques, and hands-on studio time. Classes are scheduled Monday through Friday; studios are open around the clock daily. Shorter workshops are available in the spring and in the colorful fall foliage season.

In the area, you can stroll the rock coastline, pick wild blueberries, drive to Blue Hill (where E.B. White lived after retiring from *The New Yorker*), explore the picturesque villages on the island, or, weather permitting, take a small boat to a neighbor island. Some local lobstermen will take you out to help pull their traps—of course that means waking up at 4 AM.

Accommodations vary from an open bunkhouse to a single room with bath. Bring warm clothing—Maine can be chilly at night—but if you do get cold, electric blankets are available (for a small fee) to warm you right up. *Haystack Mountain School of Crafts, Box 518, Deer Isle, ME 04627, tel. 207/348–2306, fax 207/348–2307. Topics: blacksmithing, book arts, ceramics/pottery, drawing, fiberwork, furniture making, glassblowing, printmaking, quilting, weaving, woodworking. June–Sept.: 7–21 days, tuition $275–$580, housing $155–$1,350.*

MAINE **The Woodenboat School.** Imagine pulling your oar through the water to carry yourself away from shore in a boat that you built yourself. Looking up to see the wind billowing the sail that you designed and personally sewed. Running your hand down the side of your carefully constructed canoe's perfectly bowed cedar rib. With its more than 85 boatbuilding and woodworking classes, the Woodenboat School can help you learn all you need to know to make these musings reality, whether you're a novice or a skilled woodworker and sailor. You can learn anything from basic boat design to sailmaking to marine carving; you can even work on your sailing techniques in sailing courses on both small and large crafts.

The school, in operation since 1980, occupies 64 acres on Penobscot Bay about five hours north of Boston and an hour's drive southeast of Bangor and Acadia National Park. Courses take place on the waterfront and in a converted 1916 brick barn known as the Shop, which houses three boatbuilding spaces stocked with power tools and building materials. Each year, about 600 to 700 people of all ages attend the school's one- and two-week courses which operate from June to October; in winter there are courses in California, Florida, and the Caribbean.

Most students stay on the school's grounds, either in one of two old New England inns with simple double rooms and shared baths or at a campground nearby—it's basic, with toilet and shower facilities, but no electrical outlets or tent platforms. Everyone eats together in the dining hall in one of the inns. The school can also provide a list of local B&Bs and house rentals. *The Woodenboat School, Box 78, Naskeag Rd., Brooklin, ME 04616, tel. 207/359–4651, fax 207/359–8920. Topics: boatbuilding, sailmaking, seamanship, woodworking. June–Oct.: 7–14 days, tuition $420–$745, housing $265 per week, campsites $65 per week (campers can take meals for $100).*

MASSACHUSETTS **Heartwood Homebuilding School.** Heartwood, established in 1978 to teach the skills necessary to build an energy-efficient house, offers five-day and three-week workshops for skilled builders as well as people with no previous construction experience. Your day begins with lectures and discussion in the design studio. After lunch, the class rides off to a construction site for some hands-on experience. Some of the students have had experience, some have never held a hammer, but all attend with a serious purpose in mind—they want help in designing and building their dream home. A list of tools is provided when you register, but all tools are available at the Heartwood Tool Store. The program equips you to act as your own contractor; knowing the basics helps you speak a common language with the plumbers and carpenters you hire.

Typical five-day workshops, most offered twice each summer, include timber framing, cabinetmaking, renovation, carpentry for women, drywall, and masonry. The four-member resident faculty are all licensed building contractors and architects with years of experience.

You're on your own for breakfast and dinner, and you make your own arrangements for accommodations at the hotels, bed-and-breakfasts, and campgrounds in the area, which offer special rates for people in the program.

Once you've graduated and started building your dream home, Heartwood offers a free design consultation service. You can call them to discuss and solve any problems you encounter during construction. It's almost as if you never left. *Heartwood Homebuilding School, Johnson Hill Rd., Washington,*

MA 01235, tel. 413/623-6677. Topics: carpentry, furniture making, housebuilding, masonry. May–Sept.: five days, tuition $425. Price includes lunch.

MASSACHUSETTS **Horizons: The New England Craft Program.** You probably won't find a better student-to-teacher ratio at any of the five colleges that surround Horizons, among them Smith and Amherst. Founded in 1983 by Jane Sinauer, whose large porcelain pieces have been exhibited in museums and galleries around the world, each class is limited to three students per instructor, and there are no more than 12 students and four instructors per class. The small class size offers the opportunity to explore new techniques through instruction and practice. Intensive three-, four-, or six-day studios, as courses are called, are offered once a month from April through the beginning of October; they are open to students of all levels and conducted by prominent artists and craftspeople, assisted by graduate students. Some students work late into the night given that the workshops are always open.

The intensives take an unusual approach to crafts by covering unique topics such as Japanese & African Dye Techniques, Painting and Illustrating on Fabric; Tableware, Function and Decoration: Terracotta and Majolica; and Out of the Woods: Furniture and Beyond. There's even an animation course.

Horizons is on a 50-acre farm surrounded by pastures and apple orchards in the foothills of the Berkshire Mountains. The studios occupy a complex of 12 buildings; the farmhouse was built in 1780 and is the oldest house in the valley, while the students' quarters, designed by a local architect just a few years ago, are starkly modern with high-ceiling, simple pine and white rooms, and large communal bathrooms.

At meals, everyone socializes and discusses their projects over homebaked breads, fresh vegetables, and other delicious fare. The handmade book arts intensive should come in handy. *Horizons, 108 N. Main St., Sunderland, MA 01375, tel. 413/665-0300, fax*

413/665–4141. Topics: animation, book arts, ceramics, glassblowing, photography, sculpture, surface design. Late Apr.–late Oct.: 3–6 days, complete package $300–$590.

NEW YORK **Sagamore Historic Adirondack Great Camp.** The Adirondacks have long been the playground of the discreetly rich. There was a time in the late 19th century when roughing it for the fortunate few simply meant traveling from a sumptuous Fifth Avenue setting to an equally sumptuous bucolic setting—one of the great timbered lodges called the Adirondack Great Camps. Sagamore, dating from this Gilded Age, sits among the birches and fir trees beside Sagamore Lake and is maintained much as it was at the turn of the century—no television, no locks on the doors, bathrooms in the halls, and few phones. Guest rooms, most of them doubles with twin beds, have many of the original turn-of-the-century furnishings.

Meals are served buffet-style and eaten family-style at large tables in a dining room overlooking the lake. A typical dinner tends to be chicken, turkey, or fish; lunch is soup, salad, and sandwich; breakfast always features a hot entrée. On clear evenings, dinners are often served on picnic tables at the lake's edge. The Preservation League of New York does not allow Sagamore to have a liquor license, so you should bring your own wine; smoking is too much of a fire hazard to these old wood structures to be permitted in any of the buildings.

Sagamore offers year-round classes for all ages in traditional Adirondack crafts, such as woodcarving (e.g., timber wolf, miniature loon, Adirondack St. Nick), ash-splint basketry, rustic furniture, Adirondack guide boats, birch bark baskets, handmade twig paper, and so on. There are also classes in storytelling (the "tall tales" made famous by Natty Bumppo around the campfire), exploration of other historic camps (including J.P. Morgan's Camp Uncas), and a unique grandparents' and grandchildren's summer camp (traditional crafts, canoeing, storytelling). Several weekends are also reserved for

Elderhostel participants. Some classes are two days, others last five or seven days, and, unlike most programs, materials *are* included in the cost.

When you're not in a class or workshop, you can hike (or, in winter, cross-country ski) on the numerous well-marked trails through the surrounding State Forest Preserve or bowl on the newly refinished, semi-outdoor bowling alley that dates from 1914. A word about the weather: Spring comes late to the Adirondacks and winter early, so you might want to bring something warm and weatherproof to zip into. *Sagamore, Box 146, Raquette Lake, NY 13436-0146, tel. 315/354–5311, fax 315/354–5851. Year-round: 2–5 days, complete package $235–$500. Price includes materials.*

NEW YORK **Thousand Islands Craft School and Textile Museum.** From mid-March to December of each year, you have the choice of nearly 50 workshops in the traditional arts and crafts at this school in Clayton, New York, on the shores of the St. Lawrence and just 7 miles from the International Bridge to Canada. The school, housed in a large 19th-century Victorian home, specializes in crafts such as fiber arts, basketry, and quilting, but also offers classes in early American decorative arts, jewelry, folk art, and bird-decoy carving. A popular class is theorem painting, which teaches you the techniques of painting on unlikely surfaces such as pillows, plates, and pitchers.

The school encourages a hands-on approach. You and your class of no more than 12 students work from 9 to 5, and the instructor, who might demonstrate a technique in the morning, spends the day helping and advising you as you work on your own project. Lunch is scheduled for 1, but enthusiasm for a braided quilt or a bird decoy often means that you'll work right through until the end of the day. Some workshops, such as the songbird carving class, require some intensive research; in this case, you research a bird of your choice to determine the correct body shape, pose, and feather detail. At the end of the workshop you'll have learned feather burning, acrylic painting, and how to use power carving tools with accuracy.

When you're not working, you can visit the school's textile museum, which specializes in 20th-century North American handwoven fabrics, or explore Clayton's Antique Boat Museum, Opera House, and the Thousand Islands Museum, for this was the home of Mrs. Sophie La Londe, inventor of the world-famous dressing.

The school does not provide accommodations, but a list of options, including lodging in a Victorian home in town, is provided. The only dining facilities are a small kitchen with a microwave, a coffee maker, and a sink. There are, however, plenty of restaurants, burger joints, and diners in town, and the school has a picnic area should you feel like packing a lunch. An arts and crafts program for children ages 8–13 is held every summer and includes a Children's Craft Day that concentrates on pottery, weaving, theater, and puppets. *Thousand Islands Craft School, 314 John St., Clayton, NY 13624, tel. 315/686–4123. Topics: basketry, fiber arts, folk art, jewelry, painting, quilting, weaving, and woodcarving. Mar.–Dec.: 4–10 days, tuition $135–$275. Price does not include some equipment.*

VERMONT **Camp Terra Cotta.** Sculptor Steffi Friedman has been teaching sculpting classes in her studio in Westport, Connecticut, for over 20 years. For one week each August, she picks up shop and moves to a quaint country inn in Vermont ski country. The Village Inn in Landgrove, east of Manchester and close by the Bromley and Stratton ski areas, is the perfect backdrop for the classes, held outdoors (there's a large indoor space available if it rains). Only 15 students can take the August course, which allows Friedman to individualize the eight-hour-a-day instruction. You bring your own materials and sculpt in either stone, terracotta, wax, or adobe.

You share cozy, atttractive rooms in the inn, originally built as a farmstead in the early

1800s. When the program first started 10 years ago, students pitched in and cooked the meals, but now you get to enjoy the cooking of the Snyder family at meals taken in the inn's dining room. The food includes blueberry pancakes for breakfast and delicious home-baked breads, rolls, cakes, and pies. The inn's attractively landscaped grounds have two tennis courts, a swimming pool, and a stocked fishing pond to fill the moments when you're not sculpting. *9 Yankee Hill Rd., Wesport, CT 06880, tel. 203/227–9650. Topics: sculpture. Aug.: 7 days, complete package $550.*

VERMONT **The Carving Studio & Sculpture Center.** In a 400-acre stone yard consisting of nine nonworking quarries 6 miles west of Rutland, the center, founded by Bernadette D'Amore in 1986, is housed in what was once the company store where workers exchanged scrip for food, clothing, and other necessities. Modeled after similar schools in Carrara, Italy's marble center, the Carving Studio provides space and instruction for beginners as well as experienced sculptors, with two-day to three-week programs that include figure carving, bronze casting, and wood carving and laminating, all of which run from April to November.

Classes kick off on Monday at 9 with the first of five daily half-hour demonstrations by the instructors. Here you learn about the range of tools, their uses, and the various techniques of sculpting marble including traditional hand stonework and the latest in abrasive technology as well as how to avoid flying chips. Tools are supplied, but students supply their own media; you can pick out your own piece of marble for purchase right at the site. Prices vary depending on the size and quality of the stone. The instructor to student ratio is three to five, so there's plenty of individual instruction. Classes run until 5, with a break for lunch at 12. You have the choice of three restaurants a stone's throw from the studio—a pizzeria, a greasy spoon-style diner, and a restaurant that serves soups and salads—or you can make your own lunch in the studio kitchen.

For a modest fee, students can have dinner at the studio; a typical menu might include vegetarian lasagna followed by nectarine cobbler and a Caesar salad, all prepared by the center's cook. After dinner, you have the option of sitting in on a slide show or a discussion by instructors, visiting artists, or even the students themselves, who are encouraged to show and discuss their own work. The studios are open until 2 AM, should your creative juices continue flowing through the evening, and they open every morning at 8 AM.

Lodging is not included in the price, but the center provides a housing list of over 200 area bed-and-breakfasts, inns, and hotels in the surrounding area when you first apply. *The Carving Studio and Sculpture Center, Box 495, Rutland, VT 05777, tel. 802/438–2097. May–Oct.: 5 days, tuition $350.*

VERMONT **Fletcher Farm School.** In 1947, the descendants of Revolutionary War soldier Jesse Fletcher invited the Society of Vermont Craftsmen to establish an arts and crafts school on this secluded 600-acre farm on land first settled by Fletcher in 1793. The school offers classes in July and August—many of the 56 faculty members hold teaching jobs at nearby colleges—that cover a wide variety of fine, decorative, and folk art workshops for adults of all ages and skill levels. There are also numerous classes organized especially for children.

With more than 70 workshops to choose from, you're sure to find something that sparks your interest. If you're interested in decorative arts, classes are offered in theorem painting, primitive portraiture, Ukrainian egg decorating, Norwegian rosemaling, wood graining, and marbelizing. Needlework aficionados will delight in subjects like bobbin lace, quilting, needlepoint, and knitting. Other craft classes include rug hooking, dollmaking, bandboxes, paper marbling, book arts, basketmaking, and even lampshade construction.

Three-, five-, and seven-day workshops begin with an evening buffet. These casual suppers allow you to mingle with the instructors, get acquainted, and discuss the upcoming week's activities. An orientation acquaints you with the physical layout of the school so that you can take full advantage of its many acres of natural woodlands, criss-crossed by miles of pine-needle-carpeted hiking trails. The Green Mountain National Forest is less than a 10-minute drive and the nearby villages of Proctorville and Ludlow have wonderful historic houses—Ludlow's landmark-designated historical museum is well worth a visit.

The two dormitories, known as the Roost and the Nest, give you a choice of single or double rooms (with twin beds), all of which share bathrooms. Breakfast, lunch, and an afternoon snack are included in the rates, but dinners are used as a time to explore the variety of Ludlow's restaurants.

The 200-year-old barn vibrates with class-room activity. A typical day begins with an early breakfast, followed by hands-on work-shops from 9 to 5. During the lunch breaks, you can take a picnic into the woods or stop in at the charming crafts shop to admire or buy the handcrafts made by instructors and other members of the Society of Vermont Craftsmen. In the shop, you might find a flo-ral hooked rug, a log-cabin quilt, or numer-ous other objects that, after a week at the Fletcher Farm School, could have your signature one day. *Fletcher Farm School, RR1, Box 1041, Ludlow, VT 05149, tel. 802/228–8770. Topics: bobbin lace, book-binding, braiding, calligraphy, doll-making, glasswork, painting, paper cutting, photog-raphy, rug-making, stenciling, theorem, weaving, woodcarving. Late Jun.–late Aug.: 2–5 days, complete package $140–$425.*

VERMONT **Yestermorrow.** Planning to restore an old house? Gathering stamina to design and build one from scratch? If either is true, this is a great place to start. Yester-morrow, founded by John Connell, a licensed architect, is one of the only schools that integrates home design with building skills. Here, the way in which you want to live takes an integral role in what course will be right for you. Students of all levels,

from ground zero on up (so to speak), range from 18 to 80 years old—70% of whom are men—and come here to help solidify not just how they're going to build their house, but the reasons why they want it that way. The faculty comprises licensed architects, registered builders, designers, and wood-workers, many with graduate degrees, all of them interested in helping your dream house come true.

The curriculum offered is divided into two general categories: layperson and profes-sional; although the nonprofessional is encouraged to cross the line into more advanced work and the professional to pick up a new skill. Classes are intimate, with five to 10 people per course. The one- and two-week courses offer a remarkable array of subjects covering almost every aspect of design and building: interior design, non-toxic construction, cabinetry, electrical wiring, power and hand tools, architectural crafts, and historic restoration, to name a few. At the end of some of the courses, you and four other students design and com-plete a group project.

If you choose a course in the Layperson's Curriculum, you stay at the White Horse Inn in Fayston, about 8 miles from the school. The inn provides a substantial breakfast, a bag lunch to take to school with you, and dinner. Students in the Professional Cur-riculum stay at condominiums in Warren and prepare their own meals.

The school is housed in a three-story converted barn in central Vermont's Mad River Valley, an area that's peppered with typical New England small towns—with the church, the inn, a few imposing houses, and courthouse squaring off across the village green. In an area well-known for its skiing—Mad River Glen, Sugarbush, Stowe—there are also hiking, swimming, bicycling, and horseback riding possibilities in the area. *Yestermorrow Inc., Box 76A, Warren, VT 05674, tel. 802/496–5545. Topics: architec-tural crafts, cabinetry, ceramics, drafting, electrical wiring, faux marbling, furniture design, landscaping, power & hand tools,* *woodwork. Year-round: 7 days, complete package $1,030.*

THE MID-ATLANTIC

NEW JERSEY **Peters Valley Craft Center.** In the Delaware Water Gap in northeast New Jersey and bordering the Delaware River, the Peters Valley Craft Center, surrounded by waterfalls, ponds, and well-maintained hiking trails (including a segment of the Appalachian Trail), offers 10 to 15 workshops over five to 12 days in a wide variety of subjects. Classes include house hardware, forged furniture, weaving, hand papermaking, black ash tatting basketry, cedar canoe building, furniture restoration, and painted furniture design. Ceramic classes also run, ranging from functional pots to architectural ceramics, from contemporary ceramic jewelry to the traditional art of once-fired salt glaze.

One accomplished professional craftsperson in each discipline is selected for a year-round residency position to manage a studio, plan programs, and earn a living at their craft. Two additional instructors in each discipline are hired each summer, making for such a varied choice of subjects. Most programs are open to all levels, but some are specifically designed for beginning, intermediate, or advanced students.

The center is spread over several miles, and some studios are on the edge of the property, so carpools are organized between students and the center to facilitate the movement of participants who did not bring their own transportation. Classes run from 9 to 5 every day. Following a demonstration of a new skill by the instructor, you begin work on your project, and throughout the day the instructor moves from student to student answering questions and offering advice on technique. The courses are largely run in a classroom setting, but as the class never exceeds 10 students, personal attention and a spirit of familiarity make it more of a workshop than a class.

Accommodations for a maximum of 20 students, based on double occupancy, are available in one of the center's farmhouses, some of which are on the Historical Register. Other options, including B&Bs, inns, hotels, motels, hostels, and even campgrounds are on an alternative housing list provided by the center, which will organize external accommodations for students when they register. If you do not have your own transportation and wish to avoid carpooling, you are advised to organize a room at the center; most of the external lodging options are between 7 and 13 miles from the center. Meals are served in a communal dining hall; if you are staying at the center all meals are included in the accommodations price; otherwise, you can buy a meal plan for about $20 a day.

There's also an 11-day ceramics workshop in which your work is fired in an anagama (wood-fueled) kiln. The students live together, share cooking facilities, and work together for six days making pots for a four-day firing. Children's and parent-child workshops are very popular. Topics include ceramics, jewelry, and silkscreen on fabric (usually T-shirts). *Peters Valley Craft Center, Layton, NJ 07851, tel. 201/948–5200, fax 201/948–0011. Topics: blacksmithing, ceramics, fine metals, photography, textiles, and woodworking. May–Aug.: 5–12 days, tuition $275–$400, housing $205–$560.*

PENNSYLVANIA **Sawmill Center for the Arts.** Founded in 1975, this rural arts center is located in the middle of the 6,000-acre Cook Forest State Park. From May to October, more than 130 workshops are offered, covering a wide variety of crafts from calligraphy to teddy bear making.

Most workshops meet from 9 to 4 daily with a generous lunch break and are open to all levels of experience. Enrollment is usually limited to 12 students per instructor. Woodworking is popular with students, and some typical workshops might include: Woodcarving in the Round; Realistic Bird Carving; and Advanced Power Woodcarving, a class in which students carve a miniature carousel horse.

The center has no accommodations or dining facilities, but due to its location in the state park, there are an abundance of B&Bs, inns, hotels, motels, and campgrounds in the vicinity. A directory of housing options is available upon request. For week-long classes, you have the option of ordering specially catered meals daily; menus are posted every morning in the workshop.

Bordered by the Clarion River, the park has 30 miles of hiking trails and a virgin forest that's a Registered National Natural Landmark. The center also sponsors the Nuthole Children's Craft Program, Elderhostel weeks, and a variety of other activities, including crafts markets and live theater performances at the Verna Leith Sawmill Theater. *Sawmill Center for the Arts, Box 180, Cooksburg, PA 16217, tel. 814/927–6655 or 814/744–9670. Topics: basketry, block printing, calligraphy, origami, picture framing, quilting, rug braiding, spinning, teddy bear making, and woodcarving. Late May–late Oct.: 5 days, tuition $180–$250.*

■PENNSYLVANIA■ Touchstone Center for Crafts. This 63-acre mountain retreat operated by the Pioneer Crafts Council, 10 miles east of Uniontown and 60 miles southeast of Pittsburgh, offers more than 70 intensive (weekend and five-day) workshops from June to September for all levels, from preschoolers on up. A wide choice of regional, national, and international crafts are emphasized: You have a choice of classes encompassing anything from how to forge a Damascus steel knife to making Japanese *momigami* paper for bookbinding.

A typical day begins with a hearty breakfast, followed by classes from 9 to 4 with a 1½-hour break for lunch that allows plenty of time for exploring the woodland trails on Touchstone's grounds. The workshops combine lectures, demonstrations, and hands-on experience. You work on and complete a project that you can take home after the session.

Accommodations are in rustic cabins or in stream-side campsites on the grounds. Neither have showers or bath, so if you need a little more in the way of creature comforts, there are several affordable hotels nearby. Many of these offer discounts to Touchstone students; a list is available. A variety of meal plans, served cafeteria-style in a brand-new dining hall, are available; these can be bought as a weekly package or on a meal-to-meal basis. You can expect a menu that might include roasted chicken, broiled fish, and hamburgers for the kids. Cooking is forbidden in the campsite, so the meal plan remains one of your few options. After dinner on Thursday evenings, there's always a musical or theatrical performance by guest artists.

Nearby attractions include Frank Lloyd Wright's masterpiece "Fallingwater," Fort Necessity National Battlefield (a French and Indian War-era fortification), several state forest preserves with excellent hiking trails, and local glass factories that host tours. Special prices for senior citizens and family rates are available. *Pioneer Crafts Council, Touchstone Center for Crafts, Box 2141, Uniontown, PA 15401, tel. 412/329–1370. Topics: basketry, blacksmithing, ceramics, drawing, fiber arts, metalwork, painting, and woodworking. June–Sept.: 5–7 days, tuition $150–$180, housing $50–$120. Price does not include meals.*

■WEST VIRGINIA■ The Basketry School. Connie and Tom McColley make functional and art baskets from the abundance of natural basketry materials surrounding the school, including white oak, hickory, and honeysuckle. Week-long and two-week classes are taught in the couple's spacious home and studio in the Appalachian foothills 52 miles east of Charleston.

Classes are run in a large, well-lighted studio with plenty of space for you to work in. A friendly, concentrated atmosphere is created by the relatively small class size of 10 students. During the course of the week, you will learn everything about white oak basketry—how to select and gather the right tree; then how to trim it, bark it, split it, shave, and shape it. Along the way, you'll also learn the history of traditional and contemporary basketry through discussions, demonstrations and slide presentations.

Two- and three-person cabins, each with bath, are available or the meadow around the school can be used for tent camping. Electricity, water and shower facilities are available for campers. The school also has a dining hall, which serves three meals a day. *The Basketry School, Rte. 3, Box 325, Chloe, WV 25235, tel. 304/655–7429. Topics: basketry. May–July: 5 days, tuition $250, housing $200–$275.*

WEST VIRGINIA **West Virginia Augusta Heritage Center.** Associated with Davis & Elkins College, this center is on 170 wooded acres at the edge of the Monongahela National Forest in the mountains of central West Virginia. Summer week-long workshops offer intensive classes in the folk arts, including in-depth "theme week" classes that focus on a specific cultural theme like woodcarving, music, or dance. Most workshops are a week long and open to all levels, but a few are geared to more advanced levels. Three of the summer sessions include separate workshops on folk arts for kids ages 8–13. A one-week workshop features mountain games, songs, square dancing, storytelling, and crafts. There are also several classes on musical instrument construction, open to students familiar with woodworking tools. These classes complete a guitar, banjo, or an Appalachian dulcimer.

Daily schedules vary from class to class; most meet mornings and afternoons for four to six hours daily and work in intensive small group sessions with 15 students and one instructor. Some music classes, including banjo, contra dance, piano, and dulcimer classes, meet for fewer hours, allowing time for practice or individual instruction.

Housing for Augusta students is available in the Davis & Elkins College residence halls. There are semiprivate rooms, common bathrooms, furnished lounges, and laundry rooms. Housing is co-ed, with the bathroom on each floor designated either male or female. Wholesome meals are served cafeteria-style in the dining hall; they are an opportunity for the students and master folk artists to mingle informally.

The surrounding countryside offers whitewater rafting, canoeing, caving, rock climbing, and hiking. The campus has recreational facilities that include tennis courts, swimming pool, fitness trail, and Nautilus center. *Augusta Heritage Center, David & Elkins College, Elkins, WV 26241–3996, tel. 304/636–1903, fax 304/636–8624. Topics: basketry, blacksmithing, broom making, bobbin lacemaking, chip carving, fiddle & bow repair, log home construction, pottery, quilting, stained glass, treenware (handmade functional wooden utensils), stonemasonry, weaving. July–mid-Aug.: 5 days, tuition $255–$490, housing $190.*

THE SOUTH

FLORIDA **Priscilla's Studio by the Sea.** The founder of the National Society of Tole and Decorative Painters, Priscilla Hauser is part teacher, part performer, and all business. In addition to putting out countless books and videos, she teaches her painting method in intensive 5½-day seminars at her Studio by the Sea in Panama City, right on the Gulf of Mexico in the Florida panhandle. The range of seminars, offered throughout the year, begins with Basic I, which covers the fundamentals of her techniques. You paint a variety of fruits, flowers, and leaves in acrylics or oils on surfaces such as wood and metal, glass and fabric. More advanced seminars include faux finishes, painting on lace, Christmas items from poinsettias to gingerbread people, and roses, Priscilla's specialty.

Seminars usually begin with orientation on Sunday from 4 to 9 PM. On weekdays, the studio opens at 7:30 AM, so you can come in early to practice before class starts at 9. Coffee and a hot lunch (casserole, salad, and dessert, for example) are provided. Priscilla's instruction ends at 5 (4 on Friday, the last day), but her assistant stays on, so you can continue to practice or work on a project until 9, when the studio closes.

You may either bring your own supplies, such as brushes and paints, or purchase them at the studio. A fee is assessed for each seminar's set of project materials. You are responsible for your own lodging, though Priscilla sends recommendations of nearby inns, beach houses, and RV parks, some of which give discounts to her students. Classes, filled on a first-come, first-served basis, are limited to 20 students but are open to all levels and all ages. The ratio of women to men is about 10 to one. Workshops are also offered in Oklahoma, Georgia, California, and Canada. *Priscilla's Studio by the Sea, Box 521013, Tulsa, OK 74152–1013, tel. 918/743–6072, fax 918/743–5075. Topic: decorative painting. Year-round: 5½ days, tuition $325. Price includes lunch.*

GEORGIA **Callaway School of Needle Arts.** Since 1972, the annual Callaway School of Needle Arts has been held at Callaway Gardens, a 14,000-acre resort in the foothills of the Appalachians southwest of Atlanta. The school offers four-, two-, and one-day classes within a framework of two consecutive five-day sessions in January. Courses are primarily for the intermediate or advanced stitcher and are open to no more than one or two dozen. Just look through the catalogue and pick a project that interests you—perhaps an Oriental fan in Japanese embroidery, a drawn-thread sampler, or a butterfly made with traditional needlepoint stitches.

Though you are in class much of the day, generally 8:30 to 4:30, there's plenty to occupy your off hours. You can go to a home room to visit and share ideas with other participants, see the needlework exhibit, or attend merchandise night, held once each session. If you've had enough of tiny stitches, you can indulge in any of Callaway Gardens' many recreational activities: golf on three championship courses, tennis, biking, swimming, boating, fishing, or walking around its lush gardens and wildlife-filled woodlands and lakes. In fact, this is a great vacation getaway for the whole family; guest and golf packages are available specifically for the noncrafter.

Classrooms and accommodations are in the four-star, full-service Callaway Gardens Inn, and meals are buffet style in the hotel's Plantation Room. The comprehensive fee not only covers tuition, room (single or double occupancy), and board (including a reception, banquet, and coffee breaks), but also use of the fitness center and entrance to the gardens. A list of the basic equipment and supplies needed is sent to you ahead of time, so you can bring them from home or buy them at the school's boutique. A kit fee covers the materials used in class. *Callaway School of Needle Arts, Box 2000, Pine Mountain, GA 31822–2000, tel. 706/663–5060 or 800/763–3353, fax 706/663–5068. Topic: embroidery. Mid-Jan.: 5 days, complete package $717–$913.*

GEORGIA **Timber Framing in Southern Appalachia.** When you see a barn raising, such as the one in the movie *Witness,* what you're seeing is timber framing—the method used centuries ago to build houses and barns. Large timbers, used sparingly and placed symmetrically, are bound together by mortise and tenon joints and secured by wooden pegs to construct the frame. During the 20th century, the need for quick and economical housing production caused sturdy, but labor-intensive, timber-frame construction to fall out of favor; today, however, it's enjoying a bit of a resurgence, and people who want a more craftsmanlike approach to home building are rediscovering the skill.

Near the northeast Georgia town of Clayton, John Koenig, a second-generation timber framer, founded Upper Loft Designs. Since 1987, it has offered intensive, hands-on, product-oriented timber-framing workshops in addition to its home-building services, and previous students have ranged from building tradespeople and architects to people who have gone on to construct their own home or have one built for them.

Though courses range from the two-day Timberframe Design and Planning Seminar to the three-week Comprehensive Timberframe Training, the curriculum's core course is the six-day Introductory Workshop in Timberframing. You arrive on Sunday evening so you can start at 8 AM Monday. Typical days begin with an hour of discussion, followed by eight or more of hands-on work integrated with lectures, slides, and more discussion. A lunch period breaks the day. You can work as late as you like, and by week's end you may very well be toiling well into the night. On Saturday, you raise a completed frame. Class sizes run from 6 to 18, and though most participants are men, women are quite welcome. Spouses may watch or take part for no additional charge.

If you're willing to do some primitive camping (i.e., no showers), you're free to do so at the workshop site; otherwise, Koenig provides a list of local B&Bs and hotels that offer a discount to Upper Loft students. Snacks are provided, and there's generally a party at some point. For courses of six days or longer, you need to bring your own minimal tool kit, but otherwise all you need are a notebook and pencil, the willingness to expend some physical energy, and the desire to learn and build. *Upper Loft Design, Inc., Rte. 1, Box 2901, Lakemont, GA 30552, tel. 706/782–5246 or 800/242–7474 in the Southeast, fax 706/782–6840. Topic: home building. Year-round: 6 days, tuition $295; 3 weeks, tuition $775.*

NORTH CAROLINA Faux Finishing. Fe Fi Faux is the warehouselike shop of husband-and-wife faux finishers Kevin and Cheryl Rutan, but about once a month it serves as the setting for four-day workshops in their craft. During eight-hour days, you learn all about faux finishes, from base coat to finish coat. After an introduction, which covers glaze formulas and choosing background colors, you spend the rest of the first and second days learning marble and stone finishes. Day three is dedicated to wood grains. Kevin teaches these classes and provides demonstrations of some more difficult methods, such as strie, silk moiré, and linen look, while you practice basic techniques on high-gloss paper. On the fourth day, Kevin and Cheryl take you to a local home to put your newly acquired wall-glazing skills to the test. The group of 10 to 15 students works in two groups, applying a mottled, simulated suede finish and the cloudy, less-dense French brush.

The only thing you have to bring is clothes you don't mind getting dirty. Materials, handouts, and a box lunch with sandwich and salad are included. You are responsible for your accommodations, though many participants stay at two local hotels that offer special rates to Fe Fi Faux students. A camaraderie tends to develop, and chances are you and the rest of the group might spend some of your off hours together. Workshops have been attended by designers, housepainters, housewives, and retirees, from curious beginners to more advanced decorative painters who wish to improve their technique. *Fe Fi Faux, 337 S. Davie St., Greensboro, NC 27401, tel. 910/272–3289. Topic: decorative painting. Year-round: 4 days, tuition $400. Price includes lunch.*

NORTH CAROLINA John C. Campbell Folk School. Founded in 1925 to preserve the handicrafts and music of local mountain people, the folk school is tucked away on 365 acres in a scenic valley in the southwestern tip of the state. The campus consists of 42 historic buildings, some built in a romantic European stone-and-wood style, others more typical of Appalachian farmhouses. Instructors are nationally recognized folk artists, many of whom are second-generation craftspeople whose families have been associated with the school for years. Others have moved to the area and maintain their own studios nearby.

The list of workshops is voluminous. For example, there are 46 different basketry classes, which can teach you how to make baskets of native vine or white oak or a Shaker cat-head or traditional Cherokee basket. Similar variety is offered in fields from blacksmithing and book arts to weaving and woodworking, and there are even classes in broom making, felting, and kaleidoscopes as well as noncrafts courses in dance, folklore, gardening, music, and nature studies. Most of the workshops are a week long (from supper and orientation on Sunday to Saturday breakfast), but some span a weekend, a short week (ending at Friday lunch), or two weeks.

A typical day begins with Morningsong, an informal session of singing and discussions of local folklore and history. Then comes breakfast, followed by classes until lunch. Afternoon classes end at 4:30, when you can take part in an optional planned activity, such as a historical tour or a visit to a neighbor's home and workshop. Reflecting the regional cooking of southern Appalachia, the family-style dinner comes complete with vegetables fresh from the garden and memorable home-baked wheat bread. Afterward, you can continue to work on your project or, perhaps, visit a nearby planetarium, attend a concert of Appalachian music, or drive to the Cherokee reservation (35 miles away). White-water kayaking and rafting are also popular diversions.

You can stay in a dorm room that sleeps up to eight people or in a double room, both with shared baths; a limited number of doubles with private baths are available. There's also a small 12-site campground with bathroom facilities, but board isn't included for campers. Meals can be purchased separately, however. Instructors keep track of the materials you use during your workshop, and you are billed for them on the last day of class. Many folk school courses are also available through Elderhostel, so if you're over 60, you may be able to register through that organization at a substantial savings. *John C. Campbell Folk School, Rte. 1, Box 14A, Brasstown, NC 28902–9603, tel. 704/837–2775 or 800/365–5724, fax 704/837–8637. Topics: basketry, beadwork, blacksmithing, book and paper arts, broom making, calligraphy, caning, ceramics/pottery, design/printing, dollmaking, dyeing, embroidery, enameling, felting, furniture making, glasswork, jewelry, knitting and crocheting, lace, metalwork, painting, photography, quilting, rug making, spinning, weaving, wood carving, wood turning. Year-round: 5–6 days, tuition $190–$225, housing $165–$249; camping $8 per day. Camping price does not include meals.*

NORTH CAROLINA **Penland School of Crafts.** This artists' community, founded in 1929, is set on 450 wooded acres and nestled right up against the Blue Ridge Mountains of western North Carolina. Gifted visiting artists and resident professors offer classes for all levels of experience in all kinds of media: clay, fiber, glass, iron and other metals, paper, and wood. A sampling of recent courses includes Marriage of Hot & Cold (glassworking), User-Friendly Beads (traditional and contemporary beading techniques), and Books, Boxes, and Pockets (variations on bookbinding). Most summer classes run two weeks, though a one- and a 2½-week session are held as well; fall and spring workshops are eight weeks. Because of the energy demands, glasswork classes are more expensive than the others.

The intensive program emphasizes hands-on learning, so most of your day is spent in the well-equipped studios in classes of no more than 11. (Instructors may request that you bring certain items from home, such as old photos or collage materials, but most supplies are covered by a studio fee.) Should the muse strike, you can continue work into the evening, as studios are open and in use 24 hours a day. Or you can attend slide shows or dances, visit nearby studios, or take a walk in the beautiful countryside. An occasional volleyball game or, on a hot day, a refreshing dip in the North Toe River are just the ticket. Asheville, world-renowned for its late 19th-century megamansion Biltmore House, is only a few miles away along the scenic Blue Ridge Parkway.

On-campus housing—dorms, semiprivate rooms, and private rooms with bath—is modest and rustic, but this only adds to Penland's considerable charm. The dining room buffet features a wide variety of good food, including numerous vegetarian dishes, and the leisurely meals are a springboard to conversations that extend the learning experience. You can also choose to live and eat off campus at any of a number of B&Bs and hotels. *Penland School of Crafts, Penland, NC 28765–0037, tel. 704/765–2359, fax 704/765–7389. Topics: book and paper arts, ceramics, drawing, fiber arts, glasswork, metalwork, photography, printmaking, woodworking. Late July–early Sept.: 7–18 days, tuition $240–$740, housing $200–$1,120.*

NORTH CAROLINA **Woodworking in the Appalachians.** On Drew and Louise Langsner's secluded mountain farmstead, not far from the Appalachian Trail and the Tennessee border, the expert craftspeople of Country Workshops have been teaching traditional woodworking with hand tools since 1978. Much of the work is done with a wood lathe, carving knives, drawknives, hewing axes, and hollowing adzes. Six-day summer workshops focus on such varying techniques as spindle turning and 17th-century joinery and on such varying projects as end tables and boats. Summer always brings one class each in ladderback and Windsor chair making as well as more exotic courses—perhaps Japanese woodworking, carved Swedish woodenware, or Swiss cooperage, practically a lost art. Workshop director Drew Langsner apprenticed to a master cooper (barrel maker) in Switzerland.

Arrive the afternoon before your workshop; classes run from 9 to 6 each day, though they often end earlier on the last day. In most workshops, several evenings are devoted to slide shows and lecture-discussions. Bring work clothes and basic tools; specialized tools are provided, and an extra fee covers materials used. You can camp on the farm for free or stay in the dorm or guest cabin at an additional cost. (Bedding is provided in the guest cabin but not the dorm.) Louise loves to garden and cook, so while you help with dishes and table setup, she incorporates freshly harvested fruits and vegetables into three delicious meals daily. You can even arrange to stay for dinner after

your workshop is over or through breakfast the following morning. Spouses and other guests are welcome for an extra charge.

Summer classes are composed of 8 to 12 students, primarily men ages 25 to 70. All skill levels can be accommodated. Together you are practically sequestered, with nowhere nearby to go and nothing to see save the inspiring mountain views. Besides, after all that hewing and chopping, you don't have much energy for sightseeing.

In the winter, Drew offers five-day tutorials for two people. The subject matter is similar to that of summer workshops but is more customized. The comprehensive fee includes heated lodging and meals at the family table. *Country Workshops, 90 Mill Creek Rd., Marshall, NC 28753–9321, tel. 704/656–2280. Topics: boat building, furniture making, wood carving, wood turning. Jan.–Apr.: 5 days, complete package $575. June–Sept.: 6 days, tuition $410, housing $10–$16.50 per night, camping free.*

TENNESSEE **Appalachian Center for Crafts.** Five-day workshops in five areas—clay, fibers, glass, metals, and wood—are held at this Middle Tennessee crafts center, which is part of Tennessee Tech. The variety within those areas is enormous. Clay includes hand building, wheel throwing, and raku; fiber courses range from papermaking and bookbinding to painting on silk. Glass comprises both hot (glassblowing and casting) and cold (stained glass and kaleidoscopes), and metal classes might find you in a blacksmith's forge or a jewelry studio. Within wood are furniture making and carving, but the emphasis is on wood turning.

Though weekend classes are available all year, the more in-depth, weekday workshops wait for summer, when the college is not in session. One set of courses is offered through Elderhostel (for information on them, see Sources in the Campus Vacations chapter). The other workshops are for teens on up to senior citizens. For these, you arrive on Sunday, and from 9 to 4 Monday through Friday you attend classes, which have 10 or 12 students and are taught predominantly by visiting craftspeople, some nationally and internationally known. The incredibly well-equipped studios stay open until 11, in case you want to work late, which is not uncommon. Most participants want to make at least one finished piece during their stay; in some fields, such as basketry and bookbinding, you can complete several.

If you want to do something other than work, you don't have to look far. Evenings frequently have slide lectures. The countryside around the beautiful 180-acre hillside center is full of waterfalls and caves, and tree tours, revealing such local species as papaw and ginseng, are conducted in the woods. The July 4th weekend brings the Smithville Jamboree, a celebration of bluegrass. On your way to the center, you may want to visit Knoxville, 140 miles to the east, or Nashville, 70 miles west and site of the nearest major airport.

While at the center, you stay in chalet-style cabins, which have clusters of double-occupancy bedrooms and shared baths. The air-conditioned lodgings come with linens. Meals are served cafeteria-style in a dining hall. Also on campus are a library and a supply store, where you can buy materials if you didn't bring them from home; only occasionally are supplies included in tuition. *Appalachian Center for Crafts, 1560 Craft Center Dr., Smithville, TN 37166, tel. 615/597–6801, fax 615/597–6803. Topics: basketry, beadwork, blacksmithing, book and paper arts, ceramics/pottery, dried floral arrangement, dyeing, fiber arts, furniture making, glasswork, jewelry, metalwork, quilting, weaving, wood carving, wood turning. May–July: 5 days, tuition $175–$200, housing $180–$200.*

TENNESSEE **Arrowmont School of Arts and Crafts.** On 70 acres of wooded hillside just 3 miles from the entrance to Great Smoky Mountains National Park, Arrowmont sponsors more than 60 one- and two-week courses each summer, covering the gamut of arts and crafts disciplines. Typical workshop titles are Mixed Media Quilts, Claiming the Past in Fiber, Watercolor Marbling: Traditional and Beyond, Coiled Baskets, Narrative Weaving, and Fun, Functional Pottery. The 50-member faculty comprises prominent visual artists and craftspeople. You can audit a class or, in some fields, receive undergraduate or graduate credit.

You and other adults of all ages and abilities are in class Monday through Friday from 9 to 11:30 and 1 to 4. Should you wish to work late, studios, as well as the resource center and gallery, remain open until midnight. Slide lectures, musical performances, and demonstrations along with the recreational opportunities of the national park and the town of Gatlinburg provide respite from the intensity of course work.

Living arrangements range from dorm-style cottages that accommodate 10 to 12 students to a new air-conditioned building whose rooms have private baths. Prices vary accordingly, but all come with home-style cooking in a common dining area from Monday through Saturday breakfast. Lab fees are charged for expendable materials used in the studio, but you are encouraged to bring other supplies and tools from home. *Arrowmont School of Arts and Crafts, Box 567, Gatlinburg, TN 37738, tel. 615/436–5860, fax 615/430–4101. Topics: basketry, beadwork, ceramics/pottery, doll making, drawing, enameling, fabrics, fiber arts, glasswork, jewelry, metalwork, painting, papermaking, photography, quilting, sculpture, stained glass, weaving, wood turning. Early June–mid-Aug.: 7–14 days, tuition $185–370, housing $130–$700.*

THE MIDWEST

OHIO **The Loom Shed School of Weaving.** If you're an absolute beginner looking to come to grips with the principles of basic weaving, an expert who wishes to brush up on Moorman technique, or just an amateur who weaves for fun, master weaver Charles Lermond will create a curriculum tailored to your needs. Founded by Lermond in 1980, the school, housed in what was once a slaughterhouse, is on the edge of Oberlin, a town 35 miles southwest of Cleveland.

There are no schedules here other than the ones set by Lermond and the students. Classes usually run from 9 to 5, but you are free to organize your day to suit your needs and habits. Beginners start on Monday morning in front of a pre-warped loom and then learn to warp a loom for their project; part of Lermond's belief in the need for getting people weaving before they learn the intricacies of the art. For the more advanced student, the course is designed to focus on a particular technique such as warping and drafting, blockswitching, summer/winter, doubleweave, overshot, and computer-assisted draft analysis. The instruction is project-oriented, so the goal is for you to leave at the end of the week with a finished piece.

Room and board are available for a maximum of three nonsmoking students at the Lermond ranch, a couple of minutes from the school. Other accommodations options include area B&Bs and motels, which the school can arrange. If you're staying in the Lermond house, breakfast and dinner are included in the price, with lunch for all students available from a nearby deli. *The Loom Shed School of Weaving, 14301 State Route 58, Oberlin, OH 44074, tel. 216/774–3500. Topic: weaving. Year-round: 5 days, tuition $200, housing at the Lermond ranch $125.*

WISCONSIN The Clearing. The Clearing, a series of rustic log and stone cabins, was built in the woods of Wisconsin's Door County in 1935 by Jens Jensen, a distinguished landscape architect and a friend of Frank Lloyd Wright. Five-day to one-week courses are offered from May to October for all levels and ages. A five-day mini-folk art school, offered twice in October, features a choice of courses, such as Carve and Paint a Songbird, Create a Crazy Quilt, and Whittle a Whirligig.

The group usually meets on Sunday evening for a get-acquainted supper. A 7 AM bell on Monday calls you to breakfast, after which classes begin for a full-day's work with a break for lunch at noon. Classes never have more than 20 students, and many have as few as 10. The amount of instruction varies, depending on the class; some instructors offer lectures and demonstrations followed by full-time supervised instruction, while others provide a morning demonstration and then allow the class to develop their projects individually, offering advice and critique. Of course, you are not confined to working during class hours alone; the studios are open until late evening. There are no art stores in the area, so you need to bring all of your own materials and equipment.

Use the evenings to relax. After dinner, served in the main lodge, you can read or play the piano. If it is warm enough, there's a marshmallow roast around a campfire, accompanied by the inevitable ghost stories. Accommodations are in stone and log cabins at the center, where you have a choice of a bed in a three- or six-bed dormitory, or a hotel-style room in which you must share with one other person.

Door County, a spit of land that sticks out from Green Bay into Lake Michigan, is Wisconsin's premier vacation spot if you like to sail, fish, camp, hike, and cycle. There's swimming too, if you can take the cold water. It's a rustic area comprised of small colonies of gray-shingled and white-clapboard summer houses in picturesque towns, with names like Fish Creek and Egg Harbor. The Clearing is within a brisk walk of the Door County Maritime Museum, a short drive from Chief Oshkosh Indian Museum, the Pioneer School Museum, and the ferry to Washington Island and Rock Island State Park. *The Clearing, Box 65, Ellison Bay, WI 54210, tel. 414/854-4088. Topics: hand-painted china, Navajo silversmithing, quilt making, and woodcarving. May–Oct.: 7 days, complete package $465–$505. Price does not include one dinner.*

WISCONSIN Dillman's Sand Lake Lodge. On a 250-acre peninsula on White Sand Lake in northern Wisconsin, Dillman's Lodge, built in 1935, is a family-owned and run, family-oriented resort complex of rustic lakefront lodges and cabins. More than 80 one- to six-day visual arts workshops are offered from May to October each year. Most run for five days and are open to all levels, with a few geared to the intermediate or advanced student. Instructors are all well-known professional artists and craftspeople.

All classes run from 9 to 5, with a one-hour break for lunch. Mornings usually include a demonstration or a lecture, depending on the individual instructor. Some instructors give an afternoon lecture or a critique; others prefer to let the participants pursue their individual projects with relatively little interference. The average class size is 15, with one instructor per class.

The studios are open 24 hours a day, so you can work into the night if you want to, but there's plenty to do each day: tennis, trout fishing, water skiing, archery, horseshoes, or hiking on hunting trails used by the Lac du Flambeau Indians hundreds of years ago. There are also several golf courses within a short drive. In the mornings, children meet in the Round House for games and activities, leaving the parents free to attend workshops or participate in the available sporting activities. In the evenings there are visiting professional puppet shows in the dining room, classic movies in the Round House, or an Indian powwow in nearby Lac du Flambeau. Most classes reserve one night for a slide show of artists' work—including your own.

Dillman's offers three lodging options, all equally priced: You can stay in the family-oriented log cabin, the motel-style annex, or the North Shore condo units added to the grounds in 1992. All breakfasts and dinners are included in the tuition price, but you can sign up each morning for a box lunch of sandwiches, salad, and fruit.

A series of mini-workshops on Wednesday mornings focuses on local lore and craft. Students of all ages—sometimes including parents, grandparents, and grandchildren—gather for two hours to create (and finish) a project like cattail mats, masks, and twisted baskets, using grasses and twigs. *Dillman's Sand Lake Lodge, Box 98, Lac du Flambeau, WI 54538, tel. 715/588–3143, 715/588–3110 or 800/359–2511. Topics: birch bark crafts, calligraphy, intaglio carving on gems and glass, painting, quilting, woodcarving, and woven boxes. May–Oct.: 5 days, complete package $695–$925. Price does not include lunch. See also the Painting Workshops chapter.*

WISCONSIN **Sievers School of Fiber Arts.** Sievers School of Fiber Arts occupies the refurbished Jackson Harbor School on remote Washington Island in Lake Michigan. Established in 1979 as a natural outgrowth of a successful mail-order loom design and kit business, the school now offers more than 50 classes each year in textile-related subjects: weaving, spinning, dyeing, quilting, creative sewing, and basketry. The classes are mainly geared toward beginners, although every year several are designed for more advanced students. Two-, five-, and seven-day classes, of between eight and 10 students and one instructor, are held from May through October. The 30-member faculty is made up of midwestern fiber artists who teach in schools or colleges or are in a related business. In addition, distinguished professional weavers and other fiber artists are invited to teach each season.

After a long day of workshops, students retire to a 90-year-old landmark building, with hand-hewn beams and exposed lumber construction, that serves as Sievers School's dormitory. The sleeping area has bunk beds and portable, curtained room dividers. There are complete kitchen facilities with all cooking and eating equipment and utensils needed for meals. The dormitory is for women only; male students have to take lodgings in one of the nearby B&Bs, motels, or campgrounds (a list of area B&Bs is provided when registering).

Washington Island (population 650) is reached by a 30-minute car ferry over a narrow strait originally called "Door to Death" by the Indians because of its treacherous currents. The island has a riding stable, tennis courts, three historical museums, and several beautiful beaches. On Sunday in the summer, there's baseball with teams from Door County, and the centrally located Red Barn hosts evening music and theater productions. There are also weekly displays of the instructors' and students' work. *Sievers School of Fiber Arts, Jackson Harbor Rd., Washington Island, WI 54246, tel. 414/847-2264. Topics: felt making, bound weave rug techniques, fabric jewelry, Hawaiian hand appliqué, and new color in rag rug weaving. May 15–Oct. 15: 2–5 days, tuition $110–$210, housing $100.*

THE SOUTHWEST

ARIZONA **Book Arts in Bisbee.** Near the Mexican border, 1½ hours from Tucson, and just down the road from Tombstone is Bisbee, a colorful cross-cultural town where you can read the history of the old West in the ornate facades of turn-of-the-century buildings or hear it firsthand from veterans of copper-mining days. Bisbee is jammed with antiques, boutiques, quaint inns, galleries, and live theater. It is here in this southeastern Arizona community that Pat Baldwin, owner of Waterleaf Mill & Bindery and Pequeño Press, gives private workshops in the book arts to adults, regardless of experience. Materials are provided.

Pat works with you one-on-one in four-hour afternoons—four days in bookbinding or five (weekdays) in hand papermaking or book production. Two intensive days of marbling instruction are also offered. During mornings and evenings, you can explore the area's many attractions, and Pat is happy to advise you on sightseeing and transportation. She can even make arrangements with one of the charming and reasonably priced lodgings nearby. *Waterleaf Mill & Bindery, Box 1711, Bisbee, AZ 85603, tel. 602/432-5924, fax 602/432-3065. Topics: bookbinding, papermaking. Year-round: 4–5 days, tuition $100–$185.*

ARIZONA **Fiber Arts in Bisbee.** In the southeast corner of Arizona, the southwest corner of the United States, Joan Ruane runs the appropriately named Southwest Corner, a retreat center that offers scheduled classes and customized instruction in the fiber arts. Most of what is taught is spinning and weaving, but you can also study beading, quilting, or dyeing.

Joan is joined in teaching by outside artists, many from Bisbee itself, the quaint little artists' community that was once a mining town. Most scheduled classes last three days, but some are as long as five days. Though the former, for groups of 15 to 20, are offered as classes alone, the latter, for a minimum of six people, are generally part of a package with lunch and lodging at a B&B. Depending on class size, workshops may be taught at a local inn instead of in the Southwest Corner studio. A catalogue lists scheduled classes, given fall through spring, or, if you and friends are interested, you can arrange for your own workshop.

Another option, available all year, is to set up a personalized program with Joan. You can receive a full day (six hours) of one-on-one instruction or take a one-hour or longer lesson and spend additional time just working at a loom by yourself. You are responsible for your own accommodations and meals, though Joan happily points you to charming B&Bs, one right next door. You don't need to bring your own supplies, as you may buy whatever you need—yarns, fabric, or beads—at the studio. Either way, when you're not weaving, you can discover the delights of Bisbee and the surrounding area. *Southwest Corner, Box 418, Bisbee, AZ 85603, tel. 602/432-3603 or 800/879-8412. Topics: beading, dyeing, quilting, spinning, weaving. Oct.–early May: 3 days, tuition $125; 5 days, complete package $450. Instruction year-round: $15 per hour or $50 per day. 5-day package price does not include dinner.*

ARIZONA **Spin 'N Weave.** In a classroom attached to a shop that sells wool, spinning wheels, and looms, a whole variety of fiber workshops are given, but the emphasis is on weaving. Five-day classes, taught by instructors from Tucson and beyond, range from clothing design to rug weaving. In addition, weekend courses might cover silk painting, dyeing, tapestry, or marbling, while other topics—knitting, crocheting, and spinning to name a few—are taught a day each week for several weeks. If you want to immerse yourself in fiber arts, you can stay a few weeks and take a number of these classes.

From fall to spring, when Tucson is not scorchingly hot, classes are given from 9 to 4 with a break for lunch. You can continue to work after hours as long as the shop is open or the instructor stays. If you haven't finished your project when the workshop is over, you can use the facilities until it's completed. Some materials are furnished, but others you must purchase. You may use Spin 'N Weave's looms or bring your own. For accommodations, there are local B&Bs and motels; recommendations are provided. *Spin 'N Weave, 2927 E. Grant Rd., Tucson, AZ 85716, tel. 602/321–0588 or 800/266–6245 ext. 8311 for automated mailbox. Topics: dyeing, knitting and crocheting, spinning, weaving. Sept.–May: 5 days, tuition $100–$200.*

NEVADA **Tuscarora School of Pottery.** Dennis Parks, a well-known and widely exhibited potter, chose this nearly deserted old mining town (population 20) as the site of his pottery school in 1966 because of its quiet and isolation. At 6,400 feet, it sits under clear skies, perched on the side of Mount Blitzen in the high desert of northern Nevada. Summer workshops, geared to adults from advanced beginners to professionals, are taught by Dennis along with his son Ben and other distinguished visiting artists. Different aspects of earthenware, stoneware, and porcelain, both wheel-thrown and hand-built, are covered. Work is glazed raw and single fired in kilns fueled by diesel and used crankcase oil. If you're interested, you can experiment with local materials, such as native rocks, exotic earths, and sagebrush ash. Kick wheels are provided, but you are welcome to bring an electric wheel if you wish.

The summer program consists of four two-week sessions, and you may attend from one to all four. Due to its popularity, however, there are often waiting lists, and priority is given to students staying four weeks or more. Arrive the day before your session. You can arrange to be picked up in Elko (50 miles away), the nearest town with air and bus service and site of the original Cowboy Poetry Gathering.

The workshops at Tuscarora are a little less structured than at many other pottery schools. Classes consist of dialogue and demonstration rather than lecture, and instructors are always ready to provide individualized attention. The well-equipped studios are open 24 hours a day. In your spare time, you can have fun fishing, cycling, backpacking, or hiking in the surrounding countryside—sagebrush-covered hillsides, grassy valleys, and canyons with cottonwood and aspen. The area is dotted with lupine, sego lily, and Indian paintbrush and inhabited by fauna from chipmunks to coyote, orioles to eagles.

An easy camaraderie comes from working and living together in relative isolation. You are housed in "the Hotel," a rustic 19th-century building that once served as a boardinghouse for gold-panning miners. You and the other students help with chores, and Dennis's wife, Julie, cooks hearty meals that are made with vegetables from the garden and served in the lace-curtained dining room. The fee covers room and board, instruction, glazing, and firing; the only thing you pay extra for is clay. *Tuscarora Pottery School, Box 7, Tuscarora, NV 89834, tel. 702/756–6598. Topic: ceramics/pottery. Mid-June–mid-Aug.: 14 days, complete package $790; 28 days, complete package $1,420.*

NEW MEXICO **Fabrile Workshops.** About three times annually, the artists of Fabrile Studio offer five-day workshops for six to eight students, and though the dates and sites may change from year to year, the subject matter remains the same: Navajo weaving or hand papermaking. Kim Knight Mumbower restores Navajo textiles and teaches Navajo and tapestry weaving techniques. In a typical weaving workshop, you learn to design and weave a small Navajo rug, using traditional tools and wool from the Navajo-Churro sheep of the Southwest. Coralie Silvey Jones is an artist who uses handmade paper in most of her work, in addition to owning and operating Sage Papers and Printers along with her husband. Her courses explore different papermaking processes as well as a brief history of the craft.

Workshops run Monday through Friday from 9 to 5 with a break for lunch. Lectures, like the work itself, are interwoven into the fabric of the day. Most equipment and materials are provided, but part of your time might be spent building your own loom or mould and deckle.

What to do after hours is up to you, and Taos certainly offers many options. Though room and board are not furnished, a list of suggested local lodgings is. *Fabrile Studio, Box 1551, Taos, NM 87571, tel. 505/751–0306. Topics: papermaking, weaving. May–Oct.: 5 days, tuition $300–$350.*

NEW MEXICO **Plum Tree Seminars.** Located right on the banks of the Rio Grande, Pilar is a centuries-old town of wood and adobe buildings. As in much of this part of New Mexico—Taos is just 16 miles to the northeast and Santa Fe is a bit farther to the south—the village is teeming with craftspeople who, like painter Georgia O'Keeffe and potter Juan Hamilton, have been drawn here by the magnificent scenery and the unique quality of light in the high desert.

The Plum Tree is a compound consisting of a café, a low-key bed-and-breakfast, a dorm-style hostel, and a seminar program in the visual arts and "the fine art of living." Although some of the more than 15 classes offered each year are in watercolor, landscape painting, and photography, many focus on crafts. Examples are Japanese ceramics, Pueblo pottery, contemporary Chinese woodblock printing, and papermaking using local plant material, such as sagebrush and cattails. Instructors are regionally and nationally known artists. Their work is exhibited in numerous Taos and Santa Fe galleries, and many have taught at colleges and arts schools. Their most important credential, however, is their enthusiasm.

The hands-on seminars, open to 12 participants, are held in summer and fall. The latter is particularly lovely in Pilar, thanks to the spectacular colors of cottonwoods and tamarisks. You are in class Monday through Friday from 9 to 5, which is not to say you are in classrooms. Much of your time is spent out of doors, whether gathering vegetation to use in making paper or learning to identify clay bodies. Indoor facilities are also employed, and you are sent a list of supplies to bring from home. The cost of materials is generally very modest.

Seminar participants often develop close bonds, so it's not unusual for them to get together after hours for a Mexican pot-luck dinner or a dip in the hot tub. Some evenings bring slide lectures. If you prefer to continue work on your own, you can; facilities remain open after classes. Alternately, you can explore the sights away from the Plum Tree. With the Sangre de Cristo Mountains on one side and the Rio Grande Gorge on the other, there's no shortage of recreational opportunities: swimming, hiking, biking, and white-water rafting. Outfitters are plentiful in Pilar and neighboring villages. An easy drive away you find Taos Plaza; Ranchos de Taos and its famous, much-photographed church; Ojo Calliente hot springs; the Millicent Rogers Museum; Native American petroglyphs; and several pueblos.

You can of course stay at the B&B or the hostel, which has shared baths and a kitchen, or you may choose to camp or take other lodgings in town. *The Plum Tree, Box 1A, Pilar, NM 87531, tel. 505/758–4765. Topics: ceramics/pottery, painting, papermaking, photography, sculpture, woodblock printing. May–Oct.: 5 days, tuition $250–$350.*

NEW MEXICO **Taos Institute of Art.** The 60 courses the institute offers each year cover topics from gold- and silversmithing to writing pearly prose, but the focus of each is the uniqueness of the northern New Mexico culture and environment. Favorites include Navajo weaving and pueblo pottery. Nationally recognized, professional artists provide multilevel teaching, accommodating the beginner on up to the advanced. You and five to 11 others spend 40 hours, Monday through Friday, not in classrooms but in the artist's own studio or in the field. Most courses can be taken for advanced undergraduate or graduate credit.

Tuition includes most materials, though occasional fees are added to cover expensive items like precious metals. You are responsible for making your own housing and dining arrangements; however, the institute distributes a 10-page guide to local lodgings that would do a chamber of commerce proud. *Taos Institute of Art, Box 2469, Taos, NM, 87571, tel. 505/758–2793. Topics: ceramics/pottery, jewelry, painting, photography, weaving. Late June–early Oct.: 5 days, tuition $275–$400.*

NEW MEXICO **Turley Forge Blacksmithing School.** Master ironworker Frank Turley used to be the conservator for the Museum of New Mexico, specializing in the restoration of Spanish colonial ironwork and firearms. Now five times a year he teaches three-week courses—with instruction five days per week—in traditional blacksmithing techniques. Enrollment is limited to six students, who work at their own forge and anvil. Essential techniques developed are drawing, upsetting, fullering, twisting, bending, forge welding, forge brazing, striking with sledge, power hammer use, hot rasping, and hot filing. Early on you make a fire rake and shovel, which you use during the course, and move on to steel tools, hinges, scrollwork, and fancy rivets. Specific instruction is given in the tempering of handmade tools. About half your time is spent in lab and half in demonstration and lecture. Tools and materials are furnished.

The forge is approximately 5 miles west of the center of Santa Fe, which, at 7,000 feet, is cool in spring and fall and bright and cold in winter, when it snows intermittently.

Most students stay in local apartments or motels with kitchenettes. Though you make arrangements for your own housing, a list of reasonably priced lodgings as well as campgrounds in the nearby mountain ranges is furnished. *Turley Forge Blacksmithing School, Rte. 10, Box 88C, Santa Fe, NM 87501, tel. 505/471–8608. Topic: blacksmithing. Early Feb.–late Apr. and late Aug.–early Nov.: 15 days, tuition $1,200.*

TEXAS **Southwest Craft Center.** The Southwest Craft Center is located on the grounds of the old Ursuline Academy and Convent, built as a girls' school in 1848. The secluded parklike grounds and historic buildings are situated on the scenic River Walk, nestled in among the skyscrapers of downtown San Antonio. In addition to ongoing courses, the center offers one- to four-day workshops, Thursday through Sunday, in its autumn and spring sessions. Well-known visiting craftspeople teach approximately a dozen workshops each session in the center's six studios: ceramics, fibers, metals, papermaking, photography, and surface design.

Almost all the workshops, which have maximums of 6 to 15 students, are hands-on, and each usually has an attached slide lecture, open to the public. You work in the studio from about 10 to 4 and after hours can enjoy the two exhibition galleries, gift shop, and the musical events and evening lectures that are occasionally held. Of course, you can also take advantage of the pleasures of the River Walk and surrounding San Antonio.

The center readily gives suggestions of places to stay within walking distance, many of which offer special rates to center students, as well as places to dine. For a convenient lunch, you can eat on the grounds at the Copper Kitchen, open weekdays. A varying lab fee covers your materials. *Southwest Craft Center, 300 Augusta, San Antonio, TX 78205–1296, tel. 210/224–1848, fax 210/224–9337. Topics: basketry, beadwork, ceramics/pottery, decorative painting, drawing, dyeing, embroidery, fiber arts, jewelry, knitting and crocheting,* metalwork, painting, papermaking, photography, quilting, spinning, stained glass, weaving. *Sept.–May: 4 days, tuition $120.*

UTAH **Rocky Mountain Painting Faux Finishing Workshops.** Chuck James, who does faux finishing professionally when he isn't teaching, holds a five-day, 40-hour workshop in a different city each month. Chicago, Detroit, Los Angeles, Miami, New York, Philadelphia, and Washington, D.C., are typical locations, and once a year, the site is Salt Lake City, Rocky Mountain Painting's home base. Call for a schedule to see if a workshop is being offered in a place you'd like to visit.

Designed to teach all aspects of faux finishing—graining, gilding, marbling, wall glazing, and stencil work—workshops are set up for people with a basic understanding of color theory and painting but are open to everyone. Class size, which averages 15, is limited to 24, and the student-to-instructor ratio is eight to one. Each day is filled with instruction and hands-on practice, and by the time the workshop is over, you will have completed 20 to 24 sample boards, each an example of a faux-finishing technique. All materials are included in tuition.

A catered lunch is served, but other than that you're on your own to eat and enjoy the sights of the city however you wish. A list of accommodations close to the workshop site is provided. The cost of tuition is lower for more than one participant signing up together. *Rocky Mountain Painting, 5390 S. Cottonwood La., Salt Lake City, UT 84117, tel. 801/277–8097 or 800/527–9284, fax 801/272–0685. Topic: decorative painting. Year-round: 5 days, tuition $795. Price includes lunch.*

THE ROCKIES

COLORADO **Anderson Ranch.** In 1966, the developers of Snowmass Village invited ceramist Paul Soldner to choose one of seven ranches in the valley for an art center. He chose the Anderson family's sheep ranch for the wonderful view it commands from the head of the valley and for its rustic old log barns and ranch house. On the present-day ranch, renovated log cabins and barns have been joined by new buildings that were designed in keeping with the historical setting.

More than 80 summer workshops are taught annually by respected professional artists from all around the country. Typical courses include basic woodworking, canoe construction, faux and painted finishes, trompe l'oeil painting, classic European carving, clay construction, Japanese woodblocks, and mixed media. Numerous classes and even field expeditions are offered in painting, drawing, and photography as well. Workshops are limited to 12 participants, of varying skill levels. There is usually an equal number of men and women.

Sessions run one or two weeks, from Sunday to Saturday, and classes themselves are Monday through Friday from 9 to 5. On evenings and weekends, you can continue to work (studios are open 24 hours), or you can attend demonstrations or slide lectures by visiting faculty. Snowmass Village is just west of Aspen, which hosts the Aspen Music Festival, Dance Aspen, and the International Design Conference. World-class restaurants, art galleries, and repertory theater companies abound. There is also hiking, cycling, mountain biking, and fishing.

Accommodations at the ranch are in a dormitory, and the room and board fee includes meals in the cafeteria-style communal dining hall. If you wish, you can make arrangements, through the ranch or on your own, to stay at other nearby lodgings, including condominiums with kitchen facilities. If you do live elsewhere but would like to eat at the ranch, you can purchase a weekly meal ticket.

In addition to the regular workshops, open to adults 18 and over, there's an extensive children's program for two age groups, 6 to 8 and 9 to 12. Limited to 14 kids per class, these one- and two-week courses are held mornings or afternoons and range from weaving and mask making to a study of Native American crafts. Unlike the adult workshops, they include materials. *Anderson Ranch Arts Center, Box 5598, Snowmass Village, CO 81615, tel. 303/923–3181, fax 303/923–3871. Topics: book arts, ceramics/pottery, decorative painting, drawing, furniture design, painting, photography, printmaking, sculpture, video, wood carving, writing. June–Aug.: 5–10 days, tuition $375–$600, housing $245 per week.*

COLORADO **Needlework Seminars.** Each fall, the Embroiderers' Guild of America, founded in 1958, offers its members an annual week-long seminar series. More than 50 one-, two-, and four-day classes for all ability levels are offered, covering all sorts of techniques: canvas, pulled thread, surface embroidery, silk and metal on silk, crewel, and quilting, to name a few. Seminars are in a different city each year; in 1995 it's Denver.

The first event is the opening banquet on Sunday. Classes take place on Monday, Tuesday, Thursday, and Friday, so, for example, you can opt to take two 2-day courses, with a day off between, or a four-day course that brackets the week. You are in class from about 9 to 4, with an hour and a half for lunch. Otherwise, your time is your own; peruse the seminar's education exhibit, fiber forum, bookstore, and boutique or enjoy the diversions of your surroundings. On Wednesday, you can take one of the planned tours or an extra one-day workshop, both for additional fees, or just leave the day free to do what you want, which for many participants means spending time with their spouse or family.

Membership in the guild includes its magazine, and it's in the March edition that you find details on that year's seminars. List several choices when you apply, as classes frequently fill early. When you receive your class assignment, you also get a list of supplies to bring, usually hoops and other standard needlework equipment. Materials provided during the course are covered by a

separate fee. The magazine also gives information on the host hotel, and though you make lodging arrangements directly with it, a group rate is offered. If you choose not to stay at that hotel, an additional commuter fee is assessed. Meals, too, are your responsibility. *Embroiderers' Guild of America, 335 W. Broadway, #100, Louisville, KY 40202, tel. 502/589–6956, fax 502/584–7900. Topics: embroidery, quilting. Sept.–Nov.: 4 days, tuition $270. Price includes 2 banquets.*

THE WEST COAST

CALIFORNIA **American School of Japanese Arts.** The San Francisco Zen Center at Green Gulch Farm in Muir Beach is the serene setting of the unique, 10-day Japanese Arts Seminar and has been every summer since 1987. Modeled after the Oomoto School of Traditional Japanese Arts in Kyoto, the seminar gives 20 to 25 students the unique opportunity to learn traditional tea ceremony, calligraphy, *Kyogen* (comic theater), and *Shintaido* (sword movement). Each are covered for one-and-a-half hours daily, complemented by demonstrations in flower arrangement and tea-bowl pottery—you make the tea bowls used in the final tea ceremony. The four instructors are all well-versed in the history and teachings of Japan but their Western backgrounds smoothly bridge the gap between the two cultures. Evening lectures given by the instructors on topics such as Japanese clothing, printmaking, and woodblock prints provide you with a well-rounded look at the traditions of Japan. To get you in the mood for a Zenful experience, you wear traditional Japanese clothing—so leave the suit at home.

The 100-acre Green Gulch Farm is in a valley 25 minutes outside of San Francisco. The full-time monastery is a practicing Zen community, but opens its doors as a community center year-round. There's a traditional Japanese-style teahouse on the grounds, along with a facility built using traditional Japanese joinery (no nails) where you sleep in either single or double rooms.

Vegetarian meals are prepared using home-grown produce. In your free time, which isn't too often, a five-minute's walk gets you onto the beach, and hiking is available in the hills around the center. *The American School of Japanese Arts, 606 Wilson St., Santa Rosa, CA 95404, tel. 707/578–8014. Topic: Japanese arts. Late July–early Aug.: 10 days, complete package $1,250. Price includes supplies, equipment, and traditional Japanese clothes.*

CALIFORNIA **The Fabric Carr Sewing Camp.** In 1981, Roberta Carr, realizing that 40% of all stitchers live in California, established The Fabric Carr Couture Sewing Camp in her private studio just outside of San Jose. To guarantee personal attention and an informal atmosphere, Ms. Carr, producer of seven videotapes on couture techniques, has limited the week-long classes to five students, all of whom must at least know how to read a pattern and run a sewing machine. There are 12 sessions per year, each highlighting a different theme, among them tailoring, casual couture, drafting patterns, and perfection of couture. In addition, there is a week called "Art to Wear," where you learn how sewing can be useful as an art form, as well as a professional week, limited to those in the business of making or repairing clothes. In the morning, you attend a three-hour lecture that presents the techniques you work with in the afternoon's four-hour master class. The week's work emphasizes technique, and you may leave with 50 new ones under your belt. Rather than having you work to finish one specific project, Ms. Carr wants you to master the different techniques demonstrated by working with you on a number of projects. The evenings are unstructured and you are free to continue your work or to relax your hands and minds in any way you choose.

Ms. Carr not only takes care of your sewing for the week, she also takes care of you. You are made to feel at home from day one, which begins with cocktails and dinner. From then on in it's three gourmet meals a day, with the exception of a night out at the San Jose Country Club. There's maid service at Ms. Carr's New Orleans–style house high in the hills where wrought-iron balconies and decks overlook the Santa Clara Valley. You sleep two to a room and have full run of the house, which you may not want to leave when the week is up. *The Fabric Carr Sewing Camp, Box 32120, San Jose, CA 95152, tel. 408/929–1651. Topic: sewing. Year-round: 7 days, complete package $1,350. Price includes materials and equipment.*

CALIFORNIA **Quilt Camp Shaver Lake.** Don't let the name fool you—it's not all quilting at the Quilt Camp, established in 1977. In fact, the emphasis here is on surface design and new techniques for fabric design. There are three six-day seminars covering a wide range of topics such as silk-screen painting, photo emulsion silk screen, printing through copy machines and thermofaxes, and Cyanotype (blue printing). Jean Ray Laury, a quilt maker and writer, and Joyce Aiken, an art professor at CSU-Fresno, give hands-on training to approximately 30 students of all levels in two daily demonstrations, and in personal guidance in the studio. You are free to create whatever you like in the open studio time. Evenings are set aside for slide shows, lectures, viewing each other's work, and socializing. You bring your own fabric, but all other materials are provided.

The camp is held in a large, well-lit studio at the community center of Shaver Lake, a resort town 5,000 feet above sea level in the High Sierra range one hour outside Fresno. As this is a ski area, the town isn't crowded during the summer so you have a variety of housing options. The camp will rent a room or bed for you in a chalet that sleeps two to four or a cabin that sleeps five to eight and tack it onto the price for the week, or you can fend for yourself and either camp or rent on your own—which might be good if you want to bring your family along to enjoy the scenery. Healthy buffet-style meals are cooked by the house chef, except for the two nights that dinner isn't served—there are a number of small restaurants scattered around the town to fill the gap. The High

Sierras provide the perfect place for backpacking, just make sure you bring along your needle and thread in case you get inspired by the view. *The Quilt Camp, c/o Jean Ray Laury, 19425 Tollhouse Rd., Clovis, CA 93611, tel. and fax 209/297–0228. Topic: fabric design, silk screen. July and August: 6 days, tuition $335, housing $430–$545. Price does not include two meals and fabric.*

OREGON **The Creative Arts at Menucha.** Every August since 1966, the Creative Arts Community has held a two-week residential workshop, inviting students and artists of all skill levels to learn about subjects such as Native American drum making, furniture as canvas and sculpture, ceramics, the art of jewelry, paper sculpture, and printmaking. There are 10 workshops to choose from in all. There are different instructors each week, so if you've enrolled for a two-week workshop you'll be taught the same subject from two different angles. You attend any of the 10 workshops from 9 to 4, Monday through Friday, and the studios are open 24 hours a day. The instructors are mostly local artists and professors, and with classes kept small—only eight to 10 students—they are able to give you a lot of attention. At night the instructors present their works in slide shows or give lecture demonstrations, and on Friday night they guide you on a studio tour through the many different art forms covered here. Upon applying, you will be given a list of supplies you will need to bring with you for your particular course; there is also a supply store on site.

The workshop takes place in studios in Menucha, the former estate of the Meiers, a prominent local family, but its heritage still shows even though it was converted into a conference center in 1950. Just 20 minutes east of Portland, the setting is rural, and facilities include jogging trails, tennis courts, an outdoor swimming pool, and meditative gardens, as well as a fantastic view of the Columbia River Gorge. Both students and instructors sleep in the dormitory rooms, but there are a few private rooms for couples and families. The home-style fare is heavy on homemade breads and fresh vegetables, and lean on meat. *The Creative Arts Community at Menucha, Box 4958, Portland, OR 97208, tel. 503/760–5837 or 503/236–4109. Topics: ceramics, drawing, drum making, jewelry, painting, sculpture, watercoloring, writing. Mid-Aug.: 7–14 days, complete package $475–$875.*

OREGON **Pacific Northwest College of Art.** The extension program of Pacific Northwest College of Art, a four-year accredited institution affiliated with the Portland Art Museum, opens its doors in the summer to inexperienced but interested students for five interesting and original five-day workshops. In an evening workshop entitled "Releasing the Spirit," an art therapist helps you to release your inhibitions through your creativity, rather than by focusing on a specific project—you don't take anything home with you, but you leave your creative blocks behind. In two different Native American beading workshops, which may be taken concurrently as one is during the day and one is at night, you learn techniques such as the lazy stitch, the zipper stitch, and the running stitch, which you use to create a miniature belt pouch or medallion using brain-tanned moose or deer hide and glass beads. A daytime printmaking workshop entitled "Monomania," which covers both oil- and water-based media, brings three local artists together with state-of-the-art presses to help you develop your monotype technique. The Japanese woodcut workshop, taught by an accomplished Japanese artist, lets you discover the tools, carving methods, and history of traditional and contemporary Japanese woodblock printmaking through both practice and by viewing old and new Japanese prints. These classes are open to students and artists of all levels, but are geared more to beginners. At the end of the week, your work is critiqued. The average class size is 12, and the average age of students is 30. For most classes you will need to bring supplies, but there is a fully equipped supply store down the block if you don't want to carry everything with you.

As this is an urban campus, in downtown Portland, there's plenty to do and see when you feel like a break from all that creating. The Portland Art Museum, attached to the professional studios where your classes are held, has one of the best print collections in the Northwest; there's ballet and theater up the road; and a stroll in the beautiful city park is just a few paces away. Since the program doesn't come with room and board, you can stay in the YWCA across the street, a hotel, or a wide range of bed-and-breakfasts around the city. A couple of small brew pubs nearby provide the perfect place to hang out with your fellow classmates, as do the restaurants that populate the area. *Pacific Northwest College of Art, 1219 SW Park Ave., Portland, OR 97205, tel. 503/226–0462 or 503/226–4842. Topics: bead making, Japanese woodcutting, printmaking. Mid-June– July: 5 days, tuition $120–$300.*

WASHINGTON **Pilchuck Glass School.** The well-respected Pilchuck Glass School has conducted rigorous glassblowing programs every summer since 1971, where both novice and advanced glassblowers come together to learn design techniques from the very best. In the five intensive 18-day sessions each summer, leading figures in glassworks, such as master craftsman Pino Signoretto, explain in detail hot glass sculpture, fusing, casting, flame working, neon, mosaic, engraving, cutting, and enameling, to name a few. You pick one of the five different classes offered in each session. Some classes are juried, requiring you to submit slide samples for admittance, but the majority can be taken by any level of serious glassblower.

The studios have state-of-the-art machinery, and all forms of hand tools are provided; the school store sells the books, special tools, glass, and other supplies. Sessions are limited to 50 students, and there's plenty of one-on-one instruction from the 50 faculty members, resident artists, and staff. You attend lectures and demonstrations throughout the day and evening according to your instructor's schedule, and nightly programs, such as slide shows, panels, critiques, and readings are presented by a faculty or staff member. As this is a highly intensive program, it is not uncommon to be working well into the night on various projects relating to your class. Class is not held on Sunday but the studios and library are open for students who wish to work independently.

In the middle of a 15,000-acre tree farm one hour north of Seattle, students sleep two to a room in cottages and dormitories that sit on the hillside meadows overlooking Puget Sound. The homey three-story Pilchuck Lodge houses the extensive reference library, the gallery where student and faculty works are displayed, and the gathering place where you dine on the three vegetarian-style meals prepared daily by the kitchen staff. Every studio on campus comes equipped with a beer-filled refrigerator for those long hours into the night you spend blowing and sculpting glass. As this is a highly intensive and serious workshop, there is little free time to explore the surrounding wilderness or drive into Seattle for some alternative fun, but you might not want to stray from the campus and all of its charm anyway. *Pilchuck Glass School, 1201 316th St., NW, Stanwood, WA 98292, tel. 206/445–3111 (May–early Sept.); 315 Second Ave. S, Suite 200, Seattle, WA 98104, tel. 206/621–8422 (Sept.–early May). Topic: glassworks. May–early Sept.: 18-days, complete package $1,725–$2,825.*

SOURCES

ORGANIZATIONS Every state and many cities have arts councils that can lead you in the direction of arts and crafts workshops.

PERIODICALS AND BOOKS *The Guide to Arts & Crafts Workshops*, published by Shaw Guides, covers arts and crafts workshops, travel programs, residencies, and retreats throughout the United States giving program descriptions and other helpful information.

ALSO SEE If taking a workshop or just reading about one has sparked your interest, and you'd like to try your creative hand at other crafts, *see* the Painting Workshops and Photography Workshops and Tours chapters, or look into the Writing Conferences and Workshops chapter.

Birding

By Paul M. Konrad

 ne of America's fastest-growing activities, birding, is attracting people of all ages who come from all walks of life. Although birding can be a solitary endeavor, a guided group tour provides a good way to explore an area you are not familiar with, meet other people who share your interest in birds, and let someone else take care of the non-birding aspects of the trip.

Along with operators who deal exclusively in birding tours, many nature tour packagers cater to birders. There are birding tours to every region of the country, to nearly every state, and to many destinations worldwide. Outfitters plan the itinerary, arrange lodging and usually meals, provide the transportation, and employ one or more professional guides who know the local birdlife.

There are three points to consider when planning a birding trip: What birds do you want to see? When do you want to go? And where do you want to go? The answers to these questions are interconnected, because specific species are found in particular parts of the country only at certain times of the year.

On some tours you concentrate on a given area and stay fairly close to it, perhaps even lodging in the same hotel the entire time. More common, however, is a tour that moves to different locations daily, sometimes traveling great distances, covering vastly different terrain, and relocating to a new hotel every night or so. Travel time is usually arranged so that it does not interfere with prime birding hours, but occasionally you must spend much of a day in transit.

Your daily activities on a group birding tour vary. You may spend much or all of a day visiting every inch of a wildlife refuge or bird sanctuary at a leisurely pace, or you may stop at several birding locations for short periods of time. Nearly every tour offers some predawn birding or owling after dark, but these excursions are optional, unless the group does not plan to return to the hotel for breakfast before going back into the field. Tours generally run from 5 to 14 days, with most going to readily accessible areas. The walking and hiking are rarely very strenuous, and the pace is almost always easygoing.

Birding tours range in cost from $100 to almost $300 per day, but none of these tours offers luxury. You spend most nights at budget or moderately priced hotels and motels that are part of national chains or at comparable local establishments. You eat in modest restaurants for breakfast and dinner, and often help prepare your own picnic lunch.

CHOOSING THE RIGHT TOUR

Because there are so many birding tours to choose from, when you are trying to pick one, it is best to ask a lot of questions. Start with these.

What birds or species do you aim to see on this trip? Tours are often planned around a particular bird or species, although on most

Professional ornithologist and editor of WildBird *magazine, Paul M. Konrad lives, works, and birds in southern California.*

tours, the leader will happily stop for a look at any interesting birds that you come across. Very few tours focus so single-mindedly on one bird that all others are neglected, and very few have you indiscriminately chasing after any bird you see. Ideally you want a tour that is focused but flexible.

How long has the company been in business? As a general rule, stick with an outfitter who has been around for several years. This is not a slam at new enterprises, but a company with a few years in its wake has already addressed the questions and challenges that you are likely to present to it.

How long has the company conducted this tour? If the company has not done this tour before, scrutinize the credentials of the designated tour leader all the more carefully.

What are the guide's qualifications? A birding guide might be a professional ornithologist or very knowledgeable local birder, but whatever his or her professional training, the guide should be well-informed about the ecology of the area you are visiting and the birds you are seeking out. It also helps if the guide is personable and knows enough about the area to lead you to the best places to eat and sleep.

What's the cost and what's included? Most operators include lodging and meals in the price of tours, but some cover only lodging. Unless otherwise noted, the tour prices listed in this chapter are per person and include double-occupancy lodging and meals. You must room with another birder or pay a single supplement for a private room. Transportation between birding destinations once the tour is under way is always included in the price.

What are the accommodations like? Most tours use reliable national or local chain hotels and motels that are clean and comfortable but not fancy. Sometimes, however, tours go to areas where there are more interesting inns and bed-and-breakfasts.

Will laundry service be available? If your trip of choice is in a hot, humid climate or involves slogging through mud, the availability of laundry service will help you cut down on what you pack.

What is the food like? No tour operator provides gourmet dining, but most try to find local restaurants that serve good food, including regional dishes that you will not find at home. Many operators arrange for catered hot lunches or picnics so that you do not have to leave your birding spot at midday.

What kind of transportation is used? Most companies use vans outfitted to carry up to 15 people in relative comfort. Since you spend quite a bit of time in the van, make sure you do not have to share it with too many people. It is better to find an outfitter that uses two vans per trip rather than filling one to capacity.

How far in advance do I need to book? Most outfitters ask that people reserve at least a couple of months in advance; you may, however, want to book earlier to make sure you are not left out of popular tours. Still, as long as the tour is not full, you will be welcome to sign up.

Do you have references from past guests? It is often helpful to talk with someone who has already taken a trip with the outfitter you are considering. That person can supply an unbiased view.

MAJOR PLAYERS

FIELD GUIDES Founded in 1985, this operator does only birding tours. It offers a dozen trips in the United States and about 70 more worldwide. Field Guides prides itself on the dedication of its tour leaders, most of whom are full-time employees (a rarity in the birding world) and many of whom are part owners of the company.

On most Field Guide trips, there are two leaders and no more than 16 people transported by 15-passenger vans. The pace is always leisurely, although you may walk three or four hours per day (Box 160723, Austin, TX 78716, tel. 512/327–4953, fax 512/327–9231).

VICTOR EMANUEL NATURE TOURS In business since 1976, Victor Emanuel Nature Tours offers about 50 natural history and birding tours in the United States, out of about 140 worldwide. The company's expert birding guides are either professional ornithologists or naturalists with years of field experience and a good working knowledge of the area through which they tour.

Groups consist of up to 18 birders, who are transported from site to site in 15-passenger vans, as well as planes, ferries, boats, and trains when necessary. The amount of daily walking varies from tour to tour, but the pace is usually moderate enough for people of all ages who are in good health. Children must be at least 14 years old to participate (Box 33008, Austin, TX 78764, tel. 512/328–5221 or 800/328–VENT, fax 512/328–2919).

WINGS This tour operator was founded in 1973 as Northeast Birding and has expanded its offerings to more than 40 tours in the United States and another 100 in Canada, Europe, the Middle East, and Asia. Wings has a worldwide network of 28 field experts, many of whom live in the area they are touring.

Groups range from 6 to 18 participants, with one leader for every 8 to 10 birders. Transportation is via 15- and 22-passenger vans as well as larger coaches. There is some moderate physical activity on this company's tours, including some walks that last up to four hours and shorter ones before breakfast. Uneven and wet terrain are not unusual. Although the walking is rarely strenuous, on trips with more than one leader you may be split up into faster and slower groups.

Lodging is included with all tours, but in North America, meals are not. Time is allowed for grocery shopping for those who want to make their own lunch or dinner rather than paying for restaurant meals. There are no organized group activities outside of your daily touring, and nightlife is virtually nonexistent because Wings tends to bird in places that are far from commercial development (Box 31930, Tucson, AZ 85751, tel. 602/749–1967, fax 602/749–3175).

FAVORITE TOURS

THE MID-ATLANTIC

NEW JERSEY AND PENNSYLVANIA Fall Migration of Hawks from Cape May. This eight-day tour revolves around the fall migration of hawks, but you also see other birds of prey, as well as waterbirds and waterfowl. You travel around the two best places to see the migration: Cape May State Park, on the New Jersey coastline; and Hawk Mountain, near the Delaware River in southeastern Pennsylvania. You may view up to 15 species of birds of prey flying above the vivid autumn colors of the region, including *Accipiter* and *Buteo* hawks, falcons, golden and bald eagles, and ospreys. Some days you may see more than 1,000 individual birds.

Many other species migrate along the Appalachian Mountains and Atlantic Coast at this time of year, and your skills are tested trying to identify fall warblers, thrushes, orioles, tanagers, and shorebirds. In addition, you visit the wetlands of Forsythe National Wildlife Refuge, north of Cape May, where there are a variety of waterbirds and waterfowl ranging from terns and shorebirds to ducks and geese.

Eight-hour days and fairly easy walking typify this tour, but the rocky trails through Hawk Mountain Sanctuary require good balance. The tour leaves from Philadelphia, where you gather for a welcome dinner and do some local birding early the next morning before driving to Cape May. You spend three days at Cape May, then take a day to drive to Nottingham, your base for two days at Hawk Mountain and its environs. On the morning of the last day, you can take an optional excursion at no additional cost to Conowingo Dam on the Susquehanna River, where bald eagles can sometimes be seen feeding on the fish that pass through the dam's power turbines.

You stay at Cape May's Montreal Inn, amid the gingerbread Victorian architecture of the old-fashioned seaside resort town. Expect to eat at least one version of the blue-claw crab, a local favorite. Near Hawk Mountain, you spend three nights at the Nottingham Inn, in the heart of Pennsylvania's mushroom-growing region. Be sure to try one of the many dishes made with fresh mushrooms. *Victor Emanuel Nature Tours, Box 33008, Austin, TX 78764, tel. 512/328–5221 or 800/328–VENT, fax 512/328–2919. Early Oct.: 8 days, $1,075. Sign up 3 months in advance.*

THE SOUTH

FLORIDA Tropical Birdlife of the South and the Dry Tortugas. Spring is an exciting time for birding in south Florida. On a good day, you can spot reddish egrets, roseate spoonbills, black-crowned night herons, snail kites, limpkins, Florida sandhill cranes, and short-tailed hawks—along with plenty of gators. During this tour, many resident birds are nesting and migrants are arriving daily.

The 12-day tour starts in Miami, then heads for the area's wealth of birding hot spots, including Loxahatchee National Wildlife Refuge, with its mottled ducks, smooth-billed anis, and purple gallinules; and Corkscrew Swamp, a mysterious-looking wetland landscape of bald cypress trees covered with Spanish moss that attracts swallow-tailed kites and wood storks among resident and migrant raptors and wading birds.

Around Key West, you listen for Antillean nighthawks at dusk, after watching wading birds and shorebirds in area ponds and burrowing owls near the airport. In the lower Keys, you search for rare mangrove cuckoos, along with more common white-crowned pigeons, black-whiskered vireos, and gray kingbirds.

From Key West, you set sail on a 100-foot motorized vessel for the seabird nesting colonies of the Dry Tortugas, about 70 miles west. On Bush Key, the activity of thousands of sooty terns and brown noddies is an overwhelming sight, but watch for rarer species like black noddies, masked boobies,

and brown boobies. Ft. Jefferson, a long-deserted 19th-century fortress; Loggerhead Key; Middle Key; and the smaller Keys are also explored as you look for migrant warblers and other songbirds making their way across the Caribbean Sea. On the way to and from the Dry Tortugas, you are kept busy watching for seabirds such as magnificent frigate birds, bridled terns, Audubon's shearwaters, and roseate terns. While in the Dry Tortugas, you stay aboard the ship for a couple of nights. This can get a bit cramped, but the sight of masked boobies and the sound of the songs of migrating warblers and thrushes make it worthwhile.

Back in Miami, you spend some time watching introduced species: red-whiskered bulbuls, common mynahs, spot-breasted orioles, and an unbelievable variety of parrots.

Expect 10- to 12-hour days, with the earliest reveille at 5 AM. Aside from the boat and one night in the Clewiston Inn, an antebellum-style hotel built in the 1920s, lodging is in comfortable if unremarkable hotels. The garlic poppyseed rolls at Donzanti's Italian restaurant in Homestead are considered one of the culinary high points of this tour. *Wings, Box 31930, Tucson, AZ 85751, tel. 602/749–1967, fax 602/749–3175. Late Apr.–early May: 12 days, $1,800. Price does not include meals; sign up at least 2 months in advance.*

SOUTH CAROLINA Spring Migration around Charleston. Spring migration along coastal South Carolina offers a look at many species of songbirds in the forests and waterbirds along the coastal marshes. On this tour, you go on outings from your base in Charleston to sample the rich variety of birdlife in the area.

If you are lucky, you might spot endangered red-cockaded woodpeckers or a rarely observed Swainson's warbler. More common birds in these parts include red-shouldered and red-tailed hawks, pileated woodpeckers, beautiful yellow prothonotary warblers, and, appropriately, Carolina wrens.

Some of the birding locations you visit during this nine-day trip are Francis Marion

National Forest, Cape Romain National Wildlife Refuge, Cypress Gardens, and I'On Swamp. You also see many historic Old South locations, such as Ft. Sumter, Magnolia Gardens, and Boone Hall Plantation. The coastal wetlands and low-tide mudflats attract a variety of migrating shorebirds— plovers, oystercatchers, and sandpipers, along with terns, skimmers, gulls, and brown pelicans. In the woodlands, you monitor the spring migration and see different kinds of warblers, tanagers, orioles, thrushes, vireos, and other birds.

You stay at the Vendue Inn in the heart of Charleston's historic district, just a block from the city's waterfront park. The inn is furnished with 18th-century reproductions and serves a Continental breakfast in your room each morning and wine and cheese most afternoons. The hotel's elegant restaurant offers everything from pasta to seafood. *Wings, Box 31930, Tucson, AZ 85751, tel. 602/749–1967, fax 602/749–3175. Early Apr.: 9 days, $1,700. Price does not include meals; sign up at least 2 months in advance.*

THE MIDWEST

MICHIGAN AND ONTARIO **Spring Migration on Lake Ontario.** This nine-day trip begins by crossing the border at Detroit to visit one of Canada's premier birding locales, Point Pelee, on the western shore of Lake Ontario. Exhausted migrants stop along this peninsular funnel of land, so you see a variety of songbirds, including warblers, thrushes, vireos, tanagers, orioles, grosbeaks, and many others. Shorebirds, ducks, Canada geese, and birds of prey are also abundant here at this time of year. Almost every species of bird found in the eastern forests and wetlands of North America can be sighted.

After three days at Point Pelee, you spend two days in Long Point, a peninsula that extends into Lake Erie. You then return to the United States and the jack pine forests of central Michigan, the only nesting area of the endangered Kirtland's warbler. The cool shadows of the Upper Peninsula's forests

hide other warblers, and common loons can be spotted at area lakes. You can also find displaying blue grouse and visit a sharp-tailed grouse lek, while keeping an eye peeled for nesting northern saw-whet owls along the way. At this point, you work your way back to Detroit.

Although you do move around a lot, eight-hour days and travel in 15-passenger vans keep this trip from being strenuous, and the organizers say almost anyone can keep up. Most participants are eager to get up before sunrise for the optional expedition to catch the dawn chorus of birdsongs, and just as anxious to go out again after sunset for the best owling.

You stay in modest motels such as the Point Pelee Motor Inn and comparable places in the Upper Peninsula. Breakfast and lunch are sometimes eaten in the field; if so, you can look forward to baked goods brought in from the home base of Field Guides in Austin, Texas, and such fare as tortellini salad, shrimp salad with poppyseed dressing, and wild rice salad. Dinners are at local restaurants. *Field Guides, Box 160723, Austin, TX 78716, tel. 512/327–4953, fax 512/327–9231. Mid-May: 9 days, $1,300. Sign up 10 weeks in advance.*

MINNESOTA AND NORTH DAKOTA **From Duluth in Search of Nesting Birds.** This late-spring tour in the dense pine forests of Minnesota and North Dakota offers a chance to see both familiar and sought-after birds nesting and in full song and full breeding plumage. At this time of year, the forest and lake country blooms with the sounds of ruffed and spruce grouse, northern saw-whet owls, black-backed woodpeckers, and boreal and black-capped chickadees.

The 10-day tour begins (and ends) in Duluth, Minnesota, on the southwest shore of Lake Superior. You spend about eight hours a day in the field, but it is fairly easy going; you hike only 1 to 2 miles at a slow pace in level forested areas (bring insect repellent). More than 20 species of warblers can be seen in these remote northern forests, along with least, alder, and yellow-bellied flycatchers and other passerine birds. You spend time in such prime birding spots as Sax-Zim Bog, McGregor Marsh, Solon Springs, Grand Marais, and Superior National Forest, and on the Gunflint Trail. There is also a 100-mile drive along Lake Superior, with stops for a look at common loons and Peregrine falcons, as well as an optional night excursion into a wetland in search of yellow rails (bring your own flashlight).

Accommodations are in modest motels. Although this tour is not renowned for its gourmet dining, trip leaders say a good bet is always the fresh fish, especially walleyed pike, which will appear on many restaurants' menus. *Victor Emanuel Nature Tours, Box 33008, Austin, TX 78764, tel. 512/328–5221 or 800/328–VENT, fax 512/328–2919. Mid-June: 10 days, $1,395. Sign up at least 3 months in advance.*

NEBRASKA **Spring Migration of Cranes.** The sight and sound of the thousands of sandhill cranes that fill the springtime sky along the Platte River in Nebraska is an awesome thing to experience. Nowhere else on earth is there such an aggregation of cranes, which are joined during spring migration by countless waterfowl: Canada geese, white-fronted geese, snow geese, and a variety of ducks that are most abundant in the wetlands south of the river.

Other early harbingers of spring in this region include western meadowlarks, red-winged and yellow-headed blackbirds, American robins, ferruginous hawks, and northern harriers. A few wintering birds may also linger, including bald eagles, rough-legged hawks, northern shrikes, snow buntings, and, maybe, a snowy owl.

This five-day tour starts and ends in Omaha, and you spend a couple of nights in Grand Island. Shorter days in March make rising before dawn routine (among this trip's highlights is the cacophony of birdcalls that breaks the morning silence). You spend all six or seven hours of daylight out in the field. Accommodations are in Ramada and Holiday Inn properties. The weather at this time of year is wildly unpredictable, so be prepared for anything from a balmy 70°F to snow. *Victor Emanuel Nature Tours, Box 33008, Austin, TX 78764, tel. 512/328–5221 or 800/328–VENT, fax 512/328–2919. Mid-Mar.: 5 days, $700. Sign up by mid-Jan.*

THE SOUTHWEST

ARIZONA **Hummingbirds from Tucson to the Mexican Border.** Southeast Arizona offers the chance to see as many as 15 species of hummingbirds—more than in any other single area of the United States. On this midsummer tour, you see varieties more commonly encountered in Mexico and Central America, including blue-throated and magnificent hummingbirds, as well as migrating species—such as Anna's and Allen's hummingbirds—that nest along the West Coast. In addition, you see many species indigenous to the Southwest and get to take in this region's grand scenery in the bargain.

The six-day tour starts in Tucson with a visit to a natural history museum for a quick lesson in the local flora and fauna before heading into the field. You visit Madera Canyon, where, along with hummingbirds, you see painted redstarts, black-throated gray warblers, and varied buntings. Also on the itinerary is Nogales, at the Mexican border, for a couple of days birding in and around the nearby Huachuca Mountains to explore and bird in Cave Creek Canyon, where you see some of the rarer birds.

Accommodations are in modest motels. At Cave Creek Ranch (where you stay for two nights), near Portal, Arizona, you can watch hummingbirds at feeders just outside the cabins. More memorable meals, which are included in the cost of the trip, come at the Portal Cafe, a favorite haunt of the locals for its burgers and Mexican dishes. *Victor Emanuel Nature Tours, Box 33008, Austin, TX 78764, tel. 512/328–5221 or 800/328–VENT, fax 512/328–2919. Late July–early Aug.: 6 days, $875. Sign up at least 3 months in advance.*

ARIZONA AND UTAH **Canyonlands in September.** Birds almost take a backseat to the dramatic southwestern landscapes of this 12-day trip—Zion and Bryce Canyon national parks, Monument Valley, Petrified Forest National Park, the White Mountains, and the Grand Canyon. Still, the birding in these parts is outstanding. You can expect to spot black-headed grosbeaks, Clark's nutcrackers, pinyon and Steller's jays, prairie falcons, and Lewis's woodpeckers, along with many migrating species that pass through the region in fall.

Although some 10 hours each day is spent in the field, the pace is easygoing, sometimes slow. The longest walk is only about half a mile. The days can be very hot in September (summer comes early and stays late in the Southwest), but most of the tour is at moderately high elevations (5,000 feet to 8,000 feet) so conditions are comfortable.

Lodging varies from unremarkable if adequate hotels to two-person cabins at a rustic guest ranch on the banks of the Colorado River in Springerville, Arizona. Transportation is by van. In addition to the local wonders of nature, you visit historic sites in the heart of Navajo country and have a chance to sample at least one authentic Native American meal (if you like it, there are more where that came from). *Wings, Box 31930, Tucson, AZ 85751, tel. 602/749–1967, fax 602/749–3175. Early Sept.: 12 days, $1,425. Price does not include meals; sign up at least 2 months in advance.*

TEXAS **Edward's Plateau and the Big Bend.** Birders on this tour through Big Bend National Park encounter many of the nearly 450 species of birds that have been documented in this desert canyonland, including Lucifer hummingbirds, Montezuma quail, elf owls, gray-breasted jays, hepatic tanagers, varied buntings, and zone-tailed hawks, and some species found nowhere else in the United States, such as colima warblers.

Although most of this nine-day tour is spent in Big Bend, the first two days are in Concan, some 50 miles west of San Antonio, in the west Texas hill country of the Edwards Plateau. Here you see golden-cheeked warblers and black-capped vireos; both have recently been added to the endangered species list. You also witness dramatic evening flights of Mexican free-tailed bats as they emerge by the tens of thousands from their hillside cave entrances.

The weather on this tour varies; although daytime on the desert floor can be hot, you are also at an elevation of some 6,500 feet for part of the time. Come prepared for hot days and cool nights. The walks are all pretty easy, except for one somewhat more strenuous hike at Big Bend, but it is optional.

You stay at the Chisos Mountain Lodge, near Big Bend, and eat in its restaurant, which serves such basic dishes as chicken-fried steak and burgers. Lunches are usually picnics in the field, with sometimes elaborate fixings (pasta, shrimp) prepared by the tour leaders and, as always with Field Guides, delicious baked goods from their headquarters in Austin. *Field Guides, Box 160723, Austin, TX 78716, tel. 512/327–4953, fax 512/327–9231. Late Apr.–early May: 9 days, $1,450. Sign up by mid-Feb.*

TEXAS AND NEW MEXICO **Spring Birding at High Elevations.** Held during the nesting season, this tour zigzags through southern New Mexico, starting from El Paso, Texas, and winding up in Albuquerque, to seek out hepatic tanagers, gray vireos, phainopeplas, crissal thrashers, Virginia's warblers, black-chinned sparrows, and white-throated swifts. On day hikes through the mountains surrounding Santa Fe, you may glimpse Lewis's woodpeckers, Clark's nutcrackers, zone-tailed hawks, and lazuli buntings.

Among the rarities you may come across in the southwest corner of New Mexico are gray-breasted jays, red-faced and olive warblers, painted redstarts, bridled titmice, and common black hawks. Other wildlife you encounter along the way are herds of pronghorn antelope and, occasionally, mule deer.

The hikes on this 11-day trip are not considered difficult, but they are at very high elevations, so it's easier to get winded. The high point of the trip (literally) is when you dine at the restaurant atop 11,000-foot Sandia Peak near Albuquerque; you get to the restaurant via a tram from the 6,000-foot level. Lodgings are in Holiday Inn, Hilton, and Best Western hotels. Along with the birding, you visit historic Native American sites and spend some time sightseeing in Santa Fe. *Victor Emanuel Nature Tours, Box 33008, Austin, TX 78764, tel. 512/328–5221 or 800/328–VENT, fax 512/328–2919. Late May–early June: 11 days, $1,615. Sign up by early Apr.*

THE ROCKIES

COLORADO **Breeding Prairie Grouse in Spring.** This nine-day tour from Pueblo to Denver takes in Pawnee National Grasslands along the way and provides new additions for many people's life lists: mountain plovers, McCown's and chestnut-collared longspurs, prairie falcons, upland sandpipers, ferruginous hawks, and burrowing owls, among others. The main attractions are the fascinating breeding displays of prairie grouse seen here at this time of year.

The wild dancing and strutting behaviors of each of the four plains species—sharp-tailed and sage grouse along with greater and lesser prairie chickens—are highlighted by the bizarre sounds that emanate from each of the rival males' inflated neck sacs. In the Rocky Mountains near Steamboat Springs, you should see blue grouse along with mountain bluebirds, Williamson's sapsuckers, and, perhaps, a golden eagle or two. In the cactus-studded foothills near Pueblo are species more common to the Southwest; you may even spot a greater roadrunner, the real-life version of Wile E. Coyote's nemesis (beep beep).

You move around a lot on this tour, with a good deal of daytime driving, broken up by frequent stops. You also travel from prairie grasslands to fairly high elevations in the Rocky Mountains, so prepare for cool evening temperatures. Lodging is in Holiday

Inns, Days Inns, and comparable local hotels, and meals are adequate if unremarkable. *Victor Emanuel Nature Tours, Box 33008, Austin, TX 78764, tel. 512/328–5221 or 800/328–VENT, fax 512/328–2919. Late Apr.: 9 days, $1,235. Sign up 4 months in advance.*

WYOMING **Birds of Summer in Yellowstone and the Grand Tetons.** The sight of birds does not prompt the same sense of awe as Old Faithful or a herd of bison, and they certainly are not the reason that most people visit Yellowstone and Grand Teton national parks. Birds are, however, a part of the richness of these dramatic showplaces of the western landscape, and a wide variety of western mountain species can be seen here.

In the pine-dominated forest, you might see three-toed and black-backed woodpeckers, Steller's jays, Clark's nutcrackers, and Williamson's sapsuckers. Meadows of wildflowers attract calliope and broad-tailed hummingbirds and mountain bluebirds are common as well. Along watercourses are American dippers, common mergansers, and, sometimes, harlequin ducks. At lakes, watch for cinnamon teal, Canada geese, and giant white trumpeter swans. Other waterbirds in the area include western and Clark's grebes, American white pelicans, common loons, and sandhill cranes. A few surprises are always in store for Yellowstone birders; keep an eye out for a blue grouse, an immature bald eagle, or even a great gray owl hunting along a forest edge.

Even with one 10-hour day, this nine-day tour is not particularly strenuous; you travel by van to sighting locales within each of the parks, and the longest walk is 2 miles. As part and parcel of your birding, you take a ride on an aerial tram and a raft trip on the Snake River.

You spend four nights in the town of Jackson, just south of Grand Teton National Park, a couple of nights in two-person cabins in the park, and another two nights in Yellowstone's historic Old Faithful Inn. For dining, Dornan's, a restaurant on the Snake River in Grand Teton, is a perennial favorite (there is an all-you-can-eat menu for $11). The hearty fare is cooked in a Dutch oven; the short ribs are highly recommended. *Wings, Box 31930, Tucson, AZ 85751, tel. 602/749–1967, fax 602/ 749–3175. Mid-June: 9 days, $1,250. Price does not include meals; sign up at least 2 months in advance.*

THE WEST COAST

CALIFORNIA Winter Birding in the San Francisco Bay Area. The varied terrain around San Francisco Bay attracts a diversity of birdlife. On this seven-day Field Guides tour of the Bay Area and environs, you see resident and wintering birds in freshwater and saltwater marshes, Pacific beaches, oak savannas, redwood forests, and mixed conifer woodlands.

Four days of this trip are spent in and around Monterey Bay and Carmel, south of San Francisco. Along the coast, you concentrate on shorebirds and coastal species: black turnstones, surfbirds, black oystercatchers, rock sandpipers, and a variety of gulls, terns, sea ducks, loons, cormorants, and grebes. In the coastal grasslands and oaks of the Penoche Valley, you see yellow-billed magpies, black-shouldered kites, mountain bluebirds, and Nuttall's woodpeckers. On a boat trip into the open sea from Monterey Bay, you may spot species of albatross, shearwaters, auklets, murrelets, loons, grebes, scoters, and other wintering seabirds. You also get a chance to observe harbor seals, sea otters, dolphins, whales, and California sea lions.

The last couple of days of the trip, you head back to San Francisco for a look at the birdlife of the bay and Point Reyes National Seashore. You travel by van, and very little strenuous walking is required; expect to be out and about for six to eight hours each day. There is little predawn or nighttime birding on this trip.

Lodging is in moderately priced chain or similar local hotels, albeit sometimes infused with a little more native charm. The mealtime possibilities are tremendously varied, and you can expect a mouth-watering selection of choices. Few meals are eaten in the field because even the most remote birding sites in this area are close to good eateries. In Carmel, the Rio Grill's roast chicken with honey glaze, ribs, or fresh fish are considered musts. *Field Guides, Box 16073, Austin, TX 78716, tel. 512/327–4953, fax 512/327–9231. Mid-Feb.: 7 days, $900. Sign up at least 2 months in advance.*

CALIFORNIA AND ARIZONA Desert Birds in Winter. When cold weather blankets most of the country, many birders join this Wings tour to the balmy environs of the deserts of southern California and southeastern Arizona, traveling from San Diego to Tucson.

In and around San Diego, you can hope to see California gnatcatchers, wren-tits, and Clark's grebes among the abundance of birds that regularly winter here. As you move east, you may encounter sage and LeConte's thrashers, Scott's orioles, lesser and (maybe) Lawrence's goldfinches, and verdins. Inland, around the Salton Sea, a huge saltwater lake in the California desert, are wintering flocks of snow and Ross's geese, a variety of wintering ducks, cattle egrets, white-faced ibis, long-billed curlews, and burrowing owls.

In the deserts of Arizona south of Phoenix, you see Harris's hawks, phainopeplas, cactus wrens, and Gila woodpeckers. The area southwest of Tucson—Madera Canyon, Patagonia, and Nogales—is one of the finest birding locales in the nation, and where you might see vermilion flycatchers, gray-breasted jays, bridled titmice, and yellow-eyed juncos. You could easily spot more than 200 species on this 10-day tour.

You rise at about dawn and press on for most of the day, although you have the option of taking the early part of the morning off, because the group returns to the motel for breakfast before heading to the next birding locale. Most viewing is done from within sight of the vans, so only a few short walks are called for. Among the variety of cuisines available on this trip, there is a plenitude of high-quality Mexican food to be had in the region. *Wings, Box 31930, Tucson, AZ 85751, tel. 602/749–1967, fax 602/749–3175. Late Jan.: 10 days, $1,150. Price does not include meals; sign up at least 2 months in advance.*

OREGON Coast and Forest Birds. Malheur National Wildlife Refuge in southeastern Oregon is a great location for viewing the migration along the Pacific flyway, and it is the grand finale of this trip, which covers a wide range of bird habitats, from Oregon's rocky coast inland through broken woodlands, farming areas, wetlands, coastal forests, eastern deserts, and high mountains.

Despite the amount of ground covered on this 13-day trip (you change locales and hotels every couple of days), the pace is relaxed, in keeping with the easygoing manner of Field Guides trips. You can expect to rise before sunup on only a couple of mornings, and generally days in the field are not overly long—about eight hours is average, although energetic birders will have the chance for owling some nights. You also take a boat trip 30 miles offshore in search of seabirds. Traversing these varied landscapes and habitats, you can expect to see about 200 species in all. Birds commonly sighted on this tour include sandhill cranes, Canada geese, trumpeter swans, a variety of ducks, American white pelicans, four species of grebes, Wilson's phalaropes, and a range of birds of prey.

You stay in local hotels and motels along the route, each clean, comfortable, and characteristic of its surroundings (seaside motel, mountain lodge). Meals are often eaten in the individual hotel's restaurant, such as the elegant establishment in the Inn at Face Rock, in Bandon, which offers a wide selection, from pepper steak to fresh chinook salmon and homemade soups, or at local restaurants that trip leaders know are good and interesting. You start and finish this tour in Portland. *Field Guides, Box 160723, Austin, TX 78716, tel. 512/327–4953, fax 512/327–9231. Mid-Sept.: 13 days, $1,750. Sign up 5 months in advance.*

WASHINGTON From Coast to Mountaintop in Fall. This 13-day tour runs from the alpine tundra above the timberline on snow-capped Mt. Rainier to the temperate rain forests of the Olympic Peninsula and the rocky Pacific coast beyond. It is timed to take advantage of the relatively dry, warm weather when native flowers are still in bloom.

You head east from Seattle (also the final stop) for the Cascade Mountains, then on to the Yakima Valley, for a look at such resident birds as chestnut-backed chickadees and American dippers; you also may spot golden eagles and canyon wrens. The tour next moves you south toward the Columbia River for western and Clark's grebes, summering white pelicans, and chukars, phalaropes, Brewer's sparrows, and open-country hawks. As you travel through the various terrains, you get a look at a range of migrants (vireos, warblers, western tanagers) and such resident birds as gray partridges, chestnut-backed chickadees, varied thrushes, Townsend's warblers, rufous hummingbirds, and white-headed woodpeckers in the forests; and black oystercatchers, ruddy and black turnstones, and surfbirds, among others, on the coast.

On the coastal portion of this tour, several boat trips take you about 40 miles out to sea to the edge of the continental shelf to spot species of albatross, storm petrels, jaegers, shearwaters, auklets, gulls, terns, and other seabirds. These excursions also allow you to see a variety of whales and dolphins.

The final days of the trip are spent in the varied terrain of the Olympic Peninsula, either in the temperate, mountainous rain forest, where you can see blue grouse, falcons, winter wrens, and finches, or along the coast of the Strait of Juan de Fuca for a look at tufted puffins, pigeon guillemots, golden-crowned sparrows, and Hutton's vireos.

For the most part, you stay in modest motels and hotels, but you spend two nights in Mt. Rainier National Park at the Paradise Inn, built in 1916 and now a historic landmark. There are no phones or TVs in any of the guestrooms, which most people think only adds to the hotel's rustic charm, but not every room has its own bath—a feature many regard as less than charming. Both formal dining and less formal (and less expensive) cafeteria-style food are available at the hotel. *Victor Emanuel Nature Tours, Box 33008, Austin, TX 78764, tel. 512/328–5221 or 800/328–VENT, fax 512/328–2919. Late Aug.–early Sept.: 13 days, $2,150. Sign up at least 3 months in advance.*

ALASKA

SOUTHEAST **Denali's Special Species.** Denali National Park has abundant big game, including moose, caribou, Dall sheep, wolves, and grizzly bears, but on this tour you come to see the birds, a number of which you cannot see in the lower 48 states.

Field Guides offers a 10- and 11-day trip (which can be combined for a 21-day excursion) through Denali and the Pribilof Islands. The trip takes place at the beginning of the Arctic summer, when the islands' coastlines teem with nearly 3 million nesting seabirds, including tufted and horned puffins, murres, kittiwakes, and auklets. You can often spot Asian strays, such as bluethroats, northern wheatears, white wagtails, and Arctic warblers, that have flown off course and landed here. At Denali, sightings of gyrfalcons, northern hawk owls, willow ptarmigan, and arctic terns compete with the continent's tallest peak, Mt. Denali, for birders' attention. Alaskan summer days are long, and birders make the most of it, spending 8 to 10 hours in the field, with some optional night birding.

You stay at the King Eider Inn on St. Paul Island during the Pribilof Islands leg of the trip. The hotel has no rooms with private bath. Although the inn's restaurant is pretty good, this area is not exactly renowned for its fine dining, so organizers supplement what is available locally with baked goods from Austin and provide simple meals of granola, yogurt, and fruit in the field. While in Denali National Park, you stay at the Kan-

tishna Roadhouse, a lodge with 50 rooms and 24 cabins. Despite the ruggedness of the terrain, this trip does not require difficult walking and people at all fitness levels should be comfortable with the pace.

During the second, 11-day trip excursions are made to Nome, Barrow, Seward, and the Anchorage area, offering chances to see a variety of nesting waterfowl, including emperor, brant, Canada, and white-fronted geese; king, common, and spectacled eiders; willow and rock ptarmigan; red and red-necked phalaropes; and a variety of forest birds. There is also a boat trip to Kenai Fjords National Park to see nesting seabirds along the rocky cliffs of the rugged coastline. *Field Guides, Box 160723, Austin, TX 78716, tel. 512/327–4953, fax, 512/327–9231. June: 10 days, $2,945; 11 days, $2,995; 21 days, $5,745. Sign up 3–4 months in advance.*

SOUTHEAST **Photographing Bald Eagles in the Chilkat River Valley.** There is simply no better opportunity to see and photograph bald eagles than during the November salmon runs along the Chilkat River in southeast Alaska. The largest concentration of eagles anywhere on earth can be seen when as many as 3,000 bald eagles congregate to feed on and fight over the plentiful fish against a dramatic backdrop of snowy scenery. The tall spruce and cottonwood trees that line the river serve as the eagles' perches.

From the hotel in Haines, the 16 participants on this five-day Joseph Van Os Photo Safaris tour share a school bus jitney with other nature tour groups for the 30-mile ride to the best eagle-viewing spots at open areas of the mostly frozen Chilkat River. The birdlife around here is accustomed to lots of traffic and is not particularly scared when approached. Because daylight is limited during this season, with perhaps only six hours a day (9 AM–3 PM), little time is spent hiking around.

You stay in the Captain's Choice Motel in Haines, and meals are provided by a local bakery that specializes in catering. There are alternatives, should you want to strike out on your own, but fine dining is simply not available in town.

Expect overcast—even snowy—weather, and try to get from Juneau to Haines a couple of days early, because fog can delay flights between the two towns for days at a time.

Led by renowned naturalists and photographers, this company's photo safaris teach you how to take high-quality photographs of birds rather than have you merely document on film the birds you encounter. You move around less and spend more time seeing fewer birds than on most other tours. *Joseph Van Os Photo Safaris, Box 655, Vashon, WA 98070, tel. 206/463–5383, fax 206/463–5484. Mid-Nov.: 5 days, $1,400. Sign up at least 6 months in advance.*

HAWAII

OAHU, MAUI, THE BIG ISLAND, AND KAUAI **From Tropical Forests to the Sea.** Amid the lush tropical beauty of four of the Hawaiian Islands—Oahu, Maui, Hawaii, and Kauai— are many indigenous and many endangered birds, such as nene geese, crested honeycreepers, and iiwis. This 15-day tour includes special access to rarely seen native tropical forests, several boat trips for a look at seabirds, and visits to protected refuges, as well as excursions to the forested beauty of the Nature Conservancy's Waikamoi Preserve and the Hakalau Forest National Wildlife Preserve. On the coast of Kauai you go to Kilauea Point National Wildlife Refuge to see coastal seabirds such as tropic birds, boobies, and frigate birds.

On the Big Island, you are sure to be overwhelmed by the spectacular view of the volcano during your four-night stay in Volcano House, perched on the edge of Kilauea Crater in Volcanoes National Park. The hotel's restaurant offers tasty enough food (try the prime rib or the scampi) to nearly distract you from the dining room's view of the crater.

Be prepared to get wet fairly often on this tour, which includes a boat trip, a visit to

Wailua Falls in Kauai, and a hike through a wet mountain forest; bring waterproof shoes and some rain gear. If you are game for more challenging hikes, you can wade through the sometimes knee-deep mud in pursuit of elusive crested honeycreepers in Maui's Waikamoi Preserve. *Victor Emanuel Nature Tours, Box 33008, Austin, TX 78764, tel. 512/328–5221 or 800/328–VENT, fax 512/328–2919. Late-Oct.–early Nov.: 15 days, $3,375. Sign up at least 3 months in advance.*

SOURCES

ORGANIZATIONS The **American Birding Association** (Box 6599, Colorado Springs, CO 80934-6599, tel. 800/634–7736) is the major organization for birders; it has about 10,000 members and acts as a clearinghouse for information on a variety of topics of interest to birders.

PERIODICALS *WildBird* magazine (Box 5060, Mission Viejo, CA 92690, tel. 714/855–8822) is the only monthly birding magazine available. It prints regular columns and feature articles about topics from natural history and travel to photography techniques and equipment descriptions. *Birder's World* (44 E. 8th St., #410, Holland, MI 49423, tel. 800/753–4873) is a bimonthly magazine featuring articles of general interest to birders. *Birding,* published bimonthly, is the magazine of the American Birding Association (*see* Organizations, *above*). *Birdwatcher's Digest* (Box 110, Marietta, OH 45750-9977, tel. 800/879–2473) is a small-format, general-interest birding magazine published six times a year. *Living Bird* (159 Sapsucker Woods Rd., Ithaca, NY 14850, tel. 607/254–2425) is the quarterly publication of the Cornell Lab of Ornithology.

BOOKS There are many reliable field guides; among the best known are *Field Guide to Eastern Birds* and *Field Guide to Western Birds,* by Roger Tory Peterson, published by Houghton Mifflin. The Peterson's series is the granddaddy of all birding field guides. The edition covering the western United States was updated in 1990; the updating of the eastern edition is under way. *Field Guide to the Birds of North America,* published by the National Geographic Society, is overall the most up-to-date guide. Its design makes this book easy to use, with a range map on the same page as the picture of each bird and pertinent information about it. *A Guide to Field Identification—Birds of North America* (Western Publishing) is an old standard, recently expanded, that has a range map and sono-gram for each bird. *The Audubon Society Master Guide to Birding* (Alfred A. Knopf) is a three-volume set with photos (other field guides depict the birds in paintings) that is really more of an at-home reference work than a portable field guide. However, the Audubon Society also produces two paperbacks, *An Audubon Handbook: Eastern Birds* and *An Audubon Handbook: Western Birds,* by John Farrand, Jr. These both feature photographs, too.

Campus Vacations

By Carole Martin

hether you frequently wax nostalgic for your carefree college days or are simply in need of a bit of personal enrichment, a campus vacation may be just the restorative you need this summer. Want to know more about Victorian England? Tin Pan Alley? Capitalism in China? Film noir? The Information Superhighway? All you need to do is head for your favorite campus and choose a subject. Continuing education divisions and alumni offices at colleges and universities across the country have developed scores of special programs that allow inquisitive nonstudents to spend their vacations exploring new intellectual horizons in an academic setting, in the spirit of Chautauqua—the granddaddy of all such programs, founded in 1874 in western New York State and still offering a rich schedule of classes, lectures, and other educational programs. The number of people going to campus for personal enrichment rather than a degree grows from year to year.

The beauty of one of these campus vacations, whether at a bucolic little college or amid the hallowed halls of a great university, is that there are no tests or grades, and you rarely have homework. Instead, you listen to experts lecture on a topic, read as much or as little as you want to supplement the lecture, and then discuss the pros, the cons, and the nuances with your peers beneath leafy boughs beside the quad or at spur-of-the-

moment pizza parties in the dorm. There are no admission requirements beyond a desire to expand your mind in a collegial atmosphere and an ability to pay the fees, which range from under $300 for five days at the Big Ten's Indiana University to around $1,200 for eight days at Stanford University in California. These prices include not only tuition but also a single room in a dorm, usually with shared bath, and two or three basic institutional meals a day.

The idea that intellectual growth needn't stop with graduation has become more than conventional wisdom in the second half of the 20th century. In 1956, the first Great Books group was formed in Chicago by University of Chicago president Robert Hutchkins, and others soon followed; people liked the idea of spending two hours in the hands of a leader trained to ask questions to spark discussions examining an author's words, meaning, and lessons. After World War II, night-school courses flourished to serve the needs of returning veterans; they attracted substantial numbers of students well into the 1960s and 1970s.

In the mid-1960s, Brown and Dartmouth adapted the idea of continuing education to vacation-length programs; they were a novel way to allow graduates to revisit and reacquaint themselves with their alma maters while strengthening the schools' ties with alumni—and encouraging alums to provide increased financial support. Cornell Univer-

Carole Martin's lifelong passion for learning has taken her from a career as a journalist and travel writer and editor to her current job as a teacher in the New York City public school system.

sity soon joined Brown and Dartmouth. The mid-1970s saw a host of schools across the country opening their doors to lifelong learners, people who thought immersing themselves in the classics or exploring the latest scientific breakthroughs with leading academicians might be the best of all possible vacations. Other institutions, both public and private, jumped on the bandwagon, sometimes as part of their outreach efforts to their communities. Surprised by the extent of interest they found, these colleges and universities responded by offering even broader arrays of self-contained courses, running from several days to several weeks.

Although today's learning vacations vary from campus to campus, all share a few basic characteristics. They tend to attract people who have been away from campus for years, not only alumni but also other people who love learning, ranging in age from 30 to 65 (with some as young as 18 and as old as 80). Unlike programs for regularly matriculated students, they last just a week or two. They use the same campus facilities, however: dorms, dining rooms, classrooms, auditoriums, and other venues. They also use existing faculty: Professors who teach regular summer school classes have a lighter load than usual, and those who have the summer off are often delighted to teach short-term courses in their areas of expertise.

All campus vacations offer the chance to exercise your mind and spend time with other people who are energized by discovering new interests and new ideas. Whether you participate in a program at a huge university like Indiana or at a tiny school like Maine's Colby College, the campus can seem like an oasis, far removed from the concerns of day-to-day life. Which is just what a vacation should be.

CHOOSING THE RIGHT PROGRAM

Beyond subject matter, a number of things will affect whether your campus vacation turns out to be the kind of experience you expect. You need to ask some key questions before deciding whether a particular program is right for you.

Who's teaching? Most colleges and universities showcase their own faculty at their campus vacation programs. However, depending on the theme or topic, prominent guest lecturers or visiting professors from nearby colleges and universities may supplement the home-campus staff.

What are the accommodations like? What's available can range from rather Spartan dormitories, with two twin beds to a room and communal bathrooms that serve an entire floor, to on-campus inns, conference centers, or even hotels—where all rooms have private baths, television sets, telephones, and other amenities. Somewhere in the middle are the dormitory situations sometimes called suites, where two to four rooms share a bathroom. Not all dorms have air-conditioning, and in certain parts of the country, you need it. In hot, humid areas, window fans may be provided—or you may be asked to bring your own.

There are usually a few commercial motels right on the periphery of college campuses, and some institutions block off rooms in them for summer program participants who wouldn't call it a vacation without 24-hour room service.

You may or may not need to bring soap, towels, sheets, and television sets, and other things that hotels commonly provide. Ask what's supplied and pack accordingly.

Can you earn academic credit? Although most of the summer programs are designed for edification, not certification, a few can award academic credit—a consideration if you are a teacher or are working part-time toward a degree.

How much of the day do you spend in the classroom? The more academic the program, the more hours you are likely to spend in the classroom. Generally, classes are scheduled for only part of the day to allow free time for physical activity, visits to nearby cultural centers, and informal discussions among students.

How large are the classes? Class size can range from as few as half a dozen for hands-on classes in the arts or computer technology to 75 for lectures. The norm is 15 to 25.

How much work is required outside the classroom? A few programs send enrollees reading lists before arrival, with the expectation that they'll complete some or all of the books. During the course, some require at least minimal homework. However, most are designed to allow students to complete their study within the classroom, and reading lists are handed out at the end of the program by way of suggestion to those who wish to pursue a subject off campus.

What other campus facilities can you use? As a student in residence, you usually have free run of the college, including the library and athletic facilities—tennis courts, golf courses, swimming pools, weight rooms. Some colleges have more to offer than others. Make sure that the campus provides what matters to you.

How big is the campus, and how easy is it to get around? Strolling through the bucolic grounds of a big university can be exhilarating. It also can be tiring if the campus is hilly and the places you need to go are at opposite ends of the grounds. Really big universities often have some type of van or bus system; some have bicycles for rent (or you might want to bring your own).

What's the cost and what's included? As a rule, there is a single all-inclusive price for college and university vacation learning programs, covering tuition, housing, and all meals. This is the case for the programs described here, unless otherwise noted. However, a number of colleges and universities either include only two meals a day or charge separately for tuition, rooms, and meals—an appealing price structure if you prefer to live off campus and eat in restaurants.

What is the food like? Almost everyone who has been out of school for a while remembers institutional cafeteria food with something less than enthusiasm. But things have improved a great deal on most college campuses. In addition to mystery meat and other blue plate specials, you'll frequently find salad bars and campus grills. If you have specific food preferences, make sure they can be accommodated.

What programs are available for nonparticipating family members? A number of campuses coordinate programs for children and teenagers who accompany their parents. Find out if an accompanying but nonparticipating traveling companion will also be able to take advantage of the university athletic facilities.

How long has the college been running these programs? For the most part, a young program can be as well designed and energizing as some of the more established ones. But chances are that a program that has been around a few years has ironed out all the kinks and has already answered the questions and met the challenges that you throw at them.

How far in advance do I need to register? Brochures describing the programs are typically available around January. Often, priority is given to alumni and parents of current students. Because these programs sell out fast, don't wait to sign up once you have decided what you want.

FAVORITE PROGRAMS

THE NORTHEAST

MAINE **Colby College Summer Institute.** In August, about 250 people from across the country head for this pretty little Waterville, Maine, campus to immerse themselves in great works of literature at a summer institute run by Wachs Great Books Forum, Inc., a New York-based nonprofit corporation. Each year the program focuses on a different theme, and you read and talk about an eclectic group of six or seven books relating to the topic. In past years, themes have included solitude, truth, destiny, and female writers (one year, the institute was devoted entirely to Plato). When you register and mail your

$100 deposit, Wachs sends you paperbacks of the books to be discussed so that you can read them before arrival. On campus, you're assigned to a group of 15 to 18 for two-hour conversations led by instructors trained to lead discussions of books using Great Books methods, which involve asking specific questions in order to encourage participants to talk about an author's words and their meaning and implications. Afternoons are free, and institute participants can take advantage of the college tennis courts, pool, and other facilities. In the evenings there are films, dancing, and concerts. Colby is all classic Georgian buildings and well-kept lawns; its relative isolation makes it an ideal spot for getting away from it all. Lodging is in dorms, which have window fans but lack air-conditioning (a feature you don't usually need anyway). And although the food served in the campus dining hall is modest, there is one feast, the celebratory outdoor lobster bake that ends each session. A program for children aged 4 through 15 is available. Brochures about the coming summer's program are prepared by January. *Colby College Summer Institute, Box V, Harvard, MA 01451, tel. 508/456–3505. Aug.: 6 days, $396; sign up 3–4 months in advance.*

NEW HAMPSHIRE **Dartmouth Alumni College.** Despite its academic rigor, this campus vacation program has proved very popular. It has taken place every August since the mid-1960s in Dartmouth's copper-top Colonial frame buildings, which surround a classic New England green. Each of its two five-day sessions is a series of lectures and discussions addressing a different theme, such as the riddles of creation or great books. Taught primarily by Dartmouth faculty with occasional guest lecturers, sessions usually involve two hour-long talks each morning and another at 4 PM, which are attended by all. After each of these, the audience breaks up into groups of about 15 for an hour's discussion.

Students take their academic pursuits seriously; since they eat breakfast and dinner with faculty in the campus cafeteria, there's a tendency to continue outside the class-room the debate that started inside. Afternoons are free for hiking or biking in the White Mountains or for exploring New England villages and area back roads, but you may not have time, given that there are reading assignments to be completed and, in the evening, special lectures or films, concerts, and plays related to the session's theme. Each year's program opens with a Sunday banquet and a guest speaker and closes with a picnic. The program is limited to 250 students, about half of whom attend both weeks' sessions.

Dorms offer singles, doubles, and suites, but they're simple, and although some do have air-conditioning, others have only fans; the college-owned, air-conditioned Hanover Inn is the place to stay if you like your comforts. Brochures for each summer's Alumni College usually are mailed out by March, and alumni, financial supporters, students' parents, past participants, and other friends of the college have priority; registration is not open to the general public until mid-May. A youth program, a scaled-down Alumni College with more recreation, is also available. *Dartmouth Alumni College, Department of Continuing Education, 309 Blunt Alumni Center, Hanover, NH 03755, tel. 603/646–2454, fax 603/646–1600. Aug.: 5 days, $400 for 1 session, $700 for 2. Price does not include lodging ($173–$350 for 1 session, $414–$700 for 2) or meals ($100 for 1 session, $225 for 2); sign up 4–5 months in advance.*

NEW YORK **Cornell Adult University.** Begun in 1968, this is one of the oldest campus vacation programs in the country: It's also one of the most extensive. Each July, four five-day sessions are held on the sprawling, hilly upstate New York campus. The array of courses is eclectic, covering a range of topics from the world of forensic science, Tin Pan Alley, and the American family to how to use the Internet and how to interpret poetry, from Homer to T. S. Eliot.

Some courses are lectures for 40 people or more, but there are also workshops and hands-on classes limited to 12 to 14 people.

Some 100 to 150 people sign up annually, and Cornell faculty members teach all the courses, which meet mornings, afternoons, and sometimes in the evening as well. If you're dedicated, you can log up to 35 hours of classroom time during the week. Attendance is not required, of course, and there are no homework assignments.

Away from class, there are squash and tennis courts, a state-of-the-art fitness room, a Robert Trent Jones–designed golf course, and two swimming pools. You can also go horseback riding, hike the hills of a 3,000-acre nature reserve or the stream-crossed Cornell Plantation, or look for the waterfalls and ravines high above Cayuga and Ithaca lakes.

Cornell, which has a strong academic program for hotel and restaurant management, has a reputation for serving some of the best college food in the country. Ice cream is homemade, and menus offer everything from eggs to order to Healthy Heart selections. Housing options range from dormitories with communal bathrooms (not air-conditioned but equipped with 20-inch box fans) to air-conditioned dorm rooms with private baths to quarters in a full-serice hotel on the campus; the fancier your accommodations, the greater your program fee. You might also opt to lodge at the Sheraton Inn, 3 miles off campus. A well-developed youth program for children aged three to sixteen runs concurrently with the Adult University. The brochure is available in February. *Adult University, Cornell University, 626 Thurston Ave., Ithaca, NY 14860, tel. 607/255–6260, fax 607/255–7533. July: 5 days, $735–$975. Price does not include 1 dinner; sign up 3–4 months in advance.*

NEW YORK **Summer Six at Skidmore.** Saratoga Springs, where Skidmore College is located, is the summer home of the New York City Ballet and the Philadelphia Orchestra. So it's appropriate that the arts are the focal point of virtually all the summer programs at this college in the foothills of the Adirondacks. Skidmore's highly regarded Summer Six art program draws

150 to 250 people who want to try something new or sharpen rusty skills and sensibilities. A number of shorter workshops lasting five days or more are available in figure modeling in clay, jewelry making, and monotypes and watercolor. Five-day workshops meet between 9 and 4 daily. There are usually between 10 and 15 students in each course.

In addition to the cultural activities in Saratoga Springs, students have access to the school's swimming pool, racquetball and squash courts, weight rooms, and 850 acres of attractively landscaped grounds. Summer students can stay on campus in modern, air-conditioned dormitories and take meals in a dining hall, the spa, or a snack bar. Although accommodations near campus are heavily booked in summer because of Saratoga Springs's popularity as a resort area, you can also stay off campus. The Summer Six brochure is available in late March. *Summer Six, Skidmore College, Saratoga Springs, NY 12866, tel. 518/584–5000, fax 518/584–3023. Late May–June and July–early Aug.: 5 days, $250. Price does not include lodging ($140 per week) or meals ($135 per week); sign up 3–4 months in advance.*

RHODE ISLAND **Brown University Summer College.** Brown was one of the pioneers in campus learning vacations, and this program, started in the 1960s, is a more intense intellectual experience than most. It involves a series of lectures and sophisticated discussion groups that focus on and develop a single topic—in recent years, ethnocentrism in history; the breakup of Eastern Europe; the Maya, Aztec, and Inca; and the legal system (in a program entitled The Law is an Ass). Although the idea of the summer college is to showcase Brown's own faculty, outside experts from business, government, and academe, such as Arthur Schlesinger, Jr., have participated.

The format usually calls for between five and seven hour-long lectures each day, which are attended by all participants; each is followed by a discussion in groups of about a dozen people. At one point, Brown officials considered making the program less rigorous, but the message from previous participants was "Don't baby us." In addition to the academic program, Brown schedules evening performances of theater, music, film, and dance that relate in some way to the theme or topic under study.

Intellectually demanding or not, Brown's summer college is frequently oversubscribed. Because the number of participants is limited to between 100 and 130, registration is offered first to alumni and parents of current students, then to the general public. Housing is in campus dormitory suites, which share bathroom facilities and are not air-conditioned; a more expensive choice is a new air-conditioned residence hall with singles in suites with living room and semiprivate bath and double rooms with televisions and daily maid service. The program brochure is usually available in early November. *Summer College, c/o Brown's Continuing College, Box 1920, Brown University, Providence, RI 02912, tel. 401/863–2474, fax 401/863–2785. June: 4 days, $725–$875 ($525 without lodging and dinner); sign up 3–4 months in advance.*

THE MID-ATLANTIC

PENNSYLVANIA **Penn State University Alumni College.** The five-day program held every July at this 540-acre campus in the shade of Mt. Nittany, in a scenic Appalachian valley, ordinarily shows off two of the university's colleges or schools: One year may highlight subjects typical of those studied in Penn State's School of Communications and its College of Engineering, for instance. Of the nine or so courses offered in a summer, you can generally sign up for two, each lasting three hours per day, unless you opt for a lecture course, which may run for a couple of hours with a short break. All classes are held in the morning; afternoons are reserved for tours of campus facilities, such as the biotech lab, or for an organized physical activity, which can be as accessible as rollerblading or as challenging as spelunking. The size of classes varies; while lectures may have 30 to 40 students, courses involving hands-on instruction, as with computers, and those that demand individualized attention, as in writing, are much smaller. The program draws between 70 and 100 adults each year. Although there are no assigned books or homework, professors provide bibliographies of related material so that you can pursue a subject further after the program has ended.

As students in residence, participants have access to all campus facilities, including two 18-hole golf courses, an Olympic-size swimming pool, tennis courts, and bowling lanes. During the Alumni College, Penn State also operates a day camp for children aged 6 to 13 and sports camps for teenagers. Lodging is in the Nittany Suites, the university's only air-conditioned dorm; food is wholesome and adequate, except for the ice cream, made on the campus, which is top-notch. Dinners are always on your own, but you may decide against taking the college meal plan—although at $27 for five days of breakfasts and lunches, it's a steal. The program brochure is usually available in mid-April. *Penn State University Alumni College, 105 Old Main, University Park, PA 16802-1559, tel. 814/865–7679, fax 814/865–3589. July: 5 days, $235. Price does not include lodging ($21 a night) or meals ($27 for five days' breakfasts and lunches); sign up 2–3 months in advance.*

THE SOUTH

NORTH CAROLINA **University of North Carolina Vacation College.** This is one of the nation's oldest universities, and its 730-acre campus is lovely in summer with its lush lawns, ancient trees, shaded walkways, and spacious quadrangles. Redbrick Federal buildings dating from the early 19th century predominate, but the architecture ranges from Palladian to postmodern; the nationally famous Morehead Planetarium is among the campus focal points.

Vacation College, sponsored by UNC's Program in the Humanities and Human Values since 1980 and held from mid-June through early August, consists of six or so 2½- to 5-day courses on cultural, societal, and moral topics, which can range from mythology and a look at the current state of the world to the Civil War and the American short story. About 250 to 300 people sign up each summer, and classes vary in size from 30 to 65.

Courses here tend to be fairly academically focused, but the most intensive of all are the courses that last just 2½ days; these include two hour-long lectures in the morning and one in the afternoon, each followed by a half-hour discussion period. In the five-day courses, there is usually one lecture and discussion period in the morning and one in the afternoon. In any case, you can schedule only one course at a time. Most instructors are UNC professors, but the faculty occasionally includes guests from nearby Duke University and North Carolina State. You are sent suggested reading lists before courses start, as well as bibliographies for follow-up reading. On the schedule of evening activities are films, receptions, and special dinners.

Vacation College students can use all campus facilities, including the swimming pools and tennis courts. Accommodations are in a new air-conditioned residence hall, Lenoir Hall, which has clusters of four rooms that share a bathroom; you can also stay at a university-owned motel next to the campus, the Carolina Inn, which is air-conditioned, although not as well as the dorms (fans have been handed out in the past). There's no meal plan, but in both accommodations, cafeterias offer three meals daily, including blue plate specials, burgers, pizza, salads, yogurt, and fruit; in the Carolina Inn, there's also a table-service restaurant that serves slightly better food (but is not open for breakfast). In addition, you can find a number of good eating spots nearby along Chapel Hill's main street. Brochures for each summer's Vacation College are generally available by March. Registration is open right up until the start of class, but some courses fill up early. *Vacation College, Humanities Program, CB#3425, Alumni House, University of North Carolina, Chapel Hill, NC 27599, tel. 919/962-1544, fax 919/962-4318. Mid-June–early Aug.: 2½–5 days $140–$240. Price does not include lodging ($30 a night in dorms, $54–$90 in motel) or meals; sign up 3–4 months in advance.*

THE MIDWEST

INDIANA **Indiana University Mini University.** For five days every June, from a Sunday through a Thursday, some 350 students attend the annual Mini University at this Big Ten school in the rolling southern part of the state. The program, which got its start in 1975, is a smorgasbord of lectures, with IU faculty members talking on as many as 100 individual topics clustered in seven categories: the arts, business, domestic issues, humanities, health and fitness, international affairs, and science.

Many classes, particularly those on current events, vary from year to year, but some favorites are repeated, such as the one about *Porgy and Bess*—IU is renowned for its music school—and the one that probes the nuances of body language. Morning classes last two hours, afternoon classes about an hour; you can sign up for one each morning and two each afternoon, or more than a dozen during a given summer week. Classroom discussion is encouraged, and while there are no tests or homework, you get reading lists of books and articles for future reference.

In the afternoon, instead of lectures, you can participate in tours of university facilities such as the science building; or you can take advantage of the two 18-hole golf courses, tennis courts, weight rooms, and several swimming pools, one of which is Olympic-size—IU is also known for its swimming program. The library is one of the largest in the country, and you can visit an I. M. Pei–designed modern art gallery. The campus itself sprawls with high-rise labs and dorms surrounded by parking lots but also has beautiful lawns anchored by huge old trees and late-19th-century buildings. Evening activities range from theater trips and movies to faculty receptions and recitals.

Most people stay either in the air-conditioned campus hotel, which is in the same building as the lecture halls and has private baths, or in an air-conditioned student residence hall with shared baths that is four shuttle-served blocks away. It isn't mandatory to stay on campus; if you stay in the residence hall, however, you can choose a package that includes your meals as well as your accommodations. If you bring your children, you have the option of signing them up for a day camp with age-graded programs at the IU Alumni Family Campus near Lake Monroe (it can accommodate youngsters aged 4 to 16). Brochures for the Mini University's annual offerings are available in March. *Mini University, Indiana University Alumni Association, Fountain Sq. 219, Bloomington, IN 47402-4822, tel. 812/855–9263 or 800/824–3044, fax 812/855–5959. June: 5 days, $98. Price does not include lodging (at varying prices depending on the quarters) or meals (available for $185 to those staying in residence hall); sign up 2–3 months in advance.*

OHIO **College of Wooster Summer of . . .** Begun in the 1970s, this alumni college is rooted in the strong liberal arts foundation and in the core curriculum of philosophy, art history, English, and music of the College of Wooster, the very picture of a small, traditional college with its English Collegiate Gothic–style buildings and 320 green acres of ash, elm, maple, oak, and sycamore trees. Every year for seven days in June, some 50 to 65 students come to the school for its summer program, which involves five courses; past topics have included Coping with Mental Chaos in the Age of Anxiety, Eastern Europe after Communism, Chicago in the Late 19th Century, John Chinaman as Sambo, Marriages, Family, and Community in the Middle Ages, and Fractals: Computer-generated Pictures of the Geometry of Nature. College of Wooster faculty members do the teaching and may assign readings in

advance and provide bibliographies for those who want to continue their studies after the program concludes. The name of the session changes every year to incorporate the current year—e.g., Summer of '95 or Summer of '96.

Each course involves three hour-long lectures, scheduled so that you can attend all five courses. In the afternoon, there's time for organized off-campus excursions to nearby attractions such as the art museum in Cleveland and the Blossom Music Center near Akron; these complement the academic program. You also have use of the college pool, golf course, tennis courts, running track, game room, and personal conditioning room. After dark, there are frequently performances by the Ohio Light Opera Company, in residence at the college in summer, as well as films and other activities.

Lodging options are an air-conditioned residence hall with shared baths or the Wooster Inn, which has private baths as well as air-conditioning. Food at the campus cafeteria is simple institutional fare, but good. The program brochure is ready in late March. *Summer of '95, Office of Alumni Relations, College of Wooster, Wooster, OH 44691, tel. 216/263-2324. June: 7 days, $340. Price does not include lodging ($120 in residence hall, $360 in inn but without breakfast); sign up 3–4 months in advance.*

THE WEST COAST

CALIFORNIA **Stanford University Summer College.** This eight-day program operated by the university's alumni association takes a multidisciplinary approach to a different broad general theme each year—in the past, good and evil, power and intimacy, and the environment. Professors from different areas, which in a given year might include geology, biology, literature, and political science, examine the general topic in lectures from the perspective of their particular discipline. These instructors are primarily Stanford faculty, but occasionally they are joined by outside experts who are Stanford graduates or otherwise connected with the university.

As a rule, three or four lectures of approximately an hour each are scheduled each day; there are 24 in a week. You can attend as few or as many as you wish. Usually the lectures, which are held in large halls and are open to all participants, are followed by small-group discussions led by the individual professors. There is no required reading and there are no tests, although some preparatory materials may be mailed in advance, depending on a particular year's theme. Professors may provide bibliographies and other text for participants to take home at the conclusion of the program. About 200 to 225 students attend summer college each year; it's an older than usual group, with most people from 50 to 70.

In your free time, you have access to most campus facilities, including the outstanding library, a swimming pool, tennis courts, and a golf driving range. The program also includes organized tours of some of Stanford's more specialized facilities, movies, and other cultural programming related to the theme.

You have the option of staying at Stanford in one of the university's newer, air-conditioned residence halls, which has its own dining facility. Or you can decide to stay off campus in any number of establishments ranging from bed-and-breakfasts to chain motels and hotels. When you pay tuition only, you only get lunch. The summer college brochure is ready in early May. *Summer College, Stanford University, Bowman Alumni House, Stanford, CA 94305-4005, tel. 415/725–1093, fax 415/723–3145.*

August: 8 days, $1,230 ($805 without lodging, breakfast, and dinner); sign up 2–3 months in advance.

SOURCES

ORGANIZATIONS There is no central registry of campus vacation programs, and even colleges with long-standing programs do little to publicize them outside of alumni publications and local media.

To find out about other campus learning vacations, a good first step is to make a list of colleges or universities that you wish you could attend (don't forget your own alma mater!), or of institutions in regions you'd like to visit. Then contact their alumni offices or extension program offices and ask if they offer a summer learning program that's open to the general public. If they don't, they may be able to refer you to schools that do.

Elderhostel (75 Federal St., Boston, MA 02110, tel. 617/426–8056), a nonprofit educational organization founded in 1975, offers a vast array of inexpensive, short-term academic programs at educational institutions around the world. The hitch: You must be at least 60 years old to participate, and your spouse or companion, if you bring one, must be no younger than 50.

ALSO SEE If enriching your mind in a traditional educational setting appeals to you, check out the chapters on Foreign-Language Immersion Programs, Writing Conferences and Workshops, and Painting Workshops. Want to associate with professorial types? Look into Garden Tours and Cultural Tours, led by experts in their fields.

Cooking Schools

By Sean Elder

or many of us, the desire to cook comes late in life and is the result of a lifetime of bad food. Unless you hail from one of those fortunate families that takes cooking seriously—that knows the importance of fresh basil, say, or the virtues of blackened tuna (as opposed to Charlie Tuna)—you probably grew up thinking of cooking as a necessity rather than an enjoyable hobby. I came from the latter type of home, and when I set out on my own I attempted to avoid the kitchen completely. The problem with this approach was that eating in restaurants required money, which I had even less of than I had cooking skills. I was left with no choice but to don an apron and learn to feed myself, and so I did. Not very imaginatively, at first, and not very well, but I persevered. I was lucky to be living in San Francisco, where on those rare occasions when I could afford to eat out, the food was so varied and international that it intrigued my awakening abilities and challenged my culinary limitations. Repeated visits to the Hunan Restaurant finally convinced me to buy a wok and Henry Chung's cookbook. In lieu of frequent repasts at Chez Panisse, I bought Alice Waters's collected pasta recipes and learned the difference between arugula and endive.

Years have passed, and I no longer cook because I'm broke; I cook because I enjoy it. Most of my days are spent in front of a computer, writing myself into corners, and cooking provides me with a simple form of relaxation that is almost pre-lingual in its logic: "Chop garlic. Heat oil. Put garlic in oil. Brown. Chop anchovies. Add. Don't burn." And so on. Once you know the basics, from sautéing to baking, you can do anything. The benefits of my culinary efforts are quite tangible, for my family as well as myself, and cooking is one of those harmless hobbies you can pursue while savoring a glass of wine.

For those who cook all the time, a cooking vacation might sound like a busman's holiday, but cooking schools can go beyond the techniques they teach and provide a culinary window to a new world. Explore New York through the produce of Chinatown or the fish market on Fulton Street, or discover the Southwest through its Native American–Mexican cooking heritage. The schools also give you the chance to meet like-minded chefs of all abilities; all classes listed below are open to everyone, from the rank amateur to the seasoned pro.

Going to a cooking school can also make cooking more fun by freeing you from dependence on recipes. Once you know the basic cooking techniques—knife skills, sauces, roasting, sautéing, puff pastry, baking, and so on—you can use cookbooks only for ideas, with the confidence that your meal will not only be good, but original as well. And once you thoroughly understand your kitchen and the local market, you can improvise with what you have and what's in season—not at all like the painstaking pro-

---

Sean Elder lives in Brooklyn with his wife and two children. His writing has appeared in many publications, but his cooking appears only in his own kitchen.

cess of following instructions that might as well be in Greek and hoping everything turns out all right. You may learn to savor the whole production, from picking out produce to choosing wines, and do all of this while seeing a new part of the country and eating some tasty homework.

CHOOSING THE RIGHT SCHOOL

Most courses do not include accommodations and involve a lot of free time, so be sure there are other things you want to do in the area. Also, be sure to double-check all course information: A good school will vary its programs just to keep things interesting.

Here are some questions you should ask when selecting a school:

What is the cost and what's included? The prices given here are for courses of at least four days and include the cost of all cooking ingredients and equipment, unless otherwise specified. Most courses include at least one meal a day (often lunch), which is prepared during class. For the classes in this chapter, we have noted any meals not provided. Prices do not include accommodations, transportation to and from the school, or other entertainment, unless otherwise noted.

What are the instructors' qualifications? Many of the instructors in the schools listed here are professional chefs and authors of cookbooks. Find out how long an instructor has been teaching, and take a look at any books he or she has written. The International Association of Culinary Professionals (IACP) certifies cooking professionals and teachers, but there are many qualified chefs and teachers who are not members, so ask about experience, education, and philosophy.

How long has the school been in business? The more experience a school has, the more likely it is that your course will run smoothly.

What are the accommodations like? Many schools offer only suggestions on accommodations in the area. If accommodations are included in the price of your course, find out if rooms and bathrooms are private or shared.

What is the food like? If, as at the majority of cooking schools, you prepare some of your meals in class, the course description should give you a good idea of what you'll be eating. You're probably on your own for at least one meal a day, so find out what the dining options are in the area.

What is the teacher–student ratio? The size of the class and the number of instructors is important to the quality of the course. Make sure your instructor will have time to observe you individually.

Is the class participation oriented or demonstration oriented? If you really want to get up to your elbows in flour, make sure you'll have the opportunity. In some courses you simply watch and take notes. If it is a demonstration class, make sure you get printed recipes and ample time to take notes and ask questions.

How is the kitchen designed? A good teaching kitchen will feature an overhead mirror, so everyone can see what the instructor is doing, and a work station for each participant. This means counter space and preferably somewhere to stash your knives and cooking utensils. In a smaller class, and a smaller kitchen, these things are less essential.

What do I need to know to participate? Most schools will answer "nothing," but make sure that's what they mean. If you don't know the difference between sautéing and broiling, it might make for some communication problems.

FAVORITE CLASSES

THE NORTHEAST

MASSACHUSETTS Macrobiotics in Massachusetts. For advocates of macrobiotic cooking, the books of Michio Kushi are something close to religious texts. In titles such as *The Macrobiotic Way* and *The Cancer Prevention*

Diet, Kushi and his wife, Aveline, give the guidelines for a diet that's low in saturated fat and high in fiber, natural vitamins, and minerals. At the Kushi Institute in Becket, Massachusetts, in the heart of the Berkshire Mountains, you learn not only how to change your diet, but also how to use exercise to lead a more healthful lifestyle. You are encouraged to attend seminars here with someone who can help you stick with the changes you make when you go home. You can take a weeklong cooking seminar or opt for the Way to Health seminar, which includes exercise classes as well as cooking instruction.

Fifteen students—usually of all ages and from diverse backgrounds—attend each cooking seminar. The rigorous daily schedule begins at 7 AM with some light morning exercise, followed by breakfast. There are two daily cooking classes, from 10 AM to 1 PM and from 7 to 9 PM, in which you learn how to select and prepare a variety of fish, how to use tofu and tempeh, how to make hearty soups and stews, and how to prepare healthful snacks and desserts. The afternoon, from 2:30 to 5:30, is filled with lectures and discussions, chaired by Kushi Institute graduates such as Charles Millman and John Kozinski. In these sessions you study the relationship between diet and health and get practical tips on how to use what you've learned, including how to eat healthfully on the road and how to prepare macrobiotic meals quickly.

All you have to bring to the seminar is a notebook and pencil; everything else you need is provided. Accommodations are in a turn-of-the-century hunting lodge, set amid 600 acres of secluded meadows, woodlands, and streams. You share one of eight simply furnished rooms with one other student, and there are three shared bathrooms. Private rooms are available at an extra cost, if the lodge is not full. All meals are included in the price of tuition, are prepared on the premises, and are, of course, macrobiotic. *Kushi Institute, Box 7, Leland Rd., Becket, MA 01223, tel. 413/623–2102, fax 413/623–8827. Year-round: 7 days, $985. Sign up anytime.*

NEW HAMPSHIRE **Cook and Ski.** Exercise and cooking classes are a near perfect combination. What better reward for a hard workout than a good meal? Steven Raichlen, author of *High-Flavor, Low-Fat Cooking,* had just this thought when he designed his four-day Cook and Ski course. You, and a group of 18 to 20 other skiers, split your time between schussing down the slopes of Attitash in New Hampshire's White Mountains (or skiing cross-country at the Jackson Ski Touring Center) and taking cooking lessons at the Snowvillage Inn. Raichlen figured that people who want to spend eight hours in the kitchen go to Cordon Bleu or La Varenne (he's attended both).

On Sunday night Raichlen gives a demonstration on how to make healthy substitutes for fatty ingredients. For instance, you learn to replace oil with stock, without losing flavor. Monday morning half the group gives the new techniques a try, spending three hours under Raichlen's supervision, cooking lunch for the other half of the group to eat when they return from the slopes. On Tuesday the roles are reversed. Dishes prepared may include Tuscan bean soup, Mongolian hot pot, stews, and a low-fat chocolate souffle. You also learn the importance of improvisation, adapting recipes to use the freshest ingredients available and using recipes only as a guideline. At the end of the course you collaborate with the other students to create a menu with whatever happens to be in the kitchen.

The red-and-white clapboard Snowvillage Inn was built in 1919 and has commanding views of the surrounding mountains. You can spend evenings relaxing with the other students by the living room's manorial fireplace. The 19 chalet-style guest rooms are each appointed differently; each has a private bath, and three have fireplaces. You can pay extra for a private room, or share with one other student. Austrian innkeeper Trudy Cutrone prepares Continental breakfasts and five-course dinners that include such dishes as Wiener schnitzel, gingersquash soup, and Austrian fruit torte.

All you need to bring to this class are warm clothes and any skiing equipment that you don't want to rent. Students range from beginners to pros, but are usually weekend warriors who fall somewhere in between. Noncooking spouses or partners get a special rate that covers just the skiing and the meals. Nearby North Conway has outlets ranging from Ralph Lauren to Scandinavian Design. Raichlen also offers a spring course in St. Bart's in the French Caribbean. *Steven Raichlen, 1746 Espanola Dr., Coconut Grove, FL 33133, tel. 305/854–9717, fax 305/854–2232. Late Feb.: 4 days, $475. Price includes two lift tickets; sign up at least 3 months in advance.*

NEW YORK Chinese Fusion. They call it Chinois, this meeting of French and Chinese cuisine, and Wolfgang Puck and others in California were some of the original practitioners. New York-based Chinese chef and caterer Karen Lee has been making her own inroads in this cuisine. After studying for five years with Madame Chu, the woman who brought Chinese haute cuisine to the West, Lee wrote her popular cookbook, *Chinese Cooking for the American Kitchen.* It was the editor of this book who suggested that Lee do something a little more nontraditional—say, stuff wonton with goat cheese—and a fusion-chef was born. The style she's developed has strong Oriental influences with French and Italian overtones. If the idea of a Szechuan steak au poivre or Chinese risotto appeals to you, come spend five days in her Manhattan apartment's kitchen developing a fusion style of your own.

Classes are 2½-hour learning lunches, each a combination of demonstration and participation. You eat dishes as they are completed, and sample wines selected to accompany your meal. You and the other seven or eight students in the group spend a lot of time around a 6-foot-by-3-foot butcher block table, because, as is the tradition in Chinese cooking, about two thirds of the work is preparation. You begin by learning the importance of choosing good ingredients, and may even take a field trip to Chinatown for some firsthand experience. Equally important is learning techniques, such as stir frying, dry cooking, steaming, and deep fat frying. Dishes prepared range from wild mushroom spring rolls to parchment salmon in ginger-saffron sauce.

No previous cooking experience is required. In fact, this cuisine is so original that even the most advanced cook is unlikely to be bored. Although Lee's apartment is near 59th Street and Central Park, land of top-dollar hotels, she's happy to help you find more reasonably priced accommodations. *Karen Lee, 142 West End Ave., Apt. 30V, New York, NY 10023, 212/787–2227, fax 212/496–8178. Oct. and May: $500. Price does not include breakfast or dinner; sign up at least 2 months in advance.*

NEW YORK Fundamentals of Healthy Cooking. This 10-day class is designed for those committed to learning the fundamentals of healthy cooking and learning them *now—*very New York. It's offered by the Natural Gourmet Institute of Food and Health, which has been running courses on cooking and food theory since it was established in 1977. You are taught by a team of teachers, each with at least 10 years of professional cooking experience, and each with a different area of expertise.

Each day you have two 2½-hour classes, separated by lunch. While the Natural Gourmet is not exclusively macrobiotic, you do learn about such macro staples as tofu, seiten (wheat gluten that has been cooked and rinsed of starch, so you're left with chewy high protein, "a little bizarre" admits one convert), and tempeh (made from whole soy beans, it is called "the Roquefort cheese of soy beans"). These foodstuffs provide the basic structure for countless healthy meals. Other class topics include knife skills, herbs and spices, grain identification and cooking techniques, soups, salads and dressings, whole grain bread making, and sea vegetables.

Classes are a combination of demonstration and participation. Although shopping trips aren't part of the course, you do learn what to look for when you're on your own. Groups are limited to 30 students, with one teacher and several apprentices circulating to observe and give individual help. Lunch is a kind of daily review session: On a day when fish is being discussed, you might make a salad from the previous day's vegetable class, and so on. Your day ends at 4 PM, leaving you with plenty of time to explore downtown Manhattan and the many, largely nonorganic pleasures the city has to offer in the summer.

Classes are held in the institute's two teaching kitchens. All you need to provide is a knife, preferably a Japanese cutting knife, which can be bought or rented at the school. Although the school has no accommodations of its own, there are many hotels in Midtown Manhattan. *The Natural Gourmet Institute for Food and Health, 48 W. 21st St., 2nd floor, New York, NY 10010, tel. 212/ 645–5170. July or Aug.: 2 weeks, $1,100. Price does not include breakfast or dinner; sign up by June 11.*

NEW YORK **Spa Style in a Week.** What is spa-style cuisine? It's low in fat, cholesterol, and salt, yet high in flavor, and it's becoming more popular as more and more studies link fatty diets to heart disease. This five-day course, offered three times a year by the New School for Social Research, teaches you how to prepare foods that meet these healthy standards. It's taught by Arlyn Hacket, a former chef at the Pritikin Longevity Center in Santa Monica, California; author of *Can You Trust a Slim Chef?*; and host of the PBS series "Health Smart Gourmet Cooking."

The course is limited to 14 students. You meet each afternoon from 2 to 5 PM in kitchens in the New School's main building, a 150-year-old town house that's part of the Greenwich Village Historic District. Before you start cooking, you spend an afternoon learning to shop for everything from fruits and vegetables to packaged foods. Other classes teach you how to replace oil-based cooking methods, such as deep frying and sautéing, with water-based methods such as

poaching and steaming, and other low-fat alternatives, such as broiling. Juices, wines, and herbs are used as flavoring substitutes for sugars, salts, and fats. Each class includes demonstrations and participation, and you always finish by eating what you've made. Dishes vary seasonally, and may include strawberry-rhubarb crisps and twice-cooked salmon with apricot glaze in the summer, and potato-and-bean soup and chili in the winter. *New School for Social Research, Registration Office, 66 W. 12th St., New York, NY 10011, tel. 212/229–5690, fax 212/229–5648. Spring and late fall: five days, $380. Sign up at least 1 month in advance.*

NEW YORK **A Week of French Cooking.** Peter Kump's New York Cooking School has an international reputation for excellence. When you read that another school has an instructor that studied at Kump's, you know you're in good hands. Kump himself studied in Europe and New York under such renowned chefs as James Beard, Diana Kennedy, and Marcella Hazan, before he began giving classes in his New York apartment in 1974. Today, Kump's school takes up two floors of a former carriage factory on Manhattan's Upper East Side; it has four teaching kitchens and a baking and pastry classroom. A staff of 12 instructors and 30 assistants teaches a variety of courses for professionals and amateurs. The student–teacher ratio is never greater than 12 to one, so you get a lot of personal attention.

For the nonprofessional, Kump's offers five-day, no-prerequisite courses on French cooking, pastry and baking, bread, spa cuisine, and Italian cooking. The classes meet Monday through Friday, from 10 AM to 5 PM, and have curriculums designed to teach you the basic techniques of your chosen subject. The course on French cooking is the most popular, and for good reason. Within minutes you're up and cooking, learning everything from souffles to sauces. You walk out knowing it all (or at least enough to impress your friends).

The daily itinerary varies according to the instructor (all Kump graduates), but each lesson is a combination of demonstration and participation. You start small, with a lesson on knife skills, and progress to braising, roasting, sautéing, and other techniques. By the end of the week you're preparing roast tarragon chicken, sautéed rib lamb chops, butter braised leeks, and salade niçoise. Practice recipes are handed out in class for those who are going home to a kitchen.

You must bring two knives (10-inch chef's knife and 3-inch paring knife), an apron, and a dish towel to class each day. The school is not far from Central Park and the museums (including the Metropolitan Museum of Art and the Guggenheim) that dot upper Fifth Avenue. An information sheet with restaurant and hotel recommendations is provided to visiting students. *Peter Kump's New York Cooking School, 307 E. 92nd St., New York, NY 10128, tel. 212/410–4601 or 800/522–4610. Late May: 5 days, $290, plus $235 material fee. Price does not include knives, apron, dish towel, breakfast, or dinner; sign up one month in advance.*

VERMONT **Fundamentals at a Farmhouse.** Teacher, chef, and restaurateur Tom Chiffriller offers custom-tailored cooking lessons at his rustic Vermont bed-and-breakfast. You and up to five other students spend five days learning to cook just about any type of cuisine: Mexican is the only one Chiffriller doesn't teach. You start with a basic curriculum—learning how to make a meal from what's in your kitchen (as long as it's not one beer and some peanut butter!), how to streamline recipes to save time, and basic techniques, such as making a cream sauce without lumps. From there Chiffriller adapts the course to the interests of the group, showing you how basic techniques can be adapted to many different cuisines.

Tom gleaned his own knowledge while studying restaurant management at the University of Vermont, working as a teacher at the Culinary Institute of America and the New England Culinary Institute, managing the food services for Bryn Mawr College,

and establishing the Butternut Tree Restaurant in Woodstock, Vermont. The Farmhouse 'Round the Bend bed-and-breakfast is his latest venture, and he's been offering classes there since 1991.

Each morning, you gather in the kitchen, where Tom whips up breakfasts of scones, muffins, and apple Betty. Next it's four hours of demonstration and participation. Preparing such dishes as Szechuan shredded cabbage and pork and Portuguese paella with seafood and chicken, you learn not just how to cut vegetables and make sauces, but also the skill of menu-planning. Self-sufficiency and improvisation are emphasized. Lunch each day is a sampling of the dishes prepared. Afternoon field trips include visits to a local winery, a wholesale produce company, and a local vegetable farm.

Chiffriller restored the 1844 Greek Revival farmhouse himself, and your tuition includes lodging (private or shared) in one of the three guest rooms, decorated with early 19th-century antiques. The house is a five-minute walk from the historic village of Grafton, settled in 1780. There are also miles of trails for biking, walking, and skiing; a few local shops such as the Grafton Village Cheese Company; antiques and art shops; and sheep, lots of sheep. *Farmhouse 'Round the Bend, Box 57, Grafton, VT 05146, tel. 802/843–2515. Year-round: 5 days, $650–$750. Price does not include dinner; sign up at least 1 month in advance.*

THE MID-ATLANTIC

MARYLAND **Primary Skills of Cooking.** What sauce goes with what? What technique should be used to cook this as opposed to that? Who knows? François Dionot does, and he should. A native of Reims, France, Dionot studied at the College Techniques de Barbezieux in Charentes, and L'Ecole Hôtelière de la Société Suisse des Hôteliers in Lausanne, Switzerland. Decrying the lack of a European-style culinary arts school in the United States, Dionot founded

L'Academie de Cuisine in Bethesda in 1976. What began with one simple course in French cooking is now a celebrated school educating countless chefs in the fine art of fine food, from purchasing to preparation, with a little philosophy thrown in for flavor. Past students include the chefs at Red Sage and Palladines in Washington, D.C., and the pastry chef at the White House.

For the amateur enthusiast, L'Academie offers the four-day Primary Skills of Cooking course. Three-hour classes start at 9:30 AM, 2 PM, or 6 PM, depending on which of four summer sessions you attend. The first day covers meats, the second poultry, and the third and fourth fish and shellfish. You learn to make stocks and sauces to go with each meat or fish and get lessons on handling, preparation, boning, and stuffing. Roasting, braising, sautéing, poaching, and searing are also covered. The philosophy at L'Academie is that once you know the proper techniques for cooking each type of food, you can work without a recipe.

The course is limited to 21 pupils. Pascal Dionot, François's brother and a veteran chef of such venerable Washington restaurants as Rive Gauche and Sans Souci, is the primary instructor and has three assistants. The class is held in a working kitchen, set up with five rows of counter-top-covered individual work spaces. Around the perimeters of the room are stoves, a convection oven, and a large broiler. In the front is a demonstration counter. The school has a discount package with a local Holiday Inn, and your free time can be spent exploring the nation's capital, or nearby Bethesda. *L'Academie de Cuisine, 5021 Wilson Ln., Bethesda, MD 20814, tel. 301/986–9490 or 800/445–1959, fax 301/652–7970. June–July: 4 days, $250. Price does not include meals; sign up 2 months in advance.*

WEST VIRGINIA **French Cooking in Luxury.** This is the Cadillac of cooking schools. Anne Willan, founder and president of the highly acclaimed La Varenne cooking school in Paris, offers five- to seven-day programs at the posh Greenbrier Hotel, where

spa treatments and afternoon tea are part of the package. You and the other 50 or so students are welcomed with a champagne reception, and it only gets better from there. This class is demonstration only, but what demonstration: Teaching with Willan have been guest chefs such as Julia Child, Barbara Tropp of China Moon, and Jamie Shannon and Dickie Brennan of Commander's Palace in New Orleans.

La Varenne at Greenbrier, which began in 1991 has a ritualized schedule, which begins upon your arrival, when you receive a notebook with a roster of the week's activities and events. Classes begin each morning at 9 AM and are taught by Anne Willan or a guest presenter. You always have a printed recipe to follow along with, and questions are freely asked and answered.

The first morning Willan teaches a class on Mediterranean cooking; the results make a lovely buffet lunch. In fact, each day's demonstration is followed by a tasting of the foods that have been prepared. Willan spends another class sharing recipes from her rare cookbook collection, dating back to the 16th century, giving you an unusual opportunity to sample dishes from Renaissance and medieval times. On other mornings, various visiting chefs and authors use their own signature dishes to teach such techniques as sautéing, steaming, and puff pastry.

The second daily class is from 1:00 to 2:30 each afternoon. One day this is a show-and-tell by Greenbrier executive chef Robert Wang, followed by a tour of the hotel kitchen. Eric Crane, the Greenbrier Executive Pastry Chef for 34 years, presents specialty desserts, spins sugar, and decorates cakes; and Mark Liebendorfer, Director of Dining Services, and Werner Stoessel, Wine Sommelier, conduct a tasting session pairing white wines with five different menus. Several members of the Greenbrier staff also pick one afternoon to team teach a lesson on food presentation.

You have free time in the afternoon to golf (there are three championship golf courses), play tennis on one of the 20 courts, shoot trap and skeet, go horseback riding, or visit the health spa. Dinner each night is in the Main Dining Room, including Thursday's Gold Service dinner, a black-tie optional, seven-course grand finale to the course. Friday morning you have one last class with Willan on current cooking trends and receive your La Varenne at The Greenbrier certificate as a memento of your stay.

The course is offered during eight separate weeks, from late February through late April or early May. The stiff price, $1,575 per person, includes accommodations, breakfast and dinner daily in the Main Dining Room (lunch in class), and the plethora of hotel amenities. Amtrak stops right at the front gate. *La Varenne at Greenbrier, White Sulphur Springs, WV 24986, tel. 304/536–1110 or 800/624–6070, fax 304/536–7834. Late Feb.–early May: 5 days, $1,575. Sign up at least 3 months in advance.*

THE SOUTH

GEORGIA **Paris Trained, Georgia Bound.** Diane Wilkinson studied French cuisine at the Cordon Bleu and La Varenne in Paris and Italian cuisine with Marcella Hazan in Bologna. Since 1974 she's been teaching five-day courses in her native Georgia. Wilkinson believes that knowing the basic French techniques equips you to prepare almost any other cuisine, so here you'll learn the French approach to making stocks, pastries, breads, pastas, and poultry.

Classes are held from 10 AM to 6 PM each day in Wilkinson's kitchen and are a combination of demonstration and participation. Lunch and dinner preparation provide the structure for the lessons. One day you may prepare crispy skinned salmon with capers for lunch, learning how to sauté. For dinner you may make lamb shank with confit of Vidalia onions and sweet garlic, which teaches you how to braise. The kitchen opens up into a large room with plenty of counter space. There is a six-burner wood stove, a four burner electric cook top, a bak-

ing oven, and a specially designed wood-burning fireplace, specially designed for grilling.

Each course is limited to eight students, and groups are often friends who have planned their trip together. The school is near Atlanta, west of the fashionable Buckhead district. There are several shopping malls nearby, but after all the eating you do, the walking trails along the nearby Chattahoochee River may be a wiser choice for free-time activities. Diane can recommend hotels in the area. *Diane Wilkinson's Cooking School, 4365 Harris Trail, Atlanta, GA 30327, tel. 404/233–0366. Year-round: 5 days, $650. Price does not include breakfast; sign up 2 months in advance.*

THE MIDWEST

ILLINOIS **The Art of the Cake.** If you've longed to do more than write "Happy Birthday" on a double-layer angel food cake, take the Wilton School of Cake Decorating's five-day, 40-hour course for the total decorator. Here you learn the Lambeth Method of making piping, shells, scrolls, and scallops— that layer upon layer look that you've marveled at before, wondering, "How do they do that?" This is a hands-on, up-to-your-elbows course, and although it's not just for professionals, a fundamental background and some knowledge of cake decorating is required.

The school was founded in 1929 by Dewey McKinley Wilton who had learned the craft of cake decorating in Europe and wanted to bring the art to the United States. His first-things-first philosophy has remained the school's: You learn the fundamentals, then build on (or break) the rules of traditional cake-decorating in order to achieve greater self-expression. (If you think self-expression and cake decorating have nothing to do with each other, check out the Wilton School.)

The five-day, 40-hour Lambeth Method course, offered twice a year, is the mother of all cake-decorating courses. Sue Matusiak, a

Wilton graduate and a veteran cakemeister, guides your 15-student class through the paces of decorating two killer cakes. The 6-inch cushion cake will be used to teach you how to create a puffy "cushion" effect by layering icing. The 12-inch sampler cake is divided into quarters that will each have a different design: violet, forget-me-not, pansy, and orange blossom. Classes are a combination of demonstration and participation. Your instructor demonstrates a skill—for instance, making an intricate piping border—then you practice on your cake until you get it right. There's a lot of scraping and starting over!

All work is done in the school's teaching kitchen, where you are given plenty of room to work and a drawer to store your supplies. All class materials are provided and included in the cost of the course, as is the *Wilton Way of Cake Decorating, Vol. II*, the Big Book of the Lambeth Method. There is also a Wilton retail store here, where you can buy everything you need to work your new magic at home. There are several hotels and bed-and-breakfasts near the school; ask secretary Laura Lane for suggestions. *Wilton School of Cake Decorating and Confectionery Art, 2240 W. 75th St., Woodridge, IL 60517, tel. 708/963–7100, ext. 211. May and Aug.: 5 days, $300 plus $50 application fee (refunded if you are not accepted). Sign up 3 months in advance.*

THE SOUTHWEST

NEW MEXICO **Spring Thing in Santa Fe.** This five-day course goes beyond cooking lessons to give you an education on the rich culinary culture and history of the Santa Fe area. Susan Curtis, who founded the Santa Fe School of Cooking in 1989, schedules field trips to wineries, museums, micro-breweries, tortilla factories, and farms. She also invites such experts as Deborah Madison, author of *The Greens Cookbook,* Cheryl Jameson, author of *Texas Home Cooking,* and Kathi Long, author of *Mexican Light Cooking,* to join the school's staff of six chefs in giving cooking demonstrations.

These busy days are followed by free evenings for you to explore Santa Fe.

Your week begins on Sunday at 6:30 PM when you join the staff for a tapas reception. You can mingle with the other 20 to 30 students, while listening to a strolling guitarist. On Monday morning at 10, you meet in the school's large teaching kitchen where a guest chef, usually Kathi Long, gives a demonstration on traditional New Mexican foods—chile sauces, tamales, tortillas, enchiladas. This is followed by a long lunch of the food prepared.

Tuesday morning, Cheryl Jameson or one of the School's staff members gives a demonstration on contemporary Southwestern cuisine. Traditional techniques and dishes are combined with non-indigenous ingredients to create such dishes as polenta with smoked jalapeño, pork tenderloin with chili and black peppercorn, and grilled salmon marinated with chili. After eating the results, it's off to El Rancho de Los Golondrinas living history museum, where you see reenactments of the daily lives of the Spanish colonists of the 18th and 19th centuries, including their farming and baking techniques. Wednesday's schedule is light. Deborah Madison usually gives a morning demonstration on using regional vegetables, such as the many beans used in Southwestern cooking, and the afternoon is free. You may want to use the time to rest up for the next day.

Thursday starts with a visit to La Chirapada Winery, where the vintners talk to you about the wine-making process and then let you sample as many as 18 vintages. Next, it's on to Embudo Station, a former stop on the Chile Line (a railroad line that carried crops south to Taos). The Station, on the banks of the Rio Grande, is now a smokehouse and microbrewery. The proprietors give you a lecture on smoking meat and feed you a lunch of samples that you wash down with some of their other products, hearty ales and lagers. Your journey continues (don't worry, the bus driver hasn't been sampling the same beverages you have), perhaps to

Leona's Tortilla Factory in Chimayo, or to a farm in Dixon where jams and jellies are produced. Finally you return to Santa Fe and sober—er, rest—up, before attending a reception at the school and a grand finale dinner at one of the city's famed restaurants, such as Coyote Cafe or Santacafe.

There are no prerequisites for the course, and non-cooking traveling companions can accompany you to everything but the demonstrations and lunches for a reduced price. Curtis usually works out a deal with a local hotel to give participants a discounted rate on accommodations. *Santa Fe School of Cooking, 116 W. San Francisco St., Santa Fe, NM 87501, tel. 505/983–4511, fax 505/983–7540. Late April: 5 days, $795. Price includes transportation to all field trips, but does not include breakfast or dinners (except for last night); sign up at least 2 months in advance.*

THE ROCKIES

COLORADO **Basic French in Boulder.** Offered five times each summer, this beginning French cooking course at the Cooking School of the Rockies emphasizes organizational skills along with cooking techniques. You learn how to strategically plan your meal preparation so everything is ready at the proper time. You also learn the art of *mis en place*, setting up all your ingredients and equipment before you begin cooking. Each day you prepare a four-course meal, which lets you practice these skills while learning the basics of sauces, omelets, soups and stocks, poaching, and roasting, grilling, sautéing, and braising.

Poached pears in spiced red wine sauce, salade niçoise, grilled tuna with orange-basil beurre blanc sauce, bananas flambé, roasted tarragon chicken, and lemon mousse with red currant sauce, are a few of the dishes you may prepare. The techniques you learn while making them can be adapted for use in day-to-day cooking. Each day's menu also provides a lesson on mixing and matching dishes and sauces and making wine and cheese selections. You get a notebook with recipes and detailed instructions and spend ample time taking notes before the hands-on portion of class. At the end of each session, you and the other nine students sit down and enjoy the meal you've created. The bonus here is that after this less-than-diet-conscious French feast, you can hike off the extra calories in the beautiful surrounding mountains.

The teaching staff here is well trained. Joan Brett trained at Peter Kump's New York Cooking School, studied with Julia Child, and is a member of the International Association of Culinary Professionals; Sue Dubach is a career teacher, food writer, and caterer; and Michael Comstedt was the executive chef at the Greenbriar Restaurant. Each instructor has two assistants to aid with preparation and cleanup. Classes are held in a full professional kitchen, with ten burners, three ovens, personal work stations, and a cook island and mirror so that no matter where you are you can see what's going on. You need to bring a 10-inch chef's knife, a 3-inch paring knife, and an apron. The School provides a list of accommodation recommendations. *Cooking School of the Rockies, 637 S. Broadway, Suite H, Boulder, CO 80303, tel. 303/494–7988, fax 303/494–7999. 5 times each summer: 5 days, $345. Price does not include knives and apron or breakfast and dinner; sign up at least 2 months in advance.*

THE WEST COAST

CALIFORNIA **Culinary California.** Hugh Carpenter's six-day Napa Valley Food and Wine Adventure is a grand excursion to some of the region's best wineries and restaurants, with cooking courses along the way. Carpenter has taught over 2,000 courses throughout the United States and Canada since 1975. He specializes in fusion cooking that combines elements of Asian, southwestern, New Orleans, and Caribbean cuisines with indigenous American ingredients, and is the author of several cookbooks, including *The Fusion Food Cookbook* and *Chopstix.*

Your adventure begins on Sunday evening, with a reception held at Carpenter's home in Oakland, California. You mix and mingle with the other 15 students in your group, while munching on Asian-Californian appetizers—gravlax with spicy Thai sauce, pan-fried shrimp dumplings in chipolte chili sauce. Then it's on to dinner at Tra Vigne, an Italian restaurant that looks like it was imported intact from Tuscany.

In the morning, you convene in the kitchen of the Cakebread Cellars winery, where Carpenter guides you through the preparation of such dishes as papaya and avocado salad, Caribbean prawns with cinnamon and pineapple, and Santa Fe cornbread sticks. You eat the lunch you've created, with the accompaniment of Cakebread wines, then you're free until the class gathers at Newton Vineyard, in the evening. This prestigious small winery, perched on a mountain ridge over St. Helena, is famous for its merlot, cabernet sauvignon, and chardonnay. Tour, tasting, and hors d'oeuvres fill the evening.

Day three begins with another class at Cakebread, taught by Carpenter and Cakebread's chef, Brian Streeter. The class breaks up into teams to prepare appetizers, salad, two entrées, and dessert. The afternoon is free, and the early evening finds you at the Meadow Resort for an annual croquet tournament. Dressed in whites, you ply yourself with wine and appetizers to sustain you through a grueling croquet match. If you've recovered by morning, you attend a chardonnay tasting hosted by Janet Trefethen at the Trefethen Winery. Lunch is at the revered Mustard's Grill in Napa (this is a no-host, you-pay meal), and in the afternoon there's a food and wine seminar at Beringer Winery.

On day five you tour Opus One Winery, then take a bus to Sonoma to visit Iron Horse Vineyards, famous for its pinot noir and chardonnay. Lunch is cooked by Opus One chef Mark Malicki, and followed by a tour of the winery, the historic Victorian home, and

flower and vegetable gardens. In the afternoon you go on a tour of the Laura Chenel goat cheese factory.

The last day starts with lunch at Catahoula. In the afternoon, you take your final class at Cakebread. If you're attending the July course, you prepare a picnic dinner—freshly smoked quail, chilled prawns, homemade chocolate truffles, and champagne—to be eaten at an outdoor concert at Robert Mondavi Winery. May, August, and October classes prepare dishes such as grilled Sonoma lamb, fresh San Francisco Dungeness crab, and Asian dishes from Carpenter's cookbook, and enjoy the repast in the winery's idyllic garden.

The course is limited to 16, and no previous cooking knowledge or experience is required. Carpenter is happy to recommend hotels, though the Vintage Inn in Yountville is his first choice. *Creative Food Concepts, Box 114, Oakville, CA 94562, tel. 707/944–9112, fax 707/944–2221. May–Oct.: 7 days, $860. Sign up 3 months in advance.*

SOURCES

ORGANIZATIONS The **American Institute of Wine & Food** (1550 Bryant St., Ste. 700, San Francisco, CA 94103, tel. 415/255–3000 or 800/274–2493), a nonprofit educational organization, was founded in 1981 to help food and wine enthusiasts exchange information and to foster food and wine research and education opportunities. The tax-deductible membership fee includes subscriptions to *The Journal of Gastronomy* and the *American Wine & Food* newsletter.

International Association of Culinary Professionals (IACP, 304 W. Liberty St., Louisville, KY 40202, tel. 502/581–9786) endorses cooking schools, and professional instructors and can give you a list of amateur, short-term courses.

Cultural Tours

By M.T. Schwartzman

ave you ever stood before a famous landmark, contemplating its architectural details, wondering about its story, and wishing that you knew an expert who could tell you all about it? If you were on a cultural tour, that expert would be your guide. Cultural tours focus on the many expressions of civilization: the visual and performing arts, architecture, literature, folk traditions, and historic sites. While many explore aspects of Native American culture, topics range from railroads and petroglyphs to burial mounds and textiles. In some cases, you may even have the chance to live the way people would have during the period you are studying—you may spend the night in a tepee or eat meals prepared as they would have been in the era covered by the tour.

Guides may be writers, archivists, researchers, scholars, curators, or historians but are always recognized authorities on the topic covered by the trip. They have a lot to teach. Their knowledge is firsthand: On one past trip from Travel America, for example, historian Edward Bearss led an excursion to the restoration of the ironclad USS *Cairo*, a Civil War–era wreck that Bearss personally located and helped salvage. Usually, the expert leaders can share with you a wealth of knowledge collected during a lifetime of work: On one popular Alaska trip from James Henry River Journeys, a wilderness literature forum examines the oral histories of the native Tlingit, which leaders Nora and Dick Dauenhauer have been collecting and translating for 20 years.

On cultural tours, your learning takes place not in a classroom environment, as on other study programs, but in the world at large while moving from place to place. On a typical motorcoach trip, the most common kind of cultural tour, you get up early each morning, breakfast in your hotel, then head out for a day of sightseeing that ultimately leads you to your next overnight destination. The Smithsonian Institution's Route 66 tour covers 2,400 miles in eight states over 12 days.

Depending on how much ground your tour covers, you may use one or two hotels or camps as a base and make day trips from there, or you may change hotels daily, as on traditional escorted tours. Private behind-the-scenes tours of museums and historical districts and visits to sites not normally open to the public are a hallmark of cultural tours. Occasionally, special receptions are organized exclusively for your group, as are lectures and slide shows, depending upon the facilities at the sites you visit.

Cultural tours are essentially run by two types of groups: commercial tour companies that specialize in educational travel, and not-for-profit organizations such as museums, trusts, societies, research centers, and alumni organizations. Often, a nonprofit

---

M.T. Schwartzman began his writing career at the American Museum of Natural History in New York, one of the country's oldest operators of educational tours. He is a frequent contributor to Fodor's *travel guides.*

sells a trip but does not run it; in an arrangement known in the travel industry as private labeling, the institution develops the itinerary and selects the expert leaders but leaves the actual travel arrangements to an outside operator. It's especially common for cultural institutions to charter small ships; their itinerary is the same as for cruises sold to the general public but the ship sails with the institution's own experts on board. In other cases, a cultural organization books space on a larger vessel; on these programs, you sail with other passengers, who may be individual travelers or members of cultural tours from other institutions.

Often, the opportunity to join cultural tours run by a nonprofit group is considered a benefit of membership. However, although some institutions limit participation in their travel programs to members who contribute between $250 and $500 or more annually, most make their tours available to anyone willing to join the sponsoring institution, at a cost of $15 or $20. This money helps to support the organization's work and may be tax-deductible.

Whether sponsored by a nonprofit group or a commercial operator, cultural tours are not cheap: Groups tend to be small and destinations out-of-the-way and therefore costly to get to, and lodging, often in historic properties, can be pricey (as can meals, too, when they're provided). Which is not to say that you must be rich to join a cultural tour. While the price of some packages reaches $3,000 a head for a week, there are worthwhile programs for less than $1,000 per person.

Before giving your money to anyone, shop around. Don't book the first trip that suits your fancy. There are many players in the field, and often their programs visit a few of the same sites. Call or write for brochures and look for the program that best suits your interests. Remember that the expertise of the operator is just as important as the qualifications of the expert who travels with you. Some institutions, particularly larger ones, are generalists in the field of cultural tours. Because they have a broadly stated mission

and a large membership to satisfy, they must produce trips that cover many fields. The advantage is that you will have the greatest choice of programs, and many trips may be interdisciplinary. If you have a specific interest, look into tours from smaller institutions and commercial operators, which tend to have a more limited focus. Many are mom-and-pop operations. You are likely to get more personalized service and may even be accompanied on your trip by the organization's founder or director.

CHOOSING THE RIGHT TOUR

Cultural tours share certain characteristics with other group tours. They also have qualities that are unique to educational travel. Among the questions you should ask are:

What's the cost and what's included? Like all group tour packages, those for cultural tours vary. Generally speaking and in those described below, unless otherwise noted, cultural tours include all accommodations, activities, transportation during the tour, and breakfast. Be sure to ask whether transportation between your home and the trip's starting and ending points is included; it usually isn't.

How many experts accompany the group? The number of lecturers and guides, especially as compared with the number of travelers, determines how much personal attention you can expect. A single expert usually accompanies most cultural tours, but some have two full-time experts plus guest speakers, who join the group for special presentations at successive destinations.

Do the experts mingle and dine with the group? Perhaps the most fulfilling aspect of a cultural tour is the chance for informal conversation at special receptions, over dinner, or afterward. The more you are on your own for meals, especially dinner, the fewer the chances for this informal social interaction.

Are there escorts other than the expert guides? It can be helpful to be accompanied by a professional tour director whose sole responsibility is seeing to your group's needs during the trip; he or she handles the logistics and confirms hotel and restaurant reservations, coach timetables, and site visits—and solves problems on the spot should they arise. Sometimes this role is filled by a representative of the sponsoring organization or the tour operator.

What are the qualifications of the tour leaders? Experts with impressive credentials lead the most serious cultural tour. They have earned advance degrees, written books, and otherwise established themselves as recognized authorities. However, sometimes a nonacademic representative of the sponsoring organization is the tour's only escort. Know what you're getting before you make a commitment. Experts should be more than museum administrators or volunteers.

How long has the institution been running cultural tours? How long has the operator been in business? Choose a trip from an organizer that has significant experience in planning and operating the type of tour that interests you. Ask both when the institution or operator was founded and how long it has been running cultural tours. A museum may be a century old but could have gotten into the tour business only recently; fledgling operations do not have a track record that you can judge their performance by. If the museum is relying on a commercial venture for the travel arrangements, find out the name and history of that operator. As a general rule, book with an outfit that has been in business for at least five years. If an organization or operator is new on the scene or if you're unsure of its expertise, make a special point of asking for references from past travelers.

Do you have references from past participants? To clarify your ideas about what the trip will be like, there's no substitute for a talk with someone who has followed the itinerary, slept in the beds, and eaten the meals.

What lectures and enrichment programs are planned? An important distinction between a cultural tour and a typical escorted program is the depth of the learning experience. Ask how many educational presentations will be held daily or during the trip as a whole. Find out how they will be tied in to the program—will there be lectures and slide shows in your hotel or informal talks at the sites to be visited?

How many people are in the group? Although all groups tend to be small—usually no more than 20—the exact number will shape your experience and affect your opportunity to meet one-on-one with the experts.

How will the group travel? A cultural tour may be by land or by sea. Most move from place to place by motorcoach, but minivans may be used when the group is small; some tours involve long and perhaps strenuous hikes.

What are the accommodations like? Lodging may be in modern chain hotels or historic inns. You may camp in campgrounds. Or you may live and sleep in nontraditional surroundings as part of the living-history experience. Don't let yourself be surprised.

If you're staying in hotels, inns, or motels, find out exactly what the rooms are like. Will there be double beds or twins? Antique furnishings or standard Formica pieces? Private baths or shared? Be sure to ask about anything that matters to you—fitness center, swimming pool, phones or cable TV in the rooms, or the like.

If you will be sleeping in the open air, find out who supplies the camping equipment. If the operator provides it, make sure it's of a quality you'll be happy with; you don't want a sleeping bag that isn't warm enough or a tent that you have to wrestle with to set up. Also ask about the campground facilities—what are shower and latrine arrangements?

What are meals like? Meals may be served outdoors or in fine restaurants. Sometimes, restaurants are selected to reflect the tour's theme. The National Trust for Historic Preservation, for example, often schedules meals in historic taverns, inns, or houses along the tour route. Cuisine can be as varied as cultural tours themselves: On an itinerary that explores Native American history or lifestyles, you may eat dishes representative of the tribes you are studying. On a tour of New England, seafood and shellfish may be more likely to appear on your menu. Experiencing the lively restaurant scene in Santa Fe is a highlight of the Smithsonian Institution's annual trip there.

Be sure to find out how many meals are included and how they are served. For meals that are included, ask whether they're sit-down or buffet and whether you can order anything on the menu or have a more limited selection. If you have special dietary needs or culinary preferences, make sure that they can be taken care of.

How much free time will there be? Most cultural tours schedule time for you to explore on your own, especially in the evenings. However, some tours keep to a very demanding schedule, so time for independent activity is limited.

How far in advance must I book? You must ordinarily sign up at least three to four months in advance, although some organizers recommend booking as much as a year ahead if you want to be sure of a space. Tours that are new for an institution with a loyal following, such as the Smithsonian, tend to fill up the most quickly. Once you find out about a trip and make up your mind to go, don't dawdle about signing up—you may never again have the opportunity to travel with this particular leader and this particular group.

MAJOR PLAYERS

Virtually every major museum and college or university runs a travel program of some kind: There are some 800 members of the Network for Educational Travel (*see* Sources, *below*), an association of travel sponsors and suppliers. The following operators were selected for their stature, the extent of their domestic programs, and the

unusual nature of the niche they fill. The list below includes some of the cultural world's most famous institutions—but not all. Some run few or no domestic tours and their programs fall outside the scope of this book. Others do offer domestic cultural programs, but in activities covered elsewhere in this book, such as birding and whale-watching, whose focus is predominantly on natural history (*see* Sources, *below*).

GENERALISTS

JAMES HENRY RIVER JOURNEYS This outdoor specialist, founded in 1973, schedules a few culturally oriented tours annually. Wines, fine cuisine, music, and literature are the focus of these river rafting trips, which travel through Oregon, Idaho, and Alaska. Vintners, chefs, musicians, and poets host the groups. Destinations remain the same each year, but themes and itineraries may change according to the experts signed up to accompany the trips. You might discuss literature about the wilderness in southeast Alaska or sample different wines during the stops on a trip down Idaho's Salmon River. Tours last from four days to two weeks; participants are a mix of singles, couples, and older and younger travelers. At night, the operators set up camp along the rivers and, around the campfire, discuss literature or hold recitals or readings. Although meals are cooked over the open fire, the menus are surprisingly sophisticated: At dinner, there might be chicken flavored with orange juice, ginger, and soy sauce; barbecued lamb marinated in olive oil, lemon and orange juice, garlic, and honey; or barbecued salmon, with brownies for dessert. Most prices include all meals (Box 807, Bolinas, CA 94924, tel. 415/868–1836 or 800/786–1830, fax 415/868–9033).

NATIONAL TRUST FOR HISTORIC PRESERVATION Art and architecture of cultural and historic significance are the emphasis of tours from this organization, the nation's premier preservation society. Chartered in 1949 by an act of Congress (and 20% funded by federal subsidies), the trust began its travel program in 1970 and now takes members exploring New England, the South, and the West by land and by sea. Itineraries vary from year to year, but half of the dozen or so domestic trips run annually may be repeated. Most last eight to 10 days; leaders include writers, educators, architects, and society directors past and present. In addition to these expert guides, a representative of the National Trust for Historic Preservation accompanies each tour, along with a special escort who handles travel arrangements. Groups number 20 on average but never include more than 30 participants—largely, it seems, women aged 65 to 70. Accommodations are often selected from among participants in the National Trust's Historic Hotels of America program, which means that they're of architectural and historical significance; many are designated national historic landmarks, and lunch stops are often made at sites of historical importance, including Colonial inns and even historic homes, where the kitchen lays on a meal for the occasion. To participate, you must join the National Trust ($15; 1785 Massachusetts Ave., NW, Washington, DC 20036, tel. 202/673–4000 or 800/944–6847, fax 202/673–4038).

THE SMITHSONIAN INSTITUTION The Smithsonian, founded in 1846, has been running what it calls study tours since the mid-1960s and now has more trips than almost any other cultural organization. Like the great museum's collections, its tours cover virtually every topic; travel destinations range all over the United States. In the Smithsonian's semiannual catalogue, you're sure to find something that piques your interest. Cruises along inland waterways and overland tours to sites and regions of historic importance are among the wide range of choices. Native American art, American painting, urban architecture, and western folklore and settlement are just some of the topics explored. Itineraries change from year to year, but perennial favorites are repeated just as new trips are introduced. Tours last a week to 12 days. A representative of the Smithsonian

accompanies each group to act as escort, organizer, and all-round arranger, and there's also at least one expert on hand and sometimes two—here known as study guides—who are often joined by guest speakers. Leaders and lecturers include writers, historians, and professors. Trips never include more than 30 participants, most of whom are around 55, with a mix of couples and single women. Accommodations and restaurants are often chosen to tie in with the theme of the particular tour. Menus are often preselected with a limited number of choices; lunches may be served buffet style. A reading list is provided before the start of each trip. You must join the institution to take part ($22; Smithsonian Study Tours and Seminars, 1100 Jefferson Dr., SW, MRC 702, Washington, DC 20560, tel. 202/357–4700, fax 202/633–9250).

TRAVEL AMERICA Tours from this commercial operator travel through battlefields and other historic sites of the South, West, and Northeast in their study of U.S. military campaigns and, occasionally, of other famous and infamous episodes from our nation's past. Founded in 1990 to concentrate on the Civil War, Travel America has expanded its programs to include the Indian Wars and the American Revolution. Itineraries are repeated every three or four years. Group leaders include distinguished historians who are recognized authorities in their specific field; a Travel America tour manager also accompanies some trips. Tours generally last nine days and include between 20 and 30 participants, although some have run with as few as eight. The average participants are men in their late 40s; Civil War enthusiasts or history buffs, they want to see the sites they've read so much about. Lodging is in first-class hotels or the best available—tours sometimes stop in towns with few lodging options. Travel America packages are among the few cultural tours that include dinner as well as breakfast daily; you're on your own for lunch (131 Dodge St., Suite 5, Beverly, MA 01915, tel. 508/927–4543 or 800/225–2553, fax 508/927–5140).

WHITNEY MUSEUM OF AMERICAN ART Founded in 1930, the Whitney began sponsoring trips in 1986. Today's programs highlight major art exhibitions on view in the East of interest to members; recent trips have toured Maine and North Carolina. Artists, curators, and collectors guide the group through the featured exhibit, while architectural historians or other experts act as leaders for local sightseeing. In addition, two escorts—an expert and a tour manager—are always on hand. The Whitney's four- to five-day tours are all-inclusive—trip fees cover even round-trip airfare from New York City (the cost of which is deducted from the tour price for travelers who don't originate in New York, or who use frequent-flyer mileage to cover their transportation). Groups range in size from 12 to 18; most participants are between 45 and 50, and half are men, half women. Lodging is in first-class hotels. Meals, served in restaurants, may be from a fixed menu or one with limited choices. You must be a member to participate ($55; Whitney Museum of American Art, Membership Department, 945 Madison Ave., New York, NY 10021-2790, tel. 212/570–3641, fax 212/606–0205).

NATIVE AMERICA SPECIALISTS

Native American culture is a popular theme of cultural tours, and a number of operators schedule such trips—among them the following.

THE ARCHAEOLOGICAL CONSERVANCY Of the archaeological foundations that run cultural tours, the nonprofit conservancy's program is perhaps the most wide-ranging. Founded in 1980, the conservancy began its tour program in 1986. Of the eight trips sponsored each year, about six are domestic. Most concentrate on Native American and Spanish colonial historic sites in the Southwest, but there are also river raft trips to Utah that explore prehistoric cliff dwellings and other ruins. Basic itineraries are rotated every couple of years. Various anthropologists lead the tours—different experts may join

the group en route, and several may participate in any particular trip. One conservancy staffer is also in attendance. Groups are limited to 20 to 25 people; most average in their mid-50s, although the conservancy attracts everyone from kids to senior citizens, singles and couples, men and women. Lodging is in first-class hotels and motels on land-based trips, or the best available; you camp out on river trips. Lunches are always included; on bus tours, you often have box lunches and on raft trips, meals are cookouts. You automatically join the conservancy when you book one of its trips; the cost is included in the price ($100; 5301 Central Ave. NE, Albuquerque, NM 87108-1517, tel. 505/266–1540).

CROW CANYON ARCHAEOLOGICAL CENTER Best known for its classroom-style seminars and archaeological digs open to vacationers, this center in the Colorado desert, founded in 1984 for research and education, also offers a series of what it calls cultural explorations: seven- to 12-night academically oriented tours, led by native guides and non-native scholars, that examine the pre-history of the ancient inhabitants of the desert Southwest's Four Corners region. The first of these trips ran in 1988, and new explorations are added each year; some favorites are repeated annually, while others may retain the same theme or topic but follow a different or expanded itinerary. Because some 35% to 40% of tour participants are repeaters, the center tries not to run any particular program more than two or three years in a row. Groups set out with between 10 and 20 participants, most in their mid-40s to early 50s (people from their 20s through their 80s have participated). There are usually singles as well as couples, and more men than women. The center's 70-acre, mountain-ringed campus, full of adobe buildings, is the base camp; you journey into the desert each day and return to the center each night. Although some programs have you overnighting at campsites in the desert, lodging is usually in Navajo-style hogans—small cabins that accommodate up to four (although on tours, only two or three individuals are housed in each unit); if you come solo, they assign you a roommate. On-campus meals, served cafeteria style, include both basic American fare such as baked chicken and pasta and such southwestern specialties as burritos and enchiladas; there are always fresh fruits, vegetables, and salads. Off-site meals may be brought in from the cafeteria or prepared in the open air. Membership is required to participate; proceeds help support the center's efforts to educate the public about archaeology and Native American culture ($40; 23390 Country Road K, Cortez, CO 81321, tel. 800/422–8975, fax 303/565–4859).

FOUR CORNERS SCHOOL Another educational center well-known for its on-site workshops, the nonprofit Four Corners School sponsors seven- to 10-day cultural tours every year both in its cultural studies series and its archaeology series. Sometimes cosponsored by such institutions as the Durango Arts Center, Denver Museum of Natural History, and the Heard Museum, tours in both series explore the folk traditions of native Navajo, Pueblo, Hopi, and Ute peoples, and are led by anthropologists; you take in museums, cultural centers, historic cities, and dance performances. Destinations and basic itineraries in the Southwest remain constant from year to year. Eight to 15 individuals are in each group; typical participants are 30 to 35, and there's an equal mix of men and women. You overnight in hotels and motels en route, and eat in restaurants, except for the occasional picnic, box lunch, or traditional native meal. Founded in 1984, the school is more advocacy-oriented than most other cultural tour operators—it's deeply involved in studying and preserving the flora and fauna of the Colorado Plateau—and the school encourages you to get involved. Membership is not required for any Four Corners tour (Box 1029, Monticello, UT 84535, tel. 801/587–2156; *also see* Archaeological Digs).

JOURNEYS INTO AMERICAN INDIAN TERRITORY
Tours of this organization, founded in 1988 with the goal of furthering communication between Indian and non-native peoples, focus exclusively on the heritage of Native America. Some itineraries examine the history and pre-history of America's native peoples, while others concentrate on their folk music, crafts, and dances, or the spiritual life of the continent's original inhabitants. Programs are designed for those who want not just to view Native American ways of life but also to experience them: You live in a tepee for the duration of the tour and the menu includes Native American as well as institutional fare. On some itineraries, you return to the same encampment each night after making day trips to tribal settlements in the surrounding area, while on others, you move from one encampment to another. These eight-day trips visit significant native sites in Oklahoma and southern Arizona; specific itineraries often vary from year to year. The non-native anthropologist who founded the firm, Robert Vetter, leads the tours, assisted by a Native American staff. There are between 10 and 20 participants in each group, mostly women and primarily in their late 30s through their 50s, although there are many students as well as children and senior citizens (Box 929, Westhampton Beach, NY 11978, tel. 516/878–8655 or 800/458–2632, fax 516/878–4518).

SACRED SITES The cultural tours from this nonprofit group reflect the organization's unusual mission: to preserve sacred places and the practices of the cultures that created them. Their way of living in harmony with the environment constitutes part of the subject matter of the tours. While the foundation's travel program extends from Alaska in the north to Peru in the south, many of its domestic programs concentrate on the desert Southwest—this is the only destination that consistently appears on the foundation's annual list of programs. Other offerings vary from year to year, with the most popular itineraries repeated and new ones added. Groups consist of between 12 and 20 participants; they're led by anthropologists and other scientists—an ethnobotanist, perhaps—and accompanied by not only a tour escort but also a representative of Sacred Sites and, on occasion, members of the native tribes being studied. Most participants are professional women in their 40s or retirees, but there are couples as well as single travelers. Overnights are in basic motels and dinners generally in restaurants; there are box lunches or picnics in the field at noontime. Menus tend to be low in sodium and fat, and there's always a vegetarian option. Founded in 1990, Sacred Sites began offering tours a year later. The price of each includes a contribution to the foundation (1442A Walnut St., #330, Berkeley, CA 94709, tel. 510/540–0671, fax 510/525–1304).

FAVORITE TRIPS

Most nonprofit operators change their programs annually: Since they draw participants from a limited pool—namely, their members—they must vary their offerings to fill their tours. However, commercial tour operators tend to repeat itineraries year after year. In addition, among both nonprofit and commercial operators, the most popular tours are repeated regularly—offered for a few years in a row, then dropped and brought back later. And when the same program runs in consecutive years, the exact itinerary and leaders may vary. The following tours are representative. If the one that interests you is not available when you call, a talk with the operator (or those listed among our Major Players) may well yield information about similar or equally intriguing programs.

THE NORTHEAST

MAINE **Painterly Landscapes.** Art and architecture of the rugged Maine coastline are the focus of this eight-day trip from the National Trust for Historic Preservation. In Prouts Neck, you visit the studio of Winslow Homer, who painted many of his most important works in Maine. You also visit Rockland, where Andrew Wyeth painted. The work of Maine artists of the past is on view at the

Farnsworth Art Museum and Homestead, in Rockland, while at the Maine Coast Artists Gallery, also in Rockland, you view—and can buy—the work of present-day Maine painters. At the Spring Point Museum in Portland, you can see the remains of the clipper ship *Snow Squall* and examine Maine's long seafaring past and present. Camden, another stop, is home to a fleet of two- and three-masted schooners. Lunches, dinners, teas, and receptions are sometimes held at the private homes of art dealers or other local families; other meals include a clambake and a lobster dinner at a local lobster shack. Three nights in Portland are spent in a converted summer cottage now operated as an inn. Accommodations for the remaining nights are in the Ledgelawn Inn in Bar Harbor, another converted summer cottage that has retained the charm of the original home. Leaders change from year to year. In 1994, they included an architectural historian, a curator, and a preservationist; the group was joined by the director of the Maine Historic Preservation Commission and other local experts, including a representative from Greater Portland Landmarks, as part of a tour of historic neighborhoods there. Sold out in 1993 and 1994, it may be offered again in 1995. (At press time, the Smithsonian Institution has a similar tour planned for 1995.) *National Trust for Historic Preservation, 1785 Massachusetts Ave., NW, Washington, DC 20036, tel. 202/673–4000 or 800/944–6847, fax 202/673–4038. Late Sept.: 8 days, $1,695; price includes 3 lunches and 5 dinners; sign up 9–12 months in advance.*

MASSACHUSETTS AND RHODE ISLAND **Mansions and Music.** The anchors of this 10-day study tour sponsored by the National Trust for Historic Preservation are Newport, Rhode Island, known for its grand seafront mansions, and Massachusetts's Berkshire mountains, abuzz with cultural activities all summer long; the tour is scheduled to coincide with the area's annual summer festivals. En route, the director of the Newport Historical Society and a resident Berkshires expert join the group. In Newport, where you spend four nights, eight historic homes open their doors to you for tours; four mansions are the venue for classical music recitals. In the Berkshires, you attend six performances by symphony orchestras and dance and theater groups, and visit the re-created rural New England town of Old Sturbridge Village, the completely restored Hancock Shaker Village, the Norman Rockwell museum and studio, Edith Wharton's summer mansion, and the house where Herman Melville wrote *Moby Dick*. Some lunches or dinners are at historic sites or private clubs. Lunch might consist of lobster and mango salad and zabaglione with Grand Marnier and fresh berries; dinner might start with vichyssoise and a green salad, then move on to swordfish grilled with lime and pepper or an aged sirloin in a brandy-pepper cream sauce. Accommodations are in a harborfront Newport hotel with private bath, and in Victorian bed-and-breakfasts in the Berkshires, also with private bath. *National Trust for Historic Preservation, 1785 Massachusetts Ave., NW, Washington, DC 20036, tel. 202/673-4000 or 800/944-6847, fax 202/673-4038. Mid-July: 10 days, $2,840. Price includes 6 lunches and 4 dinners; sign up 9-12 months in advance.*

NEW YORK **The Hudson Valley School.** Scheduled to show off the landscape during foliage season, this seven-day Smithsonian-sponsored tour, surveys the mountains and valleys of the Catskills and Adirondacks. The historian-leader shows the way to the villages and scenic retreats that inspired 19th-century writers and painters. In the Adirondacks, where you spend three days, you tour several camps, built as summer places by the tycoons of the era, and visit the Adirondack Museum, which has extensive displays on area history. In Cooperstown, where you spend two days, you explore the Baseball Hall of Fame, the Fenimore House, and the Farmer's Museum and Village Crossroads living-history museum; the town was named for the father of novelist James Fenimore Cooper, who used many local images in his *Leatherstocking Tales*. You stay at the elegant-rustic Sagamore Lodge on Raquette Lake in the Adirondacks, built by the Van-

derbilts and now on the National Register of Historic Places, and at the posh Otesaga Hotel on Otesaga Lake in Cooperstown. All guest rooms in the Otesaga Hotel have private bath; some in the Sagamore share. Meals are family style: filet mignon, broiled halibut, and chicken Cordon Bleu, with salad and homemade bread. At press time, this trip had just been cancelled for 1994—but if it interests you, check with the Smithsonian to see whether anything similar has been planned. *Smithsonian Institution, Smithsonian Study Tours and Seminars, 1100 Jefferson Dr., SW, MRC 702, Washington, DC 20560, tel. 202/357-4700, fax 202/633-9250. Late Sept.: 7 days, $1,245. Price includes 5 lunches and 6 dinners; sign up 5-7 months in advance.*

NEW YORK **Indians and Colonists.** The early conflicts between the British, the French, and Native Americans in the Hudson and Mohawk valleys are the subject of this nine-day Travel America tour through New York and Vermont. Guided by a curator of history from the New York State Museum in Albany, it takes place at the end of fall foliage season. Restored and ruined forts as well as Revolutionary-era battlefields are the centerpieces of the itinerary, which also examines rural Colonial life through visits to museums and living-history exhibits. Overnights and meals are in first-class hotels, the best available, in Albany, Cooperstown, and Saratoga Springs; you may order from the regular menu. *Travel America, 131 Dodge St., Ste. 5, Beverly, MA 01915, tel. 508/927-4543 or 800/225-2553, fax 508/927-5140. Late Sept.–early Oct.: 9 days, $1,295. Price includes 5 lunches and 8 dinners; sign up 3-4 months in advance.*

THE MID-ATLANTIC

VIRGINIA **Grand Houses and Plantations.** Famous homes of America's founding fathers are linked together on this seven-day tour of the first of Britain's American colonies. Sponsored by the National Trust for Historic Preservation, it is led by architectural historian William Kloss, and takes in such architectural treasures as Mount Vernon, George Washington's ancestral estate; Montpelier, home of president James Madison; Sherwood Forest, president John Tyler's plantation home; and Monticello, Thomas Jefferson's masterpiece. On many of these visits, you see buildings or rooms not normally open to the public. A Colonial cooking demonstration shows how and what our forefathers ate. An actor dressed as an 18th-century gentleman joins you for dinner by candlelight at the Mount Vernon Inn to bring the 1700s to life. Other dining experiences include lunch at the Willow Grove Inn, which dates from 1778, and dinner at the private Commonwealth Club, founded in 1890. At Sherwood Forest, you can enjoy a glass of President Tyler's favorite wine. Overnights are in the Hay-Adams Hotel, an Italian Renaissance-style hotel in Washington, DC, whose south-facing rooms have a picture-postcard view of the White House, and in Richmond's Jefferson Hotel, a National Historic Landmark with a grand lobby and a staircase straight out of *Gone with the Wind*. All accommodations have private bath. *National Trust for Historic Preservation, 1785 Massachusetts Ave., NW, Washington, DC 20036, tel. 202/673–4000 or 800/944–6847, fax 202/673–4038. Mid-Apr.: 7 days, $1,410. Price includes 6 lunches and 2 dinners; sign up 9–12 months in advance.*

THE SOUTH

LOUISIANA TO TENNESSEE **The Mississippi Campaign.** On this nine-day Travel America tour out of New Orleans, Civil War buffs follow in the footsteps of General Ulysses S. Grant as he campaigned to control the Mississippi River and split the Confederacy in two. From the Crescent City, you make your way upriver to Vicksburg National Military Park, where the ironclad USS *Cairo* is on view along with 1,000 artifacts salvaged from the ship. (The historian who led the 1994 tour participated in locating and recovering the ship, which was sunk during

the Vicksburg campaign in 1862.) Along the way, you'll visit Natchez, a prosperous antebellum town, and Grand Gulf, site of two well-preserved forts and some of the Civil War's best-preserved trenches and gun emplacements. The excursion ends with a tour of the battlefield at Shiloh, site of a pivotal Union victory and one of the war's turning points. Overnights are in Holiday Inns and similar properties. Meals are not fancy: lunches of soup, sandwiches, and salad, and dinners in hotel dining rooms, with a choice of menu. *Travel America, 131 Dodge St., Suite 5, Beverly, MA 01915, tel. 508/927–4543 or 800/225–2553, fax 508/927–5140., Late Oct.–early Nov.: 9 days, $1,295. Price includes 7 lunches and 8 dinners; sign up 3–4 months in advance.*

THE MIDWEST

MINNESOTA TO MISSOURI **Steamboatin'.** On this nine-day trip sponsored by the Smithsonian, you join a contingent from the organization rolling down the Mississippi River and its tributaries aboard the *Delta Queen*— one of the last steam-powered paddlewheelers still in service, a National Registered Historic Landmark that serves as both a floating hotel and classroom. The length, itinerary, and theme of the cruise vary each year: In 1993, the trip was down the Ohio from Pittsburgh to New Orleans; a historian and a specialist in the specific topic both accompany the group, lecturing aboard ship and joining the passengers ashore during visits to historic plantation houses and Civil War sites. The *Delta Queen* provides the perfect way to travel through the antebellum South. Between stops, you can relax in a rocking chair on deck, like a country gentleman, or settle back into a plush leather wing chair in one of the boat's parlors. Accommodations are in small but homey wood-paneled cabins for two; price varies according to the size of the cabin and its facilities. Meals are served in two seatings; cuisine is Continental with some Cajun seasonings. (This trip is also usually available from the National Trust for Historic Preservation.) *Smithsonian Institution, Smithsonian Study Tours and Seminars, 1100 Jefferson Dr., SW, MRC 702, Washington, DC 20560, tel. 202/357–4700, fax 202/633–9250. Mid-Sept.: 9 days, $2,525–$4,885. Price includes 7 lunches and 8 dinners; sign up 5–7 months in advance.*

MISSOURI TO NEVADA **Route 66.** This 2,400-mile odyssey, a Smithsonian-sponsored trip last offered in 1994, follows one of America's most celebrated roads, crossing eight states in 12 days and taking in its many curiosities, taste treats, panoramas, drive-ins, and tourist attractions old and new. Traveling with you are writer-photographer Suzanne Wallis and Michael Wallis, author of *Route 66: The Mother Road,* considered the definitive book on this historic road, one of the first inter-state highways. Numerous guest speakers join the group en route. In Springfield, Missouri, you meet the man who invented the drive-through restaurant. In Oklahoma City, you visit the National Cowboy Hall of Fame. On the way to Santa Fe, you see Amarillo's pop art monument, Cadillac Ranch, a row of 10 vintage cars buried nose down in the desert. And in Albuquerque you can photograph examples of Route 66's renowned neon signs. Many participants take along copies of the book to have them autographed en route by the various local characters profiled in its pages. Lodging is in simple mom-and-pop motels with names like the Big Texan; meals include barbecue feasts, a steak cookout at a ranch, and a dinner in a fancy restaurant. *Smithsonian Study Tours and Seminars, Smithsonian Institution, 1100 Jefferson Dr., SW, MRC 702, Washington, DC 20560, tel. 202/357–4700, fax 202/633–9250. Late June: 12 days, $1,550. Price includes 7 lunches and 7 dinners; sign up 5–7 months in advance.*

NORTH AND SOUTH DAKOTA **Legends of the West.** This nine-day trip from the Smithsonian Institution, new in 1994, travels through the legendary American West in the company of a Western historian and several guest speakers. You visit Sitting Bull's home, George Armstrong Custer's final command

post, and the site of Crazy Horse's last stand, plus important railroad centers, historic trading posts, and the Gold Rush territory of South Dakota's Black Hills. Three nights of the trip are in Rapid City's historic Alex Johnson Hotel. As a grace note, a covered wagon expedition, which includes a chuck wagon cookout, gives you a taste of pioneer life on the Oregon Trail. *Smithsonian Study Tours and Seminars, Smithsonian Institution, 1100 Jefferson Dr., SW, MRC 702, Washington, DC 20560, tel. 202/357–4700, fax 202/673–4038. Late July–early Aug.: 8 days, $1,475. Price includes 2 lunches and 6 dinners but only one breakfast; sign up 5–7 months in advance.*

OKLAHOMA **Indian Elders and Tepees.** From Journeys into American Indian Territory, this nine-day annual trip brings you face to face with not only young Native Americans but also Indian elders—many of whom lived through major episodes of Indian history. The tour takes in Indian museums, pow-wows, and dramatic performances of the Trail of Tears, a play that interprets the Cherokee's forced migration and resettlement. There are three different encampments; you stay in tepees in all of them and are served meals that often feature traditional native dishes. A non-native anthropologist leads the group, accompanied by three Native American staffers, each from a different tribe. *Journeys into American Indian Territory, Box 929, Westhampton Beach, NY 11978, tel. 516/878–8655 or 800/458–2632, fax 516/878–4518. Early–mid-July: 8 days, $795. Price includes 7 lunches and 7 dinners; sign up 4–8 months in advance.*

THE SOUTHWEST

ARIZONA AND NEW MEXICO **Native Art Past and Present.** How present-day Native American artists are using traditional skills with new materials to express traditional ideas is the focus of this nine-day study tour from the Smithsonian Institution, slated to run again in 1995. On the schedule are visits to private homes and studios and meetings with Navajo, Hopi, Zuni, and Pueblo artists as well as stops at archaeological ruins such as those in Chaco Canyon National Historic Park, and takes in some of the most dramatic mesas in North America. A study leader accompanies the group; in addition, local anthropologist Charlotte Beyal lectures on the culture gap between Indian and non-native societies, and you will meet innovative Native American artists who are using traditional skills to create artifacts out of nontraditional materials. Accommodations are in hotels in Flagstaff and Albuquerque; one of your meals is a traditional Hopi dinner, and another is in the home of a local art collector. *Smithsonian Study Tours and Seminars, Smithsonian Institution, 1100 Jefferson Dr., SW, MRC 702, Washington, DC 20560, tel. 202/357–4700, fax 202/633–9250. Late May and early–mid-Oct.: 8 days, $1,575. Price includes 4 lunches and 4 dinners; sign up 5–7 months in advance.*

ARIZONA, NEW MEXICO, AND UTAH Rock Art. Many of the petroglyphs you see in remote desert locations on archaeologist-led Jeep excursions during this 11-day Archaeological Conservancy tour are not open to the public. That's one of the features of the program, which was last offered in 1993; you also visit ancient cliff dwellings and Spanish colonial missions, plus nearly half a dozen national monuments. Lodging along the way is in Sheratons, Best Westerns, and similar properties in major cities, such as Albuquerque and Santa Fe. Other lodgings include a night at the Inn of the Mountain Gods on the Mescalero Apache reservation, and two nights at the Thunderbird Lodge at Canyon de Chelly. Box lunches are provided in the field; breakfast and dinner are up to you. *The Archaeological Conservancy, 5301 Central Ave., NE, Albuquerque, NM 87108-1517, tel. 505/266–1540. Early–mid-June: 11 days, $1,595. Price includes lunches; sign up 6 months in advance.*

NEW MEXICO Santa Fe Music and Gardens. Typical of Smithsonian tours, this week-long extravaganza, a perennial favorite slated again for 1995, is not strictly horticultural. Instead, it takes in not only gardens

but also galleries, concerts, and opera. Leading the group is Charles Mann, a professional photographer specializing in garden imagery and horticultural subjects; he is joined by several guest speakers, including garden designers and expert gardeners. You start the tour with lunch at the home of a local artist and have time to tour the Museum of International Folk Art, which houses the world's largest collection of its kind, with some 100,000 objects ranging from rugs to dolls. Turning your attention to plants and flowers, you then visit several gardens where you learn about Xeriscape, a method of conserving water for plantings in arid and semiarid climates, and a vegetable ranch, whose fresh produce is sought after by restaurants all over the country; owner Elizabeth Berry cultivates antique varieties of plants for their seeds. Evenings, you attend performances at the Santa Fe Opera, at the Santa Fe Chamber Music Festival, and by the Santa Fe Desert Chorale. You also explore the city's celebrated restaurant scene, where Pueblo, Spanish colonial, and Mexican and American frontier culinary flavors commingle; you may be invited to the home of a local artist or to an area ranch for lunch. Accommodations are at a downtown Santa Fe hotel within walking distance of galleries and museums. *Smithsonian Study Tours and Seminars, Smithsonian Institution, 1100 Jefferson Dr., SW, MRC 702, Washington, DC 20560, tel. 202/357–4700, fax 202/633–9250. Late July: 7 days, $1,785. Price includes 4 lunches and 2 dinners; sign up 5–7 months in advance.*

THE ROCKIES

COLORADO Ancient Astronomers. This eight-day tour through the desert of southwest Colorado, near the Utah, Arizona, and New Mexico state lines, takes you from the Crow Canyon Archaeological Center to ancient observatories and other sites of cosmic significance to native stargazers. Under the direction of a University of Colorado professor of astrophysics, the program has been so popular that there was a waiting list in 1994, the fifth season it was offered. One night is spent camping along the river in the desert; the other evenings are spent at the center's Cortez Colorado campus. *Crow Canyon Archaeological Center, 23390 Country Road K, Cortez, CO 81321, tel. 800/422–8975, fax 303/565–4859. Late Apr.–mid-Nov.: 8 days, $1,825. Price includes 7 lunches and 3 dinners but not 3 breakfasts; sign up 6–8 months in advance.*

COLORADO **Southwest Weavers.** The Four Corners School sponsors this seven-day survey of Native American weaving traditions, led by a textile scholar. The tour, new for the school in 1994, begins in Durango, Colorado, and visits public and private collections of textiles, where you see extensive collections of Navajo and Pueblo work and learn about the prehistoric and historic weaving traditions of the Southwest. On a visit to a Navajo reservation, you watch a weaving demonstration and explore a historic trading post. So that you don't go home empty-handed, the tour makes stops at local crafts cooperatives and a rug auction. Accommodations are in motels in Durango, Mesa Verde, and Canyon de Chelly, all with private bath, and meals are mostly in restaurants, where you have a choice of American, Mexican, New Mexican, and California cuisine. *Four Corners School, Box 1029, Monticello, UT 84535, tel. 801/587–2156, fax 801/587–2193. Late May: 7 days, $1,350. Price includes 5 lunches and 6 dinners; sign up 2–3 months in advance.*

IDAHO **Good Wine and Fine Food in the Wilderness.** During a six-day paddle trip down the Main Salmon River, through rugged central Idaho, sumptuous California-style meals cooked at river campsites headline each evening. Dinners include pleasures like caviar pie, peppers Provençal, grilled Alaska king salmon with pineapple-mango salsa, and fresh summer fruit compote with biscotti prepared by chef Bob Miller, along with the zinfandels, chardonnays, and cabernet sauvignons of Sonoma, California's, Ravenswood Winery, poured by owner-winemaker Joel Peterson, named one of the world's fifteen outstanding vintners by the prestigious *Wine Advocate.* The morning after, you and your five to six fellow rafters, working under a professional guide, man the raft to paddle through 10- to 15-foot roller-coaster waves in early summer and the less spectacular but still technically challenging waters that characterize the stream in late August. New in 1994 from James Henry Wilderness Journeys, the trip was the latest addition to a series of four wine, food, and music trips down this Idaho river. *James Henry River Journeys, Box 807, Bolinas, CA 94924, tel. 415/868–1836 or 800/786–1830, fax 415/868–9033. June–late Aug.: 6 days, $935. Price includes all meals; sign up 4–6 months in advance.*

IDAHO AND MONTANA **The Indian Wars.** In 1863, the Nez Perce fled Idaho looking for safety—only to surrender to pursuing federal troops 40 miles from the Canadian border. This tour from Travel America, led by historian and archivist Edward Bearss and last offered in 1994, retraces the natives' flight through Idaho, Oregon, and Montana, visiting the historic battlefields and trails that were the scenes of violent encounters and strategic retreats. In all, the tour covers 1,700 miles in nine days. Accommodations are in Best Western, Radisson, or similar hotels and motels. Lunch usually consists of hot soups, sandwiches, and salad and may be a buffet; dinners are in hotel dining rooms, where you have a choice of menus. *Travel America, 131 Dodge St., Suite 5, Beverly, MA 01915, tel. 508/927–4543 or 800/225–2553, fax 508/927–5140. Late Oct.–early Nov.: 9 days, $1,195. Price includes all lunches and dinners; sign up 3–4 months in advance.*

IDAHO AND OREGON **In the Wake of Lewis and Clark.** The small-ship cruises offered by many institutions have a naturalist focus (*see* Environmental Cruises); those from the National Trust for Historic Preservation concentrate on history. This cruise down the Columbia and Snake rivers follows the entire route of explorers Meriwether Lewis and William Clark, who forged a pathway to the West during a three-year expedition across uncharted wilderness to the Pacific and back. Unlike Lewis and Clark, who traveled over this terrain in wagons and rafts, you will have the benefit of Zodiacs—motorized rubber landing craft—to explore the river's side canyons and rugged shoreline. In the company of a historic preservationist and a local historian native to Oregon, you make excursions to such early settlements as Astoria, Oysterville, the Whitman Mission, and Walla Walla. Your vessel is Special Expeditions' 70-passenger *Sea Bird,* a favorite among educational tour groups. Accommodations are in small cabins for two, designed for little more than sleeping. Meals, served family style in a single seating, include both typical American fare and the traditional northern European dishes favored by the crew. *National Trust for Historic Preservation, 1785 Massachusetts Ave., NW, Washington, DC 20036, tel. 202/673–4000 or 800/944–6847, fax 202/673–4038. Early May: 8 days, $2,190–$3,250. Price includes all meals; sign up 9–12 months in advance.*

■WYOMING■ **Cowboys: Myth and Reality.** A writer-storyteller regales participants with tales of Butch Cassidy and the Sundance Kid as well as other Western legends throughout this 12-day Smithsonian trip through Wyoming. The state's high and wide plateaus were not the home of the Cheyenne, but of the cowboy and his nemesis, the outlaw—cattle rustlers and horse thieves—and the mythology related to this American icon is the trip's theme. A rodeo kicks off the program, whose schedule also includes visits to a working ranch and a saddlery; the Buffalo Bill Historical Center, a memorial to the late-19th-century figure who is most responsible for popularizing the American frontier period in American history; and the American Heritage Center, a research institute devoted to the cowboy that displays western art and cowpoke artifacts. Overnight accommodations include a night in Cody at the frontier-style turn-of-the-century Irma Hotel, named for Buffalo Bill Cody's daughter, and two nights in rustic luxury at Yellowstone's Old Faithful Inn, a sprawling turn-of-the-century log con-

struction. Meals are in local restaurants and hotels, and include a barbecue dinner. Although the trip had been cancelled for 1994 at press time, it may be worth your while to check with the Smithsonian on whether a similar tour is on offer. *Smithsonian Study Tours and Seminars, Smithsonian Institution, 1100 Jefferson Dr., SW, MRC 702, Washington, DC 20560, tel. 202/357–4700, fax 202/633–9250. Late July–early Aug.: 12 days, $1,660. Price includes 7 lunches and 5 dinners; sign up 5–7 months in advance.*

■WYOMING■ **Tracks of the Transcontinental Railroad.** The entire state of Wyoming is redolent of America's western heritage. On this 10-day National Trust for Historic Preservation tour, you explore the landmarks that create that atmosphere: preserved stagecoach stations, ghost towns, railroad depots, forts, and cattle ranches. Led by the director of Wyoming Parks and Cultural Resources, in 1994, when it was last offered, the tour loosely follows the route of the Union Pacific Railroad, which was constructed between 1862 and 1869 and which transformed the face of the frontier. Much of the tour highlights the role that the railroad played in the settlement of the West. In Cheyenne, Wyoming's capital—a town built by the Union Pacific Railroad—restoration work is underway on the 19th-century train depot, engine shop, and roundhouse where trains changed tracks and took on additional carriages. From there, you follow the right-of-way to Laramie, passing by the highest point (8,247 feet) of the original transcontinental railroad. You also stop in Hole-in-the-Wall Valley, where Butch Cassidy and the Sundance Kid once hid out between train robberies. Accommodations include the antique Sheridan Inn in Sheridan and the Irma Hotel—both once owned by Buffalo Bill Cody. *National Trust for Historic Preservation, 1785 Massachusetts Ave., NW, Washington, DC 20036, tel. 202/673–4000 or 800/944–6847, fax 202/673–4038. Early-mid-June.: 10 days, $1,650. Price includes*

7 lunches and 5 dinners; sign up 9–12 months in advance.

ALASKA

SOUTHEAST **Tlingit Tales.** The Tlingit, the original inhabitants of this part of the state, created Alaska's famous totem poles. But they have no written language. Their oral history is the focus of this two-week river trip along the region's forest-bordered Tatshenshini and Alsek rivers, from James Henry River Journeys. Billed as a wilderness literature forum, it is one of the outfitters' most popular tours and is repeated yearly, always with an anthropologist and a poet as leaders. You camp along the river banks and dine on salmon, halibut, and other local specialties; the food has a certain California flair in its unfussy presentation and the freshness of the ingredients. In summer, temperatures range from 50°F to 75°F by day down to the 40s at night; rain is common. *James Henry River Journeys, Box 807, Bolinas, CA 94924, tel. 415/868–1836 or 800/786–1830, fax 415/868–9033. Late June–early Aug.: 13 days, $2,295. Price includes all meals; sign up 4–6 months in advance.*

SOURCES

ORGANIZATIONS The **Network for Educational Travel** (329 Main St., SW, Ronan, MT 59864, tel. 406/676–2255), a coalition of 800 museums, universities, historical societies, and other nonprofit and commercial tour operators, maintains a database on educational travel. If you're interested in booking a cultural tour, you can request information by destination, interest, or sponsoring institution. The network will provide you with an up-to-date list of what's available and the tours' durations and prices.

A few other organizations include some domestic cultural tours on their roster of mainly international trips: the **Art Institute of Chicago** (111 S. Michigan Ave., Chicago 60603, tel. 312/443–3600), which has a different domestic trip every month; the **Denver Museum of Natural History** (2001 Colorado Blvd., Denver, CO 80205-5798, tel. 303/370–6304), which covers the Southwest and other regions; and the **National Geographic Society** (Box 96090, Washington, DC 20090-6097, tel. 202/857–7500), which also offers trips to the southwestern United States as well as stateside cultural cruises.

University- and college-sponsored tours allow you to learn as you travel in the company of fellow alumni. To find out more about school-sponsored trips, contact your alma mater's alumni relations office.

SEE ALSO Culture, as in horticulture, is another option (*see* Garden Tours). For a look at life in ancient times, check out Archaeological Digs. Also see Environmental Cruises, Photography Workshops and Tours, Volunteer Vacations in Research, and, if you don't mind staying in one place, Campus Vacations.

Environmental Cruises

By Melissa Rivers

nvironmental cruises are wilderness expeditions for travelers who want to heed the call of the wild but don't cherish the thought of bug bites, pitching tents, cooking out, lugging gear, and taking cold showers or none at all. The cruise ship is a more civilized means of exploring nature: All the comforts of home (and then some) float into areas untouched by modern development.

You can have a relaxing vacation on an environmental cruise and come away with a lot more than a good tan. You get the chance to see the stuff of *National Geographic* specials, firsthand. Picture the ship cutting through the water, the wind ruffling your hair as you keep a lookout for wildlife. Suddenly a black-footed albatross soars overhead, a whale spouts in the distance, or a shoal of dolphins dance in the water so close that you can hear them breathe. Then, before you can say "Ah!" you're racing across the deck to see the action on the opposite side of the ship.

There are hundreds of cruises to choose from—and the options are multiplying as more and more cruise lines, seeing trips sell out between 6 and 12 months in advance, recognize the demand and add additional departures. Such factors as the focus of the cruise, the size of the ship, and the itinerary mean that no two environmental cruises are alike.

Some present an overview of the biological, geologic, and historical makeup of the region visited; others concentrate on the wildlife there. Depending on the program, you may spend most of your time on the ship watching the passing scenery or you may make frequent excursions to explore onshore or collect specimens. Motorized inflatable rafts, often Zodiacs, may be used to convey you and your fellow passengers to dry land or to move you closer to whales and other marine life.

Some cruises explore several areas—for instance, cruises that travel throughout the Pacific Northwest. Others stick to just one, such as Alaska. If you want to study wildlife and animal habitats in depth, choose one of the latter. Cruises on the northeastern seaboard and in Alaska and the Pacific Northwest are good examples of this type; they usually include frequent sightings of cetaceans (whales, dolphins, and porpoises), pinnipeds (seals, sea lions), fish life (including flying fish, a popular sight), and various pelagic birds (those whose habitat is the open ocean). On cruises that travel inland—for instance, up the Columbia River in Washington and Oregon or along New York's Erie Canal—you can expect to learn about the history and geology of the shore area, as well as the plants, mammals, and birds that spend their lives there.

Perhaps the greatest difference among environmental cruises is the intensity of the focus on the natural world. True, all such cruises sail with a naturalist aboard (and

Writer Melissa Rivers has cruised the world over in ships of all sizes and particularly enjoys the learning experiences provided on small ships.

most of these experts have postgraduate degrees and are affiliated with a professional research or educational institution). But the naturalist lectures and other activities are the main events on some cruises, while they're just one of many activities on others. When you're deciding upon an environmental cruise, the first thing to ask yourself is whether you could possibly get bored sighting the umpteenth bald eagle or whale. If you want to learn about the tiniest facets of an orca's breeding habits, go for it. If not, you'd better pick a cruise that gives you plenty of other things to think about.

To a great extent, your options in this area depend on the size of the ship you sail on. Most environmental cruises use small, yacht-size, motor-driven ships that accommodate between 75 and 100 passengers; they feel intimate, the lifestyle aboard is decidedly casual, and the wildlife focus is pervasive. Announcements of wildlife sightings and lectures on passing flora and fauna are often made over ship-wide public-address systems, so you can hear them wherever you go. Hours of observation may be broken only by morning and afternoon lectures on area flora and fauna or daily field trips for shore observation and the gathering of plant specimens. The ships themselves have features that make it possible to get breathtakingly close to wildlife: A shallow draft lets them sail very close to shore, and powerful bow thrusters help them maneuver in bays, fjords, inlets, and other tight areas that larger ships can't manage safely. Because they are small, you are physically fairly close to the water, so you see marine life at closer range than you can from a large cruise ship. Shore excursions and the use of binoculars while on board are usually included in the cost of your trip on these small ships. Moreover, an open-door policy often prevails regarding visits to the bridge—fascinating if you're interested in navigation.

Other aspects of these small ships may or may not appeal to you. Schedules are tight and group-oriented, with set meal and activity times. Cabins tend to be compact, with a shower in a tiny head which is sometimes shared. Finally, meals are generally served family style at open seatings and consist of basic steak, pasta, chicken, and fish dishes. After dark, there are informal lectures on upcoming sites and the occasional dance, film, or night of casino games.

Large cruise liners accommodating from 1,000 to 1,500 passengers, which also make environmental cruises, offer an entirely different experience. Because of their size, large ships can't give you the close encounters with nature possible aboard more maneuverable vessels; what you see is usually very far away—some of these ships are as high as a 14-story building. Yes, there is generally a naturalist on board. But you're on your own to learn more about the wildlife. The PA systems are used only for occasional park ranger talks and whale sightings. You have to select those shore excursions that highlight the natural environment, and sometimes you may have to explore on your own. The naturalist activities are only one of a huge range of diversions: several restaurants serving a variety of cuisines, lounges, snack bars, courts for various sports (paddle tennis, basketball, volleyball, and such, depending upon the ship), swimming pools and Jacuzzis, spas, casinos, theaters, and discos. Most of these large ships also offer a supervised children's program. Shore excursions usually cost extra. The creature comfort quotient is greater than on small ships. Staterooms have such amenities as a bathtub, minibar, and TV. The passenger-to-crew ratio is lower than on small ships, so the service is more personalized. Only you can say whether the buzz of a thousand other cruisers and the wealth of comforts and activities on board will enhance your experience of nature—or diminish it.

For any given destination, you usually have a variety of options. Most lines that cruise in North America reposition their ships seasonally, spending winter in the Caribbean, summer in Alaska, and spring and fall on inland waterways or on the Panama Canal and along the Atlantic or the Pacific seaboards.

The greatest number of options, however, are available for cruises to Alaska, particularly the Inside Passage, the 1,000-mile waterway stretching from Seattle, Washington, and Skagway, Alaska. Alaska is the single most popular destination of environmental cruises. Some Alaska cruises start in the south and head north; these are the hottest tickets because the beauty of the sights seems to grow exponentially along the way. Others head south, taking in the same sights but in a different sequence; reservations for these trips are easier to come by, and so are discount fares. Typical stops include the colorful gold rush boomtowns of Wrangell and Skagway; Juneau, the capital city; the small seaport of Seward; Switzerland-like Valdez; Russian-influenced Sitka; and Alaska's wettest town, Ketchikan. Alaska cruises also typically stop in Victoria, known for its gardens.

Regardless of destination, the average cruise lasts about eight days and costs $2,000 per person based on double occupancy—and up. Prices on any given ship will vary by cabin category and sometimes by sailing date. In Alaska, for instance, early- and late-season departures are less expensive than mid-season sailings.

CHOOSING THE RIGHT CRUISE

While some smaller operators allow you to book a cruise directly, most major cruise lines only accept reservations from travel agents. No matter who you are dealing with when you are choosing your cruise, be sure to ask the following questions:

How large is the ship? The size of the ship determines whether your cruise is a luxury vacation with an environmental motif or an intense nature experience with a few of the comforts of home. The smaller the boat, the more maneuvering the crew can do to get you closer to the wildlife.

On the other hand, large ships are a better bet for a number of cruisers. You'll prefer a large ship if the environmental aspects of the trip are only one of your vacation interests. The same is true if you have any hearing impairment, because the sound quality of loudspeaker systems aboard small ships tends to be poor and announcements difficult to understand. Large ships are better, too, if you have a mobility problem: Small ships typically lack the ramps, handrails, and elevators commonly found on large ships. Unless the cruise you are contemplating is on rivers and other protected waterways, you may also want to stick with large ships if you suffer from motion sickness. (To further reduce the chance you'll be afflicted, book a cabin at the true center of the ship—on a midlevel deck halfway between the bow and the stern, and avoid alcoholic beverages, which further irritate upset stomachs and magnify feelings of imbalance.)

What are the qualifications of the naturalists leading the cruise? The experience and ability of your guide or guides greatly affect your learning experience. Make sure that they have the background to provide the kind of information you expect to get when you sign up for an environmental cruise.

What will the naturalist contribute? Find out exactly what the naturalists will do. They might simply point out and identify the wildlife along the shore. Or, at the time of sightings, they might lecture informally on the animals' habits and habitats. They might lecture on area flora and fauna by day or after dark. Sometimes naturalists are constantly available to answer your questions; sometimes they have a few set hours. On larger ships, you are much less likely to receive the personal attention of a naturalist, who may have to answer questions from 1,000 or more people.

What is the focus of the trip? Find out if you'll primarily be observing wildlife, studying the geographic features of the area, or learning about the region's natural history.

How much time is spent observing and learning about nature? Especially on larger ships, you may spend most of your time enjoying sports and other activities not related to the environment. On small ships, the environment is the star of the show, and virtually all activities aboard ship and ashore revolve around observing and exploring it.

Are Zodiacs or other landing craft available so you can get off the ship and explore frequently? If getting up close and personal with the wildlife and environment around you matters, make sure that Zodiac excursions are an integral part of the program.

What is the itinerary? Ports of call vary, as does the amount of time in each port—typically between three or four hours and a full day. Boston and Montreal are frequent stops on itineraries through the Northeast, and San Francisco, Portland, Seattle, and Vancouver, British Columbia, on cruises along the West Coast. Virtually all Alaska itineraries include stops in Juneau, Sitka, and Ketchikan.

What's the cost and what's included? It's typical for cruise fares to be per person, based on double occupancy, and to include (like all prices quoted in the following cruise reviews unless otherwise noted) all meals, lectures, and evening entertainment but not airfare to the port of embarkation or from the port of disembarkation, port taxes, optional shore trips, gratuities to the crew, and baggage or trip insurance. Be sure to ask whether your fare covers alcoholic beverages, snacks, and shore excursions. It varies from one cruise to the next.

A simple way to compare costs of different cruises is to look at the per diem—the price of a cruise on a daily basis per passenger, based on double occupancy. Also, look at what you get for the per diem, since this varies from ship to ship.

If you plan to arrive a day or two early at the port of embarkation, or to linger a few days for sightseeing after debarkation, estimate the cost of your hotel, meals, car rental, sightseeing, and other expenditures. Cruise lines often sell packages for such pre- and post-cruise stays. These may or may not cost less than arrangements you make independently, so shop around.

What are accommodations like? Make sure you know what you're getting into. Will you be sleeping in a tiny cabin or a luxury stateroom? If you care about the size of your bathroom or whether it's down the hall, ask. If you don't relish cold showers, make sure that hot ones are available. If you don't mind taking cold showers, make sure that the water is at least fresh; some of the simpler ships let you rinse off in seawater. If you must have a lower bunk, a double bed, or a window, make sure that the ship can provide it.

What are meals like? A smaller ship has a smaller galley, a smaller staff, and, therefore, a more limited menu. On large ships, you have a selection of restaurants and snack bars serving a variety of foods. The quality of food varies from ship to ship; in general, the better the ship, the better the food, and the more you'll spend for the cruise.

Find out if there are table assignments and whether there are one or two seatings; ask when these are arranged. You may be able to do it when you book, or you may have to wait until you board.

Many small ships have open seating for all meals, which means you may sit anywhere at any time. However, on many larger ships dining rooms are not big enough to accommodate all passengers at once, so mealtimes are divided into two seatings, usually from 1½ to 2½ hours apart. Dinner, for example, is often between 6 and 6:30 for early seating, between 8 and 8:30 for the late seating. On some ships, these seating times are strictly observed, and the dining room doors close 10 to 15 minutes after the scheduled mealtime; on other ships, you may enter the dining room at your leisure, but must leave by the end of the seating.

Make sure you know what the policies are on the ships you are considering, since meals play such a big part in the cruise experience.

If it matters to you, ask about the ship's policies on serving liquor. Some of the smaller ships don't serve liquor at all or serve only wine; you're expected to bring your own.

To what degree is shipboard life scheduled? As a general rule, the larger the ship, the more choice you'll have in how you spend your time.

What other onboard activities are offered? If you don't want to spend all your time nature-watching, make sure you pick a ship that gives you something else to do. Even smaller ships offer a few diversions, but they may be limited to a library for reading or a small exercise room.

What is the typical makeup of passengers? Each cruise attracts a specific audience. Find out what it is before you book, and make sure you'll be comfortable in that company. (This is especially important on small ships, where the group is smaller.) The number of cruising families is on the rise, accounting for 25% of cruise passengers. Alaska itineraries tend to have a majority of passengers who are older than 55, while on California, New England, and Caribbean cruises, the average age is lower and couples mix with families. Single travelers are usually in the minority.

What programs and facilities are available for families traveling with children? You must shop especially carefully for an environmental cruise if you plan to sail with children. Some ships don't allow children, usually those under eight; the material covered by the naturalists is too advanced. However, some cruises do provide special children's programs and activities. If these are available, question the cruise line closely to find out what they're like. Ask the same questions about activities, schedules, facilities, and supervision that you would of any day care provider. But also find out what ages of children are accepted (some require that participants be out of diapers or at least three); what hours the program runs (it may cover you for only parts of days, and it may or may not be available after dark); and whether baby-sitting is available (and from whom).

How formal is the cruise? Some cruises require fancier attire than others. On some, you will never need anything dressier than chinos and sweaters; on others, there may be one dressy evening, or several. On a select few, men tend to wear jackets and ties to dinner every evening.

Will laundry service be available? You may be able to pack lighter when traveling on a large ship with laundry service or a laundromat. Most smaller ships don't offer laundry facilities, but these ships' more casual atmosphere doesn't require an extensive wardrobe.

How long has the company been in business? Try to stick with an operator who has been in business for several years. Experience is some insurance, though not a guarantee, that the trip will run smoothly.

Do you have references from past guests? If you have doubts about whether or not you'll enjoy a given cruise, there's no substitute for a conversation with another traveler. Ask the travel agent for names of previous clients. It's a good way of judging the agent's expertise and advice, as well as the merits of a particular cruise line or ship.

How far in advance do I need to book? As environmental cruises attract more and more people, ships are sailing near or at capacity. In Alaska, cruise lines begin selling their next year's sailings as soon as the current season is underway. Departures on the most popular itineraries and sailing dates begin selling out between 6 and 12 months in advance. To make sure that you get the accommodations you want on the sailing of your choice, it's imperative to reserve well ahead of the sailing date.

MAJOR PLAYERS

ALASKA SIGHTSEEING/CRUISE WEST This operator, founded in 1973, has the largest fleet of small-ships in North America and the highest number of annual cruises in the Pacific Northwest. Three vessels—the 101-passenger *Spirit of '98*, the 82-passenger *Spirit of*

Alaska, and the 84-passenger *Spirit of Discovery*—make a variety of seven-day trips. Because of the size of these ships, you can reach areas that you can't get to in larger ships. Cruises travel between Seattle and Alaska in spring and summer; in fall, they go around the San Juan and Gulf islands and down the Columbia and Snake rivers in Washington, Oregon, and Idaho. A fourth ship, the *Spirit of Columbia,* will be positioned on the Columbia and Snake rivers, beginning March 25, 1995.

The Cruise Coordinator on each trip is trained to teach you about the flora, fauna, and geologic features that you encounter en route. Over the public address system, he or she alerts you to sights that range from a bald eagle soaring overhead to unusual plants growing in the semi-rain forest climate of Columbia Gorge. When you're following the path of the Lewis and Clark expedition, you get some history lessons, too.

Life aboard ship is fairly unstructured: Arrivals and departures, meals, and occasional evening entertainment are the only firmly scheduled events. The close quarters create a sense of camaraderie among the passengers, but you won't get the comfort and service you do on larger ships. Cabins are small and simply decorated, and most have windows and doors that open to the sea breezes. Meals are basic but well-prepared; the small galley and prep staff limit the selection. Two entrées are offered for dinner, and you must make your choice in advance. Local foods, including salmon and fresh fruit and berries are often served. Entertainment is limited—perhaps a dance and casino night. Trips are designed for adult participants; bringing children is not encouraged. American owned and operated, this outfitter has young and energetic American crews. Prices start at $1,595 (4th & Battery Bldg., 2401 4th Ave., Suite 700, Seattle, WA 98121, tel. 206/441–8687 or 800/426–7702, fax 206/441–4757).

AMERICAN CANADIAN CARIBBEAN LINE This was one of the first lines to offer cruises on small ships. In 1964, Captain Luther H. Blount of Blount Marine Shipbuilders predicted the growth in demand for smaller ships and started designing yachtlike ships with shallow drafts and bow ramps to provide direct access to the shore. Thus was born the small fleet of American Canadian Caribbean Line: the *Caribbean Prince,* the *Mayan Prince,* and the *Niagara Prince,* the last being 1994's addition to the line. These ships, almost identical, cruise along the eastern seaboard and the Florida coast, through the Erie Canal and the bayou country of the Gulf Coast, and around the U.S. Virgin Islands. Trips focus on both the cultural and natural history in these areas.

Cabins are simple and small, measuring just 8 by 10 feet, but they're air-conditioned, with built-in berths and private bathrooms with toilet and handheld shower. Rates tend to be low, and as a result ACCL offers few traditional services and facilities—sheets and towels are changed every *other* day, for instance, and it's even suggested that you pack your own beach towel. Hearty homemade fare, such as sandwiches on fresh-baked bread, and classic pastas are interspersed with such gourmet treats as chilled peach soup and crab-stuffed pastry. Generally speaking, cuisine is basic American, and many offerings use fresh seafood and produce picked up in ports along the way. Meals are served family style at a single open seating (dinner at 6); breakfast is a buffet. No alcohol is sold on board, although you are free to bring your own. Mixers and other nonalcoholic drinks are available free from the bar at all hours. Cruises are narrated by the captain, who points out the flora, fauna, and historical sites along the route; and authorities on local history and wildlife are frequently brought on board to share their insights and expertise. A cruise director arranges evening entertainment; he or she may play the piano or bring in a steel drum band or guest lecturer. The minimum age on ACCL cruises is 14, but the average guest is over 55. These no-frills cruises are an excellent value, with the cost of a twelve-day cruise ranging from $1,622 to $2,599 per person

(461 Water St., Box 368, Warren, RI 02885, tel. 401/247–0955 or 800/556–7450, fax 401/245–8303).

CLIPPER CRUISE LINE This company offers naturalist-led cruises in more areas of North America than any other, including the United States, Canada, and Central America. It offers two distinct styles of cruising: Clipper Classic cruises and Clipper Adventure cruises. Classic-series cruises focus on destinations with cultural and historic appeal, while adventure cruises sail to regions renowned for their scenic beauty and wildlife-viewing opportunities. On adventure cruises, Zodiacs ferry passengers to remote beaches, pristine forests, small villages, and wildlife refuges; a team of naturalists and lecturers conduct seminars on board and unusual walking tours ashore. Classic cruises moor at marinas or at town piers, eliminating the need for tenders or taxis. Clipper is more sophisticated and service-oriented than most other small ship lines; and its passengers are wealthier and better educated than the average cruise passenger, and older (typically in their mid-sixties).

Clipper operates three shallow-draft vessels: the yachtlike 138-passenger *Yorktown Clipper* and 100-passenger *Nantucket Clipper,* and the larger (138-passenger), older expedition ship *World Discoverer.* The *Clippers* look more like yachts than cruise ships. The trademark design, dominated by a large bridge and big picture windows that ensure bright interior public spaces, is sleek and attractive. There are only a few public rooms, and deck space is limited. The glass-walled Observation Lounge is small enough to foster conversation that can be heard anywhere in the room, so it's usually quite a friendly place. The ships' coziness can engender camaraderie or claustrophobia, but generally passengers are made to feel like invited guests. Staterooms are cozy and pleasantly decorated, with lower beds (no bunks), individual thermostats, and private bathrooms. The *World Discoverer,* built for adventure-travel, has, among other features, a hardened hull that enables it to plow through ice-choked channels. In 1985, the ship made the first Northwest Passage crossing by a passenger ship.

On all three ships, meals are cooked by chefs trained at the Culinary Institute of America and are served in a single open seating. Fresh salmon, Alaska king crab, Chesapeake soft-shell and blue crabs, gumbo, fresh tropical fruits, and other regional specialties are highlighted, and all entrée selections are cooked to order. Fresh chocolate chip cookies are available every afternoon. There are two dressy evenings on each cruise, but they don't require formal attire.

Shipboard life on the vessels is unregimented, with no crowds and a more casual pace than found on many larger ships. Crews are young, cheerful, and as quick to please as the naturalists and historians are to answer questions.

Clipper cruises are designed for those 18 and older. Prices range from $1,100 to $4,200 on itineraries that range in length from 6 to 15 days (7711 Bonhomme Ave., St. Louis, MO 63105, tel. 314/727–2929 or 800/325–0010).

HOLLAND AMERICA LINE This line, founded in 1873, is one of the few in the luxury class that has highly trained naturalists aboard to lecture on the fabulous flora and fauna of the Inside Passage. Each summer you can choose from over 90 Alaskan cruises on five modern Holland America liners, which depart from Vancouver, British Columbia. The MS *Nieuw Amsterdam,* her twin the MS *Noordam,* and the MS *Statendam* cruise the Inside Passage, making calls at Ketchikan, Juneau, Glacier Bay, and Sitka; while the SS *Rotterdam* and the MS *Ryndam* cruise the Glacier Route, which includes stops at points farther north, including Hubbard Glacier, Valdez, and Seward. Although these are typical luxury cruises, there is always a naturalist on hand, showing films, lecturing, and standing watch on deck at regular intervals to help you spot wildlife and to answer questions.

Each ship is a floating city. Nautical antiques and memorabilia, from historic artifacts to nostalgic soap boxes, reflect the line's 100-year-plus seafaring heritage. Cruises are conservative affairs, renowned for their grace and gentility. No money changes hands (you sign for everything), and loudspeaker announcements are kept to a minimum. Accommodations are luxurious: On the line's newest ships (MS *Statendam* and MS *Ryndam*), even standard cabins come with a small sitting area with a sofa; outside cabins have tubs in the bath, inside cabins just showers. On all the Holland America ships, breakfast and lunch are open seating; dinner is served at two assigned seatings (6:15 and 8:15). Food is good by cruise-ship standards and is served on Rosenthal china. The emphasis is on American cuisine, with an occasional Dutch or Indonesian dish for variety. Dinner menus often include fish fresh from the market in that day's port of call, and every menu has a spa selection. Once during each cruise there's an Indonesian lunch and an outdoor barbecue dinner, and each day there's a lunch of barbecued hot dogs and hamburgers, pasta, stir-fries, and make-your-own tacos on the Lido deck, which is also home to a self-serve ice cream and frozen yogurt parlor. Youth counsellors accompany each ship to supervise school-age children. The movies, scavenger hunts, and games of the children's program are not nature-related. There are two formal evenings each week and loads of entertainment: big-band sounds, comedy, magic and dance acts, revues, dance orchestras, a piano bar, string trios, and jazz quartets. The Filipino, Indonesian, and Dutch crew members are extremely attentive and adept at pampering passengers, who number as many as 1,100 to 1,500 on each ship. Despite all this, prices are affordable, starting at $1,195 and $2,490 for 7- and 14-day cruises, respectively (300 Elliott Ave. W, Seattle, WA 98819, tel. 206/281–3535 or 800/426–0327, fax 206/281–7110).

OCEANIC SOCIETY EXPEDITIONS This nonprofit organization affiliated with Friends of the Earth, a global environmental advocacy group, has specialized in educational eco-travel since it was established in 1972. All proceeds exceeding expenses go directly toward environmental causes, from research projects to conservation efforts. The expert naturalists who lead the trips follow a strict code of ecotourism ethics—conducting tours that do not disturb wildlife or harm sensitive habitats, properly disposing all wastes, and minimizing impact on the cultures that are visited. The leaders, trained in interpreting wildlife reaction to tour groups, can avoid triggering animal escape behaviors, thus allowing closer observation.

Destinations include New England, Alaska, the Pacific Northwest, and California (with excursions to Baja), as well as numerous foreign countries. In each area, ships are chartered for one or two journeys a year; sailing vessels are chosen for their minimal impact on the environment. Although each is different, you can usually count on compact cabins, simple meals served family style, and shared heads with freshwater showers—some cold ones, however. Schedules are quite flexible; activities are organized according to the presence of wildlife and to the whims of the weather. Although one program for teens is offered each year, most Oceanic Society cruises are for adults only. Trips range in length from 7 to 19 days and cost between $800 and $3,900 (Ft. Mason Center, Bldg. E, 2nd Floor, San Francisco, CA 94123, tel. 415/441–1106 or 800/326–7491, fax 415/474–3395).

SPECIAL EXPEDITIONS The fact that such top institutions as the Smithsonian, the Audubon Society, the World Wildlife Fund, the American Museum of Natural History, the Museum for Comparative Zoology, and the California Academy of Sciences hire Special Expeditions to run their natural history cruises is persuasive evidence that it's the best in the industry. Special Expeditions has grown steadily since it was founded in 1979 by Sven-Olof Lindblad, son of adventure travel pioneer Lars-Eric Lindblad.

Like Clipper Cruise Line, Special Expeditions operates a collection of shallow-draft vessels designed to explore nature and visit remote ports. The yachtlike, 70-passenger

Sea Bird and *Sea Lion* are tiny, and even the 84-passenger *Polaris* is among the smallest of expedition ships. While all carry Zodiacs for landings almost anywhere, none of these vessels—not even the *Polaris*—has an ice-hardened hull. Very different is the meticulously restored, four-masted, 70-passenger *Sea Cloud,* perhaps the most beautiful barque afloat, built as the *Hussar V* for heiress Marjorie Merriweather Post and financier E. F. Hutton and for a time the world's largest privately owned yacht. It's truly a sight to watch crew members scamper up the 20-story masts to unfurl the ship's 29 billowing sails (which cover 34,000 square feet).

Cruises aboard Special Expeditions ships have a friendly atmosphere and tend to draw a slightly younger, less affluent, more easygoing crowd. The company employs about 150 naturalists and historians, in most cases experts in the historical, natural, and geographic makeup of the areas that the ships visit. Between four and eight naturalists accompany each cruise to lead shore excursions during the day and present lectures and slide shows in the evening; no other line provides so many experts per cruise. Unlike guest experts on some ships, who are treated either as employees or celebrities, specialists on Special Expeditions cruises eat and socialize with passengers. You'll feel less like a paying spectator and more like part of a grand adventure.

Cruises have flexible schedules. Sometimes the captain makes the decision about where to go next; at other times, passengers vote—say, to decide whether the ship should follow a pod of whales or head for a nearby fishing village. Shipboard activities consist mainly of lectures by the naturalists and historians on the wildlife and cultural history of the ports of call.

Individual cabins are functional and extremely compact. Public areas aboard the ships, though still small, give a little relief. For instance, the *Polaris*'s main public room is more like an oversize living room than a cruise-ship lounge, and a smaller lounge in the stern doubles as the library, which is well stocked with reference books, best-sellers, and atlases. The dining rooms of the *Sea Lion* and *Sea Bird* command a magnificent view of the sea. Hearty meals draw on ingredients available in ports along the way and are heavily influenced by Northern European cooking traditions. They're served in single, unassigned seatings, so guests can mingle during the voyage. There are no special facilities for children but no restrictions about who can cruise. Note that the lilliputian *Sea Bird, Sea Lion,* and *Sea Cloud,* while very friendly and homey, rock so noticeably in rough waters that packets of Dramamine are kept in a bowl outside the purser's office. However, most itineraries are on protected inland waterways, where you won't have a problem. The outfitter's trips range in length from 4 to 28 days and start at $860 per person (720 5th Ave., New York, NY 10019, tel. 212/765–7740 or 800/762–0003, fax 212/265–3770).

FAVORITE CRUISES

THE NORTHEAST

MAINE **Figaro Cruises Coastal Maine.** Plenty of pleasure craft depart the picturesque harbor of Camden for cruises of the New England seaboard, but cruises aboard the comfortable, 51-foot sailing yawl *Figaro IV* are unique, with their vegetarian meals, plentiful exercise (from hoisting sails to hiking on shore), and loads of educational opportunities. Other than set departure and return times, your entire six-day itinerary is unstructured, so you and the other five passengers that the craft can accommodate are free to go where the wind blows, visiting coastal Maine's wooded islands, quiet coves, and quaint villages.

With their master's degrees in environmental education, coleaders Jen Martin and Barry King are well qualified to tell you about the wildlife that inhabits their cruising ground, between Boothbay Harbor and Acadia National Park on Mount Desert Island. You spend a portion of every day sailing from island to island, learning basic seamanship and sailing skills. Once anchor is dropped, you can take a small dinghy ashore for hikes and informal lectures on the area's natural and cultural history. Jen and Barry also give informal classes on the maritime history of towns visited, such as Castine, site of a major British naval victory during the Revolutionary War. Yoga instructor Dean Learner comes on two cruises each year to give lessons on Iyengar-style yoga. You can also lend a hand in the galley, learning to prepare sesame tempeh, eggplant Parmesan, quiche, and other vegetarian dishes; seafood is available on request.

Accommodations include two cabins with double beds, two semiprivate single berths separated by curtains, and two communal heads (one with a hot freshwater shower). The deck is spacious enough for you to practice yoga, work on your tan, or stretch out under the stars in a sleeping bag (bring your own). Families with small children are welcome if they book all six passenger spaces; otherwise, 15 is the minimum age allowed. *Figaro Cruises, Box 1336, Camden, ME 04843, tel. 207/236–8741 or 800/473–6169. May–Oct.: 6 days, $700. Sign up 1 month in advance.*

RHODE ISLAND **Cruising the Erie Canal and Saguenay Fjord.** Because there are so many historical sites to see in the Northeast, very few cruises here concentrate exclusively on nature; this one from the American Canadian Caribbean Line is no exception. The captain—who does double duty as the naturalist on these trips—talks not only about flora, fauna, geography, and ecology of the places you visit but also about the events that took place there.

For almost 30 years, ACCL ships have cruised the winding route from Warren, Rhode Island, through Long Island Sound, past the Statue of Liberty and New York City, up the Hudson River, through the Erie Canal, across Lake Ontario, and into the St. Lawrence Seaway past Montreal, into the magnificent Saguenay Fjord and its scenic Baie Eternité. Because of the retractable pilothouses aboard its ships, the ACCL is the only cruise line able to negotiate the narrow, bridge-covered waterways along this route.

The Erie Canal follows the Mohawk, Seneca, and Oswego rivers, hemmed in by steep cliffs and gentle foothills covered with hardwood trees. You often see large beaver mounds near the water's edge. The Mohawk River Valley is a prime habitat for otter, mink, great blue heron, egret, and ibis; and coho salmon make their way up fish ladders in the Oswego River to spawn. As you sail through the canal, the captain talks about the ecology of the region and how it has changed since the canal opened. Along the St. Lawrence River, he discusses the numerous historical sites relating to the early French and native settlers. Guest speakers occasionally come on board—a diamond miner, for instance, joins you in Little Falls, New York, to discuss geology. You make frequent trips ashore, visiting villages along the canal and spending two days each sightseeing in Montreal and Quebec.

If you have an interest in whales, plan your trip for summer, when humpback and minke whales congregate at the confluence of the Saguenay and St. Lawrence to feed on the rich supply of fish. If you are more interested in the bold changing colors of the oak and maple trees that line the route, book one of the fall sailings, which add West Point and Clayton, New York, in place of Saguenay ports of call. A bus trip through the scenic White Mountains back to your starting point ends each journey. *American Canadian Caribbean Line, 461 Water St., Box 368, Warren, RI 02885, tel. 401/247–0955 or 800/556–7450, fax 401/245–8303. Early June–Oct.: 12 days, $1,675–$2,299. Sign up 3 months in advance.*

THE WEST COAST

CALIFORNIA AND BAJA **San Ignacio Lagoon.** Oceanic Society Expeditions runs several natural history cruises from California along the Pacific side of Baja California. Some focus primarily on the whales, while others, like this one, include lessons on the rich geology, habitats, and wildlife of the peninsula. Naturalist Greg Meyer is well prepared to guide this leisurely nine-day cruise; his degree in environmental studies and his experience managing an observation station in the Sea of Cortez and researching baleen whales and the seabirds of Baja and the Sea of Cortez have given him a lot of insight to share. He presents an orientation at the beginning of the cruise and slide shows each evening to prepare you for what you'll see during the next day. He also leads shore hikes and bay excursions, telling you about the abundant wildlife you encounter.

Starting from San Diego, the trip heads south, following the migration path of gray whales. On Todos Santos Island, rocky cliffs provide nesting sites for brown pelicans, egrets, herons, ibis, cormorants, ospreys, and other migratory species. On the San Benitos Islands, off the coast of central Baja, you explore tidal pools and giant elephant seal rookeries and discuss the area's ecosystem. Perhaps the highlight of the trip is the several days you spend 150 miles farther south in San Ignacio Lagoon, the winter breeding and calving grounds for gray whales. Here you board 22-foot Mexican *panga* boats, piloted by local fishermen, for close encounters with these inquisitive creatures, which sometimes come close enough to touch. Opportunities for gray whale observation, beachcombing, and birding in the mangroves of the lagoon round out the voyage, which returns to San Diego.

The ship is the 86-foot *Spirit of Adventure*, a long-range motor cruising vessel with 14 small, air-conditioned cabins that can accommodate up to 28 passengers in doubles, triples, and quads. It has four heads, three hot showers, and an air-conditioned salon. Meals, prepared by a professional cook, feature American cuisine with a few spicy Mexican touches. *Oceanic Society Expeditions, Ft. Mason Center, Bldg. E, 2nd Floor, San Francisco, CA 94123, tel. 415/441–1106 or 800/326–7491, fax 415/474–3395. Mid-Feb.–Mar.: 9 days, $1,750. Sign up 6 months in advance.*

PACIFIC NORTHWEST Coastal Waterways. Most of the hundreds of cedar- and fir-clad islands that dot Puget Sound, the Strait of Juan de Fuca, and Georgia Strait are accessible only by private boat and remain unspoiled. Special Expeditions's six-day fall cruises aboard the MV *Sea Bird* and MV *Sea Lion* out of Vancouver, British Columbia, visit Tongass National Forest, Alaska State Park lands, and rustic port towns throughout the region, en route to Seattle. Naturalists and historians lead the trip, giving talks on the ecology of Princess Louisa Inlet (a seldom-visited fjord) and about Johnstone Strait, the San Juans, and the historical background of ports of call including San Juan, Victoria, Vancouver, and Seattle.

The sheer abundance of wildlife typically seen on this trip makes it stand out. Here, you observe harbor seals and sea lions stretched out in the sun on rock outcroppings; there, you catch sight of black-and-white Dall porpoises, often mistaken for baby killer whales, cavorting in the sea, or bald eagles diving from the sky to snatch fish from the water. Sightings of killer whales are not unusual, since several pods live in the deep channels between the islands. Twice a day you can take Zodiacs out to remote, protected islands for hikes through thick forests of Douglas fir to waterfowl habitats with ducks, puffins, cormorants, herons, and marbled murrelets. *Special Expeditions, 720 Fifth Ave., New York, NY 10019, tel. 212/765–7740 or 800/762–0003, fax 212/265–3770. Sept.: 6 days, $1,350–$2,000. Sign up 6 months in advance.*

PACIFIC NORTHWEST Exploring the Columbia River, Olympic Peninsula, and British Columbia. The annual 11-day fall passage of the 138-passenger *Yorktown Clipper* covers more of the Pacific Northwest than any other cruise and provides the best view of its many facets. The cruise departs from Seattle and makes its way among the islands in the salmon-rich waters off the coasts of Washington and British Columbia, where you watch bald eagles, sea lions, harbor seals, and porpoises feeding. Ports of call include the Gulf Islands, Vancouver, and the

San Juan Islands. Zodiac landings on some of the smaller islands of the San Juan chain, such as Matia and Sucia, give you a close look at grebes, ducks, murrelets, and great blue heron. Because several pods of killer whales live in the region, chances are very good that you'll see them at some point before you leave the straits of Georgia and Juan de Fuca. Next, you wind around the Olympic Peninsula, where you can opt to take an all-day excursion into the amazing rain forest of Olympic National Park.

The itinerary also includes stops at sites of historical and cultural interest such as Victoria, British Columbia's capital city; Washington's Port Townsend, a national historic district notable for its Victorian architecture; and the Makah Indian Reservation in Neah Bay, at the northwesternmost tip of Washington, where an ancient village was preserved by a mudslide over 500 years ago. Toward the end of the voyage, you retrace the journey of Lewis and Clark up the Columbia River, beginning in Astoria on the Oregon coast and cutting through the majestic Cascade Range at the beautiful Columbia Gorge. The balmy, clear days of September, when the trip runs, are perfect for exploring the orchards and canyons of the Hood River valley at the foot of snowcapped Mt. Hood before making the journey downriver to Portland. *Clipper Cruise Line, 7711 Bonhomme Ave., St. Louis, MO 63105, tel. 314/727–2929 or 800/325–0010. Mid-May and early Oct.: 11 days, $2,550–$3,850. Sign up 6 months in advance.*

PACIFIC NORTHWEST **In the Wake of Lewis and Clark.** Special Expeditions' weeklong spring and fall cruises aboard the M.V. *Sea Bird* and M.V. *Sea Lion* follow the westernmost leg of the historic expedition of Meriwether Lewis and William Clark, who set out in 1804 on a two-year journey to map the newly purchased Louisiana Territory and the Oregon Territory for President Jefferson. The cruise is accompanied by three regional specialists—a historian, a naturalist, and a botanist—who teach you about the Pacific Northwest of today, and that seen by the expedition almost 200 years ago.

Your cruise begins in Portland, Oregon. Cruising up the Columbia River, on the way to your first stop at the Umatilla Wildlife Refuge in eastern Oregon, you pass through the Blalock Islands Wildlife Refuge, where you see meadowlarks, western tanangers, Canadian geese, Great Blue Heron, grebe, and cormorants. At Umatilla, you can choose to take a bus into a nearby Washington vineyard for a tour, or go on a naturalist-led hike through the Refuge.

You continue up the Columbia River to the Snake River, where you stop in Clarkstown, Washington, and move to several twin-engine jet boats for an all-day excursion through the rapid waters of Hell's Canyon. There you see Rocky Mountain bighorn sheep, mule deer, raptors, and maybe even a rattle snake. Next you follow the Snake to its confluence with the Palouse River. You stop for a day in Palouse Canyon, where you can take a leisurely hike, or follow the more strenuous route along the rim of the Canyon to Palouse Falls.

Cruising back into the Columbia River Gorge, you make a stop in the town of Hood River and take a ride on the Mount Hood Scenic Railroad through coniferous forests and pasture lands. Then it's back on the river for a trip to the Bonneville Dam, where you observe the salmon migration on the fish ladders. Cruising on to the mouth of the Columbia, at the Pacific Ocean, you stop at the city of Astoria. The Columbia River Maritime Museum here is a good place to learn about the historical significance of the waters you've cruised, including their role in the Lewis and Clark expedition. The exploring party spent a winter at nearby Fort Clatsop, where another guided nature walk introduces you to the animals and medicinal and edible plants that sustained the expedition team. After your visit here, it's back to Portland and the end of the journey.

This is the most popular Special Expeditions itinerary, in part because of the in-depth look it gives at the history, geology, flora, and fauna of this richly diverse region, and in part because the route passes through eight fascinating dam locks on the Columbia and Snake Rivers, rising to 725 feet above sea level. *Special Expeditions, 720 5th Ave., New York, NY, 10019, tel. 212/765–7740 or 800/762–0003, fax 212/265–3770. Late-Apr.–May and early Sept.–Oct.: 7 days, $1,900–$2,960. Sign up at least 6 months in advance.*

PACIFIC NORTHWEST **Sailing the San Juan and Gulf Islands.** Small sailing yachts provide one of the best ways to explore the Pacific Northwest, and the *Island Roamer* is a good example of why this is true. This 68-foot ketch carries 16 passengers on six-day expeditions out of Victoria, British Columbia, through the San Juan and Gulf Islands. The itinerary is generally flexible: You go where the wildlife is. The captain, naturalist, and passengers make itinerary decisions together; most trips visit Brethour, Mandarte, Jones, Sucia, San Juan, and the Orcas islands off the coasts of British Columbia and Washington. You spend your days sailing from island to island, dropping anchor in a new area each night. Along the way, you observe wildlife, study sailing, and get experience in steering the boat, navigating, and rigging sails. Years of practical field experience, as well as their backgrounds in marine biology, ecology, ornithology, and anthropology, qualify the crew to tell you about the region's natural history, and there's lots to talk about. Moreover, because the yacht moves so quietly, it doesn't frighten wildlife away. As you cruise through protected waterways, it's common to see tawny-hued Steller's sea lions, speckled harbor seals, killer and minke whales, Dall porpoises, bald eagles, and great blue herons.

Kayaks are available for paddling along the islands' quiet shorelines, and large Zodiacs are used regularly to go ashore to visit area villages and hike through the forests and along the shore to look at plants, birds, and intertidal life. After dark, there are slide shows and lectures by the naturalist about local wildlife and their habitats.

Below deck are eight double-occupancy cabins, three heads with hot showers, a library, and a well-equipped galley, where local produce and seafood are transformed into tasty meals. A maximum of 16 guests are accommodated per trip; there is no minimum age, but only one or two young children are allowed per sailing.

This trip is chartered once a year (in late September) by Oceanic Society Expeditions, when one of their own expert naturalists leads the journey. *Bluewater Adventures, Suite 202-1656, Duranleau St., Vancouver, BC V6H 3S4, Canada, tel. 604/684–4575, fax 604/689–5926. Late Sept.–Oct.: 6 days, $875. Sign up 3–6 months in advance.*

ALASKA

SOUTHEAST **Alaska Yacht Cruise.** Morning, noon, and night, the focus of this trip is observing nature—they'll even send someone to wake you at first light if whales are near. The 101-passenger *Spirit of '98*, flagship of the Alaska Sightseeing/Cruise West fleet, can slip into constricted areas such as Desolation Sound, Le Conte Bay, and Tracy Arm Fjord, a wilderness area in Tongass National Forest. It can nose up close to spectacular waterfalls and inch close to glaciers and shorelines. In protected areas such as Misty Fjords National Monument, park rangers join the group for briefings and question-and-answer sessions.

In tiny Petersburg, a fishing village with a strong Norwegian heritage, educator-turned-fisherman Syd Wright comes aboard. From his duffel bag, he pulls out a native rattle, shaking it fiercely as he relates native folklore. He passes around fishing nets, describing Alaska's highly regulated fishing industry. He reads poetry relating to the state, explains how it came to join the Union, and relates the origin of Alaska's gold-on-blue state flag, singing a song in its honor that resounds with the pride and determination of the state's settlers.

The *Spirit of '98* is named for the famous gold fever that swept Alaska in 1898, and the ship's turn-of-the-century decor and distinctive lines recall those of coastal steamers of the day. The staff members are friendly and quick to respond—they fetch fresh-from-the-oven cookies and steaming cocoa when you get chilly on the outside decks. After all, most guests spend the entire week perched at the railing, listening to the cruise director's commentary (over the ship-wide public address system) on dolphins swimming in the bow wake or a humpback whale feeding just yards away. Aside from a few nature lectures, occasional guest speakers, evening socials, and shore excursions in Ketchikan, Juneau, Petersburg, and Sitka, there are few activities to draw your attention from the scenery. *Alaska Sightseeing/Cruise West, 4th & Battery Bldg., 2401 4th Ave., Suite 700, Seattle, WA 98121, tel. 206/441–8687 or 800/426–7702, fax 206/441–4757. Mid-May–Sept.: 8 days, $2,095–$3,795. Sign up 6–12 months in advance.*

SOUTHEAST **Exploring Alaska's Coastal Wilderness.** Four to six top naturalists lead this 10-day Alaska cruise from Special Expeditions, and each is an authority on a different area: ornithology, marine biology, glaciology, botany, history, and the like. Two ships make the trip, the MV *Sea Lion* and the MV *Sea Bird*, one northbound and the other southbound. Each carries four Zodiacs, and there are one or two shore excursions a day, each led by a different naturalist and focusing on that leader's specialty: An ornithologist may lead hikes to look for land and sea birds, a biologist may take you beachcombing, or a geologist may motor out for a discourse on icebergs.

Another unique feature of trips with Special Expeditions is their flexibility. Rather than follow rigid schedules, itineraries hinge on what presents itself along the way. Time is spent in the areas that are most compelling. You may visit a tribal house in Haines, a community with a strong Tlingit native heritage; cruise the glassy waterways of Misty Fjords National Monument looking for mountain goats, black-tailed deer, and black bears; or drift through the iceberg-choked waters of Le Conte and Glacier bays, Tracy Arm, and Frederick Sound, prime feeding grounds of humpback whales, dolphins, sea lions, and sea otters. If there is an unusual amount of wildlife to see in a specific area or if guests are more interested in one area than another, the captain and expedition leader keep the ship there longer.

The price is on the high side for this cruise, because of all the special service and expert guidance and because each ship can accommodate only 70 passengers. The fare also includes overnight accommodations in Seattle at the beginning of the trip. *Special Expeditions, 720 Fifth Ave., New York, NY 10019, tel. 212/765–7740 or 800/762–0003, fax 212/265–3770. May–Aug.: 10 days, $3,130–$4,360. Sign up 6 months in advance.*

SOUTHEAST **Inside Passage Cruise.** Holland America is the choice to make if you are looking for a traditional ocean voyage through the Inside Passage with a good dose of natural history; this seven-day cruise aboard the elegant, newly commissioned MS *Statendam* is accompanied by a naturalist who is well qualified to teach passengers about the flora and fauna seen en route. He or she gives several slide presentations during the cruise and is available during the day to answer your questions. Stops along the way include Ketchikan, Juneau, and Sitka. The high point of the trip for most people is remote Glacier Bay National Park, where you will have a good chance of observing puffins, bald eagles, humpback whales, and brown bears. During the rest of the trip, you'll watch for marine mammals along the distant shoreline with binoculars (don't leave home without them).

The ship's strong suit is luxury. Staterooms are plush, the international staff courteous and extremely attentive, and the cuisine decidedly gourmet, with more selections than anyone could possibly try—it sometimes seems that there's something being served around the clock. All kinds of facilities and activities draw passengers away from nature observation: a casino, a spa, sports courts, swimming pools, and whirlpools; and, after dark, dances, shows, and karaoke. Plus there's a challenging fitness program, with awards for participation at the end of the trip, and a children's program. *Holland America Line Westours Inc., 300 Elliott Ave. W, Seattle, WA 98819, tel. 206/281-3535, fax 206/281-7110. Mid-May–Sept.: 7 days, $1,295–$3,945. Sign up 6–12 months in advance.*

SOUTHEAST **Sailing the Panhandle.** Once a year, Oceanic Society Expeditions charters the 68-foot *Island Roamer* for an 11-day sailing expedition out of Prince Rupert, British Columbia, through Alaska's Inside Passage. The region is famous for its glaciers, fjords, mountain ranges, forested islands, and abundant wildlife. This expedition, which sails with a dozen passengers, is devoted to exploration, from poking around in native villages (some of them abandoned) to looking for brown bears, bald eagles, waterfowl, mountain goats, and porpoises. Oceanic naturalist Michael Moran is along to share his enthusiasm and expertise.

After an orientation meeting in Prince Rupert, you are transported by floatplane to the ship's dock in Petersburg, where the journey begins. From that point the itinerary is flexible—you make schedule decisions with the naturalist, according to where the most interesting wildlife is. You spend several days in Frederick Sound, the summer home of up to 100 humpback whales, and stop to view the glaciers in Le Conte Bay and the totem poles at Ketchikan's Totem Heritage Center. You also visit Misty Fjords National Monument, Wrangell Narrows, Prince of Wales Island, and, possibly, the U.S. Forest Service bear observatory in Anan Bay, to see brown and black bears fishing for salmon. To hike on the various islands en route and explore the intertidal zone, you make frequent shore excursions in kayaks and inflatable rafts.

Back on board, you can get involved in sailing the yacht and learn navigation, knot tying, and seamanship from the crew, most of them old salts with 20 years of sailing experience. Facilities include eight double cabins, three heads with hot showers, a library, and a well-equipped galley, where a cook prepares meals using local produce and seafood. Wine is served with dinner, otherwise it's BYOB. Most guests are between 20 and 60 years old, active, highly educated, and well traveled; there are more women than men. Because presentations and excursions are designed for adult learning capacities and attention spans and the quarters are tight, the trip is not particularly suited to families—discuss your plans with the Oceanic Society office before proposing this trip to your kids. *Oceanic Society Expeditions, Ft. Mason Center, Bldg. E, 2nd Floor, San Francisco, CA 94123, tel. 415/441-1106 or 800/326-7491, fax 415/474-3395. Late July: 12 days, $2,895. Sign up 6 months in advance.*

SOUTHEAST **World Explorer Cruises.** During the academic year, the 550-passenger SS *Universe* cruises the globe as college at sea, sponsored by the Institute for Shipboard Education in cooperation with the University of Pittsburgh. Since 1978, this midsize ship has spent her summers in Alaskan waters, carrying vacationers on educational cruises along the state's south-central and southeastern coasts. So comprehensive is the program on this 14-day cruise that you can earn college credit in history, geology, and anthropology for taking it. A faculty of professors and other Ph.D.'s from universities all over North America leads seminars covering the region's culture, arts, history, botany, geology, and anthropology. In addition, the *Universe* stops in more ports of call than any other Alaska cruise—nine, including Wrangell, Skagway, Juneau, Seward, Valdez, Sitka, Ketchikan, and Victoria, as well as Vancouver, the ship's home port. There are over 40 optional shore excursions to these cities and villages. In Wrangell and Seward, park rangers lead botanical walks; you gather specimens and learn to identify area flora.

No Alaska cruise would be complete without glaciers. On this trip, you can see the water turn from deep ocean blue to milky brown caused by the presence of glacial silt, as you approach Hubbard Glacier, near Valdez, and inch close enough to Glacier Bay's Margerie Glacier to hear the deep boom and see the splash when huge chunks of icebergs shear off into the sea. You learn the difference between tidewater, alpine, galloping, and valley glaciers in the shadow of these white giants.

Despite the educational content of this trip, there are also many opportunities for play: You can tour the wheelhouse, sign up for art workshops (and put your youngsters in the special Junior Cruisers program), play bingo and bridge, watch first-run movies, work out in aerobics classes, and, after dark, enjoy groups performing everything from South American folk music to opera. Facilities include a theater, five lounges, two bars, a fitness center, a launderette, and a 12,000-volume library, larger than that in any other ship at sea, with a librarian to help you find what you want. Meals include well-prepared American, Continental, and Asian offerings, and are served at two assigned seatings. The cabins are simply furnished but comfortable. Considering the length of time you spend at sea on this cruise and the caliber of the instruction, entertainment, and service, the price is exceptionally reasonable. *World Explorer Cruises, 555 Montgomery St., San Francisco, CA 94111-2544, tel. 415/393–1565 or 800/854–3835, fax 415/391–1145. Late May–Aug.: 14 days, $2,395–$4,095. Sign up 2 months in advance.*

VIRGIN ISLANDS

REGION-WIDE **Caribbean Nature Cruise.** This eight-day cruise through the U.S. and British Virgin Islands and eastern Puerto Rico immerses you in the Caribbean's wildlife. From Fajardo, Puerto Rico, the 100-passenger *Nantucket Clipper* cruises in and out of secluded bays beyond the main shipping lanes to cover Culebra, Tortola, Norman Island, Virgin Gorda, Jost van Dyke, St. John, and St. Thomas. The captain drops anchor frequently in shallow coves and near protected reefs to let you swim, snorkel, and view the abundant marine life. You can also take Zodiacs to shore to hike and explore

the tropical flora and fauna. Trained naturalists are along to provide information about the wildlife of the region. They even teach you to snorkel, so that you can view the colonies of corals and sponges, stingrays, moray eels, silver barracuda, and other fish that tend to dominate the talk at drinks and dinner.

The ship ties up at several marinas along the way, so you can also enjoy the islands' powdery, white sand beaches, their lively bars, and their small boutiques. Optional excursions include a shopping trip in St. Thomas and an island tour of St. John that takes in its scenic vistas and historical sites. *Clipper Cruise Line, 7711 Bonhomme Ave., St. Louis, MO 63105, tel. 314/727–2929 or 800/325–0010. Mid-Dec.–Feb.: 8 days, $1,770–$2,670. Sign up 6 months in advance.*

REGION-WIDE **Tall Ship Nature Expedition.** If you want to leave motorized craft behind and see the U.S. Virgin Islands under sail, turn to Dirago Cruises. In conjunction with World Nature Cruises, this line offers an annual seven-day nature expedition aboard the schooner *Harvey Gamage,* led by Dr. Donald Messersmith. A naturalist and expert ornithologist, he acts as a guide for birding excursions to Mangrove Lagoon and Magens Bay on St. Thomas, where you can see the colorful plumage of the Antillean crested hummingbird, loggerhead kingbird, brown-throated parakeet, mangrove cuckoo, green-throated carib, banana quit, and other species.

Also on the program is snorkeling along the underwater trail at Trunk Bay, St. John, and around the reef of Buck Island, off St. Croix. Brain and antler corals, sea fans, sea urchins, and sea stars are just a few of the creatures that populate the protected reef waters. On the islands you'll tour mountains covered in lantana, frangipani, and other flowering tropical plants such as mountain guava and cocoplum. Every evening, Dr. Messersmith lectures on the flora and fauna you saw during the day.

The itinerary is generally flexible, although you begin and end in St. Thomas and stop in

St. John and St. Croix at some point during the week. All nature excursions, snorkeling, shopping trips, and sailing lessons are included in the package price; an optional scuba trip costs $50. Although this is not a luxury cruise—facilities include 14 compact cabins with upper and lower berths and a washbasin, shared heads with cold water showers, a small library, and a salon where meals are served family style—the simplicity of the quarters means that costs are low. There is no bar; you must bring not only your own wine and hard liquor but even your own soda. However, lemonade, snacks, and fruit are available around the clock. *Dirigo Cruises, 39 Waterside La., Clinton, CT 06413, tel. 203/669–7068 or 800/845–5520, fax 203/669–3737. Mid-Mar.: 7 days, $695. Sign up 4 months in advance.*

SOURCES

ORGANIZATIONS The **Cruise Line International Association** (500 5th Ave., Suite 1407, New York, NY 10110, tel. 212/921–0066) can answer most questions on cruising and provide general information on cruise lines and comparison charts of itineraries, but it doesn't handle bookings. The **Department of Health and Human Services** (1015 N. American Way, Room 107, Miami, FL 33132, tel. 800/772–1213) can supply a free sanitation inspection report on any cruise ship sailing in American waters.

PERIODICALS *Cruise Travel Magazine* (Box 342, Mt. Morris, IL 61054, tel. 815/734–4151 or 800/877–5893), published every two months, has photos and features on cruise ships and ports of call. "Ocean & Cruise News" (World & Ocean Cruise Liners Society, Box 92, Stamford, CT 06901, tel. 203/329–2787) profiles a different ship each month. The quarterly *Specialty Travel Index* (Alpine Hansen Publishers, 305 San Anselmo Ave., San Anselmo, CA 94960, tel. 415/459–4900) lists tour operators and outfitters that offer special interest, learning, and adventure vacations around the globe.

BOOKS *Fodor's Cruises and Ports of Call* gives general advice on cruising and specific descriptions of lines, ships, itineraries, and ports of call; the Alaska chapter describes several environmental cruise options. *Traveling on Your Own,* by Eleanor Berman, gives advice to singles on choosing the right cruise and what to expect in the way of singles activities and pricing.

ALSO SEE If you enjoy relaxing breezes off the water and close encounters of the wildlife kind, turn to the Whale-Watching Cruises chapter.

Foreign-Language Immersion Programs

By Mary King Nash

 onjour, hola, konnichiwa, guten Tag, god dag, ciao, zdravstvuyte, ni hao ma, bom dia. Hello, in other words. Although this greeting is a good way to start a conversation in any country, it doesn't exactly constitute a dialogue. Reaching back to high school French, Spanish, or Italian, you may come up with *c'est un livre, qué hora es?* or *mia gatta è bianca,* but comments on books, the time, or your white cat won't get you very far.

If you want to have a real conversation with people from another country, you have to learn their language. Many travelers find that doing so makes a vacation or business trip much more enjoyable: It gives them the opportunity to make friends and do business with the locals, order food not on the tourist menu, and venture off the beaten path. At the same time, even people who don't plan to step foot outside the United States anytime soon can benefit from language courses. Teachers might learn to communicate with Spanish-speaking parents; food lovers might learn to order from a fancy French menu.

There are various ways to get a better handle on a language that's foreign to you: You can take a refresher course through a high school or college continuing education department, meeting at least once a week for an entire semester with as many as 20 students; or choose one at a language school, such as Berlitz, Alliance Française, and the Goethe Institute, where classes are smaller and you meet once or twice weekly for six or more weeks. You could also hire a private tutor for 10 hours a day at $30 an hour through one of the InLingua schools or the International Center for Language Studies in Washington, D.C., or Houston. Or you could really immerse yourself by signing up for, what else?, a language immersion program, either in the United States or abroad.

Because this book is about interesting ways to spend your vacation within the United States, we cover language immersion programs in this country only. These provide a sort of college-cum-summer-camp experience and are fun and relatively inexpensive. During the one to four weeks that you are enrolled in such a program, you spend every waking moment practicing the language—even when you're playing Ping-Pong or volleyball—because speaking English is generally forbidden.

The programs are often based on college campuses, where you sleep and eat along with your instructors and classmates. Every day, you attend at least four hours of classroom sessions—in the morning and sometimes in the afternoon. You're grouped according to fluency level in small classes (usually fewer than eight students) that allow for a lot of personal attention, and your entertainment also revolves around the language. There are foreign films, lectures, evenings of folk dancing and singing, and games of foreign-language Scrabble.

Mary King Nash, a freelance writer and editor who lives in New York City, has a fascination with foreign cultures.

Depending on your fluency level when you start, you can walk away from an immersion program with various skills. Beginners usually master basic travel survival tactics; they should be able to ask questions, order from menus, tell a little about themselves, and, in general, explore on their own in a country where the language is spoken. Intermediate students often enter the realm of writing and reading, in addition to speaking. Advanced students work on writing skills and are given the opportunity to discuss current foreign affairs with other fluent speakers; they also read great literature in the original language. Everyone in an immersion program should at least find a few new language-loving friends.

Most programs also try to meet your specific language needs. They may offer a drill of medical terms if you're planning to study medicine abroad, or business phrases if you're an entrepreneur who wants to make foreign investments. Just tell the program director what your needs are before classes begin. Remember, however, that you can't expect a roomful of potential travelers to spend hours reviewing medical terms or negotiating business contracts.

Immersion programs use many learning tools, including cassette tapes and instructional videos. Foreign-language newspapers, books, magazines, and films all contribute to bringing a foreign culture to life. Some programs have satellite hookups that transmit television programs from other countries and computer networks that link you to students overseas. Instructional foreign-language software programs are starting to appear at some schools, but right now these are designed only for advanced students. Be sure to pack a foreign-language dictionary and thesaurus as well as a portable cassette player and several blank tapes. You can use these to record class sessions. Using a cassette player, you can also listen to yourself speak, which is a good way to work on improving your accent.

Although the first few days of a language program can be strenuous, especially for beginners, you're likely to gain enthusiasm thanks to patient and encouraging teachers, the camaraderie of your classmates, and the fact that you will, eventually, learn. Language immersion programs work: If you hear and speak foreign words for hours on end, in a variety of settings and with everyone you meet, it won't be long before you're discussing books, forgetting about the time, and using your white cat as a true conversation piece.

CHOOSING THE RIGHT PROGRAM

Here are some questions to help you determine if a foreign-language program will suit your needs.

What languages are taught? Some programs teach only a few languages, while others teach up to 20. Make sure the language you want to learn is part of the curriculum.

How long has the program been running? Like any business, programs with a few years behind them are more likely to run smoothly and efficiently than new programs.

Is English spoken in the program? The general rule with immersion programs is that students are asked to leave their English at the door and speak only in a foreign tongue for the remainder of the program. If this makes you uncomfortable, try to find a program in which some English is used.

How many fluency levels are there? Most programs have beginning, intermediate, and advanced courses, but those with lots of students may divide these levels further, separating beginning intermediates from more advanced intermediates, for example. This makes it easier for you to find an appropriate class with students of comparable ability.

How are students placed? Can students switch classes if their original placement doesn't work out? Novices and fluent conversationalists are easier to place than those who fall somewhere in between. Language immersion programs usually have someone on staff to help you select the right class, and they often use written and oral tests to place students. If you still end up in a class that is either too easy or too difficult, you should be able to switch to a more appropriate class; make sure the program allows this.

What are the teacher's qualifications? Is he or she native-fluent in the language? Teaching a language is very different from merely speaking it. Find out if the instructor is trained to teach and how many years of teaching experience he or she has. In addition, make sure the instructor is native-fluent, that is, has a command over the language equivalent to that of a native speaker (someone who was raised with the language).

This gets tricky when you're learning a language that's spoken in many parts of the world. For example, the Castilian Spanish of Barcelona is quite different from Mexican Spanish, so if you're going to Mexico you want a teacher who is aware of those differences.

If you take a course to prepare for a trip, make sure the teacher can discuss the country's history, customs, cultural nuances, and current events. Find out how much time he or she has lived and traveled in that country; someone who has spent a few years in a place will have more insights than someone who has only traveled there, no matter how many times.

How many teachers and teaching assistants (if any) are there, and how many students? What is the student-to-teacher ratio? A program with five or six hours of daily language instruction per class may have three or four teachers and teaching assistants who rotate from class to class throughout the day. It is often easier to keep plugging away at a language if a new face—a teacher with a fresh supply of enthusiasm—periodically pops up. It also helps if classes are kept small, with no more than 10 students. The student-to-teacher ratio should be no higher than five to one.

How many hours are devoted to formal instruction and how long are the breaks? If you haven't attended school lately, you may not realize how *long* a classroom hour can seem, and some programs schedule six hours of formal instruction a day. It is up to you to decide how much you can take. Learning a language shouldn't be a punishment, so don't sign up for the most intensive class unless you're sure you can sit still. Beginners are strongly discouraged, often barred, from participating in these classes, because it is simply no fun for them to spend hours upon hours going over grammar and vocabulary drills.

Can the classes be altered to address my special needs? So you want to go to Germany to sell automobiles, and you need to learn some German car-talk. Make sure the teacher will spend some time going over the special terminology you need to learn.

Is there a language lab, and what hours is it available to students? Every worthwhile language immersion program should have a language lab where you have access to foreign-language books, newspapers, magazines, and instructional videos and cassette tapes. Some programs also provide satellite broadcasts of foreign telecasts and instructional foreign-language software.

What's the cost and what's included? Language programs range in cost from $495 to more than $6,000, although most are under $2,000, including meals and lodging. Unless otherwise noted, prices here are per person and cover instruction, double-occupancy lodging, three meals a day, a textbook, and cultural programs, such as foreign films and lectures. When a program charges different prices for single and double rooms, the two prices are given.

What are the accommodations like? Most programs are held on university campuses, and you sleep in a sparsely furnished dormitory room with a shared bath. You are usually assigned a roommate, but you can often get a single if you are willing to pay more for it. Some programs provide linens and towels; others don't, so be sure to ask. A few programs make use of pleasant hotels, and a few expect you to make your own arrangements.

Will laundry service be available? Most campuses have laundry facilities. This could save you a suitcase—if you have time to do the wash.

What is the food like? Again, because these programs are on college campuses, the food is mostly standard college fare: sandwiches, fresh fruit, a salad bar, and a choice of unexciting entrées at dinner. Be sure to ask if there are restaurants in the area and if you can opt out of the meal plan.

How much free time is there? Don't be surprised if the answer is none. Language immersion programs take it for granted that you want to practice the language every minute, in a variety of settings, both formal and informal.

What additional planned activities are there? You may not have free time, but you should certainly have fun time. Most programs schedule sing-alongs, acting skits, and walks off campus to help you develop an informal vocabulary. Lectures, music performances, and foreign films usually dominate the evenings.

What recreational facilities are available? A college campus usually has tennis courts, a gym with a swimming pool, a weight room, a running track, and basketball courts. Finding time to use them is another matter.

Do you have references from past students? To clarify your perception of instruction, lodging, and food, there's no substitute for a talk with someone who has done the drills, slept in the beds, and tasted the meals.

How far in advance do I need to register? Most programs expect you to sign up one to three months in advance, but often a program's less popular classes have openings until the last minute, and there's always a chance of a last-minute cancellation for even the most sought-after class.

FAVORITE PROGRAMS

THE NORTHEAST

NEW HAMPSHIRE **Accelerated Language Programs.** Expect the unexpected when you tackle the highly intensive Accelerated Language Programs (ALPs) at Dartmouth College. These bear the stamp of their creator, Dartmouth French professor Dr. John A. Rassias: They are active, enthusiastic, and determined to teach. You may find yourself shouting, crying, laughing, frowning, smiling, whispering, jumping, crouching, or using whatever theatrical gesture it takes to communicate foreign words and concepts without using English.

Under the direction of Dr. Rassias, this immersion program follows the Rassias method, a language-learning approach he developed based on his work teaching languages at Dartmouth and his experiences with the Peace Corps in the 1960s. Held each summer since 1982, the fast-paced classes cover beginning, intermediate, and advanced French, Spanish, German, and Italian, as well as beginning Japanese, Chinese, Russian, and modern Greek. The goal here is to learn a language in just 10 days.

The Rassias Method—at times referred to as the Rassias Madness—is described as "an all-out assault on the emotions and the senses, as well as the intellect" in "The Rassias Connection," a newsletter that provides the latest news on Rassias-related developments.

Your days begin with a 7:15 breakfast and continue well into the night, following a regimented schedule that allows only three 20-minute breaks. You experience the core of the program—the Master-class and breakout-group combination—twice a day. During these sessions, the Master instructor (one per fluency level) teaches a lesson to the group as a whole (maximum 15 students) for 50 minutes. Then, groups of four or five students gather with a teaching assistant (three or four assistants rotate among the groups each day) for 50 minutes of fast-paced oral drills, during which students are called on every minute. These exercises reinforce material from the Master instructor's lesson. Repetition, positive rewards, rhythmic pacing, and role-playing help keep students actively involved in language learning without *thinking* too much about the process.

You may find the first days to be strenuous and stressful, but the energy of the one-on-one interaction is contagious and gets the adrenaline flowing. Eventually your mind clicks on the language and your tongue follows; you begin responding automatically, knowing a correct word, phrase, or idiom without knowing exactly how you picked it up. A textbook provided by the program reiterates the lessons. Songs, skits, and poems also teach you the language, as do cultural activities, such as a Japanese tea ceremony and a French cooking class.

Although ALPs accept day students, you're encouraged to reside on campus, where the accommodations are spartan. You get a private dorm room equipped with a single bed, a desk and chair, a lamp, and a phone. Linens are provided, and there are laundry facilities in each dorm. Meals become extensions of the classroom, as teachers, teaching assistants, and students dine together in the campus cafeteria. Students from different fluency groups mingle at tables determined by language. Three meals a day are included (with lunch only for day students). Salads, sandwiches, or a choice of entrées are standard fare, but a few dishes with a foreign flavor are available at some meals.

In the evening, both instructional and educational films are shown in all the dorm common rooms. At the end of the program, you are expected to perform in a skit made up by your drill group. Your schedule here is packed, so you don't have much time to take advantage of the language resource center with its cassette tapes, language videos, and foreign books, magazines, and newspapers. You may also find it hard to schedule a visit to the campus tennis courts, the golf course, or the gym with its running track,

swimming pool, and basketball courts, but you should try—physical fitness can help greatly as you scale the ALPs. *Language Outreach, ALPS, Dartmouth College, 6071 Wentworth Hall, Hanover, NH 03755-3526, tel. 603/646–2922 or 603/646–3155, fax 603/646–3838. June and July: 10 days, $1,800. Price includes single room; sign up 1–3 months in advance.*

NEW YORK **Language Immersion Institute.** For a no-frills language-learning bargain, sign up for a summer workshop at the Language Immersion Institute of the State University of New York, College at New Paltz. These are some of the cheapest classes available, and you still get 50 hours of instruction—five hours a day, Monday to Friday for two weeks—the equivalent of a one-semester three-credit undergraduate course.

You can choose from classes in 20 languages—American Sign Language, Arabic, Chinese, Czech, Dutch, ESL (English as a Second Language), French, German, Greek, Hebrew, Hungarian, Italian, Japanese, Polish, Portuguese, Russian, Spanish, Swedish, Ukrainian, and Yiddish. Courses have a minimum of 6 students, a maximum of 15, and one instructor per class.

The native-fluent teachers create a supportive and nonthreatening class atmosphere that is conducive to learning. They are trained language professionals who teach at various schools and universities in the tri-state metropolitan area. Conversational skills are stressed at all levels, but beginners learn basic survival skills for travel, intermediate students tackle reading and writing, and advanced speakers practice complicated conversations and work on written compositions. You buy your own textbook, usually priced under $60. Cassette tapes complementing the text can be checked out of the language laboratory or purchased.

The program begins with an orientation meeting on Sunday evening. You attend weekday classes from 8 until 1, when you break for lunch. Students generally eat lunch with their instructor. After lunch, you are free to explore New Paltz and surrounding areas, do homework, or work in the language lab. Since meals are on your own, you may pick a restaurant off campus, but if you don't mind cafeteria-style food, the campus snack bar serves hot and cold dishes, including vegetarian fare. Weekly meal plans at the college dining hall can be purchased through the institute. At the end of the day, entertaining foreign films with English subtitles are shown in campus dorms.

Students sleep in dormitory double or single rooms, where linens are supplied but blankets, pillows, and fans (bring one; it's hot) are not. Bathrooms are shared. You receive a temporary I.D. card that lets you use college facilities: the library, tennis courts, a running track, and a gym with a swimming pool, racquetball courts, and exercise equipment. In your free time, you can take a tour of New Paltz, settled by French Huguenots in the 17th century; the Huguenot Historical Society (tel. 914/255–1660) has summer tours in the area.

Dr. Henry Urbanski, director of the institute, developed this program in 1981 and has honed the teaching methods to ensure rapid language acquisition. Fluent in seven languages, he is also professor of Russian Studies at SUNY New Paltz, and he organizes a one-week session at the historic Mohonk Mountain House (*see below*). *Language Immersion Institute, Faculty Tower 916, SUNY, College at New Paltz, New Paltz, NY 12561, tel. 914/257–3500 or 914/257–3501, fax 914/257–3569. June–Aug.: 13 days, $625. Price does not include lodging ($325 single, $275 double), meals, or textbook; sign up 1 month in advance.*

NEW YORK **Tower of Babble.** If you seek a language program in a first-class setting, look no farther than the one held at Mohonk Mountain House, a towering, turreted 277-room hotel in New Paltz. Each January, Mohonk invites the Language Immersion Institute from the SUNY, College at New Paltz (*see above*) to host a week of classes in 11 languages: American Sign Language,

Arabic, Chinese, French, German, Hebrew, Italian, Japanese, Russian, Spanish, and Yiddish.

You can choose from classes at four levels of proficiency (Elementary I, Elementary II, Intermediate, and Advanced), but there must be at least six students signed up or the class is canceled; sometimes, however, to meet the minimum of six students, classes of different levels are combined when two small groups of students are fairly close in terms of proficiency. The maximum class size is 12, with one instructor per class and no teaching assistants; instructors are native-fluent speakers and trained language professionals who teach at colleges and universities.

You arrive at the hotel at 4 PM on a Sunday, when you meet your instructor and classmates. Classes are conducted throughout each day, beginning with breakfast and ending after dinner with evening entertainment; a few hours every afternoon are left open for you to rest and recharge.

You might take an afternoon walk with your instructor among the grounds, learning the language in a beautiful setting. Evening entertainment includes foreign-language films with English subtitles. After hours and hours of listening to and speaking a foreign tongue, you begin to "live" that language— and sing it, act in it, and play games using it. Some students perform in a five-minute skit during the Bon Voyage luncheon on Friday afternoon.

Your home for the week is a stone-and-wood Victorian extravaganza, built between 1869 and 1910 and now listed on the National Trust for Historic Preservation's honor roll of Historic Hotels of America. Victorian and Adirondack-style period furnishings fill the hotel's nooks and crannies. You pay separately for your room and board at the resort. There are both single and double rooms within a range of prices that corresponds to escalating levels of luxury; the most elegant guest rooms contain working fireplaces, balconies with lake or mountain views, and claw-foot bathtubs.

All meals, included in the cost of your room, are taken in one of the resort's dining rooms: buffet-style breakfast and lunch, afternoon tea at 4, and dinner with a choice of several well-prepared entrées and decadent desserts. The food here is much closer to gourmet cuisine than what you find at language programs held on college campuses. Since you share a dinner table with your classmates and instructor all week, you continue to learn throughout the evening.

The hotel has views of Lake Mohonk (a glacial lake), the Hudson River Valley, and the Catskill and Shawangunk mountains. The sprawling grounds take in 2,200 acres of lawns, 85 miles of winding trails, formal and informal gardens, and 127 gazebos. In your free time, from 2 to 4 daily, you can take advantage of the hotel's sports facilities; there's tennis, golf, swimming, ice skating, cross-country skiing on 35 miles of groomed trails, and horse-drawn carriage rides. *Mohonk Mountain House, Lake Mohonk, New Paltz, NY 12561, tel. 914/255–1000 or 800/772–6646, fax 914/256–2161 (register at: Language Immersion Institute, Faculty Tower 916, SUNY, College at New Paltz, New Paltz, NY 12561, tel. 914/257–3500 or 914/257–3501, fax 914/257–3569). Jan.: 6 days, $450. Price does not include meals and lodging ($165–$277 single, $259–$359 double per night) and only includes use of textbook during program; sign up as much in advance as possible.*

RHODE ISLAND Deutsche Sommerschule am Atlantik. If German is the language you want to study, you might choose the German Summer School of the Atlantic at the University of Rhode Island (URI), which offers a three- or six-week summer immersion program in conjunction with the Goethe Institute, a German cultural organization. This language program has enough social and recreational activities to make it resemble a summer camp, but its classes are rigorous and you must speak German at all times.

An encouraging camaraderie quickly develops among the program's 60 students, the native-fluent professors, and the teaching assistants and tutors, who share meals and meet for social events. Professors and assistants are from URI and from the Goethe Institute; some tutors are students from German universities.

Students are separated according to fluency level (beginning, intermediate, advanced intermediate, and advanced) for intensive classes held from 8 to noon Monday through Wednesday and Friday and Saturday. All classes stress speaking and listening skills. Novices concentrate on basic vocabulary, intermediates practice speaking and writing, and advanced students discuss German news and current events after reading German newspapers and watching satellite broadcasts of German television programs. If you're at the intermediate or advanced level, you can sign up for supplementary classes held in the afternoon three times a week at no extra charge. These include a business class, which covers vocabulary and terminology needed to conduct business in Germany; a theater workshop; and a language-learning technique class.

All students have access to the language lab, where a computer network links URI to the Universität Bochum in Germany 24 hours a day. Students in Germany who are learning how to teach German and English serve as long-distance tutors. You can transmit your essays, letters, or even simple sentences, which the German tutors correct and return. This service has paired many pen pals, who continue communicating after the summer program ends.

Campus housing and a meal plan are mandatory and are included in the cost of the program. You stay in a sorority house in shared double rooms with shared baths or in single rooms at an extra cost. Rooms are equipped with basic dorm furniture—beds, desks, lamps, dressers. You eat in the house dining room, where breakfast and lunch are served buffet style and dinner is family style. Fresh fruits and vegetables are always available, and you can try a few German entrées offered at some meals. The meal plan does not include Saturday dinner or Sunday meals. For those meals many students go to the coast for fresh seafood, though there are restaurants closer to campus.

Afternoon recreational activities—picnics, volleyball, and soccer games—help alleviate the morning brain drain of classes. The campus is only 5 miles from the Atlantic Ocean, and beach trips are popular on Thursdays. German feature films and lectures about German cultural and political events fill evening hours, as do sing-alongs and German Scrabble games. *German Summer School of the Atlantic, University of Rhode Island, Department of Languages, Kingston, RI 02881-0820, tel. 401/792–5911, fax 401/791–4964. June–July: 20 days, $1,150 single, $950 double. Price does not include some meals or textbook; sign up at least 2 weeks in advance.*

VERMONT **The Russian School at Norwich University.** There isn't a single Tom, Dick, or Harry at the Russian School; instead, you'll find Ivan, Gregor, Olga, and Katrina. From the moment you exchange your name for a Russian one and pledge to speak only Russian, you know you're part of something exceptional. An extension of Norwich University, the Russian School has two- and three-week crash courses at the beginning and advanced levels, in addition to eight-week undergraduate and graduate classes scheduled each summer. The Russian School has a master's program during the regular academic year.

Classes here are small, with four to six students, allowing for a lot of one-on-one coaching from the instructors. You're in class six hours a day, every day, with no weekend breaks, so three or four instructors rotate daily among classes to keep the teaching varied. Because conversational skills are emphasized, by the end of the program even a beginner should be able to communicate comfortably with a native speaker.

Each day is divided into lessons that cover the following: A grammar session introduces vocabulary words and phrases that are repeated throughout the day; exercises in role-playing help develop conversational skills; and another session teaches you how to phrase questions. In reading sessions, you learn word formations and sentence structure as well as words you might encounter while traveling; and by watching videos of Russian advertisements, cartoons, and television programs, you strengthen your listening and comprehension skills. During the free conversation session, students talk with one another under the observation of an instructor who keeps the dialogue ball rolling when necessary.

The school's language lab contains instructional videos and cassette tapes and has a satellite hookup that brings in Russian television news programs, and the university library has an extensive collection of Slavic newspapers, journals, books, and magazines. A Russian ensemble, made up of several members of the Russian School's staff, teaches folk singing and dancing, and the Russian School choir gives performances of Russian Orthodox choir singing.

Language students stay in two handsome brick dormitories with both single and double rooms. Each room is sparsely furnished with twin beds (linens are not provided), wardrobes, desks, and desk chairs, and you share hall bathrooms. You dine with fellow students and instructors in the campus dining room. The menu sometimes includes entrées with foreign accents —such as Mexican beef or bean burritos, Chinese vegetable lo mein and sweet and sour pork or chicken, British fish and chips, and of course, Russian beef Stroganov and chicken Kiev. A fresh-fruit and salad bar is standard.

From 7 PM to midnight, students gather at the on-campus Russian Café for coffee and Russian cookies, even more Russian conversation, and, while it's still light, a picture-window view of the Green Mountains. The university's rural Vermont setting (15 miles from Montpelier and 50 miles from Burlington) makes hiking a favorite activity, and all wanna-be Russians learn to ask directions to the lake in nearby Brookfield, where they can go swimming. The campus has tennis courts, a gym with an indoor swimming pool, a racquetball court, a basketball court, and a weight room. *The Russian School, Norwich University, Northfield, VT 05663, tel. 802/485–2000 or 800/468–6679, ext. 2165, fax 802/485–2580. June–July.: 10 days, $495; 20 days, $750. Price does not include textbook; sign up 3 months in advance.*

THE WEST COAST

CALIFORNIA **Custom Language Services.** Just one of the programs offered by the renowned Monterey Institute of International Studies, the Custom Language Services (CLS) allows you to tailor a class to your needs and schedule. Private tutorial sessions work best, but up to four people at the same level can sign up together, reducing the cost substantially.

The basic CLS program is six hours of instruction each weekday for six weeks; it can be compressed to four weeks by adding three class hours each Saturday, or you can lengthen or shorten the hours and days to fit your timetable. A class of two weeks or less is recommended only as a refresher for those who already know the language or as a way to learn basic travel survival skills.

The Monterey Institute, a world leader in the field of foreign-language studies, attracts students from around the globe to its undergraduate and graduate programs as well as its eight- and nine-week summer language courses. Although the institute was established in 1955, the CLS program started in 1972 as a way to prepare corporate personnel and their families for relocation to foreign countries; it is currently used by people with both business and personal reasons for learning a foreign language.

Given at least three weeks' notice, CLS's program director and instructors plan a class based on how you intend to use the language. They use a questionnaire and phone interview prior to your arrival to help determine the current level of your language proficiency. Your input regarding goals and interests helps chart the course. In summer 1994, classes were offered in Arabic, Armenian, Chinese, ESL (English as a Second Language), Japanese, French, German, Italian, Korean, and Spanish. Depending on student interest and faculty availability, a class in practically any language is possible.

The course coordinator chooses instructors for each program, depending on goals and circumstances. Taken into consideration are the home country of the instructors, student's current level of ability, and specialty areas for specific jargon and terminology. If the program is set for six hours of class daily, the common arrangement is a team of three instructors, each for two hours daily. The coordinator ensures communication among the team members and divides areas of responsibility.

When you're not in class, you can use the wealth of multimedia language-learning resources at the CLS center; you can even get a key to use the facility after hours. Textbooks, audio cassettes, and video programs, such as the popular "French in Action, Russian "Let's Get Acquainted," and Spanish "Destinos" programs are in the CLS library. Satellite news broadcasts from 35 countries are of interest to intermediate and advanced students. Broadcasts can be viewed in the student center, and videotapes can be checked out from the Audiovisual Center. The Center for Language in Education and Work (CLEW) has a MacIntosh computer housed on the CLS floor, which can be utilized for drilling with language software. Programs are currently available in Chinese, Japanese, Russian, and Spanish.

Authentic materials are used in the language programs, as well. For instance, if you're planning a trip to a particular foreign region, you may practice with magazines, maps, menus, brochures, and train tables from that region. If you're a medical student planning to study in a foreign country, you are taught medical terms in the language you'll be using. CLS also tracks down foreign medical journals and articles that deal with the country's hospital system and medical customs.

The institute's campus, always abuzz with foreign and foreign-minded students, makes it easy for you to find a new pal who speaks the language you're studying. During the regular school year, language clubs invite CLS students to join their social and cultural activities such as picnics, yoga classes (taught in French), concerts, and visits to museums and the local aquarium. Off-campus trips are often part of your instruction. Russian-language students, for instance, enjoy playing chess with opponents at the Defense Language Institute, also in Monterey, which teaches languages to military personnel. Even a simple trip to the farmers' market becomes educational when your instructor teaches you the names of fruits and vegetables.

Accommodations are not available through CLS, but among the places to stay are nearby hotels that offer rooms to CLS students at a good weekly rate. You're also on your own for meals. The institute snack bar is open for breakfast and lunch, and the campus is only three blocks from Fisherman's Wharf and downtown, where there are many good restaurants. *Custom Language Service, Monterey Institute of International Studies, 425 Van Buren St., Monterey, CA 93940, tel. 408/647–4115 or 800/995–8403, fax 408/647–3534. Year-round: 20 days, $6,600; 10 days, $3,300. Price does not include meals and lodging; sign up at least 3 weeks in advance.*

CALIFORNIA **Residential Foreign Language Institutes.** There aren't too many places where you can soak in a rock-lined hot sulfur spring pool while practicing verb conjugation, but Napa Valley is one of them. If you have at least 10 college credits of French, Spanish, or Italian, you can sign up for a language immersion program at the 330-acre White Sulphur Springs Resort and Spa, about an hour's drive from San Francisco. Sponsored by the University of California Berkeley Extension, these so-called Residential Foreign Language Institutes—La Maison Française, La Casa Española, and La Casa Italiana—each take over the resort for one week every August.

English is verboten during all programs, which start with a get-acquainted meeting over aperitifs at 4 PM Sunday afternoon and end after breakfast on Saturday. You are separated into groups of 10 to 12 students based on your level of fluency, and two or three professors from well-respected colleges and universities—including the University of California Berkeley, San Francisco Conservatory of Music, Inter-American University in Puerto Rico, and New York University in Spain—rotate among these groups. Classes concentrate on vocabulary and comprehension, and since beginners are not admitted to the programs, instructors can focus on improving your conversational skills by working on the nuances of intonation, idiom, and accent.

In general, your mornings are devoted to formal classwork, with grammar review, oral presentations, skits, and discussion, while your afternoons are set aside for cultural and literary lectures, guest lecturers, oral presentations by teachers, and other structured activities, such as singing and reading plays.

Textbooks are used as reference material for the Spanish and Italian programs but are generally eschewed in favor of handouts with stories, songs, and poems. You don't use many instructional videos or tapes, but you do see films in the language you're studying. Students are encouraged to bring their favorite books, musical cassettes, and periodicals to share with classmates. Guest speakers lecture on such subjects as early Italian comic theater and 17th-century French theater and painting. There are also evening music and dance performances: You might learn Italian folk songs from professional singers or hear a piano recital of 20th-century Spanish music or watch a flamenco dance demonstration. You can take tours conducted in French of nearby wineries, including Domaine Chandon, which specializes in sparkling wines.

White Sulphur Springs Resort was the first mineral spring resort in California, built in 1852. Your accommodations are either in the white wooden inn or the carriage house, each of which has 14 single rooms. Rooms at the inn have half-baths, with showers in a separate bathhouse; the carriage-house quarters share hall bathrooms. All students have private rooms with quilt-covered queen-size beds but without televisions or telephones. You're provided with linens and towels.

You eat in a dining room with your professors and fellow classmates. Your meals are prepared by a chef hired by the school to cook only foods from the country of interest, such as beef bourguignon, seafood paella, and veal piccata. Dinner wines are from France, Spain, or Italy.

Outside the classroom, you continue speaking in your new language during games of volleyball, badminton, horseshoes, and croquet, or while walking on trails that pass by redwood, fir, and madron trees. Those who spend too much time pouring over foreign-language books, magazines, and newspapers may find relief in a massage, mud bath, or herbal wrap, which the resort will schedule for an additional charge. And, of course, there is always the hot spring.

The 33 spots for French week tend to fill up quickly, with a long waiting list; students are slower to line up for Spanish week, with a maximum of 33 people, and Italian week usually attracts only 10 or 12 participants, so it is sometimes run at the same time as other language weeks, such as a second section of Spanish week designed for teachers of Spanish and bilingual teachers who teach in Spanish. *Residential Foreign Language Institutes, University of California Berkeley Extension, 2223 Fulton St., Berkeley, CA 94720, tel. 510/642–1062, fax 510/642–0374. Aug.: 7 days, $1,050. Price includes single room; sign up 3 months in advance.*

SOURCES

ORGANIZATIONS It is not easy to find information on foreign-language programs in the United States that teach more than ESL classes for foreign students; the **Center for Applied Linguistics** (1118 22nd St. NW, Washington, D.C. 20037, tel. 202/429–9292) and the **Modern Language Association of America** (10 Astor Pl., New York, NY 10003, tel. 212/475–9500) can be helpful, although the information they have is not always current.

PERIODICALS "Rassias Connection" (6071 Wentworth Hall, Dartmouth College, Hanover, NH 03755-3526, tel. 603/646–2922, fax 603/646–3838), a free newsletter published by the Rassias Foundation, a nonprofit organization at Dartmouth College, follows developments in language learning using the Rassias method. The Rassias Foundation also publishes *The Ram's Horn* (same address and tel. no. as "The Rassias Connection"), an annual periodical with articles and commentary on language teaching and the Rassias Method by professors from American, European, and Asian colleges and universities.

BOOKS *Opportunities in Foreign Language Careers* (VGM Career Books), by Wilga Rivers, gives advice on language education and how to get jobs in foreign-language fields. It also discusses some of those fields, such as world trade, travel and tourism, and civil service. Appendices include lists of language associations and travel, study, and exchange programs.

Garden Tours

By Mary Myers

lose your eyes, take a deep breath, and imagine this: The sweetness of roses fills the air, mixed with the sharper scent of lavender and catmint. The clean aroma of fresh-cut grass is unmistakable. The sun feels warm on your skin and your ears pick up the lazy drone of a bumblebee. When you open your eyes, you are in a sea of color—the brilliant reds of oriental poppies, lush pinks of peonies and roses, deep purples of salvia, soft blue of catmint, and clear yellow of coreopsis. In the distance, tall trees cast dappled shade over a smooth green lawn. Have you fallen into an impressionist painting? No. These are the sights and smells of a well-tended garden. And you don't have to travel to Europe to experience them.

There are dozens of magnificently designed gardens all over the United States. And because of the mushrooming public interest in gardening, a number of organizations offer special tours to these preserves. Some programs are offered by tour packagers, others by botanical organizations and horticultural societies (you sometimes have to join these institutions in order to take their tours, and the tour price may be higher). A few operations custom design garden tours for individuals or groups. Group tours typically last about a week and cost between $135 and $275 a day per person based on double occupancy, depending on the qual-

ity of the accommodations and meals. A number of short one-of-a-kind tours are also available, usually sponsored by large cities' major botanical gardens. If you plan to travel in the vicinity of one of them, call ahead to see if anything is scheduled at the time of your visit.

No matter which tour you choose, you are likely to be surrounded by sympathetic and knowledgeable people. Gardeners love to exchange information (and plants), and the touring milieu stimulates conversation. Personal experiences with growing and propagating plants, and questions about layout, relentless weeds, and the latest hybrids are likely to be discussed on buses or during free time. You are certain to learn something from your fellow travelers as well as from the tour guides.

Occasionally a tour focuses on a specific period of gardenmaking. However, most tours focus on a specific region or locale and cover a gamut of garden styles there.

In a Colonial garden you might tread the soft gravel walkways of a *physick* garden—a collection of medicinal plants like mint, tansy, plantain, and others. The plants are laid out in an orderly fashion, the paths usually straight and edged with a crisply sheared low hedge. The strict symmetrical layout of many early American gardens illustrates the close connection between Europe and the

Mary Myers is coordinator of the Landscape Design Certificate program at the New York Botanical Garden and is also principal of a landscape architecture firm in Hastings-on-Hudson, New York. The firm's projects include city rooftop gardens, public-school play areas, residential landscapes, and estate masterplans.

colonies. For example, the gardens at the Governor's Palace in Colonial Williamsburg, Virginia, are a series of hedged parterres (from a French term meaning "on the earth"), composed of low-growing plants arranged with inert materials, such as gravel or coal, in elaborate carpetlike patterns.

Several of these very pleasant Colonial gardens (both domestic and grand) are in the re-created towns of Colonial Williamsburg, in Virginia, and Old Sturbridge Village, in Massachusetts. On your own, you will be able to wander down the back streets for a look at kitchen gardens, as there is usually ample free time.

Garden tours also take in preserves designed during the Country Place Era, a prolific period for American landscape architecture that ran from the mid-19th century until the onset of the Depression, when bankers, industrialists, and others who had suddenly amassed great fortunes commissioned grand houses and gardens. Often these estates were conceived as a single entity, the landscaping interlocked with the design of a mansion and its outbuildings. Some of these estates were planned by Frederick Law Olmsted, the father of American landscape architecture, and by his son and stepson, who worked as the Olmsted Brothers, as well as by such notable designers as Marian Coffin, Ellen Shipman, and Warren Manning. Their works are often huge and might contain terrace gardens, rose gardens, rhododendron or conifer collections, fountains, pools and other water features, and acres of pasture or cropland.

Many of the properties that you visit on garden tours are open to the public; the advantage of seeing them on a garden tour is that you're in the company of like-minded travelers and knowledgeable guides, who can enrich your experience immeasurably. Some garden tours (and these tend to sell out early) also allow you to visit private contemporary gardens—gardens not open to the general public. These were usually designed within the past 50 years, although some are the culmination of several generations of one family's loving care; they tend to display the most current approaches to garden design, not to mention state-of-the-art maintenance techniques. The owner is often available to discuss problems posed by the garden and their solution and to provide a personal touch. Occasionally the tour includes a meal or cocktails among the plantings.

Reflecting the trend toward incorporating ecologically sound garden design—that which is self-sustaining and does not require human intervention in the form of chemicals, pesticides, herbicides, and the like—botanical gardens and tour agencies regularly offer regional landscape tours. On walking tours of the Rockies, for example, you can hike through scenic meadows and inspect alpine environments. You might visit large public preserves such as the national parks of the western United States and Canada in the company of accomplished naturalists, horticulturists, or ecologists.

CHOOSING THE RIGHT TOUR

To help you choose a company whose trips will please you, ask a lot of questions. Then put on your sturdy walking shoes and prepare to stroll down the proverbial garden path.

What is the focus of the tour—plants, landscape design, a specific design period, or regional landscape and scenery? Any trip can be interesting, but some may be more relevant than others to your own gardening interests. However, on all tours, a passion for gardening unites participants, and both novices and experts mingle freely.

What are the qualifications of your guides? Professional geologists, naturalists, historians, landscape architects, or horticulturists sometimes accompany trips or give lectures at pertinent stops. Resident experts often meet groups to speak on their own areas of knowledge.

What lectures and enrichment programs are planned? Sometimes there is running commentary en route; sometimes the talks and other programs are restricted to your stops. Slide shows are often on the schedule.

How many people are in the group? Groups are quite small, usually ranging from 15 to 30 participants.

How will the group travel? By van, car, or bus? Most groups use a deluxe coach, equipped with air-conditioning, restrooms, and sometimes a VCR. As the name suggests, Rail Travel Center tours go by train but use coaches for certain transfers. To move the group from one trailhead to the next, companies that deal in walking tours occasionally use shuttle buses or water taxis.

What sorts of accommodations and meals are provided? Most garden tours use lodgings that are at least comfortable; some operators stick to more luxurious digs with a greater range of facilities. As for meals, they can be adventures in new American cuisine—or simply solid regional fare. In general, the more you pay, the fancier and more sophisticated the food and lodgings.

Is the trip fully escorted or locally hosted? On a fully escorted trip, a guide travels with you every step of the way and can help you unsnarl such problems as lost room reservations. On a locally hosted tour, you're met by a guide at each stop—and you're more or less on your own to work out any problems that may come up en route.

How much free time will there be? A little advance research into the area you're headed for will usually turn up other attractions that can enormously enhance the trip, even for those who love to tramp all day through herbaceous borders. Find out whether the free time is scheduled so that you can use it to pursue the other area offerings that interest you.

What's the cost and what's included? Be sure that this is spelled out in detail. Find out how many nights of lodging the trip price includes, and how many meals. Most tour prices—and all of those quoted for the trips described below, unless otherwise noted—include all meals (lunch on single-day trips), lodging (on multi-day trips),

transportation during the tour from the point of origination, and the services of guides and experts, but not gratuities to the guides, or beverages. Sometimes you must join the sponsoring organization or make a donation as well.

Are garden tours only a sideline with the tour company, or are they a well-developed specialty? Although specialty companies are more likely to offer a trip to a specific garden you'd like to visit and to have a supply of knowledgeable guides to tap, other tour companies often market very appealing trips, too.

How long has the company running the tour been in business? In general, it's best to stick with experienced operators. The company with a few years of garden touring behind it will have worked out the kinks in its programs. At the very least, make sure that those in charge have the experience it takes to orchestrate group trips and keep things moving smoothly.

Do you have references from past guests? If you have doubts or questions about a specific operator or trip, a fellow garden buff may be able to resolve them in ways that the operator cannot. If a company refuses to give you some names, you may well wonder why.

How far in advance do I need to book? Many of the specialized garden tours run just once, so if the program is one that excites you, don't wait to sign up. Although you can always try at the last minute in hopes of snagging a cancellation, you simply can't count on being successful.

MAJOR PLAYERS

BACKROADS This operator, established in 1979, is well-known nowadays for its bike tours; however, it also offers a range of walking tours through the mountains, wildflower meadows, canyonlands, and deserts of six American states and two Canadian provinces. Although tours don't deal specifically with gardens and don't attract garden buffs exclusively (your companions represent a mix of professions and intellectual interests), guides are knowledgeable about local flora and fauna and there are local experts on hand as well—naturalists, geologists, historians, and artists—so these trips can be wonderful if you're interested in regional flora and ecosystems. Moreover, unlike many operators that focus more exclusively on garden tours, Backroads may have more than one departure for each trip and usually repeats successful trips in successive years.

Routes typically cover between 6 and 10 miles per day, but you may opt to walk only 3 to 6 miles—or tackle up to 15 miles. A sag wagon is on hand to give you a lift whenever you want to ride (and to transport your luggage and pick up purchases made along the way; you carry only a day pack with rain gear, a snack, and water). Group size ranges from 14 to 20, with a balance of singles and couples. Most six-day trips are at the high end of the scale but do include all meals, with fairly sophisticated cuisine, as well as accommodation at inns or rustic lodges with private bath. Camping trips are also available; participants are put up in four-person tents, but with a maximum of two people per tent. Amenities are basic but comfortable—Backroads can rent you a sleeping bag and pad unless you've brought one along, and most campsites have showers. Lunches are usually on the road, and are either prepared by the rolling kitchen that is the company's trademark, or by the leaders themselves, who serve up a lavish picnic of sandwiches made on the spot. Dinners on inn-based trips are in a variety of restaurants and inns, but in each case the emphasis is on regional fare prepared with the freshest ingredients. Destinations include California's northern coast, the rain forests of Washington's Olympic Peninsula, and the black sand beaches and fern groves of the emerald highlands of Hawaii's Big Island; prices range from $200 to $250 a day depending on the program. *1516 5th St., Suite B122, Berkeley, CA 94710-1740, tel. 510/527–1555 or 800/462–2848, fax 510/527–1444.*

EXPO GARDEN TOURS This operation's tours, which range throughout North America, from the gardens of the antebellum South to the prairies of the Midwest, take in not only public parks and gardens but also private estates and commercial growing and breeding operations. The company also arranges symposia with well-known garden designers and writers, sometimes as part of a tour, and sometimes there are dinner receptions at historic plantations or other properties. Specific itineraries vary from year to year, but each is researched by a horticulturist or landscape architect and each group is accompanied by such an expert. Michael Italiaander, who founded the business in 1988, sets aside 1% of its net profits for the maintenance and preservation of the sites visited. Tours are first-class, not deluxe; the cost runs around $200 a day. The lodgings are good, clean, comfortable hotels, but it's the gardens that make the trips. The welcome and farewell dinners are special; other meals consist simply of tasty regional fare: fish gumbo in New Orleans, salmon in the Pacific Northwest, scrod in Massachusetts, barbecue in the South. Destinations have included gardens and rhododendron and bonsai collections in the Pacific Northwest, homes and gardens of the Brandywine Valley in Pennsylvania, and Louisiana in spring. *145 4th Ave., Suite 4A, New York, NY 10003-6913, tel. 212/677–6704 or 800/448–2685, fax 212/260–6913.*

LEARNED JOURNEYS This company runs tours for botanic gardens around the country as well as for Garden Journeys, a consortium of botanic gardens and societies that collectively offer garden travel programs. Specific offerings vary from year to year, and there may be only one or two departures for each trip, because they are timed to coincide with the most colorful blooming periods, which are short. Learned Journeys carefully researches its tours, and itineraries are reviewed by top professionals in such fields as horticulture, history, architecture, and geology; small groups and expert backup—authorities in the field, who accompany the group—are hallmarks. Since the company arranges trips for many organizations, its price levels vary widely, as do the accommodations and meals. Learned Journeys tailors its tours to each individual group, planning carefully so that every hotel and restaurant stop complements the theme of the tour. Accommodations are in charming, luxurious inns and lodges; all have private baths and many have a garden. It's rare that the tour price includes all meals, but those that are provided are in restaurants and inns with strong regional character. Expect to have your fill of scrod and lobster around Boston, grilled trout in the Rockies, and pralines, jambalaya, and chicken with creole sauce in New Orleans. You must sometimes join the sponsoring organization. Destinations have included gardens in Hawaii, the Pacific Northwest, New England in autumn, and the South in spring; the schedule has also included Mississippi River cruises aboard the *Delta Queen*, a restored circa-1926 steam-powered paddlewheeler. *3412 Calle Noguera, Box 30626, Santa Barbara, CA 93130-0626, tel. 805/682-6191 or 800/682-6191, fax 805/682-4154.*

MAUPINTOUR This travel industry giant, known for its deluxe fully escorted tours, offers a broad spectrum of programs that include gardens while concentrating on the history, local color, and scenery of the regions visited. Although the tours do not include lectures by garden specialists, many of them do take in noteworthy public gardens. They also offer more than one departure annually, and the successful trips tend to run for several years. Because Maupintour is generalist in approach, its trips are good if your traveling companion doesn't share your green thumb. All are $250 to $350 per person per day, and average group size is about 30, with a maximum of 44. Itineraries include gardens in northern New England; Lake Placid, New York; Old Sturbridge Village, Massachusetts; Longwood Gardens and the Amish Country, in Pennsylvania; and North and South Carolina. Accommodations are in either first-class chain hotels, such as the Hyatt and Hilton, or in deluxe local inns and rustic lodges

with pronounced regional personality. Although dining options vary from group to group, à la carte menus are often available, but not always; when they're not, Maupintour tries to offer regional specialties with some culinary interest. *1515 St. Andrews Dr., Lawrence, KS 66047, tel. 913/843-1211 or 800/255-4266, fax 913/843-8351.*

RAIL TRAVEL CENTER TOURS Classic Quests offered by this company focus on gardens, historic homes, and regional history, and combine train travel with transport by bus, boat, and ferry; tours have been running since 1982 and are mostly by rail. Lodging is in historic inns and medium-priced hotels, and all rooms have private bath; restaurants typically serve good regional cooking, so participants tackle barbecue on Beale Street in Memphis and cajun fare in New Orleans, to the accompaniment of appropriate music. Most meals en route are in a dining car, where you usually have a choice of three entrées. Itineraries often repeat from year to year; destinations include the Pacific Northwest, gardens in the Northeast, and the plantations and gardens of the antebellum South. *2 Federal St., St. Albans, VT 05478, tel. 802/527-1788 or 800/458-5394, fax 802/527-1780.*

TOURS A LA CARTE Because owner Jean Lenehan does not reveal names in her brochure, Tours à la Carte has gained entrée to private gardens that you could probably never visit on your own. Garden buffs like that. They also appreciate the organization's attention to detail and the fact that it makes a dry run of each trip ahead of time. The company was founded in 1973 to provide custom-planned itineraries. Lenehan's trip to Savannah, Charleston, and nearby plantations was typical: Arranged for the Pennsylvania Horticultural Society, it traveled under the guidance of a local horticulturist, visiting several private gardens. Groups are usually limited to 30, and lodgings are usually first-class hotels and inns with a local flavor, such as the Beekman Arms in Rhinebeck, New York; the Lodge Alley Inn in Charleston, South Carolina; and the White Hart Inn in Salisbury, Connecticut.

Although Lenehan usually includes only breakfast and one other meal per day, she tries to make them interesting: In South Carolina, she served up a picnic—salad, sandwiches, and southern fried chicken—in straw baskets lined with flowered napkins; in the Hudson River valley, meals were at the Culinary Insitute of America and at the Beekman Arms, whose chef is C.I.A.-trained. Occasionally, there are lunches in private homes large enough to cater to a group, or, when in Newport, Rhode Island, in a large public house such as Longwood Mansion. Lenahan's group trips usually cost around $200 per day, sometimes with an additional sum required to join the organization for which the journey was designed. *Spread Eagle Village, 503 W. Lancaster Ave., Wayne, PA 19087, tel. 610/687–4185, fax 610/688–2421.*

REPRESENTATIVE TOURS

Although organizations such as Backroads and Maupintour do repeat tours to destinations of interest to gardeners, specialized garden tour companies and botanical institutions do not run the same tours year after year. Instead, they offer a different menu of tours annually. Only group size, accommodations quality, and price levels remain similar from one year to the next. The following tours are representative. Most last about a week, but a few are only a day long—included, although they're beyond the usual scope of this book, simply because they're interesting enough to warrant planning an entire vacation around. If the one we describe isn't offered when you want to travel, it's entirely possible that the sponsoring organization will have something similar and equally intriguing to offer you. By all means, call.

THE NORTHEAST

CONNECTICUT Herbal Delights. The Nutmeg State is home to a number of fascinating herb gardens. One flanks an 18th-century farmhouse, which also has a wildflower garden, and another has an extensive collection of scented geraniums and a replica of an Elizabethan knot garden. Yet another, Gilbertie's, has theme gardens containing over 200 varieties of herbs. This daylong NYBG outing, one of several sponsored every year by the active Education Department, visited all three of these, and at Gilbertie's, the manager led a tour to illuminate the high points of the collection. *New York Botanical Garden, Education Department, Bronx, NY 10458-5126, tel. 718/817–8747, fax 718/220–6504. June: 1 day, $74–$81; sign up 2 weeks in advance.*

MASSACHUSETTS TO MAINE Autumn in New England's Forests and Gardens. This nineday trip from Learned Journeys—put together in 1993 for a consortium of organizations, including the California Arboretum Foundation and the Friends of San Luis Obispo Botanical Garden—explored the landscape and botanic gardens of New England in early October, when the woods are ablaze with color. The group traveled in the company of a horticulturist and was met by local historians and naturalists at key points. The itinerary ranged from Harvard University's Arnold Arboretum, with its collection of 7,000 varieties of plants, to such period plantings as Sedgwick Gardens in Long Hill, Massachusetts, and the Colonial gardens in Old Sturbridge Village, Massachusetts, and at the Moffatt-Ladd House in Portsmouth, New Hampshire. Other stops: Stowe, Vermont, and L.L. Bean in Freeport, Maine. And every day there was afternoon tea. *Learned Journeys, Box 30626, Santa Barbara, CA 93130, tel. 805/682–6191 or 800/682–6191, fax 805/682–4154. Oct.: 9 days, $1,443, not including most meals; sign up 3 months in advance.*

MASSACHUSETTS TO MAINE VIA NEW YORK New England Fall Foliage. Although you can visit period gardens at historic Fort Ticonderoga in upstate New York and at central Massachusetts's Old Sturbridge Village, this nine-day journey from Maupintour, an annual favorite, is really designed to show off the region's spectacular landscapes in their autumnal best. You explore the Maine coastline in Acadia National Park; admire the Old Man of the Mountains and the forests of Franconia Notch, New Hampshire; and pass through New York's Adirondack Mountains, where you take a ferry ride on Lake Champlain and make a stop in Lake Placid, host of the 1932 and 1980 Olympics. As is usual with this operator, you are not accompanied by a garden specialist. *Maupintour, 1515 St. Andrews Dr., Lawrence, KS 66047, tel. 913/843–1211 or 800/255–4266, fax 913/843–8351. Mid-Sept.–mid-Oct.: 9 days, $1,508–$2,053. Price does not include some meals; sign up 4 months in advance.*

NEW YORK **Great Estates of Long Island.** For many years the New York Botanical Garden has run a tour of great estates on this jumbo barrier island, which buffers the southeastern Connecticut shoreline from Atlantic surf and has long been a favorite summering spot for New York City residents. A recent daylong NYBG trip visited two estates. One had a rose garden with over 300 varieties of roses, an annual garden, a woodland walk, a perennial garden, an orchard, and more than 200,000 bulbs—all on just 6 acres. The other was The Point, one of the mansions that inspired F. Scott Fitzgerald's settings for *The Great Gatsby*. The house was designed by Alexander Jackson Davis, a leading American architect of the mid-1800s; landscape architect Ralph Weinrichter laid out the grounds at the turn of the century, providing sweeping views of Long Island Sound, one of the island's largest privately owned collections of azaleas, and giant specimen trees. The current owner, an avid gardener herself, chatted with the tour group. In the past, meals on this tour have included a choice of teriyaki chicken, whole wheat penne, and grilled vegetables. *New York Botanical Garden, Education Department, Bronx, NY 10458-5126, tel. 718/817–8747, fax 718/220–6504. June: 1 day, $95, not including NYBG membership ($35–$45); sign up 2 weeks in advance.*

NEW YORK **June Is for Roses.** The sometimes frustrating rose was the focus of this daylong NYBG visit to Long Island. The main event was a trip to Old Westbury Gardens (*see* Gardens Worth Visiting, *below*), where the director of horticulture led a tour of the formal rose garden to show off the 600 roses surrounded by climbing roses. The group also visited three choice private rose gardens, whose owners were on hand to provide tips; one is a consulting rosarian. The meal was a choice of ham, cheese, or chicken salad sandwiches. *New York Botanical Garden, Education Department, Bronx, NY 10458-5126, tel. 718/817–8747, fax 718/220–6504. June: 1 day, $71–$80; sign up 2 weeks in advance.*

THE MID-ATLANTIC

PENNSYLVANIA **The Dutch Country.** Rural scenery and Amish farms and markets are constants on this eight-day Maupintour trip, offered in spring and fall out of Philadelphia. But for garden buffs, the highlight may be Longwood Gardens, one of the country's great public gardens (*see* Gardens Worth Visiting, *below*), where you stop early in the trip. The contrast between its formality and the gently rolling fields and farms around it is particularly striking. Stops include an Amish homestead, Lancaster's farm market, Philadelphia, Valley Forge, and Gettysburg. *Maupintour, 1515 St. Andrews Drive, Lawrence, KS 66047, tel. 913/843–1211 or 800/255–4266, fax 913/843–8351. Mid-Apr.–mid-May and mid-Sept.–mid-Oct.: 12 days, $2,778. Price does not include some meals; sign up 4 months in advance.*

PENNSYLVANIA **Philadelphia Flower Show.** Every year the New York Botanical Garden assembles a group for a day trip by bus down to America's largest indoor flower show, one of the premier horticultural events in the country. The event's former floor manager hosts the tour there, and there's a private lunch with some of the notable floral exhibitors, privately catered in a convention center meeting room, with your choice of chicken Véronique or vegetarian lasagna, plus green salad and white chocolate mousse. Breathtaking exhibits by nurseries and horticultural organizations as well as floral designs by 700 individual exhibitors highlight the show. *New York Botanical Garden, Education Department, Bronx, NY 10458-5126, tel. 718/817–8747, fax 718/220–6504. Mar.: 1 day, $95. Price does not include NYBG membership ($35–$45); sign up 1 month in advance.*

VIRGINIA **Christmas in Old Virginia.** Since the nation's earliest years, Virginians have celebrated the Yuletide with great passion, as was evident on this eight-day Learned Journeys tour with stops at Richmond, the James River plantations, Colonial Williamsburg, and Mount Vernon—all particularly notable in their festive holiday dress. Participants also spent four nights at a luxurious inn near the mouth of the Rappahannock River along the western shores of Chesapeake Bay, with free access to the inn's private gardens. On Christmas Day, a buffet of roast turkey and ham was served aboard the inn's private yacht, followed by a cruise along some of the rivers that flow into the Chesapeake, their shores anchored by imposing country estates flanked by sweeping lawns. All in all, a splendidly merry Christmas. *Learned Journeys, Box 30626, Santa Barbara, CA 93130, tel. 805/682–6191 or 800/682–6191, fax 805/682–4154. Dec.: 8 days, $1,495, not including some meals; sign up 3 months in advance.*

THE SOUTH

GEORGIA AND SOUTH CAROLINA **Gardens and Plantations of the Colonial South.** This eight-day trip from Learned Journeys, offered in 1993, coincided with the time that the area's dogwoods, magnolias, jasmines, azaleas, and other flowering plants were in bloom—and with the annual festivals of homes and gardens in Savannah and Charleston, when you could see many private gardens. You also visited the formal landscapes of Middleton Place plantation,

which has one of the most beautiful gardens in the South, with gentle terraces rising up out of the nearby river; it is one of the oldest still functioning in the United States. Other highlights included Magnolia Plantation just outside Charleston and Brookgreen Gardens in Murrell's Inlet, two hours north of Charleston on the coast. An old-fashioned garden party was included in the trip. *Learned Journeys, Box 30626, Santa Barbara, CA 93130, tel. 805/682–6191 or 800/682–6191, fax 805/682–4154. Late Mar.: 8 days, $1,394, not including some meals; sign up 6 months in advance.*

LOUISIANA **Landscape Lagniappe.** This Expo Garden Tours program, offered in 1993, was especially designed for amateur and professional gardeners. You traveled in the company of a professor of horticulture and former director of the South Carolina Botanical Garden, along with a tour manager who handled day-to-day issues. The program included a two-day workshop and symposium with guest speakers, among them, garden writer Rosemary Verey. You also had the chance to tour New Orleans's Garden District and inspect the French Quarter's patio gardens, and to stop at showy plantations, such as Shadows-on-the-Teche, home of boxwood hedges, seasonal flower beds, and 200-year-old live oaks lavishly draped with Spanish moss. An afternoon exploring a Louisiana bayou by canoe revealed the natural side of this exotic landscape. *Expo Garden Tours, 145 4th Ave., Suite 4A, New York, NY 10003-4906, tel. 212/677–6704 or 800/448–2685, fax 212/260–6913. Mar.: 7 days, $1,099, not including some meals; sign up 45 days in advance.*

NORTH AND SOUTH CAROLINA **Plantation Gardens and the Blue Ridge.** The grounds of Biltmore, the Asheville, North Carolina, home of George Vanderbilt, were designed by Frederick Law Olmsted, and they represent one of the country's best examples of the landscape design of the Country Place Era. Here, the father of American landscape architecture created acres of luxuriant gardens with beautiful views of the surrounding mountains. But there are other notable stops on this trip. You also visit Boone Hall Plantation, redolent of the flavor of South Carolina's Low Country; Middleton Place; and the Grand Strand in South Carolina, one of the longest sand beaches along the Atlantic coast. The route takes you along a portion of the famed Blue Ridge Parkway, with splendid mountain views. *Maupintour, 1515 St. Andrews Dr., Lawrence, KS 66047, tel. 913/843–1211 or 800/255–4266. Mid-Apr.–early May and Oct.: 8 days, $1,438–$1,469. Price does not include some meals; sign up 2–3 months in advance.*

THE ROCKIES

REGION-WIDE **Antebellum Sojourn.** This eight-day trip out of Mobile, Alabama, spotlights southern gardens at their springtime best, including 65-acre Bellingrath Gardens in Theodore, Alabama; 2,500-acre Callaway Gardens, near Atlanta, where you get a special guided tour; and the stately Drayton Hall and Middleton Place plantations near Charleston. By the time you arrive in Macon, Georgia, the city's 145,000 cherry trees should be in bloom. Travel is via motorcoach and Amtrak's *Gulf Breeze* and *Palmetto* trains. *Rail Travel Center Tours, 2 Federal St., St. Albans, VT 05478, tel. 802/527–1788 or 800/458–5394, fax 802/527–1780. Mid-Mar.: 8 days, $999. Price does not include some meals; sign up 2 months in advance.*

MONTANA **Majestic Glacier National Park.** On this six-day walking trip from Backroads, you can look for 18 species of orchids among the ferns and pines and explore a stunning ice field. Glacier National Park, the focus of the trip, hugs the U.S.–Canadian border and has more than a million acres of mountain ranges, wildflower meadows, and dense forests. The trip sets off down the trail in summer, when the beautiful wildflowers are in bloom and the weather is usually warm and bright by day and cool at night. Hiking is one of the best ways to explore this spectacular natural environment. On this trip, paths skirt turquoise lakes and penetrate groves of western red cedar, Douglas fir, and western hemlock. Although there are some short steep sections, ascents and descents are mostly moderate, and vans take you to the highest elevations, such as 6,680-foot Logan Pass on the Going-to-the-Sun Road, which winds upward through forests and past lakes to the Continental Divide. Depending on which departure you choose, lodging is in luxurious inns or comfortable Glacier National Park campgrounds with hot running water and showers; on camping trips, Backroads provides four-person tents that sleep two and can rent sleeping bags and pads. Groups number between 14 and 20. *Backroads, 1516 5th St., Suite B122, Berkeley, CA 94710, tel. 510/527–1555 or 800/462–2848, fax 510/527–1444. June–Sept.: 6 days, $738 (camping) or $1,295 (with inn lodging); sign up 12 months in advance.*

THE WEST COAST

CALIFORNIA **The Classic North Coast.** On this six-day Backroads trip, you can breathe in the pungent scent of the bay trees as you hike along the San Andreas Fault zone, explore wildflower meadows, and stroll through stands of native oak and fir and clusters of stately iris, not to mention the famous Muir Woods, 485 acres of virgin redwood forest. You also tread the cliffs of the Coast Trail of Point Reyes National Seashore, just north of San Francisco, where meadows filled with wild oats alternate with dense groves of conifers and madronas. Ascents and descents are mostly moderate, although there are some short steep sections. Lodging is in rustic lodges and inns, including the Mountain Home Inn, where all rooms have private terraces with a view of Mt. Tamalpais and the surrounding range. Meals are either in the hotel or in restaurants; the cuisine is usually California style. Groups range in size from 14 to 20 people. *Backroads, 1516 5th St., Suite B122, Berkeley, CA 94710, tel. 510/527–1555 or 800/462–2848, fax 510/*

527–1444. June–Oct.: 6 days, $1,295; sign up 12 months in advance.

HAWAII

▮THE BIG ISLAND▮ **A Natural Side of Paradise.** This six-day Backroads walking tour for nature lovers explores the island's stunning black sand beaches, cascading waterfalls, emerald highlands, and stark volcanoes. You walk through the rich green pastureland of the isolated Waipio Valley, once a center of ancient Hawaiian civilization; through lush jungle past the remains of ancient villages and groves of richly scented fruit trees; and to the ruins of ancient temples, ranged along an interpretive trail, where you can picnic among the palms. Other highlights include hikes around the summit of the active volcano Kilauea, with extraordinary views of the molten lava, and in Hawaii Volcanoes National Park, where you smell the sulfur, see bubbling pools of molten rock, and hear steam hiss through rock fissures. Fern groves and beautiful beaches are also among the trip's pleasures. Hikes are mostly moderate, with only a few short steep sections, although some hiking is at 4,000 feet. Group size is between 14 and 20, and accommodations are in comfortable inns, although families may opt for a campground, whose amenities include hot showers and recreational facilities for children. Meals are in restaurants where the menus are long on fresh seafood and locally grown fruits and vegetables. *Backroads, 1516 5th St., Suite B122, Berkeley, CA 94710, tel. 510/527–1555 or 800/462–2848, fax 510/527–1444. Nov.–Apr.: 6 days, $698 (camping), $1,295 (with inn lodging); sign up 6–12 months in advance.*

GARDENS WORTH VISITING

Certain notable American gardens frequently put in an appearance on the itineraries of garden tour specialists. Here are some destinations that no aspiring Gertrude Jekyll should miss.

THE NORTHEAST

▮MASSACHUSETTS▮ **Naumkeag.** This Stockbridge garden highlights two eras' approaches to garden design: the formalism of the Country Place Era and the experimental modernism of the 1930s and 1940s. Nathaniel Barrett designed the older parts of the garden—the Linden Allée and the Evergreen Walk. Fletcher Steele, one of America's best-known landscape architects, began working here in 1925 and continued to reshape the place over the next 30 years. Two of his most successful designs are the Afternoon Garden, patterned after an Italian terrace, and the famous Blue Fountain Steps, a compositional masterpiece. The steps themselves were made of concrete block, with risers and treads of varying dimensions, supposedly measured to suit Steele's own stride. The balustrades are curved pipe rails painted white; the landings are interplanted with specimen birch trees; and the narrow water channel is painted blue. The overall effect is that of an Art Deco painting come to life. The Afternoon Garden also illustrates Steele's flair for modern materials and composition. It contains an oval pool lined with black glass and parterres with patterns of pink and green stones and black coal. The garden is surrounded by gaily painted "gondola posts," old pilings dredged up from Boston Harbor, and there are beautiful views out over the distant Berkshire Hills and nearby fields. Stockbridge was once known as the inland Newport because of its numbers of affluent summering families. Edith Wharton's place, The Mount, is nearby, as is Chesterwood, home and garden of sculptor Daniel Chester French. *Naumkeag, Box 792, Stockbridge, MA 01262, tel. 413/298–3239, fax 413/298–5239. Open Memorial Day–Columbus Day, Tues.–Sat. Admission: $4.*

▮NEW YORK▮ **Brooklyn Botanic Garden.** This showcase garden at the edge of the borough of Brooklyn's graceful Prospect Park (itself worthy of a visit) educates the public in 14 specialty gardens and a new conservatory.

Labeling is excellent, and a 2-acre Local Flora Section showcases nine native ecological zones, careful re-creations of natural habitats at various times in the past. The BBG is at the height of its beauty in early spring, when, on the famous Cherry Esplanade, hardy old Kwanzan cherries bloom near narcissus, hyacinth, and other bulbs. The Japanese Hill and Pond Garden, built in 1914, is a perennial favorite with visitors. Its flowering cherries, quinces, Japanese maples, azaleas, and tree peonies are laid out around a pond in traditional asymmetrical Japanese style with stone pathways and places to stop and meditate. Under soaring domes, a new conservatory houses the largest bonsai collection in the country, along with palms, ferns, and cacti. Other noteworthy plant collections include shrubs, magnolias, roses, and hedge plants. *Brooklyn Botanic Garden, 1000 Washington Ave., Brooklyn, NY 11225, tel. 718/622–4433, fax 718/857–2430. Open year-round, Tues.–Sun. Admission free.*

NEW YORK **The Gardens at Mohonk Mountain House.** A pristine setting in the Shawangunk Mountains, on the edge of the Catskills, is only one of the distinctions of the old-fashioned gardens at the celebrated 19th-century Mohonk Mountain House resort. Mohonk's 2,500 acres are contiguous to another 5,000 acres of preserved land, where mountain laurel, native rhododendron, columbine, hemlock, oak, and maple line a number of varied and interesting hiking trails. Go in early June to see the mountain laurel in bloom. Or visit in May to admire the old-fashioned favorites in the cultivated gardens near the hotel. The honeysuckle, wisteria, spirea, and lovely old white and purple lilacs bloom in mid- to late spring. The Victorian flower beds, with masses of such annuals as salvia, marigolds, pansies, and impatiens, look best in late summer or early fall; and in autumn, the maple, beech, oak, and sumac are a chorus of riotous color. Some of the trails are ideal for cross-country skiing in winter, when vistas of the surrounding mountains are spectacular.

At the time Mohonk was built by two Quaker brothers, Albert and Alfred Smiley, in the late 1800s, all the earth for the gardens had to be trucked in to cover the mountains' bare bones. The place still retains the ambience of a 19th-century family resort, and the focus is definitely on outdoor activities: hiking on the mountain trails, swimming and boating on the clear mountain lake, croquet, tennis, strolling in the gardens, and lolling on the rustic cedar benches in the arbors and gazebos around the grounds. The hotel rooms are pleasant but not luxurious (although some have fireplaces that are kept stocked with wood), and the food is tasty and bountiful but not fancy. You do not need to stay overnight; day passes allow entrance to the gardens and grounds (and picnicking), but not the hotel. Reservations are required for overnight stays and for meals; if you come for lunch, the cost of the meal includes the day pass. There are regularly scheduled garden walks and lectures, a well-stocked flower shop, and a greenhouse. *Mohonk Mountain House, Lake Mohonk, New Paltz, NY 12561, tel. 914/255–1000 or 800/772–6646, fax 914/256–2161. Gardens open year-round, Tues.–Sun. Admission: $5 weekdays, $8 weekends.*

NEW YORK **New York Botanical Garden.** At this world leader in botanical research and horticultural education, more than 20 beautiful plant collections create a parklike environment on 250 acres in the New York City borough of the Bronx, next to the Bronx Zoo and Fordham University. The magnolias are laid out in a grove and backed by statuesque oaks. The daffodil, rose, viburnum, azalea, rhododendron, and other collections make it an enchanting place in spring. Go to see Daffodil Hill in April or the extensive tulip display in early May. Among the well-maintained specialty gardens are a beautiful perennial garden, a nicely designed herb garden, and a rock garden begun in the 1930s. The Peggy Rockefeller Rose Garden, designed by landscape architect Beatrix Jones Ferrand in 1915 but not built until 1988, is informative as well as beautiful; its thousands of roses are laid out in parterres, radiating from a picturesque gazebo, and handouts and labels rate all the roses for fragrance, color, bloom time, and the like. In the Native Plant Garden, the wet meadow is at its best in August and September, when hibiscus, butterfly weed, goldenrod, and asters are in bloom; in autumn, the pine barren habitat is one of the highlights. Several demonstration gardens are particularly interesting for amateurs: There's one for shade, another designed to attract birds and butterflies, and yet another created around unusually fragrant plants, as well as an ornamental vegetable garden. Also of note is the 40-acre Hemlock Forest, the last remnant of the natural forest that once covered the New York City area. There's also a wonderful library and herbarium facilities that keep and classify seeds; the elegant turn-of-the-century Enid Haupt Conservatory contains palms, cacti, and seasonal displays. *New York Botanical Garden, 200th St. and Southern Blvd., Bronx, NY 10458-5126, tel. 718/817–8700, fax 718/220–6504. Open year-round, Tues.–Sun. Admission: $3 donation suggested, $4 parking.*

NEW YORK **Old Westbury Gardens.** From 1900 to 1925, some 300 estates, complete with opulent houses and gardens of every description, went up along the stretch of Long Island's North Shore that came to be known as the Gold Coast. This 100-acre estate, built in 1904 by the Phipps family, is the one that started the frenzy of building, and it is one of a handful of the dozen that survive to remain open to the public. The Phippses lived at Old Westbury for 55 years, and the garden continues to have much of the feel of private grounds. In the house, fresh flowers decorate rooms where fine English furniture and paintings by Reynolds and Gainsborough depict the gracious, unhurried life of a bygone era. The well-cared-for gardens, with their flowers and peaceful woodland, do the same. The beech-lined entrance drive, dark and mysterious, opens up into a spacious, brilliantly sunny hillside lawn. Then the openness gives way to a geometric, architectural series of "gar-

den rooms": the Lilac Walk, Rose Garden, Boxwood Garden, Primrose Path, and Autumn Walk, as well as a Ghost Walk of feathery hemlock trees and a spectacular Walled Garden. The walled garden contains a wisteria-covered pergola of intricate chinoiserie design, whose striking image is mirrored in the lotus pond below. Old Westbury is smashing in spring, with its beds of various bulbs in formal parterres. Look for bluebells and tulips, lilies and forget-me-nots. Later on, you will find irises, peonies, phlox, and roses. There is rarely a week without color during the growing season. *Old Westbury Gardens, Box 430, Old Westbury, NY 11568, tel. 516/333–0048, fax 516/333–6807. Open daily May–Dec. Admission: $5 ($8 including house).*

NEW YORK **Wave Hill.** So skillfully has Marco Polo Stufano managed the 10-acre garden he has directed for the last 20 years in the affluent Riverdale section of the Bronx that, though technically a public park, it still has the character of a private estate. His interest is in residential gardening, and he experiments tirelessly with different techniques that amateurs can use at home—for instance, transforming concrete cinder blocks into planters. The original Greek Revival mansion, built in 1843 for William Morris on a ridge overlooking the Hudson, has been much enlarged and modified. Mark Twain rented the estate, and Teddy Roosevelt summered here, as did the Perkins-Freeman family until the property was acquired by the City of New York. The setting remains serene and pastoral. Grand specimen beech and oak trees adorn the wide lawns; the rugged cliffs known as the Palisades loom across the Hudson, by turns framed by elegant pergolas and hidden along curving pathways. Spring in the hilly Wild Garden is particularly beautiful, as the early blooms of narcissus give way to cranesbill geranium and iris. In the ever-changing Perennial Garden you might discover such old-fashioned favorites as larkspur, heliotrope, and dahlias. Take a break and sit down in the rustic arbor, entwined with clematis and roses, or relax on the comfortable, movable seats you'll find throughout the grounds (a rarity in public parks in New York, where most seating is fixed). The Wave Hill Foundation holds seminars and symposia on landscape design in the house, free outdoor concerts are given in summer on the lawn, and there are changing art exhibits both inside and out. *Wave Hill, 675 W. 252nd St., Bronx, NY 10471, tel. 718/549-2055, fax 718/884-8952. Open daily year-round. Admission free.*

THE MID-ATLANTIC

DELAWARE Winterthur. This is a garden made for spring! Its creator, Henry Francis du Pont, used azaleas, flowering dogwoods, quinces, rhododendrons, and lilacs with masses of daffodils, bluebells, and other bulbs to great effect. Du Pont studied horticulture at Harvard at the turn of the century, and his gardens, apparently a work of nature, were laid out with care and precision; bloom sequence and color were carefully considered. Here pastel colors dominate, and bright color is used as an accent—a valuable lesson for the suburban gardener: Too much color kills the scene. Plant collections with names like Winter Hazel Area, Pinetum, Azalea Walk, and Magnolia Bend, laid out on 60 of Winterthur's 1,000 acres, are equipped with instructional labels and contain many hybrids and cultivars (plants bred for specific qualities). Marian Coffin, a well-known landscape architect of the Country Place Era, created the Reflecting Pool Garden, a quiet glade designed in the manner of the Italian Renaissance, and the Sundial Garden, which is bounded by very tall evergreens now over 100 years old. Don't miss either on your tour, and be sure to visit the gallery next to the house at Winterthur, which is known around the world for its American decorative arts; the collection of furniture, lamps, textiles, and pictures is without peer. Guided garden tours are available (phone ahead). *Winterthur, Winterthur, DE 19735, tel. 302/888-4600. Open year-round, Tues.–Sun. Admission to gardens and gallery: $7.*

PENNSYLVANIA Longwood Gardens. Millions of visitors make their way every year to these 350 acres in the rolling hills of the Brandywine River valley, near Philadelphia and not far from Wilmington, Delaware: Longwood is one of the premier public gardens of the United States. The sheer scale of the place, its very high level of maintenance, and its diversity keep you from noticing that it lacks a comprehensive, unified design. Each special garden is a world unto itself. Only at Longwood would you find such enormities as the immense Old-Fashioned Flower Border, over 600 feet long. There are also 11,000 different kinds of plants and 20 indoor gardens under glass. The use of water is one of the most striking aspects here: The acres of water gardens are full of moats, canals, fountains, woodland streams, and formal Italianate pools. Water shows are held every afternoon in summer, dramatic displays of thundering jets, crossing arcs, spouts, and massive sheets of water. Children (and others) love to run through the spray on hot days. There's also the Festival of Fountains, a computerized display of water, light, and music staged on summer evenings. The curtain in an open-air theater is made of water. In addition, there are formal gardens starring roses, peonies, wisteria, heather, and topiary, and 3½ acres of conservatories, whose spectacular displays are a pleasure to visit anytime, but never more than during the Christmas season—your spirits will get a real lift from the thousands of poinsettias, lights, and fragrant flowers. Spring and summer bring extravagant displays, and there are outdoor theatrical performances and fireworks in peak season. *Longwood Gardens, Box 501, Kennett Square, PA 19348-0501, tel. 215/388-6741, fax 215/388-2079. Open daily year-round. Admission: $10 (Tues. $6).*

VIRGINIA Colonial Williamsburg. More than 100 gardens flourish in Colonial Williamsburg, the reconstructed 18th-century Colonial capital in the Virginia Tidewater. The restoration of the town, funded by John D. Rockefeller beginning in 1926, has taken decades to accomplish. It comprises not only 500 buildings spread over 173 acres, including 88 original houses, taverns, shops, and public buildings, but also 90 acres of well-kept gardens and greens. Planted with species known to the Colonial inhabitants, the gardens duplicate those of the 18th century as accurately as possible. Best documented were those of the Governor's Palace, where remains of walls and walks were unearthed, and an early engraver's plate found in England provided details of the plantings. According to English custom, many of Williamsburg's gardens are green gardens, created using evergreen material that requires minimum maintenance and looks attractive year-round. Yaupon, American holly, live oak, southern magnolia, and boxwood are widely seen, along with evergreen ground covers such as periwinkle. In early April, such small ornamental trees as flowering dogwood and eastern redbud bloom together, and at about the same time, masses of tulips, anemones, and daffodils are studded among the formal evergreen plantings. Later in the spring, you will see the catalpa, horse chestnut, and magnolia trees in bloom; in summer, look for crape myrtle (its vibrant pinks are difficult to miss!). Autumn's palette of gold, tan, and russet with some touches of scarlet is more subdued here than that in New England, because oak dominates rather than sugar maple. Herb and vegetable gardens have been planted throughout the town, and corn, tobacco, cotton, flax, and sorghum, mainstays of the Colonial economy, are grown as field crops. Colonial Williamsburg offers nearly 40 exhibitions and activities; costumed interpreters relate stories of 18th-century Virginia society and culture, and you can watch many trades being practiced with the tools and methods of the time. *Colonial Williamsburg, Box 1776, Williamsburg, VA 23187-1776, tel. 804/229–1000 or 800/447–8679, fax 804/220–7729. Open daily year-round. One-day admission to*

trades and historical buildings and museums: $24.

THE SOUTH

MISSISSIPPI Crosby Arboretum. This arboretum on the Pearl River, a major stream emptying into the Gulf of Mexico, comprises 11 associated natural areas on more than 1,700 acres. The Crosby gives you the opportunity to study the native plants of the coastal plain of the Pearl River watershed in their original habitats—over 700 species of indigenous trees, shrubs, wildflowers, and grasses. Natural areas include beech-magnolia forests, a white cedar swamp, evergreen hammocks, a cypress swamp, pine savannas, and hardwood-forested bottomlands. The arboretum protects many rare and endangered plants and animals, and the several lovely pitcher plant bogs also contain many orchids. Around the lake are water tupelo and bald cypress trees, along with turtles, great egrets, and kingbirds. Most activities are at Pinecote, the 64-acre native plant and interpretive center; the wonderful pavilion there, designed by architects Fay Jones and Maurice Jennings, seems to float above the lake. *Crosby Arboretum, Box 190, Picayune, MS 39466, tel. 601/799–2311, fax 601/799–2372. Open year-round, Tues.– Sun. Admission: $2 donation suggested.*

THE MIDWEST

ILLINOIS Chicago Botanic Garden. There are 18 garden areas in this 300-acre preserve in Glencoe, 25 miles north of downtown Chicago. In the Aquatic Garden, you can see water lilies and other water-loving plants from a boardwalk over a lagoon. The English Walled Garden contains six garden rooms, examples of English gardening style. The Heritage Garden is modeled after Europe's first botanic garden in Padua, Italy. The small Prairie peaks in August. The Rose Garden contains more than 5,000 rosebushes, and the Japanese Garden, called Sansho-En, "the garden of three islands," displays carefully styled plants and judiciously placed stones. Native Illinois plants fill the Naturalistic Garden, where woodland, prairie, and bird gardens show off the special beauty of the local flora. The Dwarf Conifer Garden, very popular among homeowners, demonstrates the ways small evergreens can be used in domestic plantings. And three greenhouse areas display a Temperate Collection, Desert Collection, and Rain Forest Collection. Gardening enthusiasts can easily spend most of a day. *Chicago Botanic Garden, Box 400, Glencoe, IL 60022, tel. 708/835–5440, fax 708/835–4484. Open daily year-round. Admission free; parking $4.*

ILLINOIS **Morton Arboretum.** The hardiest, most attractive trees, shrubs, and vines of the Midwest are displayed in this garden, established in 1922 by Morton Salt Company founder Joy Morton on his 1,500-acre estate 25 miles west of Chicago. An expression of his lifelong interest in trees (his father, J. Sterling Morton, originated Arbor Day), it displays more than 3,000 types of plants from around the world. This is one of the few public gardens that you may tour in your car; it takes about an hour to drive the 8-mile-long route. There are also 25 miles of walking trails, most between 1 and 3 miles long. The Illinois Trees Nature Trail features meadows, woodlands, and spring wildflowers in the best surviving oak-maple forest near Chicago, and the Prairie Trail winds through a reconstructed pre-pioneer grassland. Among the plant collections are a pinetum, a hedge garden with more than 100 formal hedges, a dwarf shrub garden, a "sand beds" garden of plants for sandy soil, a rose garden, a fragrance garden, and a low-maintenance perennial garden. Wildlife watching and bird observation are also rewarding here: More than 160 bird species have been sighted, and you might see deer, raccoons, wild turkeys, and foxes. *Morton Arboretum, Lisle, IL 60532, tel. 708/968–0074, fax 708/719–2433. Open daily year-round. Admission free.*

MISSOURI **Missouri Botanical Garden.** This venerable institution, which opened to the public in 1859, stands out for its excellent displays, botanical research, and striking modern buildings, including the Shoenberg Temperate House and its famous Climatron, a half-acre, geodesic-domed greenhouse. As you enter it, you are immediately in the tropics: You see a small native hut, sparkling waterfalls, rocky cliffs, and the dense green foliage of tropical rain forest plants. (The garden's tropical botany research program is notably active, primarily in Central and South America, where many of its 50 botanists race against time to seek out, document, and classify the world's unknown tropical plants before they become extinct.) The Climatron displays some 1,200 tropical species, including banana, coffee, and cacao plants, and an orchid collection with more than 10,000 specimens. An imaginative electronic exhibit called the Talking Orchid not only speaks to visitors but sips water from their hands. The Shoenberg Temperate House exhibits temperate-zone species from the southeastern United States, China, Japan, and Korea; most plants in this area are thematically displayed in a Moorish Walled Garden, a Biblical and Economic Collection, a Wildflower, Rock and Vine Collection, and a collection of riparian plants (adapted to the edge of rivers and streams).

Elsewhere in the Missouri are flowering cherries, azaleas, chrysanthemums, peonies, lotus, and other Asian plantings arranged around a 4-acre lake. You can tour the display gardens by tram: the Azalea-Rhododendron Garden, which peaks in late April; the Bulb Garden, which shows off thousands of tulips, hyacinths, narcissus, and giant flowering onions, as well as summer- and fall-blooming bulbs; the Scented Garden, whose raised beds let you easily smell and touch the plants, with signage in Braille; the Hardy Succulent Garden, full of such plants as sedum, yucca, hardy prickly pear, and cobweb live-forevers, a kind of sedum, that survives outdoors in Missouri with minimal protection; and the 14-acre Japanese garden, Seiwa-En ("garden of pure, clear harmony and peace"), the largest of its type in the

Western Hemisphere. The display gardens also include the Rose Garden, Rock Garden, Desert House, Herb Garden, and Woodland Garden. There are also displays on home gardening, and two dozen residential-scale gardens will open in 1996. Also here you can arrange a guided tour of the Missouri's Shaw Arboretum, a 2,500-acre nature preserve and wildlife center southwest of St. Louis. *Missouri Botanical Garden, 4344 Shaw Blvd., St. Louis, MO 63166, tel. 314/577-5100, fax 314/577-9598. Open daily year-round. Admission $3 (free Wed. and Sun. 9–noon, Mon.–Thurs. 5–8 PM).*

THE SOUTHWEST

■ **ARIZONA** ■ **Arizona–Sonora Desert Museum.** This marvelous exhibit of the flora and fauna of the desert region, 14 miles west of Tucson, concentrates entirely on the local ecology and attempts to explain the complex relationships between the area's plants, animals, climate, and terrain. More than 1,200 kinds of plants and more than 200 living animals are on display in naturalistic settings. There's a Riparian Habitat, where river otters cavort, and a Mountain Habitat, with Mexican wolves and black bears. The unusual reptiles and invertebrates of the Sonoran Desert, from centipedes, tarantulas, and scorpions to Gila monsters, snakes, and lizards, are also on exhibit. A Cave Walk reveals an underground limestone cavern where you can inspect the beautiful mineral specimens of the region, and trained volunteers give demonstrations and talks throughout the grounds every day and are on hand to answer your questions. Do not miss the nearby Saguaro National Monument, which preserves a magnificent forest of this distinctive cactus. There you see tall, ancient specimens, their great age shown by the number and size of their arms, or branches, which can take up to a century to develop. Walking on one of the trails through the forest, you'll begin to get a sense of the timeless quiet of the desert; it is an experience you will never forget. Try to visit the museum early in the day, when it is cooler and the animals are more active. *Arizona-Sonora Desert Museum, 2021 N. Kinney Rd., Tucson, AZ 85743, tel. 602/883–1380, fax 602/883–2500. Open daily year-round. Admission: $8.*

THE WEST COAST

■ **CALIFORNIA** ■ **Filoli.** Formality blends with the natural vistas and surroundings of northern California at this meticulously maintained estate, 25 miles from San Francisco. Originally built between 1915 and 1917, the house and its gardens are a remnant of the Country Place Era and express the elegant style of the period. They were deeded to the National Trust for Historic Preservation in 1975. The 16 landscaped acres, originally laid out by Bruce Porter and augmented in 1936 by Isabella Worn, were designed to enhance the natural beauty of the site. The Sunken Garden is an example of Worn's hallmark use of color. It contains crisply sheared pillows of silvery olives; beyond them rise the inky, dark columns of tall yews. The lemon yellow of a sunburst locust terminates the formal garden view but draws the eye past it to the soft green of the native hillside. The Sunken Garden is just one in Filoli's succession of garden rooms, which also includes a Woodland Garden, with rhododendrons set among native oaks; a Yew Allée, with espaliered apple and pear trees; and a Walled Garden, containing the delicate Chartres Cathedral Garden, depicting a stained-glass window, with boxwood borders representing the lead outlines, an English holly hedge standing in for the masonry between the windows, and colorful annuals and standard roses supplying the myriad hues. Look for the climbing hydrangea on top of the south wall of the Bowling Green—a rarity in western gardens. Note the stately trees throughout Filoli's grounds: the magnificent magnolias along the front drive, the very old coast live oaks to the north of the house, and the specimen trees outside the Walled Garden—among them copper beech, American hornbeam, and dawn redwood. And don't miss the canopy of Camperdown elms to the south of the pool pavilion. What a pleasant respite from the bright rays of the sun! Filoli has splendid floral displays throughout the year, and you can make advance reservations for a docent-led tour that takes in the mansion, too. Several days each month the public can take self-guided tours of the house and gardens at their leisure. *Filoli, Canada Rd., Woodside, CA 94062, tel. 415/364–2880, fax 415/366–7836. Open mid-Feb.–early Nov., Tues.–Sat. Admission free.*

CALIFORNIA **Huntington Botanical Gardens.** Railroad and real estate magnate Henry Huntington founded this garden in San Marino, 12 miles northeast of downtown Los Angeles, in 1919. The estate is well-known as the home of one of the finest libraries in the world and a splendid collection of British art (although only the latter is open to the public). The gardens are famous for their 12-acre Desert Garden, which displays 2,500 species of xerophytes (plants that have adapted to a limited supply of water). But there are also 14 other gardens, where 14,000 different types of plants are arranged in a parklike setting of rolling lawns. The Camellia Collection, in two gardens, is one of the largest in the country, and the Japanese Garden has a bridge supported by empty oil drums, a furnished Japanese house, and a tranquil, sand-and-rock Zen Garden. The plants and colorful flowers in the Shakespeare Garden were cultivated during the writer's time; they bloom year-round. You can trace plant development in the Rose Garden, where nearly 2,000 cultivars are arranged historically. A cursory tour of the gardens takes about an hour. *Huntington Botanical Gardens, 1151 Oxford Rd., San Marino, CA 91108, tel. 818/405–2100, fax 818/405–0634. Open year-round, Tues.–Sun. Admission: $5 donation suggested.*

OREGON **Hoyt Arboretum.** One of the largest conifer collections in the United States is a notable feature here in the hills west of Portland, and a number of the trees were grown from seed. Visitors marvel at the collection's 60-year-old coast redwoods and giant sequoias, both from California. There are also dawn redwoods, a species once thought extinct, reintroduced from China during the 1940s; it was a Hoyt Arboretum specimen that produced the first cones in the Western Hemisphere in 50 million years. Ten miles of gentle trails wind through the 175-acre arboretum. Dispersed among the towering native trees are such exotics as the Chilean monkey puzzle tree, the North African cork oak, and the Australian eucalyptus. You'll pass through the interesting Weeping Tree Collection, where groves of Himalayan weeping spruce grow, along with weeping cedar, European weeping beech, and the rare Brewer's weeping spruce from Oregon's Siskiyou Mountains. Although the magnolias, crabapples, cherries, and dogwoods are spectacular in springtime, many visitors think that the peak time at the Hoyt is fall, when maples, tupelos, poplars, larches, and witch hazels burst into color. There are free guided tours every Saturday and Sunday from April through October. *Hoyt Arboretum, 4000 S.W. Fairview Blvd., Portland OR 97221, tel. 503/228–8733, fax 503/823–4213. Open daily year-round. Admission free.*

WASHINGTON **Bloedel Reserve.** Designed by landscape architect Richard Haag, the Reflection Garden at this 150-acre expanse of forests and gardens on Puget Sound's Bainbridge Island is one of the most striking and elegant garden spaces in the country. A serene reflecting pool, created by excavating into the existing, very high water table, is surrounded by dark evergreens, its pristine geometry contrasting sharply with the lushness of the native forest. Western azalea, blood currant, red osier dogwood, spirea, and moosewood viburnum attract birds in the Bird Refuge. Under the tall evergreens of the Glen, rhododendrons thrive; it is particularly beautiful when they bloom in late spring and early summer, but thousands of perennials, bulbs, and wildflowers succeed one another in bloom among the shrubs at other times of year. The Bloedel's enormous swath of more than 15,000 fluttering cyclamens is one of the largest plantings of them in the world. And there are two Japanese gardens: One is enclosed and composed of wood, stone, and sand, and invites introspection and meditation; the other draws you to think of the world outside yourself with its many beautiful views. Allow at least two hours. You need a reservation to visit; call a week in advance. The reserve is accessible by ferry from Seattle and by car from the Olympic Peninsula (use the Agate Pass Bridge). *Bloedel Reserve, 7571 N.E. Dolphin Dr., Bainbridge Island, WA 98110-1097, tel. 206/842–7631, fax 206/842–8970. Open year-round, Wed.–Sun. Admission: $4.*

SOURCES

ORGANIZATIONS Many garden tours are sponsored by horticultural societies and botanical institutions. Of these, a few stand out for the breadth and depth of their activity nationwide. The **American Horticultural Society** (7931 E. Boulevard Dr., Alexandria, VA 22308-1300, tel. 703/768–5700 or 800/777–7931) focuses on the exchange of information through its two publications, *American Horticulturalist Magazine* and *American Horticulturalist News Edition.* Its reciprocal admission program means that members can visit gardens throughout the country for free or at a discount. The **Botanical Society of America** (New York Botanical Garden, Bronx, NY 10458, tel. 718/817–8700) fosters education by means of publications and a plant information hot line. The **Garden Club of America** (598 Madison Ave., New York, NY 10022, tel. 212/753–8287) has many local chapters that sponsor various educational programs in the gardening field. The **Garden Conservancy** (Albany Post Rd., Box 219, Cold Spring, NY 10516, tel. 914/265–2029) aims to preserve exceptional American gardens by helping them change from private to nonprofit ownership, by fundraising, and through legal research. Members receive a newsletter and can join day tours of worthy private gardens.

PERIODICALS Listings of garden tours as well as of courses and other programs can typically be found in the publication of your local botanical institution. Also consult *Fine Gardening* (Taunton Press, Inc., Box 355, Newtown, CT 06470, tel 203/426–8171), a good general bimonthly by and for home gardeners, and *Horticulture* (98 N. Washington St., Boston, MA 02114, tel. 617/742–5600), which publishes articles and ads of general interest to gardeners 10 times a year. Many other publications and books are available at the stores and bookshops of botanical institutions and public gardens.

BOOKS For excellent descriptions of public gardens, often with color illustrations, see *The American Garden Guidebook: East* and *The American Garden Guidebook: West,* by Everitt L. Miller and Jay S. Cohen; *American Gardens: A Traveler's Guide,* edited by Claire E. Sawyers (Brooklyn Botanic Garden, Brooklyn, NY 11225); *Glorious Gardens to Visit,* by Priscilla Dunhill and Sue Freedman; *Public and Private Gardens of the Northwest,* by Myrna Oakley; and *The Traveler's Guide to American Gardens,* edited by Mary Helen Ray and Robert P. Nicholls.

ALSO SEE If it's the idea of traveling in the company of an expert that appeals, look into Cultural Tours. If it's natural ecosystems that fascinate you, turn to the Environmental Cruises and Nature Camps chapters.

Music Programs

By Ben Sandmel

aybe you bought a dulcimer and need a good teacher. Or you play the saxophone and want to team up with a jazz band. Or you have studied classical guitar and want to try your hand at the blues or a musical style that simply isn't taught in your region, such as Appalachian folk music. Or you're a violinist in need of a group with which to practice your chamber music repertoire.

Then perhaps this year you should spend your vacation in one of the many music programs nationwide. They are held at prestigious music schools as well as at college campuses, conference centers, and even state parks. Some programs emphasize technical training on one instrument, such as piano, guitar, or dulcimer. Other programs address a particular musical style or tradition—the Baroque period, Celtic music, blues, or opera, for example. When the program focuses on a specific ethnic heritage or culture, there may also be classes in such associated arts as folk dancing or basketry. The cost ranges from $120 for three days up to as much as $1,500 for three weeks.

You don't have to be a professional musician, although rudimentary knowledge of an instrument is usually assumed. Most programs accept musicians of all ability levels and even have classes for beginners; the aim is simply to provide as much playing and performance experience as possible. Usually you are placed with other players of similar experience and ability upon arrival or after an audition. Although many programs are geared to adults, several also welcome students from junior and senior high schools. Programs designed for professional musicians and aspiring professionals expect students to have a serious commitment to their studies and require an audition tape, a list of repertoire, and letters of recommendation. The atmosphere tends to be competitive.

Faculty at music camps customarily consists of professional musicians, music educators, or both. West Virginia's Augusta Heritage Center and North Carolina's Swannanoa Gathering attract master folk artists—experts on the musical traditions of certain parts of the country. Most schools give you a choice of instructors so you can learn a variety of playing styles.

Daily routines vary from program to program. Typically you spend about four hours a day in classes; these are small and focus on technique, playing styles, or learning new works. Some schools also offer master classes, group lessons led by instructors of greater than usual renown. The rest of the day may be filled with ensemble rehearsals, performance critiques, private lessons, practice, or lectures on music theory and history. Some programs impose a rigid daily schedule while others let you plan your own time. After dark there may be jam sessions or faculty concerts. Many programs culminate in student performances.

Ben Sandmel is a New Orleans–based drummer, journalist, and folklore researcher whose articles have appeared in such publications as the Atlantic Monthly, Esquire, and Rolling Stone.

Consider what you want out of your vacation when selecting a program. You may not want an intensive one with classes all day and concerts at night if relaxation is what you have in mind; you might be happier being in class for only part of each day. If you're not accustomed to spending time with teens, stick to programs that accept only adults. If you want to improve your performance ability, make sure that there are performance critiques. Perhaps you've always wanted to learn about Cajun music: Try a program that not only has instrumental instruction but explores Cajun culture as well. If you want interaction with other musicians, find out if you'll have a chance to attend classes other than those in your own discipline. Some programs expect you to play with ensembles; make sure you want that kind of experience before you sign up.

No matter which you pick, you should be able to immerse yourself in practice and lessons without the distractions of friends, family, or work. Not only will you be surrounded by fellow students who are as enthusiastic about music as you, you're bound to learn new skills and repertoire that you can take back home.

CHOOSING THE RIGHT PROGRAM

The specific focus of the program is the first decision to make. If you want to study dulcimer, some programs will have immediate appeal. If jazz is your interest, you'll go for others. Beyond that, the answer to certain key questions will help you differentiate among your options.

What's the cost and what's included? Most programs have one fee for tuition and another for on-campus room and board, which is usually quite economical. For these programs, we give separate prices for tuition, which covers instruction and other program-related activities, and housing, which includes three meals a day as well as lodging based on double occupancy, unless specified differently. (When singles are available at another price, that figure is also given.) Some programs charge an all-inclusive fee (designated as "complete package") for tuition, room, and board, and unless otherwise noted, they don't offer discounts for staying or eating elsewhere. All prices are per person.

What levels of ability are accepted? Most programs accommodate beginners to advanced students. A few do not accept beginners and expect you to submit an audition tape or résumé with your application.

How are programs structured, what is the daily schedule, and how much free time is there? The answers to these questions help you determine how intense the program is. Find out how many hours are devoted to formal instruction and rehearsal and ask about the length of breaks between classes. Some programs keep you very busy for as many as 15 hours a day, with only short breaks for meals; others occupy you merely most of the morning and afternoon and leave plenty of time for relaxation. Programs that accept teenagers as well as adults plan many activities to keep students amused. The important thing is to know in advance how strict a daily schedule you're expected to follow.

What is the relative importance of performance vis-à-vis technique in the program? Some programs put a lot of weight on technique; others emphasize performance; and still others fall somewhere in between. Make sure that the program's emphasis is right for you.

What are the teachers' qualifications? Make sure that they are credible and that the instructors have the background to teach you what you want to learn. Remember too that personal style is often as important as virtuosity or even teaching experience. Regardless of the teacher's credentials, if you don't like the way you're taught, you won't enjoy learning. If possible, try to talk to the instructor personally ahead of time to make sure your questions are answered and you are comfortable.

How large are the classes and what is the student-to-teacher ratio? The actual "classes" you'll be in can range from private lessons to orchestra rehearsals, with most workshops falling in the 10- to 20-student range. What's important is to find out how much personal attention you're likely to get. Sometimes larger classes have several instructors, so the number of students per teacher is still relatively small. Look for a program with a low student-to-faculty ratio—between 5:1 and 12:1 is typical.

Are private lessons available? Is the cost included in the program fee or must you pay extra? Several programs offer individual instruction, and it may or may not be included in the fee. If it is, you may get only a specified number of lessons or be left to your own devices to make the arrangements—to get private time with an instructor, it may be up to you to persuade someone. When private lessons cost extra, the fee may be under $10 an hour—or it may be more like what you're used to at home, perhaps $45 or $50 an hour.

How much interaction is there between students and teachers? Associating with professionals in the field is part of the learning experience. Yours will be much richer if you spend time with instructors at meals and in casual jam sessions as well as in class.

What are the accommodations like? Most programs provide sparsely furnished double dormitory rooms with shared baths; a few have singles, which may or may not cost extra. (If you stay in a double room, you are generally paired with a roommate if you don't bring your own.) Ask about air-conditioning. If it's not available or if you want more privacy or more comfort than a dorm affords, you may want to consider lodging in a nearby hotel or B&B. In fact, many programs can help you find suitable off-campus quarters. In dorms, linens are usually provided, but not always; you may have to bring your own pillows, sheets, towels, or blankets.

What is the food like? Most programs offer typical cafeteria fare: sandwiches, fresh fruit, a salad bar, and a choice of hot entrées at dinner. If this doesn't sound good to you, make sure that there are appealing restaurants nearby.

Do I need to bring an instrument or is one provided? Most programs expect you to bring your own instrument, at least the portable ones. Pianos, harpsichords, and organs are usually provided, as are some of the more exotic instruments you might want to try out. If, on the other hand, you'd like to study a small and conventional instrument and you don't have one, you have to consider renting one on your own. Many programs do have a few instruments of every type on hand, however, and lend them on a first-come, first-served basis.

How far in advance do I need to book? Most programs expect you to sign up one to four months in advance. But if you make your plans late, there's always a chance of a last-minute cancellation.

How long has the program been in operation? If the program is new, ask about the qualifications and experience of the people in charge. Make sure that the program seems well conceived and well organized.

Does the program provide references from past students? To clarify your impressions about instruction, food, and lodging, it always helps to talk with someone who has studied with the teachers, slept in the beds, and eaten the meals.

What facilities and activities are available for your nonmusical traveling companions? Because the intensive nature of music programs leaves very little free time, students don't usually bring their families along. If you'd like to, however, it's certainly possible, though some programs are better than others. Those held at resorts or vacation areas with a lot of recreational opportunities are your best bet. Ask what housing arrangements can be made or whether recreational facilities are available to your companions.

FAVORITE PROGRAMS

THE MID-ATLANTIC

WEST VIRGINIA Augusta Heritage Center. Elkins, a small mountain town (pop. 8,000) on the western edge of the panhandle in east-central West Virginia, is the site of the country's largest and most comprehensive folk music program, established in 1972. In April, July, August, and October, you can take your pick of several seven- to eight-day theme weeks devoted to bluegrass, blues, swing, singing, and dulcimer, Appalachian Mountain, Cajun and Creole, and Irish music. In July and August, there are also seven-day classes concentrating on specific instruments, including Autoharp, banjo, fiddle, guitar, hammered and mountain dulcimer, piano, and piano accordion; in addition, there are seven-day workshops in Celtic band, contra dance piano, group playing, and old-time string band. You must bring your own instrument.

For the seven-day instrument sessions, you register for one course per week, which usually meets Monday through Friday for four to seven hours daily. Classes are available for beginning, intermediate, and advanced students and are kept small, averaging 12 students per teacher. In most cases, you spend your days with one instructor in intensive group sessions, which usually concentrate on technique, playing styles, and repertoire, but some classes spend less time in group sessions to allow for practice.

Sessions focusing on a particular theme provide you with a wide selection of courses. Bluegrass week offers eight instrument courses, for instance. Every morning, you meet in small groups of 12 to 15 for instrumental instruction; afternoons, you work with students in other classes as part of a bluegrass band. All students enrolled for the week convene periodically for meetings with guest artists and workshops in harmony and bluegrass history. In addition, you can sign up for one of the 90-minute mini-classes that meet four times during the week; they cover instrument construction, barn dancing, weaving, movement awareness, and other topics.

Most Augusta Heritage Center students come in summer, and each week there are about 100 representing a range of backgrounds, ages, and interests. All instructors are accomplished musicians, and some are designated by the program as master folk artists, experts in traditional folk music who have devoted most of their lives to preserving the music from a particular culture. Some instructors are outstanding artists who are little known outside their own communities.

Classes are held on the wooded, 170-acre campus of Davis & Elkins College, a small private liberal arts institution. In summer, you stay in double dormitory rooms with no private baths or air-conditioning; housing for the spring and fall weeks is in a nearby motel. Typical cafeteria fare is provided in the college dining hall. Alternatively, you may choose to eat at one of the many restaurants in town or to stay nearby in an inexpensive bed-and-breakfast or motel.

After dark, you're surrounded by musical activities—impromptu recitals by students and instructors, concerts by master folk artists, and continuous jam sessions. There are also storytelling evenings, slide shows on crafts, and dance performances. Or you can simply join fellow classmates for conversation at the campus beer hall, once an old icehouse, or at the no-smoking, no-alcohol coffeehouse. You're free to use the college tennis courts, swimming pool, fitness trail, and Nautilus weight machines, and there is canoeing, white-water rafting, and hiking in the surrounding forests. In summer, the center also sponsors Elderhostel programs, folk arts classes for youngsters ages 8 to 12, and classes in dance, folklore, and arts and crafts. *Augusta Heritage Center, Davis & Elkins College, 100 Campus Dr., Elkins, WV 26241, tel. 304/636-1903, fax 304/636-8624. Mid-Apr.–late Aug. and early Oct.: 7 days, tuition $255–$265, housing $115 in spring and fall and $190 in summer. Spring and fall housing price does not* include meals ($50–$85 for cafeteria meal ticket); sign up 6 months in advance. See also *Arts and Crafts Workshops*.

■**WEST VIRGINIA**■ **Buffalo Gap Camp for the Cultural Arts.** Since 1972, some of the best folk and ethnic music and dance programs in the country have taken place at this 200-acre music mecca in the mountainous West Virginia panhandle, 100 miles west of Washington, D.C. The three-, four-, and seven-day programs, offered in the summer and fall, consist of both performances by professional musicians and group instruction in such instruments as fiddle, guitar, banjo, and accordion as well as in styles of folk music and dance. Each week there is a different theme (usually covering a geographic region), and instructors are professional musicians who are specialists in that area, often coming from the region itself.

Examples of themes are Scandinavian week, which offers instruction in couple dancing and stringed instruments; Western music week, which comes with a hoedown; and the Balkan Music and Dance Workshop, which is under the aegis of North Carolina's Eastern European Folklife Center and covers the folk music and dance of Albania, Bosnia, Bulgaria, Croatia, Greece, Romania, and Serbia; here you work with accomplished musicians, most of them from Eastern Europe, on such regional instruments as the *kaval* (reed flute), *tupan* (drum), *gaida* (Bulgarian bagpipes), and tambura (a stringed instrument resembling the lute). Other notable programs focus on English country dance and song, Cajun and Creole music and dance, and swing.

Classes are open to students of all levels, except the Scottish dance week, which is for the intermediate to the advanced. There are usually two or three workshops per week, and the total number of students attending at a time is about 300. The student-to-teacher ratio varies from 10:1 to 15:1. Everyone's urged to bring their own instrument.

You are generally in class from 8 to 6, with an hour for lunch. Instruction is informal but informative. No one is pressured to learn in the casual and social atmosphere of group instruction. Private lessons are not offered formally, but if there is enough free time, you can set up individual instruction with your teacher. (The fee for this varies by the instructor.)

After classes are over each day, there's dinner and free time until 8, when there's a dance, focused on the theme of the week. Finally, at midnight, the chef sets out a huge buffet, and a big bonfire is lit, around which students and instructors have a jam session. On some nights, instructors stage a performance instead.

Buffalo Gap does indeed feel like the summer camp it once was. You sleep bunkhouse-style, eight per cabin, with separate quarters and bathrooms for men and women. In your free time, you can hike, fish, go horseback riding, or swim in the camp lake. However, there's plenty that also makes Buffalo Gap a vacation place for adults. Meals, served in the main lodge, are fairly sophisticated, themed in keeping with the program of the moment—Eastern European fare during the Balkan workshop, Cajun food during the bayou week, shepherd's pie during the English program, and so forth. Two of the classrooms are 7,000- and 10,000-square-foot dance halls with superlative sound systems. If you don't feel like hiking or fishing, you can avail yourself of the camp's licensed massage therapist or the European-style sauna and beach, where clothing is optional. The camp has stocked refrigerators, governed by the honor system; take out a drink, place a check by your name on a list, and pay up at the end of the week. *Buffalo Gap Camp for the Cultural Arts, Box 291, Capon Bridge, WV 26711, tel. 304/856–3309 or 301/585–9247, fax 304/856–3466. Late May–late Sept.: 3–7 days, complete package $120–$250. Sign up 3 months in advance.*

THE SOUTH

■**NORTH CAROLINA**■ **The Swannanoa Gathering.** This organization, founded in 1992, focuses on traditional folk music during five separate seven-day programs. Sessions are held in July and August on the campus of Warren Wilson College, which borders 600 acres of forested mountains, 15 minutes from the town of Asheville. Most courses incorporate instrumental and vocal instruction at beginning to advanced levels and deal with a particular musical heritage or style. Instructors come from around the world and are experts in their fields; many of them teach, perform, and record regularly. Classes are limited to 20 students per teacher, and no more than 100 students are enrolled each week.

Celtic Week brings together traditional Scottish and Irish music and folklore with classes in such instruments as fiddle, *bodhrán* (a large, tambourine-like drum), bouzouki, tin whistle, *uilleann* pipes (similar to bagpipes, but air is pumped with the elbow instead of blown), accordion, concertina, harp, guitar, and dulcimer. You can also study traditional Irish songwriting, Scottish folklore and folk song, and Scottish folk dancing.

The gathering's most popular program, the Old-Time Music and Dance Week, investigates the music, singing, dance, and storytelling of the southern Appalachians via more than two dozen courses. Singers can study southern Appalachian singing, unaccompanied singing, and shaped-note spirituals, for example. Instrumentalists can sign up for everything from beginning, intermediate, and advanced old-time fiddle, guitar, banjo, and string band to Appalachian longbow fiddle, mandolin, Autoharp, hammered and mountain dulcimer, bass, and more. Clogging, buck dancing, and square and contra dancing are also on the schedule. A children's program, which runs concurrently and is open to youngsters ages 6 to 12, comprises classes in storytelling, music and dance, and crafts ($50 per child).

Mountain Dulcimer Week gives you the chance to learn from some of the top players from around the country. To expose you to several playing styles, each day's afternoon session has a different teacher.

Blues Week is devoted to the music of such stylistic regions as Mississippi's Delta and North Carolina's Piedmont; you can study and perform slide and gospel guitar, harmonica, torch songs, and blues vocals, and explore songwriting and the gospel roots of the blues.

During Contemporary Folk Week, a series of workshops aimed at folk performers, there are classes in songwriting, performance, singing, and sound and recording. The faculty critiques your work, coaches you on how to become a more confident performer, stages panel discussions on business matters, shares their knowledge of the recording industry, and provides tips on getting your music published.

Most students sign up for one or two courses in the program they're attending. Things get going on Sunday with supper, an orientation session, and socializing. From Monday through Friday, you spend most of your mornings and afternoons in classes, which last 45 to 90 minutes each. You may also meet with your instructor in the evening for performance critiques, rehearsals, or jam sessions. Other evenings bring concerts by instructors, dances, and open mike nights, followed by jam sessions. You're expected to bring your own instrument, although some are available for rent.

To foster a sense of community, the program's directors encourage students to lodge on campus in the dorms' double rooms; singles are not available. (The nearest alternative accommodations are 15 minutes away in Asheville.) Meals are served buffet-style in the college student center.

During free time, you can use the campus gym, aquatic center, tennis courts, and nature trails; explore its working farm; and make a kayak run on Swannanoa River. Off campus, you may visit the Biltmore Estate (*see* Garden Tours), Pisgah National Forest, Great Smoky Mountains National Park, and other area attractions. *The Swannanoa Gathering, Warren Wilson College, Box 9000, Asheville, NC 28815, tel. 704/298–3325, ext. 426., fax 704/299–3326. Mid-July–early*

Aug.: 7 days, tuition $245, housing $165. Sign up 4 months in advance.

THE MIDWEST

INDIANA **Indiana University School of Music.** The 1,860-acre campus of Indiana University is located in lively, sprawling Bloomington (pop. 80,000), in the hilly southern half of the state. Its School of Music has long been considered one of the country's best and is especially famous for its opera and vocal program. From June through August, it opens its doors to students, teachers, advanced amateurs, and professionals for intensive four- to 12-day workshops devoted to such topics as solo piano literature, chamber music, early music and opera performance, natural horn, fortepiano, recorder, and violin. The early music performance, natural horn, and fortepiano workshops run simultaneously to allow students in all three classes to work together. Three 3-day opera master classes are held consecutively, so you can elect to stay for more than one of them to expose yourself to different teaching styles. If you play regularly with an ensemble, you can apply together for certain workshops.

Instructors include some of the most distinguished and most widely respected musicians and professors of music in the United States. In past years, pianist Menahem Pressler, early music specialist Thomas Binkley, forte pianist Bart van Oort, violist and string director Mimi Zweig, conductor and vocals director Joan Dornemann, singer and diction coach Nico Castel, vocals teacher Virginia Zeani, and natural horn and early music instructor Richard Seraphinoff joined the school's summer faculty.

Each day, you have about eight hours of master classes, lectures on music theory and technique, sessions to demonstrate and build on your repertoire, ensemble rehearsals, and/or private lessons (for no additional charge). Most classes meet all day, and there may be mandatory performances to attend at night. Each class contains approximately 20 performing students as well as auditors, who may attend for a reduced fee. Some courses require prospective students to submit audition tapes or a list of repertoire they expect to perform. The university has a few instruments to lend.

Indiana University's School of Music complex encompasses four buildings with more than 110 offices and studios; 260 practice rooms, including 80 soundproofed rooms in a separate practice building; a recital hall; and a huge library with more than 380,000 books, scores, and periodicals as well as some 160,000 recordings. At the state-of-the art, 1,500-seat Musical Arts Center, you attend musical performances, many of them part of the university summer concert series, in which faculty members perform.

Although you may want to lodge in a hotel—a good option for couples and families—individuals find it most convenient to stay in one of the university dorms, which cost $27 a night for a single. (For families, a space might be made in family housing on campus by arrangement.) You can sign up for the meal plan, which allows you to eat breakfast, lunch, and dinner in the dorm's cafeteria. Or you can eat in off-campus restaurants—everything from fast-food chains to one-of-a-kind vegetarian spots.

During free time, you can visit the university art museum or use the campus billiards room, bowling lanes, running tracks, indoor and outdoor pools, golf course, or tennis, squash, racquetball, and basketball courts. *Indiana University School of Music, Office of Special Programs, Merrill Hall 121, Bloomington, IN 47405–2200, tel. 812/855–6025, fax 812/855–4936. Mid-June–mid-Aug.: 4–12 days, tuition $200–$600, housing $108–$324. Housing price does not include meals ($16 a day for cafeteria meal ticket); sign up 6 months in advance.*

KANSAS **Great Plains Jazz Camp.** This six-day June program, established in 1978, is an ideal place to get some performance and improvisation experience. You're surrounded by jazz in many different styles, ranging from bebop to fusion, and most of your time is spent playing and interacting with others with a passion for jazz. The teachers are leaders in their field, several of them professional musicians who have performed with premier jazz bands. Master classes are offered in saxophone, trumpet, trombone, guitar, bass, drums, and piano, as well as a course in jazz history.

On Sunday night, after an audition, you're assigned to a jazz combo of between five and eight musicians, based on your improvisational skills, and to one of four or five big bands of about 20 players each. From Monday through Thursday, you practice with your combo for two and a half hours and with your big band for two hours, both times under the guidance of an instructor. Then, between 2 and 3:30, there are master classes dealing with each instrument's basics, complexities, and techniques and information about its past and present masters. Class size varies, depending on the number of participants on a particular instrument when you attend. All of this occupies you between 8:30 and 3:30. After that, your time is free to practice, jam, and work in the camp's computerized MIDI (musical instrument digital interface) system, which allows you to compose a piece, score it to as many instruments as you want, and play it back right away—without having to round up six or seven other players to perform it. This is also the time that students rendezvous for private time with instructors who are willing to share their expertise with students who go to the trouble to seek it out. In the evening there are faculty concerts. Although most of the 78 to 85 campers who sign up every year are high school and college students, participants range in age from 12 to 67, and the program is open to students of all levels.

The site is 200-acre Emporia State University, located in the town of Emporia (pop. 25,000), surrounded by prairie and historic ranches in the Flint Hills, 50 miles east of Topeka and 100 miles west of Kansas City. You stay in modern, air-conditioned dorms in standard single or double rooms; there are chain motels and bed-and-breakfasts in town. All meals are served cafeteria-style in the student union cafeteria, which overlooks the campus lake, and the fare is strictly institutional. Alternative choices include the comfortable faculty restaurant and various local eateries. You have access to the campus athletic facilities, including a pool, weight room, and racquetball courts. *Great Plains Jazz Camp, c/o Dr. James South, Emporia State University, Division of Music, Box 29, Emporia State University, 1200 Commercial, Emporia, KS 66801–5087, tel. 316/343–5431, fax 316/341–5073. Mid-June: 6 days, tuition $185, housing $100 ($135 for a single). Sign up 3 months in advance.*

MISSOURI **The Heartland Dulcimer Camp.** Instructors at this six-day July program, which was established by internationally known dulcimer expert Esther Kreek in 1993, have a high profile in the dulcimer world: Texan Linda Lowe Thompson and Virginian Madeline MacNeil contribute regularly to *Dulcimer Player News,* Janita Baker builds dulcimers and guitars, and all have taught at various workshops and universities around the country. To give students the greatest possible contact with teachers, Ms. Kreek abides by the philosophy that less is more and restricts admission to 75—five classes of 15 each. You can study hammered and mountain dulcimer, autoharp, and accompanying vocals. Although the program is open to players of all levels of ability, you do need your own instrument.

Most of each day is devoted to instruction. Morning sessions last two and a half hours. Beginners learn tuning, left- and right-hand techniques, chord and harmony positions, and how to play simple tunes. Intermediate and advanced classes cover such topics as group playing, solo improvisation, tuning variations, embellishing, and arranging and adapting. Subjects that aren't covered in the morning are considered during 90-minute afternoon classes, which are taught by other teachers to expose you to alternative playing styles. Afterward, you can practice or relax.

The small size of the program allows time for private, 15- to 30-minute afternoon help sessions for those who need it. The cost of these is included in your tuition. In the evening, concerts showcase the talents of students or instructors; there's also a get-acquainted dance.

The program takes place at a large Presbyterian conference and retreat center, built in 1989 on 316 rolling acres near the Missouri River, 20 miles from Kansas City. A youth camp is held concurrently on a portion of the grounds. Accommodations are in two home-style lodges, which are air-conditioned—welcome, since summer temperatures soar into the 90s—or, when those fill up, in a dorm-style building with fans. Usually two people share a room with bath, but a very limited number of singles are available on a first-come, first-served basis at no extra cost. Lasagna, baked ham, and other hearty fare are served on the premises. For still other culinary options, you can make the easy drive to Kansas City. You can also ride horses ($9 per hour), go swimming in a pool ($2.50 per 90 minutes), hike, or play volleyball or basketball. *Heartland Dulcimer Camp, c/o Esther Kreek, 1156 W. 103rd St., Kansas City, MO 64114, tel. 816/942–6233. Late July: 6 days, tuition $115, housing $165. Sign up 3 months in advance.*

NORTH DAKOTA **International Music Camp.** This June and July camp began in 1956 as an educational summer retreat for high school band and choir students. Today it is open to adults, too, and its two dozen classes cover art and dance as well as music at all levels. You can choose from seven separate seven-day music sessions that focus on piano, guitar, piping and drumming, band, jazz and stage band, orchestra, vibes and marimba, handbells, or choir and show choir. All programs follow a rigorous schedule with about 11 hours out of each day in ensemble rehearsals, classes in music theory and technique, repertoire reviews, private lessons (at an extra $7.50 per lesson), and master classes set up to improve your performance and instrumental techniques. The faculty, recruited mainly from area universities, is made up of experienced musicians and teachers; there are only about 12 students per class. All instruction culminates in student performances at the end of the week.

You're housed in double rooms in modern dormitories, one for men and another for women; one dorm is reserved for adults. No singles are available, and bathrooms are communal. Married couples are not allowed to stay together. A few cabins for four, furnished with bunk beds or cots to sleep two to a room, are an option during some weeks. Built in the 1940s, these cabins lack the modern amenities of the dorms, but they do have private baths and are quieter, since they're a mile away from the classrooms. You can also camp nearby, though there's no reduction in price for campers. Three cafeteria-style meals of typical institutional fare—meat and potatoes, burgers, pizza—are served daily.

The camp convenes at the 2,300-acre International Peace Garden, on the border of North Dakota and Manitoba, roughly the geographical center of North America. There's hiking, volleyball, soccer, and swimming in the area, but your schedule doesn't leave much time for it. Taps is played at 10:30 PM (and the younger students do tend to retire then); reveille is at 7 AM for all. *International Music Camp, 1725 11th St. SW, Minot, ND 58701, tel. and fax 701/838–8472; during June and July, Box 116A, Dunseith, ND 58329, tel. 701/263–4211, fax 701/263–4212. June–July: 7 days, complete package $180–$200. Sign up 4 months in advance.*

OHIO **Baroque Performance Institute (BPI).** From mid-June to early July, as part of its year-round schedule of high-quality classical music training, the prestigious Oberlin Conservatory of Music sponsors an intensive two-week event concentrating on Baroque music for voice, flauto traverso, recorder, oboe, bassoon, harpsichord, organ, fortepiano, violin, viola, cello, and treble, tenor, and bass viol. Students of all ages and skill levels may enroll; about 110 sign up annually. In addition to daily master classes, the program includes sessions that help refine performance skills, provide coaching for chamber music ensembles, and give the opportunity to play in a baroque orchestra. The program fills your time for about eight hours a day, plus optional lectures and concerts at night.

The faculty consists of 18 distinguished baroque specialists from around the country and the world. The four-member Oberlin Baroque Ensemble is also in residence during the program. Each summer, BPI also invites a guest artist; in 1994, Christopher Hogwood, director of the Academy of Ancient Music, conducted BPI students in a performance of Purcell's *Dido & Aeneas*.

In addition to classes, which are limited to 10 to 15 students, BPI schedules faculty concerts, student recitals, lectures, and other events. Private lessons are available ($40 per 45 minutes). You have access to the resources of the Oberlin Conservatory of Music, including its extensive library and its 40 studios for private lessons, 10 classrooms, 153 practice rooms, and two performance halls. Several baroque instruments are available for loan, and there is a large collection of harpsichords, organs, and fortepianos for student use.

The Oberlin Conservatory of Music is in the northeast part of the state 30 minutes from Cleveland's Hopkins International Airport and 40 minutes from downtown Cleveland. You can lodge in standard single or double rooms in a newly restored Victorian dorm across from the conservatory or in local houses off campus (BPI can provide a list of landlords). Most students choose to cook on their own, either in their off-campus home or the dorm's cooking facilities, or to eat at any of the varied restaurants in the surrounding blocks, from fast-food places and diners to fancy bistros. However, you may also purchase rather average meals at the campus cafeteria. Rural Oberlin is easy to get around on foot or on a bicycle. Other conservatory summer programs, which run for one to two weeks each, are in flute, piano, vocal performance and pedagogy, electronic and computer music, and stringed instrument restoration. *Baroque Performance Institute, Conservatory of Music, Oberlin College,*

Oberlin, OH 44074, tel. 216/775–8044, fax 216/775–8942. Mid-June–early July: tuition $315 for 7 days, $615 for 15, housing $85 a week ($115 for a single). Housing prices do not include meals ($19 a day for cafeteria meal ticket); sign up 1–2 months in advance.

THE ROCKIES

COLORADO **Mile High Jazz Camp.** Many of the 25 instructors at this six-day July program at the University of Colorado at Boulder are regulars in America's leading jazz ensembles. About 100 professional musicians, music teachers, and students from junior high school to college come from all over the world to study with them every year. If you want more experience playing with jazz combos and big bands, this is the place for you. It was founded in 1985 and is still under the direction of two noted jazz educators with considerable bandstand experience, Bob Montgomery and Dr. Willie L. Hill.

You can take classes, which are all small, in trumpet, trombone, guitar, piano, drums, bass, and alto, tenor, and baritone saxophone. (Bring your own instrument.) At the beginning of the week you audition, so your skill level can be determined. Then from Tuesday through Friday, you spend about five hours a day in jazz improvisation sessions, jazz combo and band rehearsals, and master classes. From late afternoon until dinner, you're free to practice or relax. In the evening, there are faculty concerts. The week ends on Saturday with five and a half hours of student performances.

Students stay in standard double rooms in a dorm on the 600-acre campus, which is at the base of the Rocky Mountains. Three meals a day in the dorm's cafeteria are included. You have access to the College of Music's state-of-the-art facilities, which consist of a two-building complex encompassing 84 practice rooms and four performance spaces. Boulder, a short drive from Denver, is a cosmopolitan college town with a number of good restaurants and plenty of cultural activity. The mountains are nearby, and there's lots of hiking, fishing, and other outdoor activities. *Mile High Jazz Camp, c/o Dr. Willie Hill, University of Colorado at Boulder, College of Music, Campus Box 301, Boulder, CO 80309–0301, tel. 303/492–6352, fax 303/492–5619. Mid-July: 6 days, tuition $205, housing $145. Sign up 1 month in advance.*

IDAHO **Schweitzer Institute of Music.** Part of the Festival of Sandpoint, a summer-long outdoor music festival held in the northern Idaho mountain resort of Sandpoint, this three-week July and August program attracts professional musicians who come to study musical masterpieces in an environment emphasizing art over commerce. Although the four courses—conducting, composition, chamber music, and jazz—do not interact, a few group performances and many social occasions enable you to meet students in other programs and expose yourself to a variety of musical disciplines.

The institute was founded in 1985 by composer and conductor Gunther Schuller, the former director of the Berkshire Music Institute at Tanglewood. Winner of the 1994 Pulitzer Prize for Music Literature, he has some 50 years of experience as a conductor, composer, performer, educator, and music journalist. Instructors are experienced teachers and professional musicians who have received numerous awards in recognition of their work. In a recent year, they included Donald Erb, composition; Young-Nam Kim, chamber music and violin; Norman Paulu, strings (especially violin); Harvey Phillips, brass (tuba specialist); Allan Vogel, woodwinds; Joe Lovano, jazz and tenor sax; Kenny Werner, jazz and piano; Edwin Schuller, jazz and bass; and Dan Morgenstern, jazz history.

You are typically in class six hours a day, from 9 to noon and 2 to 5 for all but jazz students, who, because of late-night performances, attend from 2 to 5 and 7 to 10 PM. Class time may be used for rehearsals or outreach programs.

The conducting program, which is limited to 25 participants ages 18 to 32, is taught by Schuller himself. There are intensive seminars plus critiques of conductors' work, rehearsals, and performances. At the end of the program, up to five students share the baton in a concert.

The jazz program, which is limited to 25 students with four instructors, concentrates on techniques of jazz performance but also exposes you to jazz history and criticism. You practice improvising during performances and play both established works and new material by institute students and faculty.

The chamber music program aims to broaden your performance experience. Established ensembles are encouraged to apply as groups, and 40 students are accepted. Here, too, you study and practice classics and new compositions. The four instructors provide intensive coaching sessions and master classes; there's also plenty of rehearsal time.

The composition program, which accepts only six students, includes daily private lessons and seminars with a single composer, plus time to participate in other programs. You work in secluded studios with pianos (two composers per piano). Student works get a performance during the Festival of Sandpoint.

There isn't much leisure time, because even when you aren't in class or rehearsing, you may be playing at a local restaurant for an hour or two or attending a mandatory concert. Part of the program involves observing performances of the Spokane Symphony Orchestra, as well as of leading jazz, blues, country, pop, and rock musicians. Weekends are a bit less busy, and you may want to take advantage of hiking trails; bike rentals; and Lake Pend Oreille, the second-largest freshwater lake west of the Mississippi.

Each year about 75 to 100 students attend the Schweitzer Institute's programs, which run concurrently. You're expected to submit a résumé and an audition tape with your application; applicants to the conducting program must furnish a videotape, and composers must submit a written score. You are encouraged to send letters of recommendation.

The program venue is beautiful Schweitzer Mountain Ski Resort, which overlooks Lake Pend Oreille at 6,000 feet in the Rocky Mountains. Along with a cluster of condos, the complex has a hotel, where you stay in double rooms, though some singles are available (at an extra cost) to the first who request them. Three cafeteria-style meals are served daily, and plans for restaurant-catered meals are under way. Pianos and other large instruments are provided, but smaller instruments should be brought with you. *Schweitzer Institute of Music, Box 695, Sandpoint, ID 83864, tel. 208/265-4554, fax 208/263-6858. Late July–mid-Aug.: 21–24 days, complete package $1,200–$1,500 ($5 a meal and $10 a night at the resort). Sign up 4 months in advance.*

WYOMING **Yellowstone Jazz Camps.** This July camp in the Absaroka Range of the Rockies, not far from Yellowstone National Park, consists of two separate six-day workshops, one devoted to vocal jazz and the other to bass, drums, saxophone, trumpet, piano, guitar, and trombone. Both are open to adults as well as high school and college students at all skill levels. Up to 55 students and 11 or so faculty members attend the instrumental jazz week, 40 students and 8 instructors at the vocal week. Teachers have university-teaching or performance experience.

Both the instrumental and vocal weeks fill your time from 8:30 to 5 every day. The instrumental week starts with an audition and theory test, after which you're placed in a big band of 15 to 17 musicians and a combo of five to seven. Most mornings begin with sessions on music theory and improvisation and rehearsals of the various big bands and combos. Afternoons, faculty members give master classes and private lessons ($10 extra per 30 minutes). You're expected to bring your own instrument.

During the vocal week, you spend private time working with an instructor on an arrangement that you will perform solo, with a professional rhythm section, at the student concert. You also practice with a large group of eight to 12 and a smaller group of five to eight singers; you perform with both at a final concert in Cody. There are also listening classes that train your ear to hear different jazz styles and teach you about the important singers in various jazz traditions.

Evenings find students and instructors taking part in concerts, jam sessions, and clinics, which consist of impromptu discussions about influences, theory, styles, and personal experiences. Both weeks prepare you to perform at a Friday afternoon concert at the Yellowstone Jazz Festival, held in nearby Cody.

The venue, Northwest College's remote mountain retreat, is at an elevation of 8,000 feet and is surrounded by woods and meadows. A short walk yields a great view of Yellowstone. The main lodge has large rehearsal rooms, the camp dining room, a main room with a fireplace, and communal bathing facilities. Adjoining this building are 12 modern cabins, each of which sleeps six (in one room) and is heated by a wood stove. If you'd prefer more privacy, you can pitch your tent or park your RV on-site. Meals are prepared by a family who live in a nearby cottage and have been cooking at the camp ever since the program began back in 1987. The family-style meals typically include pancakes or waffles and sausage for breakfast, soup and sandwiches for lunch, and hamburgers or chicken and baked potatoes for dinner.

In their brief free time, most students focus on outdoor recreation: fishing, riding, hiking, ping-pong, volleyball, horseshoes, softball, and the like. *Yellowstone Jazz Camp, c/o Neil Hansen, Northwest College, 231 W. 6th St., Powell, WY 82435, tel. 307/754-6307 or 800/442-2946 in WY and MT, fax 307/754-6700. Mid-July: 6 days, tuition*

$265, housing $85. Sign up 5 months in advance.

THE WEST COAST

WASHINGTON **Centrum Music Workshops.** Centrum, a nonprofit center for the arts and creative education, sponsors three exceptional weeklong summer music programs on the grounds of 445-acre Fort Worden State Park. The park is at the tip of the Olympic Peninsula, 2 miles from downtown Port Townsend (pop. 7,000), a town full of restored Victorian-style buildings, on the banks of Puget Sound.

The seven-day mid-June Port Townsend Blues Workshop is designed for students of traditional acoustic blues. The faculty includes masters of America's blues traditions, several of them recipients of the National Endowment for the Arts' National Heritage Fellowship, awarded to artists who contribute to the preservation of the country's cultural vitality. Instructors from past years include under fiddler Howard Armstrong, pianist Maureen Del Grosso, harmonica players Mark Graham or Phil Wiggins, or guitarists John Dee Holeman, John Jackson, Jack Owens, or Mary Flower. You come into close contact with these instructors while working on technical musicianship. Instruction is offered in guitar, harmonica, vocals, fiddle, and mandolin.

In a typical year, slightly more than 100 students are taught by a dozen or so instructors, some of whom are part of groups or combos that teach collaboratively. Classes of varying sizes are open to musicians at all levels; beginning guitarists are expected to have a rudimentary knowledge of the instrument.

During the week, there are 1¼-hour classes in morning and afternoon sessions. In the morning, you usually attend two group classes, where the emphasis is on playing a particular instrument as you learn new techniques and songs. Each day you build upon skills you've learned the day before. Afternoon classes are often more spontaneous. They are taught by two or more faculty members who may not have played together before and may or may not have even decided exactly what to teach. Instead they collaborate on and improvise a lesson as they go. Evenings, there are jam sessions, dances, parties, films, and student concerts. The workshop culminates at the Port Townsend Blues Festival with three faculty concerts.

The eight-day Festival of American Fiddle Tunes workshop is also taught by expert musicians from around the United States: Recent instructors have included fiddlers Charlie Acuff and Kenny Baker, banjo players Carroll Best and Walt Koren, and accordionist Aldus Roger. The workshop—open not only to fiddlers but also to pianists, accordionists, and banjo and mandolin players at all levels of experience—exposes you to a variety of regional fiddling styles. Nearly 300 students were taught by 23 instructors in a recent year, and, as for the blues workshop, some of these "instructors" are groups or duos. Also as in the blues workshop, classes last an hour and 15 minutes and vary in size. In the morning, you take two group lessons that focus on teaching new tunes and introducing Cajun, bluegrass, old-time country, and French-Canadian fiddling. Afternoons are spent in tutorials in technique for beginners and intermediates and rehearsals of the several faculty-led bands, which perform at a Friday night dance and a Saturday morning concert. On other evenings, you can jam with fellow students and faculty members, attend faculty concerts, and dance to your heart's content.

The intensive eight-day Bud Shank Jazz Workshop, led by alto saxophonist Bud Shank, is one of the nation's premier summer workshops. This is due to the artistic stature of the dozen-odd faculty, which recently included trumpeter Bobby Shew, pianists Hal Galper and George Cables, vocalists Jay Clayton and Sheila Jordan, baritone saxophonist Bill Ramsay, tenor saxophonist Don Lanphere, drummer Jeff Hamilton, guitarist John Stowall, and jazz historian Bob Ricci. Equally noteworthy is the caliber of the program's students—some 200 amateur, collegiate, and professional trumpeters, trombonists, vocalists, pianists, bassists, guitarists, drummers, and baritone, tenor, and alto saxophonists between the ages of 15 to 70 from around the world. The program is geared to players with intermediate to advanced skills, and you're expected to have a basic technical command of your instrument as well as improvisation experience or a basic knowledge of music theory. With your application, you're required to submit a résumé detailing your musical education and performance background. Applicants under 18 must also submit an audition tape.

The workshop has you making music all week long. On the Sunday before classes begin, an audition puts you in one of several five- to eight-player combos based on your skill. Then, from Monday through Friday, you start the day with a 90-minute combo rehearsal and an hour-long class in music theory and improvisation. In the afternoon, there are one-hour master classes, in lecture and demonstration format, in which you are instructed on a particular instrument or style of vocals, as well as further 90-minute combo rehearsals and 45-minute faculty lectures and demonstrations followed by informal faculty concerts. Evenings bring hour-long arranging or jazz history classes and big-band rehearsals. The week ends with one of the West Coast's most prominent music festivals, Jazz Port Townsend, which showcases the talents of workshop faculty and visiting artists.

During these and other Centrum music programs, you stay on the Fort Worden park grounds in single or double dormitory rooms, some of which have an ocean view. Rooms are assigned in order of registration, so if you sign up late, you may not get a view or a single (which here costs the same as a double). You can opt for two or three meals a day, mostly typical cafeteria fare, in Fort Worden's typical cafeteria. There are also motels, hotels, inns and bed-and-breakfasts, and campgrounds in the area.

Fort Worden State Park has views of the San Juan Islands and two mountain ranges as well as saltwater beaches, ponds, wooded hills with trails, and old military fortifications. Nearby there's also hiking, sailing, kayaking, tennis, scuba-diving, and bicycling; 40 miles away is Olympic National Park. In addition, Port Townsend is full of restaurants, galleries, and crafts shops. *Centrum, Box 1158, Port Townsend, WA 98368, tel. 206/385–3102 or 800/733–3608, fax 206/385–2470. Mid-June, early July, late July: 7–8 days, tuition $225–$315, housing $150–$180 with 2 meals daily or $180–$215 with 3. Sign up 4 months in advance.*

SOURCES

ORGANIZATIONS The well-established **International Association of Jazz Educators** (Box 724, Manhattan, KS 66502, tel. 913/776–8744) is devoted to career training for both jazz educators and professional performers and, among other activities, offers a wealth of training programs; it also publishes the *Jazz Educators Journal.*

PERIODICALS For jazz programs, the *Jazz Educators Journal* is a prime source of information on activities sponsored by the association and other groups and has comprehensive listings of camps, clinics, summer programs, and the like in addition to its wide range of informative articles. Similar material and summer programs listings can be found in *The Instrumentalist* (200 Northfield Rd., Northfield, IL 60093, tel. 708/446–5000). The long-established magazine *downbeat* (180 Park Ave., Elmhurst, IL 60126, tel. 708/941–2030) is also a good place to look.

The best source of information on folk and ethnic music programs is the magazine *Sing Out!* (125 E. 3rd St., Bethlehem, PA 18015, tel. 610/865–5366). *Dirty Linen* (Box 66600, Baltimore, MD 21239, tel. 410/583–7973) is another fine periodical in the field.

For classical music programs, consult *Strings* magazine (Box 767, San Anselmo, CA 94979, tel. 415/485–6946), especially its annual Resource Guide. Although it concentrates on the violin and viola, it offers informed access to the classical world in general. The same applies to *Piano & Keyboard* (Box 767, San Anselmo, CA 94979, tel. 415/485–6946). Information on classical music camps and programs is also available in *The Instrumentalist* (*see above*).

ALSO SEE If melodies and harmonies are your passion, only a music camp will do. But there are other ways to express your creativity: See the chapters on Arts and Crafts Workshops, Painting Workshops, Photography Workshops and Tours, and Writing Conferences and Workshops.

Nature Camps

Melanie Roth

ature camps take place in some of America's most beautiful locations: the woods of New England, Death Valley, the Rocky Mountains, and Big Bend, Yellowstone, and Yosemite national parks. These are grown-up versions of summer camp: You spend a week camping out or sharing a cabin, eating cafeteria food or campfire cuisine, and turning in early after a full day of outdoor explorations. But no one sends you to make key chains in the arts and crafts tent or to boring archery classes. Instead you spend all your time learning about nature.

At nature camps you learn by doing fieldwork, firsthand observation and examination of your subject. You learn about a stream by wading in, taking a water sample, and examining the plants and wildlife you find. A visit to a mist net, where birds are caught and banded for tracking, provides a lesson on migration. Most camps take an ecological approach to educating you about the area, which means you learn how geology, botany, animals, birds, insects, and weather patterns interrelate. At some camps you may concentrate on one subject, wildflowers or grizzly bears, but you'll probably learn how that subject fits into the bigger ecological picture. For instance, while studying elk you might learn how a mild winter results in a higher elk population in the spring, which in turn causes a decrease in the population of the plants they eat and causes the bears who usually feed on the elk that die in the winter to wander far from their normal territory looking for food (whew!). You learn how people fit into the ecosystem and how we can have a positive effect on the environment. You may learn about local endangered species concerns or how to petition your government representative to help pass a conservation bill.

At most nature camps you spend the whole day hiking, from eight or nine in the morning until four or five in the afternoon. Other camps have you bicycling, canoeing, diving, or skiing. The hiking isn't usually strenuous; you proceed slowly, observing your surroundings and stopping often as your instructor tells you about what you see. A few camps have rough terrain or high altitudes that demand a higher level of physical fitness, and a few offer van or bus transportation.

Itineraries are flexible, because you can only learn about what you encounter, and wildlife doesn't adhere to our schedules. You could start out to look for a red squirrel nest and spend an hour watching wasps building a nest. On trips that cover a range of subjects, there is always something to slow down and take a look at. You learn to identify plants, examine the layers of rock in gorges, bird-watch, and search for animal tracks. If the camp is focused on a particular animal, be prepared to spend some time waiting for your subject to appear.

Although writer Melanie Roth loves Manhattan, living there has taught her to truly appreciate her escapes to areas of natural beauty.

Camp instructors are naturalists, experts in the subject matter and geographical area of the camp. They are often college professors or National Park Service employees. Groups are kept small, usually between 8 and 20 people, to minimize the impact on the environment and to make them manageable by one or two instructors.

In addition to fieldwork, some camps include a little time in a classroom or laboratory. You may hear a background lecture on migration before you visit a mist net, or see a slide show that gives examples of bear tracks so you know what to look for in the woods. In the lab, you relearn such high school lessons as how to focus a microscope, then use your skills to examine pond water for microscopic organisms or the chlorophyll-containing plant cells that perform photosynthesis.

Accommodations at nature camps range from tent sites with no electricity or water (you bring your own equipment) to air-conditioned dorm rooms; shared bathrooms are the norm. What you eat ranges from bring-your-own-food-and-camp-stove to basic cafeteria fare or family-style meals. Of course there are camps with exceptions in both areas, but they cost more. The basic dining and lodging options, coupled with the fact that many of the camp operators—National Audubon Society, National Wildlife Federation, Yellowstone Institute, etc.—are nonprofit organizations, make nature camps a very affordable vacation. If you're willing to camp and bring your own food, you can get a tent site and a week of instruction for under $200!

A few camps offer programs for children, but for the most part these trips are for adults. The slow pace and long periods of observation aren't suited for young attention spans. Participants range in age from 18 to 80. Most operators report that over 50% of participants are between the ages of 35 and 45, and that women outnumber men. There are usually some college students at each program, especially at camps that can be attended for course credit.

CHOOSING THE RIGHT CAMP

The following questions are important to ask when deciding which nature camp is right for you.

What are the instructors' qualifications? Remember that most of what you're paying for is instruction. Without a good teacher, you may as well be camping out and hiking on your own. Most of the instructors at the programs listed in this chapter are college professors, well-known researchers in a field of nature study, or veteran park guides.

What is the focus of the camp? Some camps focus on one topic—geology or wildflowers, for example. Others study all of the elements of a particular area's ecosystem.

How tough are the hikes? Find out if the terrain will be rough, high altitudes may be a problem, or long distances are covered each day.

What is the food like? Partial meal plans or no meal plan at all are not uncommon. At the camps that offer meals, the food is usually standard hot and cold cafeteria fare or basics like macaroni and cheese and hamburgers served family style in a dining hall. There are a few camps that provide meals in a hotel restaurant or offer more of a selection at the cafeteria; their prices are proportionally higher. Vegetarian diets can usually be accommodated; ask about any other special needs. At camps without meal plans, there may be kitchen facilities. Find out if these include cooking and eating utensils, storage space, and refrigerator space. Also ask about nearby grocery stores and restaurants.

What are the accommodations like? The types of accommodations included in the cost of nature camps vary greatly, so make sure you find out exactly what you're getting. There are rarely private rooms, and shared rooms may be shared by more than two people. Rustic cabins may have no electricity or running water. If a tent site is provided, find out if you are responsible for all your own camping equipment. Often you must bring your own sleeping bag or linens and your own towels. The bathroom set-up also varies. You'll probably be sharing a bathroom; find out how many people you'll be sharing with. Hot showers, in fact any showers at all, are not a given, especially at park campgrounds. If bathrooms don't have showers, ask where the nearest facilities are.

What's the cost and what's included? The instruction you receive and transportation to any sites you do not hike to are always included in the price of the camp. Not included is transportation to and from the camp itself. The type of accommodations at nature camps ranges from a tent site to a room at a lodge, so make sure you know exactly what you're getting (*see above*). There may be a partial meal plan or no meal plan at all (*see above*). If meals are not included, factor in what it will cost you to bring your own food or eat in local restaurants.

Is laundry service available? It's probably not, but if it is it could save you a suitcase.

How long has the company been in business? The longer the operator has been in business, the more smoothly the camp is likely to run.

Do you have references from past guests?

How far in advance do I need to sign up?

MAJOR PLAYERS

CORNELL'S ADULT UNIVERSITY Among the 40 or so courses offered each summer by Cornell's Adult University (CAU) are several five- to seven-day ecology workshops. These are like mini college courses: You work with professors, cover a lot of material, live in dormitories, and eat cafeteria food. Tuition is pricey, from $445 to $1,500. This chapter includes programs at Cornell's main campus in Ithaca, New York, and the Shoals Marine Laboratory in Appledore, Maine, but there are often CAU ecology programs in other areas of the country, too. All workshops have a busy schedule. Lectures and lab work are combined with a lot of time in the field—on hikes, bird walks, and field trips. Leaders are

experts in their field of study, most of them Cornell professors. Up to 300 people attend the summer programs at the main campus each week (20 each week at the Shoals campus), but there are never more than 15 students in each workshop.

At the 740-acre Ithaca campus, you study the ecology of the area's forests, gorges, farm fields, and lakes. Lodging in the Mary Donlon Residence Hall is included in the cost of courses here. You share a room with a fellow student, and bathrooms are down the hall. For an additional charge, you can choose a dorm with air-conditioned double rooms and private bathrooms, or opt for a nearby hotel that offers a package rate to participants. Meals in Ithaca are served in Robert Purcell Union; you can get basic hot and cold cafeteria food, as well as burgers and grilled cheese sandwiches. There's also a make-your-own sandwich bar.

The Shoals Marine Laboratory, on 90-acre Appledore Island in Maine, is an undergraduate teaching station for the university. The island is in the migration routes of both humpback whales and several species of birds, so you can study the interrelationships of these creatures and their water and land environments. Accommodations are in three 10-room ranch houses. Each room has two single beds with drawers under them and desks that are built into the walls. There are men's and women's toilet facilities in each cabin, but showers are in the common building, where the cafeteria-style meals are served.

A terrific youth program, for kids ages 3 to 16, is part of courses at the main campus. While parents attend classes, a staff of more than 30 instructors leads up to 120 youngsters through workshops and activities, including windsurfing, watercolor painting, and creative cooking. Families meet in the cafeteria for lunch and dinner. Small children sleep in rooms adjacent to their parents, while teens stay in a separate wing of Mary Donlon Hall with live-in counselors (Cornell's Adult University, 626 Thurston Ave., Ithaca, NY 14850, tel. 607/255–6260).

·

NATIONAL AUDUBON SOCIETY The National Audubon Society, founded in 1905, has been running 6- to 11-day adult summer camps since 1944. The camps combine the exploration of a specific wilderness area with lessons in political activism. The Audubon Society wants you to leave with a deeper appreciation for the environment and the motivation to write your government representatives about conservation issues, from clean air to endangered species protection.

Whether you go to camp in Maine, Minnesota, Arizona, Wyoming, or one of the many other Audubon destinations, you spend almost all of your time, from 8:30 AM to 5 PM, outside, observing and learning about the local environment—its ecology, geology, marine life, birds, mammals, plants, insects, and weather. Most camps have about 40 students and eight instructors, so several activity choices are offered for each morning and afternoon session. One group may cover half a mile, stopping frequently to dissect wildflowers, while another group hikes 3 miles, to the top of a nearby peak. Program leaders are college or university professors or naturalists.

Accommodations at Audubon camps vary from simple cabins to historic lodges and typical motels, but most are double rooms, often with shared baths. Most camps have a central dining hall where meals are served buffet or family style. Pasta, pizza, quiche, meatloaf, vegetable lasagna and other simple dishes make up the menu, and vegetarian options are usually available. Different programs provide a varying number of meals. Audubon camps are limited to participants 18 years and older, and cost from $495 to $1,075 (Audubon Ecology Camps & Workshops, National Audubon Society, 613 Riversville Rd., Greenwich, CT 06831, tel. 203/869–2017).

NATIONAL WILDLIFE FEDERATION It's hard to spend a week in one of the most beautiful, unspoiled areas of the United States without being inspired to take part in its preservation. That's what the National Wildlife Federation (NWF) is banking on with its Conservation Summits. Four different summits annually attract an average of 400 people each to such places as the Big Island of Hawaii, the Colorado Rockies, the Canyonlands of Utah, and the White Mountains of New Hampshire. A combination of nature walks, field trips, and classes are led by a staff of expert naturalists, many of them university professors and National Park Service workers. They teach about the ecology, natural history, cultural history, and particular conservation issues of each summit area, and they also touch on global environmental concerns and the ways that individuals can have a positive impact on the environment.

Each summit has a daytime youth program with field trips and classes for kids ages three and up. Teen groups may do service projects, such as clearing trails and building fire rings. Evening activities, from square dances to slide shows, bring everyone at the summit together.

Accommodations vary with location and may be in the dorm rooms of a host college or university or in the private rooms of an elegant resort. The total cost of attendance, including room, board, tuition, and the $16 NWF annual membership fee, can range from $500 to over $900 per adult (National Wildlife Federation, 1400 16th St., NW, Washington, D.C. 20036, tel. 703/790–4265 or 800/245–5484).

SIERRA CLUB Hosting wilderness excursions that stimulate interest in the environment and provide memorable group experiences has been an intent of the Sierra Club since it was founded in 1901. Today, club members can choose from more than 350 trips each year, in places all across the United States and in many foreign countries. There are bicycling, backpacking, canoeing, skiing, kayaking, and volunteering trips, and each type of trip is offered for different ability levels.

Like the National Wildlife Federation, the Sierra Club aims to teach you about wilderness preservation and environmental protection in a setting that demonstrates the need for them and inspires personal action. Because trip fees cover only the direct cost of the excursion and a portion of the administrative cost of trip organization, costs are low. A one-week exploration within the contiguous 48 states ranges from $285 to $785, plus the $23 to $43 it costs to become a Sierra Club member. Prices vary due to the type of lodging and the number of staff members accompanying the trip.

Volunteer leaders are experts in the geographic area of their trip and the trip's central activity—biking or kayaking for instance. They also have previous experience as guides and have spent time as a Sierra Club trainee. On some trips a naturalist accompanies the leader to provide more in-depth lessons on flora and fauna. Group size is limited to 18. Accommodations for most trips are in tents, either in the wilderness or at campgrounds. A few programs have lodging in rustic cabins or lodges, usually with dorm-style accommodations and shared bathrooms. Participants pitch in with daily chores, including meal preparation. The food is simple, probably easily portable freeze-dried food and other packaged food, such as macaroni and cheese.

There are some programs designed specifically for families, but children under 18 traveling with an adult can sign up for any trip for which they meet physical fitness and experience requirements (Sierra Club Outings, 730 Polk St., San Francisco, CA 94109, tel. 415/923–5630).

YELLOWSTONE INSTITUTE The average Yellowstone tourist spends only seven hours to one and a half days in the park, but the Yellowstone Institute, a nonprofit organization established in 1976, encourages you to take a closer look. You can do this by participating in one of its 90 or so yearly field courses, which focus on the park's natural and cultural history.

Fieldwork forms the core of most courses, so minimal time is spent in the classroom. Groups of up to 15 to 20 people hike in different areas of the park. You may observe elk, bison, antelope, and other park mammals as well as geysers, mudpots, and hot springs—evidence of the park's volcanic history. The things you see serve as illustrations for lessons on the interrelationships of the park environment and its inhabitants. Group leaders are experts on the area and their course topic; many are professors at area universities or full-time park employees.

The programs in this chapter take place at the institute's headquarters in the Lamar Valley, in the northeast corner of the park. Food and lodging are not included in the program fee, which is only $40 to $45 a day, but for $8 a night you can stay in one of the 16 cabins. These sleep two to four and have no plumbing or electricity. A central building contains two classrooms, three bathrooms with showers, and a communal kitchen with refrigerators, a microwave, two stoves, cooking and eating utensils, and plenty of storage space for your food. Most of the institute's programs are designed for adults; unless you attend one of the family classes, it's best not to bring children (The Yellowstone Institute, Box 117, Yellowstone National Park, Wyoming 82190, tel. 307/344–2294).

YOSEMITE ASSOCIATION FIELD SEMINARS
Since its founding in 1924, the Yosemite Association has offered a growing number of one- to eight-day adult environmental education seminars. Some seminars, such as those on wildflower pollination, giant sequoias, butterflies, and bighorn sheep, cover a single specific topic, while others, including those on the park's ecology and natural history, have a much broader scope.

Almost all seminars consist entirely of day hikes through the park. When these hikes are on trails the groups range from eight to 20 participants, but when they are off-trail group size is limited to eight. This prevents damage to the environment and keeps the groups manageable by a single leader. Although the hikes are usually only 5 to 8 miles, the high altitudes and uneven terrain can make them physically demanding. Depending on the topic you choose, your leader may stop the group along the way to identify plants, examine geological features, or observe wildlife. All of the association's staff members are naturalists and experts in the geographical area and subject matter of their seminars.

The low price of Yosemite seminars—about $180 for five days—includes the cost of a tent site. You have to bring your own camping equipment, including a camp stove, and your own food. The campgrounds have bathrooms with cold running water but no showers; a nearby concessioner offers showers for a minimal fee. Don't count on staying in one of the park's lodges; they are usually reserved at least a year in advance.

The seminars in this chapter are based at the Tuolumne Meadows campground, where a campground host is on hand to answer questions and give directions to restaurants in the town of Lee Vining, a 30-minute drive away. If you don't want to camp, there are also a range of hotels in Lee Vining. Yosemite programs are open to participants 18 years and over (Yosemite Association, Box 230, El Portal, CA 95318, tel. 209/ 379–2646, fax 209/379–2486).

FAVORITE CAMPS

THE NORTHEAST

CONNECTICUT **Connecticut Ecology Workshop.** The National Audubon Society's 485-acre wildlife sanctuary in the New England woods of Greenwich, Connecticut, is the setting for this six-day workshop. You learn about forest and meadow habitats as you hike along the sanctuary's 15 miles of trails, and you explore intertidal zones, beaches, and salt marsh habitats on a field trip to Long Island Sound.

Each day your group of up to 30 participants is divided into four field groups for two half-day sessions. A deciduous forest, old field communities, freshwater communities, and a hemlock gorge are each explored in single sessions. To fill the rest of your time, you choose from a list of electives covering such topics as wildflower identifica-

tion, entomology, mushrooms, geology, and ornithology. You might spend the morning studying the wildflowers of the meadow and the afternoon observing meadow insects. Or you could spend a whole day walking in the forest, splitting your time between botany studies and watching some of the more than 100 species of birds in the sanctuary. Evening lectures, discussions, and slide shows highlight local and global conservation issues.

Accommodations are in double-occupancy rooms with twin beds and private bathrooms, in a lodge set in the forest. Hearty meals are served buffet style in a main dining hall, and a vegetarian option is always offered. This workshop is run seven times each summer. *Audubon Ecology Camps & Workshops, National Audubon Society, 613 Riversville Rd., Greenwich, CT 06831, tel. 203/869–2017. Early July–Mid-Aug.: 6 days, $495. Sign up 3 months in advance.*

MAINE **Coastal Ecology.** The National Audubon Society's Hog Island camp, off the coast of central Maine, has been a base for summer ecology programs since 1936. The spruce-fir forest, rocky shoreline, and intertidal and mudflat habitats of the 330-acre wildlife refuge are good places to study the interrelationships of plants, fungi, and animals with the water, soil, rocks, and air of their environment.

Each day at the camp is divided into morning and afternoon fieldwork sessions. Up to 40 people can participate, but they are broken up into four field groups led by instructors specializing in such topics as botany, marine life, and ornithology. Over the course of the six-day camp, you spend time at each of the different island habitats, observing everything from rock formations to harbor seals. You may spend the morning seining water from ponds and streams to study their plant and animal life through magnifying hand lenses. In the afternoon, a boat trip may take you to one of several offshore seabird nesting sites.

Audubon tries to teach you about the impact of humans on the ecosystems you visit and coaches you on how to protect global life-support systems by living more compatibly with your environment.

There's an environmental and natural history library and a marine lab with tanks, a herbarium, hundreds of study skins, and microscopes. One afternoon is left open for relaxation, hiking, swimming, volleyball, or use of the camp's learning facilities. Evening talks and workshops are given on topics such as environmental activism, colonial seabird research, astronomy, and marine ecosystems.

Accommodations are in three wood-frame buildings, two for women and one for both couples and single men. Rooms are double, with either a private or shared bath. All meals are included in the price for this camp and are served buffet or family style in a main dining hall. *Audubon Ecology Camps & Workshops, National Audubon Society, 613 Riversville Rd., Greenwich, CT 06831, tel. 203/869–2017. July: 6 days, $650. Sign up 3 months in advance.*

MAINE **Natural History of the Gulf of Maine.** Cornell University's Shoals Marine Laboratory on 90-acre Appledore Island is a rich and varied setting for ecological study: Shallow waters attract schools of feeding fish, the Atlantic Ocean off the coast here is the summer feeding ground of humpback whales, and the island is a fueling stop for a host of migratory birds. In this six-day workshop you learn about the area's ecology, including its historical significance and its role in the local economy.

The workshop is led by Richard Fischer, a professor emeritus of environmental education at Cornell, and the founder and former director of the Shoals Laboratory. There is a maximum of 15 students. This keeps the group manageable by one leader and makes sure you have plenty of opportunity to ask questions.

The daily routine begins around 9 AM, but if you can rouse yourself by 5, you can join Professor Fischer on his early morning bird walks, when he demonstrates how mist nets

are used to catch birds for banding. The island hosts more than 170 species of birds during the late summer and early fall migration season. After breakfast, you may hear a lecture on the migration of butterflies or the effects of water temperature on ocean ecology, spend some time in a laboratory learning how to focus a microscope, or work in the wet lab studying the life found in water samples.

Most days include a field trip to nearby seal and seabird colonies, rocky intertidal zones, or the continental shelf, where whales are often sighted. After dinner you attend another lecture. On some evenings, a researcher at the lab may come to share his or her findings or bring everyone outside to see a particularly interesting catch in one of the mist nets.

There's not much free time in the workshop schedule, but if you do find yourself with a spare moment, there are hiking and walking trails, a volleyball net, and a shallow tidal pool for swimming.

Accommodations are in dorm-style cabins with shared bathrooms. Showers are in the common building, along with the kitchen and dining room. Meals are cafeteria style, and special diet needs can be met with advance notice. There is no children's program at the Shoals campus, but teenagers are welcome when accompanied by an adult. *Cornell's Adult University, 626 Thurston Ave., Ithaca, NY 14850, tel. 607/255–6260. Late Aug.–early Sept.: 6 days, $775. Sign up 3 months in advance.*

NEW HAMPSHIRE **Landscape of the Northern Woods.** The Appalachian Mountain Club (AMC), founded in 1876, works with the University of New Hampshire to offer three or four annual field seminars in environmental science and conservation, including this six-day study of the Northern Forest. The seminars attract many college students and teachers and are more strictly academic than many ecology camps. Fieldwork fills the bulk of your time, but background lectures and daily reading assignments on scientific theory are also part of each seminar.

The Forest's 26 million acres stretch through northern Maine, New Hampshire, Vermont, and New York and include a diverse landscape of mountains, woods, and waterways. You spend each day, rain or shine, in the field, studying the interrelationships of the various ecosystems. For example, you may learn about the link between forest and water ecosystems by observing the effect forest management has on aquatic plant and animal populations. You also look at the role people play in the landscape, from the forest management systems we employ to the impact of our settlements.

The group is limited to 12 students and is led by Daniel Smith, AMC's conservation educator. Smith has a Master's of Forest Science from the Yale School of Forestry and Environmental Studies and has been leading AMC trips for two years.

During the seminar, you stay in the lodge at Pinkham Notch Visitor Center. More than 100 people are accommodated in two-, three-, and four-bunk rooms, and there are large shared bathrooms on each hall. Breakfast and dinner are served in the lodge dining room and included in the price of the seminar, and bag lunches can be purchased at the lodge. There are no special facilities or activities for children, but they may attend the seminar if accompanied by a parent or guardian. *Appalachian Mountain Club, White Mountains Workshops, Pinkham Notch Visitor Center, Box 298, Gorham, NH 03581, tel. 603/466–2727, fax 603/466–2720. Late Aug.: 6 days, $430. Price does not include lunches; sign up 3 months in advance.*

NEW YORK **Birding in the Finger Lakes.** For years Cornell University's campus in Ithaca, New York, has attracted researchers interested in the varied bird life of the Finger Lakes region, and the school's Laboratory of Ornithology is world-famous. The field observation that you do during this weeklong workshop is part of your study of avian ecology, habitat conservation, and bird population monitoring.

Workshop leader Bill Evans has been doing bird research at Cornell for seven years and specializes in the sounds that migrating birds make at night. The workshop usually includes a field trip to Cornell's Library of Natural Sounds, which began as a collection of recorded bird sounds and has grown to include thousands of other sounds, such as those made by whales and elephants.

You can begin your days by joining Bill on his 5 AM bird walks, or wait for the scheduled activities to begin at 9. Lectures on such topics as the local bird population, migration, and migrating birds as indicator species for the health of the environment are combined with field trips. In addition to the visit to the sound library mentioned above, you explore the campus bird sanctuary and travel to different observation areas throughout the Ithaca area and other parts of New York, including the Montezuma National Wildlife Refuge. On some days a guest presenter may talk to the group about banding birds for tracking or about the ecological factors that affect bird populations. These activities continue until 3:30, with a break for lunch.

Evenings you're free to participate in Cornell's active summer campus life. There are films, concerts, and guest speakers on a diverse selection of topics. Bill Evans will probably invite you on at least one owl prowl, too. Most participants in Cornell's workshops stay in double dorm rooms and eat in the cafeteria. *Cornell's Adult University, 626 Thurston Ave., Ithaca, NY 14850, tel. 607/255–6260. Early July: 7 days, $735–$855. Sign up 3 months in advance.*

NEW YORK **Natural Life in the Finger Lakes.** During this Cornell Adult University seven-day workshop, Richard Fischer, a professor emeritus of environmental education at Cornell, teaches you about the many different environments and inhabitants of the Finger Lakes region. You spend most of your time exploring the fields, bogs, forests, creeks, meadows, lakes, and gorges around the Ithaca campus.

Daily walks and hikes are more like museum tours than aerobic workouts. You progress slowly, observing your surroundings and stopping while Professor Fischer talks about what you find. He points out how the plant life at the top of a gorge differs from what is found near the stream at the bottom. You compare the trees, undergrowth, insects, and birds found in older sections of forest with those in meadows that are becoming forested. In streams, you use dip nets to examine the algae and insects of the water.

Lectures in the field teach you about plant adaptation: Did you know that walnut trees have a chemical in their roots that prevents the seeds of other plants around them from germinating? You also learn to identify wildflowers, and you participate in discussions about human impact on the environment. Your fieldwork and occasional background lectures fill the day from 9 AM to 3:30 PM, with a break for lunch.

In the evening you're free to take advantage of the films, lectures, and concerts on campus. Accommodations are in one of the campus residence halls, and dining is cafeteria style in the student union. *Cornell's Adult University, 626 Thurston Ave., Ithaca, NY 14850, tel. 607/255–6260. Early July: 7 days, $735–$855. Sign up 3 months in advance.*

THE MID-ATLANTIC

PENNSYLVANIA **Family Camp.** With nature walks, reptile presentations, and lots of recreational activities, the four-day camp at the Pocono Environmental Education Center is enjoyed by kids and parents alike. Located in the National Park Service's Delaware Water Gap National Recreation Area, the 38-acre campus has access to more than 200,000 acres of public land with a variety of habitats—pine plantations, hemlock gorges, and deciduous forests. You are sure to spot some of the many warblers that live in the area, and you may see an eagle or a hawk.

Days begin with a morning walk at 7:45, followed by breakfast in the dining hall. The rest of the day is filled with four 1½-hour activity sessions with two or three different activities planned for each. The camps may be attended by as few as 20 guests, but they are more likely to be filled with up to 100. There are canoe trips, wildflower walks, pond and stream studies, fossil hunts, and classes on constellations, botany, birds of prey, and environmental issues. To break up your nature studies, PEEC offers classes in tie-dyeing, papermaking, candlemaking, and other crafts. There are 14 instructors on staff, and each has some expertise in a different nature topic.

After dinner you may hear a guest speaker talk about whales, or you might choose to participate in a square dance. Each family (up to six people) stays in a one-room cabin with bunk beds and a full private bathroom. You can bring your own sheets and towels or rent them. A main building contains the arts and crafts center, an indoor pool, a dance floor, and the dining room, where meals are served buffet style. PEEC also offers many three-day family weekends. *Pocono Environmental Education Center, R.D. 2, Box 1010, Dingmans Ferry, PA 18328, tel. 717/828–2319. July and Aug.: 4 days, $154. Sign up 3 months in advance.*

THE SOUTHWEST

NEVADA **Death Valley Ecology Workshop.** Most people don't realize that Death Valley National Monument is hardly a sea of endless sand dunes; instead, it encompasses an area that ranges from the sub-sea level Badwater Basin to the 11,000-foot peaks of the Panamint Range. During this seven-day National Audubon Society workshop, you study the geologic history of the area; how plants and wildlife have adapted to the varying altitudes; the complex relationships between the land and wildlife created by the area's limited natural resources; and the area's rich cultural history, from the life of Native Americans to the business of mining.

Each day you can choose between hikes, walks, and van trips. You may spend a day identifying desert plants and learning how they can be used as indicators of the salinity, texture, and fertility of the soil. A visit to Ubehebe crater is the basis for a lesson on how exposed layers of rock reveal a history of the shaping forces of ancient seas, glaciers, earthquakes, and volcanoes. A field trip to Big and Little Petroglyph Canyons gives you a chance to see one of the densest concentrations of rock art in North America. Ruined mining towns are reminders of the early settlers and the rich borax, gypsum, gold, and silver deposits that lured them to the area. Observing the kangaroo rat, kit fox, and desert bighorn, you discuss conservation issues and learn how these mammals conserve water and food. Nature photography classes are yet another option.

The Furnace Creek Ranch, a modern motel in the center of the monument, is your home for the week. Dinner your first night and picnic lunches are included in the cost of the workshop. Other meals can be purchased at restaurants in the motel and nearby. *Audubon Ecology Camps & Workshops, National Audubon Society, 613 Riversville Rd., Greenwich, CT 06831, tel. 203/869–2017. Apr.: 7 days, $995. Price does not include breakfast or most dinners; sign up 3 months in advance.*

■**TEXAS**■ **Ecology of Big Bend National Park.** Inside the boundaries created by the Rio Grande River, Santiago Mountains, and Chihuahuan Desert, the 1,200 square miles of mountains, hills, river canyons, desert, forests, and grasslands of Big Bend National Park are home to an amazingly diverse plant and animal population. At the Audubon Society's one-week ecology workshop, you take walks, hikes, and van trips to observe the many species in their various habitats. Vans can reach certain areas, but because the park is undeveloped, walking or hiking is required to reach many interesting sites. To get the most from the trip, you should be able to walk 3 to 5 miles.

More than 400 bird species have been recorded in Big Bend. September is a particularly good time for bird observation because many migrating species stop in the park to refuel. You may spend a day visiting known feeding areas along the Rio Grande, looking for western bluebirds, vermillion flycatchers, golden eagles, ladder-backed woodpeckers, painted buntings, and many other species. Many animals, including the prong horn antelope, desert mule deer, gray fox, and the small, piglike javelina, can also be observed in the park. You may study the animal populations of the different park habitats, and learn how food sources effect species distribution. Plant studies may include species that are unique to the park, such as the lechuguilla, or a general study of tree adaptation to different altitudes. For an additional charge, you can take a full- or half-day raft trip on the Rio Grande.

You spend the first and last nights of the trip at the Gage, a small inn in Marathon, Texas, in the northern section of the park. Rooms here are double occupancy; some have shared bathrooms. The other nights are spent at Chisos Mountain Lodge, near the center of the park, in basic motel rooms with private bathrooms. Dinner the first night, all lunches (some restaurant, some picnic), and one early morning breakfast are included in the cost of the trip. The rest of your meals must be purchased in local restaurants. *Audubon Ecology Camps & Workshops, National Audubon Society, 613 Riversville Rd., Greenwich, CT 06831, tel. 203/869–2017. Mid-Sept.: 7 days, $995. Price does not include breakfast or most dinners; sign up 3 months in advance.*

■**UTAH**■ **Canyon Lands Summit.** Southern Utah University, in the southwestern part of the state, is the base for this seven-day National Wildlife Federation (NWF) program, which explores Bryce Canyon, Zion, and Cedar Breaks national parks. You spend a week learning about the ecology, natural history, and cultural history of the area, with over 400 other participants and 70 NWF leaders.

Everyone comes together for meals, but a long list of morning and afternoon activity choices splits the group into many smaller units of 10 to 40 people. You may hear a morning lecture on the reptiles and amphibians found in Bryce Canyon National Park, break for lunch, then spend the afternoon on a guided nature walk, seeing these creatures firsthand. There are classes on local geology, plant studies, astronomy, and photography, as well as on how to set up a recycling program in your office or community and which cleaning products are environmentally safe. Field trips cover such topics as the role of erosion in canyon formation and the bird life of the parks. Both nature walks and bus tours are offered, so you can decide how physically strenuous your day is.

Mini versions of the adult programs are offered for various children's age groups, along with arts and crafts activities and team skills workshops. Everyone gets together in the evening for country line dances, cookouts, slide presentations by park rangers, and more.

Accommodations on the campus include single and double dorm rooms with large shared bathrooms, and apartment-style housing, where three double rooms share a bathroom and kitchen. Rooms are also available off-campus at a nearby inn. You must buy at least a partial meal plan, which includes five lunches, two cookouts, and a grounds and administrative fee, and you can opt for the full cafeteria meal plan. *National Wildlife Federation, 1400 16th, NW, Washington, D.C. 20036, tel. 703/790–4363 or 800/245–5484. Early Aug.: 7 days, $520–$865. Sign up at least 6 months in advance.*

THE ROCKIES

COLORADO **Exploring the Alpine Tundra.** During six days of fieldwork on this Rocky Mountains Seminars camping trip, you learn about the unique alpine tundra landscape of Rocky Mountain National Park, shaped by plant and animal ecology, climate, geology, and human impact. Your instructor is Dr. Paul Kilburn, who has taught plant identification and ecology courses for the University of Colorado and the Denver Botanic Gardens.

On daylong hikes, he shows you how to identify the small plants and animals of the tundra and explains the adaptations that these life-forms have made to survive in this primarily treeless, windswept, high-altitude environment. Keep in mind that hiking at these altitudes—up to 12,000 feet above sea level—requires physical fitness and a willingness to brave some inclement weather.

The course is based at the Hidden Valley Center in the eastern section of the park, about 10 miles from Estes Park. A central building contains a seminar room for pre-hike lectures, but you stay outdoors, camping in your own tent. The campground has only pit toilets, and you must bring your own food and cooking equipment. *Rocky Mountain Seminars, Rocky Mountain National Park, Estes Park, CO 80517, tel. 303/586–3565, ext. 265. Mid-July: 6 days, $160. Price does not include indoor lodging or meals; sign up 2 months in advance.*

COLORADO **Rocky Mountain Ecology.** This six-day workshop given by the Rocky Mountain Nature Association is a good introduction to the many ecosystems of Rocky Mountain National Park, a 417-square-mile area of montane meadows, valleys, forests, alpine tundra, and mountains. Founded in 1961, the nonprofit organization offers many other one- to seven-day workshops. All are limited to 15 students and led by an expert naturalist, in this case, Dr. John Emerick, an associate professor of environmental science at the Colorado School of Mines who specializes in mountain ecology.

Each day, from 8 AM to 5 PM, you hike in one of the park's ecosystems. During a day in the alpine tundra you learn about the small, low-to-the-ground plants that survive in the treeless, windy environment. In the moist, cool montane zone, just below timberline, you learn about the large coniferous trees that dominate the area and the elk and deer that populate it. Excursions to various areas of the park include lessons on how climate, soil composition, fires, and other factors affect the ecosystem. You also make trips to view park wildlife, such as the beavers who make their homes in ponds and streams. Although the frequent stops for discussion give the hikes a leisurely pace, the high altitudes and unpredictable weather demand some stamina.

You and your group camp at the drive-in or hike-in sites of the Kawuneeche Campground. The camp fee is included in the cost of the program, but you must bring your own tent, cooking equipment, and food. A central building has bathrooms with showers. *Rocky Mountain Nature Association, Seminar Coordinator, Rocky Mountain National Park, Estes Park, CO 80517, tel.303/586–1265. Late June: 7 days, $160. Price does not include indoor lodging or meals; sign up 2 months in advance.*

MONTANA **Fins, Feathers, and Fur: Glacier's Wildlife.** This six-day seminar, one of 31 offered by the Glacier Institute, is set on the 2.5 million acres of Glacier National Park and the surrounding wilderness. The Institute was founded in 1983 to promote an appreciation of the area's beauty and an understanding of ecosystem management and sustainability issues.

During this seminar you study the park's wildlife—wolves, wolverines, mountain goats, mountain lions, salmon, and salamanders—and learn what part they play in the park's ecosystem. You spend each day, from 9 to 5, on moderately strenuous hikes, so assess your physical fitness before choosing this trip. Wildlife biologist David Shea, who leads the 16-person group, has a master's degree in resource conservation and has been a summer employee of the park for 25 years. While you're exploring he teaches you about the effect of predator-prey relationships on the ecosystem, the importance of endangered and abundant species, and the survival needs of each animal. He also discusses species interrelationships and wildlife management policies.

Accommodations are in rustic wood cabins that sleep four to five, at the Glacier Park Field Camp, near West Glacier. A common building contains a classroom for quick background lectures, bathrooms with hot showers, and a communal kitchen with cooking and eating utensils. You can either bring food and cook your meals, or eat at local restaurants. Participants in the program must be at least 16 years old. *The Glacier Institute, 777 Grandview Dr., Box 7457, Kalispell, MT 59904, tel. 406/756–3911. Mid-Aug.: 6 days, $235. Price does not include lodging ($10 a night) or meals; sign up 2 months in advance.*

MONTANA **Mountains, Valleys, and Glaciers.** During this five-day Glacier Institute field seminar, you learn about the geologic forces that shaped the northern Rocky Mountains of Glacier National Park. The group leader is Dr. Lex Blood, who has a degree in geologic engineering and has taught at Flathead Community College for 19 years. On day hikes he teaches you to look at the landscape for clues to its geologic past. You observe the valleys and moraines created by glaciers, as well as fossilized algae and mud cracks that provide evidence of the erosion caused by ancient seas. You also study the ongoing effects of ice and water on the topography of the park. You hike every day, and the uneven terrain makes a few days strenuous.

Accommodations are in cabins at the Glacier Park Field Camp; bathrooms with hot showers are in the common building (*see above*). Meals are not provided, but a communal kitchen with cooking and eating utensils is available, and there are several restaurants nearby. *The Glacier Institute, 777 Grandview Dr., Box 7457, Kalispell, MT 59904, tel. 406/756–3911. Early Aug.: 5 days, $235. Price does not include lodging ($10 a night) or meals; sign up 2 months in advance.*

WYOMING **Animal Behavior.** Teton Science School (TSS) has been offering a variety of natural science field seminars since it was founded in 1967. It uses the mountains, aspen forests, and grasslands of Grand Teton

National Park and Elk Refuge as its classroom. With antelope, coyote, beaver, moose, red squirrel, digger wasps, wolves, osprey, bears, dragonflies, eagles, and bison as inhabitants, it is an ideal location for this five-day study of animal behavior.

Each day, from 8 AM to 4 PM, you and a group of up to 11 others, are in the field observing wildlife; developing your observation skills is one of the main objectives of the course. Your instructor is Dr. Allen Stokes, professor emeritus of the University of Utah and a well-known ethologist. He teaches you to recognize the nuances of animal behavior and adaptation. You learn to use the observations you make of an animal's behavior to make deductions about its species' survival strategies.

When class is over, you can visit the field science lab, natural science library, or Murie Natural History Museum at the TSS campus. Teton Science School seminars do not include accommodations or meals. The closest lodging is Dornan's Spur Ranch Cabins, about 8 miles away in Moose, Wyoming. There are one- and two-bedroom cabins, laundry facilities, and a restaurant here. Many other hotels and lodges are found in and around the town of Jackson, Wyoming. The Gros Ventre and Forest Service campgrounds are also nearby, but offer no showers, electricity, or food services. You need to bring a bag lunch each day. Teton Science School courses are open to participants age 18 and older. *Teton Science School, Box 68, Kelly, WY 83011, tel. 307/733–4765, fax 307/739–9388. Late July: 5 days, $250. Price does not include accommodations or meals; sign up 3 months in advance.*

WYOMING **Audubon Camp in the West.** The majestic Grand Tetons are the setting for this weeklong National Audubon Society workshop on mountain ecology at the Whisky Mountain Conservation Camp, near the town of Dubois in northwestern Wyoming. The daily schedule of two half-day activity sessions is the same as that of other Audubon camps, but at the Camp in the West you have as many as six choices for each session, including classes, hikes, and field trips.

Exploring mountain meadows, pine and sagebrush hills, forests, and creek and river bottoms, you can study geology, plant life, wildflowers, petroglyphs, insects, birds, and mammals. Elk, moose, deer, otter, mink, beaver, antelope, and bison are just some of the mammals in the area, and the bird population includes bald eagles, white pelicans, osprey, trumpeter swans, and three-toed woodpeckers. One day is spent on a field trip to Grand Teton National Park, where you take a float trip on the Snake River, discuss geology and ecology, visit the Indian Museum at Colter Bay, hike to Lake Taggert, and maybe hit some birding hotspots.

You can supplement what you learn in the field with classes on invertebrates, botany, nature sketching, environmental education, Native American culture, medicinal plants, and environmental activism. Evenings, there may be stories around a campfire, a square dance, or a lecture on endangered species or wetlands and forest preservation.

Accommodations are in dormitory-style cabins that sleep two to five people. Some cabins have private baths, while others share a central bathhouse. There are a few cabins with private rooms and baths for couples. Meals are served buffet style in a main dining room, and vegetarian diets can be accommodated. The workshop is offered six times each summer. *Audubon Ecology Camps & Workshops, National Audubon Society, 613 Riversville Rd., Greenwich, CT 06831, tel. 203/869–2017. Late June–early Aug.: 7 days, $695. Price does not include one dinner; sign up 3 months in advance.*

WYOMING **Bears: Bones, Signs, and Stories.** The team teaching of this five-day Yellowstone Institute course gives you a thorough education on the bears of Yellowstone National Park. You spend time in the classroom with Dr. Elaine Anderson, a research associate in zoology at the Denver Museum of Natural History, learning about the evolution of carnivores. Dr. Jim Halfpenny, author of *A Field Guide to Tracking in North America,* takes you into the park to map bear trees (those marked with scratches) and other evidence of bear activity as part of a research project on bear distribution in the park. Naturalist and folklorist Jim Garry uses observation of the bear and its habitat to explain its place in Native American myth and storytelling.

Early mornings and evenings are spent looking for bears, since this is when they tend to be most active. You observe from a distance, often with binoculars, because the bear's cuddly appearance belies his ferocity. In the afternoon you may search for bear tracks and trees, or spend time in the classroom studying the muscular structure of bears and comparing different bear skulls and teeth.

Accommodations are available for $8 a night at the institute's headquarters in cabins with no electricity or plumbing. Bathrooms and kitchen facilities, including cooking and eating utensils, are in the common building. You bring your own bedding, towels, and food. With the exception of special family weeks, Yellowstone programs are for adults only. *The Yellowstone Institute, Box 117, Yellowstone National Park, WY 82190, tel. 307/344–2294. Late June: 5 days, $225. Price does not include accommodations or meals; sign up 3 months in advance.*

WYOMING **Geology and Human Culture.** You learn two disciplines during this unusual five-day seminar offered by the Teton Science School and taught by Charles Love, a professor of geology and anthropology at Western Wyoming College. You should have a basic understanding of geology before you sign up.

Professor Love has done extensive research on the archaeology of Jackson Hole and teaches you how 10,000 years of prehistoric peoples used the resources of the area and how modern man is using the area today. On daily hikes, he points out houses being built

on active landslides and at the bottom of avalanche tracks. You also visit sites where geologists and archaeologists are working together to discover early settlement and cultural patterns.

Accommodations and meals are not provided by the Teton Science School, but there are many hotel and camping options in and around the town of Jackson (*see above*). *Teton Science School, Box 68, Kelly, WY 83011, tel. 307/733–4765, fax 307/739–9388. Early Aug.: 4 days, $200. Price does not include accommodations or meals; sign up 3 months in advance.*

WYOMING **Mammals Great and Small.** The elk, bears, bison, ground squirrels, coyote, and other mammals that populate Yellowstone National Park are the subjects of this five-day Yellowstone Institute program led by Don Streubel, a biology professor at Idaho State University. Professor Streubel teaches a group of 15 students about the role of these animals in the ecosystem of the park.

Streubel leads some early morning bear walks, but most mornings start around 8:30, with a background lecture in the common building. You may spend from 15 minutes to an hour in the classroom, hearing the plans for the day's fieldwork or seeing a slide show on the history of mammals. You spend the rest of the day in the field, hiking to nearby observation areas or riding in a van to other parts of the park. You may have to wait and watch for a couple of hours to see a grizzly, but it's a rare day that you come home disappointed.

The lesson plan is determined by the animals. If you observe a coyote feeding on an elk, you learn about the role that predator-prey relationships play in the natural control of the animal population. Finding a red squirrel's stash of pine cones may prompt a lesson on hibernation or the effect of animals on the plant population.

Accommodations are available in cabins with no electricity or plumbing at the institute's headquarters (*see above*). Bathrooms and kitchen facilities, including cooking and eating utensils, are in the common building. *The Yellowstone Institute, Box 117, Yellowstone National Park, WY 82190, tel. 307/344–2294. Mid-June: 5 days, $220. Price does not include accommodations or meals; sign up 3 months in advance.*

THE WEST COAST

CALIFORNIA **Designs and Strategies: Flowers and Their Pollinators.** There's more to the study of wildflowers than identification. At this four-day Yosemite Association seminar you discover how each flower's structure is adapted for a different pollinator—bees, butterflies, moths, hummingbirds, and the wind.

The course is led by Richard Keator, who has a Ph.D. in botany from the University of California, Berkeley, and is the author of numerous books on the flowers and plants of California. You take day hikes through alpine, meadow, subalpine forest, and scree habitats, examining the diverse flower population, including black-eyed Susans, bull thistles, lupine, and others. You study flower shape, color, arrangement, pistil and stamen position, and nectar and pollen production.

Most evenings are free, but one night there is a lecture and slide show. A tent site at the Tuolumne Meadows campsite is included in the cost of the seminar, but you have to bring your own camping equipment. There are central bathrooms, but no showers. You can also stay in a motel in Lee Vining, about a half hour's drive away. Meals are not included, so bring a camp stove or be prepared to drive to local restaurants. *Yosemite Association, Box 230, El Portal, CA 95318, tel. 209/379–2646, fax 209/379–2486. Late July: 4 days, $155. Price does not include accommodations or meals; sign up 3 months in advance.*

CALIFORNIA **Spring into Nature.** The Sierra Club's rustic Clair Tappaan Lodge is your base camp for this 7-day trip in the High Sierra. As winter snows thaw and spring flora comes to life, you explore the Pacific Crest Trail, Donner Pass, Castle Peak, and the many streams, lakes, and meadows near the lodge. Leader Sy Gelman, who has been leading Sierra Club trips for more than 20 years, crafts an itinerary to suit the group and the weather. Naturalist and botanist Tim Messick comes along on your daily hikes to help you identify the plants and birds you encounter along the way.

Mornings begin with breakfast and a group clean-up. The first day is usually spent hiking to the ridge, about 3½ miles behind the lodge. From here you have a great view of Donner Lake and the surrounding area. One day is spent at Donner Memorial State Park, where you learn the history of the ill-fated Donner Party, a group of 89 westward-bound pioneers who were trapped here in the winter of 1846–47 in snow 22 feet deep. You hike through the park, stopping along streams to look at beaver dams. Other days are spent hiking along the Pacific Crest Trail, driving to Tahoe to explore, and climbing Donner Summit or one of the other nearby peaks.

Professor Messick talks about the flora and geological features found in each area. He explains how plants have adapted to altitude and discusses the role of glaciers in shaping the mountains. As an expert on the local bird population, he can point out Steller's jays, golden eagles, and the rare gray owl.

You return to the lodge by 3:30 and have a few hours to shower and relax before dinner at 8 PM. In the evening, Tim may give a slide presentation on the ecology of the Sierra Nevada or talk about conservation concerns. If you're so inclined, you can drive to nearby Tahoe or Reno. One former guest claims to have won back the cost of his trip on his evening forays.

The dormitory rooms with double and triple decker bunk beds (the top ones are rarely used) and the shared bathrooms of the lodge are far from posh, but the showers are hot, and there's an indoor hot tub. You bring your own bedding and towels. A professional chef cooks the meals, and vegetarian alternatives are always available. *Sierra Club Outings, 730 Polk St., San Francisco, CA 94109, tel. 415/923–5630. Mid-June: 7 days, $475. Sign up 3 months in advance.*

CALIFORNIA **Stars and the Nighttime Sky.** This Yosemite Association seminar takes place under the brilliant night sky, leaving you free during the day to explore the park on your own. For five nights, 20 students gather at 7:30 to observe the stars, moon, Saturn, globular clusters, and nebulae and to listen to lectures given by Ron Oriti, director of the Santa Rosa Junior College Planetarium.

Because the course is planned for a time when the sky is particularly dark, you can view the stars with your naked eyes and binoculars, as well as with a telescope. You learn about the motion of the stars and planets, how to use the sun and stars to determine direction, and how to identify stars and constellations. Professor Oriti's lectures cover topics from the ancient Greek myths about the constellations to the modern discovery of black holes. Classes are scheduled to end at 10:30, but fascinated groups often stay up looking and talking until after 1 AM.

A tent site at the Tuolumne Meadows campsite is included in the cost of the seminar. You can also stay in a motel in Lee Vining, about a half hour's drive away. Meals are not included, so bring a camp stove or be prepared to drive to local restaurants. *Yosemite Association, Box 230, El Portal, CA 95318, tel. 209/379–2646, fax 209/379–2486. Early Aug.: 5 days, $180. Price does not include accommodations or meals; sign up 3 months in advance.*

CALIFORNIA **Where the Glaciers Roamed— Geology of Yosemite.** In this five-day seminar you learn about the creation of Yosemite National Park—the volcanic activity, glaciers, erosion, ancient seas, and great Sierra uplift. Leader Doris Sloan is a lecturer in environmental sciences at the University of California, Berkeley, where she earned her M.S. in geology and Ph.D. in paleontology. She's been leading trips in the Sierras for 20 years.

You spend your days hiking, from 8:30 to 5, mostly in the Tuolumne Meadows area of the park. You cover only about 5 miles a day, at a relatively slow pace, but because the elevation ranges from 8,600 feet to 11,000 feet, you must be in good physical condition. The high country scenery is dramatic: You hike among rounded granite domes, steep cliffs, waterfalls, and deep valleys, identifying rocks and minerals, observing the shapes created by glaciers and volcanoes, learning about the effects of plate tectonics, and learning about the history of mining in the area.

You camp at the Tuolumne Meadows campsite (*see above*). Nights are spent cooking over your camp stove, before retiring to your tent under the stars. *Yosemite Association, Box 230, El Portal, CA 95318, tel. 209/379–2646, fax 209/379–2486. Mid-Aug.: 5 days, $185. Price does not include accommodations or meals; sign up 3 months in advance.*

WASHINGTON **Birds and Butterflies from Sagebrush to Snow.** During this four-day North Cascades Institute field seminar you study the birds and butterflies of northern Washington's Methow Valley and the surrounding highlands, an area of subalpine, hill, marsh, pine gorge, and riverside habitats.

Spending time in each habitat, you learn how to identify butterfly species, such as the two-tailed tiger swallow tail and Lorquin's admiral, and bird species, including several species of tanager. You also learn how preserving the various environments results in a more diverse wildlife population. Leaders Libby Mills, a wildlife biologist and illustrator, and Saul Weisberg, executive director of the North Cascades Institute, ecologist, and writer, share their expert knowledge of the local environment and its wildlife. You are out in the field all day, hiking to different ecosystems and catching butterflies, so be prepared for the Northwest's infamous rain.

Accommodations for the seminar are in Goatwall Cabin, a large cabin near the town of Mazama, at the edge of the wilderness area. There are beds, a bathroom with a shower, and a kitchen. The institute, established in 1983, offers field seminars throughout the Pacific Northwest aiming to raise awareness about the relationships between living things and their environments. *North Cascades Institute, 2105 Highway 20, Sedro Woolley, WA 98284, tel. 206/856–5700, ext. 209. Mid-June: 4 days, $195. Price does not include meals; sign up 1 month in advance.*

WASHINGTON **Marine Science Camp.** A 45-minute seaplane ride from Seattle or Vancouver brings you to Spieden Island, the base for this weeklong camp sponsored by the Island Institute, founded in 1990 to educate people about the marine life and natural history of the Puget Sound area. On this trip you observe firsthand the whales, otters, porpoises, and marine birds of the island and explore their habitats, from the shoreline to the depths of the sound.

There are different sessions for adults, youths (ages 9–18), and families, but the teaching staff is consistent: Four core instructors with degrees in natural science fields, an assistant instructor, a boat skipper, and a kitchen staff.

An uninhabited 556-acre member of the San Juans, Spieden Island is home to herds of European fallow deer, mouflon sheep, and Asian sika deer as well as bald eagles and at least 68 other species of birds. Your days are spent hiking, sea kayaking, and exploring tidepools, and one day is reserved for a cruise aboard the institute's 43-foot charter boat looking for otters, seals, whales, and porpoises. The last two days of the camp are left open for you to spend more time at your favorite activity.

You're free from 3:30 to 6 PM each day, time that you can use to hike, relax in the Jacuzzi, or do research in the nature library. In the evening, the staff gives talks and presents slide shows that relate to the day's activities.

Accommodations for the camp are in 10 safari-style tents with wood floors and cots. Each tent is shared by two to four adults or three to five children. A rustic cedar lodge central to all of the tents contains the shared bathrooms and hot showers, the dining area, the library, and the swimming pool and Jacuzzi. The gourmet food (a rarity at ecology camps) is served buffet style and includes seafood and vegetarian entrées and fresh baked goods. *Island Institute, Box 661, Vashon, WA 98070, tel. 206/938–0345, fax 714/744–6920. Mid-June–mid-Aug.: 7 days, $695–$867. Sign up 2 months in advance.*

HAWAII

THE BIG ISLAND **Hawaii Summit.** This seven-day National Wildlife Federation summit focuses on the volcano, coastal, and rain forest ecosystems of the Big Island as well as its 20 or so different climate zones. As with most NWF summits, the 400 participants are broken up into smaller groups by their selections from a wide variety of morning and afternoon classes and field trips. Topnotch leadership of both adult and children's programs is provided by 70 to 80 staff members.

You can choose from classes on the ecology of coral reefs, the use of alternative energy in the Hawaiian Islands, tropical birdlife on the Big Island, Hawaiian history, and the adaptation of wildlife to varying island altitudes. Bus tours and nature walks may focus on the geology of Volcanoes National Park, the waterfalls and plants of the Hamakua Coast, or the insects of the Puna Coast rain forest. There are even snorkeling field trips to explore the ecology of coral reefs. You get a taste of the local culture, with evening programs of Hawaiian music and traditional storytelling.

Dormitory and apartment-style accommodations are available on campus, and the Hilo Hawaiian Hotel offers special rates for summit participants. You must purchase at least a partial university meal plan, which includes five lunches and six dinners in the cafeteria, a luau, and an administrative fee. *National Wildlife Federation, 1400 16th St., NW, Washington, D.C., 20036, tel. 703/790–4265 or 800/245–5484. Late July–Early Aug.: 7 days, $555–$1,085. Sign up at least 6 months in advance.*

SOURCES

ORGANIZATIONS The best sources for information about nature camps are the nonprofit organizations listed in the Major Players section of this chapter.

ALSO SEE If you enjoy spending your days outdoors observing wildlife you may want to peruse the Bird and Whale-Watching Cruises chapters.

New Age Centers

By Melissa Rivers

o be healthy and happy, you must attend both to your spiritual and to your physical needs: That's the underlying philosophy of the country's many New Age centers, institutions that show you how to make permanent changes in the way you live—changes the centers vow will improve your health, give you a sense of fulfillment, and renew your spirituality.

To do this, they draw on philosophies of living espoused by the New Age movement, which incorporates Eastern and American Indian spiritual practices, holism, and concern for nature. New Age centers often use modern techniques like biofeedback and psychotherapy along with ancient practices such as meditation, yoga, tai chi, vision quests (a rite of passage involving seclusion and fasting in the wild), and sweat lodges (a purification ritual). Their locations, often in beautiful countryside, are chosen to help you reconnect with the natural environment; and their menus, usually vegetarian and macrobiotic fare, aim to benefit your health and provide another way to commune with nature.

Some of these New Age centers concentrate on spiritual awareness and emphasize meditation; others focus on holistic health and pay more attention to healthy cooking and exercise. But no matter what their specialty, all these centers emphasize the need for balance between mind and body. So you eat vegetarian meals while you meditate, and you take time out to meditate between organic gardening and macrobiotic cooking classes. Many centers have a specialty—fitness, spiritual development, weight loss, health rejuvenation, recovery, or stress management—and some centers offer a variety of programs.

At most centers, you follow a daily schedule that incorporates yoga, aerobics, day hikes, meditation sessions, and classes on nutrition, self-awareness, stress management, Native American spirituality, natural medicine, and other topics. There's also bodywork—physical treatments such as Swedish and shiatsu massage, aromatherapy, herbal body wraps, reflexology, and rolfing. The amount of free time differs from center to center; some have you up before dawn and scheduled throughout the day, while others allow you to decide how much you want to participate. At many centers, too, you can set up a personal retreat; you decide how long you want to stay, which scheduled activities you want to join, and how much time you want to relax, read, meditate, sunbathe, or explore your surroundings. The centers listed here also have various rules for guest conduct: Some stress celibacy; some allow nudity; several call for volunteer work; and many do not allow smoking or drinking. Most centers discourage bringing children along, because they

Writer Melissa Rivers began her New Age journey in Japan, with the study of Zen Buddhism. Over the past decade she has continued to explore the body-mind-spirit connection through studies in herbalism, massage, meditation, Native American Spirituality, and yoga.

disrupt the peaceful environment and can't participate in most activities.

Accommodations run the gamut from tents to posh hotels. Simple, shared accommodations in dormitories are the most common option. Meals are often served buffet style; regimens may be lacto-vegetarian, ovo-lacto vegetarian, or vegan vegetarian, or even more restrictive—either macrobiotic or organic. Centers that focus on fitness or weight loss may also offer spa cuisine, which is low in calories, and supervised juice regimens and fasts, meant to cleanse your body of impurities.

The cost of a stay at the different centers in this chapter varies widely, usually based on accommodations and the time of year you visit. A holistic health or spiritual awareness vacation can be quite a bargain, if you don't mind sleeping in a dorm room with 9 other people or sharing a bathhouse with 50 other campers. Of course there are centers that offer accommodations in luxury resorts, but the price, up to $450 per night versus the $25 a night you can pay to camp out, certainly reflects the additional comforts.

Staffs include everything from doctors to Buddhist monks. In general, they are supportive, understanding, and willing to go out of their way to help you make what are sometimes difficult lifestyle changes. Staffs at centers that emphasize the physical aspects of holistic health tend to include a higher percentage of health care professionals: doctors, nurses, nutritionists. Participants come from all professions and religious persuasions. Usually college-educated people from the ages of 20 to 70, they come to get fit, lose weight, explore their spiritual beliefs, recover physical and mental health, learn to manage stress, or find more meaning in life; or simply to rest and relax, get some exercise, lose weight, or be pampered. They also come away with their spirits uplifted, and with a better understanding of themselves and a deeper appreciation of nature. Changes like these may last until your next vacation—or far beyond.

GLOSSARY Many terms used in this chapter, from types of bodywork to elements of Zen meditation, may be unfamiliar. The following is a list of the terms that appear most frequently:

Aromatherapy: Massage with oils from essences of plants and flowers intended to relax the skin's connective tissues and stimulate the natural flow of lymph.

Asana: The physical postures that constitute one of the three principal yogic practices.

Biofeedback: Monitoring and control of physical functions such as blood pressure, pulse rate, digestion, and muscle tension with an electronic sensing device.

Bodywork: Umbrella term covering massages, facials, hydrotherapy, and other similar physical spa treatments.

Hatha yoga: One of the four chief Hindu disciplines; a system of physical exercises for the control and perfection of the body.

Holistic health: A nonmedical approach to the healing and health of the whole person that seeks to integrate physical and mental well-being with lifestyle factors.

Hydrotherapy: Underwater massage; alternating hot and cold showers; and other water-oriented treatments.

Kinhin: Walking meditation.

Lacto-vegetarian diet: Vegetarian diet that permits dairy products.

Macrobiotics: Vegetarian diet low in fat and high in antioxidant vitamins.

Organic diet: Diet free of any chemically treated food.

Ovo-lacto vegetarian diet: Vegetarian diet that includes eggs and dairy products.

Pranayama: The breathing techniques that constitute one of the three principal yogic practices.

Reflexology: Massage of the pressure points on the feet, hands, and ears; intended to relax the parts of the body.

Reiki: An ancient healing method that teaches universal life energy through the laying on of hands and mental and spiritual balancing. Intended to relieve acute emotional and physical conditions.

Rolfing: A bodywork system developed by Ida Rolf that improves balance and flexibility through manipulation of rigid muscles, bones, and joints. It is intended to improve energy flow and relieve stress.

Satsanga: "In the company of truth." A gathering for chanting, meditation, and inspiration.

Shiatsu: Massage technique developed by Tokujiro Namikoshi that uses finger (*shi*) pressure (*atsu*) to stimulate the body's inner powers of balance and healing.

Sweat lodge: Native American ritual of purification through time in a steam-filled hut or teepee.

Vegan vegetarian: Strict vegetarian diet that uses no animal products.

Vegetarian diet: A regime of raw or cooked vegetables and fruit, grains, sprouts, and seeds; natural foods with no additives.

Vision quest: Native American rite of passage involving seclusion and fasting in the wild.

Zazen: Seated meditation.

CHOOSING THE RIGHT CENTER

Every New Age center is different. To understand exactly what a stay at each one involves, it helps to probe beyond the brochures, which tend to be general, and ask many specific questions, such as the ones that follow.

What is the center's philosophy, and how will it affect my experience there? Although the goal is usually to help you attain a balance between your mind and body, centers have their own philosophies about how to do this, resulting in very different programs. One center may promote the use of meditation and vision quests to achieve holistic health, while another may advocate spa cuisine and yoga classes. Programs may be very

physical, either fitness- or weight-loss oriented; or very spiritual, involving much meditation and various rituals; or very pampering, providing a great deal of bodywork. Some programs combine several of these approaches. Know exactly what you're getting into.

How large is the facility, and how many guests can it accommodate? If personal attention matters to you, choose a center that offers a small-group experience. If you want to meet more new people, pick a center where you can interact with larger groups.

How structured is the program? Programs range from workshops with full schedules of required activities and little free time to personal retreats in which you determine how you spend your time. Find out whether you must participate in all scheduled events.

What personal services are offered? Most centers offer various types of bodywork, and many centers offer nutritional, psychological, spiritual, or lifestyle counseling. Make sure the center you choose offers the services you want, and find out what they cost.

What's the cost and what's included? The cost of a stay at one of these centers can vary greatly according to where you stay, when you visit, and what program you choose. Costs listed here are by day or by program, depending on the center's offerings, and are for one person in accommodations that range from shared tents and dormitory-style rooms to private rooms in luxury resorts. Unless otherwise noted, the cost also covers meals, use of a center's facilities, and participation in regularly scheduled classes. Special seminars or workshops generally cost more. Be sure to find out what transportation is included; although fees for programs described here never include transportation to the center, a transfer from the nearest airport may be available at no extra charge. Some centers, where accommodations are more basic, ask that you bring bedding and towels. If you want to camp, you may have to furnish your own camping gear.

Are there any hidden costs? There may be additional fees for individual bodywork, beauty treatments, counseling, and child care.

What is the setting of the center? Although locations are usually peaceful, surroundings range from isolated countryside to luxurious resort areas.

What are the accommodations like? Accommodations can be anything from a shared tent and bathhouse to a private room and bath in a resort hotel. Most centers have few private rooms and baths. Know all of your options.

What type of food is served? If the diet is vegetarian, as is common among these centers, you may want to ask about nonvegetarian options or special weight-loss diets.

Will laundry facilities be available? Probably not, but if it is, it could save you a suitcase.

How long has the center been in business? Although there are no guarantees, an experienced staff is more likely to be well-prepared for any questions or problems you may have.

Do you have references from past guests?

How far in advance do I need to book? How far in advance you must book to attend a particular center may vary according to which of its programs you choose.

FAVORITE CENTERS

THE NORTHEAST

MAINE **Northern Pines Health Resort.** Marlee Turner became a believer in holistic health care when it helped her through a bout with thyroid cancer. In 1980, she opened the Northern Pines Health Resort, focusing on lifestyle management. The Northern Pines regimen of meditation, yoga, and aerobic exercise is designed to promote general good health and to teach you to manage stress. With this program—along with a diet of fresh fruits, vegetables, and whole grains—you nourish your mind and spirit as well as your body. How long you stay is up to you; once there, you can pick and choose your activities from the resort's full daily schedule, which includes early morning meditation, followed by stretch class, walks and hikes (or cross-country skiing), aerobics, and yoga. You may also attend a class, a discussion session, and an evening presentation on nutrition, Native American spirituality, cooking, vitamins, herbs, meditation, or other holistic health–related topics. In your free time, you may go canoeing or swimming, take advantage of the sauna or hot tub, or spend a little extra for a Swedish massage, reflexology session, aromatherapy, beauty treatment, clear light therapy, or time in the flotation tank.

The cabins that dot the wooded, 68-acre lakefront property can accommodate up to 30, but there are usually no more than 15 guests on hand each week—mostly well-traveled, educated women who are often doctors, nurses, teachers, or therapists. Vegetarian dishes of natural foods are served at the communal meals; you can also opt for a supervised juice fast. Children are welcome to participate with parents, and child care can be arranged. *Northern Pines Health Resort, 559 Rte. 85, Raymond, ME 04071, tel. 207/655–7624, fax 207/655–3321. Year-round: daily, $140–$230. Price does not include personal services; sign up at least 1 week in advance.*

MASSACHUSETTS **Kripalu Center for Yoga and Health.** Some 14,000 visitors a year come to this nonprofit educational and spiritual center in the Berkshires. Built as a Jesuit monastery in 1957, the center is on 320 acres of verdant woodlands and scenic meadows overlooking Lake Mahkeenac. Here, under the direction and guidance of Yogi Amrit Desai, and with the encouragement of the center's 300 permanent residents, you work to deepen your self-awareness. Toward this goal, the center offers workshops and personal retreats.

Three-, four-, and seven-day workshops include Kripalu-style yoga, meditation, massage and other bodywork, raw juice fasting, and aerobic dance movements known as DansKinetics, as well as exercises to balance energy and to help you be more loving and manage stress; 14-day workshops certify you to teach yoga or the Kripalu holistic lifestyle. In any of the center's workshops, mornings include a hike and classes in yoga, meditation, and DansKinetics; afternoons, there are classes, too, but the specifics vary from one workshop to the next. You have free time to practice yoga and meditation, explore the grounds, and have a massage or a facial, or a session of shiatsu, reflexology, or energy-balancing. An evening gathering called a *satsanga* brings residents and guests together for chanting, meditation, and inspiration.

Personal retreats, known here as Rest, Renew, and Relax, include daily meditation, yoga, DansKinetics classes, and satsanga in the evening, as well as free time for private meditation. One of the center's year-round residents will help you plan your visit. You must stay at least two nights on these (three nights between early September and late June).

The Kripalu Center accommodates up to 300 guests in an array of Spartan dormitories and private rooms; all but a few more spacious deluxe rooms have shared baths. The vegetarian cuisine is high in protein and fiber, and low in fats and sweeteners. Meals are eaten in meditative silence, either in the dining chapel or outside in the gardens. Children are welcome, and there are special programs to keep them occupied. *Kripalu Center for Yoga and Health, Box 793, Lenox, MA 01240, tel. 413/448–3400 or 800/967–3577, fax 413/448–3384. Year-round: daily, $56–$170; 3–14 days $140–$2,145. Sign up anytime.*

MASSACHUSETTS **Kushi Institute.** Since 1978, the Kushi Institute has been in the forefront of research and education in the field of macrobiotics. Two seven-day programs are available: The Way to Health workshop gives you an introduction to macrobiotics, with cooking lessons, exercise classes, and massage therapy; the Personal Transformation course, led by founder Michio Kushi, puts you on the road to holistic health through classes on macrobiotic eating, fitness, massage therapy, and healing spiritualities from Christianity to Tao Te Ching.

In both programs, days begin at 7 AM with *do-in*, simple stretching exercises, and continue until 9 PM with meditation and classes on such topics as home gardening, shiatsu, food preparation, and stress relief. Macrobiotic meals—brown rice, miso soup, beans, vegetables, tofu dishes, sushi, noodles, and pasta—reinforce your instruction in this style of eating. Three one-hour breaks give you time for short hikes on the center's nature trails or a swim in the nearby lake.

The center is in the Berkshires on 600 acres of woodlands and meadows. The Way to Health workshop is limited to 16 students, who stay in a former Franciscan lodge; the kitchen there is used for cooking classes. The Personal Transformation workshop accepts up to 45 students, and uses dormitory accommodations. In both cases, most rooms and bathrooms are shared. *The Kushi Institute, 308 Leland Rd., Box 7, Becket, MA 01223, tel. 413/623–5741, fax 413/623–8827. Year-round: 7-days, $995. Sign up anytime.*

MASSACHUSETTS **Rowe Camp and Conference Center.** The roster of programs here includes workshops on Judaism, Native American spirituality, mindfulness and compassion, psychodrama, natural medicine, the lessons of the natural environment, dealing with love and anger, healing relationships, and how to live from the heart. Although the camp is affiliated with the Unitarian Universalist Association, programs and staff don't proselytize; the goal is merely to provide an environment for personal exploration, spiritual growth, and mental healing. To make the camp accessible to the widest possible audience, fees are pegged to participants' incomes.

Each workshop draws well-known authors, lecturers, and specialists in the field, who lead two educational sessions daily—these may be lectures, discussions, writing workshops, or music or movement classes. In your free time, you can hike, relax in the cedar sauna, or take in nearby Williamstown, local art museums, and nearby ski areas.

The vegetarian meals, served family style, are delicious, and the conversation then is one of the nicest parts of a stay here; beer and wine are available at an extra charge. Accommodations in the center's 200-year-old farmhouse and two newer buildings have private rooms with shared baths; some rooms are wheelchair accessible. You can also bunk in one of several truly summer-camp-style cabins, which share a communal bathhouse; here you must bring your own linens and a flashlight.

Rowe also hosts gatherings for men and women, and recovery camps for AA members, codependents, incest survivors, and others with special concerns, as well as summer adventure camps for children. Weekend programs are available between September and mid-June. *Rowe Camp and Conference Center, Kings Highway Rd., Rowe, MA 01367, tel. 413/339-4954, fax 413/339-5708. Mid-June–Sept: 6–7 days, $195–$425. Oct.–mid-June: 3 days, $180–$320. Sign up anytime.*

NEW YORK Omega **Institute for Holistic Studies.** This center, 100 miles north of New York City, is a kind of New Age mecca, where you can strive to achieve balanced physical and mental health with help from people on the leading edge of preventive medicine and holistic health. Staff counselors are specialists in nutrition, stress management, and holistic medicine. Guest lecturers and faculty who lead the 250 two- to seven-day workshops here—on such topics as Native American studies, wellness and stress management, holistic health, bodywork, recovery, intuitive development, relationships, art, sports and fitness, and spirituality—comprise a veritable *Who's Who* of the human potential movement.

Several times each year, in addition to the workshops, there's a Wellness Week program, where you learn the importance of diet, nutrition, exercise, and a positive attitude in developing and maintaining good health. In this program, days start before breakfast, when small groups form to practice yoga or tai chi; lectures, massage sessions, yoga, group support meetings, movement and meditation classes, and more tai chi fill the rest of the time. After dark there are concerts, dances, and films.

On the campus, you'll find hiking, canoeing, basketball, tennis, volleyball, a theater, a café, and the Wellness Center, which has a sauna, massage rooms, flotation tanks, and consultation rooms. There are simple dormitories, cabins, and campsites, accommodating up to 350. Meals, served buffet style, are primarily vegetarian, with some fish and dairy options. Omega offers one family week each summer and provides an optional child care program throughout the season. In addition to what's available at the New York campus, which is in full swing in summer and early fall, there are programs in New England and in winter at Maho Bay, on St. John in the U.S. Virgin Islands. *Omega Institute for Holistic Studies, 260 Lake Dr., Rhinebeck, NY 12572, tel. 914/266-4444 or 800/862-8890, fax 914/266-4828. June–mid-Sept.: 2–7 days, $75–$450. Sign up 2–4 weeks in advance.*

NEW YORK Zen **Mountain Monastery.** This Zen monastery, in a state forest preserve in the Catskill Mountains, is the only such place in the country that offers programs for visitors year-round. Founded in 1980 as a residential artist center with a spiritual basis in Buddhism, the monastery became a year-round retreat for monastics and laypeople training in Zen in 1983. Traditional arts are still practiced here, but they are integrated with martial arts classes and traditional Zen training in self-realization, morality, and social responsibility.

At four- and five-day programs, repeated several times a year, you can attend classes on poetry, calligraphy and brush painting, cooking, music, and *aikido* (a Japanese martial art). You might be treated to a cup of green tea in a Zen tea ceremony, explore the subtleties of *ikebana* (flower arranging), or enjoy a concert of the music of the *shakuhachi* (Japanese flute).

Another option here is *sesshin*, an intense, weeklong silent meditation retreat; the monastery's Introduction to Zen training weekend is a prerequisite. The sesshin schedule is highly regimented. Days begin well before sunrise, are spent in silence, except for Buddhist chanting services, and include lecture sessions with monastery abbot Daido Loori and senior students, walking meditation, short periods of community work, *and* 8 to 10 hours of *zazen* meditation.

A four-story stone-and-wood structure built earlier in the century by Norwegian crafts-people and Catholic monks houses the dormitory, library, dining hall, classrooms, and *zendo* (meditation hall). Men and women lodge in bunks in sex-segregated rooms that sleep 10; bathrooms are shared. The three meals served daily, buffet style, are vegetarian, with occasional dairy, egg, and fish dishes (and a meat alternative always available); the venue is the main dining hall except during sesshin retreats, when you eat in meditative silence in the zendo. *Zen Mountain Monastery, S. Plank Rd., Box 197PC, Mt. Tremper, NY 12457, tel. 914/688–2228, fax 914/688–7911. Year round: daily, $40–$45; 4–7 days, $185–$325. Sign up 2 weeks in advance.*

THE MID-ATLANTIC

PENNSYLVANIA The Himalayan Interna-tional Institute of Yoga Science and Philos-ophy. Indian yogi Sri Swami Rama, author of numerous books on yoga and meditation, founded this nonprofit institute in 1971 to teach his holistic approach to living, which combines biofeedback, aerobic exercise, breathing, meditation, diet, fasting, and yoga. According to Sri Swami Rama, medi-tation and relaxation enable you to gain con-trol of your body and mind.

Each year, hundreds of weekend seminars on topics such as homeopathy, vegetarian-ism, meditation, creative learning pro-cesses, movement and energy, *pranayama*, and spiritual awakening are conducted by members of the institute's excellent interna-tional faculty, most of whom hold M.D. or Ph.D. degrees. You can create a seven-day work-and-study retreat by combining a weekend seminar with a five-day program of personal meditation, community service, and relaxation. In addition, Sri Swami Rama leads weeklong meditation workshops. There are also 14-day health transformation programs that include daily medical consul-tations, biofeedback sessions, exercise and stretch classes, cooking, and self-awareness classes.

Days begin at 7 AM with hatha yoga and fin-ish after dinner with a lecture. Schedules and class topics vary from workshop to workshop, but each day includes exercise, close to two hours of yoga, and silent time for meditation. In your free time, you can hike, socialize in the tea lounge, help with community work, play tennis, or swim in the pond (or skate on it); bring your own sports equipment. You are asked to observe silence from 10 PM until 8 AM and to avoid emotional relationships and other distrac-tions during your stay.

Accommodations are in the main building, set on 200 acres of woods and meadows in northeastern Pennsylvania's Pocono Moun-tains. You have a choice of dorm rooms with bunk beds or austere double or single rooms with sinks and shared bathrooms and show-ers. Low-fat, sugar-free vegetarian meals, with lots of grains and vegetables, are served buffet style in the dining hall; all baked goods, tofu, and yogurt are made on the premises. *Himalayan International Insti-tute, R.R. 1, Box 400, Honesdale, PA 18431, tel. 717/253–5551 or 800/822–4547, fax 717/ 253–9078. Year-round: 2–14 days, $165– $2,100. Sign up 2–4 weeks in advance.*

VIRGINIA Yogaville. This permanent com-munity of 200 residents was founded by the Reverend Sri Swami Satchidananda to teach the philosophy and practice of Integral Yoga, which combines the three principal yogic practices—meditation, *asana*, and pranayama—to strengthen the connection between mind and body. During weekend workshops and on personal retreats here, you join the community's daily schedule of yoga classes and meditation, which begins at 5 AM and continues until 7:30 PM, interrupted only by meals; weekend workshops also include a daily lecture on topics such as meditation, stress management, naturopathy and yoga, and inner exploration and transformation. On Saturday evenings everyone gathers for satsanga, which is led by Reverend Sri Swami Satchidananda when he is in residence.

Yogaville is in the James River valley near Charlottesville. The Lotus Inn, a wood lodge, contains a health food café and guest rooms with private baths; another two-story building contains classrooms, dormitories, and shared bath and laundry facilities. Motor homes can be parked on the grounds of the 750-acre retreat, and there is plenty of space for tent camping. You take your meals, lacto-vegetarian but with vegan alternatives, in the communal dining hall; the main meal of the day is lunch, which may include fresh fruit, steamed organic vegetables from the community garden, and legume or tofu dishes. Breakfast and dinner are usually light buffets of cereals, yogurt, low-fat milk, and herbal teas. There are special rates for children and discounts for those who make a commitment in advance to work in the garden, kitchen, or other areas of the community. *Yogaville, Rte. 604, Buckingham, VA 23921, tel. 804/969–3121 or 800/858–9642, fax 804/969–1303. Year-round: daily, $22–$80; 3-day workshops, $145–$175. Sign up at least 10 days in advance.*

THE MIDWEST

IOWA **The Raj.** The luxurious Raj health center, which opened in 1992 in the heart of Iowa's rolling meadows and woodlands, is devoted to the ancient system of preventive natural medicine known as Ayurvedic therapy. Three-, five-, and seven-day programs are available. After an assessment of your physiological makeup, a physician concerned both with your physical and your spiritual health prescribes deeply relaxing rejuvenation therapies known as *panchakarma*, once reserved for India's royal families, to restore balance in your body: massages with warm herbal oils, herb-perfumed steam baths, and gentle internal cleansings. In addition, staff experts train you in yogic positions and breathing techniques. An optional course in transcendental meditation teaches you how to increase your self-awareness and manage stress in your life.

The pace of daily activities is unhurried, the staff comforting. Concerts of classical Indian music and lectures on natural medicine, meditation techniques, self-massage, optimizing digestion, the role of intellect and the senses in maintaining health, and other health-related topics fill evenings. You can spend your free time hiking on the 100-acre grounds, working out in the exercise room, and visiting the adjacent Vedic Observatory, where ancient instruments allow you to track planetary and astral movements across Iowa's clear night sky.

Even though the daily vegetarian meals are delicious and filling, most participants lose weight on the program without counting calories. For dinner, you might typically have Indian rice or dal (spiced, puréed legumes), vegetables, cooked fruit, and herbal tea. Accommodations in private villas and the hotel are deluxe; the spacious, air-conditioned rooms and suites have French country furniture with Battenburg lace bedcovers, telephones, and large bathrooms. Families with children are encouraged to stay in the villas to preserve the quiet of the hotel. *The Raj, 24th St. NW, Fairfield, IA 52556, tel. 515/472–9580 or 800/248–9050, fax 515/472–2496. Year-round: 3–7 days, $1,350–$2,850. Sign up at least 2–3 weeks in advance.*

WISCONSIN **Sandhill School and Natural Health Spa.** Weekend seminars and Health Rejuvenation weeks here use a gentle regimen of exercise, education, and outdoor pleasures to teach you to lead a healing lifestyle. Fees include personal counseling and spa services, among them massage, colonic irrigation, acupressure, acupuncture, aromatherapy, energy balancing, and myofacial release. Surrounded by central Wisconsin farmland, the environment is stress-free. The school works in close cooperation with a spiritual retreat, the adjacent Christine Center for Unitive Planetary Spirituality.

You can meditate on your own or with the guidance of the staff, who use Eastern and Western meditative and medical practices to gain understanding of the whole person. Naturopaths and homeopaths come here for workshops that offer practical advice on family health care. Ayurvedic therapies, as well as yoga, are taught.

Two meals a day are available—brunch, served at 10:30 AM, and dinner, which begins at 4:30 PM; the food consists of vegetables, fruits, grains, legumes, nuts, and seeds, seasoned with herbs and spices. You sleep close to nature in either your own tent or a barnlike, dormitory-style structure; there are community bathrooms. *The Sandhill School and Natural Health Spa, Rte. 1, Box 261A, Willard, WI 54493, tel. 715/926–5028. Year-round: daily, $19–$37; 2–7 days, $160–$850. Sign up anytime.*

THE SOUTHWEST

ARIZONA **Global Fitness Adventures in Sedona.** This trip in the Sedona area is the most spiritually oriented program offered by Global Fitness Adventures, an outfitter specializing in fitness and well-being vacations. In an effort to gain deeper spiritual awareness and power, you visit four primary vortexes—energy sources in the Sedona area said to emit positive and negative charges that affect human physiology. You also explore Native American spirituality by participating in a drum and dance workshop, a traditional sweat lodge, and 8- to 15-mile hikes to prehistoric Native American settlements, Anasazi cliff dwellings, and stone medicine wheels.

Days begin with a power drink of puréed fruit, soy protein, and wheat germ, followed by sessions of yoga or tai chi and a long hike. After lunch there are muscle-toning classes, massages (three per week), and a meditation period on a secluded flat rock with panoramic views. Motivational talks on personal power, nutrition, and holistic health follow candlelight suppers in the main lodge. A sunset horseback ride and excursions to Sedona's historic sites and art galleries are also on the schedule.

Accommodations are in spacious, attractively decorated cabins near Juniper Oak Creek. Each has two double bedrooms, a shared bath, a living room with fireplace, and a large deck overlooking a canyon. The chef's vegetarian meals often include meatless adaptations of Tex-Mex specialties. *Global Fitness Adventures, Box 1390, Aspen, CO 81612, tel. 303/927–9593 or 800/488–8747, fax 303/927–4793. Apr.–early May and mid-Oct.–mid-Nov.: 7 days, $1,850. Price includes 3 massages; sign up 1 week in advance.*

THE ROCKIES

COLORADO **Global Fitness Adventures in Aspen.** Fitness with flair best describes the well-being program put together by former fashion model and fitness instructor Kristina Hurrel and her husband, author and holistic health authority Dr. Rob Krakovitz. Their seven-day program mixes pampering, physical challenges, and classes on holistic health, nutrition, and fitness skills to help you tune up your body and permanently improve your lifestyle.

Only a dozen guests participate each week, so the level of attention you receive is high. You are given a personal fitness evaluation and an individualized, tension-busting daily exercise routine; activities include stress-management classes, massages, white-water raft trips, hikes, horseback rides, and sessions of yoga, tai chi, and muscle toning. Days begin at 6:15 AM and follow a set schedule; an afternoon siesta gives you two hours to swim, fish, ride a bike, or loll in the Jacuzzi. You spend evenings listening to motivational talks on personal power, partnering, aging and wisdom, nutrition, holistic health, and detoxification. Available for an additional cost are a Native American sweat lodge purification ceremony, a dance and drum workshop, and personal holistic health consultations with Dr. Krakovitz.

Accommodations are in a comfortable 100-year-old ranch and cabins on 52 acres of land in the Rocky Mountains, in double rooms that cross country kitsch and Ralph Lauren. Meals are either vegetarian or spa style, with lots of salads, vegetables, and fish. *Global Fitness Adventures, Box 1390, Aspen, CO 81612, tel. 303/927–9593 or 800/488–8747, fax 303/927–4793. Mid-June–Sept.: 7 days, $1,800–$2,000. Price includes 3 massages; sign up at least 1 week in advance.*

MONTANA **Feathered Pipe Ranch.** This 110-acre ranch, nestled in the Rocky Mountains near the Continental Divide, was willed to current director India Supera in 1976 with the stipulation that she operate it as a healing center. Accordingly, she presents a series of weeklong summer workshops conducted by nationally and internationally known instructors such as Lilias Folan, Jean Shinoda Bolen, Andrew Weil, and other masters of yoga, mythology, holistic medicine, nutrition, shamanism, Native American spirituality, astrology, classical Indian music, or bodywork. The center's offerings are purposely diverse: The goal is to help participants find exactly what they need to realize their wholeness and connection to all of life.

Two- to three-hour morning and afternoon classes are separated by long lunch and dinner breaks that give you plenty of time to be outdoors. There are rolling lawns for sunning, miles of trails for hiking, caves to explore, and a 3-acre pond for swimming. Evening entertainment ranges from skits and storytelling to presentations by naturalists. Optional activities (for an additional cost) include an array of massages and a daylong river float trip.

Vegetarian meals are served buffet style in the main lodge; you can also have fish and organic chicken. Accommodations, for up to 40, are in log and stone chalets, tents, tepees, and Mongolian yurts in the forest; there are a few private rooms (some with private baths) as well as dormitory rooms that sleep four to six. The cedar bathhouse contains a hot tub, a sauna, massage rooms, and bathing facilities. *Feathered Pipe Ranch, Box 1682, Helena, MT 59624, tel. 406/442–8196, fax 406/442–8110. May–early Sept.: 8 days, $899–$1,250. Sign up 2–4 weeks in advance.*

WYOMING **Antelope Retreat Center.** The center's setting—500 acres of highland valley, in the foothills of the Rockies between Medicine Bow National Forest and Red Desert—is a key element in its programs, which focus on expanding your self-awareness as you reconnect with the natural environment. John Boyer grew up on this ranch and opened the place in 1988 because he wanted to share his love of nature and the inner peace he had found through the spiritual practices of his Native American neighbors. Rituals of Lakota and Dakota Sioux and other Native Americans, among them sweat lodges and vision quests, are a part of many of the center's programs.

You can choose three- or seven-day summer workshops on survival and nature awareness, vision quests, sacred Native American rituals, or crafts and skills; other weeklong quests aim to help women reconnect with nature and celebrate themselves, other women, and the environment. The daily schedules of each workshop vary with the topic and the group; the staff responds to the needs and interests of each group of participants. Unstructured personal retreats are available year-round; on these you are free to pitch in with ranch chores, gardening, and cooking, or to fill your time with meditation and hiking or skiing. Steamboat Springs, Colorado, is nearby.

You stay in comfortable if not luxurious quarters in the 100-year-old ranch house, in five double rooms that share a bath, or in two yurts outside, each accommodating four.

Meals are generally vegetarian, with occasional fish or fowl options. *Antelope Retreat Center, Box 166, Savery, WY 82332, tel. 307/383–2625. Year-round: daily, $36–$58. Late May–early Sept.: 3–7 days, $235–$650. Sign up 2–4 weeks in advance for workshops, anytime for personal retreats.*

THE WEST COAST

CALIFORNIA **Esalen Institute.** Founded in 1962, and widely considered the birthplace of the human potential movement in the United States, the Esalen Institute in Big Sur still offers the country's broadest curriculum focused on the areas of spiritual awareness and holistic health. In workshops, you can study biofeedback, contemplative practices, cooking, cultural arts, dreams, Gestalt therapy, hypnosis, intuitive development, martial arts, massage and bodywork, men's and women's studies, psychological processes, relationships, shamanism, social responsibility, sports, and wilderness and ecology; cost and duration of these workshops vary. When workshop participants do not fill all rooms, you can also stay at Esalen for an unstructured personal retreat.

A workshop's daily schedule depends on the rhythm your leader wants to establish. There is always free time for you to experience all that Esalen offers on a daily basis: tai chi and exercise classes, nature hikes, clothing-optional swimming in hot spring-fed pools, massages, rolfing, and other bodywork. Evenings bring lectures, concerts, films, dances, and other relaxing entertainment.

Esalen is situated on a particularly stunning section of the California coast, and some of the guest accommodations are in rustic lodges that overlook the pounding surf. Most bedrooms and baths are shared. Rooms with bunk beds are slightly cheaper, and children get discounted rates when accompanied by both parents. There are special activities and a dining plan just for kids; Esalen's Gazebo Park School, for youngsters aged one to six, runs year-round and can serve as child care (at additional cost). Meals are family style and incorporate meat, fish, dairy products, and fresh produce grown on the property; vegetarian options are always available. *Esalen Institute, Big Sur, CA 93920, tel. 408/667–3000 or 408/667–3005, fax 408/667–2724. Year-round: daily, $70–$125; 2–7 days, $350–$1,150. Sign up 1 month in advance for seminars, and at least 1 week in advance for personal retreats.*

CALIFORNIA **Global Fitness Adventures in Palm Springs.** Picturesque Palm Springs is yet another beautiful location for the physically and mentally challenging weeklong vacations put together by Global Fitness Adventures. Under the guidance of director Kristina Hurrel and her staff, you and 5 to 11 other participants will tune up physically through 8- to 18-mile hikes and yoga, aquatic aerobics, and muscle-toning classes. You explore Joshua Tree National Monument and the mountains and canyons of Palm Springs and, with a Native American guide, search for the ancient rock art, arrowheads, pottery shards, and ceremonial sites of the Agua Caliente Cahuilla people. Revitalizing massages and hydrotherapy are also part of the program, along with motivational lectures on weight control, stress management, personal empowerment, detoxification, and other holistic health and wellness issues. A sunset horseback ride through the canyons is part of all stays, and during certain weeks you can participate in a Native American sweat lodge ritual.

A chef prepares vegetarian meals of pastas, legumes, fruit, soups, salads, and, occasionally, fish. Accommodations are double rooms in small, private adobe casitas with fireplaces and are accessible to the swimming pools and Jacuzzi via flower-edged pathways. *Global Fitness Adventures, Box 1390, Aspen, CO 81612, tel. 303/927–9593 or 800/488–8747, fax 303/927–4793. Late Feb–mid-Mar., late Apr.–early May, and late Nov.–mid Dec.: 7 days, $1,800. Price includes 3 massages; sign up at least 1 week in advance.*

CALIFORNIA Green Gulch Farm Zen Center. Although it's only 25 miles from San Francisco, this work-study retreat on 200 acres of pines and open fields stretching to the Pacific seems far removed from the rest of the world; it is a peaceful spot to experience Zen Buddhist traditions. You can come here for free-form personal retreats or for more structured practice retreats.

Personal retreats can be as long or as short as you like, and you are free to come and go as you please. You can join in communal life and work on the organic farm, or quietly meditate on long walks through the nearby woods to Muir Beach. If you are a newcomer, you may want to join a "sitting" that introduces the forms, spirit, and detail of the Soto Zen way of life ($15); this includes instruction on zazen and *kinhin* and a discussion and silent meditation period with some of the community's full-time residents. You can join classes on Zen, learn to play the *shakuhachi* (Japanese flute), or take part in a meditative tea ceremony.

Practice retreats, available Sunday through Thursday with a three-night minimum stay, mix free time with participation in some community work and Zen practices. The morning schedule includes meditation, work, classes, and group discussions; afternoons and evenings are free. For lending a hand, you receive free meals and a modest discount on the lodging rate. There are also scheduled weekend workshops in flower arranging, organic gardening, and raku pottery (using clay dug on the farm).

There may be anywhere from six to 16 guests at the center at one time. Accommodations are in the Lindisfarne Guest House, constructed by hand in the Japanese temple style. It has a suite and 12 double rooms surrounding an atrium that rises to a traditional sloped roof; rates vary with room size. Vegetarian meals, cooked using produce from the farm, cost an extra $5 each if you are not taking part in a scheduled workshop or a practice retreat. There's an outdoor pool, and miles of hiking trails lead to Mt. Tamalpais and the Mill Valley. *Green Gulch Farm Zen Center, Star Rte., Sausalito, CA 94965, tel. 415/383–3134, fax 415/383–3128. Year-round: daily, $35–$80; 3 days, $270–$300. Price does not include meals on personal retreats; sign up anytime.*

CALIFORNIA Heartwood Institute. This rustic community on 240 acres of rolling meadows and fir-covered hills seeks to heal the earth by healing and nurturing its people. Masseurs, hypnotherapists, and polarity practitioners come here for further vocational training; the institute's wellness workshops and retreats are open to all. It's a place to unwind and treat yourself to some pampering, inexpensive bodywork sessions.

Weeklong workshops are one option; topics include Zen, hatha yoga, dietary healing, shiatsu, and other forms of self-help and holistic healing. In spring and summer, you can take a seven-day rejuvenation retreat designed to cleanse your body, mind, and spirit through juice fasting, massage, meditation, exercise, relaxation, and emotional release. In summer and fall, there is a nine-day polarity cleansing retreat, which involves a simple alkaline diet, eating support group meetings, and daily lessons in polarity balancing bodywork—balancing your body's energy using a combination of massage, meditation, exercise, and diet. The staff can also help you develop 2- to 22-day personalized retreats.

Ongoing classes in yoga, tai chi, and meditation are part of every stay, as are dips in the pool and hot tub and visits to the wood-fired sauna. In your free time, you can go hiking or mountain biking through the hills or observe the wild deer, turkeys, bobtail cats, and raccoons that live on the grounds. Unless you're fasting, you have three organic vegetarian meals a day (brunch and dinner only on Saturday and Sunday). Fish is served occasionally, and dishes containing common allergens such as wheat and milk are clearly labeled and alternatives provided. Accommodations are very simple, with private and shared rooms and communal baths in the log lodge and numerous campsites tucked among the trees around the grounds. *Heartwood Institute, 220 Harmony La., Garberville, CA 95542, tel. 707/923–2021, fax 707/923–4906. Year-round: daily, $55–$110. May–mid-Oct.: 7–9 days, $550–$890. Sign up 1 month in advance for workshops, anytime for personal retreats.*

CALIFORNIA **Ojai Foundation.** This center for cross-cultural and spiritual education, personal renewal, and reconnection with the land opened in 1979 on 40 acres of wilderness in the Upper Ojai Valley, north of Los Angeles. Programs here focus on social and spiritual themes, and many, including solstice and equinox ceremonies, are strongly linked to the four seasons and the land. Stays are designed to help you explore and deepen your relationships with others and achieve greater harmony with the earth. A specialty is improving your communications skills through the use of council meetings. You sit in a circle with a group and engage in dialogues, during which you strive to be a better listener and to effectively express your own thoughts.

Workshops last between two and four days and are usually held over a weekend. They may cover Zen meditation, natural healing, permaculture (sustainable patterns in human habitation), and such Native American practices as vision quests and sweat lodge ceremonies. Daily schedules vary with each workshop, but group meditation, classes on the featured topic, and council meetings are part of most days.

You can also arrange a personal retreat. This can be a time of seclusion or another program that meets your needs, which the staff can help you create. You can fill your days with meditation sessions, stretching and toning exercises, long hikes, visits to the ocean or hot springs nearby, or sessions in the ceramic studio.

Accommodations are in your own tent or in one of the foundation's wilderness hermitages—geodesic domes, tepees, or yurts furnished with a futon, table, and lamp. You supply the bedding in the hermitages. During workshops, vegetarian meals are served

buffet style in the dining room or on a sunny deck, and everyone helps out with preparation and clean-up. Food is not included in the cost of personal retreats, but you have access to cooking facilities. Families are encouraged to visit, and children are welcome. *Ojai Foundation, Box 1620, Ojai, CA 93024, tel. 805/646–8343. Year-round: daily, $18–$30. Mar.–June and Sept.–Dec.: 2–4 days, $150–$220. Price does not include meals on personal retreats; sign up at least 2 weeks in advance.*

CALIFORNIA **St. Helena Health Center.** What began in 1878 as a rural summer health retreat is now a fully accredited hospital and health care complex. Its programs combine holistic and Western medical practices to help you recover your health and learn to live a lifestyle that preserves it. Personal attention is a feature; the large staff, which includes a dietician, lifestyle counselor, respiratory therapist, and physiologist, as well as physicians and nurses, cares for just 10 to 20 guests a week. Individualized programs, a center specialty, are based on a complete medical exam and assessment of your diet and include bodywork, hydrotherapy, and a nutrition regimen.

There are also several 5- to 12-day group programs. The 5-day PrimeLife Fitness program, offered four times each year, includes fitness and nutrition education. The 7-day Smoking Cessation program, offered each month, relies on group support as well as education. Once or twice a year the center offers the renowned McDougall program, a 12-day workshop that assesses disease risk factors and focuses on prevention through nutrition, exercise, and stress-management techniques. Group discussions, individual counseling, biofeedback, relaxation and fitness training, and classes on how to shop for and prepare nutritious, low-fat, high-carbohydrate meals are all part of this program, along with massage and time in the sauna, steam room, and whirlpool.

The daily routine at the center changes with the program, but most days start with a walk before breakfast and include a health education seminar and exercise sessions in the gym, followed in the afternoon by stress-management training and perhaps aquatic aerobics sessions in the pool. Evenings bring more educational seminars, free time, and group winery tours, picnics, and shopping trips. The center is on a wooded hillside overlooking acres of vineyards. Although it has hiking and cycling trails, tennis courts, a pool, and a golf course, St. Helena remains very much a health retreat rather than a spa or resort.

Meals, served in the dining room, are lacto-ovo and vegan vegetarian; you may have low-fat desserts but no caffeinated beverages or alcohol. The double rooms in the guest lodge have motel-modern furnishings, private bathrooms, and balconies with views of the valley. *St. Helena Health Center, Deer Park, CA 94576, tel. 707/963–6200 or 800/358–9195; in CA, 800/862–7575; fax 707/963–6461. Year-round: daily, $185; 5–12 days, $1,185–$3,825. Sign up at least 1 week in advance.*

CALIFORNIA **Shenoa Retreat and Learning Center.** Shenoa was founded in 1987 by American alumni of the Findhorn Foundation in Scotland—perhaps the most famous New Age community and learning center in the world. The focus here is on personal and planetary transformation through education and increased self-awareness. Three- to 14-day workshops cover inner focusing, organic gardening, ecology, and religious studies; there's also voice dialogue training for mental health professionals. One frequently repeated seminar, called the Institute for Independent Living, teaches practical skills for living in harmony with the land; classes are on sustainable structures, nontoxic building materials, renewable power systems, and alternative energy options. A variety of three- and four-day family retreats, with workshops for parents, special activities for children, and optional short-term child care, are offered throughout the year, usually over holiday weekends. Unstructured personal retreats are another option. Up to 100 people may be on hand at any given time.

When classes are not meeting, you can take part in meditation sessions, indulge in a massage, tour the nearby vineyards, or take advantage of a list of outdoor activities that includes hiking, biking, swimming, tennis, badminton, and volleyball. The center has a beautiful setting on 160 acres of sunny meadows and cool forests bordered by the Navarro River and the Hendy Wood State Park redwood groves.

Meals are vegetarian, served buffet style in the dining lodge or outside under the oak trees. The 17 rustic cabins are decorated with handmade quilts and fresh wildflowers and have a private bath and at least two beds (but you must supply towels and bedding); single travelers must often share a cabin when it's busy. There is also a large, forested grove with campsites and communal bathhouses. *Shenoa Retreat and Learning Center, Box 43, Philo, CA 95466, tel. 707/895–3156, fax 707/895–3236. Year-round: daily, $30–$60. May–Oct.: 3–14 days, $90–$1,400. Sign up 2 months in advance.*

CALIFORNIA **Sivananda Ashram Yoga Farm.** This farm north of Sacramento in peaceful Grass Valley is the place to come for serious learning. Under the guidance of spiritual leader Swami Vishnu-Devananda, you and up to 30 other guests join the farm's 15 full-time residents in a strict schedule of meditation, chanting, and yoga to increase your awareness of the mind-body connection. Yoga classes concentrate on asana, pranayama, *dhyana* (positive thinking and meditation), and *savasana* (relaxation). Guest lecturers conduct special weekend and weeklong retreats on meditation, Native American wisdom, vegetarianism, Ayurvedic healing, and stress management.

Guests here must observe numerous rules. Participation in morning and evening meditation, chanting, and yoga classes is mandatory, and smoking and consumption of alcohol, drugs, and certain foods (including meat, fish, and eggs) are forbidden. You may be asked to help out with communal chores and share a room; accommodations include a few double rooms and several dorm-style rooms in a simple farmhouse and plenty of camping space on the property. Showers and toilets are shared. Two lacto-vegetarian meals are served buffet style each day: Brunch consists of cereals, yogurt, and fruit; dinner may include stir-fried or steamed vegetables, rice, tofu dishes, salad, and homemade soups and bread. *Sivananda Ashram Yoga Farm, 14651 Ballantree La., Grass Valley, CA 95949, tel. 916/272–9322. Year-round: daily, $25–$50; additional fees of $5–$18 per day during workshops. Price does not include camping gear; sign up anytime.*

CALIFORNIA **Tassajara.** In summer, this monastic community—established by the San Francisco Zen Center and well-known among food lovers for its cookbooks—opens its doors to those interested in studying Zen Buddhism. Its secluded location, next to the Tassajara Hot Springs in a narrow canyon filled with chaparral, sycamores, and oaks, provides a peaceful setting for Zen reflection. During your stay, you are invited to join the 40 full-time residents in meditation, receive basic Zen instruction, and attend lectures as you wish.

The community schedule begins before sunrise with zazen and includes work on the farm, yoga, meditation, and classes on various topics in Zen; during special five- and six-day workshops, there are classes on yoga, poetry, cooking, gardening, and sensory awareness. If you stay at least three days, you can participate in a practice retreat, in which you join members of the community in a half-day of work on the farm and spend time with leaders who guide you in the ways of Zen. You still have plenty of time for hiking, meditating in the gardens, relaxing in the steam room, and soaking in the natural sulfur spring plunges and tubs.

As many as 30 people may visit Tassajara at a time. Accommodations vary greatly and include austere dormitories, yurts, shared and private Japanese-style and redwood cabins, and a large two-bedroom suite with private bathroom and deck. The delicious ovo-lacto vegetarian Zen cuisine here is famous. Meals are served buffet style in the stone dining hall. *Tassajara, c/o Zen Center, 300 Page St., San Francisco, CA 94102, tel. 415/431–3771, fax 415/431–1006. May–early Sept.: daily, $65–$180; 5–6 days, $480–$1,030. Sign up at least 3–6 weeks in advance.*

OREGON **Aesculapia Wilderness Healing Retreat.** Graywolf (Fred) Swinney, noted author, philosopher, psychotherapist, and dream healer, believes that physical and psychological illness is the result of internal chaos, and that self-healing, spiritual renewal, and personal evolution can only begin when the disorder in your basic consciousness is revealed. In 1984, to help others work toward this revelation, he founded this shamanic dream healing center. Here he uses a variety of ancient and contemporary therapies and healing processes, such as rhythmic drumming, vision quests, Gestalt therapy, visualization, psychotherapy, sweat lodges, and fire rituals, to achieve a perfect balance in mind, body, and spirit. Named for Asclepius, the Greek god of healing, the retreat is on 80 verdant acres in the Siskiyou Mountains in southern Oregon.

There are usually one to four guests here at a time. Your retreat is a completely customized personal exploration. If you have two weeks, you may choose to make a River and Dreams vision quest, which involves white-water rafting and camping in the wilderness along the nearby Rogue River. Lodging options range from rustic cabins and simply furnished lodge rooms to wooded campsites; you supply linens and bedding. During your stay you help prepare the meals, which are vegetarian, and you can do volunteer work around the center. *Aesculapia Wilderness Healing Retreat, Box 301, Wilderville, OR 97543, tel. 503/476–0492. Year-round: daily, $100; 1 week, $550. Sign up at least 2 weeks in advance.*

OREGON **Breitenbush Hot Springs Retreat and Conference Center.** This holistic retreat, nestled in the Willamette National Forest, is named for the natural hot springs and artesian wells that are its major attraction. Although there are many options for soaking—clothing-optional pools in an open meadow, and tubs of varying temperatures in a medicine wheel configuration—guests don't spend all their time here in the water. A 1930s lodge contains gathering rooms where classes address issues relating to self-help, holistic healing, and spiritual growth. Other offerings include yoga, tai chi, meditation, guided hikes, metaphysical counseling, and yogalike spinal maintenance exercises known as EDGU. Certain other treatments cost extra: herbal wraps, massage, aromatherapy, and *Reiki,* an ancient healing method that involves the laying on of hands and mental and spiritual balancing. Poetry readings, drumming circles, storytelling, dances, and concerts are held frequently, and there is a sweat lodge every month.

You may choose to take advantage of these activities on a completely unregimented personal retreat; or you may opt to sign up for one of the weekend to weeklong workshops, which cover such topics as permaculture, folk dancing, nutrition, shamanism, aromatherapy, art, and writing. These workshops include a full schedule of classes on these subjects, in addition to the center's daily activities.

The community is self-sustaining and very environmentally conscious; hydroelectricity and geothermal heat provide power and warmth to all the buildings, among them the natural steam sauna, forest meditation sanctuary, and a greenhouse where organic produce is grown. The center is cooperatively managed by 50 full-time residents, each highly trained in yoga instruction, massage, counseling, or other fields. Up to 120 guests stay in a lodge, 41 simply furnished cabins (some with sinks and toilets), and 10 raised platform tents scattered around a communal bathhouse; you supply bedding and linens. Children are welcome. *Breitenbush Hot Springs Retreat and Conference Center, Box 578, Detroit, OR 97342, tel. 503/854-3314. Year-round: daily, $30–$75; 3–7 days, $90–* $600. Sign up 2 months in advance for workshops, 2 weeks in advance for personal retreats.

HAWAII

KAUAI **Hawaiian Wellness Holiday.** The objective here is to detoxify your body through rigorous exercise, massage, reflexology, chiropractic treatments, Reiki, aura balancing, and other natural therapies, as well as through a cleansing regimen involving diet and the possible use of organic laxatives and colonics. Director Grady Deal—a psychologist, massage therapist, nutritional counselor, health columnist, and practicing chiropractor—and his wife, Roberleigh—a massage therapist, yoga and aerobics instructor, numerologist, and astrologer—tailor weeklong programs for groups of 10 participants. The typical guest is between 30 and 65 and female (the ratio is three women to each man), and most want to start an exercise program in this motivational setting or are seeking major life changes because of health problems.

Here you learn to self-diagnose and treat underlying metabolic causes of health and weight problems. Instruction in yoga, aerobics, meditation, and macrobiotic cooking fill a good portion of your day. Three weekly massage or chiropractic treatments and excursions to view Kauai's colorful flowers, inviting beaches, sparkling waterfalls, and lush valleys are also on the schedule. Housing during the program is in the posh Sheraton Kauai Resort on Poipu Beach; you can choose a garden- or ocean-view room or suite, or opt to rent a condo. Meals are vegetarian, with fish and dairy options. You can take advantage of the many sports available in the resort area, including tennis, golf, scuba diving, and surfing. Children are welcome and can participate in the various activities with their parents. *Hawaiian Wellness Holiday, Box 279, Koloa, Kauai, HI 96756, tel. 808/332-9244 or 800/338-6977. Year-round: 7 days, $1,795. Sign up 3–6 months in advance for winter stays, anytime for other dates.*

OAHU **The Plantation Spa.** At this plantation on the verdant slopes of the Koolau Mountains, exercise, positive thinking, and pampering treatments help you achieve a balance of body, mind, and spirit. Instructors, all between the ages of 28 and 40, work closely with you throughout your stay; they can provide fitness evaluations and as much or as little supervision as you want.

A variety of fitness and instructional programs are available between 7 AM and 3 PM each day, including low-impact and aquatic aerobics, yoga, stretching, weight training, and meditation. You may take as many classes as you wish—or as few—and spend free time in the Jacuzzi, by the pool, on the beach, or out exploring the island. Then, until dinner at 6, you can indulge in a massage, beauty treatments, or herbal wraps. Motivational lectures on self-improvement, health topics, and positive thinking are part of the program, as are canoe trips, hikes to waterfalls, and classes in hula dancing and vegetarian cooking.

The Plantation Spa is very intimate: just 10 to 14 guests are housed each week in eight Polynesian-style rooms (some with private bath) in rustic cottages. Meals are strictly vegetarian, incorporating much produce grown on the property, and are served on the veranda or in the dining room of the main house to those who aren't on a supervised juice or water fast. You can opt for packages of varying lengths; some include a full array of pampering treatments and some don't. *The Plantation Spa, 51-550 Kamehameha Hwy., Ka'a'awa, HI 96730, tel. 808/237–8685 or 800/422–0307, fax 808/422–0307. Year-round: 7 days, $1,025–$1,490. Sign up 1 week in advance.*

SOURCES

ORGANIZATIONS The **Nutritional Health Alliance** (Box 267, Farmingdale, NY 11735, tel. 516/249–7070) can provide information on the role of nutrition in natural healing. The **International Spa and Fitness Association** (6935 Wisconsin Ave. NW, Washington, DC 20815, tel. 202/789–5920) can answer most questions on spa programs and therapies.

PERIODICALS *Body, Mind, and Spirit* (Island Publishing Company, Inc., 255 Hope St., Provincetown, RI 02906, tel. 401/351–4320 or 800/338–5216), published bimonthly, is filled with articles on spiritual growth and natural healing; it lists conferences and gatherings around the country. *Kindred Spirit Quarterly* (Kindred Spirit Publishing, Foxhole, Dartington, Totnes, Devon TQ9 6EB, England) is a guide to personal and planetary healing. *Natural Health* (Natural Health Limited Partnership, 17 Station St., Box 1200, Brookline Village, MA 02147, tel. 617/232–1000) is a bimonthly publication on holistic health issues. The *New Age Journal* (Rising Star Associates, Ltd., 342 Western Ave., Brighton, MA 02135, tel. 617/787–2005), also bimonthly, covers a broad base, touching on holistic health, spirituality, self-awareness, and the environment; Rising Star's *Holistic Health Directory*, published every other year, defines healing methods, energy and movement techniques, and forms of counseling, and includes an index of resources. The quarterly *Shaman's Drum* (Cross-Cultural Shamanism Network, Box 430, Willis, CA 95490, tel. 707/459–0486) covers experiential shamanism.

BOOKS *Fodor's Healthy Escapes,* by Bernard Burt, gives thorough reviews of spas and retreats throughout the country.

ALSO SEE If spa treatments appeal to you, take a look at the Spas and Fitness Centers chapter.

Painting Workshops

By Mary King Nash

If you have ever held a paintbrush, dipped it in color, and confronted a blank canvas, you've experienced the dream: You're Georgia O'Keeffe painting cow skulls bleached by a New Mexico sun; Winslow Homer chronicling a nor'easter off the coast of Maine; Thomas Cole examining the wonders of a forest glade in the Catskill Mountains. Your undiscovered genius could turn Rembrandt green with envy and send Picasso back to his blue period. But the first brush stroke brings back reality and, with it, some wishful thinking: "If only I had time, a few uninterrupted days, then I could really paint my masterpiece!"

Sign up for a painting workshop and your wish is granted. Obviously you could always register for a continuing education course at a local college or art school, or a summer program at a community art center. But the opportunity to really focus on your art comes in painting workshops—weeklong programs designed for masters-in-the-making and scheduled when the weather is most pleasant, usually between March and November. Here, away from your everyday environment, you can have professional instruction, inspiring settings, and perhaps even a warm bed and three square meals a day.

No two programs are quite alike. Some are at inns and resorts; others are run by professional artists for three days or longer. Some are operated for profit (these usually provide greater physical comforts), and some are not-for-profit (these are usually less expensive). Some are at centers that offer only fine art classes; other times, painting is just one of several disciplines being taught. Some programs are better for experts; others appeal primarily to novices.

Some workshops are more serious than others, or more leisurely, more instructive, more social, more expensive, more comfortable, or more scenic. Some are longer than others, or larger. Some are indoors and others are on location. You can rough it at a campground and cook your own meals; or bed down in basic dorms and subsist on mystery meat and other institutional fare; or live like a king at posh inns with antiques-filled rooms and exquisite meals. Whether you want to learn a new pastime, perfect a technique, study with a respected artist or learned professor, or simply meet and paint with kindred spirits, there's a painting workshop that's right for you.

Your choice in any one of these categories will not be limited by location; you can take a painting workshop almost anywhere in the United States. Not surprisingly, the settings that draw artists—and these workshops—are some of America the Beautiful's most beautiful: Maine's craggy coast, cool Wisconsin lakes, the green Hudson River Valley, the immense Colorado Rockies, California's lush wine country, redwood forests in the Pacific Northwest. An unusually large number of painting workshops flourish in and around Taos, one of the most art-con-

Mary King Nash, a freelance writer and editor who lives in New York City, looks forward to the day that she can render images as well as Mary Cassatt.

scious towns in America, where the light is clear and the colors vibrant. Any artist will tell you the only true way to see any of these places is from the painter's perspective.

In general, painting weeks run from Monday through Friday; participants arrive Sunday afternoon, when there's some kind of get-acquainted event, and leave Friday afternoon or, sometimes, Saturday morning. You might start off the week with a demonstration by the instructor, who establishes your goals and explains techniques; a lecture may begin each succeeding day. Some classes are a bit more freeform; instructors start you off painting what you like and then spend their days moving from one easel to another offering help, tips, and advice on the work in progress. Either way, painting days usually run from between 9 and 10 to between 2:30 and 5; most sessions end with a critique of the day's work. After dark, some centers have lectures, informal group discussions, and other get-togethers; others, especially in areas of considerable beauty, encourage you to explore the area on your own. Most centers have studios that are open around the clock, so that you can keep on painting if your muse is a night owl. Prices for five days range from $185 to $465 for five days of tuition only, $450 to $800 for a complete package that includes housing and at least some meals.

Studying the landscape of whatever area you visit and noting particulars of season, color, and light there—experiencing the moment in brilliant, living color—will reveal more about it than you could ever learn when sightseeing. And the painting you complete will recall more about your stay than any postcard or photograph. It's the perfect souvenir.

CHOOSING THE RIGHT WORKSHOP

The painting workshops below all offer an attractive location, a respected program, knowledgeable teachers, and a variety of choices. Before donning smock and beret and grabbing your portable easel and paints,

though, it's wise to do a little investigating to find the program that suits you best.

What subject matter and medium does the instructor teach? Although landscapes are the most popular topic, some instructors touch on figure painting, still life, or portraiture. Most workshops concentrate on a single medium, usually the one that the instructor is most comfortable with; some, however, leave the decision to you. Watercolor, although hard to master, lends itself to the immediacy of outdoor work, since its translucence reproduces some of the qualities of light you see in many landscapes and seascapes. Oils, although messy, slow, and hard to transport, are also lush and forgiving of mistakes; the colors are opulent and infused with light. You can find some classes in acrylics.

What is the class level? A novice needs to learn the basics, and programs that include daily demonstrations and a lot of supervised instruction best meet a beginner's needs. Intermediate and advanced painters usually want to get right to work; they want less structured classes that allow them to paint on their own, with individual critiques to get them over the rough spots.

Some workshops are open to students at all levels. This is not a problem for a good, experienced teacher, but you may find it irksome. If you're a beginner, you must judge whether you will find it stressful or stimulating to be around more advanced painters. An experienced painter might find beginning-level lectures boring—or might want to learn a thing or two by going back to the basics.

What are the instructor's qualifications? The instructor plays a significant role in how much enjoyment, as well as instruction, you receive. Investigate both teaching experience and personal style. Don't take it for granted that a talented artist will be a good teacher, or that you have found the painting experience of a lifetime just because a brochure tells you so. This is especially important if you choose to sign on with an independent workshop, put together by the instructor (who do you think writes those brochures?). If possible, try to arrange a short interview to assess your rapport with the instructor before handing over your money and committing your time. Ask questions about anything that concerns you. If the instructor makes you feel uncomfortable or skirts your questions, proceed with caution.

How large are the classes? The answer to this question will help you determine how much individual attention the program provides: The more students, the less one-on-one instruction. In most workshops, class size is under 20.

How many instructors are there per class? The point is to find out how much personal attention you receive in class; this is another way of approaching the issue. There may be one or more teaching assistants if the class is large.

What are days like? Find out how the day is divided between time in the studio and outdoors, lectures, demonstrations, and free time. Some programs are more intense than others: Some are leisurely half-day sessions, others involve seven or more hours of supervised work, and others fall somewhere in between. At the most rigorous programs, you eat and sleep painting, often working late at night in studios that never close. Decide what you want, then make sure that the program can give it to you. Will you find it relaxing to spend every moment painting?

What is the location like? All the programs described in this chapter are in attractive locations, but what catches the imagination of one painter may leave another cold. If your interest is in capturing the mood of gritty city scenes, you definitely don't want a program staged by the sea. If you want to paint the sea, you don't want one on a Taos ranch.

What's the cost and what's included? Ask about tuition, meals, accommodations, and supplies. The fee structure varies widely from one painting workshop to the next. The cost for many workshops in big cities, at resorts, and at established art schools that offer intensive programs in addition to full semesters is for tuition alone; it can range from well under $150 to more than $800. At other workshops, there's a complete package that includes tuition, lodging, and most or all meals. Sometimes the workshop offers separate packages for tuition and housing; the housing price may or may not include meals. Also find out about any application fees (which may be as much as $75).

In the reviews that follow, we give the price of the complete package when such a package is available. When the workshop offers separate prices for tuition and housing, both fees are given; prices we give for housing also get you three meals a day unless otherwise noted. All prices are per person, and all-inclusive packages and lodging rates are based on double occupancy. If you are alone, you will more than likely have to share with someone, unless you are willing to pay an extra charge that is usually assessed for a single.

Note that some schools supply portable easels or field chairs; occasionally they may furnish brushes, paints, and other essentials. However, you may be more comfortable with your own supplies, so instructors usually send out a materials list.

What are the accommodations like? At workshops that provide accommodations, get a sense of the general level of comfort: Ask how large the rooms are, how they're furnished, and whether baths are private or shared. If you prefer a room of your own, make sure that singles are available. Daily maid service is not a given, except at resorts; your quarters may not have a telephone or television, again except at resorts. Accommodations can be quite Spartan at the many nonprofit arts centers that attract excellent teachers yet keep workshop costs down to enable the widest possible group of students to participate. These can be true bargains, but you may be required to have a roommate or two. In such instances, if what's provided is not to your taste, you can make your own arrangements; with the money you save on the program, you can live in the luxury that suits you. In this case, or if there are no on-site accommodations, ask for lodging recommendations; nearby options may offer discounts to workshop participants.

What is the food like? At some of the non-profit workshops that keep costs down to allow artists of all income levels to participate, food may be simple and choices may be limited. If you prefer something different, just don't buy the meal plan. Usually, menus are regionally biased (if you're painting in the Pacific Northwest, marine fare dominates menus), but nearly always include pasta and straightforward American meat and fish dishes.

What facilities and activities are available for your traveling companions who don't paint? Some programs are better than others for this. Best of all are those held at resorts and inns where other activities are available; next best are programs held in vacation areas with a lot of community activities and facilities. Some painting workshops are at centers that also offer classes in ceramics, creative writing, metalsmithing, papermaking, photography, printmaking, quilting, weaving, woodworking, or other fine or applied arts or crafts disciplines.

If you do decide to make the trip with non-painting companions and the program that interests you is residential, ask what arrangements can be made for them; can they share your room and purchase the meal plan without paying for the workshop? There may or may not be a program for your children.

How long has the workshop been running? Longevity in a workshop is a good indication that people are happy with the instruction provided—and a sign that any questions and challenges that you present to the sponsors will have been resolved, probably happily, for other students before you. However, don't dismiss newcomers out of hand, particularly if their credentials are good—say, if the principals or sponsoring organizations have been involved with other noteworthy operations.

Do you have references from past students? To clarify any questions you may have about the instruction, accommodations, and food, there's no substitute for a talk with someone who has painted with the teacher, slept in the beds, and eaten the meals. Even if you call none of the names you're given, the organization's willingness to supply you with references is a good indication that the feedback you get should be positive.

How far in advance do I need to book? Schedules for summer programs are usually set by January or February. Making your commitment this early is never a bad idea, and in some cases it's essential—as for really unusual or popular workshops, which are popular in part because their small size means a lot of individual attention. On the other hand, some schools cancel courses if they don't attract enough students. In most cases, it's safe to make your plans between one and six months ahead of the workshop date. If you can't get in one year, try for the next. If you have your heart set on a specific workshop, it's always worth your while to call, even at the last minute, when you might snag a cancellation.

MAJOR PLAYERS

ACADEMY OF REALIST ART Artist-instructor Gary Faigin believes in the basics, and he offers you a solid foundation in the traditional principles of drawing and painting—namely, how to draw and paint what you see. With his wife, Pamela Belyea, he founded the Academy of Realist Art in 1989, and they run painting programs in Seattle in fall and winter and in Santa Fe every summer. The Seattle classes are in various rented studios, while the New Mexico program is headquartered at the Immaculate Heart of Mary Retreat Center, a tranquil 40-acre estate 2 miles from the center of Santa Fe. Here, he offers a series of intense, 10-day studio workshops limited to 24 students; these concentrate on the figure, portrait, and still life. In New Mexico there are also landscape classes, which take place in some of the most spectacular locales in northern New Mexico. Typically, beginning students work in charcoal, intermediate students in chalk pastel, and more advanced artists in oil paint. Instructors are professional painters with a formal academic training, and have exhibited in well-known galleries. Although the classes are expensive, at $775 to $975, you do get 60 hours of instruction in each five-day week (weekends are paint-on-your-own) as well as evening programs and various special events. Accommodations, priced separately from tuition at about $900 to $1,150, are simple and spare (private and shared rooms with their own bath and dorm quarters with a communal bath); fees for lodging also include weekday lunches and breakfasts daily (5004 6th Ave. NW, Seattle, WA 98107, tel. 206/784–4268, fax 206/783–1410).

ANDERSON RANCH ARTS CENTER This center, which occupies a complex of 10 buildings on 4 acres of a former sheep ranch 10 miles from Aspen, offers nearly 100 one- and two-week arts workshops every summer, and the number is growing. It was founded in 1966. You can study painting, drawing, and sculpture, among other disciplines—whether you are a beginner or a longtime painter; there's even a children's workshop (Young Raiders of the Lost Art of Drawing and Painting). The ranch's 100-year-old log barns and main house have been skillfully renovated for use as classrooms, and there's a new painting and drawing center that's open 24 hours a day. All teachers are working professionals, and include renowned artists such as Susan Shatter, Mel Chin, Bailey Doogan, and John Torreano. For each workshop, two assistants are on hand in addition to the instructor, to make sure that each student gets plenty of personal attention; typically, there are up to 15 students in each class. The on-site dormitory-style accommodations, available in private as well as shared rooms, are a bargain; the price starts at $245 a week for a private room with single beds and shared bath. The weekly meal plan is also a steal at $130; at each meal, you have a choice of two or three entrées, one of them vegetarian, and

there's always a salad bar. If you want something fancier and are willing to pay $590 to $700 per week, you can stay in nearby Snowmass Resort in a luxurious two- or three-bedroom apartment with hot tub, sauna, TV, and mountain-view balcony; these digs come with kitchens, so you can cook your own meals or eat out around Aspen. Tuition costs around $375 for a seven-day workshop (Box 5598, Snowmass Village, CO 81615, tel. 303/923–3181, fax 303/923–3871).

ARROWMONT SCHOOL OF ARTS AND CRAFTS This venerable multimedia fine arts center, a complex of 11 gable-roofed buildings and wood-framed cottages that opened in 1945 on a wooded, 70-acre Gatlinburg hillside in eastern Tennessee not far from the Great Smoky Mountains National Park, offers a huge variety of one- and two-week summer workshops covering painting, drawing, and sculpture for beginners through advanced students, along with ceramics, jewelry making, wood turning, and other arts. Informative, college-level courses, they meet between 9 and 11:30 in the morning and again from 1 to 4 in the afternoon, but students can work until midnight in the many studios on campus (and most do). There are usually around 10 students in each class, and the instructors, well-known artists and professors, come from all over the world. The campus has everything you could possibly need: a store that carries books and a selection of supplies, an art gallery, an art library with more than 4,000 titles, and, throughout the summer, slide shows, demonstrations, and lectures. You are housed either in simply furnished single, double, or triple rooms in cottage-like buildings (some with porches); dormitory style in a converted barn; or in the new air-conditioned dormitory, which has a few private rooms with baths. The dining room serves three meals a day, which include vegetarian choices and lots of fruit and salads; there's a barbecue picnic every Wednesday for all Arrowmont students. Tuition is $185 for five-day programs, which usually run from Sunday night through breakfast Saturday, plus $130 to $350 for accommodations and meals and $75 to process your application (Box 567, Gatlinburg, TN 37738, tel. 615/436–5860, fax 615/430–4101).

CARRIZO LODGE ART SCHOOL Between May and October, this Pueblo-style center, founded in 1956 and secluded in the middle of a canyon 2 miles from the southern New Mexico town of Ruidoso, offers more than 70 five-day, studio and outdoor workshops in watercolor, oils, acrylics, pastels, pen and ink, and drawing and other arts. Dozens of instructors, all with solid teaching experience, work with students here; their classes, limited to 25 students, who may be beginners or serious painters, are usually filled with devotees, who follow them from workshop to workshop around the country. The roster of courses here changes so drastically from one year to the next that no specific offerings are described in Favorite Workshops, *below.* However, at all of them, the accent is on having fun, and there are lots of get-acquainted activities and evening art demonstrations. Classes usually run from 9 to 5, with an hour-long break for lunch. Accommodations, which are in modern two-story townhouses, range from single or double rooms with private baths to one-bedroom apartments with fireplaces and kitchenettes. You can buy your meals in the town of Ruidoso a mile and a half away, or at the center's own Café Carrizo, which serves sandwiches, salads, or pastas at lunch and prime rib and Mexican entrées at dinner; morning coffee and pastries are provided in the workshops. Tuition varies from one workshop to the next, depending on the instructor, but can range from $200 to $500. Accommodations $35 to $65 per day, and meals from $10 upward. The center also has hot tubs, a swimming pool, and an exercise room (Drawer A, Ruidoso, NM 88345, tel. 505/257–9131 or 800/227–1224, fax 505/257–5621).

DILLMAN'S CREATIVE ARTS FOUNDATION This 250-acre old-timer, established in 1935 on a peninsula in northern Wisconsin's White Sand Lake, is a family resort with a difference: Between May and October, it offers more than 100 weeklong workshops in drawing, oils, pastels, and watercolor, for beginners through advanced painters, in addition to the fishing, sailing, swimming, canoeing, waterskiing, hiking, biking, scuba diving, tennis, golf, Ping-Pong, bingo, volleyball, shuffleboard, and badminton that you might expect to find. Teachers are all professional artists, almost all of whom have years of experience as university or art school instructors and who make a living from doing the workshop circuit. Classes have a maximum of 20 students and usually run from 9 to 4 with an hour break for lunch. Participants stay in casually furnished lakeside log cabins (seven with fireplaces) or in suites or rooms at the lodge, a somewhat rustic new building with three large studios, a dining room that seats 80, and a lobby full of Queen Anne-style furnishings. Guest rooms are carpeted and have refrigerators and private bath with shower or tubs. The workshop price, which ranges from $595 to $900, includes not only accommodations but also breakfast and dinner (with plenty of homemade breads and pastries), and you can buy a box lunch or eat at the soup and salad bar for about $5 a day. Children under 10 get reduced rates and those under 2 are free as are programs for children accompanying their parents—arts and crafts classes, nature hikes, treasure hunts, and other activities (Box 98F, Lac du Flambeau, WI 54538, tel. 715/588–3143).

LIGHTHOUSE ART CENTER Between March and mid-November, this outpost on the northern California coast, founded in 1986 and occupying an upstairs complex in old town Crescent City known as the Downtown Plaza, attracts painters of all levels for its 50-plus five-day workshops on landscape, still life, seascape, portraiture, and figure painting, using oils, watercolor, acrylics, and pastels. There are two good reasons to attend. First is the location, within walking distance of the Crescent City harbor, two lighthouses, and a number of black sand beaches and coast redwood forests—postcard-perfect settings. The other is the excellence of the teaching staff, comprised of dozens of talented, recognized artists. Most workshops are limited to 21 students, although some advanced classes are capped at 10. Classes run from 9 to 4 with a one-hour break for lunch. Lodging is in the Lighthouse Art Center's own hostel, which can accommodate just nine (under $20 a night) and has a kitchen; the center can also provide information on other accommodations and restaurants nearby. Workshops cost between $220 and $350 (575 U.S. Hwy. 101 S, Crescent City, CA 95531, tel. 707/464–4137).

OX-BOW SUMMER SCHOOL OF ART With a serene landscape of sand dunes, rolling hills, forests, and marshes, this artists' retreat on a 110-acre site bordering Lake Michigan near the town of Saugatuck, has been attracting artists since about 1910, when Frederick Frary Fursman and Walter Clute founded it as a bohemian outpost for plein-air painters. Today, the one- and two-week summer classes available between June and August are sponsored by the School of the Art Institute of Chicago, and you will be hard put to find better courses, not only in painting but also in performance, puppetry, printmaking, sculpture, and glassblowing. Courses here are serious, reflecting the presence of first-rate Art Institute faculty and visiting artists; you spend seven hours painting each day, and there are never more than 20 in a class, beginner through advanced students. After hours, there are lectures and slide presentations, and, on Fridays, a bonfire or other social gathering that encourages a spirit of bonhomie. Also on Friday, an exhibit of a staff member's work opens in the Ox-Bow Gallery, which is in a former resort hotel built shortly after the Civil War. The dining hall is also here, along with the lecture room. Guest rooms, on the second floor, are Spartan, with twin beds and dressers and bathrooms down the hall. Meals are served buffet style and are quite good, with plenty of healthful and vegetarian entrées. One-week courses cost around $240 unless they are taken for credit, in which case they cost about $450 (c/o School of the Art Institute of Chicago, 37 S. Wabash Ave., Room 707, Chicago, IL 60603, tel. 312/899–5130, fax 312/899–1453).

WOODSTOCK SCHOOL OF ART The site of this institution, founded in 1968, was once the summer home of New York's Art Students League, and the list of artists associated with the school is long and impressive. Its bucolic 38 acres of lawn, woods, and overgrown gardens, at the foothills of the Catskill Mountains, is surrounded by rolling hills, reservoirs, streams, and golf courses— all inspiring to artists. The school's stone-and-timber buildings, commissioned as a National Youth Administration resident crafts center during the Depression, are now designated state and national historic landmarks; the studios have soaring ceilings and an abundance of north windows that flood the spaces with magnificent light. Classes in topics ranging from landscape painting to printmaking, using mediums from pencils to paints and clay, are available year-round for students at all ability levels, and the directors go to some pains to work out a schedule for each individual. Instructors are all professional artists, and include nationally known painters such as Richard Segalman, Albert Handell, Robert Angeloch, Richard McDaniel, and Staats Fasoldt, all featured in *American Artist* magazine. Typically, classes meet between one and four days a week, and although they run for anywhere from several months to an entire year, you can sign up for just a few weeks and can join at any time. You are also allowed to jump from one class to another, sampling oil painting and printmaking, say, or sculpture, or whatever combination you wish. Also available are about a dozen intensive Monday-to-Friday summer workshops, which cost a moderate $220 to $295; winter courses, at $85 to $140 per semester, are quite inexpensive. Classes tend to be small (around 10 students), to allow instructors to provide students with a great deal of individual attention. A converted barn with two bedrooms, a living area, and a kitchen can house up to four students (at $85 a week per person), but most participants look to the town of Woodstock for their rooms and meals; the school maintains a housing list for its students with information about motels, rooms in private homes, campgrounds, and other accommodations (Rte. 212, Box 338, Woodstock, NY 12498, tel. 914/679–2388).

FAVORITE WORKSHOPS

THE NORTHEAST

CONNECTICUT **American Impressionist Inspiration.** The well-respected Silvermine School of Art, founded in 1950, opens its studios to the public with a series of one-week and weekend workshops throughout the year. One favorite program has been the workshop that offers artists of all levels the opportunity to paint the favorite landscape sites of three celebrated American impressionists—John Twachtman, Childe Hassam, and J. Alden Weir—using oils, watercolors, or pastels. Students, up to 20 per class, paint on location with instruction from 10 to 2 and there are individual critiques throughout the session. Instructors are usually professional painters with wide experience in their respective mediums. If the course isn't available at the time you're ready to sign up for it, you are certain to find another of equal interest. In cold months, students meet in the studio to study figure and still-life compositions; warm months find them setting up easels around the lawns and gardens of the four-acre campus or at nearby parks and historic estates.

Typically at Silvermine, classes end at 2:30 to give you time to explore the area or paint on your own. Accommodations or meals are not included, but many painters stay around the corner at the 10-room Silvermine Tavern ($50 per night, including Continental breakfast). Meals there include New England clam chowder, broiled sole, and other New England standbys; you can also take your pick of restaurants around New Canaan. *Silvermine Guild Arts Center, 1037 Silvermine Rd., New Canaan, CT 06840-4398, tel. 203/966-6668, fax 203/966–2763. July: 5 days, tuition $235. Sign up 2 months in advance.*

MAINE **Sebasco Art Workshops.** These five-day workshops in oils and watercolor, first offered in 1985, are taught by talented, well-respected instructors at the Rock Gardens Inn, a main building and 10 shingle and clapboard cottages, housing from two to six guests each, perched on a peninsula on the coast of Maine. Classes number between 10 and 30, with five instructors, and painters at all levels are accepted, from beginning through advanced; although you do some life drawing and still life work, the focus is on painting landscapes—especially the inn's gardens, lawns, and seacoast, with its breakers and tide pools. The good food and comfortable cottages with fireplaces, private bathrooms, and sun porches keep painters coming back. You check in Sunday afternoon for a get-acquainted cocktail party, and the workshop ends after lunch on Friday. After breakfast on Monday, following a demonstration of technique by the instructor, you're given a picnic and head for a scenic spot on the grounds or nearby, where you paint until 3 or 4 in the afternoon. A critique at the inn rounds off the painting day. You have access to an Olympic-size saltwater pool, a nine-hole golf course, and grass tennis courts; you can also take boat trips, try lawn bowling, and go surf fishing. At dinner, there's always a choice of tasty dishes such as fresh salmon with dill butter, grilled lamb chops with mint pesto, and steamed lobster with drawn butter. *Sebasco Art Workshops at the Rock Gardens Inn, Sebasco Estates, ME 04565, tel. 207/389–1339. June–Sept.: 5 days, complete package $700–$800. Sign up 3 months in advance.*

MASSACHUSETTS **Capturing Cape Ann's Rocky Coast.** The Rockport Art Association, a group of 230 artists and more than 900 contributors who are hooked on the beauty of this coastal town, organizes five-day landscape workshops in summer and fall for painters at all levels who work in oils; you either concentrate on simplifying and planning compositions or on the impressionistic use of color, depending on the instructor. The association was founded in 1927 for the purpose of the advancement and preservation of the visual arts and has been offering these courses since 1986. Instructors are professional painters with nationwide workshop experience, and are noted for a wide range of techniques and styles, from the use of abstract watercolor to structured oils. The group, which usually includes about 20 participants, first gathers on Sunday evening at the association's center, part of which is a 200-year-old former tavern, for a get-acquainted wine and cheese party; you gather there again at 9 each morning to decide on a painting site—a beach, park, historic building, or other location within walking distance. Then you go out and, after a demonstration by the instructor, paint on your own, usually *alla prima* (completing the work in one sitting), with help as required, until about 3:30, when the instructor critiques each participant's work and the group breaks for lunch. Participants are on their own for accommodations and meals; there's a good selection of restaurants in town, an artsy community whose shops draw crowds of weekenders and day trippers from nearby Boston, and the association can provide a list of lodging options. *Rockport Art Association, 12 Main St., Rockport, MA 01966, tel. 508/546-6604. June and Sept.: 5 days, tuition $230-$255. Sign up 1-2 months in advance.*

■MASSACHUSETTS■ Oil Painting *Alla Prima* at the Boston Museum of Fine Arts. At this intense, college-level workshop for painters of all levels, the emphasis is on finishing your landscape, figure, or still-life composition *alla prima*, in one session. This approach helps you work faster and use paint more effectively and teaches you to go with your instincts and take risks. Classes include 15 students and run from Monday through Thursday for three weeks. Instructor Ken Beck, a Boston painter, has exhibited primarily in Boston; his work is in the collections of the Boston Public Library and the Museum of Fine Arts, whose school, established in 1876, sponsors the course. Classes meet from 9 to 1 in the painting studio; afternoons and weekends are given over

to independent painting at the school. There's no housing, but a limited number of students can stay in dormitories at other schools in the surrounding Back Bay–Fenway neighborhood; other lodgings in the area, one of Boston's priciest, cost considerably more. Alternatively, because the School of the Museum of Fine Arts is affiliated with Tufts University, registering for the workshops through Tufts makes you eligible for dormitory housing at its Medford, Massachusetts, campus just outside Boston, about 30 to 45 minutes by public transportation from the museum. A snack shop in the museum building sells soup and sandwiches; there are many other restaurants five or ten minutes' walk away along Huntington Avenue. *School of the Museum of Fine Arts, 230 The Fenway, Boston, MA 02115, tel. 617/267-1219, fax 617/424-6271. June: 12 days (Mon.–Thurs. for 3 weeks): tuition $439-$465, housing $450. Housing price does not include meals; sign up 2 months in advance.*

■NEW HAMPSHIRE■ The White Mountains in Oils and Acrylics. The Inn at Thorn Hill, located in a marvelous clapboard Victorian designed by Stanford White, makes a pleasant setting for this four-day workshop for beginner through advanced students, one of a series available for painters at all levels in watercolor, pastels, acrylics, and oils. Built in 1895 as a private residence, the house became an inn in 1908; the workshops were first offered between 1975 and 1980 and returned in 1991.

During this workshop, you assemble at breakfast to discuss the day's agenda and then set off by 9 to paint the streams, covered bridges, farms, and villages of the White Mountains, returning around 4. Although the format of classes may vary depending on the abilities of a dozen group members, students produce a couple of paintings a day after the instructor's demonstrations. Like most of the teachers here, instructors Dale Ratliff and Charlotte Wharton are drawn from the membership of such professional organizations as the North

Shore Arts Association, the Pastel Society of America, the Copley Society of Boston, the Salamagundi Club, the International Society of Marine Painters, or the American, Boston, and New England watercolor societies— many of the instructing artists here have prestigious awards to their credit. After class, there are critiques of the day's work, followed by free time for hiking, swimming in the inn's pool, or exploring the surrounding area. There's tennis, golf, and horseback riding within walking distance.

Accommodations are in the Carriage House, whose country-inspired rooms, decorated with collectibles, all have private bath; this building has a large living room with a wood-burning fireplace and a hot tub is nearby. Meals, served by candlelight in the dining room of the Victorian main inn, are four-course affairs featuring shellfish in phyllo, sautéed duck breast, poached fresh salmon, and other fairly epicurean fare. However, all but one dinner as well as bag lunches cost extra and must be arranged in advance—and you can always opt for one of the many restaurants, ranging from simple to sumptuous, within walking distance in Jackson Village. No smoking is permitted in the inn. *The Inn at Thorn Hill, Box A, Jackson, NH 03846, tel. 603/383–4242 or 800/ 289–8990, fax 603/383–8062. May–Oct.: 4 days, complete package $457–$565. Price does not include 4 dinners; sign up 5 months in advance.*

■ NEW YORK ■ **Landscape Painting in Oil.** This intensive five-day course in painting landscapes, one of many offered each summer at the Woodstock School of Art, helps you learn the process of composing a landscape from value sketches to a completed work. Class meets between 9 and 4, with a break for a BYOB lunch, either on the campus or in the surrounding countryside to paint nearby Catskills landscapes—beautiful rolling hills, with lots of streams and reservoirs. Instructor Mary Anna Goetz, author of *Painting Landscapes in Oil,* is always with the class, so you get one-on-one attention; there are usually 10 students per group,

mostly intermediate or advanced painters. Most students stay and eat in nearby Woodstock. *Woodstock School of Art, Rte. 212, Box 338, Woodstock, NY 12498, tel. 914/679–2388. July: 5 days, tuition $220. Sign up 1 month in advance.*

■ NEW YORK ■ **The New Hudson River School.** The northern Catskills and the lawns, gardens, and streams surrounding the Greenville Arms, William Vanderbilt's 1889 three-story Victorian manor house, are the subjects of student work at a series of five-day workshops, the Hudson River Valley Art Workshops, held at Vanderbilt's former manor, a country inn on 6 acres in a rural village in upstate New York. Every year from spring through fall it hosts about two dozen one-week workshops in watercolor, pastels, drawing, and acrylic and oil painting, for beginning through advanced painters, up to 20 per class. Landscape is the usual focus, but workshops in floral painting, experimental techniques, and figure are also offered, with a different well-known artist teaching each. Workshops are in session between 9 and 4 daily, but students often paint after class, since the studio is open around the clock. The program was established in 1981.

The instructor of this class is Frank Webb, a respected teacher and author of books on watercolor techniques. Classes run from 9 to 4 and are held outdoors, where he encourages artistic self-discovery rather than a particular style. Discussions of the synthesis of abstraction and realism are supported by clear and dramatic demonstrations.

Dispelling the myth that art is born of suffering, this package treats you to antique-filled rooms with bed linens dried in the sun, as they were in simpler times. The inn's chef cooks delicious country fare: At breakfast, for instance, there's homemade banana-bread French toast or blueberry-buttermilk pancakes. Guests arrive in time for a wine and cheese party on Sunday afternoon and depart after breakfast on Saturday. If you register before May 1, your name is entered in a drawing, and if you win, your whole package is free. You'll find a swimming pool, shuffleboard, and croquet, as well as bikes to rent and tennis and golf nearby. *Hudson River Valley Art Workshops, Box 659, Greenville, NY 12083-0659, tel. 518/966-5219, fax 518/966-8754. July: 5 days, complete package $649. Sign up 1 month in advance.*

NEW YORK Painting the Big Apple. The New York Studio School in Greenwich Village is a historic spot in the art world: It was the original home of the Whitney Museum of American Art and, before that, the sculpture studio of Gertrude Vanderbilt Whitney and Daniel Chester French. The school, founded in 1964 and relocated to its current address a year later, has full spring and fall semesters and offers this three-week Painting in the City course for experienced painters in all mediums—oils, acrylics, and watercolors—as part of its summer program of intensive two-, three-, and five-week courses in studio and location painting, drawing and sculpture. Like all the school's offerings, this one is open by application only: To be considered, you must submit examples of your work and you must paint at the intermediate level, or have considerable experience in drawing. If you're among the 15 to 20 selected, you have the run of the large, skylit studios between 8:30 AM and midnight. You meet here in the morning, then go out and paint until evening. The course's emphasis is on developing your pictorial language and familiarizing you with historical and contemporary landscape imagery; you set up your easels all over the city, painting where you please, as a group or individually. Critiques end each day, and evenings bring talks by art critics, historians, and visiting artists; at the end of the workshop, each painter's cumulative work gets an in-depth examination. Instructors are typically working painters with diverse attitudes. *New York Studio School of Drawing, Painting and Sculpture, 8 W. 8th St., New York, NY 10011, tel. 212/673-6466, fax 212/673-6466. July: 3 weeks (weekdays only), tuition $1,125. Sign up 2–3 months in advance; application deadline late May.*

THE SOUND

LOUISIANA Deep South Watercolor Encounters. Having taught over 300 workshops, M. Douglas Walton knows a thing or two about painting. He teaches and directs this summer program of six 12-day courses at Louisiana Tech University, in the north central part of the state. All courses are in watercolor, but each has a different emphasis—composition, creative expression, color, figure, or design. Each includes daily demonstrations, lectures, and critiques; Walton's approach emphasizes the artist's individuality of expression rather than the end product. Students from the beginner through advanced levels are eligible. Every day, class runs for nine hours. You start by making preparatory sketches, sometimes on location and always under the supervision of Walton and his assistant, then return to paint in the large studio or sketch still life in the adjoining composition room, both of which are open around the clock. (An instructor is there until about 5.) You may complete from one to three paintings per day. Each course includes no more than 30 students. The program was first offered in 1977.

Lodging is available off campus as well as in Louisiana Tech University dormitories; rooms have twin beds, built-in dressers, and either shared bathrooms with showers only or communal baths down the hall. The eclectic campus, which mixes modern and manor-style buildings, is on the outskirts of tiny, southern-rustic Ruston. Although kitchen privileges are available in the dorms, you can also eat at the college food court, which serves pizza, salads, and the like. *Louisiana Tech University, Box 3182, Ruston, LA 71272, tel. 318/251–4130, fax 318/251–5003. May–Aug.: 12 days, tuition $350, housing $10 a night. Housing price does not include meals; sign up 2 months in advance.*

TENNESSEE Watercolors in the Smokies. A five-day watercolor workshop is one of many offered at the Arrowmont School on its 70-acre mountain campus in the eastern part of the state, but the specific content varies from year to year, since it is very much a reflection of the interests of instructors, who themselves change from one semester to the next. One might have you covering drybrush–wet paper techniques, graphite and watercolor combinations, calligraphic applications and brushwork, or paint layering. With another instructor, you might concentrate on drawing, or work on location, or use a live model. Instructors tend to be from universities, experienced at teaching, and classes usually include no more than 15 students, most of them at the beginner to intermediate level but also including some advanced students. *Arrowmont School of Arts and Crafts, Box 567, Gatlinburg, TN 37738, tel. 615/436–5860, fax 615/430–4101. Mar., June–mid-Aug.: 5 days, tuition $185, housing $130–$350. Sign up 2–3 months in advance.*

THE MIDWEST

■**MICHIGAN**■ **Painting on the Banks of Lake Michigan.** The shore of Lake Michigan, with its sand dunes, rolling hills, forests, and marshes, constitutes the principal subject matter for the 20 beginning, intermediate, and advanced landscape painters who take the two-week course at this picturesque 110-acre retreat of the School of the Art Institute of Chicago. If you want to make strides with your painting, be sure to go for the two-week course, which has more than twice the instruction of the retreat's one-week courses. At times a model is brought in to compound the challenge of rendering the landscape. Classes typically meet from 9 until 5. Instructors are first-rate faculty art professors and visiting painters and teach oils, egg tempera, and other mediums.

Lodging and meals are in a former resort hotel built shortly after the Civil War. Rooms are spare, and meals include lots of granola, salads, and vegetables. *Ox-Bow Summer School of Art, Division of Continuing Studies and Special Programs, School of the Art Institute of Chicago, 37 S. Wabash*

Ave., Room 707, Chicago, IL 60603, tel. 312/899–5130, fax 312/899–1453. Mid-June–mid-Aug.: 7–14 days, tuition $240–$720, housing $312–$676. Sign up 5 months in advance.

■**WISCONSIN**■ **Landscapes in Pastels, Oils, and Acrylics.** This five-day workshop, one of about 100 visual arts programs offered between spring and fall by Dillman's Creative Arts Foundation, concentrates on teaching students to block in and layer color to express atmosphere in natural light. The painting day begins at 9 with a demonstration and discussion in the studio. In the afternoon, the class, made up of up to 25 painters of all levels, moves outdoors to paint on location with the instructor. Teachers include nationally recognized artists such as Tom Lynch and Bob Hoffman, who have years of teaching experience. Studios are open 24 hours a day.

At this 250-acre family resort on White Sand Lake in northern Wisconsin, accommodations are in lakeside log cabins and the main lodge; at meals, six different entrées are available, all served with homemade bread. *Dillman's Creative Arts Foundation, Box 98F, Lac du Flambeau, WI 54538, tel. 715/588–3143. June: 5 days, complete package $695. Price does not include lunch; sign up 3 months in advance.*

■**WISCONSIN**■ **Watercolor with Bridget Austin.** The Clearing, a retreat center that opened in 1935 and sponsors workshops in the arts, is on 128 acres of woods and meadows on the shores of Green Bay in scenic Door County. All the buildings are log or native stone, and the entire site is on the National Register of Historic Places. Founder Jens Jensen, a landscape designer and conservationist, aimed to create "a source of renewal and communion with nature, a place for clearing one's mind." Accordingly, workshops at The Clearing are informal and relaxing (never with more than 18 students), and encourage every participant to be aware of nature.

In this six-day workshop, the curriculum reflects the strengths of instructor Bridget

Austin, a watercolorist known for both her landscapes and her more intimate portraits of natural subjects. Students first sketch on location, then head for the studio to paint. Austin supervises students for six hours a day and covers many facets of the creation of a painting, from planning a workable sketch and techniques of negative painting to glazing and calligraphy. Classes are limited to 17 students, who range from the beginner to advanced levels.

Other programs at The Clearing include both independent study and organized classes in photography, weaving, wood carving, nature study, stained glass, quilting, dance, writing, philosophy, and pastels. Pressure is at a minimum here—there are no deadlines or painting schedules apart from the demonstrations by the instructor—and since studios are open around the clock, you can keep your own schedule. On the menu you might find a country-style chicken breast served with rice pilaf, an orange and spinach salad, and cherry cheesecake. Accommodations are either doubles with private bath or dormitory rooms that sleep three or six. *The Clearing, 12183 Garrett Bay Rd., Box 65, Ellison Bay, WI 54210-0065, tel. 414/854–4088. Mid-Sept.: 6 days, complete package $445–$485. Sign up 4 months in advance.*

THE SOUTHWEST

NEW MEXICO **Landscape Drawing and Painting.** In these two popular landscape workshops offered consecutively in late summer by the Seattle-based Academy of Realist Art, you spend two weeks living and working in some of the most spectacular locales in and around Santa Fe. The instructor, realist artist Gary Faigin, works with students of all levels; he offers 45-minute lecture-demonstrations daily as well as personal critiques and evening programs. Everyone paints outdoors directly from nature; beginners work in pastels while more advanced artists work in oils. The course addresses the chief problems of depicting landscapes—deciding on composition, massing-in the key elements, and creating a solid tonal structure—and gives much attention to the representation of color, light, and space. Painting days run from 9 in the morning until 4 in the afternoon, although enthusiastic students often start at dawn and continue through sunset. There are never more than 24 students in a class.

The first session begins with six days in Santa Fe, at the school's headquarters, with painting at sites in and around town. Then you move 70 miles to Ghost Ranch, the remote, 24,000-acre wilderness preserve that was Georgia O'Keeffe's home for 40 years; here, there are sunset painting trips and other fascinating scheduled treks as well as plenty of free time to roam the range. You paint for four days at the ranch, lodging on a colorful cliff above a valley in rustic bunkhouses with shared rooms and a separate bathhouse building. Meals are served in the large dining hall, and many dishes are prepared using organic local produce.

The second workshop of the summer convenes in Santa Fe for a day of orientation, but departs immediately on an ambitious itinerary through the backcountry. The next stop is Ghost Ranch, where you spend four days painting. Then you're off to quaint Taos, where you lodge in 1920s elegance at the fabulous 22-room adobe home of the late Mabel Dodge Luhan, whose comfortable guest rooms are done in Taos period furnishings with European accents; the mansion, on five acres of grounds, has housed the likes of D. H. Lawrence, Carl Jung, Willa Cather, and Aldous Huxley. You paint for a day on the estate and have the weekend free to explore on your own. Leaving Taos, you head for Cimarron, a grassy high-mountain plains settlement where you paint for five more days and headquarter at the 137,000-acre Philmont Scout Ranch, with accommodations in simple rooms or bungalows; then you move on to the St. James Hotel in town, whose rooms have a Wild West motif.

On both trips, while you're in Santa Fe, you get an American breakfast on weekdays and a Continental one on weekends. The second program includes breakfasts in Taos, full Southwest-style buffets, and in Cimarron, you are served meals suitable for Boy Scouts—but after all, you didn't come for the food. Neither program includes the cost of transportation between painting sites; you need your own vehicle. *Academy of Realist Art, 5004 6th Ave. NW, Seattle, WA 98107, tel. 206/784–4268, fax 206/783–1410. Aug. and Oct.: 10 days, tuition $875, housing $900–$1,100. Housing price does not include dinners and most lunches in Taos; sign up 9 months in advance.*

NEW MEXICO **Taos en Plein Air.** Bob Ellis, one of the many talented painters who call Taos home, conducts this five-day landscape workshop under the aegis of the Taos Institute of Art at some of his favorite painting spots in the area, including both mountains and plains. Because he himself works in different mediums and styles, you can use oils, watercolors, or pastels and paint the way you want, either tackling the landscape in abstract or representational form. The class, limited to 12 intermediate and advanced painters, meets after breakfast and usually works until dusk, to capture the evening light.

Other programs offered by the institute, which was founded in 1989, cover creative writing, local history, weaving, pottery, and photography, among other subjects. You're on your own for accommodations, but the center will make recommendations; and Taos is a good restaurant town, especially for southwestern and Spanish food. *Taos Institute of Art, Box 1389, Taos, NM 87571, tel. 505/758–2793, fax 505/758–2793. Sept.: 5 days, tuition $325. Sign up 6 months in advance.*

TEXAS **Wildflowers in Pencil and Watercolor.** During this four-day workshop at the nonprofit Hill Country Arts Foundation, you complete three paintings and numerous preparatory sketches in pencil, watercolor, or both. The emphasis is on making naturalistic interpretations of the land around the center—16 acres of wildflowers bordering the Guadalupe River at Johnson Creek, 6 miles west of Kerrville and 65 miles northwest of San Antonio. Instructors, who are mostly professional artists and exhibiting painters such as Alex Powers and Naomi Brotherton, give a painting demonstration every day. Although these are in watercolor, you can paint in whatever medium you choose, and you don't need to be an expert to sign up—students are accepted at the beginner and intermediate levels as well. There are up to 15 students in the workshop, which meets from 9 until 3, with an hour break for lunch; the painting studios stay open until 5.

The center, founded in 1958, sponsors a number of other affordable painting workshops throughout the year as well as workshops in subjects such as photography, sculpture, printmaking, jewelry making, folk art, ceramics, and drawing. You're on your own for room and board, but the center will make suggestions. Most students bring bag lunches and eat dinners in local restaurants, which serve everything from French and Continental fare to ethnic and Texas specialties. *Hill Country Arts Foundation, Box 176, Ingram, TX 78025, tel. 210/367–5121. Nov.: 4 days, tuition $160. Sign up 1 month in advance.*

THE ROCKIES

COLORADO **Watercolor: Painting the Landscape.** The Anderson Ranch Arts Center buzzes year-round, but summers are chockablock with workshops, including this 14-day landscape class for painters at all levels. All work is in watercolors, and the emphasis is on dispelling the notion that watercolors are not a sophisticated technique. Consequently, you learn dry- and wet-brush techniques as well as a method that involves overlaying yellow, blue, and red to create all the colors of the spectrum. When the day begins, at 9, you head for the Rocky Mountain hillsides; in the afternoon, the group moves back into the studio for critiques. There is always plenty of individual attention, since there are only 16 students in a class. The instructor is Susan Shatter, a Brooklyn College art professor whose work is in the collections of the Chicago Art Institute, the Museum of Fine Arts in Boston, and the Philadelphia Museum of Art. Two assistants are also on hand.

You can cook your own meals or buy a meal plan. Housing is in dorm rooms, which are extremely economical, especially since their price includes meals, and in apartments at nearby Snowmass Resort, which come without meals but have access to hot tubs, whirlpools, and a swimming pool and are more comfortable, more spacious, and more expensive. *Anderson Ranch Arts Center, Box 5598, Snowmass Village, CO 81615, tel. 303/923–3181 or 800/595–2722, fax 303/923–3871. June: 12 days, tuition $575, housing $245–$365 with meals or $550–$645 without. Sign up 4 months in advance.*

WYOMING **The Snake River in Watercolors.** The Snake River Institute, founded in 1988 and headquartered at the Hardeman Ranch in Wilson, Wyoming, 7 miles from Jackson and very near Grand Teton National Park, the setting for this five-day open-air workshop in watercolor for painters at all levels. Instructors vary from year to year, but are chosen for the passion they bring to their subject and for their ability to teach; Judith DeShong Hall and Hollis Williford, who taught not long ago, added a new dimension to the painting experience by encouraging students to chronicle their work and surroundings in an illustrated journal. Each morning you undertake painting assignments that help you hone your drafting skills amid mountain peaks, glacial lakes, and groves of cottonwoods; during the afternoon, you work individually. Classes never have more than 15 students per instructor.

This workshop is one of more than two dozen offered between April and October on topics relating to the arts and humanities, celebrating the cultures and communities of the American West; other topics range from Pueblo Indian life, art in Santa Fe, and pho-

tography in Yellowstone to storytelling and dinosaur digs. The institute can recommend accommodations; meals are available in Wilson, where your options include a deli and two American-style resturants, and in Jackson, where you'll find everything from fancy French cafés to mom-and-pop spots that serve up meat-and-potatoes fare. *Snake River Institute, Box 128, Wilson, WY 83014, tel. 307/733–2214, fax 307/739–1710. July: 5 days, tuition $375. Sign up 4 months in advance.*

THE WEST COAST

CALIFORNIA **Figurative Watercolor.** In this five-day Lighthouse Art Center class, you concentrate on learning how to paint the human body using watercolors, but you can paint in any style and even go purely abstract. Under the tutelage of Arne Westerman, an expert watercolorist and author of a book on watercoloring, you learn a three-step method that explores the subject matter from composition to design to painting; this technique frees you to focus on your interpretation of a scene rather than on the limitations of the medium. Classes, which include students of all abilities and are all limited to 20 students, meet from 9 to 4 in the studio and then move outdoors, perhaps to Battery Point Lighthouse, the harbor, or the redwood forests of Jedediah Smith State Park. There's no meal plan, but there is a nine-bed hostel that offers accommodations with kitchen privileges for about $17 a night; you must bring your own bedding and food. There is also a good choice of restaurants in the vicinity. *Lighthouse Art Center, 575 U.S. Hwy 101 S, Crescent City, CA 95531, tel. 707/464–4137. Late Aug.: 5 days, tuition $295, housing about $17 per night. Housing price does not include meals; sign up 5 months in advance.*

CALIFORNIA **Watercolor Workshop with Roger Armstrong.** This five-day summer workshop, part of the Art Institute of Southern California's continuing education program, is a good and affordable introduction to outdoor painting. The class meets from 9 until 4, with an hour-long break for lunch, and works in either one of three painting studios or at scenic sites on campus, one of them a grove of stately sycamore trees that survived the 1993 fires. You might cover the nature of color, composition, collage, transparent and opaque techniques, and techniques for working in pen and ink, pastels, and caran d'ache; you also learn how to work from sketches and how to give paintings atmosphere. There are about 12 students of all levels in every class. Instructor Roger Armstrong, an expert watercolorist, is a past president of the National Watercolor Society.

The campus of the Art Institute of Southern California, which was founded in 1961 and has been offering this program since 1989, is an oasis of lawns and gardens in the city, just 2 miles from the Pacific. Lodging is not included, but you have a choice of hotels and motels around Laguna Beach. Meals are in restaurants; you can take your pick of everything from burgers and fries to Continental fare. *Art Institute of Southern California, 2222 Laguna Canyon Rd., Laguna Beach, CA 92651, tel. 714/497–3309 or 800/255–0762, fax 714/497–4399. Mid-July: 5 days, tuition $200. Sign up 2 months in advance.*

OREGON **Experimenting with Watercolor.** For two weeks during every summer since 1965, the Creative Arts Community at Menucha, a former estate that serves as a retreat and conference center the rest of the year, has offered one- and two-week workshops in such topics as oil painting, watercolor, drawing, furniture painting, creative writing, ceramics, and poetry at this wooded, 96-acre property overlooking the Columbia River Gorge. The course, for artists at all levels, is one of several that fill up particularly early with repeaters. They come for the outstanding instructors, practicing artists and teachers, many with M.F.A.'s, and appreciate the warmth of the community and the good food, particularly the homemade bread. You meet not only on location but also in the studio, which is

open around the clock, and cover such topics as wet-on-wet, drybrush, and mixed-media combinations. Classes are in session between 9 and noon and 1 and 4 Monday through Friday (you arrive on Sunday and leave after breakfast on Saturday); there are slide shows, lectures, and other programs after dark. There are usually about 10 students in a class.

The course fee includes both good meals made with local produce and lodging in a dormitory room with three to five beds (private and semiprivate rooms are available at an additional charge). Menucha has a jogging trail, tennis court, volleyball court, and swimming pool. *Creative Arts Community, Box 4958, Portland, OR 97208, tel. 503/760–5837 or 503/243–6827. Aug.: 5–10 days, complete package $475–$875 ($628–$1,200 with private room, $568–$1,080 with semiprivate). The lowest complete package price is based on quadruple occupancy; sign up 5 months in advance.*

WASHINGTON **Seascapes from the *Zodiac*.** This nine-day movable sketching-and-watercolor feast takes place aboard the marvelously remodeled 127-foot schooner *Zodiac*, as it sails through the spectacular waters that wash Washington's evergreen San Juan Islands. There are about four hours of painting daily, followed by individual critiques. Each day's lesson has a specific goal relating to content and technique, such as techniques to use to capture the water's colors or for layering paint. Subjects include schooners, fishing boats, small villages, fir forests shrouded in soft mists, and waterfalls. The boat sails from place to place at midday, when the breezes rise; you stop to paint onshore in the early morning and late afternoon or perhaps for a surfside picnic of fresh-caught fish. Instructor Caroline Buchanan has been sailing and teaching in the area since 1984. The program admits up to 14 students of various levels, and there's space for up to six nonpainters. There are sailing classes daily, open to all.

The boat is a beauty—it's on the National Register of Historic Places and is one of the last of the working pilot schooners still under sail. It has four gaff-rigged sails, a 4,000-square-foot mainsail, and a solid mahogany deckhouse built by old-time shipwrights. But it also has such modern conveniences as electricity, showers, and comfortable berths—although the quarters are tight—and the sails are backed by full engine power. With a crew of eight, the service standards are very high, and the galley is outstanding, offering such examples of culinary wizardry as fresh roasted salmon and sautéed bay scallops with basil and white wine sauce. Accommodations are in cabins, each with four bunks. *Buchanan Watercolors, Ltd., Box 218, Olga, WA 98279, tel. 206/376–5509, fax 206/376–5509. Aug.: 9 days, complete package $1,650. Sign up 9 months in advance.*

WASHINGTON **Watercolor Painting of Water and Sky.** This five-day workshop, one of more than 60 classes offered between May and October by an environmental learning center known as the North Cascades Institute, is held on Orcas Island, one of the San Juan Islands, which are scattered around northern Puget Sound, just off the coast of Vancouver Island; the site has beautiful gardens, meadows, and forests, and the ocean is five minutes away. The class stresses the importance of observation in painting nature, and you learn a few tricks that help you capture the way color and patterns change as light shifts when you paint outdoors; you also study shapes created by waves, ripples, and dewdrops. The class convenes at Moran State Park Environmental Learning Center, a rustic building with large studios tucked into the woods overlooking an open meadow and a freshwater lake; you have lessons and discussions here in the morning and move outdoors to paint on location in the afternoon and evening under the guidance of an instructor. Each class has no more than 10 students, of all levels, and one instructor, who is chosen based on expertise and teaching ability. Although the whole approach is relaxed and

nonjudgmental, there's no shortage of instruction; there are individual critiques every day after dinner.

Accommodations are in private and semi-private rooms in rustic heated cabins, which can house up to 150; there are no private baths. Meals, which you prepare in the center's kitchen, are not included in the course fee. There's a freshwater lake for swimming. The rest of the year, the center offers classes in nature studies, photography, birding, creative writing, marine ecology, geology, and drum making. *North Cascades Environmental Learning Center, North Cascades Institute, 2105 Hwy. 20, Sedro Woolley, WA 98284, tel. 206/856–5700, fax 206/856–1934. Sept.: 5 days, package $225. Price does not include meals; sign up 4 months in advance.*

SOURCES

ORGANIZATIONS The **Visual Artist Information Hotline** (tel. 800/232–2789, weekdays 2–5 PM EST or leave message), although not a source of workshop recommendations, can help locate books, resources, and local agencies that provide assistance to visual artists.

PERIODICALS The March issues of *The Artist's Magazine* (F&W Publications, Inc., 1507 Dana Ave., Cincinnati, OH 45207, tel. 513/531–2222) and of *American Artist* and *Watercolor '94* (both from BPI Communications, 1515 Broadway, New York, NY 10036, tel. 212/764–7300) include lists of hundreds of workshops.

BOOKS *The Guide to Art & Craft Workshops*, by Shaw Guides, Inc., available in most city libraries, provides detailed notes about workshops and residency programs throughout the United States.

ALSO SEE Want to channel your creativity in other ways? Turn to Writing Conferences and Workshops, Arts and Crafts Workshops, or Photography Workshops and Tours.

Photography Workshops and Tours

By Lori P. Greene

ike insects in amber, images are held suspended within the framework of a photograph, pieces of time captured. But not every image is equal: Some elicit moods, some bring back memories, and some do nothing at all.

What is it that makes a photograph effective? The angle of the shot, the direction of the light source, the brilliance of the color, the intensity of the subject matter, the clearness or smokiness of the print. These are just some of the points that a good photographer must consider. It is not just a matter of point and shoot.

To make strong photographic statements, you must exercise your mind and cultivate your eye, then practice your technique. One of the best ways for both amateurs and experienced photographers to do this is to enroll in a photography workshop or tour.

In a *workshop* situation, you spend your time in a classroom, studio, and darkroom, and sometimes on location. You focus on specific technical skills, aesthetics, or a particular aspect of photography, such as portraiture, photojournalism, and documentary. Critiques of everyone's work are an integral part of the learning process.

On a photography *tour,* you travel to one or more destinations and spend much energy shooting in the field—landscapes, wildlife, architecture, cityscapes, and more—trying to capture the essence of what you see. You may experiment with challenging light conditions or learn how to observe wildlife patiently before snapping your shutter. If there are facilities for developing your film, there may be critiques, but sometimes you don't see your work until the tour is over.

During some workshops, you are immersed in the image-making process from dawn until late evening. If you're not taking a darkroom course, your film is usually developed overnight so that your photos may be critiqued the next day. This feedback is crucial—it can take your work in new directions—but be forewarned: Critical evaluations by instructors and fellow students are sometimes difficult to swallow. Some teachers and peers are honest to the point of insensitivity, so you must be able to stand up to harsh criticism. The feedback, good or bad, is often the most beneficial part of the course. It can teach you what you did wrong and how to fix it or build your confidence in how you shoot. Furthermore, what you learn from evaluations of other students' work can be applied to your own photography.

There are a variety of institutions that offer photography workshops and tours, in both leafy settings and urban centers. Large photography programs with workshops for students at all levels of experience are offered by such institutions as the International

---

Freelance writer Lori P. Greene takes her photography classes while on assignment with her husband, a professional photographer. Together they have crawled through Antarctic penguin rookeries and bushwhacked through the jungles of Papua New Guinea, but Greene insists that, for most people, a photography workshop or tour is an easier way to learn.

Center of Photography in New York, the Maine Photographic Workshops, and the Santa Fe Photographic Workshops. These programs cover aesthetics, printing, computer-generated imagery, hand painting, black-and-white developing, and more—all taught by a diverse faculty consisting of leading professionals.

Smaller institutions, schools, and even individual photographers have programs with a narrower scope. These often focus on a single aspect of photography, one in which the instructor has lots of experience, be it nature, landscape, or underwater photography or perhaps black-and-white printing.

Some institutions have a photography program that complements programs in other art forms. The Touchstone Center for Crafts in Pennsylvania and the Anderson Ranch Arts Center in Colorado, for example, are multi-art centers where such crafts as painting, drawing, woodworking, sculpture, and furniture design are also taught. These are good places to bring a companion who wants to study something other than photography.

Many photography tours are set up by companies that specialize in outdoor adventure. They are often led by professional outdoor photographers who work alongside you while providing advice on how to frame a picture and what exposure to use. Instruction is less formal than that of workshops, but you may be up at dawn, when the low light transforms even the most mundane scenes into visual wonders. You spend the day touring a given area and learning ways to view it, and at dusk you're still behind the camera while the light once again hangs low.

Tours are generally open to shutterbugs of all levels, but most workshops are designed for either beginning, intermediate, or advanced photographers. A beginner usually knows the basics of using a camera; an intermediate student has taken pictures for a few years and may have a portfolio of work; and an advanced photographer has shot seriously for several years and may have worked professionally.

Workshops and tours also differ in the intensity of the work at hand. You can pick a workshop in which you must spend dawn to midnight in class, in the field, and in the darkroom, with little time to relax; or you can pick one that meets for only part of the day. Photography tours tend to be even more laid-back, with photography an important part of an overall vacation. You travel from place to place, and although you do receive instruction, it is less time-consuming than the amount offered in workshops. Beginners may enjoy a tour more than a workshop, because it allows you to gain experience in a less pressured atmosphere.

Both photography workshops and tours are costly—prices range from about $325 for five days to $3,750 for two weeks—but most participants get their money's worth. These courses help you focus on the visual part of your world and turn single moments into potent works of art.

CHOOSING THE RIGHT PROGRAM

After you decide what you want to learn and whether you want to take a workshop or a tour, you should investigate all your options. Asking the following questions will help you make the right choice.

How long has the institution or operator been in business and how long has the particular workshop or tour been run? Experience is often the key to smooth programming and trouble-free workings.

What aspect of photography does the workshop or tour focus on? Make sure you sign up for a workshop or tour that addresses your needs. Maybe you want to learn more about composition or develop a new technical skill, such as color processing. Perhaps you want to gain experience shooting portraits or learn to take better scenic shots. If you've always wanted to produce the perfect black-and-white print, then a darkroom workshop is probably the answer. If you aren't drawn to a particular topic but wish to improve your overall skills, try a class that explores personal vision. If you're beyond the beginner's stage, a lighting or portraiture workshop may be right for you. Workshops that explore specific areas of photography, such as photojournalism and documentary photography; special printing techniques; or particular formats, such as view cameras, are usually geared to intermediate or advanced photographers. If you have little interest in the great outdoors, you are probably better off learning in a classroom than taking a tour to the Alaskan wilderness.

What skills and level of experience are required? Some workshops and tours are set up to accommodate photographers with varied skills and experience; others are designed particularly for students who are either beginners, experienced amateurs, or professionals. Sometimes a specific technical skill is required, and sometimes you must submit a qualifying portfolio in order to be accepted into a course.

What type of film and camera format are used? For lots of workshops and tours you must use color slide film, but there are some for fans of black-and-white images. A few classes encourage the use of many kinds of film. Almost all workshops and tours have you shooting with a 35mm camera; if you want to use another format, such as a 2¼ or 8x10 view camera, either look for a course or tour specifically designed for that format or make sure the instructor is willing and able to address your needs.

What equipment do I need to bring? You almost always are responsible for bringing a camera, film, and tripod; sometimes you must have filters and different lenses. If you are asked to bring equipment that you don't own, you may want to choose a different workshop rather than buy or borrow it.

What is the maximum number of participants? What is the student-to-teacher ratio? Most workshops and tours limit the number of participants. A class of eight is small enough to ensure that each student receives an equal amount of attention and large enough for students to learn from one another without getting bored. A maximum student-teacher ratio of 10 to 1 gives all students enough time to ask questions and have their work evaluated.

How much time is devoted to instruction? Is there free time for other activities? You must decide how much time you want to spend learning, taking pictures, or working in the darkroom. Some workshops are so intensive that you must work from early in the morning to late at night; this kind of schedule is designed to push your creativity to the utmost and improve your skills through constant practice. Other workshops and, particularly, photography tours give you more time to relax and enjoy the scenery.

Are instructors available outside of class? Can private conferences and critiques be arranged? You spend a lot of time with your instructors in class and on field trips, so you may not care to interact with them during your free time. On the other hand, you may enjoy their company and want to spend as much time as you can absorbing their knowledge. If that's the case, pick a workshop or tour in which the instructor stays in the same hotels as students and eats in the same dining hall or restaurants. Sometimes instructors will meet with students privately to discuss their work; sometimes this is not an option.

Where can I see the instructor's work? Before you sign up for any course, it's a good idea to look at samples of the instructor's work. If you like it, there's a good chance you can learn something useful from that person; if you don't, it's unlikely that you will respect what he or she has to say about your own work.

What's the cost and what's included? Workshop fees may or may not include lodging and meals, whereas fees for tours usually do. Unless otherwise stated, prices given in this chapter are per person and include lodging and meals. Lodging is either double occupancy or in multibunk rooms, unless specified differently; when single rooms are available, you must pay a supplement to get one. Whether you sign up for a workshop or a tour, you must bring your own equipment and film. Transportation between shooting locations is most often provided, but ask just to be sure.

Is there a lab fee? Many programs charge a lab fee that covers film processing or chemicals if the workshop concentrates on darkroom work. This could add substantially to the cost of your vacation.

What are the accommodations like? Some institutions have their own housing, which may consist of both private and shared rooms. On tours, you often stay in motels, hotels, or campgrounds. Find out if you must share a room with other students or a bathroom down the hall or, if camping, a tent.

What is the food like? Sometimes you eat in dining halls with cafeteria-style food; sometimes a chef is hired to cook up fancier meals. You may have to rely on local restaurants, so make sure there are enough of them that serve food that appeals to you.

Do you have references from past participants? Try to talk with at least two people who have taken the workshop or tour, but take what they say with a grain of salt. Although they can give you details not found in the brochures, keep in mind that the chemistry between a student and an instructor can greatly affect what the student gets out of the course.

How far in advance must I sign up? For some workshops and tours you must sign up months in advance, but if there's an opening, those that don't require portfolio reviews will usually accept you up until the last minute.

FAVORITE WORKSHOPS AND TOURS

THE NORTHEAST

MAINE **Maine Photographic Workshops.** Established in 1973 by David Lyman, this institution has one of the largest photography programs in the country, with 100 one- and two-week courses each year. It is based in the picturesque seaside village of Rockport on Penobscot Bay, 90 miles north of Portland and 2 miles from the lively resort town of Camden, in an isolated environment that's perfect for concentrating on creative work.

Workshops are offered for students with all levels of technical and artistic experience, from the beginner to the career photographer; each class is limited to between 16 and 18 participants. Most courses on the intermediate and advanced levels require you to submit a portfolio or tear sheets with your application.

Whether you're seeking to develop your skills in taking personal, fine art, or commercial images, you should have no trouble finding the right class. The schedule includes workshops in black-and-white and color photography, portraiture, professional development (such as Introduction to Photojournalism, Fine Art Business, and The Motion Picture Still), the studio, and digital imagery, as well as fine art, travel, stock, and documentary photography. "Foundation" workshops teach beginners the basics of techniques and aesthetics. Master classes are designed for advanced photographers and give them the chance to work with leading experts in the field; recent offerings have included Portrait and Figure Class, The Handmade Photograph, Photographing Cultures, and The World Observed.

The faculty is chosen from some of the best fine art and commercial photographers working today. Recent instructors have included Chris Rainier, Arnold Newman, George Tice, Mary Ellen Mark, Eugene Richards, Jill Enfield, and Maria Cosindas, as well as other professionals who have worked for *Life, National Geographic, Sports Illustrated,* and other major magazines, such as Jim Blair, Elizabeth Opalenik, and Bill Allard.

You should be prepared for an intensive schedule. Classes begin at 9, and mornings are busy with lectures, critiques and discussions of students' work, and technical demonstrations. Afternoons usually center on field trips and one-on-one meetings with instructors. A good part of your day is devoted to hands-on experience to learn the skills of your particular workshop. Film and slides are processed overnight so they can be critiqued the next morning. Photographers are often found working in the darkrooms until late at night (darkrooms are open from 8 AM until midnight). In the evenings, you can attend screenings and slide shows devoted to photographic subjects.

The extensive facilities include 50 enlargers in group darkrooms, a color film–processing lab, a library, a gallery, a photography supply store, and a 2,200-square-foot Studio Barn with a wide selection of lights, grip equipment, sets, and props, used mainly for the film (motion picture) program. The recently opened Ernst Haas Photographic Center contains five new classrooms, a 14-enlarger darkroom, and eight private darkrooms.

Lodging and dining are available on campus or nearby. The 100 rooms on campus, available on a first-come, first-served basis, are within walking distance of classrooms and dining. They range from basic dorm rooms with shared bath to homier rooms with TV, telephone, and private bath. Other accommodations include single and double motel rooms and rooms in private residences with private or shared baths. You can also stay at recommended inns and bed-and-breakfasts, which tend to be more expensive. Students are encouraged to take three meals a day at the Homestead, a 19th-century farmhouse, where you dine and network with staff and other workshop participants. Meals are served buffet style, and vegetarian and special diets can be catered to; on Friday night, a complete banquet is held, with lobster, steak, fresh corn, and pies for dessert. *Maine Photographic Workshops, 2 Central St., Rockport, ME 04856, tel. 207/236–8581, fax 207/236–2558. June–Oct.: 7 days, $450, plus $85–$125 lab fee; 14 days, $900, plus lab fee. Price does not include lodging and meals ($355–$625 per week); sign up 2 months in advance.*

MASSACHUSETTS **Edward Barry Photographic Services.** Since 1988, this company has specialized in travel and scenic photography workshops that provide concentrated time and new opportunities behind the viewfinder. They are designed for aspiring beginners as well as more experienced photographers. The Whale Watch and Lighthouse Excursion, a five-day workshop in Cape Ann (a peninsula on the northeastern tip of Massachusetts), encourages a supportive rather than competitive critiquing of your work as you learn from each member's knowledge and experience. In lectures or in the field, the workshop covers composition, exposure, lighting, and the effects of lenses and filters in travel and scenic photography. It is limited to eight students with one instructor; if more students wish to join the class, an additional instructor is engaged. The instructors are Edward Barry, who is a veteran photographer, a judge of photography competitions, and a professional photography teacher in New Jersey; and Gene Sellers, a published photojournalist.

The workshop is scheduled from Wednesday through Sunday, providing enough time to cover all the key sights in the area and allowing for relaxation and rescheduling of specific shoots in case of inclement weather. Field trips for photo shoots include a whale-watching expedition and visits to Thatcher Island, Rockport village and harbor, the coves near Gloucester, Eastern Point Lighthouse, and Annesquam Lighthouse. You're encouraged to develop a personal style as you receive instruction on the use of specific lenses and filters under different light conditions.

Same-day processing is available for E-6 slide film and C-41 print film. At least two evening critiques of your work by instructors and peers are scheduled. Students are expected to bring a 35mm single-lens reflex camera with manual settings, a wide angle to short telephoto zoom lens, a medium telephoto zoom, a tripod, a cable release, and a few filters.

Accommodations and the whale-watching trip are included in the workshop fee. Students stay in Gloucester at Cape Ann Marina, a modern hotel with balcony views of the harbor, a heated indoor pool, and the Gull Restaurant, which serves mainly traditional New England seafood dishes, such as lobster, swordfish, haddock, and halibut, as well as pastas, prime rib, and chicken. Except for an orientation luncheon, participants take care of their own meals and are encouraged to eat together as a group at various restaurants around Cape Ann. *Edward Barry Photographic Services, 203 Beekman La., Neshanic Station, NJ 08853, tel. 908/359–0288. Late July: 5 days, $585. Price does not include meals; sign up 1 month in advance.*

NEW HAMPSHIRE **Appalachian Mountain Club.** Founded in 1876, the Appalachian Mountain Club (AMC) promotes the conservation and enjoyment of the natural world and teaches skills needed to safely appreciate the outdoors. Besides courses in outdoor recreation (including hiking, backpacking, camping, bicycling, canoeing, kayaking, and rock climbing), the AMC offers several weekend and four-day nature photography workshops in June, September, October, and December, as well as classes in watercolor, music, storytelling, writing, and drawing.

Two four-day photography workshops in September take advantage of the rugged landscape of the White Mountain National Forest in northern New Hampshire. The Fall Foliage Photography workshop allows you to spend your days examining panoramic mountain and forest landscapes during the lustrous season of autumn color. If weather permits, you spend some time above tree line. In the evening, you discuss aesthetic and technical problems of nature photography with the instructor. The Waterlight Photography workshop keeps the mountain panorama in mind but concentrates on working with natural light and capturing the subtleties of streams, brooks, and waterfalls on film. You spend most of your day in the field. Both these fall classes are taught by one of Britain's leading landscape photographers, Philip H. Evans, who has published two volumes of mountain photography.

These courses are open to photographers at all levels of experience on a first-come, first-served basis, with a student-teacher ratio of 10 to 1. Food and accommodations are included in the workshop fee. Your lodging is at Pinkham Notch Visitor Center at the eastern base of Mount Washington on Route 16, 10 miles north of Jackson, New Hampshire. The lodge accommodates more than 100 guests in two-, three-, and four-bunk rooms. Hearty, full-course American meals are served at breakfast and dinner, and lunch, sometimes in the form of a trail meal, is also included. You can buy snacks at the center's snack bar.

The AMC sponsors photography programs in three other northeastern locations: Acadia National Park in Maine, the Berkshires of Massachusetts, and New York's Catskills. It offers other types of programs at the Mohican Outdoor Center in the Delaware Water Gap in New Jersey. *Appalachian Mountain Club, Pinkham Notch Visitor Center, Box 298, Gorham, NH 03581, tel. 603/466–2727, fax 603/466–2720. Sept.: 4 days, $325; sign up 1 month in advance.*

NEW YORK **International Center of Photography.** Started in 1974 by distinguished photographer Cornell Capa, the International Center of Photography (ICP), a nonprofit institution, has a unique workshop program that takes place within a museum environment and stresses the integration of the history, theory, and practice of photography. In a landmark building along the historic Museum Mile of Fifth Avenue on the Upper East Side of Manhattan, the ICP has an extensive collection of photographs—more than 12,000 original prints—and offers a series of exhibitions. It also has a resource library of books, periodicals, slides, and biographical files. Throughout the year, the ICP schedules a wide selection of courses for students at all levels of experience; these classes cover such varied topics as black-and-white and color photography, portraiture, lighting, photojournalism and documentary photography, professional training, printing techniques, and the use of specific materials, as well as the development of personal vision.

During the summer, the program consists of more than 45 workshops, many of them lasting four to five days. Classes usually meet daily from 9 AM to 4 PM and combine lectures, demonstrations, critiques, field trips, studio work, and hands-on experience. Many workshops beyond the basic level require a portfolio review before acceptance. Most are limited to 14 to 18 participants, with one instructor and one teaching assistant per class; students may request a private conference with the teacher should they need additional instruction.

Because of its highly regarded reputation and its Manhattan location, the ICP attracts many notable and award-winning professionals to its faculty; recent instructors and lecturers have included Arnold Newman, Jay Maisel, William Wegman, Donna Ferrato, Maggie Steber, and Gretchen Bender. The center has complete state-of-the-art facilities, including two large black-and-white teaching labs, a film development area, three in-lab classrooms, a large color printing lab, and a non-silver photography process area. The ICP does not provide student housing, and you're expected to take care of your own meals.

In addition to the summer classes in Manhattan, one- and two-week summer travel workshops are available; these include tuition, lodging, and some meals, and cost between $1,000 and $2,600. These special workshops have taken place in such areas as Cape Cod, Massachusetts, and Normandy, France. *International Center of Photography, Education Department, 1130 Fifth Ave., New York, NY 10128, tel. 212/860–1778, fax 212/360–6490. Late June–early Sept.: 4–5 days, $265–$365, plus $50 lab fee. Price does not include lodging and meals; sign up 2 months in advance.*

RHODE ISLAND **Block Island Photography Workshops.** These workshops, first held in 1984, teach the Zone System of exposure and contrast control in black-and-white printing, which was developed by Ansel Adams. The instructors encourage you to define your goals for each workshop ahead

of time, so they can help you gain the technical knowledge you need to achieve these goals as you focus your attention on the creative side of photography. Classes are open to amateurs and professionals who work in a variety of camera and film formats; to encourage interaction between participants and teachers, each workshop allows no more than six students to an instructor.

An intensive workshop is held twice a year on Block Island off the Rhode Island coast. The schedule over the four-day period combines morning lectures and demonstrations on the Zone System, early morning and afternoon hands-on field sessions concentrating on landscape photography, and evening sessions devoted to critiquing portfolios of both students and instructors. Block Island allows opportunities to shoot pictures of rugged coastline, tranquil fields and grasslands, small farmhouses, and well-preserved examples of Victorian architecture in the hotels and cottages of the harbor village.

The instructors are Jack Holowitz and Steve Sherman, two experts in black-and-white photography and printing. Holowitz, a portrait photographer for 25 years, has conducted seminars sponsored by Kodak throughout the United States and Canada. Sherman, who formerly worked in advertising, now devotes most of his energy to teaching and practicing black-and-white fine art photography. Each year, the two also offer a popular portrait, figure, and darkroom workshop (lasting two days or longer) in Springfield, Massachusetts, and a week-long landscape photography course somewhere in the Southwest; recent classes have been held in Death Valley and the canyons of Arizona and Utah.

Workshop fees include ground transportation between field and studio locations, but they do not include meals, lodging, and film-related costs. The instructors make arrangements with local hotels and motels for discount rates for participants. Students take their meals at nearby restaurants, and again, the instructors arrange for group rates. *Block Island Photography Workshops, Steve Sherman, 319 Pheasant Dr., Rocky Hill, CT 06067, tel. 203/563–9156, or Jack Holowitz, 114 Bellevue Ave., Springfield, MA 01108, tel. 413/739–3480. Apr. and Nov.: 4 days, $395. Price does not include lodging and meals; sign up 2 months in advance.*

THE MID-ATLANTIC

PENNSYLVANIA Joe McDonald's Wildlife Photography. For about 30 weeks throughout the year, this company, founded in 1985, provides a variety of wildlife photography workshops and tours for students who have a basic knowledge of 35mm photography using an SLR camera and interchangeable lenses. While some workshops are held in rural central Pennsylvania, many of the workshops and tours take place in different parts of the United States.

In workshops, the emphasis is on instruction, in the field and in the classroom. Daylight hours from sunrise to late in the afternoon are typically devoted to practicing photography, but they also involve demonstrations, occasional quizzes, exercises in composition, and plenty of discussion and field advice from instructors. Evenings are reserved for slide lectures covering photographic techniques and evaluation of students' work. You receive a number of handouts, including specific shooting guides, assignments, and exposure sheets, all designed to help you get the most out of your shoot. The instructors also cover the wildlife to be encountered in the field.

During photography tours, students receive less formal instruction and spend most of their energy taking pictures of indigenous wildlife, though instructors are always available to provide advice and solutions to problems that arise in the field. The first evening is devoted to an orientation covering wildlife subjects you are expected to see on the tour and technical information that will be useful in the field; on subsequent evenings, students' work is discussed.

Workshops are attended by 6 to 10 participants, so you receive plenty of personal attention from the two instructors, who strive to maintain a humorous and relaxed atmosphere. Still, they're quite serious in wanting you to learn how to take better photographs. Many classes are attended by past participants who were pleased by their previous experiences. The instructors are Joe McDonald, who has taken pictures of wildlife for more than 25 years and has written three guides to wildlife photography, and his wife, Mary, also a professional photographer.

The McDonalds offer an intensive weeklong nature photography course in rural Pennsylvania. Other four- to seven-day workshops and tours travel to south Florida, the Everglades, Yellowstone National Park, Montana, Arizona, Utah's Zion and Bryce national parks, and the Olympic Peninsula in Washington. Along the way, you photograph birds, wildflowers, and such diverse mammals as the cougar, bobcat, lynx, fox, wolf, otter, black bear, and grizzly bear.

During the Pennsylvania workshops, students stay at the McDonalds' rustic farm vacation home in single and double rooms. Three meals a day are included, all served family style at the home. Participants who sign up for workshops and tours at other locations around the United States stay at AAA-approved moderately priced motels. Included in the cost of these programs are breakfasts of cereal and danishes and lunches of cold cuts, salads, fruits, and desserts, eaten in the field. Dinners, which are not included, are taken as a group at moderately priced local restaurants. *Joe McDonald's Wildlife Photography, R.R. #2, Box 1095, McClure, PA 17841-9340, tel. and fax 717/543–6423. Year-round: 4–7 days, $750–$1,875. Price for workshops and tours away from home base do not include dinner; sign up 2 months in advance.*

PENNSYLVANIA Touchstone Center for Crafts. Since 1972, Touchstone Center for Crafts has educated and encouraged its students to develop technical skills and innovative expression in arts and crafts. Located 1½ hours south of Pittsburgh by car, it organizes classes, exhibitions, lectures, and demonstrations for people with a wide range of artistic experience. For 10 weeks during the summer, Touchstone usually has three five-day photography workshops in addition to classes in other crafts, such as pottery, glassblowing, monoprinting, jewelry making, paper art, metal crafts, blacksmithing, fiber arts, and painting. The program also has art classes for children ages 6 through 12 should you wish to bring your child with you.

Workshops for the novice and more experienced photographer combine lectures, discussions, and assignments to strengthen each student's skills. Classes are small, usually from 8 to 10 students. In one beginner's course, you explore basic photography techniques and learn how to develop film. Other workshops, open to all levels of expertise, teach you how to add color to black and white pictures using special development techniques or how to photograph artwork using natural and artificial light. Courses are held Monday through Friday from 9 AM to 4 PM, with studios open to students 24 hours a day. The center has one darkroom with two enlargers. The lab fee for each class covers the cost of all chemicals and photographic paper that is purchased by Touchstone and used by the students.

Courses are taught by professional artists with teaching experience. In addition to the workshops, the center presents a series of performances on Thursday evenings in July and August. Also on Thursday evenings, students and visitors alike participate in Touchstone's Student Art Auction, where arts and crafts created throughout the week are donated and auctioned, with proceeds used for studio improvements. The Touchstone Gallery features artwork by Touchstone faculty members.

A gentle stream flows through Touchstone's 147-acre campus, with tall oak trees in the mountains of Pennsylvania. A limited number of rustic cabins (two to four people per cabin) are available on a first-come, first-served basis. You can also camp at the center's tent and RV sites, which have no hookups or cooking facilities. The dining plan offers three meals a day prepared by caterers and served family style in the dining hall. *Touchstone Center for Crafts, R.D. 1, Box 60, Farmington, PA 15437, tel. 412/329–1370. Late June–Aug.: 5 days, $130–$175. Price does not include lodging ($50–$60 per week for cabin, $25 for campsite) and meals ($60 for 15 meals); sign up 1 month in advance.*

THE SOUTH

FLORIDA **Naturethics.** Founded in 1982 by naturalists John Green and Tom Tyning, Naturethics has an annual schedule of events that combines natural history observation with photography. For more than 20 years, Green and Tyning have led tours, taken pictures, and written books and articles relating to natural history. Their main goal is to provide workshop and vacation tour participants with detailed introductions to the various places being viewed. So instead of just teaching you how to photograph animals and natural settings, the two instructors increase your awareness and understanding of the subjects and environments on your trip. You're encouraged to practice patient observation during the workshop or tour to allow exceptional opportunities to see and identify the behavior and interactions of wildlife and their habitats as you encounter them.

One of Naturethics's most popular and most successful tours visits the Florida Everglades, a unique ecosystem that reveals a fascinating interaction between plants and animals. Each day you discover a different ecological environment, such as the enormous, shallow Florida Bay, freshwater sloughs, tropical hardwood hammocks, and cypress domes. Along the way you see such varied wildlife as birds, butterflies, lizards, alligators, and amphibians. Field events take place during the day and evening, both on foot and in the van provided. The daily schedule features sunrise photography shoots, bird-watching walks, a tram tour of Shark Valley, and a canoe trip.

Although there is no formal photography instruction on the trip, Green and Tyning give tips to anyone who asks. The group comprises up to 12 participants, who usually have a range of photographic experience. Most come with 35mm cameras. There are no facilities for developing film in the park, so you don't get to see your work until the tour is over.

You have the option of camping (bring your own tent and equipment) or staying in nearby cottages or motel rooms, which are not included in the price. All accommodations are in the Flamingo section of the park, on Florida Bay. Good home-cooked meals, prepared by the camp chef, are included, except for one dinner when participants eat together in a local restaurant.

Naturethics has other 7- to 12-day photography tours and weekend excursions around the United States and eastern Canada, including trips to such destinations as southeastern Arizona; New Jersey's Edwin B. Forsythe National Wildlife Refuge; the northern coast of Maine; Cape Cod; the Berkshires in Massachusetts; and Okefenokee in southeastern Georgia. *Naturethics, Box 961, Amherst, MA 01004, tel. 413/256–8739. Jan.: 8 days, $725. Price does not include cabin accommodations or 1 dinner; sign up 2 months in advance.*

FLORIDA **Nikon School of Underwater Photography.** Sponsored by Nikon for photographers who use the Nikonos System, this school provides hands-on underwater photography instruction by top professional photographers at dive locales in the Florida Keys and the Caribbean. All courses are six days and combine classroom and underwater instruction, during which you learn the use of various underwater lenses and accessories. Close-up, macro, and wide-angle lenses and TTL (through the lens) strobe exposures are all covered. Both basic and advanced courses are available only to those

with Nikonos underwater camera equipment and scuba certification.

Workshops in Key Largo are taught by Stephen Frink, a frequently published underwater photographer who leads many photo tours to dive destinations each year. Because these Key Largo workshops are so popular, they are open to 25 students; however, no more than 12 divers sign up for other courses. All courses include daily lectures, personal critiques, and dive opportunities; generally two to three hours of instruction and two tank dive excursions are provided each day. E-6 film processing is available for immediate evaluation of images, but you pay extra for film and processing.

Packages at Marina Del Mar Resort in Key Largo include seven nights' accommodations, six days of underwater photographic instruction, six days of diving, tanks, and weights, as well as a daily Continental breakfast. Other meals are taken on your own. *Nikon School of Underwater Photography, Waterhouse Photographic Tours, Box 2487, Key Largo, FL 33037, tel. 305/451–2228 or 800/272–9122, fax 305/451–5147. Early June and mid-Sept.: 6 days, $631–$987. Price does not include lunch and dinner; sign up 2 months in advance.*

THE SOUTHWEST

ARIZONA **Grand Canyon Expeditions Company Photography Expedition.** In 1964, Grand Canyon Expeditions Company began running commercial trips along the Colorado River through the Grand Canyon; it started offering special-interest excursions in 1984. Twice a year, photographers with a varied range of expertise join veteran outfitters for an eight-day photography expedition that starts at Lee's Ferry near Lake Powell, Arizona, and ends at Pearce Ferry, Arizona. Each tour is limited to 28 participants. You cover some 300 river miles and negotiate nearly 200 exciting rapids as you travel in a 37-foot S-Rig river raft that contains 20 separate compartments and enough room to transport all participants' supplies and equipment. These trips are not totally dominated by photography shoots, so a companion who just wants to experience the river journey should have an equally enjoyable trip. Travel is slow enough to allow more than enough time for swimming, fishing, hiking, and composing the perfect shot.

The expedition lends itself easily to capturing a number of beautiful images of nature. Under the guidance of an expert professional photographer, you have the chance to shoot spectacular geological formations, abundant wildlife, cacti, rushing waterfalls, Native American ruins, and wildflowers. Scenic highlights along the way include Navajo Bridge, Phantom Ranch, Red Wall Cavern, Bright Angel Canyon, Lava Falls, and Granite Park. The changing landscape and lighting conditions along with the personalized instruction provide ample challenges for you to improve your camera skills.

You begin your trip by staying one night at a hotel in Las Vegas at your own cost. After an early morning departure from Las Vegas, the company provides all transportation, camping equipment, waterproof river bags, a waterproof box for your camera and personal items, meals, and beverages. In the evening, you have time for photographic instruction. Afterward you sleep in the canyon under the stars. There is no place to have your photos developed along the way.

Meals are prepared by the boatmen. Breakfasts consist of campfire coffee, tea, juice, fruit, and a choice of breakfast foods. For lunch, you're provided with delicatessen meats, cheeses, breads, and cookies. Dinners include a meat course cooked in Dutch ovens and served with fresh vegetables, salad, biscuits, soup, and dessert. *Grand Canyon Expeditions Company, Box 0, Kanab, UT 84741, tel. 801/644–2691 or 800/644–2691, fax 801/544–2699. Mid-July and early Aug.: 8 days, $1,595. Price does not include 1 night's lodging; sign up 6 months in advance.*

ARIZONA, NEW MEXICO, UTAH **The Ray McSavaney Photographic Workshops.** Since 1990, this program has included several seven-day workshops that focus on the southwestern landscape. Starting with the premise that photography is a continuous creative process, instructors look at their students' past body of work in addition to concentrating on questions and problems that arise on location. Teachers encourage participants to consider why they chose certain subjects, how they view the world, and how their future photographic goals may best be achieved.

The workshops are open to photographers who work in different formats and have a range of experience. The daily schedule involves on-site instruction, critiques, discussions, and presentations on the aesthetic and technical aspects of photography. To ensure that each student receives an equal amount of personal attention, enrollment for each workshop is limited to eight participants per instructor. The distinguished faculty, chosen from award-winning professionals with years of teaching experience, includes Carol Brown, Philip Hyde, Ray McSavaney, John Nichols, John Sexton, and Jack Waltman.

One of the most popular workshops offered is The Southwest Landscape, which takes you to the heart of the Navajo Nation. The workshop begins early Sunday afternoon at Canyon de Chelly in northeastern Arizona, where you have the opportunity to photograph the architectural remnants of ancient Anasazi cliff dwellings. Midway through the workshop week, the group travels north into Utah to Monument Valley's sandstone sculptures. You attend specially arranged tours that allow ample time for photographing well-known sights and less famous areas in both Arizona and Utah. As you aim to gain a personal sense of the landscape, you also explore the relationship between Native Americans and their land.

Another workshop, The Spirit of the Land–Photographing Northern New Mexico, covers the visually diverse areas around

Taos, including Ranchos de Taos, Pueblo de Taos, Chimayo, the Ghost Ranch (painted by Georgia O'Keeffe), and the Taos Mesa; students take pictures of rivers, canyons, valleys, mesas, mountains, and regional architecture. This class ends the day before the renowned Indian Market occurs in Santa Fe, so you can spend the weekend visiting the market before returning home. Other workshops include The Land of Standing Rock, which explores the landscape of eastern Utah (Arches National Park, Canyonlands National Park, Fisher Towers, and the La Sal Mountains); The Visual Image, which visits Capitol Reef National Park near Torrey, Utah; and Anasazi Viewpoints, which concentrates on landscapes in Colorado associated with the Anasazi culture.

Workshop tuition does not normally include lodging and meals, except for The Southwest Landscape, which covers lunches, refreshment breaks, and a barbecue dinner. Depending on the workshop, the program makes arrangements for you to stay at motels, reasonably priced condos, bed-and-breakfasts, or campgrounds near each location. Participants provide their own transportation, and usually travel by car caravan. Ray McSavaney, who runs the workshops, will arrange car pools if necessary. *Ray McSavaney Photographic Workshops, 1984 N. Main St., Studio 402, Los Angeles, CA 90031, tel. 213/225–1730. May–Oct.: 7 days, $450–$600. Price does not include lodging and meals; sign up 3 months in advance.*

NEW MEXICO **Photo Adventure Tours.** Since 1986, this company has organized tours to destinations around the United States while providing informal instruction in the basics of photography along the way. Although the trips are open to all photographers, they are probably best suited to those with less experience who wish to improve their skills in nature and travel photography. Tours are run by professional photographers who usually have an in-depth knowledge of the destination and prior experience photographing the place.

Trips are led by two instructors and limited to 20 participants, accepted on a first-come, first-served basis. The daily schedule generally begins at sunrise so that participants can arrive at sights before other tourists. There are no lectures, classroom demonstrations, or critiques of your work (film is not always developed along the way). Although photography instruction is rather informal, you may ask in advance for individual and more intense guidance. Your tour leaders carry a wide variety of lenses that you may borrow at any time.

Two popular tours visit New Mexico in October. The four-day trip to the Albuquerque Balloon Festival allows you to take shots of the ascension of more than 600 hot-air balloons. A five-day trip covers various sights and landscapes around New Mexico, including White Sands National Monument, Lincoln National Forest, the Badlands of New Mexico, the Zuni Pueblo, Gallup and Route 66, El Morro National Monument, Acoma Pueblo and Sky City, and Laguna Pueblo. Among other U.S. destinations explored by Photo Adventure Tours throughout the year are California, the Navajo areas of Arizona, Utah's Zion and Bryce national parks, Hawaii, and the Upper Peninsula of Michigan.

Tour packages include lodging, breakfast, and dinner at chain hotels such as Best Western and Holiday Inn. Participants eat lunch, often consisting of sandwiches, on location, but it is not usually included in the cost. *Photo Adventure Tours, 2035 Park St., Atlantic Beach, NY 11509-1236, tel. 516/371–0067 or 800/821–1221, fax 516/ 371–1352. Early Oct.–mid-Oct.: 4–5 days, $435–$495. Price does not include lunch; sign up 2 months in advance.*

NEW MEXICO **Santa Fe Photographic Workshops.** Established in 1990 by Reid Callanan, who has been running photography workshop programs since the mid-70s, this program comprises more than 40 week-long summer workshops over a seven-week period. Many of these workshops involve field trips that enable you to photograph the stunning mountain and desert landscapes of northern New Mexico, a region that also encompasses three distinct cultures—Native American, Hispanic, and Anglo.

The program is based at the Workshops Center, a mile and a half from the downtown city plaza. The administrative office, three classrooms, a store, the studio, and dormitory housing are all at the center. Across the quiet, dead-end street is the Community Tent, an informal gathering place where cold drinks, coffee, and snacks are sold all day long, and an attractive adobe building nearby houses additional staff offices, two classrooms, a small darkroom, an audiovisual room, a gallery, and a workroom.

Although a few workshops are open to beginners (such as Beginning Photography, Introduction to Color Photography, and Color Imaging on the Macintosh and the PC), most courses are geared for experienced amateurs and professional photographers, who are required to submit samples of work with their application. The varied selection includes workshops in landscape, documentary, and studio photography, portraiture, figure study, photojournalism, and lighting techniques. Workshops are limited to 16 to 18 participants and are taught by established professional photographers. Recent instructors have included Nick Nichols, Karen Kuehn, Gary Gorman, Sam Abell, Eugene Richards, David Michael Kennedy, and Joyce Tenneson.

The daily schedule for most workshops involves field trips to locations around Santa Fe and northern New Mexico, critiques and discussions of students' work, and one-on-one meetings with instructors. Film and slides are processed overnight at the workshops' lab so that images can be critiqued the next day.

Several workshops focus on learning about the indigenous cultures as you take your pictures. Such workshops as Land of the Anasazi, Southwestern Landscape Adventure, and Bisti Badlands Wilderness Land-

scape involve travel with the instructors to special New Mexico locales while you investigate the aesthetic, technical, and philosophical issues of making photographs. A series of electronic imaging workshops using Adobe Photoshop software, held in association with the Santa Fe Community College, gives you intensive exposure to the techniques and technology used to create digital photography. Through lectures, demonstrations, and personal critiques, you learn image manipulation, retouching, color adjustments, and other creative techniques and then apply these skills to individual projects.

Monday and Wednesday evenings throughout the summer are devoted to slide lectures by instructors, who present their work and talk about their careers and lives in photography. Following the Friday night barbecue, students present slides of their work.

You pay extra to stay in the on-campus dorm housing across the street from the Workshops Center and next door to the studio. About 38 students can be accommodated in the simply furnished single and double rooms with shared or private bath, available on a first-come, first-served basis. You can also stay in recommended local inns, motels, and hotels.

The mandatory meal program includes a gourmet buffet orientation dinner on Sunday evening, a Friday evening barbecue dinner at a nearby ranch, and five box lunches (consisting of sandwich, salad, and dessert) that can be taken on field trips or eaten under the Community Tent. Vegetarian meals are available. You can opt to purchase a pass for buffet breakfasts for the week, but you're on your own for other meals. *Santa Fe Photographic Workshops, Box 9916, Santa Fe, NM 87504, tel. 505/983–1400, fax 505/989–8604. Mid-June–early Aug.: 7 days, $595–$795, plus $80–$125 lab fee. Price does not include lodging ($225–$350 per week), mandatory meal program (2 dinners and 5 lunches, $105 per week), and optional breakfasts ($18 per week); sign up anytime.*

THE ROCKIES

COLORADO **Anderson Ranch Arts Center.** Located on a historic campus in Snowmass Village, 10 miles west of the mountain resort community of Aspen, Anderson Ranch Arts Center provides professional and personal development workshops in photography, as well as in other art forms, such as ceramics, painting, drawing, woodworking, sculpture, and furniture design. These intensive one- and two-week courses aim to stretch the creativity of students as they learn new artistic techniques.

Photography workshops at Anderson Ranch began in 1973 and are currently sponsored by Eastman Kodak Company. Workshops are offered for beginners, seasoned professionals, and all those in-between, from traditionalists to those interested in experimenting with technique and vision. Topics include portraiture, platinum and palladium printing, landscape, the nude, view camera technique, photojournalism, and beginning, intermediate, and advanced black-and-white printing. In the past, workshops have also been offered on constructing and shooting with a pinhole camera; creating multimedia slide presentations; and shooting with the alpine light of mountain ridges and tundra.

Classes generally meet from 9 to 5 weekdays for the one- and two-week sessions. You spend your days taking photographs in the studio or on location and participating in critiques of students' work. Instructors review portfolios, provide lab and field demonstrations on technique and artistic development, and meet with students individually to address special interests. One or two faculty members along with one or two assistants lead each class; assistants work individually with students and help them prepare chemicals in

Enrollment is limited to 15 students per workshop. After you register, you fill out a questionnaire that gives the instructor information on your level of experience; the coursework is sometimes adjusted to suit your group. One or two faculty members along with one or two assistants lead each class; assistants work individually with students and help them prepare chemicals in

the darkrooms. Recent instructors have included many renowned photographers, such as Judy Dater, Jerry Uelsmann, John Sexton, Sam Abell, Barbara Crane, and Ralph Gibson.

The center's facilities contain individual and group printing labs, film processing areas, and finishing and print-viewing spaces. Black-and-white enlargers are available for 35mm, 120, and 4x5 formats. In darkroom courses, you usually are assigned your own enlarger. Labs are open 24 hours weekdays. Workshops have lab fees that cover chemicals and darkroom use but not E-6 color slide processing. E-6 color film is processed at a nearby professional lab during the day and overnight at students' own cost.

Anderson Ranch is situated on 4 acres next to a golf course and encompasses renovated log cabins and barns alongside new buildings. Students have the option of staying in the on-campus dormitory or nearby condominiums; in both places, shared and private rooms generally share a bath. Participants can sign up for a meal plan providing three cafeteria-style meals a day at the on-campus dining hall; faculty and students dine together. A children's art program is run concurrently with the adult program.

The center also sponsors a Field Expeditions Program of one- and two-week workshops in the Rocky Mountains, Utah Canyonlands, and the Grand Canyon. Most of these camping trips are designed for intermediate to advanced students with some hiking and camping experience; they are led by guides and instructors familiar with the locales. Some of these workshops involve river rafting through desert country or horsepacking. Fees for the program cover tuition, guides and outfitters, lodging, meals, film pickups for processing, and transportation to sites. *Anderson Ranch Arts Center, Box 5598, Snowmass Village, CO 81615, tel. 303/923–3181, fax 303/923–3871. Early June–late Aug.: 6- to 12-day on-campus workshops, $350–$825, plus $35–$100 lab fee. Early May–early Oct.: 8- to*

14-day field expedition workshops, $970–$2,500. Price of on-campus workshops does not include lodging and meals ($245–$365 per week), but field expedition workshops includes lodging and meals; sign up 2 months in advance for all workshops.

■**MONTANA**■ **Rocky Mountain School of Photography.** Opened in 1987, this Missoula-based photography school has a 10-week summer career training program and more than 20 weekend and weeklong workshops year-round in Missoula and other destinations around the United States.

Several of the weeklong workshops involve nature and landscape photography in Montana, and others concentrate on photographic technique. Most of these workshops are designed for intermediate and advanced students who work with a variety of formats. The daily schedule involves field shooting, lectures by instructors, demonstrations of photographic techniques, and critiques of students' work. All classes are limited in enrollment; the maximum number of students for workshops ranges from eight to 18.

The school has one darkroom with 15 enlargers. This facility is available for just a few courses, and then only during scheduled times. For most workshops, students may have E-6 color film processed locally to allow discussion of photographs taken during the class.

Typical workshops explore the Montana landscape during different seasons. Springtime in Potomac Valley, based in western Montana, includes such shooting locations as small historic towns, wildflower meadows, glacier-draped mountains, a gold-mining ghost town, and the Great Plains. The course covers advanced methods of exposure for color and black-and-white close-up photography, composition, and the use of particular films and filters. The Montana Field Workshop takes in the varied wild landscape of northwestern Montana in summer, including three days amid the dramatic environment of Glacier National Park and another day at the National Bison Range.

The Black-and-White Zone System of Exposure concentrates on the technique devised and practiced by master photographer Ansel Adams to produce fine art black-and-white pictures. The workshop provides darkroom experience in film processing and printing and covers such topics as previsualization; exposing for shadow placement; altering film development; using filters to control contrast; and archival processes of mounting and toning images.

Documentary Portraiture concentrates on the techniques and aesthetics involved in making an exceptional portrait and capturing the unique spirit of a location. The class combines slide lectures, critiques, photographing in the studio and in the field, and darkroom printing.

Other weeklong workshops are held in such diverse locations as Okefenokee Swamp in south Georgia; the desert canyonlands of Arizona; the mountains of Ouray, Colorado, known for its canyons, waterfalls, and wildflowers; Yellowstone National Park; and Martha's Vineyard, off the Massachusetts coast. Instructors are all professional nature· photographers and experienced teachers; the school's founders, Neil and Jeanne Chaput de Saintonge, are permanent staff members, and recent instructors have included Bruce Barnbaum, Jim Bones, Alison Shaw, Dennis Darling, and Jay Dusard.

You're responsible for your own lodging and meals. The school helps students make arrangements for moderately priced lodging at local hotels, motels, and inns. When you register, you receive a form asking about your lodging preferences. *Rocky Mountain School of Photography, Box 7605, Missoula, MT 59807, tel. 406/543–0171 or 800/394–7677. Year-round: 6–8 days, $395–$975. Price does not include meals and lodging; sign up 1 month in advance.*

THE WEST COAST

■**CALIFORNIA**■ **Ambient Light Workshops.** Started in 1990, Ambient Light Workshops gives both the novice and the more advanced photographer one-on-one instruction and hands-on experience in the field. During a seven-day period, each student learns about composition, exposure, lighting, Zone System concepts, the uses of various kinds of films, lenses, and selecting the right subject. The instructors are proficient in a number of camera and film formats, so you can bring along 35mm, 4x5, or 8x10 cameras. Each course is limited to 10 students and the student-teacher ratio is 5 to 1, so you receive a lot of personal attention. Workshops are scheduled to avoid high tourist seasons.

During mid-September, Ambient Light has a one-week workshop that covers Yosemite National Park, Mono Lake, and Bodie Ghost Town, with a variety of outdoor subjects along the way. The program provides all ground transportation in a stretch minivan for the entire week, starting from Oakland International Airport. In Yosemite, you shoot pictures of waterfalls, giant redwoods, and mountainous landscapes; at Mono Lake, the tufa rock formations, standing 15 feet above water, make interesting subjects, especially beautiful at sunrise and sunset. One day of the workshop is devoted to Bodie Ghost Town, with its late 19th-century buildings well preserved on the eastern edge of the Sierras near Nevada. This workshop is taught by John Mariana, the founder of Ambient Light and an experienced, award-winning landscape photographer who specializes in teaching the use of the simplified Zone System for 35mm and medium-format cameras.

Fees include your lodging inside Yosemite in private multibedroom mountain homes, with a fireplace, balconies, a kitchen, and laundry facilities. Singles and doubles are available, and all rooms have their own bathroom. You're responsible for your own meals, so stops are made at grocery stores, restaurants, and cafeterias along the way. Students usually have dinner together at local restaurants for around $10 per person.

Ambient Light Workshops has other week-long workshops in the Southwest; one travels to Monument Valley, Mesa Verde National Park, and Shiprock, while another visits Durango, Chaco Canyon, the Anasazi ruins, Bisti Badlands wilderness landscape, Great Sand Dunes National Monument, Rancho de Taos Church, Santa Fe, Taos, and Taos Pueblo. *Ambient Light Workshops, 5 Tartan Ridge Rd., Burr Ridge, IL 60521, tel. 708/325-5464. Mid-Sept.: 7 days, $950–$1,500. Price does not include meals; sign up 1 month in advance.*

ALASKA

STATEWIDE **Alaska Up Close.** Since 1984, Alaska Up Close, based in Juneau, has organized customized photography, wilderness, and natural history tours for groups and independent travelers. One of its most popular photography tours for travelers on their own is A Gathering of Eagles, which goes from Juneau to the 49,000-acre Chilkat Bald Eagle Preserve in Haines. Between late October and January, as many as 3,500 bald eagles congregate along the Chilkat River to feed on the late salmon run. On the tour, you photograph these special birds from a nearby roadway. The steep-walled Chilkat Valley is also home to moose, wolves, mountain goats, lynx, coyotes, foxes, and mink; brown bears often use the area for feeding during the night.

Hyde with Eagles, an eight-day guided group trip to the eagles' meeting place, (called the Eagle Council Grounds), takes place in mid-November. You receive hands-on field instruction in wildlife photography, including advice on how to shoot pictures of the bald eagles in flight and during feedings. Lectures and informal discussions during the week address such topics as wildlife behavior and low-light and winter photography. The program leader also provides information on outdoor photography in the whole state of Alaska during all seasons.

You travel between Juneau and Haines via a half-day cruise on Lynn Canal and have four days for photography in Chilkat Valley.

Each day in Haines, your group arrives near the Eagle Council Grounds by bus at the crack of dawn to observe the birds' feeding activity and to prepare for photo opportunities as day breaks. Hot lunch is served in the field to take full advantage of the daylight. The trip includes a visit to Mendenhall Glacier near Juneau for additional nature shots.

Limited to 10 participants, the program is open to anyone with a basic knowledge of 35mm photography; a telephoto lens of at least 300mm and sturdy tripod are recommended equipment for the trip. John Hyde, a cinematographer and professional wildlife photographer whose work has appeared in such magazines as *National Geographic*, *Outside*, and *Smithsonian*, leads the tour with the help of a local naturalist guide and briefings by a state biologist.

You stay in local lodges, small hotels, or motels with restaurants on the premises or nearby. The only meals provided as part of the tour are dinner on the night you arrive in Haines and four lunches at the Chilkat Bald Eagle Preserve.

Alaska Up Close arranges several other tours around the state for photographers and wildlife enthusiasts, but none of these is escorted. The 10-day John Muir's Alaska, held from late May through August, follows in the footsteps of the famous naturalist as it covers Southeast Alaska's Inside Passage, with its jagged snowcapped mountains, massive glaciers, and luxuriant rain forest. The 10-day Rites of Spring tour in May explores Southeast Alaska's nature highlights of spring migration as well as an early fish run in the Stikine and Chilkat valleys and Medenhall Wetlands State Game Refuge; the 14-day Alaska's Parklands, conducted from June through August, visits Denali, Glacier Bay, and Kenai Fjords national parks. *Alaska Up Close, Box 32666, Juneau, AK 99803, tel. 907/789–9544, fax 907/789–3205. Mid-Nov. (Hyde with Eagles): 8 days, $1,595. Late-Oct.–mid-Dec. (A Gathering of Eagles): 7 days, $1,030. Price for Hyde with Eagles does not include all breakfasts, 4 lunches, and most dinners; price for A Gathering of Eagles does not include most meals; sign up at least 1 month in advance.*

STATEWIDE Joseph Van Os Photo Safaris. With an emphasis on wildlife and nature photography, this company, started in 1980, offers both workshops and photo safaris open to photographers with all levels of experience. On photo safaris, you concentrate on shooting while the company handles the travel details. Guides are well acquainted with the specific destination being covered so that they can show you some of the most notable places in the area to take memorable pictures. You shoot alongside some of America's leading outdoor photographers, who are always nearby to provide pointers on how to get your best shot.

On many of these tours, limited to 16 participants, you spend most of your day taking pictures, aside from lunchtime siestas during hot weather. Companions simply interested in the great outdoors might also enjoy these trips.

On most safaris, you stay in pleasant first-class inns and hotels or tented camps. Your meals are included in the package price; you usually dine in restaurants, though sometimes picnics are provided in the field.

Several of the most popular photo safaris travel to various areas of Alaska. You can photograph brown bears at Katmai National Park, bald eagles near the Chilkat River, and big game, such as bear, moose, and caribou, in Denali National Park. One trip, The Best of Alaska, covers the diverse landscapes of Denali and Kenai Fjords national parks, as well as the Anan Bear Preserve, part of the Panhandle.

Other destinations visited on safaris include Yellowstone National Park and the Grand Tetons, Colorado's San Juan Mountains, and Zion and Bryce Canyon national parks in southern Utah. Four separate trips concentrate on photographing wildlife—birds of prey in Colorado and predatory mammals in Montana and California.

The company also offers about five photo workshops around the country each year. These courses provide an intensive learning experience concentrating on technique. To allow ample time for field shooting and indoor slide lectures, the workshops are usually based at a single site near a number of wildlife and nature subjects. Workshops are limited to 12 to 20 participants. Although most of these courses focus on the fundamentals, you can arrange with the teachers for advanced instruction and special areas of study. A typical workshop involves critiques of work and discussions relating to equipment and marketing your photographs. Film is processed locally at an extra cost. The price of the workshop does not include meals and lodging, but the company can suggest restaurants and places to stay. Likely locations for photo workshops are Olympic National Park in Washington, Acadia National Park in Maine, Saguaro National Monument in Arizona, and Sanibel Island in southern Florida.

Both safaris and workshops are usually led by two instructors. Recent faculty members have included such experienced outdoor photographers as director Joseph Van Os, Perry Conway, John Shaw, Renee Lynn, Tim Davis, Jeff Lepore, Rod Planck, Wayne Lynch, David Middleton, and Jim Zuckerman. *Joseph Van Os Photo Safaris, Box 655, Vashon, WA 98070, tel. 206/463-5383, fax 206/463-5484. Year-round: 6-day workshops, $645; 5- to 13-day safaris, $1,295–$3,750. Price for workshops does not include lodging and meals, but price for safaris includes lodging and meals; sign up several months in advance.*

SOURCES

ORGANIZATIONS **Photographic Society of America** (3000 United Founders Blvd., Suite 103, Oklahoma City, OK 73112, tel.

405/843–1437) is comprised of mostly amateurs but has members at all levels of experience; it aids camera clubs and publishes *PSA Journal.*

PERIODICALS *American Photo* (1633 Broadway, New York, NY 10019, tel. 212/767-6000 or 800/274–4514) is a magazine for advanced amateurs and professional photographers. *Outdoor Photographer* (12121 Wilshire Blvd., Suite 1220, Los Angeles, CA 90025-1175, tel. 310/820–1500) covers outdoor, adventure, and travel photography. *Photo District News* (1515 Broadway, New York, NY 10036, tel. 212/536–5222 or 800/669–1002) is a trade magazine designed for professionals and those who wish to learn more about all aspects of the photography industry. *Popular Photography* (1633 Broadway, New York, NY 10019, tel. 212/767-6000 or 800/274–4514) contains the latest information about cameras, film, and other equipment as well as articles about photographic techniques.

BOOKS *The Guide to Photography Workshops and Schools* (ShawGuides, 625 Biltmore Way, Suite 1406, Coral Gables, FL 33134) contains listings for workshops, tours, residences and retreats, organizations, and schools in the United States and Canada. *Photographer's Market* (Writer's Digest Books, F&W Publications, 1507 Dana Ave., Cincinnati, OH 45207), updated annually, lists photography workshops around the United States and suggests more than 2,000 places for selling and marketing work.

ALSO SEE To learn a different way to look at your world, turn to Painting Workshops or search for sculpture classes in the Arts and Crafts Workshops chapter.

Spas and Fitness Centers

By Bernard Burt

f you're looking for a vacation that will teach you healthier ways to live—and, in the process, restore your mind, body, and spirit—a spa may be the answer. The facilities and treatments available at today's establishments go far beyond those of the old European spas, grand hotels cosseting those who came to sip the waters. American spas reflect current trends in medical thinking. They take a holistic view of health and promote preventive medicine: They are devoted to showing you how more exercise, a better diet, and better ways of dealing with stress can make you not only look better but also feel better. You pick up lots of tips: how to cook without salt, sugar, butter, and sometimes other fats as well, or how to make portions seem larger (serve food on small plates) or mealtimes more enjoyable (slice meat thinly and fan it out). In addition, after a week of relaxed spa life, you know how good it feels to feel good. Wanting more, you may well take the spa's lessons to heart, and, like many spa guests, make some changes in the way you live when you're not on vacation.

There are all kinds of spas, some of them truly deluxe. Destination spas are really self-contained resorts totally focused on health and fitness; such bodywork as massages, facials, manicures, and pedicures are also part of most stays. Along with such services, many spas have stop-smoking or stress-control programs. Some also have alternative dining plans—you can opt for spa cuisine instead of southern fried chicken with mashed potatoes and cream gravy. Other spas have sports programs or are part of top American sports resorts; you may find sport-specific exercise classes, which, say, add boxing and tennis movements to aerobic workouts.

A few spas are New Age retreats or ranches with health and healing programs based on combinations of ancient therapies and the latest concepts in behavior modification. Other establishments show you how you can strengthen your body against illness through good nutrition and by understanding the relationship between mind and body; some centers focus on the message of Dr. Dean Ornish, author of *Dr. Dean Ornish's Program for Reversing Heart Disease* who argues for a low-fat, high-fiber diet and regular exercise, or on the teachings of Dr. Deepak Chopra, author of the best-seller *Ageless Body, Timeless Mind*, who believes that health is not merely the absence of disease but a state of well-being that infuses the entire body and mind.

Some spas are medically supervised health and fitness centers, where you are monitored by physicians, physiotherapists, and nutritionists. These centers usually give you a personalized daily exercise schedule, calorie-controlled meals, and regimented programs to help you stop smoking and learn to deal with stress and excess pounds—both at the center and after you go home.

Spas also come in all price ranges, depending on such variables as accommodations,

---

Bernard Burt, the author of Fodor's Healthy Escapes, *reviews spas regularly for various publications.*

facilities, location, services, and the amount of supervision. For a seven-day package that includes the spa program, meals, and lodging, expect to pay between $800 and $2,000 per person for a double or between $1,000 and $2,000 (up to as much as $4,000 at a really glamorous spot) for a single. If you want to cut costs, look into the seasonal specials available at some spas. (Florida spas, for instance, offer lower rates in summer.)

Different as spa programs are, similarities emerge when you take a close look. Most spas have packages that include lodging, dining, and activities. Basic spa services such as exercise and body treatments are comparable in quality from one spa to the next, and diet is important no matter where you go, although what constitutes healthful eating may vary. Some spas simply offer a low-calorie diet and a balanced selection from the basic food groups, with fish and chicken several times a week. Others cook with organically grown foodstuffs or have you eating vegetarian fare. Centers that specialize in fitness or weight loss often offer supervised juice regimens and fasting.

For your first spa vacation, try a spa with a structured program of anywhere from five days to two weeks. Typically, at such establishments, each day begins with a walk and stretching session or yoga or meditation. After breakfast, there might be lectures or workouts. In the afternoon, you may go out for a hike or another walk, or have time free to take advantage of spa services such as aromatherapy or hydromassage. At night, you can enjoy lectures by specialists in different health fields. If you don't like regimentation, look for a resort spa with plenty of activities in addition to the fitness and treatment offerings.

Study the spa's schedule in advance of your visit, and don't hesitate to ask the spa director for advice before you arrive. Several establishments offer personal consultations in such areas as fitness testing, biofeedback, and meditation, as well as one-on-one training. Such advance preparation can be the first step in establishing a personal fitness regimen. Consult your physician well before leaving home and take along medical records that will help the spa director plan your schedule.

COMMON SPA FEATURES AND PROGRAMS In order to evaluate the range of programs a spa offers, it helps to understand spa-speak. You'll hear many of the following terms frequently.

Acupressure: Finger massage intended to release muscle tension by applying pressure to the nerves.

Aromatherapy: Massage with oils from essences of flowers and other plants intended to relax the skin's connective tissues and stimulate the natural flow of lymph.

Ayurvedic medicine: 4,000-year-old Native American treatments with oils, massage, and herbs.

Herbal wrap: A treatment in which the body is wrapped in hot linens moistened with herbal infusions, plastic sheets, and blankets; the moisture, heat, and herbal essences are said to promote muscle relaxation and the elimination of toxins.

Hydrotherapy: Underwater massage, alternating hot and cold showers, and other water-oriented treatments.

Inhalation therapy: A treatment during which you breathe hot vapors or steam mixed with eucalyptus oil, either using inhalation equipment or in a special steam room. The goal is to decongest the respiratory system.

Juice fast: A juice-only diet.

Parcourse: A trail, usually outdoors, punctuated periodically by exercise stations, where you may find simple equipment and a sign instructing you how to use it.

Pilates training: A conditioning system that incorporates a set of mat exercises and muscle-strengthening resistance equipment.

Pritikin diet: Once considered austere but now more frequently followed, the Pritikin diet, developed by the late Nathan Pritikin, consists of 10%–15% protein, 80% complex carbohydrates, and 5%–10% fat. It has been shown to contribute to lower cholesterol and blood pressure.

Reflexology: Massage of the pressure points on the feet, hands, and ears; intended to relax the parts of the body.

Rolfing: A bodywork system developed by Ida Rolf that improves balance and flexibility through manipulation of rigid muscles, bones, and joints. It is intended to improve energy flow and relieve stress (often related to emotional trauma).

Salt glow: A cleansing treatment, also known as a salt scrub, using coarse salt to remove dead skin, similar to the loofah body scrub.

Shiatsu: A massage technique developed by Tokujiro Namikoshi that uses finger (*shi*) pressure (*atsu*) to stimulate the body's inner powers of balance and healing.

Sprung floor: A safe, impact-absorbing surface for aerobic and dance studios.

Swedish massage: A type of body work involving stroking, kneading, friction, vibration, and tapping that aims to relax muscles gently.

Swiss shower: A shower with several strong water jets aimed at thighs, calves, and back and leg muscles.

Thalassotherapy: A treatment first used by the ancient Greeks performed with seaweed-based products; you are wrapped, scrubbed, and soaked in marine algae. The objective is to stimulate circulation and relax your muscles.

Water aerobics: Aerobics workouts in a swimming pool, also known as aquacise, aquaerobics, aquafit, aquatics, and swimnastics, which include stretching, strength, and stamina exercises that combine water resistance and body movements.

CHOOSING THE RIGHT SPA

The spas in the reviews that follow are some of the best of their type. To choose the one where you will be comfortable and will most effectively profit from the experience, it helps to ask a lot of questions.

What is the daily schedule? You need to find out how structured the program is— will you be herded from one area to another according to the schedule of a group or a schedule set for you when you arrive, or will you have some choice from one day to the next? Some programs are tightly monitored. If you want something less regimented, choose a spa that provides several options in its daily schedule or allows for a personalized program.

How much time do participants spend exercising? If you are used to intense workouts, look for a spa with a full range of classes, one-on-one training, and personal consultation. If you want to kick back and relax, go elsewhere.

Is the spa program adaptable to my fitness level? The age group at spas ranges anywhere from mid-twenties to mid-sixties, but many spas are more suitable than others for any given segment of that range. Make sure that the program's activities can be adapted to your fitness level. If you have any questions about whether you are physically up to the program, talk to your doctor.

Are all guests spa guests? You will get the most personal attention at a destination spa where all guests participate in spa programs. Smaller spas provide more camaraderie among guests and staff.

What's the cost and what's included? Spa packages may include lodging, meals, lectures and workshops, personal services, the use of exercise and recreational facilities, taxes, gratuities, and service charges that cover charges for waiters, housemaids, and the like, and for personal services included in the packages. In order to properly compare the cost of visiting various spas, you need to find out just what a package includes.

Be especially careful to find out about fees for personal services such as massages and facials. Because these can really add up, decide which you want to take advantage of and how often, and then ask which are included in your program package. Bear in mind that a massage billed as free may turn out to be a half-hour rubdown rather than a full-hour treatment.

Ask hard questions about recreational facilities you plan to use, as well. For instance, if you plan to play a lot of golf in your free time, make sure that the greens fees are included—and at the tee times you prefer, not just at off-hours.

Taxes and gratuities represent a particularly hefty expense. Local and state taxes plus service charges for massages and other personal services can add 25% or more to the cost of your program. Ask how gratuities are handled for housekeepers and dining room staff as well as physical therapists.

Usually transportation to the resort is not part of the package, although transfers from the nearest airport sometimes are. If they're not included and you don't plan to arrive by car, be sure to check on the cost as you price out your trip.

Some spas provide exercise outfits or bathrobes; at others, you must bring your own.

Note that unless otherwise noted, prices in this chapter include lodging, meals, lectures and workshops, the use of exercise and recreational facilities, service charges, gratuities, and taxes, and are per person based on double occupancy. They are given as guidelines only for comparative purposes and change frequently.

Will laundry service be available? Daily laundry service is available at some spas at varying extra cost. Others have laundry facilities so that you can do your own washing. Know what you're getting into.

What are the accommodations like? Spas range from Spartan to luxurious. Find out about both the public spaces and the guest rooms. What is the general level of comfort? How are they furnished? If you must have a TV or telephone, make certain that it's available. If you care about having a private bath, make sure that the program price isn't based on your sharing the facilities down the hall. What arrangements will be made if you come to the spa with a non-participating friend or spouse? What are the typical arrangements for solo travelers: Are singles available, or are they assigned a roommate?

At some establishments, spa facilities and accommodations are under the same roof— a useful setup when the weather is bad. If you want more privacy, find out if lodging alternatives are available that are separated by a long walk from the main facilities.

What is the food like? Especially at spas where weight loss is a goal, you want to hear that the food is tasty and appealingly presented despite its being low in everything that has put on the pounds you're visiting the spa to shed.

If it matters to you or your traveling companion, find out whether alcohol is available. It's usually not, although you can sometimes get wine. If you are not familiar with the spa's food program, ask for more information or sample menus.

Does health insurance cover any part of the program cost? At some spas, medical tests and physiotherapy ordered by your doctor may be reimbursable under your health care plan.

What non-spa activities are available? At some, the extracurricular options include lectures and films on fitness and health matters; after dinner, most participants turn in early, totally exhausted by the physical activities earlier in the day. Other establishments are full-blown resorts, and the spa activities are only the alternatives to tennis, golf, hiking, swimming, beachcombing, and the like; after dark, there may be movies, dancing, and so on. After you have a sense of what the spa program involves, consider how you might like to spend your free time, and then find a spa that can accommodate you. A spa that is part of a larger resort, or one in a lively resort town where there are lots of other things to do, is probably a better choice if you plan to visit with a nonparticipating companion.

How far in advance do I need to book? It's necessary to reserve between 2 weeks and 6 months ahead. Often, however, you can give a call and have a room within the week.

How long has the spa been in business? A long, positive history tells you that the spa is doing something right.

Do you have references from past guests? To clarify your ideas about what it's like to stay at a given spa, there's no substitute for a talk with someone who has slept in the beds, eaten the meals, and gone through the program.

FAVORITE SPAS

THE NORTHEAST

MAINE **Northern Pines Health Resort.** During a bout with thyroid cancer Marlee Turner discovered the importance of holistic health practices. In 1980, to share with others the lessons she learned about nourishing the mind, body, and spirit, she opened this informal spot on a wooded, 68-acre lakefront property. Maine's only health spa, this is a safe place to try a spa for the first time, and many visitors return.

Ms. Turner bases her program on the teachings of Paavo Airola, who stressed a regimen of meditation and yoga and a diet of fresh fruits, vegetables, and whole grains. You can pick and choose from the full daily schedule; mornings are devoted to meditation, stretching exercises, guided walks through the woods, breakfast, and health-oriented and workout classes, leading up to noontime reflection and discussion. After lunch you may take a yoga class or go for another hike on the trails on the property. Daily classes cover topics such as nutrition, stress

management, cooking, vitamins, herbs, and meditation. Weekends feature two- or three-day workshops on a variety of subjects, among them osteopathy, art, music, and astronomy. In your free time you can go canoeing, swimming, or jogging, or, for an additional fee, sign up for special services including Swedish massage, reflexology, aromatherapy, beauty treatments, and herbal wraps. Facilities include a sauna, a hot tub, an exercise room, and a flotation tank for a sensory deprivation and relaxation session.

Although the resort has space for up to 30 weekly guests, there are usually no more than 15 visitors per week, which means lots of personal attention from the energetic staff. Well-worn lakeside log cabins dating from the 1920s can provide total seclusion for couples. Lodge rooms and cabins with two bedrooms, added in the 1980s, are on a hillside amid towering pines, spruces, and hemlocks. The cook is on hand to explain the ingredients of the vegetarian communal meals, served buffet style; you can also opt for a supervised juice fast. Most guests are highly educated, well-traveled women, a good percentage of them involved in healing and helping professions. *Northern Pines Health Resort, 559 Rte. 85, R.R. 1, Box 279, Raymond, ME 04071, tel. 207/655–7624, fax 207/655–3321. Year-round: 6 days, $504–$1,374. Price does not include 7% lodging tax or gratuities.*

MASSACHUSETTS **Canyon Ranch in the Berkshires.** The Health and Healing Department at this elegant property on 120 acres of woodland in the Massachusetts mountains teaches you how to prevent and soften the effects of aging via programs and consultations on nutrition, exercise physiology, movement therapy, behavior, and medicine. Other departments at the ranch offer some 40 classes in everything from breathing, meditation, and yoga to hiking, biking, canoeing, snowshoeing, and cross-country skiing. There are also programs that help you deal with overeating, stop smoking, or learn to control stress.

The ranch's architectural centerpiece is the late 19th-century Bellefontaine Mansion, which now houses the dining room, the library, and the health and healing and arts and crafts centers. Inside a separate ultramodern 100,000-square-foot spa and fitness center there are exercise and weight-training rooms; a 75-foot swimming pool; a jogging track; tennis, racquetball, and squash courts; and separate spas for men and women with saunas, steam rooms, Jacuzzis, and inhalation rooms. Lodging is in a modern two-story inn with 120 guest rooms and fancier suites, furnished in a functional New England style. Glass-enclosed walkways connect the mansion, fitness center, and inn; on the grounds, there are also outdoor tennis courts, an outdoor swimming pool, and walking trails. Meals are low-calorie, consisting of New England specialties cooked with a minimum of salt and fat. *Canyon Ranch in the Berkshires, 165 Kemble St. (Rte. 7A), Lenox, MA 01240, tel. 413/637–4100 or 800/742–9000, fax 413/637–0057. Year-round: 7 days, $2,040–$2,980 single, $1,750–$2,980 double. Price includes a selection of personal services but not 9.7% tax or 18% service charge.*

NEW YORK **Living Springs Lifestyle Center.** A revitalized life and control of health problems are the goals at this homelike, budget-priced retreat within easy reach of New York City. Courses, which are under medical supervision, focus on disease prevention, nutrition, weight management, stress control, and quitting smoking. After a consultation with the staff doctor, you can schedule spa treatments, enjoy the saunas, and, in warm weather, swim in the spring-fed lake. You learn how to prepare nutritious, low-fat meals, too. A medical package that involves bloodwork ($65–$115) and a 2½-hour doctor visit ($150) are not included in the price.

The retreat's own kitchen serves vegetarian buffets. The eight guest rooms with private bath are in a modern, two-level lodge. Commuter trains from Manhattan's Grand Central Terminal stop at Peekskill, where Living Springs transportation can pick you up. *Living Springs Lifestyle Center, 136 Bryant Pond Rd., Putnam Valley, NY 10579, tel. 914/526–2800 or 800/729–9355, fax 914/528–9171. Year-round: 7 days, $895 single, $695 double.*

NEW YORK **Mountain Valley Health Resort.** The desire to lose weight and learn to keep it off are the common objectives of guests at this 15-acre Catskills health resort, opened in 1992. When you arrive, you provide a brief medical history, which spa director Natalie Skolnik then uses to determine your diet and exercise program. At extra cost you can obtain a computerized analysis of your body-fat ratio. No subsequent medical supervision or consultation is available.

A supportive camaraderie prevails among guests. The days are structured but nothing is mandatory. You may want to start your day with a walk after breakfast, then go on to morning classes in toning and firming, step aerobics, or swimnastics in the indoor or outdoor pool. Each afternoon there is free time to relax in the sauna, swim, or do yoga. In addition, there are lectures—discussions on how to enjoy eating portion-controlled meals, deal with stress, and incorporate exercise into your daily life. Other services, available at extra charge, include massage, reflexology, shiatsu, manicures, pedicures, and body wraps. There are two tennis courts and hiking and cross-country ski trails; downhill skiing is nearby at Hunter Mountain.

In the attractive dining room, you can choose a 650-, 900-, or 1,200-calorie menu, or opt for a juice fast or vegetarian dishes. The chalet-style lodge comfortably houses 50 to 60 guests. Some accommodations are skylit loft rooms that accommodate four people. The resort's several porches and balconies are popular gathering spots after dinner. *Mountain Valley Health Resort, Box 395, Hunter, NY 12442, tel. 518/263–4919 or 800/232–2772, fax 518/263–4994. Year-round: 7 days, $595–$1,150. Price does not include 8% tax or 15% gratuity.*

NEW YORK **New Age Health Spa.** Creative visualization—whereby the mind leads the body naturally toward a positive outcome—

is a key tool at this establishment, which was opened in 1975 as the New Age Health Farm and became the New Age Health Spa in 1986. At that time, Werner Mendel and Stephanie Paradise took over the property and expanded its focus to include fitness, holistic health, personal growth, and spa services. Located on 160 acres in the southern Catskills, it's the closest spa of its type to New York City.

You're free to set your own pace as you pick and choose from among classes in meditation, personal awareness, nutrition, yoga, t'ai chi, weight training, stretching, and aerobics (in the pool and in the classroom); you can fill your time with supervised morning hikes along country roads and swims in indoor or spring-fed outdoor pools, and by watching videos or reading books from the library of health and wellness titles. The Challenge by Choice ropes course involves climbing a 50-foot tower; you learn the power of teamwork and the pleasure of attaining your goals. Weekend hikes into the high Catskills give you panoramic views of the Hudson River valley. Spa services range from reflexology, aromatherapy, loofah scrubs, mud treatments, manicures and pedicures, facials, and hair treatments to Swedish, shiatsu, and sports massage, along with colonics and Ayurvedic botanical detoxification, an ancient Indian treatment using oils, massage, and herbs to purify the body. Personal consultations in cooking, herbology, hypnotherapy, tarot, and astrology are also available (group sessions free, private sessions at $50 an hour).

Because the owners are usually on hand in the big farmhouse that serves as both social center and dining room, the atmosphere is homey. Graduates of the Culinary Institute of America prepare the meals along guidelines set by the American Heart Association (high carbohydrates, no sugar, and low protein, fats, and salt); many dishes are spiced with herbs grown in the greenhouse behind the kitchen. You might also opt for a supervised juice fast, a 700- to 800-calorie vegetarian diet, or a rotation diet with vegetarian, fish, and poultry meals.

There are five separate guest houses. Rooms have a country look and are small but comfortable, with private baths. The two suites have Jacuzzis. No more than 65 guests are on hand during any given week, most of them educated business people and professionals from New York City and suburban Long Island and New Jersey; some return a few times a year. Transportation to and from Manhattan is available on Sunday and Friday by reservation. *New Age Health Spa, Rte. 55, Neversink, NY 12765, tel 914/985–7601 or 800/682–4348, fax 914/985–2467. Year-round: 5 days, $965–$1,423 single, $665–$1,047 double. Price includes 2 personal services.*

VERMONT **Green Mountain at Fox Run.** Opened in 1973 by MIT-trained nutritional biochemist, Dr. Alan H. Wayler, this establishment on 20 acres in central Vermont is the country's oldest program devoted to helping women (and only women) develop a diet and exercise plan that they can integrate into their lives at home. Weeklong and five-day retreats teach participants how to control weight and emotions; instead of deprivation, moderation becomes the key. Overcoming feelings of failure is the first step in the process, according to Wayler, because so many come here after losing weight and regaining it. The staff, which includes a registered dietician, an exercise physiologist, and a behavioral therapist, helps you develop your own program. Follow-up support, provided through newsletters and a hot line, is very much part of the program. Massage, manicures, and pedicures are available at an extra charge.

The main lodge, where classes are held, has 26 duplex rooms that accommodate two to four persons and have modern baths; some singles are available. Menus allow for 1,200 or 1,400 calories per day; the food here is low in fat, cholesterol, and sodium and higher in complex carbohydrates. The lodge has exercise equipment such as treadmills, stationary bikes, a NordicTrack, a rowing machine, and free weights. Nearby, there's hiking, skiing, and biking, as well as theater, discount shopping, and historical sites.

Green Mountain at Fox Run, Box 164, Ludlow, VT 05149, tel. 802/228–8885 or 800/448–8106, fax 802/228–8887. Year-round: 5–21 days, $1,100–$5,825.

VERMONT New Life Fitness Vacations. Founded in 1978 by nutrition guru James LeSage, New Life was one of the country's first fitness-oriented vacation programs. Think of it as a luxurious camp for grown-ups; the goal during its six- and seven-day sessions, conducted at the elegant Inn of the Six Mountains, is to change your lifestyle for the better by helping you shed pounds, increase your stamina, and learn new relaxation, nutrition, and exercise skills. Assisted by a youthful and outgoing staff, LeSage takes you through active days that start out with a walk before breakfast and include stretching, conditioning, and aerobics classes; aquacise sessions; yoga; and hikes of 5 miles or more through the Vermont countryside. After dark, there are presentations on nutrition, healthy cooking, self-massage, body alignment, and relaxation as well as discussion about how to integrate what you've learned into your daily life. There are never more than 25 guests on hand. Your program is individually tailored to your goals.

The attractively presented meals are high in fiber, low in fat, and full of complex carbohydrates; they provide between 1,000 and 1,200 calories a day. The spacious, tastefully appointed rooms have private baths, televisions, and phones; some have balconies. On the property there are tennis courts, exercise equipment, a whirlpool, sauna and steam rooms, and indoor and heated outdoor pools; nearby is golf, horseback riding, mountain biking, canoeing, and antiquing. *New Life Fitness Vacations, Box 395, Killington, VT 05751, tel. 802/422–4302 or 800/228–4676, fax 802/422–4321. May–Oct.: 6 days, $1,099–$1,125 single, $980–$999 double. Price includes 2 hour-long massages but not 7% Vermont sales tax or 15% service charge.*

VERMONT Topnotch at Stowe. This classic New England mountain resort caters to sports enthusiasts and weary urbanites seeking a sophisticated escape close to nature. Its full-service spa, opened in 1989, offers a state-of-the-art exercise program as well as seminars covering such topics as bodywork, skin care and nutrition, and relaxation. There is also an extensive selection of face and body treatments—everything from seaweed wraps to salt scrubs, aromatherapy, and hydrotherapy in a special French tub lined with pulsating jets. Sport-specific classes and conditioning consultations get you in shape for tennis and skiing.

You have a choice of one-on-one training or scheduled aerobics classes every hour between 9 and 4. You can also get a personal fitness assessment, during which your body fat is measured, your blood cholesterol determined, and your flexibility, endurance, and strength tested. You are assigned to one of five levels, and your program begins. Instructors are noted for their sense of humor as well as their teaching skills. You can choose one free treatment or professional service (such as a fitness assessment) per day; for others you pay extra.

In the dining room, you can choose between spa cuisine and international fare. Meals are calorie-controlled, based on 1,000 to 1,300 calories a day for women, and 1,300 to 1,700 calories a day for men. Rooms, located in the main lodge, are furnished with antiques and a library stocked with good bedtime reading. Topnotch is a good bet if your traveling companion is not interested in spa activities. There are special rates for nonparticipating companions, for instance, and plenty of other diversions. Topnotch is known for its tennis program and has 14 courts, and it's not far from Mt. Mansfield, one of New England's best ski areas. Also on the grounds are a 60-foot heated indoor swimming pool, a heated outdoor pool with mountain views, and 30 miles of groomed cross-country trails that link up with the Catamount Trail along the ridge of the Green Mountains. *Topnotch at Stowe, Box 1458,*

Stowe, VT 05672, tel. 802/253–8585 or 800/451–8686, fax 802/253–9263. Year-round: 5–7 days, $1,210–$2,275 single, $990–$1,645 double. Price includes 1 personal or professional service daily but not 7% tax or 17% service charge.

THE MID-ATLANTIC

PENNSYLVANIA **Deerfield Manor Spa.** At this 12-acre property in the Pocono Mountains, owner-director Frieda Eisenkraft provides moderate exercise, a healthy diet, and lots of country charm. Most of the 33 guests are high-powered working women, many of whom return every year to renew friendships with each other and staff members and maintain their health. Some come for luxury treatments, and others don't miss an aerobics class; some stick to a strict menu plan while others request extra portions and snack freely.

The week's program begins on Sunday, with dinner followed by a meeting with Frieda, who started the spa in 1981. She tells you about the facilities, the food, staff members, and the fitness program, which includes aerobics, step aerobics, body toning, circuit training, stretching, yoga, water aerobics, and guided walks. After breakfast on Monday is an optional exercise orientation and weigh-in. The exercise class schedule changes daily. A few days into the week, guests staying a week can sign up for a free exercise consultation to develop a program to bring home. Every evening after dinner there is a different activity, whether it's a demonstration of healthful cooking by the chef or a handwriting analysis by a local graphologist. The atmosphere is laid back—you're allowed to come and go as you please, and all activities are optional. Caloric intake is a main subject for conversation.

One of the spa's buildings is a lovely white clapboard farmhouse dating from the 1930s; guest rooms there are full of rattan furniture and antiques. In an annex structure, rooms are newer, superclean, and airy, with Laura Ashley bedspreads and cathedral ceilings. All rooms have cable TV and private bath. Three lounges, where you can watch movies, read, socialize, and listen to music, are in the main house, as is the dining room, which serves three meals and an afternoon snack each day. You select your own menu a day in advance as part of a behavior modification program—the idea is that if you plan what you're going to eat, you'll eat less. The non-fat, low-salt entrées and side dishes consist of fresh fruit and vegetables, eggs, cottage cheese, yogurt, bran cereals, wheat bread, fish, and chicken; you consume between 800 and 1,100 calories a day. Supervised juice fasting is also available.

Fitness classes take place in a converted barn; water aerobics are in the heated outdoor pool. The main building has a sauna, manicure room, and massage rooms where, for a fee, you can experience Swedish massage, reflexology, shiatsu, or Reiki, a therapy session during which the practitioner's hands are placed for three to five minutes on each of twelve different areas of your body. Other treatments, such as facials, body buffs, and seaweed wraps, also cost extra. Two tennis courts on an adjacent property are open for matches. Or you might go hiking in the Delaware Water Gap National Recreation Area or Worthington State Park, just a short drive away. An outlet shopping center is also nearby. *Deerfield Manor Spa, 650 Resica Falls Rd., East Stroudsburg, PA 18301, tel. 717/223–0160 or 800/852–4494, fax 717/223–8270. Apr.–mid-Nov.: 6 days, $899–$999 single, $699–$799 double. Price does not include 6% tax or 15% service charge.*

VIRGINIA **Hartland Wellness Center.** This establishment, on a 760-acre estate in piedmont Virginia provides health education and exercise in a Christian environment; its 10- and 18-day programs include cooking lessons, private and group counseling, and exercise. Faculty and students of the health professions at Hartland College, with which the center is associated, help you get in shape. The dedicated doctors and educators on the staff, all Seventh-Day Adventists, focus on disease prevention; they believe that good living habits can prevent many simple ailments. Using a computer, they do a nutritional analysis and recommend a diet that takes into account your physical condition as well as your weight-loss goals. The center was founded in 1983 and now accommodates up to 23 guests at a time, many of them older and suffering from arthritis, diabetes, obesity, or cancer.

After a full-day of testing, the staff designs a schedule and recommends an exercise program. Activities begin with breakfast at 6:45 on weekdays. At the treatment center, housed in a two-story mansion adjoining the college campus, you might have hydrotherapy, which stimulates circulation by using contrasting hot and cold showers. Three low-fat vegetarian meals are provided daily. Guests stay in rooms furnished with antiques. On weekends, the center has a picnic and schedules trips to area historic sites at no extra charge. *Hartland Wellness Center, Box 1, Rapidan, VA 22733, tel. 703/672–3100 or 800/763–9355, fax 703/672–3107. Year-round: 10–18 days, $1,500–$2,700.*

VIRGINIA Integral Health Center. Staying at this institution in a large, rambling house overlooking a scenic bend in the James River near Charlottesville is like joining a small group of friends at a country retreat. Inspiration comes from Sri Swami Satchidanada, founder of the Yogaville community just down the road, and the program, under the direction of Sandra McLanahan, M.D., and Michael Sullivan, M.D., weds yogic principles with modern medicine's understanding of health and well-being. You meditate, you practice breathing, and you learn visualization, a method of directing energy in a conscious manner. Staff members, trained in holistic health sciences, consult with you and lead workshops on coping with heart disease, stress, and other illnesses.

The subject matter under consideration varies from one weeklong session to the next; the focus may be on learning to live with cancer or on preventing heart disease by using yoga coupled with Dr. Dean Ornish's diet-exercise-meditation plan. There may be between 10 and 20 participants on hand.

Massage, medical consultations, and chiropractic sessions are available at an additional charge. In your free time, you can hike to Yogaville's impressive meditation center to participate in Integral Yoga sessions.

Accommodations at the Integral Health Center are homey, with shared bathrooms in some cases, a sauna, and an outdoor Jacuzzi. The meals are simple, vegetarian, and served family style; menus typically feature tofu dishes, steamed vegetables with rice or pasta, green salad, fruit, and homemade soups and breads. *Integral Health Center, Box 1681, Buckingham, VA 23921, tel. 804/969–3121, 804/969–1451, or 800/858–9642, fax 804/969–1303. Year-round: 8 days, $1,995 single, $2,995 per couple.*

WEST VIRGINIA Coolfont Resort and Spectrum Spa. Nestled in a valley in the Appalachian Mountains near historic Berkeley Springs, this informal, camplike 1,300-acre resort and conference center has been identified with health and environmental programs since 1973. Creating the Spectrum Spa here in 1992, in two barnlike structures, was a labor of love for Coolfont Resort owners Martha and Sam Ashelman, who often join morning hikes and yoga classes or dine with program participants in the main lodge. In addition to a fitness center with an indoor springwater swimming pool, the spa has 16 private rooms for bodywork, a full-service beauty salon, a demonstration kitchen, and an aerobics studio with a sprung floor, specially designed to cushion your bouncing and help prevent injuries.

Coolfont's spa retreats, limited to 20 participants, introduce you to the latest trends in nutrition, weight management, stress control, and quitting smoking; also on the program are classes in aerobics, yoga, and body-strengthening exercises. You can book spa services as a package in conjunction with a spa retreat or à la carte; these services include massage, herbal wraps, loofah body scrubs, facials, and hair, nail, and skin care. There is a weight room with basic exercise equipment but no instruction. The pre-breakfast walk is open to all resort guests.

You can stay in the modern three-story Woodland Lodge, whose 22 rooms have fireplaces and whirlpool baths; in 20 mountain chalets with two bedrooms and double whirlpools; in the Manor House, which is listed on the National Register of Historic Buildings; or in log cabins. Tent and trailer sites are also available. There are two dining rooms; one offers bountiful buffets with a different ethnic or other culinary theme each night and no particular nutritional profile, while the other offers a fixed menu of low-fat, high-fiber meals that run 1,200 to 1,400 calories a day.

A nonprofit foundation sponsors cultural and educational evenings at the resort, including chamber music and National Gallery of Art films. In free time, you can play tennis on the resort's eight outdoor courts or, nearby, soak in the mineral water baths at Berkeley Springs State Park or go antiquing. *Coolfont Resort and Spectrum Spa, Rte. 1, Box 710, Berkeley Springs, WV 25411, tel. 304/258–4500 or 800/888–8768, fax 304/258–5499. Year-round: 6 days, $1,100–$1,395 single, $990–$1,195 double. Price does not include 6% room tax, $3.65 per night service charge, or gratuities.*

THE SOUTH

FLORIDA **Doral Golf Resort and Spa.** With its red-tile roof, rotunda-topped villa, and statuary-punctuated formal gardens, this posh spa overlooking five manicured golf courses is like a vision of Tuscany in Florida. Completely self-contained with 48 suites and 2 excellent restaurants, the spa took its inspiration from the ancient baths at Terme di Saturnia, near Rome, and mixes European and American ideas about promoting health. Programs are innovative,

built around biofeedback (for stress management) and boxing-style aerobics (for fitness); upon arrival, you can choose to concentrate on health and fitness or weight management, or just relax and get beautified. Treatments for muscular and skin problems are a specialty; fango warm mud packs from Italy's Saturnia volcanic springs are part of the massage therapy. Above the upper levels of the villa's central atrium are the sun deck, a lounge, 26 private massage rooms offering a selection of treatments, the coed beauty salon and skin-care treatment rooms, the running track, exercise class rooms, and the men's and women's locker rooms, themselves equipped with whirlpool, saunas, and steam rooms. The gymnasium and weight room are below the lobby level.

Your daily regimen is up to you. There are classes in jazz dance, low-impact aerobics, and other topics; trays of fruit and raw vegetables are set outside the studios between sessions. Staff specialists plan serious regimens only after comparing your health profile with a computerized model based on nationwide health statistics, and you can make appointments for personal services. After dark, there are lectures and presentations on various topics, including one on vegetarian cuisine by Alix Landman, the Doral's head nutritionist.

Most of the aging baby boomers who work out here relish the Italian-accented menu created by executive chef Ron Hook. He often shows up in the spa's demonstration kitchen, perhaps preparing his version of risotto, which is made with evaporated milk and porcini mushrooms and has about half the calories of the conventional version. In the dining room, favorite dishes include the thin-crust vegetarian pizza and baked zucchini stuffed with tomatoes and rice. You can specify the portion size you prefer.

When you have free time, you can borrow a feature film from the concierge to watch on the VCR in your suite, which also contains a bar stocked with fruit and Italian mineral water. Marble-walled bathrooms with his and hers toilets, robes, twin baths, and dressing areas are standard. For the ultimate fantasy, book one of the five suites, decorated to evoke regions of Italy. There are 16 tennis courts nearby. *Doral Saturnia International Spa Resort, 8755 N.W. 36th St., Miami, FL 33178, tel 305/593-6030 or 800/331-7768, fax 305/591-9268. Year-round: 8 days, $2,815-$5,805 single, $2,310-$3,850 double. Price does not include 18% tax or 18.5% service charge.*

FLORIDA **Hippocrates Health Institute.** The three-week Health Encounter at the Hippocrates Health Institute in West Palm Beach aims to make you knowledgeable about food and its relationship to health. Program director Brian R. Clements began teaching vegetarianism in Boston more than 30 years ago and moved his institute to this estate in 1985.

The program is highly structured. A typical day begins at 8 with light exercise, breakfast, a blood-pressure check, and a discussion of health and diet. Such nutritional education as well as regular exercise, massage, reflexology, detoxification, and relaxation are all part of the program, along with classes that teach you life-enhancing skills such as deep relaxation techniques. You also learn how to cook with unprocessed organic vegetables, make sprouts, and grow greens. Once a week you have a session with the massage therapist. Certain days are designated as juice fasts. Throughout the program, a psychologist and physician work with health director Anna Maria Gahns to advise you on personal problems and monitor your progress. The spa has various classrooms and therapy rooms including four swimming pools, a cold plunge pool, a whirlpool, and a sauna.

The program's 30 to 40 participants lodge in two guest cottages and garden apartments, and in the main building, a Spanish-style hacienda, with three luxury suites. Vegan fare is served buffet style at meals, with lots of nuts, seeds, sprouts, herbs, algae, and sea plants. Guests have access to an outdoor swimming pool, and excursions, for which there is no extra charge, are taken to the beach, local museums, and shopping malls. *Hippocrates Health Institute, 1443 Palmdale Ct., West Palm Beach, FL 33411, tel. 407/471-8876 or 800/842-2125, fax 407/471-9464. Year-round: 21 days, $5,900-$7,800 single, $2,600-$4,500 double.*

FLORIDA **Pritikin Longevity Center.** You can get a massage, a facial, or a manicure at this center on Miami Beach in one of those ubiquitous pink palaces of pleasure. But that's peripheral in this place, a destination where healthy people learn how to safeguard their health and those suffering from heart disease, insulin-dependent diabetes, obesity, and uncontrolled high blood pressure learn how to change the quality of their lives. Exercise, diet, stress-management training, and health counseling are the core curriculum; the program is tightly monitored and leaves little time free for more than an ocean swim or walk on the beach promenade. During the two weeks that most participants spend here, their schedule requires checkups by the medical staff, attendance at lectures, and workouts on a battery of Trotter treadmills, StairMasters, and stationary bikes. Daily sessions of aquatics and aerobics alternate with yoga and other activities. But the program's backbone is the Pritikin diet, which is 10% to 15% protein, 80% complex carbohydrates, and 5% to 10% fat; you learn about the diet both in cooking classes and at meals, which are mostly vegetarian, with regular appearances by fresh fish, pasta, and rice. Being part of the supportive group at the center helps newcomers, who range in age from 18 to 85. The staff is very accessible.

The 100 bedrooms are modestly furnished; some have an ocean view, while others face Collins Avenue. Pritikin alumni have a toll-free hot line, are welcome to return for monthly meetings, and can join support groups around the country. *Pritikin Longevity Center, 5875 Collins Ave., Miami Beach, FL 33140, tel. 305/866-2237 or 800/327-4914, fax 305/866-1872. Year-round: 13 days, $5,973 single, $2,587 double.*

FLORIDA **PGA National Resort & Spa.** Here, you can sign up for thalassotherapy,

Swedish massages, facials, hydrotherapy, reflexology, and salt-glow treatments; you can also soak in pools that contain mineral salts from the Dead Sea and the French Pyrenees. But what makes this resort different from all other spas is that it's all about sports conditioning: Here you learn how to exercise more safely and more effectively and what to do when you overextend yourself on the playing field—lessons crucial to amateur athletes. Facilities for tennis and golf players are equally strong: The resort's 28,500-square-foot health and racquet club has 5 indoor courts and 19 Har-Tru outdoor tennis courts (12 lighted for night play), and there are five golf courses. The 26-acre lake has a private beach, kayaking, paddle boating, and canoeing.

Resident nutritionist Cheryl Hartsough works with a team of spa chefs to ensure heart-healthy options in the resort's five restaurants—among them the Italian restaurant, Arezzo, and the poolside Citrus Tree, where Florida seafood is the specialty. The resort's 336 rooms are spacious; those in the main hotel have a private terrace or balcony, king-size beds and sofas, dressing rooms, remote control TV, and built-in wet bars. The 80 two-bedroom, two-bath suites are even roomier. *PGA National Resort & Spa, 400 Ave. of the Champions, Palm Beach Gardens, FL 33418, tel. 407/627–2000 or 800/633–9150, fax 407/622–0261. Year-round: 5 days, $2,387 single, $1,929 double.*

FLORIDA **Royal Atlantic Health Spa.** This newcomer, opened in 1993 and supervised by holistic medicine specialist Michael Klaper, M.D., is just the place to enjoy yourself while you learn about a healthy lifestyle and lose weight: The location, directly on the beach, is pleasant, and there's an outdoor swimming pool as well as exercise classes and lectures and workshops on stress management and nutrition.

Each day begins with a vigorous walk along the beach, followed by low-impact, step, and water aerobics. There's also an outdoor heated pool and a fitness center, equipped with treadmills, stationary bikes, step

machines, a Universal weight-training system, and free weights. To improve body awareness and flexibility, you can join a yoga or meditation session or attend classes in vegetarian cooking. In addition, a number of treatments are available, among them massages, salt scrubs, and aromatherapy. You can schedule medical and dental consultations at no extra charge.

Meals, served in the garden-level dining room, are vegetarian. Breakfast consists of fruits and juices, lunch is an extensive salad bar or baked potatoes, and dinner, served by candlelight, may include vegetarian lasagna or peppers stuffed with wild rice. No coffee or dairy products are available. Juice and water diets can be arranged.

The center can accommodate 100 guests in its three-story main building. Although rooms are tiny and motel-like, each has a private bath, TV, phone, and terrace or balcony. *Royal Atlantic Health Spa, 1460 S. Ocean Blvd., Pompano Beach, FL 33062, tel. 305/941–6688 or 800/583–3500, fax 305/943–1219. Year-round: 7 days, $1,195–$1,545 single, $995–$1,345 double. Price does not include 9% tax or 5% service charge.*

GEORGIA **The Sea Island Spa at the Cloister.** It was in 1989 that this spa opened at the venerable Cloister, the grande dame of southern seashore resorts, directly on the pristine Atlantic beach of a private 5-mile barrier island. Sports add a special dimension to this well-mannered seaside escape; the resort has 54 holes of golf, a golf center, 18 tennis courts, water sports, three skeet ranges, bike rentals, fishing charters, and a program of nature hikes and boating expeditions into the tidal creeks and marshes around the island, where bird life is abundant.

The spa tailors programs to each guest's needs and goals. A program created for golf and tennis players stresses flexibility, strength, and pre-game warm-up rituals. You can work out (with an ocean view) in the spa weight-training room and aerobics studio. A wide variety of treatments is available, among them thalassotherapy; all are performed away from the beach crowd in private rooms, each of which is used for just one guest. Treatments can be booked à la carte or as one-, two-, three-, or five-day packages. Each January the spa hosts a five-day program for women that includes workshops on interior design and fashion, information about ob-gyn and skin care, and a full complement of fitness classes. Morning beach walks and stretch classes are open to all resort guests at no charge. There are also aquacise classes in the big outdoor swimming pool.

Lodging is in handsomely decorated rooms in spacious modern lodges overlooking the beach and the Intracoastal Waterway; private cottages are also available. Meals follow the full American plan, and there's a formal dinner and dancing every night but Sunday. Some spa cuisine is available. You can enjoy fresh seafood at the beachside restaurant. *The Cloister, Sea Island, GA 31561, tel. 912/638–3611 or 800/732–4752, fax 912/638–5159. Mid-Mar.–Nov.: 5-day package, $1,965 single, $1,525 double. Price does not include 5% tax or 15% gratuity.*

NORTH CAROLINA **Duke University Diet and Fitness Center.** Since 1969, the center has provided participants with a plan for weight loss they can take home with them. Involving a team of doctors, clinical psychologists, dieticians, exercise physiologists, and massage therapists, the highly regimented course combines exercise classes, cooking demonstrations, a grocery store tour, and (at additional cost) individual psychotherapy as well as lectures and workshops about nutrition, fitness, behavior, and medical management. Participants include men and women from all walks of life; some want to lose 20 pounds while others are seriously obese or are trying to stop smoking. Many return for refresher courses. There are usually between 90 and 120 in residence.

A typical day begins with breakfast at 7:45, followed by an aerobics class in the gym or indoor pool or a walk on the treadmill or around the scenic campus. Next you might attend a stress-management lecture, and after lunch a demonstration of health-wise cooking methods. Then you might take a t'ai chi class and a small group workshop. After dinner, you can play volleyball, go to a movie, or nurse a cup of coffee and chat with other participants.

Meals, served in the dining room, are all portion-controlled and low in calories, sodium, fat, and cholesterol. Housing is up to you; the center can make recommendations. *Duke University Diet and Fitness Center, 804 W. Trinity Ave., Durham, NC 27701, tel. 919/684–6331 or 800/362–8446, fax 919/682–8869. Year-round: 14 days, $3,895; 28 days, $4,795.*

NORTH CAROLINA **Structure House.** This center founded in 1977 is one of the nation's premier residential weight-loss retreats. It attracts people with disabilities, those who are aging, and people who have 20 to 200 pounds to lose. The goal is to teach you how to control your weight over the long term. The program involves mental and physical conditioning as well as a diet. Among the programs are group sessions with a stress therapist, private counseling, classes in how to choose wisely from a restaurant menu, and instruction on the causes of obesity. Stays of two to four weeks are recommended; alumni can return for a week or more of reinforcement.

The Life Extension Center, which is on the grounds, contains the gym, weight room, treadmills, recumbent bikes, massage rooms, and the indoor pool (connected by terrace to an outdoor pool and sun deck). Select from among step, aquacise, and other aerobics classes; schedule a massage with specialists in deep-muscle therapy or a Swedish-style relaxer; or take a walk on a woodland trail through the rolling 22-acre property. Arrival is on Sunday, and there are 85 to 95 participants on hand at any given time, served by a staff of 30 professionals.

Everyone stays in modern one- and two-bedroom apartments in two-story houses on the grounds. These units have weekly maid service, a washer and dryer, telephone, and color TVs. Food plans are based on a weekly system that allows each person to plan his or her meals, according to a 5,000 calorie per day program. The food is home style. *Structure House, 3017 Pickett Rd., Durham, NC 27705, tel. 919/493–4205 or 800/553–0052, fax 919/490–0191. Year-round: 7 days, $1,400 single, $1,277 double (returnees $740 single, $612 double).*

SOUTH CAROLINA **Hilton Head Health Institute.** Here on this celebrated southern resort island is a good place to go if you need a push to make a change in your life. The medically supervised programs are designed to help you modify your lifestyle and work habits, maintain your weight, stop smoking, lower your cholesterol, and boost your stamina and overall wellness. Groups of 30 to 45 men and women attend the program for five, 12, or 26 days; each program has a specific starting date. After a medical screening (included in the program cost), you work with a team of psychologists, nutritionists, and physical fitness specialists to learn about the effects of nutrition and exercise on the body's metabolism and to deal with the effects of stress on productivity and health. Mornings usually begin with a moderately paced walk. Lectures, workshops, exercise classes, and meals are all part of the program during the rest of the day. In free time, you can take advantage of Hilton Head's beaches, golf, tennis, hiking, biking, and other recreational opportunities. Indoors at the center, you'll find a weight-training unit, stationary bikes, and treadmills.

Program activities take place in a campus-like cluster of villas on the island. Participants share well-decorated apartments, fully equipped for laundry and cooking; each person has a private bedroom and bath. You follow a diet of 800 to 1,100 calories daily during the week but can eat more on weekends; meals are varied but are always high in complex carbohydrates, moderate in proteins, and low in fat, with no sugar or salt. *Hilton Head Health Institute, Box 7138, Hilton Head Island, SC 29938, tel.*

803/785–7292 or 800/292–2440 (in Canada, 800/348–2039), fax 803/686–5659. Year-round: 5–12 days, $2,450–$3,675 single.

TENNESSEE **Tennessee Fitness Spa.** This fitness center, housed in a complex of new and old buildings on rolling terrain southwest of Nashville, takes an easygoing approach to weight loss. Conditioning takes the form of canoeing and biking trips and hikes to beautiful and historic sites in the area, and trainer John Alexander and his staff of 16 use country music and line-dancing choreography for aerobics classes. Aquacise classes take place in the 60-foot swimming pool, which is enclosed and heated in winter.

You might begin your day with a hill walk, a 2½-mile warmup to a stretch class and step aerobics. Then you could have a soak in the big hot tub, play some volleyball, or sign up for a massage, facial, haircut, manicure, or pedicure. Meals are low in fat, salt, and sugar; you regularly attend nutrition classes in the dining hall, where the spa chef demonstrates how to prepare healthy dishes. Participants range in age from 20 to 70; many come for a month or more.

Accommodations cost less than at almost any other spa in the country, especially when four people share a quad unit. In addition, there are 20 double rooms in six rustic two-story chalets. *Tennessee Fitness Spa, Rte. 3, Box 411, Waynesboro, TN 38485, tel. 615/722–5589 or 800/235–8365. Feb.–Nov.: 7 days, $799–$839 single, $529–$559 double, $459 quad. Price does not include gratuities.*

THE MIDWEST

ILLINOIS **Heartland Spa.** The comforts are down-home and the fitness program upbeat at this spa, which is surrounded by farmland only 90 minutes from Chicago; it's a comfortable place to cultivate a personal regimen that you can continue at home.

Designed for up to 28 participants, the program begins with an orientation session that helps you select exercise classes and personal services. Once a barn for prize-winning dairy cows, the main three-level structure houses a 15-meter swimming pool, massage rooms, sauna and steam rooms, and weight-training and cardiovascular conditioning equipment. On the top floor is an aerobics studio with a sprung floor.

Days begin with stretches and a brisk walk, followed by your choice of high- or low-intensity aerobics; the rest of the day, you can take step classes, yoga, or t'ai chi, or, outdoors, a ropes course. In summer you can hike or paddle boat on the estate's lake. Massages, facials, and sea salt body exfoliation are an option, although at additional charge. Every day, the spa delivers a sweat suit and workout clothing appropriate to the weather to your room. Weatherproof access to the fitness center via an underground tunnel makes getting to class easy at all times.

Meals, served in a bright, cheerful dining room, are mainly vegetarian, with 1,500 calories daily for men, 1,200 for women. The diet is high in complex carbohydrates and low in fat, sugar, and sodium. You may see waffles, banana pancakes, or egg-white omelets on the breakfast table. Typical dinner entrées are lasagna and grilled salmon.

Guests stay in a 14-room manor house dating from the 1940s, furnished with pine pieces; at night they gather near the living room fireplace. *Heartland Spa, Rte. 1, Box 181, Gilman, IL 60938, tel. 815/683–2182 or 800/545–4853, fax 815/683–2144. Year-round: 5 days, $1,625 single, $1,375 double.*

MINNESOTA **The Marsh.** In a supportive, self-contained environment close to nature, The Marsh encourages the connection of mind and body through a variety of programs that combine relaxation techniques and energy-building exercises. This "Center for Balance and Fitness" is housed in a dramatic wooden structure overlooking marshland; the interior feels residential, and everything is state-of-the-art, from cardiovascular and weight-training gyms to the 75-foot lap pool and therapy pools, one of

which is equipped with a hydraulic lift chair. Designed in 1985 as a health center to showcase innovative programs conceived by Ruth Stricker, The Marsh added accommodations in 1993 and more than doubled its space for programs. The new 27,000-square-foot structure includes a climbing wall, an art gallery, and a silo-shaped meditation tower where a "mental gym" challenges you to work out with brain-teasing games. At the center's hub is a cozy, informal café serving fresh-baked bread and muffins and low-fat breakfasts, lunches (included in the fee for overnight guests), and gourmet dinners.

Coordinated by spa director Linda Yard, your program is individualized and includes the core strength-training program, with scheduled classes in the health center, as well as bodywork in nine private treatment rooms and personal consultation with wellness specialists. The staff comprises cardiologists, physical therapists, nutrition counselors, psychologists, and personal trainers who span the fitness spectrum. Study the class schedule in advance; you can choose from among t'ai chi, yoga, meditation, Flowmotion, somatics (movements to help you manage chronic pain), centering exercises for alignment and stretching, and back therapy with physiogymnastic balls.

For solo workouts, there's a fully equipped training center, indoor and outdoor running tracks, and full lines of Cybex, NordicTrack, and Quintar equipment. The full-swing golf studio and short court racket games provide indoor sports practice. For a relaxing spa treatment, try hydrotherapy in a French Setma tub or a relaxation chamber that supplies dry heat or steam as rollers gently massage your aching muscles. The spa's specialty is a hydrotherapeutic circuit of steam room, body polish, and water-jet massage.

Guests take dinner in the Moon Terrace dining room or a café; typical dishes are fresh grilled salmon, chicken breast with wild mushrooms, and pork medallions with salsa. Dinners, not included in the accommodations charge, cost about $16 per meal. The six guest rooms have either a queen-size bed or two single beds, a private bathroom and robes, a TV, and lovely marshland views. *The Marsh, 15000 Minnetonka Blvd., Minnetonka, MN 55345, tel. 612/935–2202, fax 612/935–9685. Year-round: 4 days, $500 single or double. Price does not include tax, gratuities, dinner, or lunch.*

OHIO **Sans Souci Health Resort.** This quiet Dayton-area estate is on 80 acres crossed by 6 miles of hiking trails and borders a 600-acre wildlife preserve. It's a great location to practice the healthy lifestyle espoused by the strong but loving owner-director, Susanne Kircher, a registered nurse who acquired the place in 1978. Wakeup exercises and stretching and breathing sessions take place outdoors, where you're serenaded by the birds and cooled by gentle breezes. Mornings begin with a walk around the 1.8-mile, 18-station parcourse; meditation walks take you into the local pine forests.

Every week, six to eight guests embark on the highly structured regimen, which reflects both Kircher's European spa training and the latest thinking in stress and weight management and includes lectures, massage, yoga, aerobics, and exercise in the outdoor swimming pool. You won't find high-tech weight training, but instead long, sustained workouts. Cooking classes show you how to cut out polished rice, butter, and animal fats from your diet; you leave with a copy of Kircher's cookbook, *Sans Souci Spa Dining*. While you're here, meals are mostly vegetarian and provide 800 to 1,000 calories daily. An hour a day is set aside for rest and relaxation; some choose to visit the organic garden or the sprouting place, which supply fresh vegetables and sprouts for summer meals.

Lodging is in the manor house's rooms, which are furnished in English country style and have private baths and dressing areas. *Sans Souci Health Resort, 3745 Rte. 725, Bellbrook, OH 45305, tel. 513/848–4851, fax 513/435–4904. May–Oct.: 6 days, $1,480 single, $1,230 double.*

THE SOUTHWEST

ARIZONA **Canyon Ranch Health and Fitness Resort.** Few fitness resorts have more programs and facilities than this 70-acre former dude ranch in the foothills of Tucson's Santa Catalina Mountains; it was founded in 1979 by Mel and Enid Zuckerman, who also own a sister property in the Berkshires. The grounds are splendid—full of cactus gardens and tropical trees, with streams meandering among the casitas that cluster around the spa complex, the Life Enhancement Center, and the Health and Healing Center.

Unlike some resorts with rigid programs, the ranch lets you choose your own activities. For instance, you might opt for a cross-training program that includes hiking, biking, workouts in the nine gyms, and swimming in the indoor and outdoor pools—the mix is up to you. Or you can sign up for a more structured program such as the comprehensive eight-day program at the Life Enhancement Center, which addresses health risks; another, lasting two weeks, gathers up to 40 participants who exercise and eat together as they attempt to deal with the obstacles to good health in their lives. Cooking classes show you how to prepare healthful fare at home.

A team of 40 health professionals closely monitors your exercise and diet. In addition to such spa staples as sports, aerobics, and nutritional consultations, Canyon Ranch provides professional services such as stress-management counseling, homeopathy, hypnotherapy, and medical checkups, as well as such spa services as massage, aromatherapy, and herbal wraps; there's an extra charge for these unless you've purchased one of several special packages. You can also sign up for more challenging hikes into the canyon country, led by experienced staffers. The ranch also provides mountain bikes and transportation to trailheads at no charge.

The morning stretch and walk, open to all, is perhaps the best time to get acquainted with other guests, an interesting cross section of people ranging from young executives and television celebrities to grandmothers; up to 40% of those on hand at any one time are men, and some people return several times a year.

Meals, which use organic ingredients, are low in salt and saturated fat but high in fiber, and are prepared without refined flour or sugar. Guests have the option of lodging in single rooms known as casitas or in suites and private cottages; cottages have a kitchen, living room, and laundry. All accommodations are decorated in desert colors with southwestern furnishings. *Canyon Ranch Health and Fitness Resort, 8600 E. Rockcliff Rd., Tucson, AZ 85715, tel. 602/749-9000 or 800/742-9000, fax 602/749-7755. Mid-June–mid.-Sept.: 7 days, $2,040–$3,750 single, $1,860–$3,140 double.*

ARIZONA **Marriott's Spa at Camelback Inn.** This quintessential Arizona desert resort, established as a celebrity hideaway at the base of Mummy Mountain in 1936, has the most complete spa facilities in the Phoenix-Scottsdale area: an aerobics room, outdoor whirlpool, hot and cold plunge pools, lap pool, sauna, steam room, Swiss shower, indoor and outdoor massage rooms, and a fitness room with treadmills, Stairmasters, video monitors, four types of exercise bicycles, weight-training equipment, and even a health food restaurant. The spa, which occupies a spectacular southwestern-style hacienda and was established in 1989, also offers a variety of packages, including seven-day renewal packages, covering a variety of pampering, fitness, and wellness services. Here's your chance to try an herbal body treatment, an antiaging facial, a Parisian body polish, aromatherapy, or the like.

Typically, you begin your day with a scenic power walk or a t'ai chi class. Then, if you're on the seven-day renewal package, you can choose from among a dozen services or schedule a fitness evaluation, designed by the Cooper Aerobics Center (*see below*), or a more extensive lifestyle analysis, all of which are included. All spa guests

are supplied with workout clothing, a robe, slippers, and other amenities.

You have your choice of two restaurants that serve tasty, low-fat foods. The spa renewal week includes breakfast and lunch daily and a deluxe room in a private casita, with king-size bed or large twins, decorated in pastels and earth tones. There's a special day camp for kids. *Marriott's Spa at Camelback Inn, 5402 E. Lincoln Dr., Scottsdale, AZ 85253, tel. 602/596-7015 or 800/242-2635, fax 602/596-7018. Year-round: 7 days, $1,792–$2,695 single, $2,761–$3,685 double. Price includes 1 spa service daily but not dinner.*

TEXAS **Cooper Aerobics Center.** Dr. Kenneth H. Cooper, a pioneer in research on aerobics, established this Dallas-based center of preventive medicine in 1970 in a stately 63-room redbrick lodge on 30 acres. Today, it is also the home of a first-class fitness resort, known as the Cooper Wellness Program.

Here, the supportive and highly trained staff helps you cultivate new health habits, teaches stress-management techniques, and demonstrates healthy cooking; these sessions are part of your daily schedule, along with three exercise sessions per day and any other activities you can squeeze in. Four-, seven-, and 13-day programs, each with 15 to 20 participants, are available. Closely monitored, you team up with other guests for morning walks and runs on cushioned indoor and outdoor tracks. You also have access to four lighted Laykold tennis courts and two heated outdoor pools, six lanes wide and 75 feet long. The gym also has a pair of racquetball courts, a steam room, a sauna, a whirlpool, and Cybex strength-training equipment. A variety of medical exams are available here, all at extra cost.

The center attracts people from all walks of life, ages 19 to 75, including health-care professionals. Workshops with Dr. Cooper and other health experts help you manage stress or stop smoking, and individual counseling sessions can be scheduled to work on specific issues.

Program meals are calorie-controlled, low in fat and cholesterol. One night you visit an Italian restaurant and practice ordering a heart-healthy dinner. You have the option of staying in area motels or in the guest lodge, whose 63 rooms and suites have heavy mahogany king- or queen-size beds, wing chairs, and a balcony and private bath. *Cooper Aerobics Center, 12230 Preston Rd., Dallas, TX 75230, tel. 214/386-4777 or 800/444-5192, fax 214/386-0039 (Cooper Aerobics Center Guest Lodge, tel. 800/444-5187). Year-round: 4–7 days, $1,395–$2,595. Price does not include 6% tax, 20% gratuity, or lodging (at Guest Lodge, $88–$126 single, $95–$133 double per room).*

TEXAS **Lake Austin Spa Resort.** Crew and singles sculling were recently added to the roster of activities at this Texas Hill Country spa, the largest and oldest in the state. The lake on which it's sited is the prime year-round training camp for local and national rowing clubs. A rower in residence schedules classes for beginners; you can rent boats at $10 a day.

However, the spa's weeklong program incorporates several other exercise choices, among them 2- to 3-mile morning walks, a more strenuous 6- to 12-mile weekly trek, or 2-hour bike rides—all group outings—or, on your own, solo explorations via mountain bike along the ranch roads of the Texas Hill Country. There are also aquacise sessions in the outdoor swimming pool. In the basic package, instructors teach you step aerobics and help you work toward more advanced conditioning.

A range of services is available at extra cost. If you choose, you can start your program with a fitness assessment or hire a personal trainer. Or you might make appointments for bodywork services, including herbal skin care or herbal wraps, facials, clay body masks, thalassotherapy, or massage.

Meals appeal to southwestern tastes: Low-fat barbecued meats, enchiladas, and fajitas complement salads made from ingredients from the organic garden. Near the lake,

the resort has 40 cabins furnished with sleigh and pencil-post beds, armoires, and Shaker-style pieces; up to 80 guests can be accommodated. *Lake Austin Spa Resort, 1705 Quinlan Park Rd., Austin, TX 78732, tel. 512/266-2444 or 800/847-5637, fax 512/266-1572. Year-round: 2–3 days, $205–$220 single, $180–$195 double, per day; 4 days and up, $185–$200 single, $160–$180 double, per day. Price does not include 6% tax or $27.50 per day gratuity.*

UTAH **Green Valley Spa and Tennis Resort.** The canyon country of the southern part of the state makes an inspiring setting for the learning experience here, which begins with an introduction to how the body's weight-regulating mechanism works and includes trips to supermarkets, cooking workshops, discussion groups, bodywork, and more. In the morning, you do yoga and hike right from the resort into the red-rock hills. After an early morning hike, or after lunch, you can go to the fully equipped gym for conditioning exercises, which help you learn correct posture and body movement. Aquacise classes are given in the 13-foot swimming pool. You can do more hiking in the afternoon or play some tennis. In fact, you can play day or night on the resort's courts (a quartet of them indoors, 15 outdoors) or take classes at the Vic Braden Tennis College, which is on the premises. You can also relax in a Jacuzzi or sign up for one of spa director Carole Coombs's skin or body treatments, done with locally made natural products. Three full-body massages, one upper-body acupressure massage, one lower-body acupressure massage, a foot reflexology (a pedicure and foot massage combined), and a facial, among other things, are included in a pampering package. Additional treatments are extra.

The 50 participants each week are housed in apartments with spacious contemporary interiors, including living room, kitchen, private bath, and balcony. Meals are of nutritious, low-fat fare, prepared without sugar or salt. *Green Valley Spa and Tennis Resort, 1515 W. Canyon View Dr., St. George,*

UT 84770, tel. 801/628–8060 or 800/237–1068, fax 801/673–4084. Year-round: 7 days, $2,350 single or double.

UTAH **National Institute of Fitness.** The program at this institution, located in the red-rock canyon country near Zion National Park, is intensive and no-frills, involving lots of hikes, exercise classes, and personal instruction on state-of-the-art weight-training and cardiovascular-strengthening equipment. The goal is to start reducing elevated serum cholesterol, blood glucose, and hypertension. Having shed more than 100 pounds between them, co-owners Marc and Vicki Sorenson set a good example for the 145 participants on site at any given time.

On arrival you're given a fitness evaluation, including a cardiovascular endurance test, and assigned to one of five groups according to your fitness level. Highly structured, the subsequent daily program includes walks of 1 to 10 miles, along trails that wind up razor-edged cliffs and down to hidden Native American ruins, along rust-colored ridges and through meadows full of juniper, and desert terrain scattered with sagebrush. In addition, there are workouts in the heated indoor swimming pool, low-impact step aerobics, toning classes, and lectures. Guests with serious weight problems stay a month or more, often shedding 50 pounds. Repeaters make up a majority of the participants, who are mostly women. You have access to the spa pool when it's not being used for classes, and there's no charge to book the outdoor tennis court or indoor racquetball court. With the opening of a skylit multipurpose Megahealth Building in 1992, spa treatments and bodywork, which are à la carte, became more comprehensive than before. The spa was founded in 1974.

Meals follow a nutritionally balanced, low-fat, weight-loss plan, with controlled portions of food that is high in complex carbohydrates and low in salt, fat, and sugar; vegan diets are popular.

Lodging is in modern dome-shaped housing units with contemporary furnishings, a bath,

and four beds; in the more expensive single and double rooms, located in one of four housing units on the premises; and in the new housing unit next to the Megahealth Building, in deluxe single and double guest rooms with private bath. *National Institute of Fitness, Box 380938, Ivies, UT 84738, tel. 801/673–4905, fax 801/673–1363. Year-round: 7 days, $1,124–$1,199 single, $764–$814 double, $594 quad.*

THE ROCKIES

COLORADO **Aspen Fitness and Sports Medicine Institute.** The fitness program at this section of the tony Aspen Club focuses chiefly on weight loss and on rehabilitating sports-related injuries, but—appropriate to its setting—it's also a good spot to train for skiing or any of dozens of other outdoor sports. A personal trainer works with a team of physicians, an exercise physiologist, and a nutritionist to devise a program that works for you, one that you can continue at home. You may then be coached on how to order meals in restaurants, enrolled in Pilates training, or instructed in the use of an isokinetic exercise machine, which provides a workout for the entire body at once. Most people stay from five days to a few weeks.

The club has a well-equipped fitness center with aerobics classes, an indoor lap pool, and racquetball, squash, basketball, and indoor and outdoor tennis courts. Special sports training for children is available, including a toddler swim class, and the child-care center takes infants and children.

You have several lodging options. The Aspen Club Lodge has rooms and suites with oak furnishings, twin and queen-size beds, bath, and kitchen; Continental breakfast is part of the package, but lunch and dinner are on your own. Arrangements can also be made for accommodations in studios, condominiums, and private homes—all with Jacuzzi, fireplace, and sun deck; these cost more than the lodge and vary in price according to availability. *Aspen Fitness and Sports Medicine Institute, 1450 Crystal Lake*

Rd., Aspen, CO 81611, tel. 303/925–8900, fax 303/925–9543 (Aspen Club Lodge, 303/925–6760 or 800/633–0336, fax 303/ 920–2020). Year-round: 5 days, $1,875– $6,375 single, $1,675–$6,175 double. Price does not include lunch or dinner.

THE WEST COAST

CALIFORNIA **Cal-a-Vie.** Since they established Cal-a-Vie in 1983, Marlin and William F. Power have been combining attributes of European and American spas here, with the goal of teaching their guests how to become fitter and healthier. Terraced into a southern California hillside, the spa's 24 country villas seem lifted from an area of Provence. Yet the outdoor pool, streams, manicured gardens, and wonderful food are pure American.

The weeklong program is limited to 24 participants, and personal attention is facilitated by a ratio of four staff members per guest. There are men-only, women-only, and coed weeks. After an initial fitness evaluation, the staff recommends a diet and exercise regimen. After that, your daily routine varies little: Mornings are devoted to exercise, afternoons to bodywork and salon treatments. Each day begins with a pre-breakfast hike into the hills, followed by aerobic, body-contouring, and pool exercises: Boxercise, for instance, releases stress and builds strength and stamina, while yoga, t'ai chi, and stretch classes provide a calming counterpoint. Later, in the bath-house you sample a wide range of therapies: aromatherapy massage, clay body masks, thalassotherapy, and standard massages. Hydrotherapy tubs are infused with herbs and seaweed.

Robes, shorts, T-shirts, and sweat suits are provided, and guests have been known to wear any of them to the very casual dinner. As you go on to another activity, a fresh set of clothes is supplied. Laundry is picked up and returned daily.

One night the kitchen becomes a classroom, as the chefs demonstrate the secrets of low-fat cooking during dinner. You eat between 1,200 and 1,500 calories per day. The menu includes vegetarian fare as well as chicken and fish. Guests stay in private villas with beamed ceilings, hand-carved furniture, and king-size beds with fluffy down comforters. All guest quarters have private baths. *Cal-a-Vie, 2249 Somerset Rd., Vista, CA 92084, tel. 619/945–2055, fax 619/630–0074. Year-round (closed mid-Dec.–early Jan.): 7 days, $3,950 single. Price does not include $66.15 tax per.*

CALIFORNIA **Center for Mind Body Medicine.** This institution devoted to preventing the effects of aging sponsors week-long health retreats at L'Auberge, an elegant Del Mar beach resort; the goal is to teach you ancient and modern therapies to help you achieve total health. Under the medical direction of Dr. David Simon and inspired by the work of Dr. Deepak Chopra, author of the best-seller *Ageless Body, Timeless Mind*, the program consists of lectures by Dr. Chopra and his colleagues at San Diego's Sharp Institute as well as workshops on meditation and yoga, nutrition counseling, and daily massages. The 10 to 12 retreat participants begin with an orientation on Saturday. Then, each day starts with meditation, yoga, and a beach walk. Later, you can go for purification and rejuvenation therapies such as herbal paste and deep tissue massages, warm oil baths, herbal steam treatments, and aromatherapy, all included, as well as lectures and workshops that explore traditional Ayurvedic healing principles, the latest research on aging, and relaxation and meditation techniques that you can use to put your mind in touch with your body. Special therapies are available for correcting physical problems caused by injury. Additional spa services, available at extra cost, include body scrubs. Meals are vegetarian, especially prepared for nutritional balance. Participants eat together in a private dining room.

Arranged on one floor of L'Auberge facing the sea, guest rooms have a balcony or terrace, marble-tile baths, and televisions. *Center for Mind Body Medicine, 8010 Frost*

St., Suite 300, San Diego, CA 92123, tel. 619/541-6724 or 800/827-4277, fax 619/541-6706. Year-round: 7 days, $3,450 single or double. Price does not include 20% gratuity.

■CALIFORNIA■ **Claremont Resort.** When you work out at this 239-room resort on 22 acres of hillside gardens, you have a view of San Francisco Bay. Although the white-turreted Victorian landmark was built in 1915, the spa complex was added in 1989 and its programs are state-of-the-art. Up to 450 spa guests can be accommodated at any given time.

The Claremont's facilities include a multipurpose aerobics studio and weight room, 10 tennis courts (lighted for night play), a heated outdoor pool, a separate lap pool, and, in the locker rooms, whirlpools, steam rooms, and saunas. You can sign up for massages and facials, hydrotherapy and aromatherapy, nutrition counseling, and fitness training, in the form of aerobics, yoga, and stretching classes. Some 30 bodywork specialists are on call. The four-day spa package includes a choice of several treatments and can be taken with meals or, for a discount, without. The cost of longer stays is based on your particular program. Workout clothing is provided.

The Claremont is also the site of a highly structured weeklong retreat with Dr. Dean Ornish and specialists in stress management, nutrition, and diet from his Preventive Medicine Research Institute. At this retreat, lectures based on the best-selling *Dr. Dean Ornish's Program for Reversing Heart Disease* demonstrate how a low-stress, no-smoking lifestyle involving exercise and a low-fat vegetarian diet can reverse heart disease within a year. There are also workshops, workouts, yoga, meditation, and specially prepared low-fat meals. This program is limited to 100 participants.

Rooms are spacious, beds oversize, and all baths private. The resort menu offers a regular selection of sophisticated low-fat, low-cholesterol, low-calorie fare; menus indicate exactly how many calories you are consuming. *Claremont Resort, Box 23363, Oakland, CA 94623, tel. 510/843-3000 or 800/551-7266, fax 510/843-6239. Year-round: 4 days, $1170 single, $1812 per couple (or $20 extra per night for nonparticipating companion). Price does not include 11% tax or 17.5% gratuity.*

■CALIFORNIA■ **The Golden Door.** One of southern California's oldest and most glamorous fitness resorts, the Golden Door teaches you about a healthy lifestyle while utterly pampering you. Opened in 1959 a mile from its present location, the resort now encompasses 177 acres of canyon and orchard. Beyond its ornate brass door, it's a cross between a first-class resort and a Japanese country inn, an enchanted realm of Japanese-style gardens and buildings. The four spacious gyms have glass doors that slide open to fresh air. The graceful bathhouse contains a modern sauna, steam room, Swiss shower, and treatment rooms for body wraps and body scrubs.

During the weeklong programs, you get one-on-one training from the fitness and nutrition specialists. Each day begins with stretches outside, followed by a sunrise mountain hike. The day may include weight training, aerobics, tap dancing, tennis, yoga, and massages and beauty treatments. For returning guests, there's the four-day, eight-hour Inner Door course, at which you are secluded in a teahouse to learn visualization and meditation techniques, work on stress-management skills, and practice creative thinking. The food here is low in fat, cholesterol, salt, and sugar, but rich in fiber; you'll find lots of whole grains. Midmorning juice or broth, vegetable snacks, and nonalcoholic aperitifs are also served.

No more than 39 guests are accepted for the weeklong programs. Participants come from many backgrounds and countries, but most are middle-aged and success-oriented. Five weeks are reserved for men only, one for couples, and four are coed; the rest of the year is for women only. You stay in one-story stucco buildings patterned after old Japanese inns; rooms are done in muted colors with Japanese wood-block prints on the walls, parquet floors with rugs, sliding shoji screens in the bathrooms, and jalousie windows. Each has a private garden. All guests here have the use of sweat suits, workout clothing, bathrobes, slippers, and Japanese robes, and transportation to and from San Diego International Airport is included in the package price. *The Golden Door, Box 463077, Escondido, CA 92046, tel. 619/ 744–5777 or 800/424–0777, fax 619/471– 2393. Year-round (closed late Dec.): 7 days, $4,250 single or double.*

CALIFORNIA **The Oaks at Ojai.** Teaching good exercise habits and motivating you to keep them up at home is the focus of this high-energy spa, housed in a dignified two-story 1918 former country inn built of wood and stone, a landmark on sleepy Ojai's main thoroughfare. Although the lobby's dark green walls and wood-burning fireplace evoke a quieter, gentler era, the fitness regimen and spa cuisine are totally modern. Former professional ice skater and physical fitness instructor Sheila Cluff bought the place in the 1970s.

The no-frills program includes workouts in the large heated pool, intense aerobics classes rated for different fitness levels, and progressive stretches, along with morning hikes in the hills, brisk walks along country roads, and, late in the day, a stretch-and-relax class. You can also work out on weight machines. At day's end, you can go for a soak in a nearby hot springs or schedule an hour-long massage, one of several spa services and treatments available at additional cost. Sometimes there are cooking demonstrations or lectures after dinner.

Designed to help participants lose weight, the menu is planned to provide only 1,000 calories daily, but the foods are fresh and natural. In the morning, fruit, muffins, and vitamins are set out at the coffee bar in the main building. There is a midmorning broth break, and vegetable snacks are available in the afternoon. Dinner is casual.

Guests are diverse, ranging from young professionals to grandmothers; film industry folk, actresses, and homemakers all drop in to shape up and relax, and there are usually a few overweight women in residence for a month or more. Rooms are small and simply furnished and have showers or tubs. Cottages, another option, accommodate between one and three guests.

Ojai, located south of Santa Barbara, is an arts center and a favorite with practitioners of several healing faiths; in your free time, if you're interested, you can make appointments with psychics, astrologers, members of the Theosophy movement, and the like. *The Oaks at Ojai, 122 E. Ojai Ave., Ojai, CA 93023, tel. 805/646–5573 or 800/753–6257, fax 805/640–1504. Year-round: 5–7 days, $895–$1,323 single, $625–$1,113 double. Price does not include 10% tax or 14% service charge.*

CALIFORNIA **The Palms at Palm Springs.** The swimming pool at the center of the resort is the focal point of activities at this informal spa, also owned by Oaks proprietor Sheila Cluff, near the heart of Palm Springs. There are four sessions of water exercise daily, along with aerobics classes, which are held in a small aerobics studio and outdoors under the palms; you can choose from among 14 classes daily. Workouts' goal is to increase flexibility, burn calories, strengthen the heart, and increase lung capacity. The desert climate, the low-calorie diet, and the rigorous exercise quickly get results. If you need more structure, you can plan a weight-management program with a resident nurse or schedule one-on-one weight training. Personal services—massage, aromatherapy, and a facial—are available at extra cost.

The place appeals to women and their devoted spouses. Most participants are in their middle fifties and in good shape but want to shed a few pounds. In the recently refurbished Spa Hotel, you can soak in thermal waters and choose from a massage-sauna combination or European treatments for hair, skin, and nails.

The menu provides 1,000 calories daily; food is simply prepared and you eat lots of vegetables, pasta, and chicken. Although the resort's layout is compact, as many as 84 people can be accommodated in the 43 guest rooms, which are in a red-roof manor house and private bungalows with a Spanish colonial air. Some rooms have their own patio; others share a bath. *The Palms at Palm Springs, 572 N. Indian Canyon Dr., Palm Springs, CA 92262, tel. 619/325-1111 or 800/753-7256, fax 619/327-0867. Year-round: 5-7 days, $925-1365 single, $725-1085 double. Price does not include 10% tax or 14% service charge.*

CALIFORNIA Pritikin Longevity Center. This was the first of the country's institutions dedicated to the diet and exercise regimen developed in the late 1970s by the late Nathan Pritikin. Healthy people sign up for the strictly regimented, medically supervised programs here to preserve their health and learn to control their diet. Others come to lose weight, lower their cholesterol, or manage their blood pressure. The four-week program helps people with heart disease, insulin-dependent diabetes, and other serious health problems.

A full physical examination, with a treadmill stress test and a complete blood-chemistry analysis, marks the beginning of the program, which involves exercise, nutrition and health education, stress-management counseling, and medical services. The daily schedule packs in cooking classes and lectures along with three exercise sessions—workouts in the well-equipped gym or walks along the beach or down the Santa Monica pier. (Swimmers must use a nearby hotel pool or the ocean.) Diet is also a key to Pritikin life; chefs cook without added fat, salt, or sugar, and meals are largely vegetarian, although fish and chicken are served several times a week. The guest services desk makes appointments for massages or acupuncture sessions, which cost extra. The program lasts for 13 or 26 days, and the doctor and physiologist assigned to work with you when you arrive monitor your progress throughout.

Housed in a beachfront hotel, the center has modern rooms with private baths. The larger, more expensive quarters have a Jacuzzi tub and ocean views. Participating companions staying in the room with you get a reduced rate. *Pritikin Longevity Center, 1910 Ocean Front Walk, Santa Monica, CA 90405, tel. 310/450-5433 or 800/421-9911, fax 310/450-3602. Year-round: 13-26 days, $6,555-$11,181. Price does not include gratuities.*

CALIFORNIA Skylonda Fitness Retreat. The goals of the seven-day programs at this establishment on 16 forested acres of coastal hills south of San Francisco is to help people lose weight and recharge physically and spiritually. It opened in late 1992.

The program involves walks, yoga, meditation, weight training, aerobics, aquatic exercises, and massage. Twice a day you hike through the spectacular redwood forests and golden meadows of the South Bay Peninsula, which separates the Pacific Ocean from San Francisco Bay, a part of California rarely seen by visitors or residents. The day also includes an hour of silence and reflection. From the 6 AM wake-up call to the 9 PM close of evening programs, you interact closely with the up to 30 other guests during hikes, circuit training with PACE equipment, aquatics classes, yoga and stretch relaxation classes, and other fitness activities. Facilities include an indoor lap pool, a weight-training circuit, a spa facility with sauna and steam rooms, and an open air whirlpool. Appointments for a massage, facial, manicure, and pedicure come with the program. The imaginative cuisine of head chef Sue Chapman draws on the region's fresh organic produce, game, and fish; she pays close attention to the nutritional needs of the rigorous exercisers here but keeps the fat content of the diet to less than 10% per week.

Accommodations are in a spacious three-story log lodge with a library and stained-glass windows. Each of the 15 bedrooms has double beds with duvets and a private bath. Workout clothing is supplied, and transportation to and from San Francisco International Airport is included in the price. *Skylonda Fitness Retreat, 16350 Skyline Blvd., Woodside, CA 94062, tel. 415/851–4500 or 800/851–2222, fax 415/851–5504. Year-round: 7 days, $2,535 single or double.*

HAWAII

THE BIG ISLAND **Kalani Honua Conference Retreat and Center Institute for Cultural Studies.** Weeklong courses in traditional Hawaiian arts and crafts are the focal point of the activity at this institution, which was founded 13 years ago on the site of an old Hawaiian school and is now the state's largest retreat and conference center. But there are also classes in gourmet vegetarian cooking, bodywork, and movement practices of the East and West. In addition, you'll find a Japanese-style spa with a communal hot tub, sauna, massage rooms, and pavilions for yoga, aerobics, and meditation classes, along with tennis and volleyball courts, a fitness center with weight-training equipment, an 85-foot swimming pool, and hiking trails. Therapeutic services include acupressure, shiatsu, rolfing, and traditional lomilomi massage, the rocking, rhythmical massage of ancient Hawaiian royalty. For relaxing, there are hammocks under the palms, a Jacuzzi, and a clothing-optional black sand beach.

Meals, served buffet style on an ocean-view terrace, include fresh tropical fruits and real Kona coffee, and there is usually a vegetarian main course and a fish or fowl option at dinner. The lush seaside setting is close to Kilauea, the world's most active volcano. Many guests venture off on their own to explore craters or secluded beaches among the lava flows.

Native Hawaiians make up part of the large staff, and all have professional experience in their area of expertise. With campsites under the stars, little cottages, and private and shared rooms in two-story octagonal cedar *hales* (lodges) ranged around the secluded, manicured grounds, the retreat has space for up to 100 people at a time.

Most guests are active, college-educated men and women between the ages of 25 and 55. *Kalani Honua Conference Retreat and Center Institute for Cultural Studies, R.R. 2, Box 4500, Pahoa, HI 96778, tel. 808/965–7828 or 800/800–6886, fax 808/965–9613. Year-round: 8 days, $1,295 single, $650–$995 double, $550 triple, $370 tent site; daily rate $28–$85 per person without meals, $55–$112 with meals.*

MAUI **Grand Wailea Resort, Hotel and Spa Grande.** The 50,000-square-foot Spa Grande at this posh resort offers the state's most extensive health and fitness facilities. In addition to 10 individual and private Jacuzzi areas, there are Roman-style whirlpools 20 feet in diameter and 42 individual treatment rooms, where you can enjoy five different facials and seven types of massage, including lomilomi. The unique Polynesian sand bath has you wrapped in moist ti plant leaves topped by volcanic sand, which is heated to make you sweat. Stress management, nutrition, and fitness counseling is available, and spa director Darryll Leiman has specialists to work on a personalized program. You can also join classes in the spa's exercise studio.

Except for the classes, all spa services are à la carte. However, a variety of packages are available, among them a four-night Spa Sampler that includes hydrotherapy and traditional Hawaiian health therapies. The Terme Wailea circuit, which every package guest gets, involves treatments designed to exfoliate and cleanse the skin: a loofah scrub or Japanese goshi-goshi scrub; a Swiss shower; and skin treatments with Maui mud, seaweed, papaya enzyme, or other herbs, applied as you rest in enormous marble tubs inlaid with gold mosaic. The two- or four-day Grande Plan includes additional services and consultations, plus one adventure activity such as sea kayaking, a bike ride, or a hike to an island waterfall.

The resort's 767 rooms, located in an eight-story complex, all have an ocean view, private terrace, and modern bath. Hotel facilities include 14 tennis courts, two 18-hole golf courses, Maui's only indoor racquetball and squash courts, and a children's camp. Catamaran cruises and water sports on the beach are other diversions. At the resort's Café Kula, chef Kathleen Dealman offers spa cuisine: You might find organically grown greens from farms in the Kula region of the slopes of Mt. Haleakala. The resort also has Italian and Polynesian restaurants and a Japanese-style eatery with a sushi bar and tatami rooms. *Grand Wailea Resort, Hotel and Spa Grande, 3850 Wailea Alanui Dr., Wailea, HI 96753, tel. 808/875-1234 or 800/888-6100, fax 808/874-2424. Year-round: 4 days, $2,504-$3,437 single, $1,740-$2,405 double (additional nights $465). Spa Sampler price does not include meals; Grande Plan does not include dinner.*

OAHU **Ihilani Resort and Spa.** The spa programs at this 387-room luxury hotel on Oahu's leeward coast, 25 minutes from Honolulu International Airport, are inspired by the seaside location and by ancient Hawaiian healing therapies, among them special Hawaiian Thalasso treatments that involve seaweed, salt scrubs, and facial masks with marine algae. The spa opened in 1994.

Terraced into a hillside facing Pearl Harbor, the spa has separate sections for men and women, a coed aerobics studio and weight room, and private patios for alfresco massage. Each treatment room has a high-tech tub that circulates fresh seawater through a special water massage unit imported from France. Packages enable you to sample several therapies. The resort has an outdoor lap pool.

The kitchen here uses locally grown produce, fresh fish, and lots of herbs. Meals are low in sodium, sugar, and fat. Guests stay in spacious oceanfront rooms, some with private terraces; seven suites come with a whirlpool. Each room has a marble bathroom. *Ihilani Resort and Spa, 92-10001 Olani St., West Oahu, HI 96707, tel. 808/679-0079 or 800/626-4446, fax 808/679-0080. Year-*

round: 4-7 days, $2,022-$3,733 single, $1,533-$2,834 double.

SOURCES

ORGANIZATIONS **International Spa & Fitness Association** (informally known as I/SPA; 1300 L St. NW, Suite 1050, Washington, DC 20005, tel. 202/789-5920, fax 202/898-0484) is dedicated to enhancing the spa experience and provides consumer updates on member resorts, among other information. Association members include resort owners and managers, affiliated day spas, consultants, travel agents, educators, and suppliers of spa products.

PERIODICALS Three quarterly newsletters provide information about spas. "Custom Spas" (Custom Spa Vacations, 1318 Beacon St., Brookline, MA 02146, tel. 617/566-5144, fax 617/731-0599) lists, evaluates, and gives prices for spa vacation packages. "The Pursglove Review" (Box 19181, Washington, DC 20036, tel. 202/223-9744, fax 202/686-6427) reviews spas and covers new services, equipment, and resorts. "Spa Review" (2400 Virginia Ave., Consul 715, Washington, DC 20037, tel. 202/331-0228) assesses not only new resorts but also new treatments and products, and gives special attention to spas in California, Europe, and Asia. There is also an annual directory of spa vacations, *Spa-Finder* (Spa-Finders, 91 5th Ave., Suite 301, New York, NY 10003, tel. 212/924-6800 or 800/255-7727, fax 212/924-7240), which lists package prices and has a regional index and a glossary of spa terms.

BOOKS *Adventure Learning in a Spa Environment*, by Gregory D. Hagin (from I/SPA; *see above*), is a case study of the ropes course program at the New Age Health Spa. *The Bath,* by Diane Von Furstenberg, documents historic and contemporary bathing styles, including European and American spas. *The Bodywork Bible*, by Thomas Claire, a consumer's guide to massage and bodywork by a therapist, explains how to enjoy spa services. *California Spas*, by Laurel Olson Cook, offers a detailed survey of spas and hot springs throughout the state. *Fodor's Healthy Escapes*, by Bernard Burt, reviews, in depth, 240 spas, health resorts, retreats, and cruises in the United States, Canada, Mexico, and the Caribbean. *Hawaii Eco-T Directory*, by Shelly Addix (Leeward Community College, Community Services, 96-045 Ala Ike, AD-121, Pearl City, HI 96782), describes hikes, trip outfitters, spiritual retreats, and environmental program resources throughout the Hawaiian Islands. *Take My Body and Fix It,* by Sonnie Imer (The Taste of Tahoe, Box 6114, Incline Village, NV 89450), outlines western spa programs and provides spa recipes. *Taking The Waters*, by Alev Lytle Croutier, is an illustrated book about European and American spas.

ALSO SEE If mastering the discipline of a healthy lifestyle intrigues you, check out the New Age Centers chapter.

Volunteer Research Vacations

By Sean Elder

n Steven Spielberg's top-grossing *Jurassic Park,* the mathematician Ian Malcolm, played by Jeff Goldblum, berates the work of John Hammond, the irresponsible scientist played by Richard Attenborough, saying that a real scientist doesn't build on or borrow from knowledge gathered by others as the bad doctor clearly has in his successful attempts at reconstructing dinosaur DNA. A real scientist, Malcolm says, plunges into the dark alone, boldly going where no man has ever gone before; a real scientist is sort of an action-adventure hero—one man, or woman, against nature.

This is nonsense, of course. Nowhere outside the movies—where lab coat–clad stars are forever turning away from their microscopes or computers to cry "Eureka!"—do scientists tackle problems by themselves. Scientific discovery arises from research, plain and simple; and scientific research is plodding, methodical, and usually based on other work in the field. This is why abstracts are always such tough sledding, filled as they are with footnotes and references.

For any armchair scientist who has ever aspired to the role of scientific researcher, a volunteer research project is just the thing. These projects generally teach you new skills and allow you to employ them in the context of a disciplined research effort. In all of these projects there is a stated goal or premise, and while your part in achieving the goal or proving the premise may be small, it is as essential as that of the group leader. As a volunteer researcher you are a piece of the continent, a part of the main.

Though there is no average volunteer vacation, the ones included here typically last from two to three weeks; cost anywhere from $300 to $3,000; require no special education, background, or level of physical fitness; and are open to anyone over 18 (some programs will admit younger people with a parent's permission).

Most organizations will send you a briefing that gives all kinds of information about the trip and its objectives. It tells you about the weather, how hard the trip will be, and how to prepare, and it includes a checklist of things you're going to need.

CHOOSING THE RIGHT PROJECT

Obviously, you first need to know what type of work the project involves, whether it's dolphin monitoring or photo cataloging. Then ask the following questions before you sign up.

How long has the project been using volunteers? Chances are that a project on which volunteers have been working for two or more years will be better equipped to handle your needs than one that has just begun to use volunteers.

Who (or what) benefits from the volunteers' labor? Many of the organizations listed are

---

Sean Elder writes for many publications, and he does his own research.

affiliated with various academic institutions and international research groups and are happy to tell you what use is made of the work you do. Sometimes the information you gather is donated to one school or research center; other times it is shared by all interested parties.

Is any special background or training required? Although most trips do not demand special abilities, some do: The dolphin trips need strong swimmers, while the search for moose bones on Isle Royale calls for great physical stamina.

What will I learn by working on this project? Many outfitters promise that you will come away with a sense of accomplishment, an appreciation for the subject matter of your research, and maybe even a greater understanding of a particular ecosystem. But some projects are more like courses in which you learn specific skills: how to identify humpback whales or what the loon's various cries mean, for example.

What special qualifications does the project director and/or instructor have? Many volunteer vacations are headed by researchers and scientists noted in their field. Ask about their credentials, number of years of experience, and their familiarity with the subject that's covered.

How much hands-on experience do participants get? On some projects, the researcher does most of the interesting work and you watch from the sidelines. On others, you are encouraged, even expected, to participate.

Is there a doctor in the house? Some of the trips described in this chapter take place in wilderness conditions, miles from any hospitals or medical stations. Check to see that the leader or someone on the trip knows first aid and CPR.

What's the cost and what's included? Prices of volunteer vacations vary substantially from the generally inexpensive Wildlands Studies trips ($385) to some of the more blue-chip Earthwatch trips ($3,935). Some projects may appear inexpensive until you realize the cost does not include airfare,

accommodations, and meals. Unless otherwise stated, prices for the trips listed here include three meals daily, double-occupancy lodging, and local transportation but not airfare. Although as a rule prices include tents and cooking gear, they usually do not include sleeping bags and other personal camping gear; be sure to ask.

How are the fees used? It can be satisfying to know where your hard-earned vacation dollars are going. Earthwatch, for instance, gives you an estimate of the entire cost of the project showing a breakdown of your share.

Are fees and other expenses tax-deductible? If the parent organization is nonprofit, the chances are good that you can deduct some part of your vacation cost, including your airfare, as a charitable contribution. Also ask your accountant.

What sort of food and accommodations are provided? Since lodging varies from a comfortable bed in a mountain lodge to a patch of ground beneath a pup tent, it's best to know where you can expect to lay your head. Some trips supply their own cook, but on other projects it's catch-as-catch-can, and you can only eat so much macaroni and cheese.

Will laundry service be available? If it is, you can certainly pack lighter.

Is there free time? And what is there to do with it? Although a long day of bear-trapping may leave you too tired to consider doing much of anything come evening, whale-watching in Hawaii could well be complemented by a little night music.

Do you have recommendations from past participants? Some organizations have notes from former volunteers in their briefings, but it is even better to speak with former volunteers yourself.

How far in advance do I need to book? You must sign up for the most popular projects many months in advance, but some projects don't fill up and you can join them at the last minute.

MAJOR PLAYERS

EARTHWATCH This organization has been providing scientists with the funding and volunteers they need to address ecological problems around the world since 1972. In that time, Earthwatch has raised $26 million in capital and human resources and mobilized over 40,000 volunteers. In one year it sponsored 160 projects around the world, 37 of them in the United States. To get funding from Earthwatch, a scientist submits a proposal, then undergoes a peer-review process in which the worth and necessity of the project is evaluated. Money is raised largely through volunteers who pay for the opportunity to participate in the project. No special skills are required for any Earthwatch volunteer, just curiosity and a willingness to learn. Volunteers range in age from 16 to 85, but most are 25 to 60 years old. Group size varies greatly, from 2 to 22. Although Earthwatch is associated with the protection of endangered species, the list of disciplines its research trips cover includes art history, cultural anthropology, and paleontology. The average trip is two weeks, and your contribution—$700 to $2,400—covers food, lodging, and a portion of the project's expense. Ask for an EarthCorps Briefing, which tells you everything you need to know about any particular project (680 Auburn St., Box 403FD, Watertown, MA 02272-9104, tel. 617/926–8200 or 800/776–0188, fax 617/926–8532).

SMITHSONIAN RESEARCH EXPEDITIONS Volunteers participating in one of the Smithsonian's many research expeditions are as likely to spend their vacation indoors as out—digging through old movie stills, collecting aeronautical data, or measuring plant samples. Rest assured, though, that all research done by you and your teammates is put to good use. The Smithsonian's raison d'être is to work with scientific authorities to collect, organize, and interpret data; nobody does this better. Much of the research is done in Washington, D.C., but the Smithsonian also sponsors natural science trips during which you might map a forest in Maryland or research small animal ecosystems in the Shenandoah Valley in Virginia. To participate, you must contribute from $945 to $2,900, depending on the project; this contribution covers your accommodations, supplies, and some meals. Volunteers tend to be over 40, with a healthy percentage of early retirees in their 50s and a growing group of students and young professionals. Group size ranges from 5 to 25 but is usually around 10 or 12 (The Smithsonian Associates, 90 L'Enfant Plaza SW, Suite 4210, Washington, D.C. 20560, tel. 202/287–3210, fax 202/287–3244).

UNIVERSITY RESEARCH EXPEDITIONS PROGRAM Students, teachers, and the general public have been participating in the University Research Expeditions Program's worldwide research trips since 1976. Archaeology, anthropology, geology, marine biology, paleontology, music, art and the humanities, zoology, environmental studies, animal behavior, and sociology are all covered by the program, which has brought together more than 700 teams to date, with more than 4,500 volunteers. This program's trips last from two to three weeks; costs average around $1,300 but vary according to destination. The fee covers meals, double-occupancy lodging, research equipment and supplies, and camping and field gear when needed. Volunteers range from 16 to 80 years old, but most are between 25 and 65. A typical group is comprised of 10 or 12 people (Desk L-03, University of California, Berkeley, CA 94720, tel. 510/642–6586, fax 510/642–6791).

WILDLANDS STUDIES Since 1980, this organization has been providing volunteers with hands-on experience on wild-land field projects in the United States and Canada. Wolf habitat projects, in which you can run with the wolves or at least in their wake, have been a Wildlands Studies staple since 1982; trips of this nature are now available in Idaho, Montana, and Washington. The organization also sponsors research trips focusing on bighorn sheep, spotted owls, and grizzly bears. Volunteers are generally 19 to 35 years old, although there is no upper age limit. You can get college credits through San Francisco State University for participating in these projects, but enrollment is not limited to students. Course costs are manageable at $300 to $400, which includes lodging but not food (3 Mosswood Circle, Cazadero, CA 95421, tel. 707/632–5665).

FAVORITE PROJECTS

At press time, few sponsors knew with any certainty what projects would be available in the coming years. All the trips listed here are *likely* to be continued, but you should double-check with the organization to make sure that the trip is in fact being offered and all the information given—price, date, destination—is current.

THE MID-ATLANTIC

MARYLAND **Secret Life of Plants.** What effect will a rising level of carbon dioxide have on plants? Will it stimulate growth and photosynthesis, cause changes in species composition, reduce water loss from ecosystems? Dr. Bert Drake of the Smithsonian Environmental Research Center has made this study his own, and you can assist him in the long-term research and learn more about plant ecology in the process.

At the research center nature preserve, near Annapolis and the Baltimore-Washington International Airport, Dr. Drake measures the growth of plants exposed to elevated carbon dioxide levels. The mornings are devoted to lectures on overall climatic change (the big picture), but you spend your afternoons in marsh grasses and sedges, measuring indigenous plants and taking samplings. These are then compared to plants that have been artificially given twice the normal amount of carbon dioxide. You learn not only how to gather data but also how to record it on computers at day's end. Although a background in plant ecology is not required, you must be enthusiastic about the subject.

Teams of five volunteers spend six August days in a fully equipped mobile home. Rooms are shared, and there is some communal cooking, but, fortunately for all, you're close to Annapolis and a bevy of good restaurants. *Smithsonian Research Expeditions, The Smithsonian Associates, 490 L'Enfant Plaza, SW, Suite 4210, Washington, D.C. 20560, tel. 202/287-3210, fax 202/287-3244. Mid-Aug.: 6 days, $945. Price does not include dinners; Sign up 2–3 months in advance.*

WASHINGTON, D.C. **Of Air and Space.** Every year, the Smithsonian's National Air and Space Museum acquires thousands of historically important documents relating to the world of flight. These might include military data, photos and journals, even films of historic flights and failures. Someone must catalog all this information for the National Air and Space Archives, which currently house more than 35,000 books, 7,000 bound journals, and 700,000 feet of motion picture film. That someone could be you. Working with Archives Division staff members, you learn the basic rules of handling, labelling, and storing materials.

This is one of the Smithsonian's most popular ongoing programs, with countless repeat volunteers and a waiting list almost guaranteed. What keeps these air-and-space buffs coming back? To call fans of aeronautical engineering obsessed would be an understatement; to them, the Air and Space Museum is like Disneyland without the dwarfs. This project provides volunteers with the opportunity to work behind the scenes—and in proximity to the *Spirit of St. Louis.*

You share a room with one of seven other volunteers in a Washington hotel (a different one is used each year). There are welcome and farewell dinners, but you buy your other meals in the museum cafeteria or in local restaurants. Free time finds you in the nation's capital, with all of its charms, although the heat at the end of the summer can be mighty debilitating. Beware: archival work is more exhausting than it sounds, and days are a full eight hours. *Smithsonian Research Expeditions, The Smithsonian Associates, 490 L'Enfant Plaza, SW, Suite 4210, Washington, D.C. 20560, tel. 202/287–3210, fax 202/287–3244. Late July–early Aug.: 14 days, $1,350. Price does not include most meals; sign up in October, as soon as catalog is available.*

THE SOUTH

FLORIDA Searching for Dolphins in the Sea. Human fascination with dolphins began long before the days of Flipper: A fresco depicting a few of the sea mammals mid-frolic adorned the queen's chamber at the Palace of Knossos in 1600 BC. For anyone who's envied those Homo sapiens who swim with—and sometimes even touch—bottlenose dolphins, this Earthwatch project is a must.

It has been one of the outfitter's most popular programs since 1982. You and up to four other volunteers primarily observe, photograph, and survey dolphins that have been tagged. You gather information on the animals' social skills, sexual habits, and signature whistling.

Once a year, in June, a team of 14 to 22 volunteers assists in capturing dolphins for tagging then releasing them. The animals are captured with large nets dropped from motorboats, and occasionally handlers are called upon to jump from the fast-moving boats to disentangle one that's endangered. Consequently, your swimming skills should be strong. For that matter, *you* should be strong: Bottlenose dolphins weigh up to 600 pounds and can be troublesome during capture operations ("One female we captured in 1975 was named Killer for good reason," Earthwatch ominously notes).

The project is executed along the central west coast of Florida, near Sarasota, in the shallow bays of the Gulf of Mexico; these mild waters are well protected and abundant in sea life. Volunteers stay in a large house with a pool and dock, and you share the responsibilities of shopping and cooking.

You spend from eight to nine hours each day in the Florida sun, so sunscreen and other protection are a must. There's also a lot of bouncing about in small boats, so those prone to seasickness should be prepared or stay away. *Earthwatch, 680 Auburn St., Box 403FD, Watertown, MA 02272-9924, tel. 617/926–8200 or 800/776–0188, fax 617/926–8532. Year-round: 15 days, $1,695 (observation). June: 15 days, $2,495 (capture/release). Sign up 2–3 months in advance.*

GEORGIA The Slow Study of Turtles. Consider the lot of the loggerhead sea turtle. Every two to six years, the nesting female comes ashore on Georgia beaches, digs a nest cavity, lays about 120 golf ball–size eggs, buries them in the sand, and returns to the sea, leaving the hatchlings to fend for themselves. Those that aren't eaten in their shells—by raccoons, ghost crabs, and other predators—scramble into the brine, often to be consumed by sharks, killed by motorboats, or drowned by fishing nets. The nursery years of those that survive are spent, it is believed, floating in the Gulf Stream on mats of seaweed, unattended by adults. Small wonder that they look so tough.

Since 1973, the Caretta Research Project has been monitoring and protecting the hatchlings in a cooperative agreement with the U.S. Fish and Wildlife Service, which oversees the Wassaw Island National Wildlife Refuge. The long-term goals of the project are to learn more about the giant turtles and their nesting habits, to protect the eggs and hatchlings, and to involve the public in the fate of this species, which has been on the threatened species list since 1978.

This is a vacation for people who like the beach and who like to work at night. Volunteers are needed weekly throughout the summer for two separate seasons. In the egg-laying season, which runs from early

May through mid-August, you spend most of the night patrolling Wassaw Island's 6 miles of beaches with a team of up to eight people, searching for female sea turtles. When you find the 250- to 400-pound creatures, you tag and measure them after they have completed their nesting activities. In the hatching season—August to mid-September—your nightly job is to monitor the nests laid earlier in the summer, trying to protect the eggs from predators, and then to escort the hatchlings in their triumphant scramble to the sea. During the early August weeks, participants may see both adults and hatchlings.

Island leaders and assistant leaders school you in all necessary research techniques and acquaint you with sea turtle fact and lore. The teams of eight stay in two small cabins in the center of the island (coed arrangements depend on the male-female makeup of each group) and eat together. Meals may consist of such dishes as grilled chicken, stir-fries, and spaghetti. You are expected to help out with the housekeeping. Since almost all work is done at night, there's plenty of free time to read, relax, swim, bird-watch, and, in general, enjoy the land. Volunteers are cautioned to marshal their energies; turtle maintenance can run through the night. Remember: The Georgia coast in summertime is subtropical, and there is no air-conditioning. *Caretta Research Project, Savannah Science Museum, 4405 Paulsen St., Savannah, GA 31405, tel. 912/355–6705. Mid-May–mid-Aug. (egg-laying season): 7 days, $395. Late July–mid-Sept. (hatching season): 7 days, $350. Sign up 2–3 months in advance.*

LOUISIANA **Where Have All the Neotropical Migrant Bird Species Gone?** At one time, the Louisiana bayou was rife with exotic migratory birds such as the Louisiana water thrush, the Acadian flycatcher, and the ever-popular white-eyed vireo. In recent years, however, there have been what birders call apparent abundance decreases. And it's not just here: All over the United States, exotic migrant bird populations have been decreasing.

Many scientists believe this is at least partly because of our shrinking wetlands.

As sightings of these birds in the Louisiana bayou diminish, scientists want to establish what is keeping the birds from returning here each year. It could be nest predation, the loss of forest, or some other habitat change; ornithologists disagree.

But in order to address—and, it is hoped, redress—the problem, the decline in population must first be scientifically established. This is where you come in. Project director and principal investigator Dr. Robert Hamilton, working at the Bayou Cocadrie National Wildlife Refuge, in Concordia Parish, schools teams of two to five volunteers in the trials of nest finding, nest monitoring, mist-netting (a gentle way of catching birds for tagging), data recording, and more. You spend a lot of the two-week trip in the swamps of Louisiana—quite a sight at sunrise, when you arrive at the study site. Your field work concludes around 2:30 PM, and you should finish logging the day's activities by 4; the rest of the day is yours.

You sleep in double rooms at a nearby rented house, and you eat Cajun foods prepared for you by Earthwatch staff. The work is not strenuous, though there are mosquitoes and ticks to contend with (it's a swamp, folks), and you will get wet. For birders, it is an uncommon opportunity to see some uncommon birds—and a chance to assist scientists in understanding the changing wetlands and their importance to us and other species. *Earthwatch, 680 Auburn St., Box 403FD, Watertown, MA 02272-9924, tel. 617/926–8200 or 800/776–0188, fax 617/926–8532. May–Aug.: 14 weeks, $1,195. Sign up at least 2 months in advance.*

NORTH CAROLINA **Tracking Black Bears.** How close have you come to a black bear? How close have you wanted to come? If you want to get really close and personal, Earthwatch has a project for you. Since 1987, Dr. Roger Powell and his colleagues from the zoology department of North Carolina State

University have been actively following the black bear population of the Pisgah Black Bear Sanctuary in Pisgah National Forest. They are studying the different social organization of the males and females. It is believed that females establish their territory around food and its availability, while males organize their territory around females—and their availability. This involves tracking the bears' sexual habits, diet, and need for space, which can only be done by radio-monitoring the bears. And for bears to be radio-monitored, they must first be trapped and tagged.

There are two segments to the work at hand. If you come in May or early June, you work with 6 to 15 team members to livetrap black bears. This is as close as you can come to one without getting into bear wrestling. From late June to August, teams of no more than five help track the previously tagged bears and measure bear food eaten at bait sites you set up.

The Pisgah Black Bear Sanctuary is in the mountains of western North Carolina, near the picturesque town of Asheville. You begin your 19-day trip with several days of orientation and a drive along the Blue Ridge Parkway, which overlooks the study area. You learn the basics of tracking and are briefed on the overall goals of the project. Once in the field, you usually start each day at 8 AM, although the daily schedule of trips from late June to August is a little less rigid.

The first groups of volunteers set traps and check them on a daily basis. After all the bears in the central part of the study area are tagged, other groups spend much of their time engaged in telemetry work—that is, tracking the bears using radios. You work out of the project truck, in two-hour shifts, recording your findings on laptop computers. No experience is required for this or any other activities. There are informal daily discussions of the data and its significance.

You camp, two or three to a tent, in one of several local campgrounds and cook communally over fires and stoves. Hot showers are available at a U.S. Forest Service facility

a half hour away. The hiking involved, especially in the May and early June trips, is rigorous and physically demanding; smokers are advised not to join. *Earthwatch, 680 Auburn St., Box 403FD, Watertown, MA 02272-9924, tel. 617/926-8200 or 800/776-0188, fax 617/926-8532. May–Aug.: 19 days, $1,195. Sign up as far in advance as possible.*

THE MIDWEST

MICHIGAN **Loons of the Great Lakes.** The modern loon has inhabited the earth for 10 million years, and its relatives date back 50 million years, but today the loons of the Great Lakes region are in trouble. Their number has been dwindling, and, more distressing, dead loons have been found to have high levels of mercury in their blood.

This is bad enough for the poor loon, but it may be bad news for its neighbors as well. Project director David Evers notes that loons are an indicator species, meaning their welfare serves as a barometer of the entire ecosystem's health. In order to better read that barometer, scientists need more information about the noble bird, its demographics, and its tolerance for mercury.

Toward that end, Evers is looking for birdwatchers—serious bird-watchers—to join him at the Whitefish Point Bird Observatory in the Seney National Wildlife Refuge in a swamp south of Lake Superior, between Munising and Newberry. After a day of field training, your team of four to six volunteers whiles away the remaining nine full days at observation stations in the brush, where you can sit comfortably and watch the loons through binoculars and spot scopes. Strenuous activity is not involved. "Extreme patience and alertness are required," Evers says, and he means it. The expected work week is 40 hours. You're given a list of 20 normal behaviors, such as courtship, nest building, foraging, locomotion, resting, preening, and chick rearing, and you check off the behavior each time the loon you're observing does it.

Teams working in June and July set out in motorboats with nets to assist in capturing the birds. Captured birds are banded and weighed, and blood samples are drawn. Your job is largely to assist the researchers by holding the spotlights and the birds themselves, once they're in the boat.

A furnished house within 15 minutes of the refuge is your home for the 12 days. Usually just two people share each bedroom. Volunteers and staff share the responsibility of preparing meals, which might consist of spaghetti, a barbecue, or a local specialty such as whitefish. Evers's research partner, ornithologist Jim Paruk, plays the guitar and encourages other pickers and strummers to bring their instruments.

The song of the loon is loud enough to carry over 200 acres and varied enough to carry a best-selling album (*Voices of the Loon* sold over 80,000 copies). "When in June 1987 the last dusky seaside sparrow died, the extinction merited a news story here and there," wrote nature writer Sue Hubbell. "But when bad things happen to loons, and they do, we raise a ruckus." Long live the loon. *Earthwatch, 680 Auburn St., Box 403FD, Watertown, MA 02272-9924, tel. 617/926–8200 or 800/776–0188, fax 617/926–8532. May–Aug.: 12 days, $1,195. Sign up at least 2 months in advance.*

MICHIGAN **Moose, Meet Wolf.** In 1949, wolves from Canada crossed an ice floe and moved to moose-infested Isle Royale National Park. Rather than decimating the moose population, the wolves stabilized it and allowed the island's overgrazed vegetation to recover. A famous U.S. National Park Service study of the animals' symbiotic relationship began in 1958; this Earthwatch project is a continuation of that study. It yields evidence of the essential nature of wolf predation, at a time when wolves are once again being hunted from the air.

Those who come hoping to run with the wolves, be forewarned: Volunteers spend their days doing one thing—hiking the island looking for moose bones. About 2,400

dead moose have been recovered in this fashion in the past 35 years. Teams of up to five search for the bones and bring them back to home base. Most data recording (bones are analyzed for disease and decay) is done by a staff assistant.

Dr. Rolf Peterson, a Michigan Technological University professor of wildlife ecology who heads the program, takes great pains to warn all comers of the strenuous, demanding nature of moose-bone hunting. This is not a routine backpacking trip; in your search for bones you go over and under fallen trees, march through wetlands, traipse over beaver dams, and, in general, get wet and cold, all the while carrying 40 pounds on your back. There is no electricity or hot showers at the campsite, and toilets are of the pit type. This trip defines roughing it. Because you have to carry the food, meals are comprised of lightweight grains and powdered drinks. An oatmeal or granola breakfast is usually accompanied by coffee, cocoa, or Tang; lunch may be a hearty gorp mix, and dinner is warm and instant.

What has kept volunteers coming back for more than 30 years is the natural beauty of the island. The nation's least-visited national park outside of Alaska, Isle Royale is surrounded by the cold waters of Lake Superior. It is a haven for birds, beavers, wolves, and, of course, moose—a little piece of Eden in the Great Lakes region. If long days in primal nature appeal to you, and you don't mind getting wet and dirty, this is the week for you. Think of how good that first hot shower will feel. *Earthwatch, 680 Auburn St., Box 403FD, Watertown, MA 02272-9924, tel. 617/926–8200 or 800/776–0188, fax 617/926–8532. May–Aug.: 7 days, $750. Sign up 2–3 months in advance.*

MINNESOTA **The Lone Wolf and Its Associates.** What about that lone wolf, anyway? Does it really exist? One hypothesis of this project's leaders is that wolves traveling *from* the den tend to run with pack members, while those *returning* come in alone.

When do they lose their companions, and why? What effect does weather have on the predatory patterns of the wolf? Project leaders David Mech, Lori Schmidt, and John Terwilliger, who have extensive experience with wolves and/or the Great Lakes region, also hypothesize that wolves tend to travel less when air temperatures and wind speeds are high, but they are unaffected by rain. Go figure.

This project is being conducted in northeast Minnesota, near Lake Superior. Most of the work is radio-tracking timber wolves from one of several tracking vans. The U.S. Fish and Wildlife Service continuously livetraps and radio-collars the wolves; the agency allows Earthwatch researchers to monitor them. What is learned about the timber wolves and their habits as predators aids our understanding of the animal and ultimately will have an effect on its survival.

The trip begins with several days of orientation for the group of 7 to 10 volunteers. During this time, you learn the reasons for the study and are generally exposed to wolf culture and research. You get training in radiotelemetry, and you visit abandoned den sites. Later in the week, most days are spent tracking the wolves in six- to eight-hour shifts from 5 AM to 9 PM. The days are long but not particularly strenuous; patience and a good sense of humor will stand you in good stead here.

You stay at Timber Wolf Lodge, on a campus of Vermillion Community College, in Ely, Minnesota. There are 10 cabins that each sleep two to four and have a bathroom with hot shower as well as a kitchen. Cooking is the shared responsibility of staff and volunteers. There is some off-duty time to take advantage of the abundant fishing, canoeing, and hiking possibilities. As in most of life's endeavors, the ability to amuse yourself is a must. *Earthwatch, 680 Auburn St., Box 403FD, Watertown, MA 02272-9924, tel. 617/926–8200 or 800/776–0188, fax 617/ 926–8532. Mid-June–late Aug.: 13 days, $1,395. Sign up 4 months in advance.*

THE SOUTHWEST

TEXAS **Rock and Roll in Big Bend.** The jagged landscape of Big Bend National Park was created by volcanoes, and now, 34 million years later, it is an ideal place to study caldera formation. This trip is an amateur geologist's dream come true: You help scientists analyze the exposed layers of the earth's crust to predict the long- and short-term effects that volcanic explosions have on the earth's surface. You take rock samples and measure fragments, and you learn to use a magnetometer to measure magnetic field intensity.

Dr. Tim Duex of the University of Southwestern Louisiana specializes in igneous petrology, the study of rocks that have been melted. He is joined by Dr. Dan Tucker and Dr. Gary Kinsland—specialists in structural geology and geophysics, respectively—in the Big Bend country, where the team is working toward understanding what geologic events resulted in the formation of the Sierra Quemada Caldera, a 3-mile-wide, remote caldera that was largely uncharted until now.

The Big Bend area, though located within the United States, is more reminiscent of central Mexico, or the moon. It has a desert climate, with mostly clear, sunny days. Daytime shade temperatures are usually in the 50s in winter; in May, the mercury could climb above 100°F. You work at elevations of 4,000 to 5,000 feet in rough, barren terrain.

Three to ten volunteers form two groups. One team camps in the caldera, where it performs gravity and magnetic surveys, while the second team travels throughout the park measuring volcanic fragments and collecting rock samples. Halfway through the 10-day trip, the teams switch jobs so that everyone is given the opportunity to do everything.

The group culture here is tight: Your team eats, sleeps, and scrabbles together. While in the caldera, you camp in tents, which you or other volunteers bring, and the rest of the time you usually stay in a house maintained by the Park Service. The house has three double rooms, a kitchen, electricity, and hot and cold running water. If this house is unavailable for some reason, you camp in park campgrounds. Cooking responsibilities are shared, but most of what you consume is dried or freeze-dried.

Although the project briefing from Earthwatch makes the conditions sound almost transcendental, be forewarned: This desert landscape is treacherous. Trips are run in the winter and early spring to beat the ungodly heat; even so, dehydration and loss of electrolytes are a real concern. You should be in good physical condition. Persons with respiratory and/or heart problems would be at risk. And we haven't even begun to talk about the flora. "Almost every plant in the area wants a piece of your hide," say the organizers. "Some take it, others cling to it, and still others enter it." *Earthwatch, 680 Auburn St., Box 403FD, Watertown, MA 02272-9924, tel. 617/926–8200 or 800/776–0188, fax 617/926–8532. Jan.–May.: 10 days, $1,195. Sign up 2–3 months in advance.*

THE ROCKIES

COLORADO **How to Fix Nitrogen.** The mystery: The plant life of the American Southwest is abundant despite the arid climate and the limited amount of nutrients in the soil. The thesis: Nitrogen-fixing shrubs, such as the bitterbrush, which abound in the Southwest's piñon-juniper woodland, convert the relatively abundant nitrogen into ammonium, the soil nutrient responsible for the aforementioned abundance of plant life.

This project, sponsored by the University Research Expeditions Program, concentrates on studying the mesa plant community of Mesa Verde and Crow Canyon, in the southwest part of Colorado, but it also touches on another mystery: the disappearance of the Anasazi, who inhabited the area from AD 600 to nearly 1400. Why did the Anasazi move on to new territory after living here for 800 years? Was their departure linked to these shrubs? Pollen records suggest that Anasazi agricultural fields were established by clear-cutting these woodlands, and scientists hypothesize that this may ultimately have had an adverse effect on their crops.

The stage here is the mesa country of the famed Four Corners region of southwestern Colorado. You work in two teams of four to six volunteers, the first excavating roots with Dr. Alison Berry near Crow Canyon Archaeological Center, and the second measuring plants with Dr. Lisa Floyd-Hanna at Mesa Verde. Fieldwork begins at 8 AM and continues until 12:30. The afternoon heat forces the teams indoors after lunch; lab work and the recording of data fill the day. You learn about the Anasazi from archaeological researchers at Crow Canyon through lectures and trips to local museums, and you visit both Mesa Verde and Crow Canyon Anasazi sites.

If you want to help with this study, you should be in good health and not too sensitive to insects: The gnats drive some participants nuts. After assembling at Durango Airport, the volunteers proceed to Crow Canyon, where you stay in dormitory rooms and eat in the cafeteria. At Mesa Verde, you bunk in two- or three-person tents and cook meals in the field as a team. You can get college credit for this work. *University Research Expeditions Program, University of California, Berkeley, CA 94720, tel. 510/ 642–6586. Late June–early July: 12 days, $1,245. Sign up 2 months in advance.*

IDAHO **Meet the Mountain Lion.** Is it actually possible for mountain lions and people to get along? Human intrusion on what was once mountain lion turf has resulted in habitat fragmentation, a term used to describe a situation in which a species' habitat range is divided by human development. This has had some dire consequences: Mountain lions feed on cattle and horses, causing ranchers to hunt the lions down; and within the mountain lion community, rates of inbreeding and infanticide increase. That's right—mountain lions sometimes eat their young.

By tagging and monitoring these animals, scientists seek to determine how the mountain lion survives when its habitat is non-continuous. They hope to gain a better understanding of the effects and consequences of habitat fragmentation on the mountain lion and, by extrapolation, on other large predators.

Working in winter, in rugged country near Pocatello, Idaho, and the Utah border, teams of six to eight researchers and volunteers capture and radio-collar mountain lions. In summer, other groups of six to eight researchers and volunteers monitor those lions, keeping track of where they go and what they eat.

Teams working from January to February have a tougher go of it. They search the area for fresh kills—usually young deer—and then, with the help of local trackers and their hounds, follow, capture, and tag the lions responsible. To participate, you must be in good shape and able to hike up and down mountain slopes in the snow; it helps to have experience reading maps.

The summer teams work from July through September, radio-monitoring tagged lions. This means lots of time standing on hillsides, watching a monitor to see where the lions go (you get to know your teammates *very* well), and recording compass bearings of the lions. You are taught the necessary compass- and map-reading skills during orientation. You also learn to use a field guide to identify plants on predation sites, information that is recorded on a computer and used to determine the relationship between the size of a patch of vegetation and its usefulness as a hiding spot for mountain lions on the prey.

The work day in winter is long, starting at 5 AM and running until 9 PM. In summer, volunteers begin working the eight-hour shift at 9 AM. The winter crew stays in a ranch house owned by one of the houndmen, and meals tend to be heartier than those offered in summer, with lots of stews for dinner. Summer volunteers camp out in several two- and three-person tents and cook over an open campfire—pancakes for breakfast and meat and potatoes for dinner. In both seasons, cold sandwiches, vegetables, and fruit are eaten in the field. Earthwatch staff will lead volunteers on hikes for fun when time permits.

Esprit de corps is an important part of this project; principal investigators Dr. John Laundre, research associate and visiting assistant professor at Purdue University and Idaho State University, and Dr. Donald Streubel, professor of biology at Idaho State University, have a great love of mountain lions, and by the end of the week, so do you. *Earthwatch, 680 Auburn St., Box 403FD, Watertown, MA 02272-9924, tel. 617/926–8200 or 800/776–0188, fax 617/926–8532. Jan.–Feb.: 7 days, $1,295. July–Oct.: 10 days, $1,295. Sign up as far in advance as possible for winter sessions, 2-3 months for summer sessions.*

MONTANA **Living Crow Culture.** Your work for this Smithsonian project may include intertribal dancing with the Crow people until 3 AM, an important part of the annual Crow Fair and Family Reunion, held on the reservation near Billings since 1913. This event brings the Crow together to dance, renew acquaintances, and rejoice in their culture.

For several years, Dr. Charlene James-Duguid, a cultural anthropologist with the Smithsonian, has been collecting data on contemporary Crow culture at the fair, creating an extensive anthropological record of the community. You help with this work by interviewing people and recording the events and experiences of the fair.

Dr. James-Duguid trains you in social science research methods—interviewing, observing, and recording techniques. Then you meet with members of the community to talk about a variety of topics, including family history, work, social relationships, and the adaptation of traditional ways to meet contemporary needs. You also take part in activities at the fair and record your observations. The data is then gathered and given to the National Anthropological Archives of the Smithsonian and to the Crow community.

Groups consist of 15 to 20 volunteers, who stay at local motels and eat mostly traditional Crow foods at the fair, including fried bread and Indian tacos. Although you don't need any previous anthropological experience, Dr. James-Duguid emphasizes the need for patience and flexibility. Because the Crow view time differently from most of us, those who adhere strictly to schedules may be frustrated. This is a crash course in anthropology, a rare glimpse into contemporary Native American culture, and an excellent way to gain an appreciation of the trials and tribulations of field research. *Smithsonian Research Expeditions, The Smithsonian Associates, 490 L'Enfant Plaza, SW, Suite 4210, Washington, D.C. 20560, tel. 202/287–3210, fax 202/287–3244. Mid-Aug.: 7 days, $1,500. Price does not include all meals; sign up by March 15.*

MONTANA **The Study of Streams.** Tamer than rivers and less majestic than lakes, small streams are nonetheless important in western ecosystems. For this Yellowstone Ecosystem Studies (YES) project, you are encouraged to get your feet wet while helping researchers to understand how disturbances in the landscape, such as fires, erosion, and pollution, affect streams and the neighboring habitats.

You join research directors Andrew Marcus and Wayne Minshall as they explore the stream ecology of either Cache Creek (in 11 days) or Soda Butte Creek (in 8 days), two streams that enter the Lamar Valley in Yellowstone National Park. The scenery here is spectacular, and the fish are usually biting, so bring your rod and be sure to get a fishing license. You rub antlers with bison, elk, moose, and antelope, and the Lamar Valley is no stranger to bears and coyotes.

Each group of up to eight volunteers begins with basic training, when you collect sediment samples from flowing streams, measure the depth of pools, and estimate the fish population. You use a variety of research equipment, including traditional nets and sieves as well as hand-held computers that show a map of the area and indicate your location as you hike. This is done by transmitting a signal via satellite. You would probably never expect to see yourself vacuuming algae off river rocks, and neither would the buffalo beside you. You're in the field between 7:30 AM and 3 PM most days, and you must be able to walk up to 4 miles in that time.

You're in good hands with the research directors. Marcus has been involved in wilderness expeditions since he was two; he accompanied his father, a geographer, on research trips in high alpine settings from New Zealand to Nepal. Minshall is recognized as an international authority in the field of stream ecology; he was collecting data from the water while the Yellowstone fires raged in 1988.

The two leaders expect you to have fun. In your free time you can hike, fish, tour Bozeman, or simply sleep. On the Cache Creek you must hike 8 miles in and sleep in two-person tents at a campground in Yellowstone backcountry. On the Soda Butte Creek trip you are treated to two cabins with bunk beds, shower, kitchenette, and refrigerator in Cooke City. All meals are prepared by a staff cook using a propane stove. It's basic meat and potatoes with some vegetarian options.

You're going to get wet while working on this project, and you have to be prepared for both hot and cold weather; even in the summer, snow is not unheard of.

YES, formerly the Yellowstone Project, is the brainchild of Montana State University professor Robert Crabtree. The organization, which also tracks coyotes, birds, and grizzlies and conducts alpine lake surveys in the national park, is famous for disseminating its research. *Yellowstone Ecosystem Studies, Box 6640, Bozeman, MT 59771, tel.*

406/587–7758, fax 406/587–7590. Aug.: 8 days, $995; 11 days, $1,095. Sign up at least 2 weeks in advance.

MONTANA **Tracking the Coyote with Computers.** While many animal-tracking vacations make use of such time-tested tools of the trade as compass, binoculars, and field notebook, the Yellowstone Ecosystems Studies (YES) nine-day Little Wolf project gives you hands-on experience with equipment of the '90s: palmtop computers. Used in conjunction with traditional tracking devices, such as radio equipment and spotting scopes, these handheld PCs allow researchers to record the pack size, litter size, and den behavior of the wily coyote and transmit the information from the field directly to orbiting satellites so that the data can be shared by land management agencies, academic institutions, and nature writers.

The project's main objective is to figure out if coyotes have filled the niche in Yellowstone National Park that was vacated by the gray wolf. You and a group of up to nine other volunteers work with seasoned research biologists in locating den sites and then recording the social and feeding behavior of coyotes. You leave for the field at 7 AM and return at 4:30 PM, and you must be able to hike in moderate terrain. At least one full day is left open for you to enjoy the park however you see fit—hiking, biking, fishing, and more.

Accommodations are in Cooke City, Montana, in either a house or cabin (it varies from year to year). Usually two or three volunteers are assigned to a single bedroom, and bathrooms are shared. There is a staff cook, but volunteers are encouraged to help prepare meals. You might eat pizza, pasta salad, or barbecue chicken. You're shuttled in a Suburban to Yellowstone, a ride that could take 15 minutes or an hour, depending on where the coyotes are expected to be. *Yellowstone Ecosystem Studies, Box 6640, Bozeman, MT 59771, tel. 406/587–7758, fax 406/587–7590. Mid-May–mid-June: 9 days, $995. Sign up 2 weeks in advance.*

THE WEST COAST

CALIFORNIA **Bobcats and Foxes near the Big City.** San Francisco comedian Bob "Bobcat" Goldthwaite was probably unaware when he took that sobriquet that there was another bobcat in the vicinity, but right across the bay, where Marin County meets the Golden Gate Bridge, there are lots of them—along with gray foxes, deer, seals, even mountain lions.

The idyllic preserve known as the Golden Gate National Recreation Area (GGNRA), 750,000 acres of unsullied nature, wraps around San Francisco's northern and western shoreline and is just minutes from downtown. The extraordinary natural diversity of the place sets it apart from other wilderness areas and makes it an ideal place to study wildlife. This Earthwatch project, called California Carnivores, concentrates on the area's bobcat and gray fox populations. Its purpose is to learn more about how these two animals interact with each other and how the local human population affects them.

As a volunteer, you spend 13 days assisting project directors Dr. Judd Howell and Seth Riley as they radio-track the cat and the fox, watching the animals as they rest during the day and as they hunt and roam at night. Carnivore research is demanding and time-consuming: Your work day begins at 8 AM, when you're given your field assignment for the day, and ends after dusk. Up to 10 volunteers can sign up for each session, and they are divided into teams of two. You do a lot of hiking up and down rocky slopes, so a little aerobic preparation wouldn't hurt. You learn how and where to place cameras to film the animals and how to collect and examine the film. Some volunteers are chosen to assist in capturing and radio-collaring additional bobcats and foxes. The information you gather is used to plot the movements and habits of each species.

The housing for this project is primo: the Headlands Institute, located in the GGNRA's Ft. Mason, a former military installation at the Marin Headlands. It contains class-rooms, two dormitories with rooms that accommodate four to six people, and a dining hall. The views of the bay and the bridge are unsurpassed. Earthwatch is just one group that uses the institute, so you can expect to meet other boarders from all over the world, from kids to senior citizens.

Breakfasts and such basic dinners as spaghetti and broiled chicken are prepared by the Headlands Institute's experienced chef, and the staff makes bag lunches—cold cuts, peanut butter, and cheese, as well as fruit and yogurt for the field. At least two evenings are set aside for enjoying the pleasures of San Francisco, which, for lovers of good food and music, remain legion. *Earthwatch, 680 Auburn St., Box 403FD, Watertown, MA 02272-9924, tel. 617/926–8200 or 800/776–0188, fax 617/926–8532. Feb.–May: 13 days, $995. June–Sept.: 13 days, $1,295. Sign up 2 months in advance.*

CALIFORNIA **Look to the Skies.** When you tire of studying the earth and its inhabitants, you can join the Smithsonian in studying the stars. Or should we say the suns? On this seven-day expedition you work on the HK Project, a study begun in 1966 to learn more about how the ebb and flow of our Sun's sunspot cycles (periods of intense magnetism) affect climate and, possibly, global warming. Because a comprehensive study of the sun's 11-year cycle would take centuries, scientists are studying a group of similar stars to gather information on a wide range of astronomic behaviors.

Your work is done at Mount Wilson Observatory, founded in 1904 at the crest of the San Gabriel Mountains in the Angeles National Forest. The observatory has been the scene of some great moments in astronomy: It was here that Edwin Hubble discovered the expanding universe that so panicked the young Woody Allen in *Annie Hall.*

As an "apprentice astronomer" for the HK Project, you are taught how to measure the magnetism of sunlike stars. Your observations aid in estimating the ages of stars, data

that is used to determine the oldest stars and the ones most likely to have developed technical intelligence within their system. That's right: The HK Project is part of the Search for Extraterrestrial Intelligence (SETI) program.

This is another good project for insomniacs, since the best viewing is done in the wee hours of the morning; some volunteers choose to stay up all night. Although no special education is required—astrophysicist Dr. Sallie Baliunas teaches novices their way around the telescope—an interest in astronomy is a must.

You and the other 5–10 volunteers are housed in private rooms with shared baths in a historic building on the observatory grounds. Cooking is communal, and there are excursions to a local grocery store to buy food, which is not included in the cost of the trip.

Like most astronomers, you sleep late, eat breakfast, and attend afternoon lectures; some day trips are scheduled to local labs and museums. Free time can be spent in the observatory library or hiking in the mountains. After dinner, you settle in for a long night of sky-watching. Onward and upward. *Smithsonian Research Expeditions, The Smithsonian Associates, 490 L'Enfant Plaza, SW, Suite 4210, Washington, D.C. 20560, tel. 202/287–3210, fax 202/287–3244. Mid-July and mid-Sept.: 7 days, $1,150. Price does not include meals; sign up 5 months in advance.*

CALIFORNIA **New Dolphins in Monterey Bay.** For years, Monterey Bay has been home to Pacific white-sided dolphins and harbor porpoises, but 10 years ago, bottlenose dolphins began to appear. Surfer and marine biologist Tom Norris was the first to record sightings of the bottlenose and the first to suggest that the bottlenose presence in the bay might be permanent. With a small grant from the National Marine Fishery Service, he started the Coast Dolphin Project, which continues to this day under the auspices of Earthwatch and the directorship of Daniela Feinholz.

The goal of this project is to learn more about bottlenose dolphins in the wild and the differences in social structure between these California bottlenose and those found in Florida. Since Norris's first casual sightings, Feinholz has discovered that the Monterey Bay bottlenose dolphins are part of a larger population that stretches down to the Mexican border. It seems that these dolphins shifted their range as a result of El Niño—a warm Pacific current that appeared in the early '80s.

Your job as a volunteer is to help survey the dolphins in Monterey Bay. Working from a base in Moss Landing, your team of three or four volunteers sails each day on a 15-foot Boston Whaler into the bay, where you sight and identify dolphins and record your findings. For reasons of safety, you must be able to swim. By the end of the expedition, Feinholz boasts, volunteers can evaluate dorsal fins and identify specific dolphins, photograph moving dolphins, and even develop their own black-and-white film. You also learn to collect data, work a Loran-C (a sort of electronic boat-locater), and maintain a database on a PC.

While you're working, you share quarters in a rented three-bedroom house in nearby Castroville or Moss Landing. This house, which varies from trip to trip, acts as project headquarters. Feinholz takes food seriously—good food is essential for her good morale. Born in Italy, she likes to serve lots of pasta. Staff and volunteers take turns cooking, but a few nights are given over to the abundant local eateries. Your free time— at least two days out of the two weeks—can be spent sea kayaking, biking, hiking, and enjoying the magnificent Monterey Bay area in any number of ways. *Earthwatch, 680 Auburn St., Box 403FD, Watertown, MA 02272-9924, tel. 617/926–8200 or 800/776– 0188, fax 617/926–8532. Mar.–Oct.: 14 days, $1,595. Price does not include meals on Sat. and Sun.; sign up 2–3 months in advance.*

WASHINGTON **Don't Call Them Killer Whales.** They're orcas, as any kid who saw *Free Willy* can tell you. In fact, Kenneth Bal-

comb, vice-president of the Center for Whale Research, was involved in the campaign to free the whale that played Willy, but that's another story. When not working for the liberation of movie whales, Balcomb spends at least part of his year in Puget Sound, counting orcas. Seems there used to be more of them than there are now.

Between 1966 and 1976, 50 orcas in Puget Sound were either killed or removed to provide specimens for marine parks around the world. In 1976, Balcomb was asked to take an orca census, and his findings revealed that there were only 68 of the noble mammals left. Since then, Balcomb's Orca Survey has tallied the population on an annual basis, and since 1988, this census project has been run in conjunction with Earthwatch. Although the population of orcas has grown to 91, Balcomb still needs volunteers to help count dorsal fins and work toward gaining an understanding of the factors that affect orca numbers.

Your team of 5 to 10 volunteers and four staff members begins work off the shore of San Juan Island at 9 AM and ends about 5 PM. Weather permitting, half of you cruise the Sound aboard a trimaran and a small motorboat, photographing whales and recording your sightings in logbooks. You also assist in recording the animals' underwater mewlings. The other half of your group stays at the house and either assists with developing the photos or enters the data into a field computer. Teams rotate from day to day. The results of the survey are published in scientific papers as well as in lay texts such as *Life* and *Newsweek*.

Your base is a waterfront house on San Juan Island, a popular summer vacation retreat. There are shared rooms and baths in the house, but many people prefer to sleep in sleeping bags on the porch, which overlooks the water and can accommodate everyone. Meals are prepared by the staff with one volunteer each evening; expect fresh fish, crab, and shellfish, according to the season, as well as vegetables from the house garden. You eat in the house's dining room or outside at picnic tables behind the house.

This is a trip for the amateur naturalist; you can spend your free time admiring both the sea life of Puget Sound and the other wildlife surrounding it, including eagles, hawks, deer, raccoons, and rabbits. For those with a less rural leaning, there's an artsy movie theater in Friday Harbor, 12 miles away, and live music at a nearby tavern.

Balcomb says you should be prepared for boring, rainy days when you don't see any whales, so that you are ecstatic on those clear, sunny days when all the whales show. Those prone to seasickness should think twice about this trip. *Earthwatch, 680 Auburn St., Box 403FD, Watertown, MA 02272-9924, tel. 617/926–8200 or 800/776–0188, fax 617/926–8532. June–Sept.: 10 days, $1,795. Sign up 2–3 months in advance.*

WASHINGTON **The Grizzly Bear Truth.** The much-maligned and mythologized grizzly bear once roamed much of the western United States, but hunting, trapping, and loss of habitat have resulted in its virtual decimation. The grizzly now survives in less than 2% of its former range, and the North Cascades are part of that territory. A critically important grizzly population has been discovered here, and Wildlands Studies needs your help in determining its exact size and researching its habits.

Your group of 12 volunteers assembles in Seattle, then carpools to central Washington, where you begin hiking across the North Cascades, with their incredible views of granite peaks and flowing glaciers. You spend the first few days in backcountry field workshops, learning about bear ecology, research techniques, and backcountry survival, and also familiarizing yourself with the forested landscapes and wildlife populations in the Wildlands study area. Project leader is Bill Gaines, a specialist in the conservation of endangered species and the leader of another Wildland Studies project, the popular Wolf Habitat study (*see below*).

For the next 10 days, you assist Gaines and his wildlife specialists while backpacking through the Cascades, one of the nation's greatest mountain ranges, with jagged peaks, glaciated canyons, hanging valleys, and mountain lakes. You collect evidence of bear habitation, such as hair and scat, and document track and den locations. You also observe bear activity patterns and behavior. All findings and observations are recorded in field journals and provided to wildlife biologists involved in the preservation of the grizzly.

This trip is not for the faint of heart. Summer mountain weather runs the gamut from 90°F to the occasional snow squall. You spend 6 to 10 hours in the field, and although on most days you hike only a mile or less, every few days you must hike 5 miles to a new site. Prior research experience is not required, but you must bring binoculars and field notebooks as well as your own camping (you sleep in the backcountry) and hiking gear. A good pair of broken-in hiking boots is essential. Food is purchased locally, during scheduled group shopping trips, and cooking duties are shared.

The last two days, still in the backcountry, are devoted to workshops summing up and evaluating what has been learned. The outing ends on a festive note, with a guest speaker and a barbecue. San Francisco State University will give you credit for participating. *Wildlands Studies, 3 Mosswood Circle, Cazadero, CA 95421, tel. 707/632–5665. Mid-July: 14 days, $385. Price does not include $50 application fee or $175 for food, gas, and miscellaneous expenses; project fee due by May 25. Sign up 1–4 months in advance.*

WASHINGTON **Will the Wolf Survive?** The timber wolf (*Canis lupus*) once had the greatest range of any living terrestrial animal—with the exception of human beings. While the latter has done more than any other creature to eliminate the former, it is heartening to know that some of us are now cheering the wolf's ultimate survival. Because of the pressures of development and habitat loss, these animals have been driven to near extinction in the lower 48, and hunters have been recruited to decimate their numbers in Alaska. But field reports indicate that wolves are making a tenuous return in the mountains of Montana, Idaho, and Washington, venturing into their former habitats through narrow wildland corridors between mountains that border the United States and Canada.

Since 1982, Wildlands Studies has been monitoring the wolf's return in Idaho and Montana; in 1990, the organization launched a similar study in Washington. Headed up by Bill Gaines, U.S. Forest Service wildlife biologist and an authority on endangered species, this study is being conducted in the Cascade Mountain Wildlands. It is one of the most popular programs Wildlands offers, and small wonder: Not only do volunteers get to hike through the spectacular Cascades, but they also spend a good deal of time conducting a howling survey after the sun goes down. This means that you and the other volunteers hike and drive up backcountry service roads while howling like wolves to see what responds.

Your days are spent in more traditional pursuits: searching for tracks, scat, and other physical evidence of wolves. You collect samples and record your findings in field journals. The group of 12 generally sticks together, but for the wolf howling surveys, you break up into pairs. During the typical wolf program, research is done from both tented base camps near roads and on short backpacking trips. Free time may find you fishing or simply communing with nature.

No previous research experience is required to participate, but most volunteers are 18 to 35 years old. Curiosity and a sense of humor come in handy. All necessary skills, including howling, are taught on site under the direction of wildlife specialists from Wolf Haven International, an organization dedicated to the memory of wolves, and the U.S. Forest Service. Compass and map reading are also covered.

Camping and cooking responsibilities are shared, with meals prepared at base camp on portable stoves or over campfires. You may eat freeze-dried food, pasta, fresh vegetables, dried fruits, soups, nuts, and granola. Participants bring their own tents or share with others. The temperature in summer is usually in the 70s or 80s, with occasional showers; be sure to bring rain gear and clothing that can be layered. Many of the locations surveyed are accessible only by car, and cars are supplied by the volunteers, so getting accepted to work on the Wolf Habitat project is like getting a date in high school: Your chances are a whole lot better if you've got wheels. San Francisco State University gives you credit for joining this one. *Wildlands Studies, 3 Mosswood Circle, Cazadero, CA 95421, tel. 707/632–5665. Mid-Aug.: 14 days, $385. Price does not include $50 application fee or $100–$250 for food, gas, miscellaneous expenses, and some special research equipment; project fee due by May 25. Sign up 1–4 months in advance.*

ALASKA

SOUTHEAST **Words to Match My Mountains.** Like Alaska itself, the Wrangell Mountains Project is outsize and overblown compared to the other projects in this chapter. It pushes the envelope in terms of time (five weeks) and expense ($2,550, plus airfare), but it is well worth it, especially for those interested in science and writing.

Anyone who's ever been subjected to a first-year writing class has had to begin with the fundamentals: Describe a paper clip, a classroom, the person sitting beside you. Those enrolled in the Wrangell Mountains Project are faced with a more suitable challenge: Describe the Wrangell-St. Elias National Park and Preserve. Twelve times the size of Yosemite, surrounded by peaks that reach 16,390 feet and the continent's most active glaciers, this park is on the outer edge of Alaska's tourist future.

While most of the land within the park boundaries is federally owned, some lands around the Gold Rush–era town of McCarthy, where the project is based, are privately owned. Local landowners retain their subsistence hunting and access rights; feelings about tourism are, let us say, mixed. Part of the project's goal is to educate tourists and perhaps even a few locals about their surroundings. The project also aims to explore the complex geological, ecological, and cultural elements that have shaped this landscape, and it touches on the critical management issues that will determine the region's future.

Fourteen volunteers interested in ecology, botany, geology, and land management hone their research skills by observing nature, investigating nature in the field, and writing reports, including a required term paper. Volunteers write descriptive material and guidelines suggested for the future management of the park. All of this work is donated to the park and the project library.

The project includes two extensive (and sometimes rigorous) journeys into the backcountry. The first takes you along the 25-mile-long Kennicott Glacier, upon which you travel and camp. Studying the glacier, you and the other volunteers reconstruct ecological and geological history. You learn to recognize signs of ecological change in the rock, ice, and streams, and record your findings in logbooks.

The second trip brings you high into the alpine regions of the mountain landscapes, where you travel off-trail through meadows and tundra, in the playing fields of the golden eagle and the grizzly bear. During this time, you work on backcountry projects of your own devising, and your report is also given to the park and the project library.

In the program's headquarters is the Old Hardware Store, a National Historic Site. It houses the library and is home to a small number of graduate students, who are not working with you. Here, too, is the big kitchen where meals are cooked and eaten in communal fashion. Expect fresh vegetables, hearty pastas, and soups.

You sleep in tents (provided by some volunteers) along McCarthy Creek and have plenty of time for introspection.

Benjamin Shaine, the program's founder, has been leading research groups into the Wrangell Mountains for 20 years; he wrote a novel, *Alaska Dragon*, which is about the region and its inhabitants. Edward LaChappelle, also a project leader, is a McCarthy resident, claimed to be "one of the world's experts on snow and ice," and a writer as well. San Francisco State University gives you college credit for participating in this project. *Wildlands Studies, 3 Mosswood Circle, Cazadero, CA 95421, tel. 707/632–5665. Mid-July: 35 days, $1,650. Price does not include $900 group expenses; Sign up 2–3 months in advance (program fees due May 25, group expenses due June 1).*

HAWAII

THE BIG ISLAND **How to Identify a Humpback.** Like Shriners returning to Vegas, humpback whales return to the Hawaiian waters every winter, creating the largest concentration of humpbacks in the North Pacific. The whales come back to the Islands with but a single impulse: procreation. Adult males come a-courting, singing long, complex songs to prospective females. And since 1982 Earthwatch volunteers have joined staff researchers from the Kewalo Basin Marine Laboratory to document their annual return.

Some of the objectives of this project, called Humpbacks of Hawaii, vary from year to year, but two goals remain constant: the identification of the whale population by age and sex, and a better understanding of the dynamics of the inter-island whale migration.

One of the project scientists videotapes the whales as they cavort and compete for females underwater, and this footage is reviewed by the team each evening. You and three to six other volunteers assist in sighting and locating whales and recording data in a log. You spend a good portion of your two-week stay on board a 17-foot Boston Whaler equipped with an 88-horsepower outboard engine, taking still photographs of whales when they surface. These photos help to identify whales by such characteristic features as their tails, known as flukes, which are as distinctive as human fingerprints, if somewhat larger. Some of the team members are in contact with the boat by radiotelephone from an elevated sighting station on land.

Back at the rented house that serves as base for the project, you learn how to analyze the photos by matching them with data from previously identified whales. All volunteers take turns working with the boat team, the shore team, and the photographic analysis team.

Days are long: You awake at 7 AM, arrive back at base at 5:30, and then begin cleaning equipment, developing photos, and logging data. The communally cooked dinners—generally consisting of pasta dishes and salads—are followed by briefings and educational lectures. Staff members are knowledgeable about the area. There is at least one full day off, and you are encouraged to take in the Big Island's sights, including Hawaii Volcanoes National Park. Although this trip doesn't require volunteers to be especially fit, those prone to seasickness or sensitive to extensive exposure to heat or sunlight should think twice about joining. *Earthwatch, 680 Auburn St., Box 403FD, Watertown, MA 02272-9924, tel. 617/926-8200 or 800/776-0188, fax 617/926-8532. Late Jan.–Mar.: 13 days, $1,995. Sign up 2–3 months in advance.*

SOURCES

ORGANIZATIONS **Volunteer in Technical Assistance** (1600 Wilson Blvd., Suite 500, Arlington, VA 22209, tel. 703/276–1800) matches your skills with projects in need of volunteers. The **Points of Light Foundation** (1737 H St., NW, Washington, DC 20006, tel. 800/879–5400) can put you in touch with a volunteer center that has community-based projects near you.

PERIODICALS *Earthwatch* magazine is the house organ of Earthwatch (Earthwatch Membership Service, Box 8037, Syracuse, NY 13217, tel. 617/926–8200) and the way to find out about their projects. It's published bimonthly and is slick and (generally) well written. Its "Field Notes" section gives you a quick flavor for a variety of projects.

BOOKS *Shaw Guide to Academic Travel* (Shaw Guides) contains everything from bear treks on the Maine coast to Faulkner seminars in Oxford, Mississippi. *Volunteer Vacations* (Chicago Review Press), by Bill McMillon, is as thorough a guide to all types of volunteer trips as you will find. Its profiles of sponsoring organizations are interspersed with short, lively narratives about the experiences of individual volunteers on specific programs.

ALSO SEE If you want to volunteer, but you would rather build trails or homes than count fins, turn to the chapter on Volunteer Vacations in Public and Community Service. If you're interested in science, but rather not work so hard, look into Environmental Cruises, Nature Camps, or Whale-Watching Cruises.

Volunteer Vacations in Public and Community Service

By M.T. Schwartzman

ould you like to help build a hiking trail that stretches from New York to North Dakota? Or to help remove airplane wreckage from a mountainside crash site? And would you be willing to pay a small fee for the opportunity? If so, maybe a volunteer vacation is for you.

Spending your vacation as a volunteer enables you to give as well as to get, turning hard work into good works and getting a relatively low-cost vacation at the same time. In these days of budget cuts and belt tightening, the need for volunteers is felt in all sorts of places by all sorts of organizations that serve small communities and the public at large. Where and how you contribute depend on what you hope to accomplish. If you want to leave your office routine behind and get outdoors, you can sign on to work as a campground host in a park or to crew on a sailing ship. If you're looking for something a little more "charitable," helping the homeless and rebuilding inner-city housing are among your choices. Public service can also entail working on a model farm, helping run the museum at a state historic site, or donating time at a wildlife sanctuary.

Volunteer positions generally take the form of either construction and maintenance or education, and of the two, the former is by far the more common. Also, because park services are typically short staffed, there are lots of volunteer projects in parks, offered both by nonprofit groups and by the parks themselves. As a result, one of the most plentiful jobs open to volunteers is trail building and maintenance in national and state parks across the country and along the length of the original volunteer-built trail—the Appalachian Trail.

A typical trail-maintenance crew consists of 10 to 20 people, who work out of a backcountry field camp to which they often must hike the first day. Led by one, sometimes two, experienced leaders, crews make camp near the work site for a week or so at a time. The next few days might be spent clearing debris, improving and rerouting an existing trail, or building new trails, followed by a day for rest and relaxation. You might take advantage of the recreational opportunities of the wilderness, such as hiking, fishing, or climbing, or, if you're in a more developed setting, do a little sightseeing. (Though some volunteer projects are very work intensive, the ones listed in this chapter offer a good balance between labor and leisure; this is, after all, your vacation.) Then the cycle repeats—a few more days of work, followed by another day or two off, and finally a return to "civilization."

In return for your time and effort, you generally pay very little. Some volunteer programs charge no fee, while others cost significantly less than a similar nonworking trip. The cost of mounting the project is subsidized by charitable contributions or by

---

M.T. Schwartzman has written about the Appalachian Trail—one of the most popular destinations for volunteers—for the Appalachian Mountain Club's magazine, AMC Outdoors, *and* Fodor's *National Parks and Seashores of the East.*

park budgets. However, the same budget cuts that reduce the number of paid staff also reduce the money available for volunteer programs, and individual projects come and go with funding.

Luckily, there is usually a similar project in a similar or even the same location. For example, the Sierra Club and the American Hiking Society both organized outings to remove airplane wreckage in 1994, and both the Sierra Club and Backcountry Volunteers run an annual trip to Admiralty Island in Alaska. Sometimes groups act as cosponsors; Volunteers for Peace shares projects with both the Appalachian Mountain Club and Habitat for Humanity. In fact, checking around might save you money, since cosponsoring agencies often don't charge the same amount for the same trip (*see* Choosing the Right Project, *below*).

A little-known benefit of volunteering is the chance to meet people from many different backgrounds and cultures. Volunteer vacations are often international in character. On some programs, particularly those offered by Volunteers for Peace, as many as 80% of the volunteers may be from other countries. Many of these foreign visitors want to experience U.S. culture in a more profound way than they could as a tourist; others, like their American counterparts, might just be looking for a way to travel cheaply, to get involved in a particular type of work, or to receive school credit.

The organizations and projects listed below are happy to accommodate all ages, ability levels, interests, and time commitments. So if you're interested in a vacation not just to feel good but to do good, you can do very well indeed by joining the nationwide corps of volunteers. To paraphrase the old advertising slogan, it's the hardest vacation you'll ever love.

CHOOSING THE RIGHT PROJECT

It's important to match the right person to the right project, for both the volunteer's and the project's sakes, so the first order of business, before you apply for anything, is to take stock of your skills and interests. Because many volunteer crews have limited space and are often filled on a first-come, first-served basis, sponsoring agencies usually ask applicants to list several choices; you may very well not get your first or even second pick, so be sure to list only those projects you would truly like to work on. To know that, be ready to ask some questions:

What are my responsibilities? Like any job, you're required to perform certain tasks on a daily or weekly schedule. In addition to the project work, these may include housekeeping or cooking duties at a base camp or communal living quarters.

What are the working conditions like? Locations range from inner cities to wilderness, and work sites can be in offices or museums, dense woods or open fields. If projects are conducted outdoors, make sure you know what the climate is like, and be aware that work usually continues rain or shine.

Is physical work involved? Some, but not all, volunteer work involves manual labor. Find out how strenuous it is, and make sure that your physical fitness is up to the challenge. Keep in mind that trail maintenance is usually very physically demanding and is even harder at high altitudes. For clearing really heavy debris, though, pack animals are often employed.

What's the cost and what's included? Most volunteer programs require that you pay to join. Sometimes, this is a nominal fee to cover the sponsoring organization's administrative costs. Other projects charge up to several hundred dollars to offset the expense of meals or housing. Registration fees are payable in advance, but additional charges may be payable upon arrival at the work site. When there's a fee for the trips listed below, it covers accommodations and all your meals. When there's no fee, such as for government jobs, be sure to find out what's provided and what's not—it varies greatly. Sometimes the same organization even provides different benefits for different jobs. Transportation between your home and the project is never included. You probably need to bring your own work clothes, such as work gloves and boots, and you may be asked to buy and wear a uniform on the job; however, hard hats, safety goggles, and other tools and equipment are generally provided when needed. One of the most important "safety items" to check on is accident insurance. Some projects, usually government-run programs, provide workers' compensation insurance, while others offer no coverage and may require that you carry your own and sign a liability waiver.

One more note about cost: Different organizations that offer similar or even the same projects don't necessarily charge the same amounts. (For example, the difference in cost between two trips to Alaska's Admiralty Island, offered by the Sierra Club and Backcountry Volunteers, is more than $500.) A little shopping around can be worth your while, but make sure you know what's included in each so you're not comparing apples and oranges.

What are the accommodations like? Housing is as varied as the projects and locations where they take place. Primitive cabins or campsites are typical accommodations for backcountry work; there may be no showers or other plumbing, and the work site may be a good hike away. On other trips, home is a tent at a drive-up campground or perhaps a lodge, while in more populated settings, you often find community-style living in a dormitory. Some projects, however, make no provisions for housing, and you must locate your own, although often the sponsor can offer advice on finding a nearby campground or other inexpensive place to stay.

What is the food like? In projects where meals are provided, they differ according to setting. In the backcountry, food is usually packed in and cooked out. Often, it's vegetarian, as much for practical as for philosophical reasons. Cuisine is generally prepackaged but not freeze-dried, and there's usually fresh fruit and vegetables at least for the first few days. Closer to electric-ity, you may find more meat, but meals still run the gamut from home-cooked dinners in a private home to college cafeteria fare. On some projects, you may occasionally find yourself as chief cook and bottle washer, literally, so you and your fellow volunteers might be what determines how good the chow really is. On other trips, such as the Sierra Club's, a cook often accompanies each work crew.

What are the medical facilities like? Accidents happen, especially if you're doing manual labor. If the project is at a remote wilderness site, there needs to be, at a minimum, adequate first-aid materials and a group leader trained in first aid. Some projects, such as those sponsored by the Sierra Club, recruit doctors as volunteers for their trips.

What kind of training or instruction is there? Most volunteer work requires no previous experience, and you are trained on the job in the skill or task to be performed. In some cases, previous experience in the use of certain equipment, such as chain saws, may be preferred.

How much leisure time is there and what are the recreational opportunities? Most programs provide for personal time, but what there is to do depends on the locale. In rural and wilderness settings, you can take advantage of the opportunities for outdoor recreation. In urban jobs, entertainment is more likely to be indoors.

Can I take part if I have a medical condition or dietary restriction? If there are any special circumstances that might put you at risk or be difficult for the organizers to accommodate, be sure to ask ahead of time. For example, in trail building or maintenance, you may anger some bees along the way—not good if you're allergic to bee stings. If you follow a special diet, the food provided may not fit the bill. In both cases, you could bring along what you need (a bee-sting kit and dietary supplements), but if you're going to a remote wilderness site, you may be too limited in what you can carry or too far from medical facilities for it to be practical. A medical examination may be required for participation; if so, find out who pays for it.

Is there a minimum or maximum age? In most programs, participants have ranged from teenagers to septuagenarians; however, because of the physically demanding nature of much of the work, most tend to be in their 20s and 30s. Though organizations do not generally exclude an older prospective volunteer because of a set maximum age, they need to be sure all participants can handle a project's rigors. As for minimums, you must generally be at least 18, but in some cases, younger volunteers are accepted if they are accompanied by an adult or have the signed permission of a parent or legal guardian.

Is there a minimum time commitment? Some volunteer positions, particularly at national or state parks, require that you spend at least two to four weeks in a position. This is especially true for summer volunteers or where extensive training is involved. Most of those listed below, however, require just a week or 10 days.

Is there any religious affiliation? Some volunteer work, especially housing construction and other inner-city projects, is church sponsored, and the day may begin or end with a prayer meeting or other devotion. If you are not particularly devout, this may not be for you.

Do you have references from past volunteers? It's always helpful to ask for references. Talking to people who've worked on a project can help you understand how strenuous the work is, how well run the organization is, how good the food or housing is, or whatever else is important to you. You may not feel like following up on many, or even any, but if a sponsoring organization refuses to give you names, it should put up a red flag. It may also be a good idea to speak to whoever is leading the trip or to someone who led it in the past. Talking to the cook might help, too, if you follow a particular diet.

How long has the project been run? It probably doesn't matter how long a particular project has been running, but it might very well matter how long the organization has been running similar projects. Often, training and logistics are complicated enough that experience is necessary to put on a well-managed project. Talking to current or former trip leaders can give you a sense of how well-organized projects are.

How far in advance do I need to book? This varies by organization and, since many trips are filled on a first-come, first-served basis, by the popularity of the particular project. Where Volunteers for Peace advises you to sign up six weeks in advance, the Sierra Club recommends at least six months. On the other hand, there are many projects with plenty of room for volunteers, and not much advance notice is generally needed.

MAJOR PLAYERS

AMERICAN HIKING SOCIETY Formerly associated with Backcountry Volunteers (*see below*), this Washington-based organization, which lobbies Congress and acts as an environmental advocate on behalf of 100 affiliated clubs, now runs its own volunteer vacations program. Among its most ambitious goals is the construction of the American Discovery Trail, a path that would lead 5,000 miles from the Atlantic to the Pacific. Volunteers do construction and maintenance on a large number of trails, mainly in national parks, though a few trips are centered on the American Discovery Trail. The tasks involved include building bridges and dams, installing fences, planting vegetation, constructing outhouses, and drilling holes for dynamite placement. One group disassembled an abandoned airplane that had been left in a wilderness area.

Rustic settings are a constant, usually in heavily wooded areas in the mountains—some as high as 10,000 feet—and often near a stream or lake. Most trips have base camps with water pumps or wells and outhouses. Volunteers bring their own tents, but food is provided; group meals are cooked over a campfire.

Crew size is 10 to 12 people, and requirements for participation are the same as those for Backcountry Volunteers. There is a $50 registration fee for all trips, which are one or two weeks in length. Insurance is provided by the federal agency supervising the work. In addition to sponsoring its own projects, the society provides information on those offered by other organizations in its directory *Helping Out in the Outdoors* (*see* Sources, *below;* Box 20160, Washington, DC 20041, tel. 703/255–9304, fax 703/255–9308).

APPALACHIAN MOUNTAIN CLUB Founded in 1876, the AMC was a charter member of the Appalachian Trail Conference (*see below*) and is now its biggest member. Since 1919, the club has enlisted volunteers for trail-maintenance programs throughout the Northeast and today keeps up 1,400 miles of trail, including a 350-mile stretch of the Appalachian Trail. Historically, the club's main focus has been on its birthplace, the White Mountains of New Hampshire, but its projects now extend throughout the United States.

AMC volunteers can join one of two basic programs: Volunteer Trail Crews or Trail Service Trips. Volunteer Trail Crew projects run for a week or longer out of five base camps: Camp Dodge in the White Mountains, New Hampshire; Bascom Lodge in the Berkshire Mountains of Massachusetts; Echo Lake Camp in Acadia National Park, Maine; a camp in New York's Catskill Mountains; and the club's newest outdoor center at the Delaware Water Gap National Recreation Area, in New Jersey. Trail Service Trips are 10- to 12-day sojourns at backcountry locations nationwide. Although both programs concentrate on trail maintenance and building, the trail crews have a cushier lifestyle; lodging at the base camps includes electricity and running water, and menus are more varied, with more fresh fruits and vegetables. Members of the trail crews tend to come from the Northeast, since that's where the camps are located, but service trip participants come from all across the country. Weeklong trail crew programs typically cost $35, while service trips average $195. Tools, training, room and board, and most necessary equipment are provided for volunteers in both programs. Insurance is not provided, and volunteers must sign a waiver of liability (5 Joy St., Boston, MA 02108, tel. 617/523–0655).

APPALACHIAN TRAIL CONFERENCE Constructed in the 1920s and '30s, the 2,147-mile Appalachian Trail, which passes through 14 eastern states from Maine to Georgia, was the nation's first national scenic trail and is still the world's longest continuously marked footpath. Founded in 1925 to help build the AT, as it's known, the Appalachian Trail Conference (ATC) currently acts as a coordinator for 32 organizations that help maintain and improve the trail, including moving sections of the original route to newly acquired land. Workers are dispatched to help with local projects in conjunction with the National Park Service, U.S. Forest Service, state agencies, and member clubs.

The ATC divides its volunteer work force into four crews: Southern, Mid Atlantic, Maine, and Vermont. You can work a one- to six-week stint, and no previous trail-building experience is necessary. However, you should be familiar with rustic outdoor living, since accommodations consist of tent camps set up near the work site. The conference provides training, safety gear, tools, and meals. Each seven- or eight-person work crew is led by a staff of one or two, who act as camp coordinator and crew leader. You must be 18 or older and in good physical condition—the manual labor required can be considerable. Over the years, volunteers have come from across the country and around the world, from all sorts of backgrounds and occupations. No fees are charged to sign up or to participate, and insurance is provided by the supervising federal agency—either the park or forest service, depending on the location of the particular trail segment (Box 807, Harpers Ferry, WV 25425, tel. 304/535–6331, fax 304/535–2667).

BACKCOUNTRY VOLUNTEERS A relative newcomer to trail maintenance, Backcountry Volunteers, founded in 1979, conducts much of its physically demanding work in rugged terrain at high altitudes. You must be able to hike 5 to 10 miles a day, supply your own camping equipment, and be prepared to do hard manual labor for 10 days of a two-week vacation. Work teams usually consist of 10 to 12 individuals, led by a volunteer coordinator from Backcountry plus a representative of the supervising agency—that is, the park or forest service. Base camps include a cooking tent and sleeping tents at primitive sites without showers or laundry facilities. Food, often provided by the supervising agency, is standard meat and potatoes supplemented with salads, fruits, and vegetables. Two volunteers assume cooking responsibilities each day.

More than one-third of volunteers are returning alums. You must be at least 18 or have the permission of a parent or legal guardian; those under 16 must be accompanied by an adult. A $40 registration fee is required for all projects—quite inexpensive compared to other agencies that sponsor similar outings. Insurance is provided while you're on the job (Box 86, North Scituate, MA 02060; send a self-addressed stamped envelope).

HABITAT FOR HUMANITY INTERNATIONAL

Founded in 1976, Habitat for Humanity (HHI) became better known when Jimmy Carter's involvement brought the organization national exposure in the early '80s. The group's goal is simple: to eliminate poverty-level housing worldwide using volunteer labor and donated money and materials. Today, HHI conducts projects, nominated by local charitable organizations, in all 50 states and 40 foreign countries. Though secular in its mission, HHI's local partners are often church groups, and the workday may begin or end with prayer.

Volunteering with HHI stretches the definition of a vacation, but the hard work you put in brings immediate and visible results—the construction of a new home for someone who needs it. No carpentry skills are needed; the house leader for each team is either a professional or a very skilled amateur, and a job can be found for people of all ages and abilities. Projects cost $150 to $250, which covers meals and lodging in settings that vary from homes to dorms. Volunteers are covered by accident insurance, but must sign a liability waiver anyway.

One week a year, in mid-July, is designated as House-Raising Week; it includes the Jimmy Carter Work Project, in which the former president and first lady take part. Although the goals and work remain the same, the project moves to a different location each year—a South Dakota Sioux Indian reservation in 1994, south-central Los Angeles in 1995. If you volunteer during this annual building blitz, you may even get a chance to rub elbows, or share nails, with Carter himself (121 Habitat St., Americus, GA 31709, tel. 912/924–6935, fax 912/924–6541).

NATIONAL PARK SERVICE The park service's Volunteers in Parks (VIP) program provides opportunities to work and live in any of the 350 units under the service's jurisdiction. Each park runs its own program. From Maine to Hawaii and Alaska to Florida, in big cities, small towns, and remote wilderness areas, positions are available that are as diverse as their locations. In addition to trail-maintenance worker, you can choose to be a public information officer, living-history actor, brochure writer or designer, campground host, shuttle bus driver, cabinetmaker, librarian, photographer, computer programmer, or teacher. Living and working conditions vary according to your job, and housing is only available at some of the large parks. Some parks reimburse volunteers for out-of-pocket expenses to cover local travel, meals, and uniforms. A medical examination, paid for by the federal government, is required, and you're covered by workers' compensation. You must be 18 or older; younger participants may become VIPs at parks in their own communities or at other sites as part of a family or organized and supervised group (U.S. Dept. of the Interior, Box 37127, Washington, DC 20013, tel. 202/208–4747).

SIERRA CLUB The Sierra Club was founded in 1892 for the purposes of wilderness preservation and restoration and has been running volunteer vacations since 1957. The club's original focus was Yosemite, but today it organizes more than 80 service trips every year to destinations nationwide. Perennial favorites include Denali National Park in Alaska, Chaco Canyon in New Mexico, and Acadia National Park in Maine. Other projects are geographically mobile, such as the North Country Scenic Trail, a planned route that will stretch 2,000 miles from New York to North Dakota by the year 2000, or airplane wreckage removal trips, which rid remote locations of debris as needed.

Most projects are 7- to 10-day outings to secluded sites, where you do trail maintenance, revegetation, cleanup, or campsite restoration. Half of the days are for work, the other half for play. Since training is provided on the job, no special skills are required, but you must be physically fit and supply your own camping equipment. The club provides all other tools and equipment, as well as meals. In fact, the club emphasizes good food perhaps more than any of the other organizations listed. On many outings, the staff includes a cook, who must first attend a wilderness-cooking training seminar and assist on one outing as a trainee. A number of trips cater to vegetarians, and other special diets can sometimes be accommodated if requested in advance. Living quarters are primitive campsites near the work site with few facilities.

Work crews, ranging in size from 8 to 20 volunteers, are led by a staff of 2 to 4 Sierra Club representatives. A doctor is recruited to accompany most crews, and the trip leader has attended a Red Cross Advanced First Aid course or the equivalent. About half of the volunteers come from California, and many return year after year to complete the work they started, especially on trail-maintenance projects. The club's service trips range

from $200 to $600—among the most expensive volunteer vacations, though cheaper than the club's guided outings. (This is largely the result of the club's high profile and overhead; it incurs a lot of expenses in promoting itself and its goals.) Insurance is not included. Some service trips are cosponsored with the Nature Conservancy (Dept. 05618, San Francisco, CA 94139, tel. 415/776–2211, fax 415/776–4868).

STATE PARKS DEPARTMENTS Many states have volunteer programs similar to that of the federal government. The most common opportunities are as campground hosts, but volunteers are also needed to produce park newsletters, serve as information officers, do trail maintenance and construction, help develop interpretive programs, and perform general office work. On-site housing is often provided, especially for campground hosts, and food and utilities may be included as well, depending upon the program and your position. Training, tools, and other equipment are most certainly furnished, and some expenses for local travel may be reimbursed. There is generally no sign-up fee, and you're usually covered by workers' compensation. The only states that don't have campground host programs are Arkansas, Hawaii, Kentucky, Louisiana, Mississippi, and Rhode Island. Many of the states that do have such programs are also happy to work out a special project with you that matches your interests with a park's needs. For more information, call the parks department of the state you're interested in.

VOLUNTEERS FOR PEACE The aim of VFP is to promote volunteer work camps in the United States and 40 other countries. Its international work camp directory (*see* Sources, *below*) lists 50 or so domestic projects each year, such as helping the homeless, building houses, urban gardening, conservation, and working with underprivileged children. About half repeat annually, and many are affiliated with religious organizations. On many projects, especially those in inner cities on the East Coast, you may work with more than one local organization. Teams range from six to 12 individuals, and a leader, sometimes two, oversees each group. On 95% of the projects the work is indoors, and more than 80% of volunteers are foreigners. Those under age 18 are not accepted.

A registration fee of $150 covers room and board; a few projects, usually those in more-expensive locations, such as Alaska, also require an additional fee, ranging from $50 to $100. Some camps serve only vegetarian meals. Accommodations vary according to location, but the most common setting is a dorm with bunk beds or mattresses on the floor. Men and women are often housed in the same room, and a cooperative living arrangement prevails. In other words, you are responsible for housekeeping chores as well as your volunteer work. Accident insurance is not provided (43 Tiffany Rd., Belmont, VT 05730, tel. 802/259–2759, fax 802/259–2922).

FAVORITE PROJECTS

THE NORTHEAST

■ **MAINE** ■ **Baxter State Park.** This 200,000-acre wilderness preserve two hours north of Bangor is home to Mt. Katahdin, the northern terminus of the Appalachian Trail. Here you and 10 other Volunteers for Peace can take part in lakeshore restoration, grounds keeping, landscaping, and carpentry projects at Katahdin Stream, Kidney Pond, and Daicey Pond. Free time can be spent swimming, canoeing (canoes provided), hiking, and watching the resident wildlife, which includes moose, bear, and loons. Lodgings are primitive log cabins with neither electricity nor running water. Volunteers must bring a sleeping bag, backpack, boots, and rain gear. *Volunteers for Peace, 43 Tiffany Rd., Belmont, VT 05730, tel. 802/259–2759. Early July: 14 days, $150. Sign up 6 weeks in advance.*

■ **MAINE** ■ **Wildlife Preserves.** At two federal wildlife management areas, you and 11 other Volunteers for Peace complete environmental and historic restoration work, including improving wildlife habitats, restoring historic buildings such as lighthouses, erecting osprey nesting platforms, and building trails. The group spends two weeks at the Moosehorn National Wildlife Refuge, located in eastern Maine near the Canada border, and one week at the Petit Manan National Wildlife Refuge, a coastal and island preserve. While at Moosehorn, you sleep at refuge headquarters; at Petit Manan, you stay either in dorms at headquarters or in tents on the coastal islands, depending on the trip. Leisure-time activities—swimming, canoeing, hiking, and the like—vary by location as well. All gear is provided, and Petit Manan even has its own boat, which can be used for whale-watching excursions. *Volunteers for Peace, 43 Tiffany Rd., Belmont, VT 05730, tel. 802/259–2759. Aug.: 21 days, $150. Sign up 6 weeks in advance.*

■ **MASSACHUSETTS** ■ **Cape Cod Seashore.** Want to spend a week at the beach? On this Sierra Club service trip, you and 15 others maintain trails and boardwalks, help stabilize sand dunes, and rehabilitate cranberry bogs in the Cape Cod National Seashore. Free-time activities include a tour, led by a guide from Massachusetts Audubon, of North Monomoy Island, a national wildlife refuge that is flooded with birds on their autumn migration. You can also hike, bike, and enjoy the beach, wildflowers, sand dunes, pine forests, marsh grass, and bogs. Housing is at Paine's Campground, a private facility with hot showers located in a wooded area within walking distance of the Atlantic beach. At least once during the trip, you help prepare the day's meals and clean up afterward. *Sierra Club, Dept. 05618, San Francisco, CA 94139, tel. 415/776–2211, fax 415/776–4868. Mid-Sept.: 7 days, $325. Sign up 6–8 months in advance.*

■ **NEW HAMPSHIRE** ■ **Appalachian Trail.** Volunteers for Peace joins forces with the Appalachian Mountain Club to help maintain the section of the Appalachian Trail that winds through the White Mountain

National Forest. Five VFP participants join an equal number of foreign volunteers for brush clearing, bridge building, and erosion control. The work is hard, but the only experience necessary is backpacking. Living quarters are cabins at Camp Dodge. If you prefer and if you bring your own sleeping bag, tent, and other camping gear, you can camp in the mountains instead. *Volunteers for Peace, 43 Tiffany Rd., Belmont, VT 05730, tel. 802/259–2759. July and Aug.: 14 days, $150. Sign up 6 weeks in advance.*

NEW HAMPSHIRE **Backcountry Ranger.** Straddling the Maine–New Hampshire border, the White Mountain National Forest contains 1,200 miles of rugged trails and most of New England's highest peaks within its 763,000 acres. Because of its size, the forest needs volunteers to supplement its staff of professional rangers. As a backcountry ranger, you live in the wilderness, assist hikers, and perform first aid and rescue operations as necessary. You are provided with a campsite, equipment, insurance, and freeze-dried food, which can range from scrambled eggs for breakfast to steak for dinner. *White Mountain National Forest, Federal Bldg., 719 Main St., Box 638, Laconia, NH 03247, tel. 603/528–8721. June–Sept.: 2-week minimum, no charge. Sign up 1–6 months in advance.*

NEW HAMPSHIRE **Rural Rehabilitation.** Southwestern New Hampshire, between Keene and Hanover, is the setting for the Newport/Goshen Lempster Coalition's annual volunteer work camp. Among those attending are 12 participants from Volunteers for Peace, who help on a range of community-service projects: restoring a library, painting a community center, and cleaning up parks, to name a few. In Goshen, volunteers live in a large, solar-powered house on a mountain lake with the family of a coalition member, while in Newport, volunteers live on a farm. At either work camp site, you share in housekeeping duties, such as cooking and cleaning. *Volunteers for Peace, 43 Tiffany Rd., Belmont, VT 05730, tel. 802/259–2759. Late July–mid.-Aug.: 21 days, $150. Sign up 6 weeks in advance.*

NEW YORK **Hudson River Sloop Clearwater.** Whether you take the helm of this 106-foot replica of a 19th-century sailing ship or guide elementary school children through a series of water tests, you can help spread the word about why the Hudson River needs to be protected, what dangers it faces, and how to keep it clean. No previous sailing experience is necessary. Just sign on to crew for a week at a time, and you get training in sailing techniques, such as hoisting the sails, and other shipboard operations, like swabbing the decks. Most important, you act as a representative of the *Clearwater* in its mission of environmental advocacy.

Crews of six volunteers eat and sleep aboard ship, assisting a sailing staff of seven—the captain, mates, engineer, and cook—plus an educator and perhaps a sailing apprentice. In spring, a second boat hosts four more volunteers. Though you should be 18 or older if you're on your own, students 16 to 18 can apply through an internship program and children 10 to 15 may crew if accompanied by a parent. Team members are selected for diversity; a mix of teenagers and senior citizens is typical.

Family-style, mostly vegetarian, meals are served in a mess three times a day. At night you retire below decks to a dorm-style main cabin that accommodates 12 in twin beds or a secondary cabin that sleeps three. There is no electricity aboard ship and no shower. Water is carried aboard for bathing, and at certain docks, you can shower at the homes of members who live nearby. *Hudson River Sloop Clearwater, 112 Market St., Poughkeepsie, NY 12601, tel. 914/454–7673. Mid-Apr.–mid-Nov.: 7 days, $55. Price includes membership; sign up 8–10 weeks in advance.*

VERMONT **Green Mountain Audubon Center.** In Burlington, on the shores of Lake Champlain, the Green Mountain Audubon Center teaches environmental education. Each summer, 10 Volunteers for Peace work at the center for two weeks, performing trail maintenance, cutting wood, and perhaps doing a little painting. A third week is spent helping at a local day camp.

Housing is community style: in common areas of a Quaker Meeting House or other local church, in dorms of a nearby college, or in tent camps during trail-maintenance projects. Meals are vegetarian. Social events, such as pot-luck dinners, give you a chance to meet members of the community, and free time is allotted so you can enjoy the lake, nearby rivers, and the Green Mountains. *Volunteers for Peace, 43 Tiffany Rd., Belmont, VT 05730, tel. 802/259-2759. July: 21 days, $150. Sign up 6 weeks in advance.*

THE MID-ATLANTIC

NEW JERSEY **Genesis Farm.** On this 140-acre farm work camp in the rural community of Blairstown, 90 minutes from New York City, you can work and live as part of a group of 10 Volunteers for Peace. While you construct model solar-powered structures and composting toilets or renovate existing farm buildings, you demonstrate environmentally sound living and farming practices. Housing is in tepees, and meals, often shared with Blairstown residents, are vegetarian. Free time can be spent enjoying the outdoor recreational opportunities of the nearby Delaware Valley and, in the evenings, joining in song and dance. *Volunteers for Peace, 43 Tiffany Rd., Belmont, VT 05730, tel. 802/259-2759. Early Sept.: 21 days, $150. Sign up 6 weeks in advance.*

NEW JERSEY **Hawk Mountain Sanctuary.** The Delaware River is one of the few places in the East where bald eagles migrate for the winter. Along the Kittatinny Ridge, part of the Appalachian Mountains, 16 Sierra Club volunteers help maintain the visitor facilities at Hawk Mountain Sanctuary. Tasks include general grounds keeping, trail maintenance, gardening, and perhaps painting buildings or collecting admission fees. During free time, you can hike the Appalachian Trail and observe the fall raptor migration from a lookout. Base camp is a private campground, Christmas Pines, a few miles away in Auburn, Pennsylvania; its bathhouse has hot showers and electricity. At least one day during the trip, you help cook and clean up after meals. *Sierra Club, Dept. 05618, San Francisco, CA 94139, tel. 415/776-2211, fax 415/776-4868. Late Sept.: 7 days, $235. Sign up 6-8 months in advance.*

PENNSYLVANIA **House Building in Philadelphia.** In a project sponsored locally with the Philadelphia Yearly Friends Meeting, Volunteers for Peace sends 10 volunteers to build homes for low-income families in the City of Brotherly Love. Sometimes 5 to 10 Habitat for Humanity volunteers join the group. Carpentry, electrical, and other construction skills are helpful but not required. During your stay in the city, you are housed with a Quaker family and attend church along with the other volunteers. *Volunteers for Peace, 43 Tiffany Rd., Belmont, VT 05730, tel. 802/259-2759, or Habitat for Humanity International, 121 Habitat St., Americus, GA 31709, tel. 912/924-6935, fax 912/924-6541. Mid-July: 14 days, $150. Sign up 6 weeks in advance.*

VIRGINIA **Appalachian Trail.** "Perhaps the hardest work you have ever performed," the Appalachian Trail Conference warns about this ongoing project in southwest Virginia. You might find yourself doing trail design and construction or rough carpentry, building shelters and bridges, rehabilitating an eroded trail, or clearing and managing open areas, but be warned: Along the way you could be breaking and moving rocks, digging holes, and splitting logs.

Each trip has a base camp, where there are showers and laundry facilities, plus cabins that house two or three people in bunks. From there, you are transported by van to a field camp, which may be a primitive site or a cabin compound with a water source nearby. Here you sleep in a tent or cabin and, in addition to trail work, pitch in with such chores as cleaning, cooking, washing dishes, and sharpening tools. Meals, prepared in a tent kitchen, consist of fresh meat and vegetables; menus feature the likes of chili, chops, fish, or pasta, with side dishes of salad and rice. Plenty of fruit, candy bars, and cookies are on hand for a quick energy boost between meals. Insurance is included.

One-week schedules start with orientation and instruction on Wednesday, followed by work from Thursday to Monday. Tuesday, the day off, is spent at base camp. Free time is set aside for sightseeing, swimming, fishing, rock climbing, hiking, caving, or just loafing. *Appalachian Trail Conference Southern Volunteer Crew, Box 10, Newport, VA 24128. Late May–late Aug.: 7 days, no charge. Sign up 6 months in advance.*

WEST VIRGINIA **Holistic Holiday.** Each year, Volunteers for Peace sends 10 to 15 volunteers to the Gesundheit Institute, an ongoing work camp dedicated to building a holistic community. Located in Pocahontas County in southwestern West Virginia, the institute is set on 314 rural acres. The ultimate goal is to build a hospital where fun and art are major parts of the healing process. However, major funding is still lacking, so most of the tasks for volunteers are on the grounds— landscaping, gardening, and small construction projects. A full schedule of group activities, such as swimming outings, hiking excursions, and parties, keeps you busy even when you're not working. Home during your stay is a yurt—a round, tentlike structure. While at the institute, you're expected to pitch in with cooking and cleaning. *Volunteers for Peace, 43 Tiffany Rd., Belmont, VT 05730, tel. 802/259-2759. Late Aug.: 14 days, $150. Sign up 6 weeks in advance.*

THE SOUTH

ARKANSAS **International Learning and Livestock Center.** The Heifer Project, founded in 1944, is dedicated to easing global hunger by promoting sound livestock management practices. At the group's 200-acre livestock center, in the hills of rural Arkansas, you can help the eight full-time staff members teach the public, especially visiting schoolchildren, about the issues of world hunger. Among the displays are the Education Trail, which features a re-creation of a typical house in Appalachia, and the Guatemala Hillside Farm, 2½ acres of

steep, eroded hillside, which illustrates how small-scale farmers can use limited resources to become self-sufficient. Other sites demonstrate livestock management techniques.

Depending on your abilities and the center's needs, you can assist with farm chores, such as milking the goats, cleaning the barns, or cultivating the new organic garden; help in the community kitchen or office; guide schoolchildren on tours along the Education Trail; or work on construction projects, such as fence building or painting, that expand the facilities or keep up existing structures. Because farm work is hard and potentially dangerous, no minors are accepted. Volunteers should be healthy; those who are less physically fit can work indoors. The center accommodates up to 15 volunteers, from all over the country and the world, in furnished houses, one set up for couples and the other for individuals. *Heifer Project International, International Learning and Livestock Center, Rte. 2, Box 33, Perryville, AR 72126, tel. 501/889-5124. Year-round: 1 week–1 year, $125 a week for stays less than 1 month. Sign up 2–3 months in advance.*

THE MIDWEST

MISSOURI **Campground Host.** Want free lodging just 7 miles from Branson, the new country music center? Many do, which is why Table Rock State Park is the most popular park in Missouri's VIP program. The 356-acre park is in the Lakes Region of southwest Missouri, amid the Ozark Mountains' White River Hills, and it borders the northeast shore of 53,000-acre Table Rock Lake. As a campground host, you greet incoming campers, collect fees, act as a public information officer, perform light maintenance, and help run campground activities. Recreational opportunities within the park include hiking, boating, fishing, and swimming.

Table Rock was the pilot park in Missouri's volunteer program, which now includes 35 parks across the state. Other popular units, all with trout hatcheries, are Lebanon's Bennett Spring State Park and Cassville's Roaring River State Park, both 3,000-acre units in the Lakes Region, and Salem's Montauk State Park, 1,300 acres in the southeast. Insurance is provided. *Missouri Dept. of Natural Resources, Division of Parks, Recreation, and Historic Preservation, Volunteer Program Coordinator, Box 176, Jefferson City, MO 65102, tel. 800/334–6946. Mar.–Oct.: 4-week minimum, no charge. Sign up 12 months in advance.*

THE SOUTHWEST

NEVADA **Living History Interpreter.** Visitors to Spring Valley State Park come to hike, participate in water sports on 65-acre Eagle Valley Reservoir, and explore the pioneer ranch lands nearby. You can help bring the area's ranching past to life for them by reenacting some facet of history. Working as an interpretive assistant, you research, design, and present a living-history program, including dressing up in period costume.

There are other volunteer positions at Spring Valley, including campground host and trail maintenance worker, and there are interpretive assistant positions at other Nevada parks as well, though duties are likely to vary, from posting signs and leading hikes to developing lectures, slide shows, and self-guiding nature trails. Nevada's Volunteer in Parks program is extensive, accepting volunteers for more than 50 positions at 16 park units plus state and district headquarters. Camping space, sometimes including utilities, is provided for some positions, and workers' comp is included. *Spring Valley State Park, Star Rte., Box 201, Pioche, NV 89043, tel. 702/962–5102, or for all state parks, Administrator, Nevada Division of State Parks, Capitol Complex, Carson City, NV 89710, tel. 702/687–4370. Year-round: no minimum commitment, no charge. Sign up 4 weeks in advance.*

THE ROCKIES

WYOMING **Lodge Restoration in the Absaroka Mountains.** For several years, the Sierra Club has sent 10 volunteers to restore Anderson Lodge, a historic two-story log cabin located 30 miles east of Yellowstone Park. One of the club's most popular trips, it has attracted considerable attention from local newspapers and the PBS TV show "This Old House." Work may include fixing an outdoor stairway, installing floorboards, or excavating drainage ditches. Volunteers with carpentry skills are especially needed, although willingness to help is the most important qualification.

To reach the lodge, you hike 7 miles, carrying personal gear and cooking equipment in case the pack animals are delayed. You sleep in tents at a base camp, and food tends toward the vegetarian. *Sierra Club, Dept. 05618, San Francisco, CA 94139, tel. 415/776–2211, fax 415/776–4868. Late July: 10 days, $275. Sign up 6–8 months in advance.*

WYOMING **Museum Volunteer.** Want to be a prospector, blacksmith, or mountain man? As a museum volunteer at one of Wyoming's state parks, you get to dress in period costume and act in living-history demonstrations. The two most popular sites for volunteers are South Pass City State Historic Site and Fort Bridger State Historic Site.

South Pass, outside Lander, is a collection of 11 buildings that remain from the original capital of the Dakota Territory. Now open to the public, the whole town re-creates a frontier settlement of the 1860s. In addition to historical reenactment, you can help set up and maintain exhibits, work in the museum shop, answer visitors' questions, and assist with administrative duties.

Ft. Bridger, in the town of the same name, was the original outpost of Jim Bridger, a fur trader, trapper, and pioneer who was one of the first settlers in this area. Here work involves teaching visitors what life was like in the wild, wild West by dressing in period costume and acting as a tour guide through eight historical buildings. Volunteer opportunities in museums are also available at four other locations: Fort Phil Kearny State Historic Site in Story, Guernsey State Park in Guernsey, Trail End State Historic Site in Sheridan, and Fort Fetterman State Historic Site in Douglas. Group housing in trailers is sometimes available, depending on the site, but meals are not included. *Wyoming Dept. of Commerce, Information & Education Svcs., Barrett Bldg., 3rd floor, 2301 Central Ave., Cheyenne, WY 82002, tel. 307/777–7695. Late May–mid-Sept.: 2-week minimum, no charge. Sign up 2 weeks in advance.*

THE WEST COAST

CALIFORNIA **House Building in Los Angeles.** The annual Jimmy Carter Work Project, sponsored by Habitat for Humanity, is moving to the Watts-Willowbrook neighborhood of south-central L.A., with the goal of building 30 to 40 houses. At the same time, other building projects are being undertaken elsewhere in greater Los Angeles, including the San Fernando Valley neighborhoods damaged by the 1994 earthquake.

Jimmy and Rosalynn Carter work alongside you and about 2,000 other volunteers in the L.A. area, and together you eat the same meals, sleep in the same accommodations, and ride in the same buses. Dorms at the University of Southern California provide the accommodations. Breakfast and dinner are served at campus cafeterias; lunch is eaten at the work site. In the evenings, you are free to explore the city. Work days, which start at 7:30 at the building site, begin with prayer and song. *Habitat for Humanity, Jimmy Carter Work Project, 3580 Wilshire Blvd., Los Angeles, CA 90010, tel. 213/386–9930, fax 213/380–9960. Mid-July: 7 days, $150–$200. Sign up 1 month in advance.*

CALIFORNIA **Santa Cruz Island.** This Sierra Club vacation, cosponsored with the Nature Conservancy, is extremely popular, and volunteers have been turned away in the past. The island, the largest of the eight Channel Islands, is so biologically diverse that it has been compared to the Galápagos. It's located 25 miles off the coast of Santa Barbara, and 90% of the land is owned and managed by the Nature Conservancy. While on the island, you and nine other volunteers mostly perform trail upkeep, but there may also be general chores—painting, fence repair, and hay pitching—at the historic central ranch facility. Housing is in nearby cabins. In your free time, you can explore the ranch, the mountains, and the beaches. *Sierra Club, Dept. 05618, San Francisco, CA 94139, tel. 415/776–2211, fax 415/776–4868. Mid-Apr. and late Oct.: 7 days, $325. Sign up 6–8 months in advance.*

CALIFORNIA **Tahoe Rim Trail.** Just as the Appalachian Trail was built more than half a century ago, today a 150-mile hiking and equestrian trail along the ridge tops surrounding Lake Tahoe is being constructed thanks to a group in South Lake Tahoe. The goal is to enhance the lake's recreational opportunities while preserving its scenic beauty. Construction began in 1984, and two-thirds of the trail loop, including 50 miles that follow the existing Pacific Crest Trail, has been completed. The final leg is scheduled for completion by 1999.

Work entails typical trail-building tasks: clearing debris, raking, and using jackhammers to remove boulders. Training, safety equipment (hard hats and safety goggles), and trail-building tools are the only items provided. The rest—including work gloves and boots, insurance (a liability waiver is required), food, and lodging—is your responsibility. You can live in a nearby campground or motel or pitch a tent close to the work site.

Volunteers of all ages and abilities are welcome; there's plenty of work to go around and never enough hands. Those under 17 can take part with signed parental permission. In fact, families often volunteer together. Crews of 1 to 100 are led by at least one crew leader, and though many volunteers come from the local community, they also have traveled from as far away as England to participate. *Tahoe Rim Trail, Box*

10156, South Lake Tahoe, CA 96158, tel. 916/577–0676, fax 916/577–8602. Mid-June–mid-Oct.: 1 day–4 months, no charge. No advance registration necessary.

CALIFORNIA **Trail Revegetation in Yosemite.** Unlike most trail-maintenance projects, which build or improve trails, this Sierra Club service trip aims to give a trail back to nature. Working on no-longer-needed trails in the national park, 10 volunteers help revegetate paths so heavily used they have worn deep into the landscape, causing considerable erosion. Pack animals bring fill to the work site.

The base camp is accessible by car; from there you walk the couple of miles to the work site at 8,600 feet, carrying your tools and pack lunch. Meals tend toward vegetarian dishes. Free time can be spent enjoying the Yosemite wilderness. The club runs similar revegetation trips at Crater Lake National Park in Oregon, Canyonlands National Park in Utah, and elsewhere. *Sierra Club, Dept. 05618, San Francisco, CA 94139, tel. 415/776–2211, fax 415/776–4868. Late Aug.: 21 days, $275. Sign up 6–8 months in advance.*

ALASKA

SOUTHEAST **Cabin Care.** On Admiralty Island National Monument in the Inside Passage, known for its population of grizzly bears, Backcountry Volunteers runs an annual trip to spruce up three cabins on Hosselborg Lake, which are used for visitor rentals. Work includes general cleaning (floors, windows, and furniture) and painting, plus cutting and carrying firewood. The latter is especially demanding work, and experience with a chain saw is helpful. Food and tents are supplied, and you can spend free time hiking, fishing, and exploring. For those interested in the island but not this type of work, the Sierra Club runs a trail-maintenance trip here. *Backcountry Volunteers, Box 86, North Scituate, MA 02060. Late June: 11 days, $40. Sign up 4–6 months in advance.*

SOUTHEAST **Glacier Bay.** Here's a relatively inexpensive way to spend 10 days in Alaska's famous Glacier Bay National Park, renowned for its 16 tidewater glaciers. Part of this Sierra Club trip is spent doing trail maintenance and other varied tasks in the immediate vicinity of Bartlett Cove, at the entrance to the park and 11 miles from the town of Gustavus. During this time, you stay at the Bartlett Cove Campground. The rest of the trip you work on more remote trails; after hiking 4 to 5 miles, you set up camp near the new site. All work is done with hand tools, which must be carried to the camp along with all food and cooking gear, since there is no pack support. You and the 9 other trip members help prepare all meals, which are vegetarian. In your free time, you can sea kayak, hike, fish, or take a small-boat excursion to see the calving glaciers. *Sierra Club, Dept. 05618, San Francisco, CA 94139, tel. 415/776–2211, fax 415/776–4868. Mid-June: 10 days, $425. Sign up 6–8 months in advance.*

SOUTHEAST **Sitka Service.** In Sitka, an island community on the Inside Passage and the former capital of Russian Alaska, you and eight other Volunteers for Peace work with the Dog Point Fish Camp, Alaska Raptor Center, and Raven's Way Program doing various types of construction, maintenance, and repair. Construction experience is helpful but not necessary. The Dog Point Fish Camp is a native program that teaches local youth traditional ways and history. The raptor center is a hospital for sick and injured eagles and other birds of prey. Raven's Way is a drug and alcohol rehabilitation center for teenagers. While working in town, you are headquartered downtown at the Lutheran Church, where you eat and sleep. In your off hours, you can take advantage of the many opportunities for hiking, camping, kayaking, or looking for whales, eagles, bears, otters, and other marine and land animals. *Volunteers for Peace, 43 Tiffany Rd., Belmont, VT 05730, tel. 802/259–2759. July: 21 days, $245. Sign up 6 weeks in advance.*

SOURCES

BOOKS *Helping Out in the Outdoors* (American Hiking Society, Box 20160, Washington, DC 20041, tel. 703/255–9304, fax 703/255–9308) is an annual 128-page directory of more than 2,000 volunteer jobs and internships in parks and forests nationwide. The *International Workcamp Directory* (Volunteers for Peace, 43 Tiffany Rd., Belmont, VT 05730, tel. 802/259–2759, fax 802/259–2922) is put out every April for summer and fall volunteer placement. *National Volunteers in Parks Directory* (Solutions) is a listing of campground-host positions available throughout the United States.

ALSO SEE If you're interested in volunteering but would prefer to make a more intellectual and less physical contribution, check out the chapter on Volunteer Research Vacations.

Whale-Watching Cruises

By Melissa Rivers

 close encounter with whales in their natural habitat is a thrilling experience. Hearing the resonant whoosh of a whale exhaling and witnessing such acrobatics as spy-hopping (a whale poking its head straight up out of the water for a look around), breaching (leaping almost entirely out of the water and coming down with a thunderous splash), and skimming (feeding at the surface), you get a true sense of these magnificent animals' size and beauty. You can see whales from many spots along the California and New England coastlines, but the best way to get up close and personal with these creatures is to take a whale-watching cruise.

Whale-watching cruises generally last from 4 to 15 days. Some travel to feeding, breeding, or calving grounds, and others cruise along a portion of a whale migration route. Some boats dock in a different port each evening, some anchor in secluded natural harbors and coves, and others keep moving through the night.

The biggest difference between these cruises, however, is the boats, which range from small sail-powered vessels to full-size cruise liners. Sailboats are quiet and have less impact on the environment than motorized boats. They're generally also small and have limited passenger space, tight sleeping quarters, shared bathrooms, and tiny galleys in which simple, family-style meals are prepared. The range of motorized vessels runs from smallish cabin cruisers originally built for sportfishing to converted fishing trawlers and pleasure yachts to the largest floating hotels. The larger boats provide more space and privacy and have kitchens that can cook up more elaborate meals. The size of the boat also determines the entertainment facilities, which may include a bar (even the smallest sailboats usually have at least a liquor cabinet from which you can buy drinks), a lounge equipped with a high-tech entertainment system, a hot tub, and a pool. Small boats can go places that cruise liners can't, and when you cruise on a small boat, you are close to the water and, thus, close to the whales. On a cruise liner, you watch the whales from high above the water, but the ship is more stable than a small boat, so you may fare better in rough seas.

Because whales migrate, whale-watching is a seasonal activity, and the season changes from place to place. These huge mammals spend summer in feeding grounds in cooler climes and winter in breeding and calving grounds in warmer waters. February through April is the best time for watching whales in Hawaii, California, and Baja California, and June through August is best in southeastern Alaska, New England, and on both coasts of Canada.

Different whale species frequent different waters. Humpbacks that live in the North Pacific migrate between summer feeding

---

Melissa Rivers has written about Mexico, Canada, and the Orient. During summer, she travels from her inland Oregon home up the west coast to Alaska in search of memorable whale encounters.

grounds off Alaska to winter breeding and calving grounds off Hawaii or the coast of Baja. Humpbacks in the North Atlantic winter in the Caribbean and, in summer, move to the Gulf of Maine and the Bays of Massachusetts and Fundy, where they mingle with sperm whales, minkes, finbacks, and the rare right whale.

Pilot and false killer whales are also seen in Hawaiian waters during the winter. Orcas (killer whales) are most prevalent in Washington's Puget Sound and along the coast of British Columbia, with resident pods in those waters year-round; however, transient orca pods have been spotted from Glacier Bay in Alaska to Monterey Bay in California.

Gray whales are easily spotted along the west coast during their annual migrations from calving grounds in Mexican lagoons and Hawaiian bays to summer feeding grounds in Alaskan waters. The warm waters of Baja lagoons such as San Ignacio are now famous for encounters with gray cows and calves. A winter trip around the Baja Peninsula with stops in San Ignacio Lagoon, Magdalena Bay, and the Sea of Cortez affords your best chance for seeing the widest variety of whales (up to 10 different species, including the famous blue whale, the largest creature on earth) on one trip.

This is not your average spectator sport. It's more like a seagoing game of hide-and-seek. Whales are unpredictable, so you must be prepared to wait and watch patiently, scanning the water for signs. You may see what looks like rain spattering on the water; this is a sign that herring are surfacing—and whales are sure to follow. Sometimes it seems the whales don't want to be watched; other times they rub up against the boat. Also unpredictable are the weather and sea conditions. You can get wet and chilled (it's often 20 degrees colder on the water than onshore), and some people get seasick.

On most whale-watching cruises, you focus on observing cetaceans and, sometimes, other wildlife, but you don't spend every waking hour in pursuit of them. Your day is usually divided between active whale-watching or whale-seeking and shore excursions, snorkeling, swimming, and just lolling about. On some cruises, talks are given covering the history and culture of the ports of call along the route.

Whales are warm-blooded, air-breathing mammals that, along with dolphins and porpoises, belong to the order Cetacea, which is divided into two suborders, Mysticeti (baleen) and Odontoceti (toothed). Baleen whales, including blue, gray, humpback, minke, and right whales, are grazers, seining krill through the fringed, comblike plates that hang from their upper jaw. Toothed whales, including beaked, beluga, orca, and sperm whales, are predatory, catching fish, squid, and other marine creatures in their teeth.

Whale-watching cruises grew out of concern for the whales' welfare. By the early 20th century, many species had been hunted nearly to extinction, and by mid-century, pollution was seen as a threat to all whales. In the 1960s, people worried about humankind's effect on the environment used the plight of whales as a symbol of their cause, and the condition of whales became a bellwether for the condition of the planet. The interest in whales quickly grew, and by the late 1970s, whale-watching had become a booming tourist industry. Today people pay from $100 to $500 a day to cruise the waters looking for whales.

CHOOSING THE RIGHT CRUISE

Each whale-watching cruise is different—even trips offered by the same outfitter—so it is best to ask the following questions to determine if a specific cruise is right for you.

Which or how many species are seen on this trip? Most trips are in or through areas that attract several species, although some cruises focus on a particular whale, with any other species you come across considered a bonus.

When is the best time to take this trip? What is the record for spotting whales on this

trip? Some trips are run for several months, but if you ask, you may find out that the sighting record is better in one or two of those months.

What are the conditions of the sea? Some waters are nearly always calm and others are always choppy; some waters change from season to season. If you get seasick, the condition of the sea is a major point to consider when deciding which cruise to take.

What kind of boat is used and how many passengers does it carry? You have to weigh the pros and cons of traveling on small sailboats versus large or giant motor-powered vessels, but make sure you know what kind of boat is used for the trip you are considering. It's commonplace for outfitters to charter different boats for various trips, so even if you know the outfitter, be sure to ask about the specific boat being used. Also, the size of the boat alone doesn't mean much until you know how many passengers it carries. Because each boat is arranged and outfitted in a distinct way, it is difficult to give an ideal ratio of passengers to boat length, but a trip with 15 people is certain to be quite different from one with 150.

Is the cruise round-trip? Some cruises start and end at the same port, but just as many are one-way only and you must get home from the final stop. This can add substantially to the cost of your trip, because you may have to fly out of a different airport or travel long distances to return to the one at which you originally arrived.

What ports of call are visited? Some trips make many stops, while others hardly stop at all. If you are interested in touring Alaskan towns, choose a cruise that makes a few stops; if you prefer cruising to walking, pick a trip that keeps moving.

How long has the company been in business and how long has it been offering this particular trip? Like people, companies learn from experience, so one that has been running trips for a few years probably knows how to handle problems better than a new enterprise might. Trips that have run successfully for five or more years are more likely to run smoothly than one that's new.

What are the trip leaders' qualifications? Try to find a trip led by a marine biologist or natural historian with an expertise in cetaceans. On the better trips, this person also has knowledge of the area's other wildlife as well as its vegetation and geology.

What sort of commentary is provided? Some trips are intense short courses in all things cetacean; virtually everything that happens is narrated, and much of your time is spent being educated about what you will see or have just seen. Other trips are less formal; you get information only on whale behavior that you see.

What shore excursions are available and is there an additional fee for these? You may find that the shore excursions are the best part of the cruise you pick, but the added cost puts the cruise out of your price bracket.

What's the cost and what's included? Prices of whale-watching cruises vary considerably, depending on the type of ship, the number of days, and the destination. The best way to compare prices of cruises is to figure out the cost per diem. Unless otherwise stated, prices quoted in this chapter are per person and include lodging on board (in shared bunk rooms on smaller ships and in double cabins on cruise liners) as well as three meals a day while at sea. Transportation to the boat, port charges, and shore excursions are not included, unless stated otherwise.

What are the accommodations like? On smaller ships you must sleep in bunk rooms with other participants and share a bathroom; on cruise liners you may pay for a single cabin with a private bath; and between these two extremes, there are a variety of sleeping arrangements.

Is laundry service available? Generally, only the largest ships have laundry facilities, but always ask. Also find out if there's a Laundromat at one of the ports and whether or not you'll have the time to stop. If you can wash your clothes, you can bring far fewer of them. Except for the full-size cruise ships, no boat in this chapter has laundry service. Get the lowdown on the likely weather conditions and pack accordingly.

What is the food like? This will depend upon the individual boat—and its cook. Some outfitters, however, have established reputations for serving good to excellent meals on board. Also find out if meals are served at preset seatings with tables assigned or if you can sit where you choose. Assigned seating is great for making friends (you eat with the same people every day) but can be difficult to deal with if you and your tablemates aren't a good match.

How far in advance do I need to book? Most cruise operators ask that you sign up at least a couple of months in advance—some advise even earlier—but all sell passage until the departure date if space is still available.

Do you have references from past guests? It always helps to talk with someone who has made the trip.

MAJOR PLAYERS

AMERICAN CETACEAN SOCIETY Established in 1967, this nonprofit group is the oldest whale protection organization in the world. Through whale-watching trips, which are usually led by someone with an advanced marine-science degree, it hopes to foster interest in cetacean conservation and research. The society's whale-watching cruises were started in 1973 and now travel to Alaska, British Columbia, Baja, and the Canadian High Arctic. Different vessels are chartered in each area, so accommodations vary. Cooks make use of the best local produce to serve meals of many cuisines. Fresh fruits are available, and the homemade desserts always gain high praise on trip evaluations. Cruises last from 7 to 11 days and cost between $1,400 and $2,400 for ACS members; nonmembers either add 10% of the trip price or join ACS at $35 for a single membership, $45 per family. All ages are

welcome, but there are no special programs for children (Box 2639, San Pedro, CA 90731-0943, tel. 310/548–6279, fax 310/548–6950).

BIOLOGICAL JOURNEYS Biologists Ronn Storro-Patterson and Ron LeValley had already spent several years leading whale-watching trips in Baja California when they created Biological Journeys in 1980. Since its inception, Biological Journeys has expanded to include trips in southeast Alaska, British Columbia, and other international destinations. One of the founders generally accompanies trips; other leaders may be scientists, teachers, or another type of professional, but all are experts in particular subjects or the places visited. Alaskan expeditions are aboard the company's ship, *Delphinus,* a 50-foot trawler refitted for natural history cruises; in other regions, different ships are chartered. *Delphinus* sleeps 10 to 12 passengers in three double cabins, a four-person V-shaped berth (usually used by just two people or a family of four), and two single berths; all have small bunks, reading lights, and limited storage space. There are two bathrooms (one with hot shower); a comfortable lounge equipped with a library, VCR, and slide projector; a pilothouse; and a saloon with plenty of seats with unobstructed views. Meals are a mix of California and Continental cuisines and include homemade breads, soups, and plenty of fresh fruit. Sightings are announced over the public-address system, and video cameras and a hydrophone capture the sights and sounds of the day. Cruise lengths average 9 days, and costs range from $2,500 to $3,300. Children are welcome on selected trips (1696 Ocean Dr., McKinleyville, CA 95521, tel. 707/839–0178 or 800/548–7555, fax 707/839–4656).

FAVORITE CRUISES

THE NORTHEAST

CANADA, MAINE, AND MASSACHUSETTS From **Prince Edward Island to Boston.** This 15-day late-summer cruise in the Canadian Maritimes and along the coast of Maine is reliable for sighting minke, finback, and humpback whales. The 207-foot motor yacht *Nantucket Clipper*, which carries 100 passengers, spends several days in the Bay of Fundy and cruises along the forested coastlines of New Brunswick, Nova Scotia, and Maine; it also allows a full day at Stellwagen Bank, off the coast of Massachusetts, where sightings this time of year are virtually guaranteed.

Whales are the primary focus of this Clipper Cruise Line itinerary, but the trip takes in the culture and history of the region, too. A historian briefs you on the ports of call, which include Charlottetown, Prince Edward Island (port of embarkation), Halifax, Nova Scotia, and Boston (port of disembarkation). Optional city tours are available in each port. You can also choose to hike with the ship's naturalist through the bogs of Campobello Island, in New Brunswick, and on Mount Desert Island, part of Acadia National Park in Maine.

The *Nantucket Clipper* has staterooms of various sizes (priced accordingly), but all are narrow and have low beds and private bathrooms. Passengers gather for socializing and evening lectures in the spacious forward lounges. Meals, prepared by chefs trained at the Culinary Institute of America, are served in single open seatings; regional specialties are highlighted, and most entrée selections are cooked to order. *Clipper Cruise Line, 7711 Bonhomme Ave., St. Louis, MO 63105, tel. 314/727–2929 or 800/325–0010. Early Sept.: 15 days, $3,600–$5,400. Sign up 6 months in advance.*

MASSACHUSETTS **The Mating of Right Whales.** The primary purpose of this four-day expedition off the New England coast and out into distant water (more than 50 miles offshore) is to observe the mating behavior of the rare right whale. Named *right* because they were once the most profitable whales to hunt, these whales are believed to number only a few hundred now. On this trip, run by the Yankee Fleet and the Atlantic Cetacean Research Center (ACRC), you have an opportunity to view right whales, and you

may also see sperm whales, porpoises, and white-sided dolphins.

The 100-foot MV *Yankee Freedom* departs from Gloucester, then heads 100 miles out to sea toward Georges Bank and Browns Bank, both dependable spots for whale sightings because the shape and depth of the ocean floor in each creates an upwelling of the krill that whales feed on. The boat then loops around to Brier Island off the coast of Nova Scotia and heads across the north end of Jefferies Ledge and back to Gloucester.

Naturalist Steve Frohock, director of the ACRC, leads the trip and provides commentary. (He is often assisted by Scott Krauss, cetacean director at the New England Aquarium.) Other cetacean researchers frequently come along, which means there are usually plenty of knowledgeable people around. Videos and slide presentations are shown in the main cabin during long cruising stretches.

The *Yankee Freedom* is outfitted for up to 40 passengers but rarely carries more than 35. Accommodations include 11 bunk rooms with two to eight bunks, washbasins, and reading lights in each; shared heads; and saltwater and freshwater showers. Hot family-style meals are served in the main cabin. With so much time spent on the open ocean, young children and anyone susceptible to seasickness are discouraged. *Yankee Fleet, 75 Essex Ave., Gloucester, MA 01930, tel. 508/283–0313 or 800/942–5464, fax 508/283–6089. Mid-July: 4 days, $700. Sign up 2–3 months in advance.*

MASSACHUSETTS **Sailing a Tall Ship.** Dirigo Cruises is the only New England operator that offers multiple-day whale-watching cruises out of Boston. Aboard the two-masted 95-foot schooner *Harvey Gamage*, the six-day trips with up to 26 passengers combine whale-watching, New England history, and the opportunity to sail on a tall ship and pick up such seamanship skills as rigging, hoisting, knot tying, and splicing.

Although the itinerary may change with the wind, tide, and recent sightings, the typical cruise spends one day at Stellwagen Bank observing groups of feeding humpback, finback, and minke whales as well as the rest of the marine life and seabirds. Your other days are filled with cruising between historic coastal towns, such as Salem, Provincetown, and Gloucester. On most trips, you're in port every night but one, so there is time to go ashore and explore. A marine biologist presents daily lectures, videos, and slide shows on the wildlife found along this coast. The cruise returns to Boston.

The mainmast of the *Harvey Gamage* towers 91 feet above the water. This beautiful wooden schooner, built in 1973, is equipped with a main saloon, a galley, shared heads, and tight bunk rooms (doubles, triples, and one quad) with washbasins. You can sleep under the stars above deck if you like (bring your own sleeping bag), and the leaders try to arrange one night out at Stellwagen Bank so that, weather and moon permitting, you can see the whales at night. The showers on board are cold freshwater, but hot showers are available at the Gloucester marina, usually the second or third night's port of call. Hearty meals consisting of a variety of meats, seafood, and fresh produce are served family style in the main saloon; on fair weather days, you might have buffet-style meals on deck or even a shoreside picnic. Children of all ages are permitted, but small tots don't always fare well on a six-day cruise. *Dirigo Cruises, 39 Waterside La., Clinton, CT 06413, tel. 203/669–7068 or 800/845–5520, fax 203/669–3737. Aug.: 6 days, $795. Sign up 3–4 months in advance.*

THE WEST COAST

CALIFORNIA **Monterey Bay's Marine World.** This trip differs from the others in this chapter in that most of your time is spent on land. Shearwater Journeys, founded in 1978 by Debra Shearwater, offers a weeklong, land-based trip for up to 14 participants during which you spend sunrise to sunset learning about the rich ecosystem of Monterey Bay and especially about the whales.

The week begins with a visit to the Monterey Bay Aquarium, where Debra, who used to be a tour guide there, leads you through the various exhibits. You spend five or six days looking for whales and other marine life from the Montery Peninsula's Point Lobos State Park, Point Piños, and Año Nuevo (a breeding ground for elephant seals). For the last two days, you cruise the waters on a 60-foot motor-powered vessel during the day, returning to your motel at night. You travel past Cannery Row to Point Piños, at the southern edge of the bay. Because it juts out into the migration track of the gray whale, this point is a top spot for viewing, both from land and sea. During the whales' peak traveling time in January, it's not unusual to scan the horizon and count 50 to 100 passing whales each day. You may also see shoals of dolphins that frequently escort the migrating whales.

It is easy to get caught up in Debra's enthusiasm, not only for cetaceans but for all marine and avian life inhabiting the bay. Bring along a camera and take plenty of shots if you'd like to help researchers track and identify the migrating grays and various orcas, northern right whales, Dall porpoises, and Risso's dolphins that come into Monterey Bay. You might even get the chance to assist in hydrophone recordings of dolphin communication.

Evenings are dedicated to learning from local experts, who present slide shows and videos. Afterward you retire to your room at a small motel in Pacific Grove, within easy walking distance of the rocky shoreline of Point Piños. Family-style breakfasts are eaten at the motel; sack lunches, in the field; and dinner, in local restaurants. Van transportation between sites is provided. Children over 12 are welcome. *Shearwater Journeys, Box 1445, Soquel, CA 95073, tel. 408/688–1990. Jan.–Feb. and Aug.–Oct.: 8 or 9 days, $1,600–$1,800. Sign up at least 3 months in advance.*

CALIFORNIA TO BAJA **Baja and the Sea of Cortez.** The first portion of this 11-day American Cetacean Society cruise is much like any other trip along Baja's Pacific coast, with stops on several islands and a few days at San Ignacio Lagoon, where curious mother whales and their calves often approach boats. But rather than double back to San Diego from there, this cruise continues 150 miles south to Magdalena Bay, where gray whales calve. It then takes you another 150 miles to the southern tip of Baja, rounds it, and heads north into the Sea of Cortez (also known as the Gulf of California), whose calmer and warmer waters offer refuge to whales, dolphins, manta rays, whale sharks, and hundreds of species of tropical fish.

This trip has been run in various forms since 1973, and past participants have spotted as many as 10 different cetacean species, including several of the larger whales (finback, blue, sperm, gray, Byrde's, pilot, and humpback).

Each morning you have free time to snorkel among brilliantly colored parrot fish, damselfish, and rainbow wrasses, or to hike throughout the numerous island sanctuaries for a look at frigate birds, blue-footed boobies, royal terns, and other tropical seabirds. Afternoons are usually spent whale-watching as you sail toward the evening's anchorage.

The trip is aboard the 95-foot cabin cruiser *Searcher.* The 30 or so passengers stay in 16 cabins, each with two to four bunks and a sink. There are also four shared heads, two hot freshwater showers, a library, and a galley where meals are served family style. Slide lectures about whales and other wildlife, and a preview of the next day's activities is presented each evening. Children as young as eight have been on this trip, but there are no special activities or facilities for them. This is a one-way trip, and you arrange your own return from the final stop in La Paz, a small city on Baja's gulf coast. *American Cetacean Society, Box 2639, San Pedro, CA 90731-0943, tel. 310/548–6279, fax 310/548–6950. Mid-Mar.: 11 days, $2,350–$2,585. Sign up 2 months in advance.*

CALIFORNIA TO BAJA **To Baja with the Best.** Nearly every whale-watching outfit runs a

tour down Baja California's Pacific coast, but no one has been doing it longer than the *Pacific Queen.* Its 10-day whale-watching trip has been led by the same biologist on the same boat with the same captain since 1971. The San Diego Natural History Museum, in conjunction with Palomar College, sponsored the first whale-watching trips to Baja California's San Ignacio Lagoon; it was on these early trips that encounters were first made with the famous "friendly" gray whales, which allow humans to touch them.

Museum marine biologist Margie Stinson and another biologist now lead the trip independently, taking 25 passengers aboard the 88-foot *Pacific Queen* on round-trip expeditions out of San Diego to the lagoon, where gray whales come to mate and give birth. On the way, you stop to see Baja's desert canyons and the seal rookeries, wildflowers, ospreys, herons, and other wildlife of Todos Santos, West San Benito, Cedors, and San Martin islands. At the lagoon, you board skiffs to get closer to the gray whales, in some cases close enough to touch them.

The *Pacific Queen* is a sportfishing motorboat, outfitted with single and double bunk rooms, two hot-water showers, and three heads. The ship's cook whips up amazingly bountiful meals in a postage-stamp galley. The cuisine is a mix of American and Mexican fare, with plenty of fresh seafood. Evenings are filled with slide shows and talks presented by the naturalists. Children are allowed on a case-by-case basis. *Pacific Queen, Fisherman's Landing, 2838 Garrison St., San Diego, CA 92106, tel. 619/726–2228, 619/224–4965, or 619/221–8500, fax 619/222–0799. Mid-Feb.: 10 days, $1,500. Sign up 3–6 months in advance.*

ALASKA

SOUTHEAST **Humpbacks, Grizzlies, and Glaciers in Frederick Sound.** This 10-day Biological Journeys trip through Frederick Sound, between Juneau and Petersburg, gives you a look at humpback whales in their summer feeding grounds. Led by a marine biologist, you and seven to nine other passengers board the 50-foot MV *Delphinus* to study the intricacies of the diverse ecosystem of Alaska's Inside Passage. The educational component of this trip is taken seriously; California's Humboldt State University will even give you academic credit for taking it. Children who can handle being in this adult environment may participate.

You learn to scan the water looking for the rainlike pattern that herring make, and before long you should see a humpback shoot to the surface scooping up huge mouthfuls. You're also likely to spot orcas, Dall and harbor porpoises, sea lions, and other marine mammals.

Whales share top billing with glaciers and grizzly bears on this trip; there are shore excursions to observe bears from a tower platform over salmon-filled Pack Creek and to view the glacial areas of Endicott Arm, Ford's Terror, and Tracey Arm. Videotape and hydrophone recordings made during the day are reviewed at evening lectures, so you can see and hear anything you missed because you were watching something else. Cruises are one-way, either from Juneau to Petersburg or vice versa. *Biological Journeys, 1696 Ocean Dr., McKinleyville, CA 95521, tel. 707/839–0178 or 800/548–7555, fax 707/839–4656. July–early Sept.: 10 days, $3,295. Sign up 4–6 months in advance.*

SOUTHEAST Killer Whales in Prince William Sound. Traveling farther north than other trips, along the Alaskan coast to Prince William Sound, Alaska Wilderness Sailing Safaris makes a seven-day run in search of killer and humpback whales. You couldn't hope for more qualified leaders than Drs. Jim and Nancy Lethcoe, two naturalists who have written volumes about the glaciers, geology, and natural history of the sound and have more than two decades of experience guiding trips in Alaskan waters.

You begin your journey in Valdez by taking the 8:30 AM tour boat ($89.50 round-trip) to the Growler Island Wilderness Camp. This six-hour boat ride is narrated, and on arrival you are treated to an all-you-can-eat cookout with salmon, chicken, ribs, and vegetarian options. From the camp, the Lethcoes lead groups of three or four in search of the killer whales that reside in the sound and the humpbacks that feed here each summer. Finback and minke whales are also spotted in the area from time to time, and you can usually count on seeing porpoises, sea lions, harbor seals, sea otters, puffins, and bald eagles.

To locate the best sighting areas each day, the Lethcoes keep in contact with a network of other scientists studying this virtually undisturbed 10,000-square-mile wilderness area. Besides watching the whales and other wildlife, you visit Columbia and Meare's glaciers, go kayaking for a closer look at the shoreline, and hike in the Chugach National Forest.

The Lethcoes operate the 40-foot *Arctic Tern III*, a Nordic 40 sailboat. The boat has compact but comfortable quarters and carries three or four passengers. Bunk rooms are tiny and heads are shared, but the boat has a full galley. Menus are lowfat with an emphasis on fresh fruits and vegetables, and special menus are available on request. There is a small library of books on the history, ecology, and geology of Prince William Sound, as well as a dinghy and inflatable kayaks for guest use. Families are welcome. *Alaska Wilderness Sailing Safaris, Box 1313, Valdez, AK 99686, tel. 907/835–5175, fax 907/835–5679. Early May–mid-June, mid-Aug.–mid-Sept.: 6 days, $1,560. Sign up at least 1–2 months in advance.*

SOUTHEAST Sailing with Humpbacks into Frederick Sound. Famous for its glaciers, its spectacular scenery, its abundant wildlife, and, of course, its whales, southeast Alaska's waterways are prime feeding grounds for humpbacks. Enter the *Island Roamer,* a 68-foot sailing yacht that carries a dozen people on 11-day cruises along the coastal waterways.

You gather in Prince Rupert, British Columbia, for orientation and take a floatplane (about $225) to the boat's anchorage in Petersburg (the trip is also done in reverse, where you sail from Prince Rupert and take the floatplane back from Petersburg). The itinerary is flexible, but you are sure to spend some time in Frederick Sound, the stomping ground of minke whales and Dall porpoises, and the summer home of several hundred humpbacks. Although cetaceans are the focus of attention on this trip, other wildlife is discussed in detail when it's encountered, as are the glaciers along the route. Small inflatable boats are used to take you ashore for hiking.

The crew of four have several years of practical field experience among them, along with backgrounds in marine biology, ecology, ornithology, and anthropology. Accommodations are in cabins with two berths each. You share the three heads, which have hot showers. Meals are prepared using local seafood and produce, and wine is served with dinner. Evening discussions and slide shows focus on marine mammals of the North Pacific, and there is an extensive library on board. The price of this trip includes a shore excursion to Ketchikan. This trip is quite popular and often sells out far in advance. Children are permitted. *Bluewater Adventures, 202-1656 Duranleau St., Vancouver, BC V6H 3S4, Canada, tel. 604/684–4575, fax 604/689–5926. Mid-June–July: 11 days, $2,400. Price includes 1 shore excursion; sign up at least 3–6 months in advance.*

HAWAII

OAHU, KAUAI, MAUI, AND THE BIG ISLAND **Saving the Humpbacks.** American Hawaii Cruises's seven-day whale-watching cruise is about as far from roughing it as you can get on any whale-watching trip. As a major contributor to the humpback whale research conducted by the Center for Whale Studies, the cruise line runs several of these trips out of Honolulu aboard their luxury liners SS *Independence* and SS *Constitution.*

Humpbacks are the stars of this trip. You spend a full day in the waters off Maui, where humpbacks often breach just yards from the ship, and there are optional small-craft trips to get even closer. If you stay on

deck, you can often see the humpbacks during the week near Kauai and the Big Island, although they are usually far from the ship. Other whale-related activities include documentaries shown in the ship's theaters, shore excursions to maritime and whaling museums, and a variety of whale trivia games and contests with prizes awarded. There are also presentations on other cetaceans found in Hawaiian waters made by a local naturalist who works in humpback-whale research and is on board for the week. You make stops at Kona and Hilo on the Big Island, Kahului on Maui, and Nawiliwili on Kauai.

Fine dining is part of any luxury cruise experience, and this trip is no exception. In 1993 the cruise line began offering traditional Hawaiian specialties made with fresh local ingredients from each island. At the beginning of the week, you are assigned to a table at one of two evening seatings, so you eat dinner with the same people all week. These ships spend the rest of the year doing traditional cruises, so they are equipped with an abundance of facilities: lounges and bars, saunas, massage rooms, and a movie theater, fitness center, shopping arcade, sports deck, pool, and game room. There's a special program for kids age 5 to 16.

Cabins come in a variety of sizes—with prices to match. Each ship has a crew of more than 300 and can carry nearly 800 passengers, but even when full they don't seem crowded. (Note: At press time, American Hawaii Cruises was under new ownership, but no changes in the whale-watching and other theme cruises had been announced.) *American Hawaii Cruises, 2 North Riverside Plaza No. 2000, Chicago, IL 60606, tel. 312/258–9600, fax 312/258–9601. Jan.–Mar.: 7 days, $995–$3,000. Sign up 6–12 months in advance.*

SOURCES

ORGANIZATIONS All of the following are involved in cetacean research and education and can be contacted for more information on whale-watching in North America: **Allied**

Whale Research (College of the Atlantic, Bar Harbor, ME 04609, tel. 207/288–5644); **American Cetacean Society** (Box 2639, San Pedro, CA 90731-0943, tel. 310/548–6279, fax 310/548–6950); **Atlantic Cetacean Research Center** (75 Essex Ave., Gloucester, MA 01930, tel. 508/283–2708); **Center for Whale Research** (Box 1577, Friday Harbor, WA 98250, tel. 206/378–5835); **West Coast Whale Research** (2020 Grosvenor Bldg., 1040 W. Georgie St., Vancouver, BC V6E 4H1, Canada, tel. 604/731–2166).

PERIODICALS "Spirit of the Sound" (Box 945, Friday Harbor, WA 98250, tel. 206/378–4710), a quarterly newsletter published by The Whale Museum, covers issues affecting marine mammals.

BOOKS *The American Cetacean Society Field Guide to the Orca,* by David Gordon and Chuck Flaherty, lists orca facts, guidelines for watching, and the best viewing spots along the western U.S. coastline. *The Oceanic Society Field Guide to the Gray Whale* (Sasquatch Books) profiles the migration cycles and behavior of gray whales and lists prime viewing areas from Alaska to Baja California. *The Sierra Club Handbook of Whales and Dolphins,* by Stephen Leatherwood, Randall Reeves, and Larry Foster, is a useful reference to what you'll see in the wild, with photos, illustrations, and descriptions of various cetaceans. *Where the Whales Are,* by Patricia Corrigan, describes several species and lists North American whale-watch tour operators.

ALSO SEE If you enjoy studying nature from the decks of a boat, turn to the Environmental Cruises chapter, and it's wildlife that holds your interest, check out the Birding and Nature Camps chapters.

Writing Conferences and Workshops

By David Low

hether you're an aspiring poet, a published novelist, or a born raconteur who wants to get your stories down on paper, you may find a writers' conference or workshop a good way to learn more about the process of writing or to make contacts in the publishing world. Conferences and workshops also provide writers with the chance to meet others with similar concerns, anxieties, and struggles. And if you've started to wonder if writing is worth pursuing as a profession, as an avocation, or even at all, attending a conference may help clarify what role it will play in your future.

Most of the conferences contained in this chapter offer daily workshops in a few areas of writing, along with lectures on the writing craft and readings by faculty and participants. Some also feature panels or talks with editors, literary agents, publishers, and others from the business side of publishing. Frequently, when a program concentrates more on the technical and creative aspects of writing rather than on the business side of publishing, the term *workshop* rather than *conference* is used in the name of the program.

Workshops usually engage instructors and students in discussions of participants' work, although some also provide writing exercises or talks relating to technique. At many conferences, you bring works in progress, in hopes of getting feedback and suggestions for revisions from instructors and peers. Several programs, however, welcome beginners and offer classes on the basics of writing. Panels often deal with such practical matters as how to write a book proposal or how to get a literary agent.

Most writing conferences focus on poetry and general fiction, but several also include courses in nonfiction, essay writing, or particular genres of fiction, such as mysteries, science fiction, and romance novels. Other gatherings concentrate on particular topics, such as women's issues, or on types of writing, such as children's books and nature writing.

Conferences attract a diverse group in terms of age, race, profession, and level of experience. Some conferences accept you on the basis of a writing sample, while others are first come, first served. There are workshops for just about everyone from beginners looking for guidance to those looking to turn pro, and even for pros who want to refine or expand their repertoire. Nearly every conference or workshop included in this chapter has faculty who are published writers with teaching credentials; occasionally, instructors also include editors, literary agents, or journalists.

Although conferences may provide useful feedback and encouragement about your writing, there may be negative aspects as well. Like many artists, writers can be an eccentric, unpredictable, competitive, and

---

David Low, a published fiction writer and book editor, has attended several writing conferences.

even fairly insensitive bunch. Along with the objective commentary and helpful advice, you may well hear criticism that is not constructive and seems off-the-wall or even hurtful. There's no way to predict people's reactions, but that's part of exposing your work to the public. Many of the teachers at these conferences are adept at clearly pointing out the strengths and weaknesses of a manuscript while remaining supportive. Published writers, especially those who have achieved some fame, don't always make the best teachers of writing because they're so used to having their own egos massaged. There are even some who believe—mistakenly—that giving tough, mean-spirited evaluations of student work means that they're being honest. That old rule applies here: Being good at doing something doesn't mean being good at teaching it. Most conference directors, however, make a point of hiring writers with good reputations as teachers. You may even get lucky and get one who understands your work in a way that no one ever has before.

If you choose a program that focuses on the business end of writing, don't expect to get your manuscript read and published then and there. Generally, guest speakers from the publishing world don't spend much time with individual participants; that's not what they've been paid to do. It is generally a bad idea to force a manuscript on an editor or agent in this context. Concentrate instead on making business contacts that could prove valuable later on.

Many conferences and workshops meet on college campuses, where participants stay in dormitories and dine at central dining halls. As a result, accommodations are likely to be merely adequate, and the food unexciting cafeteria fare. Luckily, most college towns also tend to have a variety of good—or at least interesting—restaurants. Some lodgings include kitchen facilities, so you can prepare your own meals. In general, the college settings are pleasant, tranquil environments. A number of conferences, however, take place in more dramatic or festive surroundings—a mountain retreat, a remote wilderness, a seaside resort, or the heart of a big city. Accommodations may be in seaside hotels or ski lodges amid spectacular scenery. Some of these conferences also pay special attention to food, hiring their own cooks to prepare sophisticated meals.

The conferences and workshops included in this chapter vary in cost from less than $500 to over $1,500, depending mostly upon whether lodging and meals are part of the package, but based also on the reputation and location of the program. Programs at colleges tend to be less expensive; the cost of those held elsewhere tends to be higher when you add the cost of any accommodations and meals that are not included in the price.

CHOOSING THE RIGHT PROGRAM

First decide what type of instruction would most benefit your work—a workshop that concentrates on the craft of writing and will help you improve a manuscript or a conference that emphasizes the nuts and bolts of getting published—then ask the organizers the following questions.

What are the requirements for acceptance? Conference requirements vary. Some programs accept all applicants; these are usually open to anyone interested in writing. Others require that you submit a writing sample with the application; these tend to attract writers who are past the beginner's stage.

How many students attend and how big are the classes? The number of participants at a program, and the number in any given seminar or workshop within it, varies wildly. Generally speaking, the lower the student-to-teacher ratio the better, especially if you want your writing to get personal attention. On the other hand, an inspiring lecture is no less so if given before a large crowd.

How much time is spent in workshops versus lectures? If you're attending a conference to get a response to your work and advice on revisions, choose a program that allows more time for workshops going over students' writing than for lectures.

How much of the day is spent in class and is there time to write and relax? Most workshop sessions last 2½ to 3 hours—although there are some that go on for longer—and are given in either the morning or afternoon, with the other part of the day free, filled with lectures and panel discussions, or open for taking another workshop on a different topic. If your chosen workshop focuses classroom time on critiquing and editing, find out when you are supposed to do the writing or if you're meant to arrive at the program with material to work on.

Are there organized non-workshop activities? Most conferences offer after-class activities of some sort, including readings by instructors and panel discussions, but these events are often optional. If you're attending a conference to improve your writing, it's wise to choose one that allows time to absorb what you've learned in class, and has less socializing.

How long has the workshop or conference been operating? Although newer programs may be perfectly fine, one that's been around for a few years will probably have dealt with and even be able to anticipate just about any situation or questions that may arise.

Who will be on staff when you want to go? The staff should be described in the conference brochure, but don't count on past instructors being there when you go. When you know exactly who will be teaching, try to read some of their work. If you like a writer's work, chances are he or she will have something valuable to pass on to you about writing.

Are private conferences with faculty scheduled and can you choose which faculty member you'd like to meet with? Many programs include one private conference with a faculty member as part of the fee; some charge extra for private consultations, and only a very few allow for additional private meetings. You generally have your private meeting with your own workshop leader.

Are faculty accessible to students at all times or only in classes? Although some teachers are open to meeting outside of class, don't assume that this is part of the program. It's rare that a faculty member is available to students every minute during the conference.

Are there workstations available? If you're planning to write while at a conference, find out if there is space available to do so. Some conferences provide rooms with a writing desk, and a few even have typewriters and computers available. For the most part, however, you should expect to supply your own writing equipment.

What's the cost and what's included? Many conferences include tuition, meals, and lodging in one price, others offer a meal and/or lodging package at additional cost, and some expect you to take care of your own lodging and meals. Unless otherwise noted, prices in this chapter include tuition, double occupancy lodging, and meals. Some programs also charge a $30 to $50 application fee or a reading fee, ranging from $10 to $60, for manuscript evaluations or personal conferences.

Are scholarships available? Some programs offer financial aid or fellowships based on the quality of your work. Applicants for aid must usually apply far in advance of the regular deadline, and some scholarships require recommendations.

What are the accommodations like? Many conferences are at colleges, where you stay in dormitories; others are at hotels or resorts with fancier digs. Most college dorm lodgings offer both single and double rooms, with single rooms usually costing a bit more. At hotels and resorts you are most often roomed with another workshop participant, but if you are determined to have a room of your own and are willing to pay the extra money for it, chances are no one will stop you.

What is the food like? You might be served standard cafeteria fare, but sometimes a chef is hired to cook up delicious meals. The workshop's setting—college campus or resort hotel—will be your first clue as to the caliber of the cuisine.

How far in advance do I need to book? Generally speaking, the sooner the better. Some workshops accept students by the quality of a submitted piece of writing, and that takes some time. Others are on a first-come, first-served basis, and can fill up fast. In either case, however, if there's still room at the last minute, you may get in.

Do you have references from past participants? It's often helpful to talk with people who have attended the conference in the past. They may be able to tell you how much or how little they got out of it. It's best, however, to talk with more than one person, since personality and talent could have a big effect on the writer's experience.

FAVORITE PROGRAMS

THE NORTHEAST

CONNECTICUT **Wesleyan Writers Conference.** Nonfiction workshops distinguish this six-day conference, held at the Wesleyan campus annually since 1956, from those that concentrate on poetry and fiction. Here, seminars, readings, and manuscript consultations can not only expose you to writing by the authors who teach or speak at the conference but also give you new perspectives on your own work.

You can choose among daily seminars in fiction, poetry, and nonfiction; most people attend one to two seminars in a particular genre regularly and sample the others. Typical morning and early afternoon seminars deal with the novel, the short story, fiction techniques, poetry, screenwriting, literary journalism, and the memoir. Seminars are led by visiting university writing teachers and established professional authors. You register for a consultation with a faculty member.

During the late afternoon and evening, you may attend workshops, student and faculty readings, guest lectures and talks by writers, and sessions with editors, agents, and publishers. The keynote lecture features a writer of national reputation; past speakers include Joyce Carol Oates, David Halberstam, and Donald Justice.

Writers of all levels of experience, ages, and backgrounds are welcome, and about 100 people attend each year. Scholarships and teaching fellowships are awarded on the basis of work submitted; otherwise acceptance is on a first-come, first-served basis.

You stay in campus dormitories in single rooms with shared bath, and meals are provided. You also have access to the university's athletic center with tennis courts and a swimming pool, and Olin Library, with its outstanding poetry collection. Wesleyan University is in Middletown, Connecticut, 30 minutes from Hartford and New Haven and two hours from either Boston or New York City. *Wesleyan Writers Conference, Anne Greene, Director, Wesleyan University, Middletown, CT 06459, tel. 203/343–3938, fax 203/347–3996. Late June: 6 days, $680. Price includes single room; sign up anytime, but scholarship and fellowship application deadline is 3rd Fri. in Apr.*

CONNECTICUT **Writers Retreat Workshop.** This 10-day workshop welcomes approximately 14 participants who have a novel in progress or ideas for a novel. To be accepted, you must submit an application along with a description of the novel you plan to work on while at the workshop. Since it began in 1987, the Writers Retreat has been attended by writers of every level, beginners to already published authors, from age 25 to 85—all firmly committed to improving their writing skills.

Workshop leader Gary Provost has been a contributing editor and columnist for *Writer's Digest* magazine and is also the author of books for writers, as well as many works of fiction and nonfiction, from children's books to true crime. Provost conducts daily classes (usually right after breakfast) that focus on story sense and dramatic structure. After the first few days of attention to craft, sessions are used to analyze student assignments. Later in the week, you team up with another attendee and edit each other's work. You meet privately with Provost at least once during the workshop and also have a formal session with a visiting editor and/or agent. In the evenings there are informal gatherings with the workshop leader, a New York editor, or an agent, as well as movies, games, and philosophical discussions.

The Writers Retreat takes place in a three-story Victorian house in the residential Federal Hill section of the town of Bristol, about 20 miles west of Hartford. Meals are provided, and lodging is dorm style with shared baths (some singles are available). Each student gets a private work space.

Provost offers a similar workshop in Florida in February as well as others at various other locations around the country. *Writers Retreat Workshop, Write It/Sell It, Box 14067, Northeast Plaza, Sarasota, FL 34728, tel. 800/642–2494, fax 813/379–0360. Oct.: 10 days, $1,595. Sign up several months in advance.*

■**MAINE**■ **The International Film & Television Workshops.** Established in 1973, this program comprises more than 200 workshops in all aspects of filmmaking and photography, including a half-dozen 7- and 14-day writing courses for first-time screenwriters as well as published writers who want to refine their work in the company of their peers and under the guidance of a professional writer. Workshop leaders are leading Hollywood screenwriters, and recent classes have included Script and Story Structure, Creating the Film Character, Writing for Television, Screenwriter's Master Class, and Writing Television Documentaries.

Each workshop is limited to 15 writers, but enrollment is generally around 10. To be admitted to most classes you must submit a writing sample and résumé and have the specified amount of professional experience. The workshops begin at 9 AM and you stay busy with lectures, critiques, discussions, and screenings all morning. Afternoons are devoted to writing and one-on-one consulta-

tions with instructors. You spend evenings in screenings or writing your assignment for the following day.

This program is based on a 20-acre campus in the small, tranquil New England village of Rockport, on Penobscot Bay, 90 miles north of Portland and 2 miles from the lively resort town of Camden. If you opt for the lodging plan, you have your choice of accommodations in Rockport, from standard motel rooms to lodging in period houses; singles, doubles, and dorms are available. You can arrange lodging for yourself at local motels, bed-and-breakfasts, and inns. Most students take their meals at The Homestead, a 19th-century farmhouse; meals are served buffet style and include lobster on Friday nights. At mealtimes students are able to share ideas with the film, television, and writing professionals attending and teaching classes. *The Workshops, 2 Central St., Rockport, ME 04856, tel. 207/236–8581 or 800/227–1541, fax 207/236–2558. May–Oct.: 7–14 days, $495–$695. Price does not include lodging and meals ($355–$625 per week); sign up as early as possible.*

■**MASSACHUSETTS**■ **Cape Cod Writers' Conference.** Run by the Cape Cod Writers' Center (*see below*), this six-day conference, established in 1963, includes courses and lectures on the craft of writing and the path to publication. Five courses are offered, meeting for 90 minutes a day, Monday through Friday. The lecture courses, which include some group discussion, deal with fiction, nonfiction, juvenile writing, poetry, and writing for television and film. Class leaders are published writers and writing teachers. Evening lectures cover the writing process and the publishing business. You can schedule conferences and manuscript evaluations with instructors, as well as with the book editor and literary agent who are in residence for the entire program (each personal conference and manuscript evaluation costs extra).

Attendees number about 150 and have different levels of writing experience; manuscripts may be submitted in advance for evaluation, but this is not required. The program is held at the Craigville Conference Center, near Hyannis. You can choose to stay at the conference center, which has a dining room that serves three meals a day (included in the daily rate), or at one of the numerous local bed-and-breakfasts. *Cape Literary Workshops/Cape Cod Writers' Center, Marion Vuilleumier, Executive Director, c/o Cape Cod Conservatory of Music and Arts, Rte. 132, West Barnstable, MA 02668, tel. 508/775–4811. Mid-Aug.: 6 days, $70 per course. Price does not include lodging (about $70 per night at nearby inns) or meals; sign up anytime.*

MASSACHUSETTS **Cape Literary Workshops.** This six-day program provides practical discussion on how manuscripts may be revised for publication. It is comprised of four-hour morning workshops on the novel, poetry, children's book illustration, children's book writing, and script writing and has been offered since 1986 by the Cape Cod Writers' Center, which also sponsors the Cape Cod Writers' Conference (*see above*).

The program begins with a Sunday evening orientation session. Workshops meet mornings, Monday through Friday, and in the afternoon you are free to write or explore the area. Enrollment for each workshop is limited to 10 participants, both beginners and people with works in progress, and each participant gets one personal critique. Faculty members are published writers with experience in conducting workshops. You are encouraged, but not required, to send some of your current work in advance.

Workshops meet at the Saint Mary's Episcopal Parish House on Route 6A in Barnstable. You arrange for your accommodations at nearby bed-and-breakfasts or motels and eat in area restaurants. *Cape Literary Workshops/Cape Cod Writers' Center, Marion Vuilleumier, Executive Director, c/o Cape Cod Conservatory of Music and Arts, Rte. 132, West Barnstable, MA 02668, tel. 508/775–4811. Mid-Aug.: 6 days, $410. Price does not include lodging or meals; sign up anytime.*

MASSACHUSETTS **Mount Holyoke Writers' Conference.** Since 1988, this seven-day conference has developed the work of both beginning and experienced writers and promoted contemporary writing through its workshops in fiction, nonfiction, poetry, and, occasionally, writing for children. With 10 to 15 participants, these intensive workshops meet for four afternoons over the space of a week; the other days feature craft lectures and panel discussions with guests from the publishing world. You spend mornings writing or in hour-long individual conferences with workshop instructors, and evenings are devoted to readings by faculty and guest writers.

Workshop leaders are chosen for artistic achievement, commitment to helping aspiring writers, and teaching experience. Recent instructors have included Ron Carlson, Shelby Hearon, Deborah Digges, and William Matthews. Faculty fellows (those who've just published their first book) offer additional manuscript consultations. To be admitted, you must submit a sample manuscript and a brief cover letter. The 75 or so participants come from all over the country and represent a variety of ages and professions.

The conference is held on the rolling 800-acre campus of Mount Holyoke College in South Hadley, in western Massachusetts near the Berkshire mountains. The town of South Hadley is about two hours by car from Boston and three from New York City. You stay and dine on campus at Mead Hall, and you're guaranteed a single room. More dining options are readily available across from the campus in the Village Commons, which consists of shops, restaurants, and a movie theater.

You have access to the entire campus, including an athletic center, tennis courts, an 18-hole golf course, an art museum, and the school's lawns, woods, and lakes. *Mount Holyoke Writers' Conference, Michael Pettit, Director, Box 3213-T, Mount Holyoke College, South Hadley, MA 01075, tel. 413/538–2308. Early June: 7 days, $700 with* lodging and meals ($400 without). Price includes single room; sign up anytime.

MASSACHUSETTS **New England Writers' Workshop.** Both the writing craft and the business of publishing are covered in this intensive five-day program geared to novelists and short story writers. Each leader meets with up to 15 participants to discuss and evaluate student work in the morning. During the afternoon, guest authors, editors, and agents speak about their professions and answer questions. You schedule one manuscript consultation with your workshop leader.

Workshop leaders are established authors and college-level writing teachers. Recent staff members have included C. Michael Curtis, conference director and senior editor at *The Atlantic,* and Jill McCorkle and Elizabeth Cox, novelists and short story writers. Guest speakers have included novelists John Updike, Stephen King, and Tim O'Brien; Faith Sale, senior editor at Putnam; Charles Everitt, publisher, Globe Pequot Press; and literary agents from New York. Approximately 40 students attend, and most have been writing for a few years. The conference is small enough to allow all questions at lectures to be answered and for staff members to get to know the participants personally.

The workshop takes place at Simmons College in Boston, in the Fens neighborhood, near the Museum of Fine Arts, Symphony Hall, and the Isabella Stewart Gardner Museum. You can choose to stay in single or double rooms at the college residence hall or opt to arrange your own lodging elsewhere. Coffee, tea, doughnuts, and croissants are offered each morning, but you have to buy your own lunch (either at the campus cafeteria or at the Longwood Galleria, a restaurant complex only a five-minute walk from campus) and dinner. There are no scheduled evening activities. *New England Writers' Workshop, Simmons College, Jean Chaput Welch, Assistant Director, 300 The Fenway, Boston, MA 02115, tel. 617/521–2090, fax 617/521–3199. Mid-June: 5 days,*

$630 with lodging ($675 for a single; $525 without lodging). Price does not include meals; sign up at least a week in advance.

NEW HAMPSHIRE **The Frost Place Annual Festival of Poetry.** This weeklong gathering of poets, established in 1979, takes place at Robert Frost's old farmhouse on a ridge overlooking the White Mountains of northern New Hampshire. Each day of the festival is presided over by one of the guest faculty, which consists of six nationally known poets. In the past, Amy Clampitt, Maxine Kumin, Brad Leithauser, and Charles Simic have participated. Mornings are devoted to lectures. You may attend two guest faculty afternoon workshops; during one of these, you receive a critique of your work. On other afternoons, you take part in critique workshops with each of the four resident faculty, all of whom work closely with students during the festival.

The festival creates an informal, friendly environment with small workshops of six to eight participants; guest faculty classes have an additional six to eight auditors, who do not have their work critiqued. Readings by faculty and students are scheduled in the evenings.

You must submit three pages of poetry to be considered for admission; about 120 people apply each year and about 45 are accepted. Attendees are usually in their thirties and have often been writing for several years.

The Frost Place can offer suggestions about where to stay in the area, including guest houses and inns that cost from $20 to $45 a night. Keep in mind that this area is a popular vacation spot in summer, so you must book far in advance. Also in the vicinity are bed and breakfasts and accommodations with kitchens. The festival arranges six catered lunches for a special rate. *The Frost Place Annual Festival of Poetry, Donald Sheehan, Executive Director, Ridge Rd., Franconia, NH 03580, tel. 603/823–5510. Late July–early Aug.: 7 days, $375. Price does not include lodging or meals; sign up by mid-July.*

NEW YORK Feminist Women's Writing Workshops. Since 1974 these weeklong workshops have provided a supportive environment for beginning and experienced women writers of all ages and backgrounds. The weekday schedule consists of small group critiques and writing sessions, workshops, evening readings, and talks. You may work in one or more genres, including poetry, fiction, personal essay, autobiography, drama, and journal writing.

The faculty here is made up of workshop alumnae who have become published writers, performance artists, and university teachers. The gathering invites a visiting professional writer to conduct seminars and give a reading; in 1994, the visiting writer was Dorothy Allison, author of *Bastard Out of Carolina*. New applicants are asked to submit a writing sample, and the conference encourages writers with all levels of experience to apply. About 25 to 30 women attend each year.

The workshops are held on the pleasant 170-acre campus of Hobart and William Smith Colleges in Geneva, on the shore of Seneca Lake, the largest of central New York's Finger Lakes. The town is equidistant from Syracuse, Rochester, and Ithaca, each about an hour away. You share one of the campus houses with 4 to 16 women, and private rooms are available. Lunch and dinner are served at the campus dining hall, and Continental breakfast is delivered to the residences.

Campus facilities include a pool, a weight room, and tennis courts. Nearby are such sites as the Harriet Tubman House, the Women's Hall of Fame in Seneca Falls, and the Montezuma Wildlife Refuge, known for its great blue herons. *Feminist Women's Writing Workshops, Margo Gumosky and Mary Beth O'Connor, Codirectors, Box 6583, Ithaca, NY 14851, no phone. Mid-July: 7 days, $500. Sign up anytime.*

NEW YORK Hofstra University Summer Writers' Conference. At this intensive 10-day program, established in 1972, there are six 2½-hour workshops daily, conducted by distinguished professional writers in poetry, nonfiction, fiction, writing for children, playwriting, and such genres as mysteries and science fiction. Students usually attend all sessions of up to three of the workshops.

Workshop size varies from 5 to 18 participants. Leaders are established authors, who are often also teachers. One half-hour conference for manuscript discussion is scheduled with a faculty member. Free time is given over to writing and readings by guest writers, presentations by faculty, and visits from a publisher, editor, or literary agent. The conference begins with a reception to welcome students and ends with a special banquet featuring a speech by a respected writer; Oscar Hijuelos, Hilda Wolitzer, and Jeffrey Sweet are among past speakers.

Applicants who want to take the program for credit must submit a writing sample no longer than five pages to demonstrate competence in written English, but acceptance is basically first come, first served. Applicants who don't want credit need not submit a writing sample. There are about 50 participants each year, ranging in age from 19 to 70; some are beginners, and others have been published in newspapers and literary magazines.

The conference meets at Hofstra University in Hempstead, Long Island, about 25 miles from New York City. About half of the participants live nearby and commute to the conference. If you come from out of town, you can stay in the residence halls, which are furnished simply and have shared bathrooms. No meal plan is offered, although you may eat at the college cafeteria. *Hofstra University Summer Writers' Conference, Lewis Shena, Codirector, 110 Hofstra University, Hempstead, NY 11550–1090, tel. 516/463–4016, fax 516/564–0061. Mid-July: 10 days, $875 with lodging ($600 without). Price includes only one meal; sign up anytime.*

NEW YORK New York State Summer Writers Institute at Skidmore College. First offered in 1987, this month-long program, sponsored by Skidmore College and the State University of New York at Albany, is divided into two 14-day sessions with courses in fiction, nonfiction, and poetry. Each three-hour course meets three times a week and is attended by 16 students.

If you're working on a novel, you can register at no extra cost for tutorial sessions with the senior fiction fellow, who in 1994 was novelist Douglas Glover. Tuesday and Thursday afternoons are given over to roundtable discussions with visiting faculty, who in the past have included Joyce Carol Oates, Russell Banks, Susan Sontag, and Ann Beattie. The faculty consists of prominent writers and teachers; recent instructors were Bharati Mukherjee, Marilynne Robinson, Francine Prose, and Richard Howard.

You must submit a brief letter describing relevant information (previous workshop experience, degrees, special interests) and a writing sample. The program attracts about 100 students from across the country, with participants ranging in age from 19 to 68, but most are in their twenties and thirties.

The institute is held at Skidmore College in Saratoga Springs, New York, a historic spa resort about 175 miles north of New York City. Students staying on campus are housed in air-conditioned single rooms unless a double is requested; you eat in the college dining hall or at nearby restaurants. All students have access to the college swimming pool, tennis courts, and gym; the college also has an active series of summer arts events, and the New York City Ballet and the Philadelphia Orchestra are in residence at the Saratoga Performing Arts Center. If you attend the second of the two sessions, in late July, you will be around for the start of Saratoga Springs's thoroughbred racing season. *New York State Summer Writers Institute, Office of the Dean of Special Programs, Maria McColl, Secretary, Skidmore College, Saratoga Springs, NY 12866-1632, tel. 518/584–5000, ext. 2264, fax 518/581–7400, ext. 2179. July: 14–28 days, $1,015–$2,030 with lodging and meals*

($840–1,190 without). Price includes single room; sign up anytime.

NEW YORK Remember the Magic: the International Women's Writing Guild Summer Conference. This eight-day writing conference for women emphasizes the joy of creativity and personal and professional empowerment. Started in 1977, it combines writing with other art forms. Each day there are more than 50 workshops, which are 75 minutes long and are on such topics as Writing: The Nuts and Bolts of It; Writing: Mythology, Folklore, and Truths; and Writing: The Arts and Body Movement. You may take up to six workshops a day. Readings and special events are scheduled during the evening.

The conference is open to 450 women regardless of professional portfolio, age, or background. Although the week attracts a diverse group, many participants are in a transitional period of their life, having recently experienced such events as a divorce or the departure of children from home. The 50-member faculty have a variety of interests, accomplishments, and teaching backgrounds.

The program takes place at Skidmore College in Saratoga Springs, about 175 miles north of New York City. You stay in modern dorms in double rooms (or a single for a higher price) and eat in the campus dining hall, which has a wide choice of dishes, including fruits, vegetables, and salads. *International Women's Writing Guild Summer Conference, Hannelore Hahn, Executive Director, Box 810, Gracie Station, New York, NY 10028, tel. 212/737–7536, fax 212/737–9469. Mid-Aug.: 8 days, $600–$675. Sign up anytime.*

NEW YORK Robert Quackenbush's Children's Book Writing and Illustrating Workshops. This unique five-day workshop, held annually since 1982, provides the opportunity to work with Robert Quackenbush, a prolific author and illustrator of children's books with more than 160 fiction and nonfiction books for young readers to his credit, including mysteries, biographies, and songbooks.

The goal here is to learn how to create books for children—from start to finish—and to help free you from creative blocks. The workshop focuses on picture books and is limited to 10 participants.

Class meets daily from 9 to 4 with one hour for lunch. The week begins with a discussion of each individual's plan or idea for a book, and by the end of the week, participants have a project ready in manuscript and/or dummy form to submit to a publisher. Lectures and readings cover such topics as how to work with a publisher to produce a book and how to develop projects for today's children and today's market. You may work individually or in groups, and Quackenbush provides daily feedback to each student or group. Depending on the needs of the class, the workshop may include a talk with a visiting editor and trips to a publisher or a relevant local exhibition.

The class attracts both professional and beginning writers and artists of different ages from all over the world; admission is after a phone interview or a staff review of your writing samples. Many workshop alumni have had their class projects published. You're responsible for arranging your own hotel and meals, although Quackenbush can suggest places to stay and to eat in the area. His studio, where workshops take place, is on Manhattan's Upper East Side, within walking distance of several major museums and galleries. *Robert Quackenbush's Children's Book Writing and Illustrating Workshops, 460 E. 79th St., New York, NY 10021, tel. 212/744-3822, fax 212/741-0515. Mid-July: 5 days, $650. Price does not include lodging or meals; sign up by June 1.*

NEW YORK **Vassar College Institute of Publishing and Writing: Children's Books in the Marketplace.** This annual six-day conference, started in 1974, concentrates on how the children's book industry works. Leading authors, artists, editors, designers, and agents in the field come together with those who want to learn about publishing and become part of it.

Monday to Friday, you spend mornings with writers and editors of children's literature, who review and discuss your writing proposals (although submitting a proposal is not required). During the afternoon and evening, workshops and lectures deal with various aspects of the industry: The Editorial Process, Creating the Picture Book, Deciphering a Contract, and the Production Process are just a few examples. Artists' portfolios are reviewed on the last day, and there is a festive luncheon.

Past instructors and speakers have included writers Nancy Willard and Mary Jane Auch; artists Barry Moser and Ed Young; literary agent Ethan Ellenberg; Scholastic executive editor Dianne Hess; and artists' representative Dilys Evans. The limited enrollment of 40 allows for serious consideration of individual projects. Applicants aren't screened ("I want a good mix of experience and innocence," says director Barbara Lucas. "They tend to reinforce each other.").

The conference is held at Vassar College, located in Poughkeepsie in the heart of the Hudson River valley, 75 miles north of New York City. Participants are housed in dormitories and take their meals at the central dining hall. The tranquil 1,000-acre campus encompasses fields, walking paths, gardens, two lakes, and 200 species of trees. You can use Vassar's athletic facilities for swimming, squash, tennis, jogging, and golf. *Vassar College, Director, Institute of Publishing and Writing, Box 300, Poughkeepsie, NY 12601, tel. 914/437-5903. Mid-June: 6 days, $800 with lodging and meals. ($525 without). Sign up by May 1.*

VERMONT **Bennington Writing Workshops.** This workshop on the 500-acre campus of Bennington College in southwestern Vermont provides a peaceful environment in which writers can create new work and revise manuscripts. The two-week sessions offer six hours of workshops in fiction, poetry, and nonfiction per week, as well as evening readings by students and prominent authors, hour-long tutorial meetings with faculty, and panel discussions on magazine and book publishing with professionals from the industry. The rest of the time is reserved for writing. Publishers and editors are in residence for three days, offering advice on how to submit manuscripts. Faculty are selected for the quality of both their writing and teaching experience.

Approximately 90 writers, both beginning and published, attend each session, and some people stay for both; individual workshops are limited to 12 students. You must submit a brief writing sample and a summary of your related experience. Lodging is in modest single dormitory rooms and meals are served in the Commons dining hall. The on-campus Carriage Barn Café is open at night after readings for receptions for students and teachers. Good restaurants, charming country stores, and a spring-fed lake good for swimming are all within walking distance of the campus. *Bennington Writing Workshops, Liam Rector, Director, Box BR, Bennington College, Bennington, VT 05201, tel. 802/442–5401, ext. 160, fax 802/442–6164. July: 14 days, $1,270 with lodging and meals ($815 without). Price includes single room; sign up as far in advance as possible.*

VERMONT **Bread Loaf Writers' Conference.** One of the oldest (established in 1926) and best-known writers' conferences in the country, the 12-day Bread Loaf Writer's Conference offers an opportunity for sustained dialogue between established and aspiring writers, as well as teachers of writing.

Authors come here to discuss writing as a craft and a profession; you shouldn't expect to do much writing. Bread Loaf is also not necessarily ideal for a sensitive novice, but it can be enjoyable if you want to meet other writers.

During the first week, staff members lecture about writing and hold discussions. The second week is devoted to workshops in poetry, fiction, and nonfiction during which manuscripts by participants are considered. Faculty and staff members read from their own work during the afternoon and evening. Editors, agents, and publishers make brief visits to the conference and provide panels and lectures. Panels on special topics, such as biography and nature writing, are also scheduled.

The faculty is made up of professional writers who also teach; several have been instructors at Bread Loaf for many years. Recent faculty members have included Nicholas Delbanco, Donald Justice, Robert Pack, Linda Pastan, Francine Prose, Mark Strand, and Nancy Willard. You can attend as a contributor or an auditor. Contributors each have one private conference with a faculty member and must submit writing samples ahead of time. Auditors may attend all conference events but don't have private conferences with the faculty. If you want financial aid, you must submit a nomination from an agent, editor, or writer by March 1. About 230 writers, from a wide range of ages and backgrounds, attend each year.

The conference is held at Middlebury College's summer campus in the Green Mountain National Forest in Ripton, Vermont. You stay in campus houses in double rooms with shared baths. Meals are served in the Bread Loaf Inn's dining room, with food prepared by the college dining service.

Middlebury's summer campus has tennis and volleyball courts, and swimming and excellent fishing are also available locally. Nearby is hiking, riding, golf, and antiquing. *Bread Loaf Writers' Conference, Carol Knauss, Administrative Coordinator, Middlebury College, Middlebury, VT 05753–6125, tel. 802/388–3711, ext. 5286. Late Aug.: 12 days, $1,450 ($1,380 for auditors). Sign up anytime; financial aid applicants contact the Writers' Conference by mid-Feb. for guidelines.*

VERMONT **Wildbranch Workshop in Outdoor, Natural History, and Environmental Writing.** First offered in 1988, this weeklong workshop is aimed squarely at writers who want to improve and learn how to market their outdoor, natural history, or environmental writing. Some 25 to 30 fiction writers, journalists, and essayists of all levels attend. Because the resident faculty are on campus during the entire session, you have ample opportunity to get feedback on your manuscript.

Three courses involving writing, reading, and discussions of student work are given daily—recently, Getting Personal, The Natural History of the Familiar, and Is Outdoor Writing Literature?, as well as a works-in-progress course open to intermediate and advanced writers; each course is limited to 10 students. You attend one of these daily, along with lectures and workshops offered by visiting faculty, who are usually editors and professional writers or journalists; one of these sessions generally deals with the business side of nature writing. You're not required to submit a writing sample unless you plan to take the works-in-progress course.

The three resident faculty members have recently included Steve Bodio, contributing editor and book reviewer for *Fly, Rod & Reel* magazine; Gale Lawrence, naturalist and teacher; and Joel Vance, a former writer for the Missouri Conservation Department. There are usually four visiting faculty.

The workshop convenes on the Sterling College campus in north central Vermont, 1½ hours from Burlington, 4½ hours from Boston, and 3 hours from Montreal. You stay in the school's dormitories, usually in doubles, although singles are usually available at the same price; three meals a day are provided at an informal dining hall. There are ample opportunities for canoeing, hiking, bicycling, swimming, and fishing at nearby lakes and streams. *Wildbranch Workshop in Outdoor, Natural History, and Environmental Writing, David Brown, Director, Sterling College, Craftsbury Common, VT 05827, tel. 802/586–7711 or 800/648–3591, fax 802/586–2596. Late June: 7 days, $700. Price includes single or double room; sign up by May 15.*

THE MID-ATLANTIC

MARYLAND Writers' Workshops at St. Mary's. You must submit a writing sample with your application to participate in one of the three workshops offered at St. Mary's College of Maryland, in the south-central part of the state. The two-week Intensive Poetry Writing Workshop, the 10-day Writer's Community Retreat, and the 8-day Fiction Writing Workshop all concentrate on the art and craft of writing in classes of fewer than 16, with supportive instructors who are published writers as well as teachers.

The Intensive Poetry Writing Workshop consists of five hours of morning and afternoon classes in which you write and discuss your work with instructors and classmates. On weekends, some 14 guest poets give readings and run 90-minute workshops and seminars; they are also available for individual consultation. Past guest poets have included Grace Cavalieri, Lucille Clifton, and James Haba.

The 10-day Writer's Community Retreat has an unstructured format designed to allow you to work according to a schedule that you design on your own. Based on the wishes of retreat participants—and with their help—the three guest instructors organize three 90-minute workshops. The rest of the time is left for participants to enjoy the surroundings and write.

The Fiction Writing Workshop involves five hours daily of morning and afternoon classes devoted to various aspects and techniques of fiction writing, such as plotting, point of view, and character development. You study published works of fiction (usually short stories), do writing exercises, and participate in critiques of students' work. On one of the weekends of the session, there are readings, workshops, and seminars by guest authors.

You stay on campus in single dormitory rooms. You can either cook your own meals in their kitchens or eat in nearby restaurants, some of which are within walking distance of the college. St. Mary's is in historic St. Mary's City, 10 miles from the Chesapeake Bay in the heart of Tidewater Maryland. *Writers' Workshops at St. Mary's, Dr. Michael Glaser, Director, St. Mary's College of Maryland, St. Mary's City, MD 20686, tel.*

301/862–0239. Late May–early June: 8–14 days, $350–$625. Price includes single room but not meals; sign up before May 1.

PENNSYLVANIA Cumberland Valley Fiction Writers Workshop. Devoted exclusively to fiction writing, this six-day conference offers aspiring writers the opportunity to work closely with an established author and provides an intensive yet informal experience. It consists of four workshops, limited to 10 participants each, that meet five times a week from 9 AM until noon. Class time is spent discussing and critiquing the students' work. Each faculty member gives an evening reading, and an afternoon is given over to a writers roundtable, a question-and-answer session with faculty. You have at least one private conference with your workshop leader. One day during the week, you all take a hike on the Appalachian Trail and visit nearby Fuller Lake for a picnic and swimming.

The faculty includes award-winning short story writers and novelists who also teach at the university level; recent instructors have included Lorrie Moore, Madison Smartt Bell, and Robert Olmstead. You must submit a 10-page writing sample with your application, and places are awarded on a first-accepted, first-reserved basis.

Most of the 30 to 40 participants come from Pennsylvania and nearby states (and many students commute from home) but are diverse in age, experience, and occupation. Although most write serious mainstream fiction, writers of historical fiction, fantasy, or other genre fiction are also welcome. The atmosphere is congenial and supportive.

Workshops meet at Dickinson College, a small liberal arts college in Carlisle, Pennsylvania, just 20 miles west of Harrisburg, the state capital, and two hours by car from Philadelphia or Washington, D.C. You stay in the college residence hall, two to a suite with private bedrooms, a common living area, and bath. You can opt for the full meal plan at the school's dining hall or pay as you go, taking only some meals there; several restaurants and food shops are within walking distance.

You have access to the college athletic facilities, including a pool, tennis courts, and a gymnasium. The surrounding area has many historic sites of interest, and Pennsylvania Dutch Country is nearby. *Cumberland Valley Fiction Writers Workshop, Judy Gill, Program Director, Department of English, Dickinson College, Box 1773, Carlisle, PA 17013-2896, tel. 717/245–1291. Late June: 6 days, $550 with lodging and meals ($300 without). Price includes single room in suite; sign up by May 15.*

THE SOUTH

GEORGIA Southeastern Writers Association Workshop. This weeklong conference offers workshops in poetry, the novel, playwriting, the short story, mass market fiction, nonfiction, writing for children, and inspirational writing. The goal is to help the 100 participants along the path to getting published and offer the opportunity to network with fellow writers.

Although applicants aren't screened and a manuscript is not required for acceptance, you have the option of submitting one for evaluation in each of three categories. You receive a written critique and a personal consultation during the program. The faculty consists of publishing professionals who are willing to share time with students both in and out of class. Other activities include a poetry reading, a writing contest, an awards banquet, and evening lectures by guest editors and writers.

The conference takes place at Epworth-by-the-Sea, a large hotel and conference center on St. Simons Island, 60 miles south of Savannah. You have your choice of singles, doubles, and triples at the hotel, and all meals are provided. Faculty and students eat together. The conference encourages participants to bring their families. The island offers six golf courses, a pool, beaches, walking paths, historic buildings, fishing, and the restaurants and shops in St. Simons village. *Southeastern Writers Association Workshop, Nancy Knight, Director, 4021 Gladesworth La., Decatur, GA 30035, tel. 404/288–2064. Late Aug.: 7 days, $380–$595 with lodging and meals ($200 without). Sign up anytime; manuscript submission by June 1.*

KENTUCKY **Green River Writers Novel in Progress Workshop.** This weeklong conference is designed for the beginning novelist who has a work either in progress or completed and who wants a professional critique and peer support. Monday through Friday are spent in groups of five to seven participants, with each group led by a faculty member. Each workshop has a different focus—horror/fantasy, romance, mystery, other genres, and mainstream—and you schedule an hour-long private conference with your workshop leader. You choose one workshop to "major" in, and your work is scrutinized only here, but you may sit in on any or even all of the others. On Saturday morning there are lectures on such topics as publishing short story collections, writing for children, and collaborating on a novel. A panel discussion by editors and literary agents fills Saturday afternoon, after which you have a 15-minute private conference with them. The conference ends with a Saturday night buffet at which you mingle with the 30 or so other participants, instructors, and visiting panelists.

All instructors are published novelists, and most also have teaching experience. The faculty changes from year to year, although there are usually many familiar faces among both the teachers and students who have come back for more. You must submit a synopsis or outline of your novel, along with three chapters or 60 manuscript pages. Several participants have already completed novels and are attending the program for feedback and advice on how to publish their work.

The conference is held at the University of Louisville's Shelby campus in a suburban area of East Louisville. You stay in small, graduate student dorms in private or shared rooms, with shared baths. The dorms have TVs, kitchens, and dining areas. You take care of your own meals, which you can cook yourself or eat in local restaurants. *Green River Writers Novel in Progress Workshop, Sandra Daugherty, Program Director, 11906 Locust Rd., Middletown, KY 40243, tel. 502/245–4902. Early Jan.: 7 days, $275. Price does not include lodging ($14–$19 per night) or meals; sign up by Dec. 1.*

NORTH CAROLINA **Duke University Writers' Workshop.** With the aim of creating an atmosphere of generosity and support rather than competition, this program includes seven workshops, limited to 10 to 15 writers each, covering fiction, poetry, playwriting, the memoir, and writing fundamentals. Each workshop meets for three hours, Monday through Friday mornings, and includes one 30-minute conference with the workshop leader. Two afternoons are given over to readings by faculty and participants, and another two are free for writing or relaxation and guest lectures. The program, first held in 1979, ends with a group luncheon and a talk by a guest speaker, usually a local professional writer.

The faculty may not be famous, but they are all published authors and experienced teachers. Workshop sessions balance criticism and instruction—you discuss manuscripts' strengths and weaknesses, and explore possible revisions. Participants are all serious about writing but vary in experience; most workshops require a writing sample and/or a letter describing your personal goals for the workshop.

The program takes place on the campus of Duke University in Durham. Most participants stay in local hotels rather than on campus, although lodging in dorms can be arranged; there is no meal plan. The campus offers swimming, tennis, and golf. *Duke University Writers' Workshop, Marilyn Hartman, Director, Box 90703, Durham, NC 27708-0703, tel. 919/684–6259, fax 919/681–8235. June: 6 days, $295. Price does not include lodging and includes only one meal; sign up anytime.*

TENNESSEE **Sewanee Writers' Conference.**
This 12-day program of workshops and lectures on the craft of writing, first held in 1990, takes place at the University of the South in Sewanee, Tennessee. The *Sewanee Review,* a distinguished literary publication, makes its home at the school, and such celebrated authors as Robert Penn Warren, Katherine Anne Porter, Ford Madox Ford, Peter Taylor, and Jean Stafford have lived and worked in the town. The program is supported by a fund established through the estate of playwright Tennessee Williams.

On the daily schedule, lectures alternate with workshops in fiction, poetry, and playwriting. You choose one workshop to attend when you sign up and attend its five sessions; in your free time, you may also audit other workshops. There are two instructors per workshop; you meet once privately with one of them to discuss your work in progress. Afternoons and evenings are devoted to lectures or readings by workshop and university faculty, and guest writers, critics, agents, directors, and editors. One of the students' plays discussed at the conference may be developed for a future production at the university.

The workshop leaders always include several highly respected writers: Recent faculty members have been fiction writers John Casey, Tim O'Brien, Susan Minot, and Stanley Elkin; poets Maxine Kumin and Derek Walcott; and playwrights Tina Howe and Horton Foote. Guest speakers have included editors David Godine and Robert Giroux and writers Arthur Miller, William Styron, and Peter Taylor.

Applicants are selected on the strength and promise of their work. You must send in 10 to 15 pages of poetry, 20 to 40 pages of fiction, or a one-act play with your application. There are 105 participants in the program, and 15 students in each workshop.

The University of the South's rural campus, full of ivy-covered Gothic buildings, is in south-central Tennessee, 45 miles southeast of Chattanooga and 90 miles northwest of Nashville. You stay in single or double dormitory rooms with shared bathrooms. The full meal plan, served on campus, includes a salad bar, low-calorie items, and vegetarian selections. The university summer session and the Sewanee Summer Music Center sponsor films, lectures, and concerts, and you're within walking distance of tennis courts, lakes, and a golf course. Biking, jogging, hiking, rock climbing, and horseback riding are also available. *Sewanee Writers' Conference, Cheri Peters, Administrator, 310 St. Luke's Hall, University of the South, Sewanee, TN 37383-1000, tel. 615/ 598–1141. Late July: 12 days, $1,150. Sign up by early spring.*

THE MIDWEST

ILLINOIS **Mississippi Valley Writers Conference.** This six-day conference, established in 1974, provides professional guidance to writers at all levels of experience. There are eight hour-long writing workshops daily, led by professional writers, in poetry, writing for children, nonfiction, the short story, and romantic fiction; two cover the novel and there's one for beginners on basics and a photography workshop. Each workshop has 15 to 20 participants, and each gets a private conference with the workshop leader, who will critique a 10-page manuscript if it's submitted in advance. You can submit a manuscript for each and every workshop you take. Evenings are devoted to readings by faculty and students, and on the last night there's a banquet, during which students receive awards for their writing.

The conference is held at Augustana College, a liberal arts institution on the banks of the Mississippi River that serves as the area's major arts center. You stay in a campus dormitory, and although meals are in the cafeteria, it's all home cooking. *Mississippi Valley Writers Conference, David Collins, Director, or Bess Pierce, Secretary, Student Center, Augustana College, Rock Island, IL 61201, tel. 309/764–5540. Early June: 6 days, $40 (1 workshop), $75 (2 workshops), $30 for the third or additional work-*

shops. Price does not include lodging ($95 for 6 nights) or meals ($85 for 15); sign up by May 15.

INDIANA **RopeWalk Writers Retreat.** New Harmony, Indiana, now a typical midwestern small town, was the site of two experiments in communal and utopian living in the 19th century; the restored buildings built and used by their creative thinkers are the backdrop for this intellectual retreat. The aim is to provide writers with expert instruction and advice in a small workshop setting where there's plenty of opportunity for interaction among the 50 or so attendees—usually about a dozen per workshop.

The conference offers fiction, poetry, and sometimes nonfiction workshops, and you get one individual conference with your leader. Workshops meet three times a week, and lectures on technique and discussion groups are held twice weekly. Evenings are usually reserved for readings by faculty and guests.

The faculty consists of five published authors who often are also teachers. Recent faculty members have included Ann Beattie, Stephen Dobyns, Heather McHugh, and Andrew Hudgins. Only scholarship applicants' work is screened and evaluated beforehand. Full-paying applicants submit manuscripts with their applications; materials are then forwarded to workshop leaders to be read before the workshop begins. Participants are usually college educated and in their thirties and forties.

You can stay at the New Harmony Inn and Conference Center, the retreat's Shaker-simple headquarters, or choose the less expensive lodgings of the Barn Abbey, a rustic dormitory with double rooms, or any of the area's many bed and breakfasts. You take breakfast and lunch at the Barn Abbey dining room, and two dinners are provided; other nights you eat on your own in town. *RopeWalk Writers Retreat, Linda Cleek, Program Coordinator, c/o Extended Services, University of Southern Indiana, 8600 University Blvd., Evansville, IN 47712, tel. 812/464–1989 or 800/467–8600, fax 812/*

464–1958. Mid-June: 7 days, $375. Price does not include lodging ($15–$75 per night) and most dinners; sign up by mid-May (late Apr. for scholarship applications).

IOWA **Iowa Summer Writing Festival.** Home to the famed Iowa Writers' Workshop, a two-year graduate program, the University of Iowa has also sponsored this Summer Writing Festival since 1987. Perhaps the largest in the country, this noncredit program offers more than 90 workshops lasting one or two weeks, as well as some weekend options, in a variety of topics and genres, from writing of novels, short stories, poetry, essays, and plays to creative nonfiction, women's writing, writing with ethnic variety, children's books, romance novels, science fiction, and the memoir.

Workshops start with Sunday supper, orientation, and a class meeting. For the rest of the week, classes meet for three hours each afternoon. Although workshop instructors may also suggest writing exercises and readings of published work, the primary text for classes is student writing; the group discusses each writer's work, and leaders encourage and critique you both in class and in private conferences.

Monday through Friday at 11 AM is the Elevenses, a series of presentations, lectures, and panels. In the evening there are readings by guest authors, often followed by question-and-answer sessions. Mornings and some evenings, you're free to write, read, research, and meet with other writers. An open-mike night gives everyone a chance to share his work.

The faculty consists mostly of published writers, many of them University of Iowa graduates or teachers. Workshops are open to any adult—first come, first served—who wants to participate; there are classes for beginning, intermediate, and advanced writers, and all are limited to 12 students.

The University of Iowa is in Iowa City, in the southeastern part of the state. You are responsible for arranging your own accommodations, but there are several options: a campus residence hall, an on-campus hotel, and the downtown Holiday Inn, within walking distance of the school. Meals are also up to you (except for the welcome supper and the banquet at the end of the week), and again, there are many possibilities to choose from between the residence hall kitchens and cafeterias, the campus dining rooms, and nearby restaurants. The university sponsors several summer cultural programs, including theater and musical performances. *Iowa Summer Writing Festival, Peggy Houston or Karen Burgus Shootman, Division of Continuing Education, 116 International Center, University of Iowa, Iowa City, IA 52242, tel. 319/335–2534, fax 319/335–2740. June–July: 6–13 days, $310–$620. Price does not include lodging or meals; sign up by early Mar.*

MINNESOTA Mississippi River Creative Writing Workshop in Poetry and Fiction. This gathering at St. Cloud State University, established in 1974, is Minnesota's longest-running and best-known creative writing conference. The program, two weeks involving eight formal meetings, Monday through Thursday afternoons, is especially good for beginners or those who want to brush up on their creative writing skills.

Poet and short story writer Bill Meissner, who teaches at St. Cloud State University, leads the first week of workshops; he gives daily writing exercises and conducts group discussions about fiction, poetry, and nonfiction.

During the second week, you can meet and talk with four or five visiting published authors, who read from and lecture about their own work, and answer questions. Guest speakers are selected for both their writing skills and their abilities and reputations as entertaining and personable teachers; past visitors have included poet Robert Bly and novelists Jon Hassler and Kate Green.

No writing sample is required, and each year about 35 to 40 people attend, representing many ages, backgrounds, and professions; many come from the surrounding area. The group stays together as a unit throughout the program, but may be split up occasionally for discussions or class exercises.

You can stay in university student housing or opt for the reasonably priced area accommodations. You are responsible for your own meals, but there are several restaurants and eateries near the campus. *Mississippi River Creative Writing Workshop in Poetry and Fiction, Dept. of English, Riverview 106, St. Cloud State University, St. Cloud, MN 56301-4498, tel. 612/255–3061. Mid-June: 8 days over a 2-week period, $297–$320. Price does not include lodging or meals; sign up anytime.*

MINNESOTA Split Rock Arts Program. This program consists of 45 intensive weeklong workshops in both the literary and visual arts—some 16 of them devoted to writing, with topics ranging from creative nonfiction, the short story, essay writing, and journals and diaries to children's picture books, poetry, and the nature of creativity. Most of these require about 60 hours in and out of class, including some work done before you arrive. There are about 16 students in each group.

Participants are usually highly motivated and in their forties; they're typically not earning a living at their art but are committed avocational artists who come here for the opportunity to work with renowned practicing writers and artists. The faculty are all also accomplished teachers with the experience to direct and challenge their students at different levels.

The Split Rock program, which was founded in 1983, takes place at the University of Minnesota's campus in Duluth, on the hills overlooking the western tip of Lake Superior and the city's harbor. Some workshops are conducted as retreats at the university's Cloquet Forestry Center, southwest of Duluth, amid 160-year-old red pine trees.

Lodging is not included in your fee, but residences and two-bedroom apartments on campus are available. You may fix your own meals in your apartment's kitchen; eat out around Duluth; or buy a meal ticket good for any 10 meals—breakfast, lunch, or dinner—at the dining center. If you attend workshops at the Cloquet Forestry Center, your fee includes lodging at the center and meals in its dining hall. *Split Rock Arts Program, University of Minnesota, 306 Wesbrook Hall, 77 Pleasant St. SE, Minneapolis, MN 55455, tel. 612/624–6800, fax 612/624–5891. July–Aug.: 6 days, $330–$350 ($584 with lodging and meals at Cloquet Forestry Center). Price of Duluth workshop does not include lodging or meals; sign up in March.*

MISSOURI **Mark Twain Writers Conference.** At this relaxed five-day gathering, established in 1985, you can explore the intricacies of both the written word and the marketing of creative work. Each year, morning lectures explore a main theme (the Great American Novel, the Great American Short Story, the Wild Wild Midwest), while afternoon workshops and discussion groups cover both craft- and business-related topics: fiction and nonfiction, the short story, poetry, books, humor, mystery, genre writing, biography, Mark Twain, children's literature, personal and inspirational writing, book proposals, freelancing, and making the most money from your work. You may also arrange private conferences with faculty.

Evenings are for fun, and past years have brought a dead celebrities banquet, a murder mystery contest, and a toga party.

Instructors include published writers, editors, literary agents, and publishers. Recent faculty members have included James Hefley, publisher of Hannibal Books; award-winning mystery writer Nancy Pickard; and Bruce Woods, an editor at *Writer's Digest*. The 145 participants, accepted on a first-come, first-served basis, are a diverse group from all levels of writing experience and education.

The conference meets at Hannibal-LaGrange College on a bluff overlooking the Mississippi River in the northeastern Missouri town of Hannibal, Mark Twain's boyhood home. Twainees stay in college residence halls, mostly doubles, although a few singles

are available at the same price on request; you can opt to lodge at local hotels at additional cost. Meals are in the campus dining hall. In town, you can visit several sites associated with the 19th-century author; a riverboat ride and tours of Hannibal's historic district, the Mark Twain home and museum, and Twain's last public speaking site in town, are included in your conference fee. *Mark Twain Writers Conference, Cyndi Allison, Coordinator, 921 Center St., Hannibal, MO 63401, tel. 800/747–0738, fax 314/221–2462. June–July: 5 days, $375–$395. Sign up by the end of March.*

OHIO **Antioch Writers' Workshop of Yellow Springs.** This seven-day program at Antioch College, a central Ohio cultural center, creates a supportive environment for writers at all levels of experience. The conference was established in 1986.

Classes and lectures run from morning to midafternoon daily and cover the novel, the short story, poetry, nonfiction, playwriting, writing for children, and other topics. During the afternoon, agents, editors, and other publishing professionals make presentations. In the evening, there are readings by faculty and visiting writers, followed by sharing and critique sessions, in various genres, that can run until midnight.

The 20-member faculty consists of professional writers, many of them with considerable teaching experience. Of the conference's 80 participants, 30 of the more advanced participate in intensive seminars in the short story, poetry, and memoir. Because the student-to-faculty ratio is a low four-to-one, you have ready access to instructors. Manuscripts submitted in advance will be read and discussed with you privately.

Single and double dorm rooms are available at Antioch; you can get a special rate at the 8-mile-distant Xenia Holiday Inn; or you can pitch a tent at the 2,000-acre John Bryant State Park, 4 miles from Antioch. You can take your meals in the campus cafeteria on a meal plan or on a pay-as-you-go basis, or eat at restaurants in town. Dorm rooms have refrigerators and microwaves. The conference begins with a special banquet that features a keynote speech by a prominent writer.

Antioch College is 30 minutes from Dayton and an hour from Columbus and Cincinnati. The area has a number of pleasant shops, and there's a 1,000-acre nature preserve with hiking trails and a 9½-mile bike path open to cyclists, walkers, joggers, and skaters. Tuition discounts are available for repeat attendees and residents of neighboring counties. *Antioch Writers' Workshop of Yellow Springs, Susan Carpenter, Director, Antioch University, Box 494, Yellow Springs, OH 45387, tel. 513/767–7068, fax 513/767–6470. Mid-July: 7 days, $450. Price does not include lodging or meals; sign up 2 months in advance.*

THE SOUTHWEST

NEW MEXICO **Santa Fe Writers' Conference.** This five-day conference gives emerging poets and fiction writers the chance to meet well-known authors and benefit from their instruction. At the core of the conference are small, morning workshops in fiction and poetry, which are limited to 15 participants each. During these, you concentrate on manuscript editing and the creative process. You attend lectures by agents and editors in the afternoon, faculty readings of their own works in the evening.

Four poets and writers with considerable teaching experience lead workshops. Recent faculty have included poets James Tate and Dara Wier, fiction writer E. M. Broner, and novelist Robert Stone. Participants are chosen by the quality of their work; you submit 10 pages of your writing in order to be one of the 60 accepted. You may schedule one private conference with a workshop leader for evaluation of your manuscript.

Workshops meet at Plaza Resolana, a small conference center facility near Santa Fe's historic plaza. You stay in single or double rooms right at the center, where a full meal plan is provided. The neighborhood is brimming with shops, restaurants, and galleries, and you're only a short walk from art and history museums, Native American vendors selling their wares, and the landmark La Fonda Hotel. *Santa Fe Writers' Conference, Julie Shigekuni, Program Director, Recursos de Santa Fe, 826 Camino de Monte Rey, Suite A-3, Santa Fe, NM 87505, tel. 505/ 982–9301, fax 505/989–8608. Early Aug.: 5 days, $645 ($745 for singles). Sign up anytime.*

NEW MEXICO **Taos School of Writing.** This weeklong conference takes place in the dramatic mountains of the Kit Carson National Forest, 9,000 feet above sea level. First held in 1993, it is made up of small workshops on fiction and nonfiction writing (the number varying according to the number of attendees). You spend mornings in groups of no more than 12, critiquing student manuscripts; faculty rotate through all classes to keep the instruction lively and varied. Authors, editors, and agents speak in the afternoons and then stay on for two-hour group discussions. You have several hours of free time right after lunch for reading, hiking, writing, or napping. Evenings are open for writing, readings by students and faculty, and informal meetings.

Instructors include prize-winning writers, as well as a visiting agent and editor who provide valuable perspectives on the marketplace. The program also invites visiting lecturers, among them, in the past, Tony Hillerman and Roger Zelazny. When you apply, you must submit a manuscript of no more than 20 pages; although there are no restrictions on subject matter or style, poetry and screenplays are not allowed. The faculty determines admissions based on the quality of the writing. Many of the students here have been writing for several years; some have published their work or come from journalism, teaching, and writing-related professions.

The school is in the mountains in Taos Ski Valley, 23 miles north of the town of Taos and about three hours from Albuquerque. Workshops are at Thunderbird Lodge, a wood-frame ski resort where everyone stays and eats—its dining room offers some of the best eating in the area. In the area, you can go hiking or visit the Taos Pueblo, the Millicent Rogers Museum, Kit Carson's home, the D. H. Lawrence Ranch, or the awesome Rio Grande Gorge. *Taos School of Writing, Suzanne Spletzer, Administrator, Box 20496, Albuquerque, NM 87154, tel. 505/293–0303, fax 505/237–2665. Mid-July: 7 days, $1,050. Sign up by May 1.*

THE ROCKIES

COLORADO **Aspen Writers' Conference.** The craft of writing and participants and their work are the focal points of this conference first held in 1976. Mornings, there are workshops in fiction, poetry, and literary nonfiction (each limited to 15 writers) and private conferences with faculty. Afternoons, staff members give craft lectures. A business program features presentations by agents, editors, and publishers, who are available for questions. There are usually special guest speakers, often from the international literary scene. Past guests have included novelist Michael Ondaatje and poet Miroslav Holub.

The faculty is made up of accomplished writers, most of whom have taught at the university level; recently you might have studied with Alicia Ostriker, Robert Pinsky, Shelby Hearon, and Charles Baxter. You're asked to submit a poetry or prose manuscript with your application, and you should have some knowledge of contemporary literature. There are usually about 60 participants per session.

The weeklong program takes place at various sites in Aspen. The school arranges for your accommodations in area condos; you're on your own for meals. Aspen is chockablock with good restaurants, as well as with Victorian-style buildings; music, art, dance, and theater; and loads of hiking, rafting, biking, camping, horseback riding, fishing, ballooning, and other outdoor activities. The conference organizer, the Aspen Writers' Foundation, also sponsors other literary educational programs for adults and children. *Aspen Writers' Conference, Drawer 7726, Aspen, CO 81612, tel. 303/925–3122. Late June–early July: 7 days, $425. Price does not include lodging or meals; sign up at least 2 months in advance.*

MONTANA **Environmental Writing Institute.** First held in 1990, this five-day workshop is one of only a few devoted exclusively to nature and environmental writing. It's sponsored by the University of Montana in conjunction with the Teller Wildlife Refuge, the private 1,300-acre preserve 45 miles south of Missoula that is the program's venue. From Sunday through Thursday, you spend mornings in workshops discussing and critiquing one another's work. Afterward, you have free time to write, read, contemplate the scenery, or soak in a hot springs or go hiking, rafting, fishing, bird- or wildlife watching in the refuge; the nearby Bitterroot Range has some of the country's finest alpine and subalpine landscape.

You meet, lodge, and dine in remodeled rustic farm buildings. Most rooms are doubles, but there are a few singles at the same rate; all meals are homemade. Guests, including local writers and wildlife biologists, often stay for dinner and talk informally with participants. One evening, the workshop leader gives a public reading of his or her work.

To be among the 14 participants, you must apply with a résumé and a nonfiction manuscript on an environment-related or nature topic; most but not all participants seem to have written about the northern Rockies and are about 37 on average, with published work to their name. Past leaders have included Peter Matthiessen, Wendell Berry, and Gretel Ehrlich. *Environmental Writing Institute, Henry Harrington, Director, Center for Continuing Education, University of Montana, Missoula, MT 59812, tel. 406/243–6486, fax 406/243–2047. Late May: 6 days, $500. Sign up by March 31.*

MONTANA **Yellow Bay Writers' Workshop.** This informal weeklong conference sponsored by the University of Montana includes workshops in poetry, fiction, and creative nonfiction. It's held in western Montana, at the Flathead Lake Biological Research Station at Yellow Bay, 55 miles south of Glacier National Park. Flathead is the largest natural freshwater lake in the United States west of the Mississippi.

Four instructors, all professional writers, lead workshops of up to 15 students. Past faculty have included Ian Frazier, Marilynne Robinson, Thomas McGuane, James Tate, Carolyn Kizer, and Joy Williams. You attend daily workshops, along with lectures on the writing craft and readings by other students; evenings are devoted to faculty readings. Each year a guest editor or publisher leads a discussion or panel on publishing. Instructors also stay at the conference site, so you have many opportunities to converse with them. To apply, you must submit a brief manuscript and one-page biography. The average participant is 35 to 40 years old and has been writing independently for several years.

You sleep in rustic one-room cabins with shared bath—on your own if you wish (at the same price as with a roommate). Meals are served in a cafeteria on the grounds. In your free time you can go swimming, fishing, and boating or canoeing in Yellow Bay; bookstores, restaurants, galleries, and theaters are in Big Fork (15 miles away) or Polson (18 miles distant). *Yellow Bay Writers' Workshop, Annick Smith, Workshop Coordinator, Center for Continuing Education, University of Montana, Missoula, MT 59812, tel. 406/243–6486, fax 406/243–2047. Mid-Aug.: 7 days, $725–$775 with lodging and meals ($425 without). Sign up by 1st week of July.*

THE WEST COAST

CALIFORNIA **Annual Book Passage Travel Writers' Conference.** Sponsored by a lively Marin County bookstore noted for its nearly encyclopedic travel section, this four-day conference covers travel writing in all its manifestations. *San Francisco Examiner* travel editor Donald George, who has chaired the Thursday-through-Sunday event since its beginnings in 1992, covers writing for guidebooks, writing for magazines and newspapers, and writing travel literature; you learn everything from how to market yourself and break into new publications to how to develop a guidebook proposal and whether or not to hold out for electronic rights. George and a couple of other veteran travel scribes teach daily, three-hour, morning workshops that deal with topics ranging from how to prepare a manuscript (as in "Where do you put your name?") to how to tell a good story and write a query that sells. In the afternoon, two 90-minute panels each day showcase representatives from the major travel information providers, including Fodor's editorial director Karen Cure, Moon Publications marketing director Donna Galassi, Mountaineers' editor-in-chief Margaret Foster, *Condé Nast Traveler* special-projects editor Aaron Sugarman, *Travel & Leisure* senior editor Barbara Peck, and *Los Angeles Times* travel editor Leslie Ward, among others. Every participant has ample opportunity to ask questions. In 1994 the keynote speakers at the opening-night banquet were Jan Morris and Arthur Frommer.

Most participants who don't live in the area lodge at the Corte Madera Inn, a modern Best Western property with a certain California ambiance (weathered-shingle siding, a lushly landscaped courtyard, and a magnificent swimming pool complete with hot tub), where many of the workshop meetings are held. Lunches, served at Book Passage, run to pasta salads; area restaurants offer a varied choice of sophisticated California and Italian fare. Good shopping is just across the street, and the Wine Country and the pleasures of the city are a short drive away. *Book Passage, 51 Tamal Vista Blvd., Corte Madera, CA 94925, tel. 415/927–0960. Mid-Aug.: 4 days, about $450. Price excludes breakfast, all but 1 dinner, and lodging (about $85 per night including Continental breakfast); sign up any time.*

CALIFORNIA **Idyllwild School of Music and the Arts Summer Program Writing Work-**

shops. Readings, critiques, and some writing exercises fill the mornings of these weeklong adult writing courses at this renowned school's summer program, established in 1950; assignments and individual conferences take place in the afternoons and evenings. Courses are intensive, limited to 15 participants; they may include workshops in the writer's journal and creative writing in all genres. Published professional writers attend these courses alongside near novices, and classes are small enough for everyone to get individual attention.

The school is in southern California's San Jacinto Mountains, near the town of Idyllwild, a 2½-hour drive from Los Angeles or San Diego, on 205 acres surrounded by the San Bernardino National Forest. There's plenty of hiking, swimming, rock climbing, and other outdoor recreational activities nearby. Because this program covers arts other than writing, there are also musical concerts, artist lectures, theatrical performances, and gallery openings.

You can stay on campus in singles or doubles in the motellike residence halls, which have private baths, or pitch your tent or park your trailer in a campground. Meals are available at a special weekly rate at the school cafeteria but may also be purchased individually. Many writers' workshop participants eat off campus in local coffee shops and restaurants. Arts programs for children aged 5 to 18 are also available. *Idyllwild School of Music and the Arts, Summer Program, Box 38, Idyllwild, CA 92549, tel. 909/659–2171, ext. 365, fax 909/659–5463. July: 6 days, $650 with lodging and meals ($750 for singles; $375 without lodging and meals). Sign up anytime.*

CALIFORNIA **Napa Valley Writers' Conference.** This weeklong conference focuses not on getting published but on the writing process. Three workshops each in poetry and fiction; you attend one of them for two to three hours each day. In the New Poetry workshop, you create new poems and revise previously written ones; the Craft of Fiction workshop, which emphasizes storytelling

techniques, has you working with your own completed manuscripts. The schedule also includes talks by faculty on the writing craft and panels of visiting editors and agents. You get one private meeting with the instructor of your choice.

This workshop is held on the lovely Napa Valley College campus, which is surrounded by the hills and vineyards of the famous wine-growing region. With only 6 teachers and 60 to 75 participants, the conference is small enough that a faculty–student rapport grows up that you won't find at larger conferences. Evenings bring readings by faculty members at local wineries, with some of the host's vintages served at the reception.

Faculty members are chosen for the quality of their teaching as well as their writing; past teachers have included Ron Hansen, Alice Adams, Jorie Graham, and Czeslaw Milosz. Applicants submit a manuscript and a letter describing their writing background. Most participants have attended other workshops or university writing programs, although talented beginners are also accepted.

Participants generally stay in area motels, and except for the opening night reception where dinner is served and the final night's picnic, you're on your own for meals. Wonderful restaurants lines both sides of the highway through the valley; the school cafeteria serves breakfast and lunch, and several delis and fast food restaurants are within walking distance. *Napa Valley Writers' Conference, Sherri Hallgren, Managing Director, Napa Valley College, 2277 Napa-Vallejo Hwy., Napa, CA 94558, tel. 707/253–3070, fax 707/253–3015. Late July or early Aug.: 6 days, $450. Price does not include lodging and most meals; sign up by June 1 (by May 15 for scholarships).*

CALIFORNIA **Santa Barbara Writers Conference.** This eight-day conference stands out for the variety of genres its workshops cover—from poetry, fiction, juvenile writing, and biography and autobiography, to playwriting, screenwriting, nonfiction, mystery, science fiction, and humor. Each year some 360 beginning and more experienced writers come to the conference, held at the Miramar Hotel in the seaside Montecito, just outside Santa Barbara, to hone their craft and work toward getting published.

Workshops run Saturday through Thursday. From morning until midafternoon, you're in class; after that are lectures on technique and the publishing business. Personal conferences with the faculty of 29 established writers may be arranged each day. In the evening, you attend talks by such successful writers as Ray Bradbury and William Styron; in the late evening, you can pick up further pointers on manuscripts at still other workshops.

Participants are accepted on a first-come, first-served basis. Because of its size, this conference may not be ideal for a beginning writer seeking an intimate, supportive atmosphere. The seaside hotel at which you also stay has swimming, tennis, and hiking. Except for two barbecues and a wine and cheese party, meals are on your own in the hotel dining room or at nearby restaurants. *Santa Barbara Writers Conference, Barnaby and Mary Conrad, Codirectors, Box 304, Carpinteria, CA 93014, tel. and fax 805/ 684–2250. Late June: 8 days, $660–$885 with lodging ($335 without). Price does not include most meals; sign up by May 15.*

CALIFORNIA **Squaw Valley Community of Writers.** In July and August, the Squaw Valley Community of Writers, established in 1969, sponsors four separate weeklong programs devoted to poetry, screenwriting, fiction, and nonfiction. It also sponsors a program called the Art of the Wild in conjunction with the University of California, Davis. This program is devoted to writing of all forms inspired by wilderness, nature, and the environment.

Each of these programs offers small group workshops of up to 12 participants who meet in the morning to discuss and critique one another's work. Depending on the program, you spend afternoons at craft sessions; panels on editing, publishing, and

literary agents; or discussions on scripts and films. Staff and participants eat dinner together, and staff members read from their works in the evening.

The faculty are all published writers or professional screenwriters, and most of them have been teaching for years. For the fiction and nonfiction programs, the staff also includes working editors and literary agents. Recent instructors have been writers Richard Ford, Robert Stone, Pam Houston, and James D. Houston; poets Robert Hass, Rita Dove, Galway Kinnell, Sharon Olds, and Gary Snyder; and screenwriter Frank Pierson. Amy Tan is among the alumnae; she frequently gives talks and does readings. Admission to each program is based on submitted manuscripts. The program strives to have people of varying age, geographical origin, and experience in writing and wilderness travel, so that you might meet writers from many of the United States as well as Australia and Canada, ranging in age from 20 to 74. Financial aid is available.

The workshops are conducted off-season at the Squaw Valley ski resort, 10 miles north of Lake Tahoe at 6,200 feet in the Sierra Nevada. You stay in single or double rooms in houses and apartments with kitchens; camping is also available. Dinners, which are included, are served buffet style in a large restaurant; you take care of your own breakfast and lunch. There are numerous local cafés and restaurants. Sunrise nature walks in the Sierras are part of the Art of the Wild program. *Squaw Valley Community of Writers, Brett Hall Jones, Executive Director, Box 2352, Olympic Valley, CA 96146, tel. 916/583–5200 June–Aug. or 415/389–5931 Sept.–May.; for the Art of the Wild, c/o Jack Hicks, Dept. of English, UC Davis, Davis, CA 95616, tel. 916/752–1658. July–Aug.: 7–8 days, $725–$900 with lodging ($525 without). Price does not include breakfast or lunch; apply by May 10.*

OREGON **The Flight of the Mind.** Nurturing literary writing by women in a noncompetitive, feminist environment is the aim of this program started in 1984, and classes focus on the work of women writers. At two separate weeklong sessions, workshops are available in poetry, fiction, novel writing, and nonfiction; some courses address specific topics such as From Autobiography to Short Story, Investigating the Mystery, and Fantasy and Science Fiction.

For three hours each day, either in the morning or afternoon, each participant meets with her class of up to 14 students and her workshop leader. Although students do not have private conferences about their work with the faculty, leaders make an attempt to give everyone the same amount of attention; the arrangement does push you to work hard. Evenings, leaders and students read from their work, and there are occasional staff lectures.

Leaders select participants based on a writing sample and an autobiographical statement of up to two pages; they attempt to assemble a group whose cultural background and experience are as diverse as that of the nine published women authors who act as the instructors; recent faculty have included Ursula K. LeGuin, Grace Paley, Naomi Shibab Nye, and Elizabeth Woody. About 70 women attend each session, some for both weeks.

Workshops are held at the Dominican Order's retreat center, St. Benedict's, in the pine-forested foothills of the Cascade Mountains some 50 miles east of Eugene. In free time, you can go hiking, swimming, or river rafting, or have a soak in an area hot springs.

Lodging options include single or double dorm rooms or a large dorm room for six with shared baths, and private cabins; camping is nearby. The workshop organizers' own kitchen staff use lots of fresh produce and bake their own breads; desserts are low in sugar. *The Flight of the Mind, Judith Barrington and Ruth Gundle, Coordinators, 622 S.E. 29th Ave., Portland, OR 97214, tel. 503/236–9862. June: 7 days, $525–$850. Sign up by Apr. 15.*

■WASHINGTON■ Port Townsend Writers' Conference. This 10-day program aims to help aspiring writers polish their work, to develop wider audiences for good writing, and to make authors feel part of a community where writing is a vocation rather than a business. The conference was founded in 1974.

You have two workshop options. If you have some writing experience and want an intensive program, go for full enrollment; it gives you a daily two-hour manuscript workshop in fiction, poetry, writing for children, or nonfiction prose as well as one scheduled conference with your teacher. If you have less experience or if you don't want to work as hard, plan for open enrollment; you don't attend manuscript workshops, but you may attend the daily classes in writing technique, journal writing, and other topics. Some classes and the manuscript workshop run concurrently, but full-enrollment students are welcome to attend other classes as their schedule permits. Readings by faculty and lectures on the writing craft are open to all as are the receptions that follow two of these and a salmon bake on the beach on the first Sunday evening.

The faculty represents some of the country's finest writers, including Pulitzer, Guggenheim, and MacArthur award winners. Of the some 150 participants who attend annually, most range in age from 35 to 50 and have college degrees in writing or have been writing seriously for at least a couple of years; open-enrollment students are usually less experienced. There are no more than 16 students in any workshop. Admission with full-enrollment status is based on the quality of the writing samples you submit with your application; open enrollment is first come, first served.

The setting is Fort Worden, a 445-acre state park 2 miles from Port Townsend at the tip of the Olympic Peninsula, on Puget Sound; there are fine views of its islands and the distant mountains. You stay in single dormitory rooms at the park, or, if they're full, in the motels, hotels, bed and breakfasts, and campsites nearby. You may sign up for two or three meals a day at the dining hall. In your free time, you can hike the wooded hills and explore the area's ponds, saltwater beaches, and old military fortifications. Port Townsend, a historic seaport community, is full of restored Victorian buildings, restaurants, galleries, and crafts shops. *Port Townsend Writers' Conference, Carol J. Bangs, Program Director, Box 1158, Port Townsend, WA 98368, tel. 206/385–3102, fax 206/385–2470. July: 10 days, $515–$680 with lodging and meals ($260–$365 without). Price includes single room; sign up by early June; financial aid deadline is May 1.*

SOURCES

ORGANIZATIONS **Poets & Writers, Inc.** (72 Spring St., 3rd floor, New York, NY 10012, tel. 212/226–3586) is the central source of practical information for the literary community in the United States, offering current news about conferences, grants, award competitions, and readings, as well as expert advice on resources and the process of publishing creative work. Several other organizations around the country provide useful information to U.S. writers on literary conferences, events, and competitions, in addition to counseling on the publishing business; some sponsor research libraries and local workshops, readings, and other activities to promote literature in their area. The larger regional organizations include **Arizona Authors' Association** (3509 E. Shea Blvd., Suite 117, Phoenix, AZ 85028-3339, tel. 602/942–4240); **Austin Writers' League** (1501 W. 5th St., Suite E-2, Austin, TX 78703, tel. 512/499–8914); **Beyond Baroque Literary Arts Center** (681 Venice Blvd., Venice, CA 90291, tel. 310/822–3006); **Just Buffalo Literary Center** (493 Franklin St., Buffalo, NY 14202, tel. 716/881–3211); **The Loft** (Pratt Community Center, 66 Malcolm Ave. SE, Minneapolis, MN 55414, tel. 612/379–8999); **National Writers Association** (1450 S. Havana, Suite 424, Aurora, CO 80012, tel. 303/751–7844); **New Hampshire Writers and Publishers Project** (44 S. Main St., Concord, NH 03303, tel. 603/226–6649); **Poetry Society of America** (15 Gramercy Park, New York, NY 10003, tel. 212/254–9628); **Small Press Traffic Literary Arts Center** (3599 24th St., San Francisco, CA 94110, tel. 415/285–8394); **The Writer's Center** (4508 Walsh St., Bethesda, MD 20815, tel. 301/654–8664); **Writers Connection** (Box 24770, San Jose, CA 95154, tel. 408/445–3600); **The Writer's Voice** (West Side YMCA, 5 W. 63rd St., New York, NY 10023, tel. 212/875–4124); and **The Writers' Workshop** (Box 696, Asheville, NC 28802, tel. 800/627–0142).

PERIODICALS *Poets & Writers Magazine* (72 Spring St., New York, NY 10012, tel. 212/226–3586), an essential news journal for writers, features author interviews, articles on writing and the publishing industry, and information on grants, contests, workshops, and calls for manuscripts. *Poetry Flash* (1450 Fourth St., Berkeley, CA 94710, tel. 510/525–5476) contains author interviews, book reviews, and an extensive calendar of literary events, mainly, but not exclusively, in the western part of the United States. *The Writer* (120 Boylston St., Boston, MA 02116-4615, tel. 617/423–3157), *Writer's Digest* (1507 Dana Ave., Cincinnati, OH 45207, tel. 800/333–0133), and *Writers' Journal* (3585 N. Lexington Ave., Suite 328, Arden Hill, MN 55126, tel. 612/486–7818) all offer essays on the writing process and the publishing business.

BOOKS *The Guide to Writers Conferences* (Shaw Guides) and *Novel and Short Story Writer's Market* (Writer's Digest Books) both provide extensive listings of U.S. writers' conferences and workshops. Poets & Writers also publishes an annual listing of writers' conferences.

ALSO SEE If your creative spirit yearns for other outlets, see the chapters on Arts and Crafts Workshops, Painting Workshops, and Photography Workshops and Tours.

Appendix: Where the Programs Are

ALASKA

Birding, *48*

Cultural Tours, *85*

Environmental Cruises, *98–100*

Photography Workshops and Tours, *214–215*

Volunteer Vacations in Research, *260*

Volunteer Vacations in Public and
Community Service, *276*

Whale-watching Cruises, *284–285*

ARIZONA

Archaeological Digs, *9*

Arts and Crafts Workshops, *29*

Birding, *43–44, 46*

Cultural Tours, *81–82*

Garden Tours, *129*

New Age Centers, *173*

Photography Workshops and Tours, *208–209*

Spas, *233–234*

ARKANSAS

Archaeological Digs, *6*

Volunteer Vacations in Public and
Community Service, *273*

CALIFORNIA

Arts and Crafts Workshops, *34–35*

Birding, *46*

Campus Vacations, *58*

Cooking Schools, *69*

Environmental Cruises, *95*

Foreign-Language Immersion Programs,
111–112

Garden Tours, *122, 129–130*

Nature Camps, *161–162*

New Age Centers, *175–179*

Painting Workshops, *196*

Photography Workshops and Tours, *213*

Spas, *237–240*

Volunteer Vacations in Research, *256–257*

Volunteer Vacations in Public and
Community Service, *275–276*

Whale-watching Cruises, *283*

Writing Conferences and Workshops,
308–310

COLORADO

Arts and Crafts Workshops, *33–34*

Birding, *45*

Cooking Schools, *69*

Cultural Tours, *82–83*

Music Programs, *141*

Nature Camps, *157*

New Age Centers, *173*

Painting Workshops, *195*

Photography Workshops and Tours, *212*

Spas, *236*

Volunteer Vacations in Research, *253*

Writing Conferences and Workshops, *307*

CONNECTICUT

Garden Tours, *119*

Nature Camps, *152*

Painting Workshops, *189*

Writing Conferences and Workshops, *291*

DELAWARE

Garden Tours, *126*

DISTRICT OF COLUMBIA

Volunteer Vacations in Research, *247*

FLORIDA

Arts and Crafts Workshops, *21*

Birding, *41*

Photography Workshops and Tours, *207–208*

Spas, *227–229*

Volunteer Vacations in Research, *248*

GEORGIA

Arts and Crafts Workshops, *22*

Cooking Schools, *67*

Garden Tours, *121*

Spas, *229*

Volunteer Vacations in Research, *248*

Writing Conferences and Workshops, *300*

HAWAII

Birding, *49*

Garden Tours, *123*

Nature Camps, *163*

New Age Centers, *180–181*

Spas, *241–242*

Volunteer Vacations in Research, *261*

Whale-watching Cruises, *286*

IDAHO

Cultural Tours, *83*

Music Programs, *142*

Volunteer Vacations in Research, *253*

ILLINOIS

Cooking Schools, *67*

Garden Tours, *127–128*

Spas, *231*

Writing Conferences and Workshops, *302*

INDIANA

Campus Vacations, *57*

Music Programs, *138*

Writing Conferences and Workshops, *303*

IOWA

New Age Centers, *172*

Writing Conferences and Workshops, *303*

KANSAS

Archaeological Digs, *8*

Music Programs, *138*

KENTUCKY

Writing Conferences and Workshops, *301*

LOUISIANA

Cultural Tours, *80*

Garden Tours, *121*

Painting Workshops, *192*

Volunteer Vacations in Research, *249*

MAINE

Arts and Crafts Workshops, *13–14*

Campus Vacations, *53*

Cultural Tours, *78*

Environmental Cruises, *94*

Garden Tours, *119*

Nature Camps, *152–153*

New Age Centers, *168*

Painting Workshops, *189*

Photography Workshops and Tours, *202*

Spas, *221*

Volunteer Vacations in Public and Community Service, *270*

Whale-watching Cruises, *281*

Writing Conferences and Workshops, *292*

MARYLAND

Cooking Schools, *65*

Volunteer Vacations in Research, *247*

Writing Conferences and Workshops, *299*

MASSACHUSETTS

Arts and Crafts Workshops, *14–15*

Cooking Schools, *61*

Cultural Tours, *78*

Garden Tours, *119, 123*

New Age Centers, *168–169*

Painting Workshops, *189–190*

Photography Workshops and Tours, *203*

Spas, *221*

Volunteer Vacations in Public and Community Service, *270*

Whale-watching Cruises, *281–282*

Writing Conferences and Workshops, *292–294*

MICHIGAN

Birding, *42*

Painting Workshops, *193*

Volunteer Vacations in Research, *250–251*

MINNESOTA

Birding, *42*

Cultural Tours, *80*

Spas, *232*

Volunteer Vacations in Research, *251*

Writing Conferences and Workshops, *304*

MISSISSIPPI

Garden Tours, *127*

MISSOURI

Cultural Tours, *80–81*

Garden Tours, *128*

Music Programs, *139*

Volunteer Vacations in Public and Community Service, *273*

Writing Conferences and Workshops, *305*

MONTANA

Cultural Tours, *83*

Garden Tours, *122*

Nature Camps, *158*

New Age Centers, *174*

Photography Workshops and Tours, *213*

Volunteer Vacations in Research, *254–256*

Writing Conferences and Workshops, *307*

NEBRASKA

Archaeological Digs, *8*

Birding, *43*

NEVADA

Arts and Crafts Workshops, *30*

Cultural Tours, *81*

Nature Camps, *155*

Volunteer Vacations in Public and Community Service, *274*

NEW HAMPSHIRE

Campus Vacations, *54*

Cooking Schools, *62*

Foreign-Language Immersion Programs, *106*

Nature Camps, *153*

Painting Workshops, *190*

Photography Workshops and Tours, *204*

Volunteer Vacations in Public and Community Service, *270–271*

Writing Conferences and Workshops, *294*

NEW JERSEY

Arts and Crafts Workshops, *19*

Birding, *40*

Volunteer Vacations in Public and Community Service, *272*

NEW MEXICO

Arts and Crafts Workshops, *30–32*

Birding, *44*

Cooking Schools, *68*

Cultural Tours, *81–82*

Painting Workshops, *194–195*

Photography Workshops and Tours, *209–210*

Writing Conferences and Workshops, *306*

NEW YORK

Arts and Crafts Workshops, *15–16*

Campus Vacations, *54–55*

Cooking Schools, *63–64*

Cultural Tours, *79*

Foreign-Language Immersion Programs, *107–108*

Garden Tours, *119–120, 123–5*

Nature Camps, *154*

New Age Centers, *170*

Painting Workshops, *191–192*

Photography Workshops and Tours, *204*

Spas, *222*

Volunteer Vacations in Public and Community Service, *271*

Writing Conferences and Workshops, *295–297*

NORTH CAROLINA

Arts and Crafts Workshops, *23–25*

Campus Vacations, *56*

Garden Tours, *121*

Music Programs, *136*

Spas, *230*

Volunteer Vacations in Research, *249*

Writing Conferences and Workshops, *301*

NORTH DAKOTA

Birding, *42*

Cultural Tours, *81*

Music Programs, *140*

OHIO

Arts and Crafts Workshops, *26*

Campus Vacations, *58*

Music Programs, *140*

Spas, *233*

Writing Conferences and Workshops, *305*

OKLAHOMA

Cultural Tours, *81*

OREGON

Arts and Crafts Workshops, *36*

Birding, *47*

Cultural Tours, *83*

Environmental Cruises, *97*

Garden Tours, *130*

New Age Centers, *179*

Painting Workshops, *197*

Writing Conferences and Workshops, *310*

PENNSYLVANIA

Arts and Crafts Workshops, *19–20*

Birding, *40*

Campus Vacations, *56*

Garden Tours, *120, 126*

Nature Camps, *155*

New Age Centers, *171*

Photography Workshops and Tours, *206*

Spas, *225*

Volunteer Vacations in Public and Community Service, *272*

Writing Conferences and Workshops, *300*

RHODE ISLAND

Campus Vacations, *55*

Cultural Tours, *78*

Environmental Cruises, *95*

Foreign-Language Immersion Programs, *109*

Photography Workshops and Tours, *205*

SOUTH CAROLINA

Archaeological Digs, *7*

Birding, *41*

Cultural Tours, *81*

Garden Tours, *121*

Spas, *231*

SOUTH DAKOTA

Archaeological Digs, *8*

Cultural Tours, *81*

TENNESSEE

Archaeological Digs, *7*

Arts and Crafts Workshops, *25–26*

Cultural Tours, *80*

Painting Workshops, *192*

Spas, *231*

Writing Conferences and Workshops, *302*

TEXAS

Archaeological Digs, *10*

Arts and Crafts Workshops, *32*

Birding, *44*

Nature Camps, *156*

Painting Workshops, *195*

Spas, *234–235*

Volunteer Vacations in Research, *252*

UTAH

Arts and Crafts Workshops, *33*

Birding, *44*

Cultural Tours, *82*

Nature Camps, *156*

Photography Workshops and Tours, *209*

Spas, *235–236*

VERMONT

Arts and Crafts Workshops, *16–18*

Cooking Schools, *65*

Foreign-Language Immersion Programs, *110*

Spas, *223–224*

Volunteer Vacations in Public and Community Service, *271*

Writing Conferences and Workshops, *297–298*

VIRGINIA

Archaeological Digs, *6*

Cultural Tours, *79*

Garden Tours, *121, 126*

New Age Centers, *171*

Spas, *225–226*

Volunteer Vacations in Public and Community Service, *272*

WASHINGTON

Arts and Crafts Workshops, *37*

Birding, *47*

Environmental Cruises, *96–97*

Garden Tours, *130*

Music Programs, *144*

Nature Camps, *162–163*

Painting Workshops, *197–198*

Volunteer Vacations in Research, *258–259*

Writing Conferences and Workshops, *311*

WEST VIRGINIA

Archaeological Digs, *6*

Arts and Crafts Workshops, *20–21*

Cooking Schools, *66*

Music Programs, *135–136*

Spas, *226*

Volunteer Vacations in Public and Community Service, *273*

WISCONSIN

Arts and Crafts Workshops, *27–29*

New Age Centers, *172*

Painting Workshops, *193*

WYOMING

Birding, *45*

Cultural Tours, *84*

Music Programs, *143*

Nature Camps, *158–160*

New Age Centers, *174*

Painting Workshops, *196*

Volunteer Vacations in Public and Community Service, *274*

Notes

Notes

Notes

Notes

Notes

Notes

Notes

Notes

Notes

Fodor's Travel Guides are available at bookstores everywhere, or call 1–800–533–6478, 24 hours a day.

U.S. Guides

Alaska
Arizona
Boston
California
Cape Cod, Martha's Vineyard, Nantucket
The Carolinas & the Georgia Coast
Chicago
Colorado
Florida
Hawaii
Las Vegas, Reno, Tahoe
Los Angeles
Maine, Vermont, New Hampshire
Maui
Miami & the Keys
New England
New Orleans
New York City
Pacific North Coast
Philadelphia & the Pennsylvania Dutch Country
The Rockies
San Diego
San Francisco
Santa Fe, Taos, Albuquerque
Seattle & Vancouver
The South
The U.S. & British Virgin Islands
The Upper Great Lakes Region
USA
Vacations in New York State
Vacations on the Jersey Shore
Virginia & Maryland
Waikiki
Walt Disney World and the Orlando Area
Washington, D.C.

Foreign Guides

Acapulco, Ixtapa, Zihuatanejo
Australia & New Zealand

Austria
The Bahamas
Baja & Mexico's Pacific Coast Resorts
Barbados
Berlin
Bermuda
Brazil
Brittany & Normandy
Budapest
Canada
Cancun, Cozumel, Yucatan Peninsula
Caribbean
China
Costa Rica, Belize, Guatemala
The Czech Republic & Slovakia
Eastern Europe
Egypt
Euro Disney
Europe
Europe's Great Cities
Florence & Tuscany
France
Germany
Great Britain
Greece
The Himalayan Countries
Hong Kong
India
Ireland
Israel
Italy
Japan
Kenya & Tanzania
Korea
London
Madrid & Barcelona
Mexico
Montreal & Quebec City
Morocco
Moscow , St. Petersburg, Kiev
The Netherlands, Belgium & Luxembourg
New Zealand
Norway
Nova Scotia, Prince

Edward Island & New Brunswick
Paris
Portugal
Provence & the Riviera
Rome
Russia & the Baltic Countries
Scandinavia
Scotland
Singapore
South America
Southeast Asia
Spain
Sweden
Switzerland
Thailand
Tokyo
Toronto
Turkey
Vienna & the Danube Valley
Yugoslavia

Special Series

Fodor's Affordables
Caribbean
Europe
Florida
France
Germany
Great Britain
London
Italy
Paris

Fodor's Bed & Breakfast and Country Inns Guides
Canada's Great Country Inns
California
Cottages, B&Bs and Country Inns of England and Wales
Mid-Atlantic Region
New England
The Pacific Northwest
The South
The Southwest
The Upper Great Lakes Region
The West Coast

The Berkeley Guides
California
Central America
Eastern Europe
France
Germany
Great Britain & Ireland
Mexico
Pacific Northwest & Alaska
San Francisco

Fodor's Exploring Guides
Australia
Britain
California
The Caribbean
Florida
France
Germany
Ireland
Italy
London
New York City
Paris
Rome
Singapore & Malaysia
Spain
Thailand

Fodor's Flashmaps
New York
Washington, D.C.

Fodor's Pocket Guides
Bahamas
Barbados
Jamaica
London
New York City
Paris
Puerto Rico
San Francisco
Washington, D.C.

Fodor's Sports
Cycling
Hiking
Running

Sailing
The Insider's Guide to the Best Canadian Skiing
Skiing in the USA & Canada

Fodor's Three-In-Ones (guidebook, language cassette, and phrase book)
France
Germany
Italy
Mexico
Spain

Fodor's Special Interest Guides
Accessible USA
Cruises and Ports of Call
Euro Disney
Halliday's New England Food Explorer
Healthy Escapes
London Companion
Shadow Traffic's New York Shortcuts and Traffic Tips
Sunday in New York
Walt Disney World and the Orlando Area
Walt Disney World for Adults

Fodor's Touring Guides
Touring Europe
Touring USA: Eastern Edition

Fodor's Vacation Planners
Great American Vacations
National Parks of the East
National Parks of the West

The Wall Street Journal Guides to Business Travel
Europe
International Cities
Pacific Rim
USA & Canada